# THE WHICH? BOOK OF HOME IMPROVEMENTS AND EXTENSIONS

# THE WHICH? BOOK OF HOME IMPROVEMENTS AND EXTENSIONS

Published by Consumers' Association
& Hodder and Stoughton

THE WHICH? BOOK OF
HOME IMPROVEMENTS AND EXTENSIONS

is published in Great Britain
by Consumers' Association,
14 Buckingham Street, London WC2N 6DS
and Hodder & Stoughton,
47 Bedford Square, London WC1B 3DP

First edition, second printing



ISBN 0 340 33455 X

Filmset and printed in Great Britain by
BAS Ltd, Over Wallop, Hampshire
Bound by R. J. Acford, Chichester, West Sussex

## Acknowledgements

**Editor**
Jill Thomas

**Consultant Editor**
David Holloway

**Design**
John Herbert, Turner Porter Associates Ltd

**Illustrations**
Tom Cross
Hayward and Martin
Summit Art Studios

**Cover illustration**
Hugh Dixon, Spectron Artists

**Contributors**

Dave Beadle
Terence Bines
Gillian de Bono
Quentin Deane
Chris Evans
Sharon Evans
David Fowler
D Fuller
Robert Henley
Philip Houston
Andrew Jarmin
S B Johnson
Andrew Lawrence
Brian Keyworth, Dip. Arch RIBA
David Malkin
William Peskett
Ross S Taylor

**The publishers also wish to thank**
The Timber Research and Development Association
The Electricity Council
The Royal Institution of Chartered Surveyors
and its Building Cost Information Service
for advice on valuation and costs
The readers of *Which?* who took the time
and trouble to provide details of their
own home improvements and extensions
The *Which?* checkers and consultants

# Contents

## PART 1 WHAT'S INVOLVED



## PART 2 IMPROVEMENTS ROOM BY ROOM

# PART 3 EXTENSIONS AND CONVERSIONS

# PART 1
# WHAT'S INVOLVED

# Chapter 1

# THE WHYS AND WHEREFORES

It is often said that buying a house is the largest purchase or investment that most people ever make but, having bought the house, the spending rarely stops as householders continue to improve and extend their properties. The increasingly high costs of moving house have perhaps encouraged more and more householders to make the most of the houses they already own instead of 'trading up' to a bigger or better property. Nowadays some half of all planning applications are from householders intending to extend their homes and around 30 per cent of all the money lent by Building Societies goes out as loans for home improvements, conversions and extensions. Do-it-yourself is a booming activity not only because it saves money but because people enjoy doing it themselves and frequently find that they are as good, if not better, than the average tradesman.

This book covers home improvements as distinct from essential household maintenance and repair. It deals with the sorts of alterations you might make to a house or flat to make it more comfortable, better organised and, if necessary, larger. Part I is about why you want to improve, the financial implications and how you can set about things. Part II is a room-by-room manual of improvements to the existing building. Part III is about building extensions, converting lofts and creating other habitable space.

## Why you might improve

Most householders improve their homes to better their own comfort and standard of living or sometimes just to stamp their own mark on a new house. There can be financial rewards in an increased house value, especially if you buy a dilapidated house fairly cheaply and invest some effort into bringing it up to date, but such increases are rarely realised as actual cash since the extra £'s usually go towards paying for the next house.

## How you might improve

Improvements include things like installing central heating or patio doors, replacing windows and re-fitting a kitchen or bathroom. These may be adaptations of a house that's basically sound and well equipped or part of a major renovation of an older house. The Government is committed to improving the existing housing stock and, through local authorities, provides grants for a large variety of improvements, from the provision of basic amenities such as a bathroom to installing loft insulation – see page 20.

Some improvements are part of maintaining the house and involve replacing fittings which are damaged or unsafe. Rewiring because the old electrical wiring is hazardous is one example, replacing rotten or rusty windows is another. Projects like this usually provide the opportunity to upgrade as well as replace the existing fittings.

Other improvements involve replacing fittings which may still work adequately, but which look worn or out of date. New kitchen units and bathroom fittings are two examples.

Installing central heating has been a very common improvement in the last decade, so much so that around 70 per cent of all houses are now centrally heated and soon it will be time to start replacing old systems. The central heating boom has meant that lots of fireplaces have been removed and blocked up, and many houses were built without a chimney. So another 'improvement' might be to establish a working fireplace.

## Why you might extend

There are lots of reasons why you might want space, most of which have to do with a growing family: new babies need bedrooms and though young children can often double up, they begin to need separate rooms as they get older; teenagers need space to escape parents and parents need space to escape teenagers; elderly relatives may have to be accommodated at a time when there's already considerable demand for the existing rooms from younger members of the family.

It's also useful to have spaces for people to play – a model railway room, a music room, a table tennis room or a plant conservatory – and for people to work – a study, a workshop or a sewing room. If you run a business from home, specially devoted space is usually necessary. It's better if this can be separate from the main part of the house – in a loft conversion for instance. Pay special attention to sound proofing and arrange windows so that you can't be disturbed by the comings and goings of other members of the household.

## How you might extend

Building on to the existing house is the obvious way to get more space, but there are two other choices worth considering. One is re-arranging the space you already have. The other is converting or re-arranging space which is currently not habitable. Extending a house or converting existing space are alternatives to moving house. Such investments involve considerable time and money and it's important to weigh up exactly what you hope to gain, it might be better to move.

## Why not move?

Among *Which?* members, around a third of all house moves are because of changing jobs or a transfer to another place of work. Other moves are primarily steps up the house-buying ladder, where for instance a young couple will increase their mortgage in line with their expanding income, even though they may have no immediate need for the extra space. There's no alternative to this sort of move or to a move undertaken for a specific reason – to get into a different school catchment area for instance.

Moving house involves finding the new place, arranging to buy it, raising the finances and selling your own house, transporting the goods and chattels and then settling down in your new home. It's a time-consuming, nerve-racking and expensive business. If you employ a solicitor, an estate agent, a building surveyor and a removal firm to assist with the administrative and practical sides of the move, the total cost is likely to be in excess of £2000. Even if you do as much as possible yourself, stamp duty is unavoidable. On top of all that is the cost of new carpets and so on.

Extending or converting generally involves fewer other people, less legal hassle and although there may be some VAT and some additional rates to pay, there are no hefty taxes. But extending does have its own problems: finding someone to do the work, or the effort of doing it yourself; the upheaval of improving the house you're also trying to live in – the noise, the dirt and so on. It can also be expensive, with building costs typically somewhere between £250 to £400 a square metre (around £30 a square foot) if you employ outside help; perhaps half this if you do it yourself.

Although some of this outlay might be recouped when you eventually sell the house, a percentage usually has to be written off. It's generally unwise to invest in a conversion that isn't valuable to you in terms of the space or convenience it provides – see page 18.

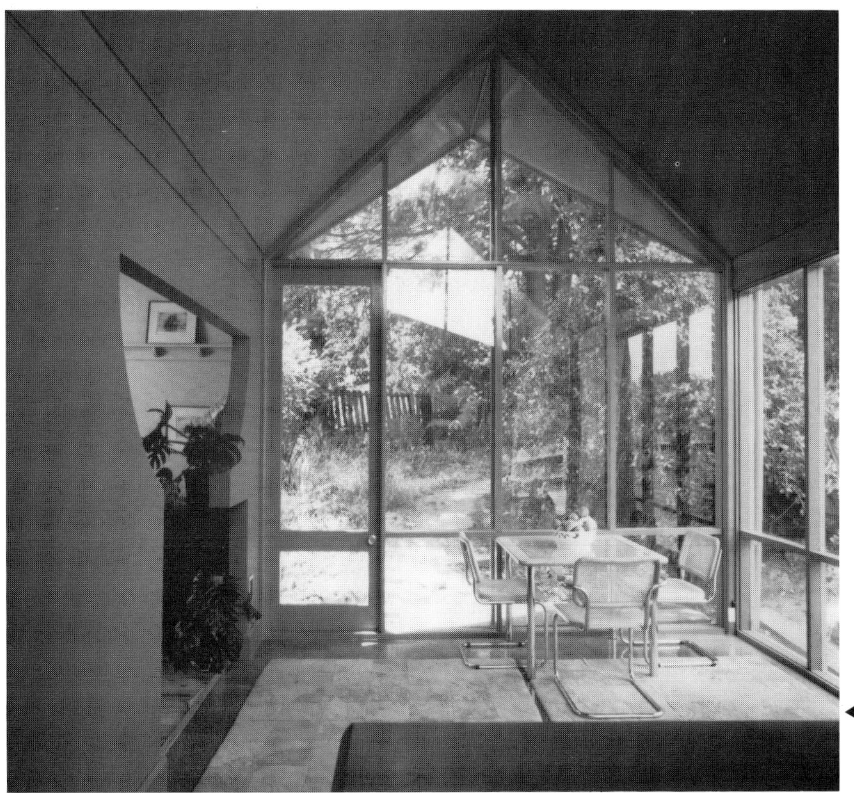

◀ This airy room is a glazed extension to the house. The opening through the original external wall has been shaped to make an unusual feature.

# Re-arranging existing space

Moving things around inside a house can be a cost-effective way of getting more space – even knocking down a dividing wall can give a little extra floor area. Moving or blocking off a door can be helpful, although it doesn't create any more space it alters the traffic routes through the house and may allow the furnishings to be arranged more effectively. Moving a door can be particularly beneficial in kitchens, which frequently suffer from badly planned traffic routes – see Chapter 3. Where two rooms have been knocked into one, one of the doors often becomes superfluous and can be blocked off. Or both can be blocked off and a new door created in a better position. Rehanging a hinged door the other way round is not difficult and can give greater flexibility. Sliding doors save space; consider them for wardrobes as well as doors between rooms.

It isn't easy to step back from your own house and think about how the existing layout could be altered effectively. Would you, for instance, consider making the upstairs of your house open-plan living space and redefining the downstairs into an entrance hall, kitchen and bedrooms? It's a radical change but could mean that you make good use of several square metres currently under-used as a landing (though an upstairs WC will usually still need some sort of lobby).

Another choice, common in small terraced houses, is to knock the front room and hall into one, but this means the front door opens straight into your living space and that can be a great inconvenience. It may also be unpopular with potential buyers.

Moving the staircase is a possibility for some houses. Changing an enclosed flight to an open one can give the impression of more space and allows you to use the area under the stairs – but if you do this you'll need to provide storage elsewhere for things like a vacuum cleaner and an ironing board. A spiral staircase isn't usually much more economical on space than a straight flight but it takes up a square

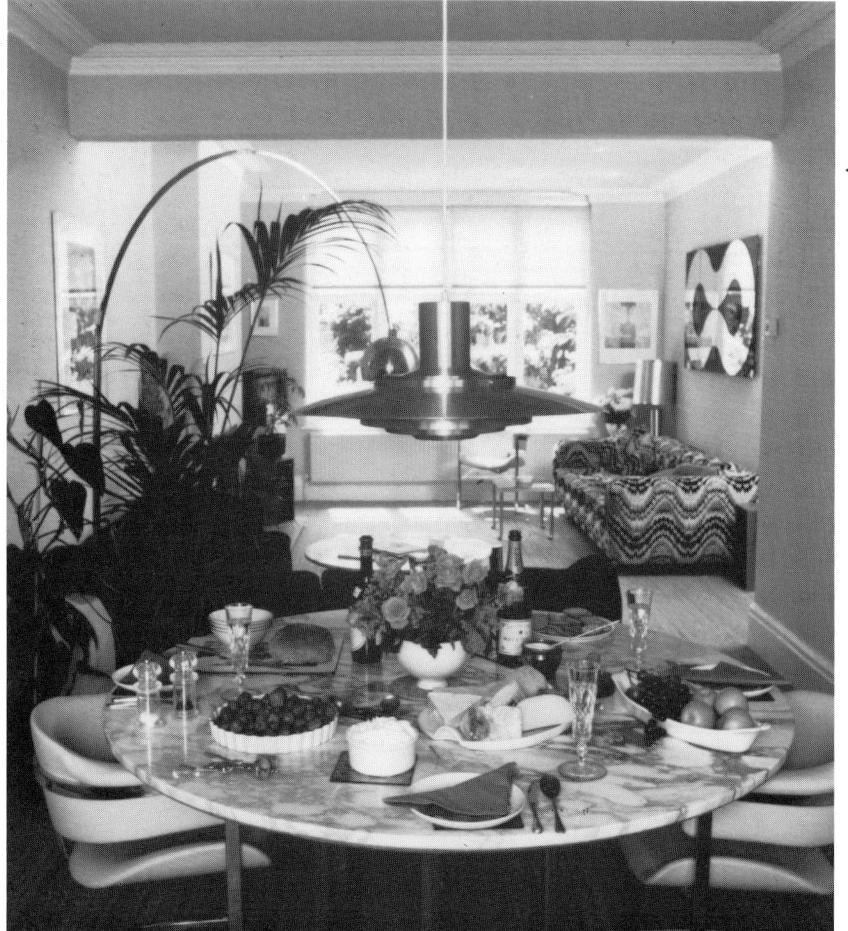

◀ Knocking down the wall between two rooms is a common internal re-arrangement of space.

The dividing wall was demolished and a lintel inserted to support the construction above.
▼

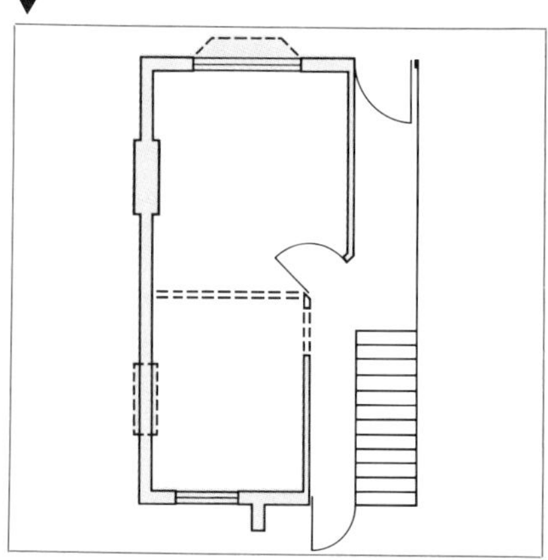

space rather than a rectangular one and so may be fitted where a straight flight couldn't be used. A spiral staircase may also give the impression of taking less space.

Knocking down a wall is a common internal change. Usually it's to create a through room of some sort, but it can also be done to move a wall between two rooms so as to make one larger and the other smaller or to allow a third room to be slotted between two existing ones. Two large bedrooms could become three or could yield space to create a bathroom accessible from one or both bedrooms.

A new room can also be created by building a partition wall across a large existing room. An extra large bathroom could be split to give two bathrooms or a large bedroom could be split to provide two smaller children's rooms. In the second case, both rooms would need window light but a second bathroom could be an internal room. Creating new rooms

▲ The space under the stairs is an enclosed cupboard in many homes. It can often be incorporated into the room below.

Open stairs can give the impression of space. ▶

Spiral stairs usually take just as much room as a straight flight. ▶

Partitions can help to create interesting shapes as well as provide storage and screen off parts of a room.
▼

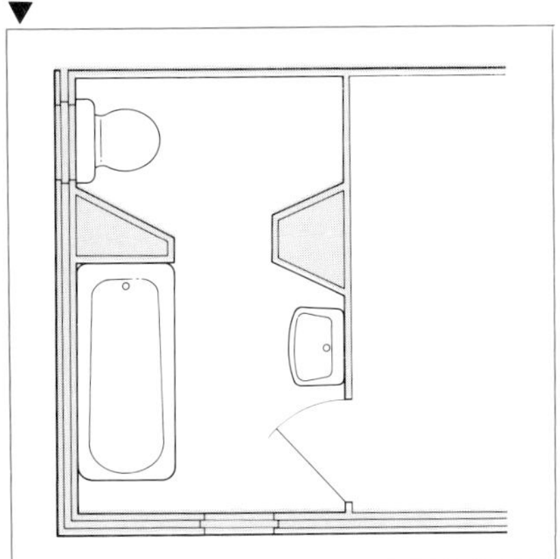

usually gives you the opportunity to make rooms interesting shapes by building partitions which zig-zag or incorporate storage or both.

Bathrooms, utility rooms and, in some parts of the UK, kitchens, readily lend themselves to small spare spaces. This is because the Building Regulations regarding ceiling heights are less stringent for these rooms. The ventilation and window light rules are also different – see Chapter 8.

Sometimes it's possible to re-arrange a house vertically – though usually this is more expensive and involves professional designs. For instance, it might be possible to build a small extra room in the tall space above the stairwell. Another radical alteration would be to sub-divide two existing high-ceilinged rooms into three new rooms with lower ceilings – see below. In a room with a very high ceiling it may be possible to incorporate a gallery floor or you may be able to do this by building up into the roof space. Even if there isn't enough height below the gallery to stand the space could be used as storage.

▲ A yard already bordered on two sides by the main house can be enclosed to give more space.

▲ A small space can be used to create an effective kitchen. The window is required by law in Scotland and Inner London, but is not mandatory in other parts of the country.

THREE ROOMS FROM TWO

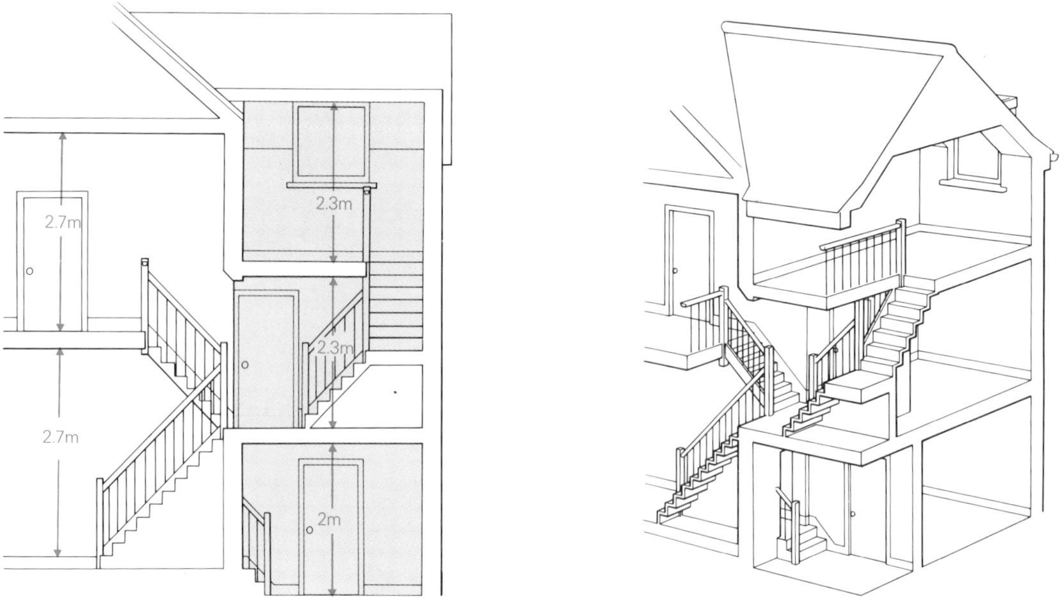

2.7m
2.7m
2.3m
2.3m
2m

By re-arranging space vertically, two high-ceilinged rooms could be converted to three rooms with lower ceilings.

# Converting existing space

In many houses and flats there are pockets of existing unhabitable space which could be converted to living accommodation. Lofts, garages and basements are the three most obvious ones, but outbuildings – such as an old outside WC – could be converted and a balcony or courtyard could be enclosed to give more room.

Creating new rooms in the loft beneath a pitched roof adds space to the house without sacrificing any ground around the house. It's a good solution for extra bedrooms or for a home office or self-contained bolt-hole. The rooms created can often have considerable character created by the sloping walls and ceilings and there may be the advantage of good views from the top of the house. A full conversion is a major structural project and so subject to the Building Regulations. It will usually involve a strengthened floor, some alteration to the roof supporting timbers, a proper staircase and windows, as well as all the finishing off – creating walls and so on. A part conversion, perhaps just boarding the floor and installing a skylight, cannot be regarded (or used) as habitable space, but may still give

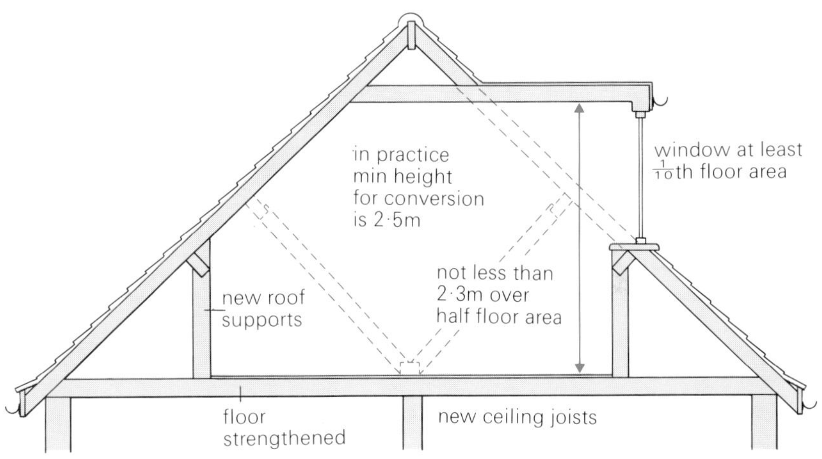


A full loft conversion is a major structural project governed by the Building Regulations – the England and Wales regulations are shown here.

▲ Roof windows can be useful to provide natural light in a loft with good headroom or in a part loft conversion (not intended for habitable use).

◀ To achieve the necessary minimum ceiling height of 2·3m for habitable rooms in a loft, a dormer window is very often required.

usable extra room – for light hobbies, for instance.

Plans to use a garage as living space can also be considered as either a full or part conversion. A full conversion is once again a major structural project to bring the building up to the standards for habitable rooms required under the Building Regulations. A part conversion may simply involve moving your washing machine to the garage or building a workshop there. Apart from access to an electricity supply (and perhaps a water supply) there's little work to be done. Part conversion could involve making the garage clean and comfortable enough to permanently house a model railway or to become a utility room. This is likely to mean some sort of heating is required (and therefore better insulation – you might need a raised and insulated floor for instance), more power sockets and better lighting.

Upgrading a basement is the third major option – if you have one. Damp, ventilation and lack of light are the three problems it's usually necessary to overcome with this sort of conversion. If the ceiling is lower than the necessary 2.3m, a part conversion may be all it's sensible and cost-effective to do. Basements can be fitted out for most of the same purposes as part conversions of garages.

An existing garage can be converted to habitable space with a new garage built alongside as above or as a separate building.

A basement conversion can be very successful; damp and lack of light are often the two major problems. Here the small basement garden area outside has been roofed with translucent material to let in maximum light, to create useful extra space which does not however meet the full requirements for a habitable room.

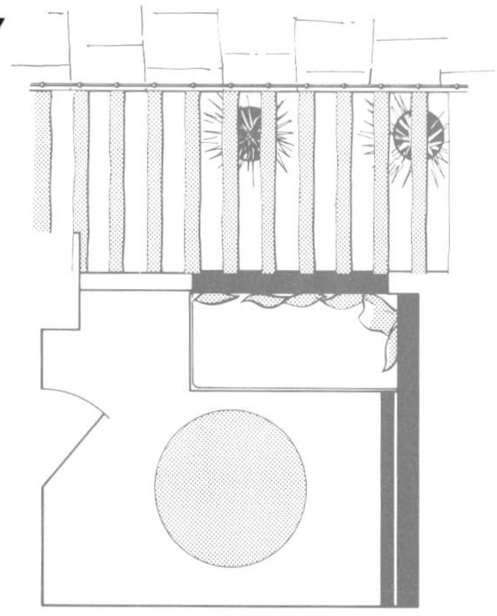

# Building on

Extending sideways is a common way to get more living space and you'll have a fairly good idea of the spaces around your home which could be used for an extension. Many extensions are single-storey, either a ground floor extension to the side or the back of the house, or a second storey added or extended over an existing garage or perhaps on piers to give a new carport beneath. Ground floor extensions can be built by any of the methods of house construction (brick, block, stone or timber-framed) or as units bought from a specialist manufacturer.

Extensions intended for living in must meet the stringent requirements of the Building Regulations, but some of these – the insulation requirements for the roof for instance – are relaxed for sun-lounges, dayrooms and conservatories with translucent roofs.

Two-storey extensions are usually constructed on site from bricks (or blocks) and mortar though they can also be timber-framed. They obviously cost more, but they're usually not twice the price of a single-storey, so £ for area gained they're better value. The advantage of an extension that's the full height of the existing building is that it can more easily be made to look as if it was always there and not just an extra appendage.

Ground floor extensions are commonly used to provide a bathroom in a terraced house or to extend the small kitchens common to many three- and four-bedroom houses. Although they eat into the ground around the house, the outdoor space lost in this way can be reclaimed on a flat-roofed extension by creating a rooftop area with access from the first floor – but the roof must be properly designed.

First-floor extensions are commonly used as extra bedrooms, extended bedrooms and bathrooms. The design of a first-storey extension needs careful thought. The gain in space may have to be offset against space effectively lost in arranging access, it's often necessary to lop a bit off an existing room – to create a corridor down one side of a bedroom for instance.

A single-storey ground floor extension is often used as a new kitchen or to enlarge a small kitchen. Garden rooms or conservatories are another common extension.
▼

A two-storey extension can more easily be made to look as if it's always been there but again access can mean some bedroom space is lost.
▼

# How much will it cost?

Your outlay on any home improvement is the cost of brick and mortar (or whatever) and labour. At 1983 prices you can reckon on paying around £300 a square metre for a single-storey extension and around £275 a square metre for each floor of a two-storey one. Note though that these are average costs and there is a great deal of variation. Also smaller extensions tend to cost considerably more a square metre – say £400. Loft conversions are also a little cheaper than single-storey extensions – around £275 a square metre on average, but again the variation is large.

When calculating whether an improvement is worth doing in financial terms you might also want to think how much it could add to the value or saleability of your home. Neither is easy to quantify, much will depend on the size and type of a house. A second bathroom for instance might be a good improvement in a four-bedroom house, but over the top for a three-bedroom one. Where a house is situated is also important. It's no good improving beyond the general tone for the neighbourhood.

**Three-bedroom semi-detached, without garage or central heating. Built in 1930's. Largish garden mostly to rear**
**Situation** In a surburban road of mixed property.
**Assumed value** £32,500

| Part-loft conversion with roof light and retractable loft-ladder (area 25m²) | |
|---|---|
| cost | around £1,500 |
| value | possibly up by £750 |
| recoup | 50% |

| Full loft conversion with permanent staircase (area 25m²) | |
|---|---|
| cost | £6,875 |
| value | possibly up by £3,000 |
| recoup | 45% |

| Full depth two-storey extension to side, to provide double garage, suite of bed/sitting room, kitchenette and WC on ground floor. Two bedrooms and a new bathroom above (area 50m²–25m² on each floor) | |
|---|---|
| cost | £13,750 |
| value | possibly up by £14,000 |
| recoup | nearly 100% |

| Single-storey extension to rear to create new kitchen area extended dining room. Former kitchen – to become dining room (existing fittings re-used) (area 20m²) | |
|---|---|
| cost | £6,000 |
| value | possibly up by £3,500 |
| recoup | 60% |

| Porch with cloakroom (WC and basin) (area 6m²) | |
|---|---|
| cost | £2,400 |
| value | possibly up by £500 |
| recoup | 20% |

| Utility room/rear lobby (area 6m²) | |
|---|---|
| cost | £2,400 |
| value | possibly up by £500 |
| recoup | 20% |

| Central heating with gas-fired boiler | |
|---|---|
| cost | around £1,500 to £2,000 |
| value | possibly up £1,000 to £1,500 |
| recoup | up to 100% |

Some improvements are almost always uneconomic – expensive replacement double-glazed windows are a glaring example – and swimming pools are often quoted as an example something that will put many purchasers off. Other improvements such as central heating are good value and will usually make a house easier to sell, provided of course that they are well designed and the standard of workmanship is high.

However, the overall message from estate agents is clear – you cannot rely on any improvement increasing the value of your home by more than the improvement cost to carry out, and the prime purpose of all your improvements should be to create the sort of house you want to live in. And, if you want a house that will be easy to sell don't make your improvements too individual.

**Two examples**

For the two example houses some common improvements are illustrated with an idea, for these specific examples assumed to be in the S.E of England, of the *cost* (based on the national averages above) and the *possible value* of each improvement. These examples are intended only to give food for thought – the exact figures will not apply to other types of house.

The example *values* assume that the house is sold immediately after, or at least fairly soon after, the improvements have been made. If a number of years elapse it becomes difficult to separate the value attributable to the improvements from the total.

For a major project it might be worth paying for a professional's valuation.

**Four-bedroom detached house, with double garage. Built in the 1970's. Open plan garden; rear garden 50ft deep.**

**Situation** On an estate of 50 or 60 detached houses of similar type. Smallish garden front and back.

**Assumed value** £65,000

| Cavity wall insulation | |
|---|---|
| cost | £500 |
| value | nil |
| recoup | nil but will save on fuel bills |

The big scare of 1982 put some people off cavity wall insulation and this could affect how quickly the house sells.

| Ground floor flat roof extension behind garage to provide utility room (area 6m²) | |
|---|---|
| cost | £2,400 |
| value | possibly up by £2,000 |
| recoup | 85% |

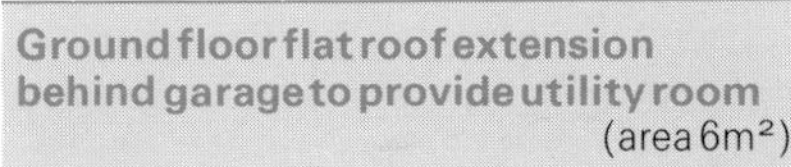

| Sun-lounge to rear (central heating not extended into this room – therefore no winter use) (area 15m²) | |
|---|---|
| cost | £3,300 [1] |
| value | possibly up by £500 |
| recoup | 15% |

[1] based on average 1983 cost of £220m²

| Replacement windows | |
|---|---|
| cost | around £3,000 in aluminium or pvc |
| value | possibly up by £1,000. |
| recoup | 35% |

The possible increase in value will apply if most of the neighbouring houses have already had this done, if the house is the only one to be improved in this way the increase may be less significant.

| First floor extension to side over garage and new utility room (foundations are good for load) to provide new main bedroom and en-suite bathroom (area 20m²) | |
|---|---|
| cost | £5,500 |
| value | possibly up by £10,000 |
| recoup | 240% |

This house is perhaps now a little top heavy with too many bedrooms for the available living space

| Conservatory in glass and aluminium to rear (area 15m²) | |
|---|---|
| cost | £1,500 |
| value | possibly up by £1,000 |
| recoup | 65% |

| Convert integral garage to new room (area 15m²) | |
|---|---|
| cost | £2,000 |
| value | possibly up by £2,500 |
| recoup | 80% |

# Raising the money

Home improvements are the sort of expenditure for which you will probably consider a loan of some sort. As the interest you pay on loans to buy or improve your home will qualify for tax relief, it usually makes sound financial sense to borrow at least some of the cost. Tax relief is restricted to loans, rather than overdrafts, not exceeding £30,000 – if you borrow more, you pay the full interest on the extra.

Some homes are also eligible for grants made by the local authority from a pool of money supplied by the government.

## Loans

If your employer gives cheap loans, this may well be the best form of borrowing for a home improvement. If you're buying your home on a mortgage, you could ask if your building society, bank or other lender will consider adding to your loan.

Borrowing from an insurance company (if you have a policy with a cash-in value) may also be cheap. And all the High-Street banks now offer home improvement loans.

The cheapest loan for home improvements is normally an increased mortgage. The lender will want details of what you intend to do with plans, quotations and so on. Make sure you ask for all the money you need – for example, builders' estimates won't include the cost of redecorations you intend to do yourself, but you might want to include these in the loan. The lender may want to revalue your house and will probably lend only enough to bring your total mortgage up to a certain percentage – typically around 80 per cent of the predicted house value once it is improved. As your house will generally be worth more than when you bought it this means they may allow a loan of 100 per cent of the improvement costs. There'll usually be some costs for the valuation and possibly for the lender's solicitor's fee to redraw the mortgage and make any necessary registration. *Which?* readers have found that lenders don't discriminate against d-i-y schemes, but won't pay till the work is finished.

### Tax relief

For the purposes of income tax relief on the interest of any loan, improvements must be permanent alterations, so ordinary repairs and decoration don't count, but extensions and conversions are obviously eligible, as are new fitted units in your kitchen and restoring a dilapidated house or converting it to flats. Installing central heating counts for tax relief but portable heating and night storage heaters don't. Tax relief is also available on interest on loans for landscaping your garden or improving the road outside your house.

## Grants

Grants for home improvements fall into two categories: *mandatory grants* which the local authority has to grant provided you can meet certain conditions and *discretionary grants* which they can withhold if they choose – if they've run out of money for instance.

### Mandatory grants

There is only one mandatory grant. It is called an *intermediate grant* and is given to help meet the cost of putting 'standard amenities' into a house which is without them. The standard amenities are an inside WC, bath (or shower), kitchen sink, wash hand-basin and running hot and cold water to all of these where necessary. The grant can also cover costs of repairs carried out at the same time. The grant is intended for basic improvements and associated repair and the council have the right to insist that the completed work will leave your house fit for human habitation. However, provided you qualify, you have a right to the grant even if you don't want to put in all the standard amenities and you can apply for another grant later if you want.

### Discretionary grants

Local authorities vary in what they'll give discretionary grants for – so check early on what your council's attitude is. There are three types – improvement grants, repair grants and special grants.

**Improvement grants** are made for a wide range of improvements to a house, or to help convert a house into flats, and for repairs you do at the same time. The house or flat must have been built or converted before 1961. You may be able to get an improvement grant for:

- putting in a damp-proof course
- installing electric power points, or rewiring if the present wiring is unsafe
- repointing
- making the front door water-tight
- taking out a fireplace or chimney breast.

There are many other alterations which may be eligible (ask at your local authority offices for details). Improvement grants are not normally available for central heating (unless it forms part of a major scheme of improvement) or for enlarging the home simply to get more bedrooms.

The repairs part of the grant can't usually be more than 50 per cent of the total grant, but this is increased to 70 per cent if the repairs are substantial and structural. The grant may be made in stages against a schedule of works agreed with the local authority.

**Repair grants** are for pre-1919 homes which need substantial and structural repairs (eg major works to the roof, walls, floors or foundations). Routine maintenance does not qualify.

**Special grants** are for putting 'standard amenities' (eg WC, bath, kitchen sink, running hot and cold water) into homes shared by more than one family, or for providing a means of escape from fire for such houses. Special grants are not available in Scotland or Northern Ireland.

### Conditions for getting a grant

Conditions vary with the different grants – but generally you must certify that you own the home (freehold or on a lease with at least five years to run), that you or a member of your family live in the home (or you rent it out). Tenants can also apply for grants (though not for special grants) – they may need to get permission from the landlord before they start work on the home. The home must come up to a certain standard (varies with the grant) after the work has been done, *and you mustn't start work without getting your grant application approved.* For improvement and repair grants, the rateable value of your house must be below certain limits (£400 in Greater London, £225 elsewhere) unless the grant is for work to help a disabled person or you live in a housing action area.

### Housing action areas

These are residential zones which have been declared special areas. If you live in such an area, the rateable value limits for houses are lifted and your house is a priority case which is eligible for a higher grant.

### General improvement areas

These are also areas identified for special attention. The local authority itself will aim to improve its own property and will actively encourage other property owners in the area to do the same. Again your house will be eligible for a higher grant.

### Other grants

You may also be able to get a grant towards the cost of:

- insulating your loft and lagging water tanks and pipes (all of which must be done). You qualify for this only if your loft is presently uninsulated.
- repairs to a building of architectural or historic interest.

For all grants, remember you shouldn't start work until the grant has been approved – and that can take some time. Information is contained in Department of Environment leaflet *Home Improvement Grants* (available at Citizens' Advice Bureaux, consumer advice centres or council offices).

### Grants for the disabled

If existing standard amenities are inaccessible to someone disabled in the home, you are entitled to an intermediate grant (whatever the house's rateable value) to put extra ones in – for example an extra WC on the ground floor. You may also be able to get an improvement grant to help with other adaptations needed to the house – for example a lift or wider doorways for a wheelchair; you may also be able to get rate relief.

These grants can be available even for handicapped people who are not registered as disabled – an elderly person crippled with arthritis may qualify, for example.

For details check with your local authority.

### Grant procedure

Grants are agreed in advance against estimates for the work that the grant is intended to help with. Remember this may be more than you originally wanted to do, because the council can insist that other things are done as a condition of the grant. Make sure that you are aware in detail of all the work the council wants done and have a grant to cover it all. Professionals' fees should also be covered. The money is normally paid when the work is completed. You can do the work yourself or employ a builder. The council won't pay until they are satisfied that the work has been carried out properly. D-i-y labour is unlikely to be included as an eligible expense.

## HOW MUCH GRANT?

The size of the grant you can get depends on how much of the work is eligible for grant aid. The cost of this work is called the *eligible expense.* In most cases, you get 50 per cent of the eligible expense, but for priority cases – homes which are unfit, lacking standard amenities or in need of substantial and structural repair or for homes in housing action areas – you can get up to 75 per cent. Higher limits may also apply in cases of hardship – up to 65 per cent and 90 per cent respectively. If the home is in a general improvement area, you can get up to 65 per cent of the eligible expense. These percentages can be changed: in 1982 the percentages for all repair grants and intermediate grants were raised to 90 per cent; they are due to revert to the percentages given here on March 1st 1984.

There are upper limits to the eligible expense on which each grant is worked out. For example (in April 1983):

- improvement grants – percentage paid on eligible expense up to £13,800 for a priority home in Greater London, £10,200 for such a home elsewhere. For non-priority homes, the limits are £9,000 and £6,600 respectively
- repair grants – percentage paid on eligible expense up to £6,600 in Greater London, £4,800 elsewhere
- intermediate grants – percentage paid on eligible expense up to a total of £3,000 in Greater London, £2,280 elsewhere if all standard amenities are required; plus £4,200 in Greater London, £3,000 elsewhere for associated repair work. There's a maximum eligible expense for each amenity.

# Who needs to know?

A surprisingly large number of people should be informed before you embark on any building project in your home. The local authority has to know because it administers the Building Regulations and the Town & Country Planning Acts – the main rules governing the building, alteration and use of houses. The lender of the money you used to buy your property should usually be informed, as should the house building and house contents insurers. It may also be necessary to tell one or more of the service authorities – electricity, gas or water – what you're doing. And if you're worried about how it might affect your rates you can get in touch with the Inland Revenue Valuation Office (the local authority will do this anyway if you apply for planning permission or Building Regulations approval).

## Planning authority

The Town and Country Planning Act of 1971 requires planning permission to be obtained for most types of development. For planning permission purposes, development is considered as:

- *building work* – such as a house extension or garage
- *change in use* – such as dividing a house into flats, starting to run a business from a house or changing a shop to an office or a dwelling
- *other work* such as a hard-standing for a car or putting up a fence or wall.

Except in certain cases, work which affects only the inside of a building, such as knocking two rooms into one, is not considered as development. Neither is work which does not materially affect the external appearance of a building, such as repointing brickwork and general repairs and maintenance. Work that affects the look of the building may be controlled.

### Permitted development

Some work is classified as 'permitted development' and can be carried out without planning permission, provided the work meets certain conditions on size and location.

The enlargement of a house by an extension is permitted as long as the total addition to the original house is not more than 70 cubic metres or 15 per cent of the volume of the original house (up to a maximum of 115 cubic metres) whichever is the greater – for a terraced house 50 cubic metres or 10 per cent. (For Scotland see page 26.) The volume of the original house is calculated from the external measurements of the house (including the roof) as it stood on 1st July 1948 or as originally built, if it was built after that. The enlargement must not be higher than the highest part of the roof of the original house and no part of the enlarged building within two metres of any site boundary should be higher than four metres. Also no part of the enlargement should project beyond the existing building line on any side of the house which faces a road and the area of the ground covered by buildings (other than the original) should not exceed 50 per cent of the available ground. These rules also apply to the construction of a detached garage within five metres of a house.

If a proposed enlargement falls outside any of these conditions, planning permission must be obtained before work starts. If the enlargement will be occupied as a separate dwelling, planning permission is also required, even if it meets permitted development conditions.

Loft conversions are often permitted development in England and Wales, since usually the only addition to the volume of the house is a dormer window. In Scotland these always need permission.

Small buildings such as garden sheds and greenhouses are permitted as long as they are not more than four metres high with a ridged roof (two sloping sides) or three metres high with a non-ridged roof. In addition, they must not project beyond the front of the house or in total cover more than half of the grounds.

Porches also come within permitted development provided the floor area of the porch is not more than two square metres; no part is higher than three metres above ground level; and no part is less than two metres from any boundary between the garden and a road or public footpath.

Planning permission may be required for central heating oil storage tanks, gates, fences and walls, hardstanding for cars and access roads or paths if they exceed their permitted development size and location.

If the proposed work will be near a road junction or intersection and likely to obscure a motorist's view, planning permission should be sought even if the work comes within the permitted development limit. The Department of the Environment leaflet – *Planning Permission: A Guide for Householders*, available free from your local planning department gives further details on all these points.

The local authority can serve an **enforcement notice** if work is carried out which exceeds the permitted development limit without planning permission, or if work carried out is not in accordance with the approved plans. The enforcement notice can require you to return the building to its original state.

### Making your application

Normally, to apply for planning permission you need to fill in four copies of the application form available from the planning department of your local authority. A professional adviser can make the application on your behalf.

WHICH ALTERATIONS NEED PERMISSION OR APPROVAL?

**Garages** within 5m of the house can be permitted development but planning permission may be needed for new access to a garage.

Building Regulations approval is required though detached garages of less than 30 sq m are exempt from some regulations.

**Loft conversions** are generally permitted development limit but planning permission may be required for dormer windows (this is always so in Scotland).
Building Regulations approval is always required.

**Porches** not more than 3m high, less than 2 sq m in area and 2m from the boundary between the garden and road (or public footpath) do not need planning permission in England and Wales. All other porches do and front porches need permission in Scotland. Building Regulations approval is always required in Inner London and in Scotland, but a porch less than 2m in area which has no complications with nearby windows, ventilation, flues or drains is exempt in England and Wales.

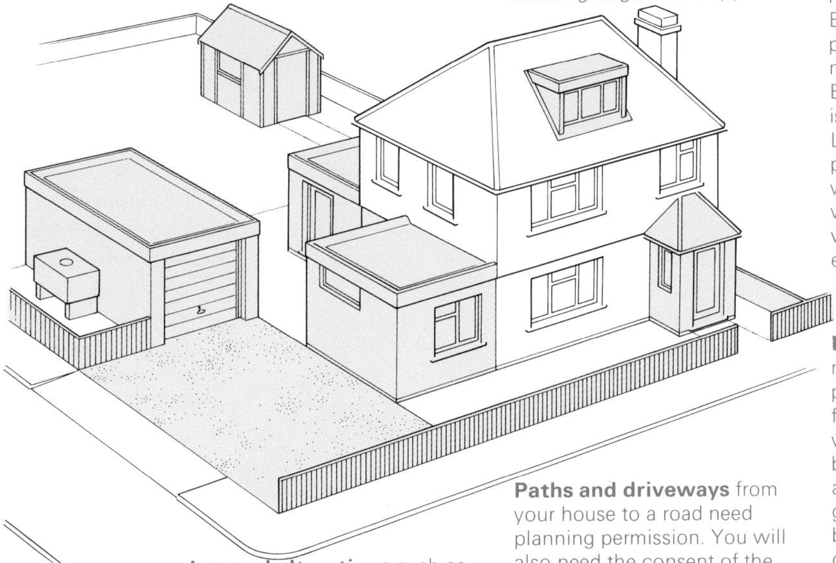

**Fences and garden walls** do not need planning permission provided that no part of the fence or wall is higher than 1m where it runs along the boundary between a house and a road. In other parts of the garden, the fence or wall may be up to 2m high as long as it does not obscure a motorist's view from a road. There may be other planning restrictions on fences and walls affecting your house – the original granting of planning permission on an open plan estate, for example. The Building Regulations do not cover fences and garden walls.

**Extensions** can be permitted development if the increased volume is within limits. Extensions forward of the building line need planning permission.

**Internal alterations** such as knocking two rooms into one or converting a bedroom into a bathroom do not require planning permission unless you are converting a house into flats.
Building Regulations approval is usually required.

**Paths and driveways** from your house to a road need planning permission. You will also need the consent of the Highways Authority if the path or driveway needs to cross a pavement or footpath along the road.
Building Regulations do not cover paths and driveways, but there are regulations on for example the protection of drains beneath a drive.

The appropriate fee – usually £22 – should accompany your application.

If you do not know whether you need to apply, or are unsure of any details, a preliminary discussion with the planning authority can be helpful. Some authorities issue guidance notes.

### Your local authority's reply

When you have made your application, the local authority will consider things like how well the proposed work will fit in with the surrounding style of architecture. They will then send you a decision notice of approval or rejection, usually within five to eight weeks of applying. The approval is then valid for five years. If the application is rejected, the local authority should give their reasons for refusal and, if accepted, they may impose certain conditions such as using materials which match the existing building so that the overall external appearance is preserved.

If you consider that the refusal or conditions imposed are unreasonable, you can appeal to the Department of the Environment (or Welsh Office if you live in Wales) within six months of receiving the decision notice. An appeal can also be made if the local authority fails to give a decision notice in time (usually two months). Further information is available from the Department of the Environment booklet called *Planning Appeals: A Guide to Procedure*.

### Other problems

The planning permission obtained when the house was originally built may restrict development such as putting up fences and walls on an open-plan housing estate.

A building registered as being of special architectural or historical interest will need *listed building consent* from the local authority for *all* work.

In some areas – Conservation Areas for example – the local authority will limit the types of development that can be carried out by serving an *Article 4 direction* on the owners and occupiers of affected buildings. In this case, planning permission may be needed for fairly small works, even though the work would normally be allowed as permitted development.

## Building control

Building control is a statutory function of the local authority who employ Building Control Officers to administer and enforce the Building Regulations. Building Control may form a separate department within a local authority but is more usually part of the Planning Department or Technical Services Department. The Building Regulations apply to England and Wales.

In Inner London the London Building Act and the London Building (Constructional) By-laws operate. In Scotland (and N Ireland) there are different Building Regulations. The regulations are to protect public health and safety by assuring minimum standards for the construction and alterations of buildings or certain works and fittings. Most buildings are covered, but there are exemptions and partial exemptions for some types of building.

At present the regulations are written in legal language and are not easy for the layman to understand. There are however plans afoot for changes which will hopefully make regulations easier to comprehend. Copies of the 1976 regulations and the 1978, 1981 and 1982 amendments can be consulted in local authority offices or in many public libraries. They can be bought from HMSO. There are also many guides to the regulations which aim to explain the complexities. However none of these is really much clearer to a layman.

Building Regulations approval should be sought from the local authority before starting any building work (including the installation of fittings such as WCs), structural alterations or extensions to existing buildings or before making a material change in use of a building or part of a building. A material change in use can be work like converting a barn into a house, a house into flats or an integral garage into a living room. To obtain Building Regulations approval, notice of intention to build and drawings have to be submitted to the local authority before work starts.

### What the regulations say

Some of the regulations lay down specific requirements or standards. Others allow some degree of flexibility by demanding a particular performance requirement or standard and then give a 'deemed-to-satisfy' method of construction which, if followed, will meet the standard required. Other methods of construction or materials may however be used to suit particular circumstances, provided they meet the performance standard and are approved by the Building Control Officer. Certain materials and methods of construction could be deemed to satisfy the Building Regulations if they conform to a British Standard or to a British Standard Code of Practice.

When planning an extension or removing a wall to enlarge a room, the relevant parts of the Building Regulations have to be taken into account. The regulations can affect the design, size, siting and materials of construction. The regulations are more severe in the case of habitable rooms such as bedrooms and living rooms.

General repairs and maintenance do not need Building Regulations approval as long as no structural work is involved.

### Relaxations

Some of the regulations may be relaxed by permission. The local authority have the discretion to relax any regulation except those that deal with fire precautions. There are official relaxations – called type relaxations – these can deal with the fire regulations (see page 290 for the inference for loft conversions).

### Making your application

To avoid possible delays when applying, and to clarify whether approval is required or not, a preliminary discussion with the Building Control Officer (District Surveyor in Inner London) can be advantageous. You should make an appointment by telephone as Building Control Officers are often out on site inspecting building work – they are most often to be found at their desks before 9.30am and after 4.00pm.

Two copies of the formal notice of an intention to carry out work which is controlled by the Building Regulations along with two copies of the drawings need to be deposited with the local authority for approval. They can be deposited on your behalf by an architect or builder. The actual number, type and scale of drawings varies with the type of job. Applications have to be accompanied by the relevant plan fee. Some authorities issue *guidance notes* on what is required, though the Building Control Officer will advise. The drawings should preferably use metric measurements as all the various Building Regulations now do.

### Fees

A plan fee and an inspection fee are chargeable on applications. If you're eligible for a home improvement or intermediate grant, you can normally recoup a percentage of the fee.

The fees are payable in two stages: the plan fees on application for approval of the building plans and the inspection fee following the first inspection of works on the site.

If the local authority fails to approve or reject the application within the prescribed time limit (five weeks, unless an extended limit has been agreed), the fee will be refunded although a site inspection charge will still be payable. Should the application be rejected and re-submitted with amendments at a later date, a second application charge will not be made, provided it is essentially the same project.

If the local authority chooses not to inspect, the inspection fee will not be charged.

The fees for England and Wales (but not Inner London) are set out in the Building (Prescribed Fees) 1982. In this document the fees are fixed according to the type of work. In January 1983 for an extension up to 20 square metres the plan fee was £6, and the inspection fee £18. For extensions over 20 square metres, and loft con-

## INNER LONDON

Inner London means the area which was under the control of the London County Council before the GLC was formed in 1965. Planning in London is controlled by the main Act which applies in England and Wales, but for historical reasons, building in the Inner London area is subject to the London Building Acts and the London Building (Constructional) Bye-laws 1972 to 1979 apply. These are laid out quite differently from the other Building Regulations and published by the GLC instead of HMSO. Many of the regulations are similar to those in other parts of the UK.

London building law is different in a number of ways, not least in that approval is not required before work starts. Instead the *builder* must serve notice on the district surveyor (DS) at least two days before work begins and the DS will respond (by formal notice) only if the proposals are unacceptable. In order to avoid possible delay at the time when you want to start work, it makes sense to send particulars to the DS in advance of the mandatory two days' notice.

Fees in London are on a fixed scale related to the cost of the work. The builder must inform the DS of the cost of the work and pay the relevant fee within 14 days of completing the work. The fee for work costing £4,500 was £56.50 in January 1983.

Any construction work which affects an adjoining building or its land is subject to a unique law outlining the rights and obligation of the building owners. This law makes it clear that a building owner has the right to carry out work on an existing party wall or fence which is on the boundary line between properties. When a building owner has the intention of doing any such work he must give notice to the owner of the adjoining building. For a party structure (eg the dividing wall between two semi-detached houses) two months' notice is required, for a boundary fence or wall one month is required. If the adjoining owner disputes the notice or does not give consent within 14 days, the matter then has to be settled by building surveyors representing the owners. This can be one agreed surveyor or two independent surveyors each representing one of the owners. Where each owner appoints his own surveyor, the two surveyors appoint a third surveyor as an adjudicator in case they do not agree.

If the boundary line is not built over and a building owner wishes to build there, he must give notice to the owner of the adjoining land and may only build if the adjoining owner consents. If consent is not given, the owner who has proposed the building can build only on his own ground, but provided he gives notice he may place footings below the surface of the adjoining land.

versions but not more than 40 square metres, the plan fee was £12 and the inspection fee £36. For porches between two and four square metres in area the plan fee was £3, the inspection fee £9. Fees for work to existing houses not in any of these categories are read from a Table which sets the fees against 70 per cent of the building costs, for instance the plan fee for work costing £4,500 is £11; the inspection fee is £33 – see above for Inner London, over the page for Scotland.

### Your local authority's reply

The local authority must approve or reject your plans within five weeks unless the time is extended (usually by an extra three weeks) by written agreement. When there is doubt as to what is intended on the application form or drawings, the applicant can be asked to clarify the proposals. When the Building Control Officer is satisfied that the work will not contravene the regulations if carried out following the plans and specification, he will recommend approval and a notice of approval will be sent to the applicant.

The local authority may provide a set of postcards to send to the Building Control Officer as notification for inspection at certain stages of the work as required in the regulations – 24 hours' notice before covering foundation excavations, foundations, a damp-proof course (dpc), any material laid over site, and drains or private sewers, and before completion of the work. If these notifications are not made the local authority can require you to cut into or pull down any work to see whether the regulations have been contravened. If the local authority does not issue cards it is still your responsibility to give the required notice.

Where work is carried out contrary to the regulations, the local authority can serve notice on the building owner requiring the work to be removed or altered. If this is not carried out, the local authority can alter the work themselves and charge the owner the cost. Notice to alter or remove contravening work can only be served within 12 months of completing the work.

If the proposed work would involve building over or diverting an existing public sewer, consent must also be obtained from the local authority (they may have plans of the drains and sewers of your property). The Building Regulations deal only with the removal of waste, soil and surface water from a house. Where proposed work will involve the plumbing system of a house, the work must conform to the water authority's bye-laws.

## SCOTLAND

The Town & Country Planning (Scotland) Act 1972 with its amendments, including the General Development (Scotland) Order 1981, regulate town planning in Scotland. Most of the rules are similar to England & Wales, but in Scotland it is the applicant's responsibility to serve a notice on his neighbours.

Extensions under permitted development can be up to 50 cubic metres or one fifth of the volume of the original house or 115 cubic metres whichever is the greater. Extensions to terraced houses 50 cubic metres, one tenth of the volume or 115 cubic metres. Appeals should be made to the Secretary of State for Scotland.

Building Control is regulated by the Building Standards (Scotland) Regulations 1981. One of the biggest differences between these and the regulations in England & Wales is that the Scottish regulations include rules for electrical installations which are based on the IEE Regulations as in England – see page 49.

In Scotland the local authority's approval is called a Building Warrant. Fees for warrants are based on the estimated cost of the operations and should accompany the application. For a project costing £4,500 the fee was £38 in January 1983.

Work can proceed when a warrant has been issued (normally within fourteen days), but notice is required in writing of the date on which work is started; when drains are to be laid or when they are to be back filled and the work is completed. Within 14 days of completion if the work is satisfactory the authority will issue a certificate.

## Lender

The mortgage of a property often restricts any modifications without the consent of the lender. So it is sensible to write early on to inform the lender of your intention to add to or to modify the mortgaged property. You should provide some detail of your plans, but a letter is generally sufficient and it is not usually necessary to provide drawings.

There is a second reason why you might want to contact the lender. He is likely to hold the title deeds to the house and it is possible that these deeds include restrictive covenants which prohibit or limit some types of work – for instance conversion of a house into flats, the building of walls or fences on open land, or the installation of an aerial or other other structure above the roofline. There may be easements regarding neighbours' drainage, gas or electricity supply, pipes and so on.

## Insurance companies

There are various reasons for telling your insurance company what you are doing to your house – it's worth informing both the house building insurer and the house contents insurer if you have separate policies. First an extension or major improvement will increase the cost of rebuilding the house if it is destroyed or damaged, and so it is usually necessary to increase the sum insured. Second, if any accidental damage – such as breaking the WC bowl while trying to refit the bath – is caused to your property during building, you may want to claim against your policy. Failure to notify the company in advance of the work could invalidate your claim in the company's eyes.

Finally many building projects involve creating temporary access to the house making it vulnerable to intruders as well as to excesses of weather. It is your responsibility to take all precautions to preclude both burglaries and weather penetration, but if something goes wrong you may want to make a claim and giving the insurer prior notice of the activity may help to convince him that you have been diligent over your responsibilities. One or two policies specifically exclude damage during the building period and, with these it would be worthwhile taking out special insurance.

## Neighbours

If your building project requires planning permission, it is usually the planning authorities' practice to contact your neighbours about any proposed development, but you may be asked to serve an official notice on your neighbours. During the time the authority considers your application it may take the opportunity to contact your neighbours either directly by post or by publishing a list of recent applications.

However it's worth talking to your neighbours yourself whatever work you're doing and whether or not the local authority makes contact. For simple jobs, you may just want to warn them that you will be making some noise or that your front garden will be turned into an unsightly builder's yard for some weeks.

For more extensive jobs it's worth talking over your plans in some detail, especially if your project is likely to be unpopular. Early friendly consultation where you take notice of your neighbour's point of view can help to avoid problems when the building work commences.

## Service authorities

Your intention to carry out any work on an electricity, gas or water supply should be notified to the appropriate service authority who may then have the right to inspect the work. In practice few householders bother to give such notice and the authorities rarely enforce it – see Chapter 2.

## Rating authority

Although it is your local authority who collects the rates, rating assessments are made by Valuation Officers employed by the Inland Revenue. You can find the address of the Valuation Officer by asking your local authority, by looking in the Telephone Directory (under *Inland Revenue*) or at a main post office. If you tell the Valuation Officer (VO) what you intend to do to your house he should be able to tell you how it will affect your rating assessment when complete.

Your rating assessment will be increased if the improvements (plus any other or previous improvements not already assessed) increase the *gross value* by more than £30. Gross values are higher than the rateable value on which the rates are actually levied and if, as is likely, you don't know what your gross value is you can find out from the *Valuation List*, a copy of which you can see where you pay your rates. Note that even if the improvements are not included immediately they will be included in your assessment when all gross values are updated.

As well as affecting your rates, a change in rating assessment will also effect the amount of water rates.

FORMS

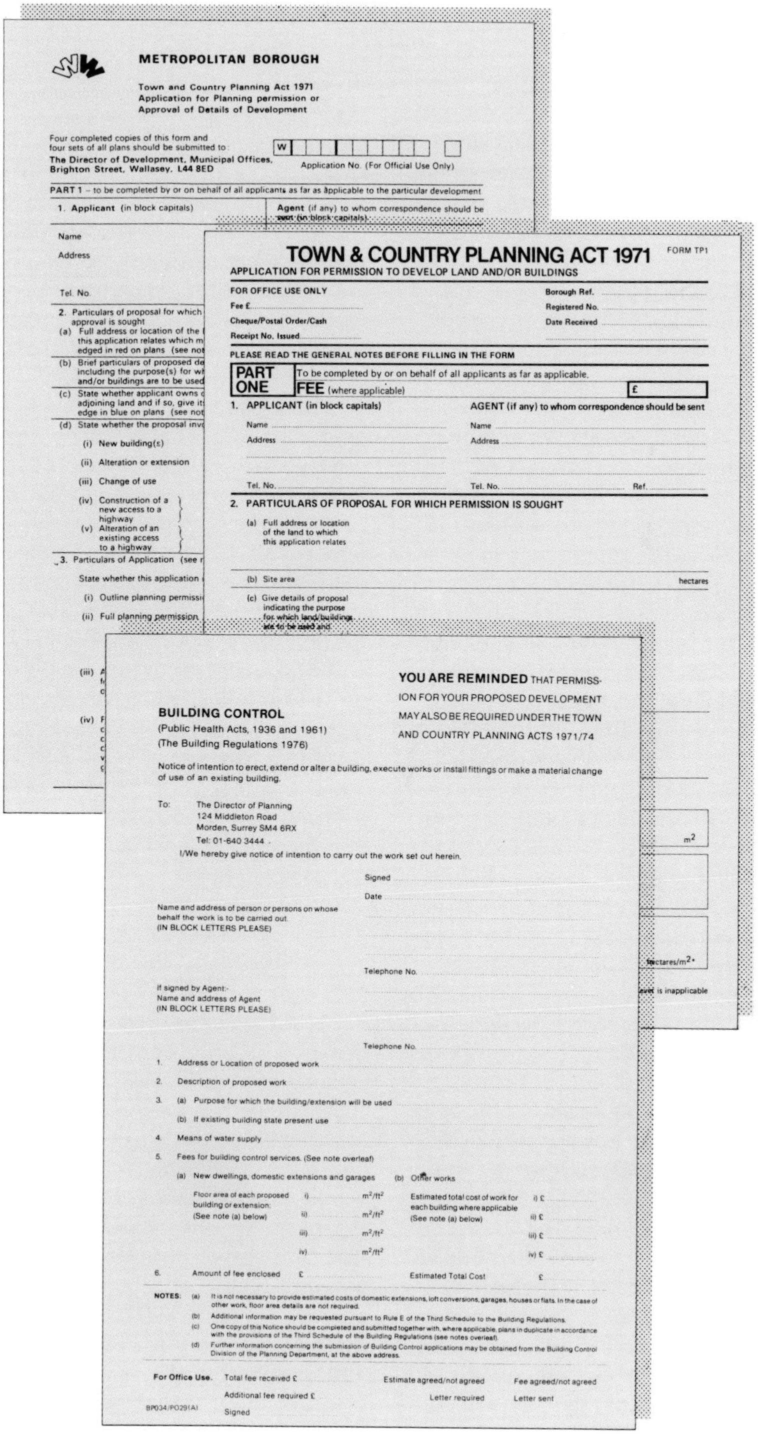

METROPOLITAN BOROUGH

Town and Country Planning Act 1971
Application for Planning permission or
Approval of Details of Development

Four completed copies of this form and four sets of all plans should be submitted to:
The Director of Development, Municipal Offices, Brighton Street, Wallasey. L44 8ED

W

Application No. (For Official Use Only)

PART 1 – to be completed by or on behalf of all applicants as far as applicable to the particular development

1. Applicant (in block capitals)
Agent (if any) to whom correspondence should be sent (in block capitals)

Name
Address
Tel. No.

2. Particulars of proposal for which approval is sought
(a) Full address or location of the land to which this application relates which must be edged in red on plans (see notes)
(b) Brief particulars of proposed development including the purpose(s) for which the land and/or buildings are to be used
(c) State whether applicant owns or controls any adjoining land and if so, give its location and edge in blue on plans (see notes)
(d) State whether the proposal involves:
(i) New building(s)
(ii) Alteration or extension
(iii) Change of use
(iv) Construction of a new access to a highway
(v) Alteration of an existing access to a highway

3. Particulars of Application (see notes)
State whether this application is for:
(i) Outline planning permission
(ii) Full planning permission

TOWN & COUNTRY PLANNING ACT 1971 — FORM TP1

APPLICATION FOR PERMISSION TO DEVELOP LAND AND/OR BUILDINGS

FOR OFFICE USE ONLY
Fee £
Cheque/Postal Order/Cash
Receipt No. Issued
Borough Ref.
Registered No.
Date Received

PLEASE READ THE GENERAL NOTES BEFORE FILLING IN THE FORM

PART ONE — To be completed by or on behalf of all applicants as far as applicable.
FEE (where applicable) £

1. APPLICANT (in block capitals)
AGENT (if any) to whom correspondence should be sent
Name
Address
Tel. No.
Ref.

2. PARTICULARS OF PROPOSAL FOR WHICH PERMISSION IS SOUGHT
(a) Full address or location of the land to which this application relates
(b) Site area — hectares
(c) Give details of proposal indicating the purpose for which land/buildings are to be used and

BUILDING CONTROL
(Public Health Acts, 1936 and 1961)
(The Building Regulations 1976)

YOU ARE REMINDED THAT PERMISSION FOR YOUR PROPOSED DEVELOPMENT MAY ALSO BE REQUIRED UNDER THE TOWN AND COUNTRY PLANNING ACTS 1971/74

Notice of intention to erect, extend or alter a building, execute works or install fittings or make a material change of use of an existing building.

To: The Director of Planning
124 Middleton Road
Morden, Surrey SM4 6RX
Tel: 01-640 3444

I/We hereby give notice of intention to carry out the work set out herein.

Signed
Date

Name and address of person or persons on whose behalf the work is to be carried out
(IN BLOCK LETTERS PLEASE)

Telephone No.

If signed by Agent:-
Name and address of Agent
(IN BLOCK LETTERS PLEASE)

Telephone No.

1. Address or Location of proposed work
2. Description of proposed work
3. (a) Purpose for which the building/extension will be used
(b) If existing building state present use
4. Means of water supply
5. Fees for building control services. (See note overleaf)
(a) New dwellings, domestic extensions and garages
(b) Other works

Floor area of each proposed building or extension: (See note (a) below) i) m²/ft² ii) m²/ft² iii) m²/ft² iv) m²/ft²

Estimated total cost of work for each building where applicable (See note (a) below) i) £ ii) £ iii) £ iv) £

6. Amount of fee enclosed £ — Estimated Total Cost £

NOTES: (a) It is not necessary to provide estimated costs of domestic extensions, loft conversions, garages, houses or flats. In the case of other work, floor area details are not required.
(b) Additional information may be requested pursuant to Rule E of the Third Schedule to the Building Regulations.
(c) One copy of this Notice should be completed and submitted together with, where applicable, plans in duplicate in accordance with the provisions of the Third Schedule of the Building Regulations (see notes overleaf).
(d) Further information concerning the submission of Building Control applications may be obtained from the Building Control Division of the Planning Department, at the above address.

For Office Use. Total fee received £ — Estimate agreed/not agreed — Fee agreed/not agreed
Additional fee required £ — Letter required — Letter sent
Signed

BP034/PO29(A)

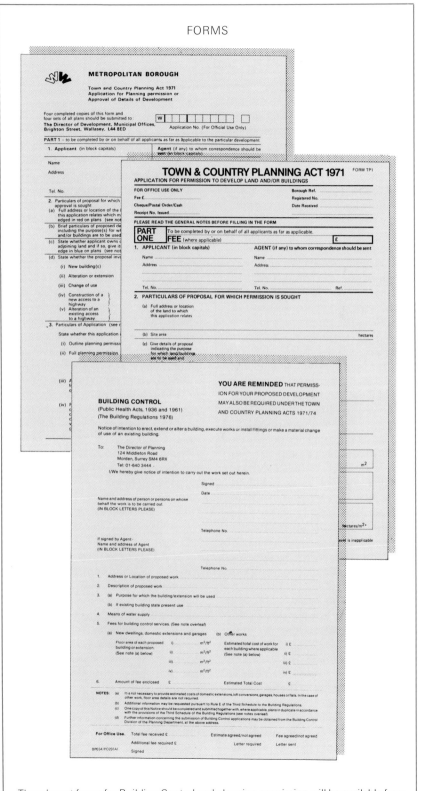

The relevant forms for Building Control and planning permission will be available from your town hall.

# Who'll do the work?

You can approach any improvement or building project in three different ways: you can leave it completely to the professionals and experts, you can do it all yourself or you can combine professional work and d-i-y.

**Employing professionals** usually means the job's done more quickly. If you've chosen your experts wisely, you have the reassurance that the job will be done competently and safely to the required standards and that if anything does go wrong you'll have some come-back. Lenders of loans for extensive or potentially difficult home improvements might be happier for work to be carried out by professionals. But employing professional help throughout a project is usually the most expensive choice and choosing the right people isn't easy.

The professionals you go to for advice and help with your project fall into two clear groups: those who plan, design and supervise and those that build and carry out the skilled or unskilled manual tasks. Finding a professional to suit your needs isn't always an easy task. Local knowledge and personal recommendations are always the best ways of finding the good firms, but if you're new to an area there are alternatives to sticking a pin in the telephone directory. Addresses for all the organisations mentioned on the following pages can be found on page 314. Even if you're fairly certain who you want to do the work, two or three (or even four) estimates should *always* be obtained, so that you can get some idea of the market price. All sorts of things can make a professional put in a high or low price for a job and, unless you check, you may pay two or three times as much as you need.

**Doing-it-yourself** means you save the labour costs and, if necessary, you can plan the work so that it proceeds in stages as and when you can afford the materials. It inevitably means that the job will take longer (usually longer than you estimate), but if you're competent, careful and patient, there's no reason why the work should be to a lower standard. In fact do-it-yourselfers often claim to be more conscientious than the average tradesman and cite this as one of the chief reasons for d-i-y.

A chief drawback of d-i-y is that you've no come-back against anyone if things go wrong, but this shouldn't be a serious problem if all your d-i-y projects are carefully planned and undertaken. Often the worst that can happen is that you spend extra time learning about and solving problems. All the improvements in this book are within the capabilities of a competent do-it-yourselfer who has the time, confidence and inclination. Some of the illustrations for the guides in this book are based on photographs of projects *Which?* readers have carried out themselves with a minimum of professional help.

If you're ever in any doubt about a d-i-y project the best thing to do is to get some advice. For any structural jobs – an extension, a loft conversion or knocking down an internal wall, for instance – some professional advice is essential, at least at the design stage. It costs a small proportion of the total to pay someone like an architect or a building surveyor to draw up a set of detailed plans and to calculate all the design loads, timber sizes and so on, that are involved. Building Regulations approval is a further safeguard.

Responsibility for designing is the minimum level of professional help you should involve in a project, but it's possible to hive off any other parts of the job that you don't feel capable of doing, don't have time to do, or simply don't like doing. One of the commonest combinations is to employ a professional designer and a builder to carry out any structural work, but to add the services and decorations inside and out yourself.

When you employ a tradesman to do a particular job – bricklaying, for instance – you can often save money by preparing the site properly for him. But don't expect any tradesman to welcome your help on site as an amateur labourer.

**Gaining d-i-y skills**
Books such as this, its sister volume the *Which? Book of Do-it-yourself* and many other do-it-yourself manuals contain valuable advice. For larger projects, books intended for building or architectural students are often helpful on the details of construction if not the techniques. Practical classes in basic skills are often run in the evenings by adult education centres. The City and Guilds Institute have recently begun summer courses for do-it-yourselfers. Video is the latest innovation – the moving pictures can be frozen to capture details.

Helping friends or more experienced do-it-yourselfers on their projects will give you useful experience as well as earning favours in return. If you have the nerve to ask, amenable builders and tradesmen on local sites may demonstrate small constructional details – you obviously can't expect basic tuition. Observing working methods from a discreet distance can also be helpful – noting where and how a bricklayer stacks his bricks, for instance.

Manufacturers of building materials, tools and equipment publish a wealth of literature which is often free and frequently very useful – the Building Centres are a good source. The various trade research and information associations provide helpful advice – much of it free – the Cement and Concrete Association booklets are especially good.

## WHICH? READERS' EXPERIENCES

In 1982, 3,241 *Which?* readers responded to a postal questionnaire about the extensions and conversions they'd made to their houses since 1980. These readers had been pre-selected from responses to a series of shorter questionnaires to a much larger random sample of readers, which asked whether they'd carried out such building work and would be willing to give more detail. Around seven per cent of the *Which?* readers surveyed had extended or converted part of their home; two-thirds of these completed the second questionnaire. Their collective experiences are illuminating.

### About the work done

■ Most extensions were cavity wall construction, but 1 in 5 of the single-storey extensions had solid walls. Bricks and blocks were used most often, but in 1 in 10 was timber frame.

■ The new rooms created were used for all sorts of purposes: downstairs, sunrooms, cloakrooms and utility rooms were most common; upstairs, most of the new rooms were fitted out as bathrooms or bedrooms or, in loft conversions, as playrooms.

■ 57 per cent of *Which?* readers' extensions have a flat roof.

■ The average time to completion was 15 weeks. Not surprisingly two-storey extensions took significantly longer – 26 weeks on average.

■ The average gestation time for an extension or conversion was 10 months.

■ The average area of a loft conversion in a semi-detached house (or bungalow) was 19·5 square metres; in a detached house (or bungalow) was 29 square metres.

■ An extension to a terraced house was typically 14 square metres in area; to a semi – 18·5 square metres; to a detached house – 23 square metres.

■ For single-storey ground-floor extensions, small building firms were quicker than larger building firms – 11 weeks on average compared to 15; d-i-y was significantly slower – 28 weeks on average – and took longer still if professional help was engaged for some parts of the job. For two-storey extensions or ones above the ground larger firms were slightly quicker – 18 or 19 weeks on average compared with 21 – d-i-y took getting on for a year.

■ Loft conversions took on average 34 weeks as d-i-y projects but mixing d-i-y with professional helped to speed things up. A typical conversion took 10 to 11 weeks if a specialist firm or building firm did the work.

■ Getting Building Regulations approval took six weeks on average; getting planning permission took six and a half weeks on average. Single-storey extensions usually got through both departments fastest; two-storey extensions and loft conversions generally took a week or so longer.

### Cost and value

■ Single-storey extensions cost on average £300 a square metre. Extensions to detached houses were usually larger and worked out cheaper on a square metre breakdown.

■ Loft conversions cost on average £280 a square metre. Conversions to detached bungalows were cheaper – perhaps this is because the job is closer to the ground and the staircase is easier to organise. D-i-y conversions cost around £100 a square metre.

■ Nearly all the *Which?* readers expected their extension or conversion to make their house easier to sell.

■ About half the *Which?* readers expected to recoup the whole cost of the building work (or more) if they sold their house.

■ Around 9 out of 10 *Which?* readers thought they'd got good (or very good) value for money. They were best pleased with the value of the d-i-y projects, slightly less pleased than average with work done by specialist extension firms.

■ Not surprisingly one/two men building firms were the cheapest for single-storey extensions. These were also the firms with whom the readers were least likely to make a written contract, probably because one wasn't offered by the builder.

### Some things to learn from

■ 1 in 3 *Which?* readers who employed a builder asked only one firm to cost the job. But when readers got several quotes the highest quote was typically half as much again as the lowest quote – a difference of about £2,250, on average.

■ 37 per cent of the *Which?* readers would do something different if they could do the job again – nearly half the people who had two-storey extensions said they'd do something different.

■ 4 out of 10 *Which?* readers asked the designer to alter the drawings he first submitted. It took on average five weeks to get agreed drawings. These changes were most likely to be made because the customer had changed his mind or because the designer has got it wrong. One in eight of the plans had to be altered to match cash limits.

■ Around half the work was done without a written contract between the householder and the builder.

■ 1 in 3 *Which?* readers had a complaint about somebody involved in the building project. This was most likely to be the builder (especially specialist firms) but the list included architects, surveyors, BCO's, planning officers and independently sub-contracted labour. As is usual with all types of home improvement work most complaints were about poor quality work, slow work (or delays) or about work incorrectly done or not done according to the drawings or instructions. Five per cent of the complaints were about damage to the property and a further five per cent involved remedial work.

### Some encouraging facts

■ 1 in 5 *Which?* readers successfully drew up their own plans for their single storey extension.

■ 2 out of 3 of the drawings submitted for Building Regulations approval were accepted as first submitted; 3 out of 4 planning permission applications were accepted first time.

■ 68 per cent of the *Which?* readers who applied for grant aid were successful.

■ 1 in 6 extensions were d-i-y with help from friends and relatives, most were single-storey.

# People who design

Architects, building surveyors and consultants offer a range of services – from the first discussion and designs, to the preparation of the necessary documents and drawings, getting approval from the various authorities, obtaining quotations and arranging contracts with builders, supervising work (to a greater or less degree) and authorising payments. You can make use of all these services, or seek professional advice at selected stages only.

To assess whether an architect, surveyor or consultant is likely to be satisfactory for your particular project, make an appointment to discuss in general the extension scheme you have in mind. Some charge a small fee for a discussion of this sort, others allow a short free period, say half an hour, of preliminary advice.

Ask to see drawings which have recently been prepared for a similar project. Ask when he last submitted drawings for such a project to the relevant local authority and whether the drawings were approved at first submission.

At this stage, any expert you approach should be able to give you a very rough idea of the approximate cost of the scheme, including an idea of his fee for the part you want him to play.

## Architects

The title of 'architect' may be used only by a person who is a registered architect. Anyone calling himself an architect has to be registered with the Architects' Registration Council of the United Kingdom and must have specific academic qualifications. Many architects are members of the Royal Insitute of British Architects (RIBA).

Some local authorities keep in their offices a list of local architects for the public to consult, and registered architects in private practice are listed in Yellow Pages. The RIBA central clients' bureau in London and RIBA regional offices will recommend architects in the area who would be suitable to carry out particular projects. Local architects may pass you to another local practice if they can't or don't want the work.

Architects are not allowed by their code of professional conduct to advertise or solicit work. What they can do is to put up a display board with their name at their office and at any site where they are undertaking work. There is no such restriction on individuals who are not registered architects, and architectural consultants generally advertise in local newspapers. In directories they may be listed under 'building consultants' or 'design consultants'.

The fees charged by members of the RIBA are determined by the extent of the services provided and are usually a percentage of the total cost (which cannot be known until the work is complete). The RIBA publishes a scale of charges to which at one time all its members had to adhere as a minimum. Now the fee can be negotiated between architect and client and the RIBA scales are merely a recommended guide.

The RIBA percentage fee scales start at a total building cost of £20,000. For work costing less than that – as most have extensions will – RIBA say an appropriate fee should be agreed between client and architect. For a full basic service which includes advising on alternative possibilities, preparing drawings for specific instructions, submitting the necessary information for approval to the local authority, drawing up specifications or other particulars required for obtaining tenders, preparing a contract, advising on the engagements of a builder and specialist consultants if required, preparing a timetable, supervising the work, issuing certificates for payment and generally seeing the job right through – you could reckon to pay around 12 per cent of the total building cost. Of course you may not need the architect to undertake all of this for your particular scheme and the percentage fee should be less for less involvement. Preliminary services – such as advising on the feasibility of a scheme – would normally be charged on a time basis.

An architect's fee is often exclusive of the cost of prints and other reproductions of drawings and documents needed for submission to authorities, and of travelling and other expenses. A separate charge may be made for these. Separate fees are charged for designs for special fittings, garden layouts and similar extras.

Other services not included in the percentage fee may be preparing any additional special drawings or handling any exceptional negotiations that may arise from an application for approval. An architect should be able to tell you in advance what he will charge for any of these services.

An architect is entitled to charge for amending drawings if you change your instructions so it is important that you give good directions at the outset. Note too that an architect's fee is charged in respect of any work included in the original drawings, even work which is subsequently not carried out.

If you keep the cost of the extension down by providing some of the materials or carrying out some of the building work yourself, you may still be expected to pay a fee based on what the work would have cost if the builder had carried it all out. So if the cost would have been £1,500 and you have reduced this to £1,200 by providing the bricks (from an old outhouse that you have knocked down, for instance), the architect may charge his percentage on the £1,500. Sort these things out before starting.

## Building surveyors

A building surveyor can be asked to perform a similar role to an architect – designing, preparing drawings, submitting applications, supervising the builder – according to your requirements. To be sure of approaching the right kind of surveyor (there are several kinds of surveyor and some are not qualified in design and building work), you can write to the Royal Institution of Chartered Surveyors (RICS), the Chartered Institute of Building, or to the Incorporated Association of Architects and Surveyors and ask for names of members of the Building Surveyors' Division in your area.

The basic charges of building surveyors are similar to those of architects. Details for Chartered Surveyors are available in a booklet *Conditions of engagement for Building Surveying Services* sold by the RICS. In June 1982 the recommended scale fees for a Building Surveyor's involvement in a project involving building work in an existing building was 13 per cent for a project costing up to £2,500; 12.5 per cent (with a minimum charge of £325) for a project costing between £2,500 and £8,000. You should ask during your initial discussion how much the surveyor would charge for the work you want him to do.

Building surveyors are perhaps better known for their role as consultants when a structural survey is required to establish the condition of an existing house. There are no recommended scale fees for this sort of work but most surveyors will quote over the telephone on hearing a description of the size and age of the property.

There are two types of survey – a full structural survey, which is a detailed technical inspection of the house including where possible, an under-floor inspection and close inspection of the roof face, and a limited scope and therefore cheaper survey – known as the *House Buyers Report and Valuation*. See also page 40.

The Incorporated Association of Architects and Surveyors issues a booklet, which a member of the public can buy from the IAAS, setting out the terms of employment and minimum charges for their building surveyor members. Members of the IAAS also offer a limited scope type of survey.

## Consultants

There are also firms and individuals who carry out work similar to that of registered architects but who are not registered and are therefore prohibited from describing themselves as architects. These individuals carry on business under titles such as architectural consultant, building design consultant or architectural surveyor. They are not forced to adhere to any professional codes or conditions. No criterion for their degree of competence is laid down; their work could be very good or useless.

Many of these people advertise in the local press. Sometimes they are Building lecturers working freelance in their spare time. There are also architectural technicians who normally provide a technical back-up service in architects' offices, but may work freelance.

Fees charged by individuals who are not members of one of the professional bodies are not controlled in any way. They are often considerably less than the RIBA scale fees for similar services. Check whether the individual has professional indemnity insurance.

## Building control officers

(BCO) – including Inner London District Surveyors.

Although they're not in your employ, most offices that administer the Building Regulations (see page 24) have an active policy of assisting do-it-yourselfers and householders as far as is practicably possible. *Which?* readers have generally found them constructive and provided you don't overdo the questioning they are a good source of advice on local building practice and how to interpret and meet the Building Regulations. A BCO may be willing to tell you if an idea for building is feasible for your house. He may do this by a quick inspection or, if your house is post-war construction, he may be able to refer to plans kept in his office. Once plans are approved and building work starts the BCO will visit the site to inspect at certain pre-set stages although he is not obliged to inspect.

## Packages

Apart from all the independent experts you can employ, there are firms who specialise in one type of improvement, extension or conversion and offer a complete design and build service.

One advantage is that you have to deal with only one firm for everything, and, if anything goes wrong, they cannot shift the blame. Also for a special type of improvement you are dealing with a firm likely to have a lot of experience in that special field – a loft conversion for instance. The main disadvantage is that you are putting all your eggs into one basket, you have no independent professional adviser and the builder is virtually drawing up his own instructions.

The price quoted for a package covers everything involved in the job. Because this includes design work and because the firm is quoting a price before it has detailed drawings or specifications to go on, the quotation may be higher than one submitted by an ordinary builder for carrying out the construction work only.

Package firms often have detailed contract forms and before committing yourself you should read any form of contract very carefully, especially the small print. Some contracts absolve the firm from responsibility for any alterations to the original plan, and consequent additional expense, that may become necessary once work has started. This condition could apply even if the alteration were due to a deficiency in the drawings which the firm itself had prepared, or to any miscalculation in design or specifications. If a contract appears too one-sided, you should insist that counter-conditions are incorporated.

# People who build

On major projects builders and other tradesmen usually work to drawings and schedules drawn up by somebody else. These form the *builder's brief* on which he bases his costs, estimates, his materials and so on.

## Builders

The names of local builders can be found in directories and local advertisements and on sign boards. Regional branches of the National Federation of Building Trades Employers and regional offices of the Federation of Master Builders (FMB) can be asked for the names of local builders who might be suitable for extension projects. The FMB have a small register of member builders who are in their Warranty Scheme which provides extra insurance for the client. The National Home Enlargement Bureau's (NHEB) register of Bonded Builders is another scheme intended to help the consumer find good builders. The customer has the option to make his contract the subject of a Contract Completion Guarantee – backed by insurance. The scheme was introduced in late 1982 so it's too early to say how helpful it will be.

Local professionals – including architects, surveyors, consultants and building control officers – should know about the competence and expertise of local building firms. Before engaging a builder ensure that he is familiar with and capable of carrying out the type of scheme envisaged: ask whether he has recently carried out any similar scheme, and where you can see some of his work.

It is wise to approach prospective firms well in advance of the time when you would like work to be started: six months' notice is not excessive.

A builder calculates the approximate cost by multiplying either the net floor area or the net cubic content of the new structure by a rate per square or cubic metre. The rate varies considerably, depending on all sorts of factors. A more precise costing is achieved when the quantities are priced accurately and labour costs are calculated at known rates.

You should allow the builders about a month to send their quotes to you. You will receive either an estimate or a quotation. An *estimate* is a guide to the price that will be charged when the job is finished – it may turn out to be more or less. A *quotation* is a price which the builder offers to do the work for. It may be a fixed price or subject to fluctuations in the cost of labour and materials. In either case there may also be provision for variation due to unforeseen problems.

For very large jobs, it is a good idea to have a list called a Bill of Quantities. This list sets out each stage of the work and may include entries like: building a blockwork wall, plastering, supplying and fitting a bath and so on. Some items may be marked as *prime cost*. Usually, this is an approximate price set aside to cover the cost of special items; when you have eventually decided on which special item (a bath, for instance) you want, you will be charged the actual price (which will probably include the builder's profit). Make sure you know who is buying these special items – you do not want the builder turning up expecting you to have bought the bath ready for him to install when you thought he was buying it.

### Start and finish dates

If you want all the work done within a certain time, ask the builder for a time schedule stating when the work will start and finish. But be wary: jobs often take longer than builder's estimate and if you change your mind or otherwise hamper the builder's progress he'll have a good excuse for not completing on time. Find out from the builder how much of the work is going to be sub-contracted. Delays can often be caused by plasterers or electricians not turning up on time for instance. With jobs which involve lots of different trades, you might be better off using a firm of builders who can carry out most of the work themselves. Always have a written contract – see page 312 for the clauses it should contain.

## Electricians

Electrical contractors are listed on the roll of the National Inspection Council for Electrical Installation Contracting (NICEIC); they may also be members of the Electrical Contractors' Association (ECA). These contractors are qualified (and required) to work to the IEE Wiring Regulations. You can get a list of local NICEIC contractors from your public library, Citizens Advice Bureau or Electricity Board Showroom – the Electricity Boards are themselves affiliated to the NICEIC. Or you could look under electrical contractors in local directories.

With most improvements and alterations you probably have a clear idea of exactly what needs doing and can give the person you employ a specific brief. Electrical work isn't always like that. Even if you think you just want a new socket-outlet installed, an electrician may find that there's a lot more to do on your wiring than that and if he's competent he should refuse to add to or alter an existing system that's at all suspect. So before you employ an electrician to do any alterations to your electricity circuits it's best to have an inspection made.

In the past *Which?* has found that the Electricity Board often does the most thorough (but also the most expensive) inspections. In practice of course you could expect an electrician to quote for the new work and any remedial work on the basis of the one wiring inspection.

## Plumbers

There's no shortage of plumbing firms advertising in local newspapers and shop windows or with entries in local directories. The problem is choosing one that will give you good service at reasonable cost. There are various sources of information that may help you. The Institute of Plumbing (IP) is the professional body of the industry with over 5,000 registered plumbers on their books and will supply a list of those in your area. These have satisfied the Institute with their qualifications and experience that they are competent plumbers. Some firms use the IP symbol in their advertisements and you can check whether a plumber is registered by asking to see his pocket certificate.

The *Business directory of registered plumbers* should be available at a public library or the office of your local water authority. You can contact the National Association of Plumbing, Heating and Mechanical Services Contractors, or the Scottish and Northern Ireland Plumbing Employers' Federation, for a list of their members and the Federation of Master Builders has some members who are plumbers.

In a survey of *Which?* readers carried out some years ago, we found that, when looking for a professional plumber, most people turned to one they'd used before, or had a plumber recommended by a builder, a d-i-y or hardware shop, or by a friend. With plumbers getting three estimates is often quite difficult, but perhaps all the more necessary for that.

For a straightforward plumbing job, such as installing pipes and taps in a new extension, a quotation may be the better sort of costing to agree to. On the other hand, replacement plumbing or work in older buildings which might involve hidden problems may encourage plumbers to make higher quotations to allow for such difficulties – and you still have to pay the agreed price even if the job goes smoothly – so an estimate is probably better in these circumstances.

After the job is done, if you have any complaints about the standard of the work done (or if you think you have been grossly over-charged) by a member of the Institute of Plumbing or any of the trade associations; they will investigate your case.

If you've got a water leak which is wasting water, your local water authority may help with the repair. The work is usually done free of charge, but is likely to be limited to rewashering of taps and cold water storage cistern ball valves (not WC cisterns); and water authority plumbers won't come to council houses – if you're a council tenant, contact your local housing office about plumbing repairs.

## Gas fitters

CORGI – the Confederation for the Registration of Gas Installers – is governed by a National Council with representatives from British Gas and from building, plumbing and heating trade organisations. It provides a register of firms considered capable of performing installations or servicing in compliance with Gas Safety Regulations, relevant British Standard Codes of Practice and Building Regulations. (For a list of those on the register, ask at your local gas showroom, Citizens' Advice Bureau or public library.)

All work carried out by CORGI registered firms can be inspected at any time by CORGI inspectors, either as part of routine monitoring or as a result of a customer complaint. The work of every registered installer is examined at least once every year. Although using a CORGI firm cannot guarantee you good workmanship, it is a useful safeguard because of the registration and inspection requirements. And CORGI will deal with complaints about the work of installers on their register: they have a local office in each gas region.

Registration with CORGI is not compulsory for firms installing or repairing gas appliances, though by law gas installations must be made by a 'competent' person and must comply with the Gas Safety Regulations and the relevant building regulations.

## Other tradesmen

A small building company will often subcontract part of the work to specialist tradesmen, and there's nothing to stop you doing this direct if you can find tradesmen who are interested. For these sort of people local knowledge may be not only your best, but your only source. As well as the main trades of plumbing and electrical work, trades like joinery, bricklaying and plastering can be contracted out. *Which?* readers who've done it have usually been successful, but it's an unorthodox way of building which carries an element of risk. Ask for a fixed price based on your designer's drawings and make sure the price includes everything on the drawings – it's worth putting a clause in your agreement to this effect. Always get an agreement in writing. A letter simply confirming your verbal agreement is all that is required.

## Replacement window installers

It's often the builder who installs the windows in a new building as it goes up. Replacement window installers are another group, normally engaged to remove and replace the windows in an existing house. They are usually suppliers of double-glazed windows in aluminium or plastic. Within this trade, there are a number of household names who have a large share of the market as well as numerous local firms – who tend to be cheaper and may also do the job sooner.

When you engage one of these firms to carry out the work for you, there'll be no question about a written contract, but it will be on the installer's terms and you should read his standard form very carefully before committing yourself and handing over a hefty deposit. Window installers rarely undertake to do any building work in connection with window replacement, if you want any opening decreased or enlarged you'll normally have to have a builder in and in that situation it's worth considering whether you'd be better off using a builder for the whole job. In the past *Which?* readers have been less often disappointed by window installations carried out by local builders.

## Deposits and stage payments

Your agreement with any firm or individual carrying out work on your behalf will inevitably include a clause on the method of payment. Most people will want some sort of interim payment. This may be in the form of a large deposit or a stage payment when part of the work is complete, with the balance on completion.

Firms who are contracted to provide made-to-measure components – such as a prefabricated extension or replacement windows – will usually want a deposit as a condition of the sale. They claim the deposit covers the cost of the materials and fabrication. A deposit is a sign of your good faith and means that the firm doesn't lose out if you rescind your agreement, but if there are long delivery dates as there often are with replacement windows for instance, it means that the firm has use of your money for some time before they begin work on your order, and in the meantime you lose the interest, and risk losing the deposit altogether if the firm goes out of business. A few 'rare' firms operate a bonding scheme for deposits which seems fairer; if a deposit is unavoidable you could try suggesting to other firms that any deposit is held in independent hands until it is needed.

A builder or tradesman may also ask for an initial payment to buy materials. It's generally considered unwise to agree to this (because a reliable builder will be considered credit worthy by local merchants), but it is acceptable to pay in stages for work that has been completed. Stage payments are best based on an agreed percentage of the total cost. Whatever the arrangement it should be clearly stated in the contract.

LOOK OUT FOR THESE SYMBOLS

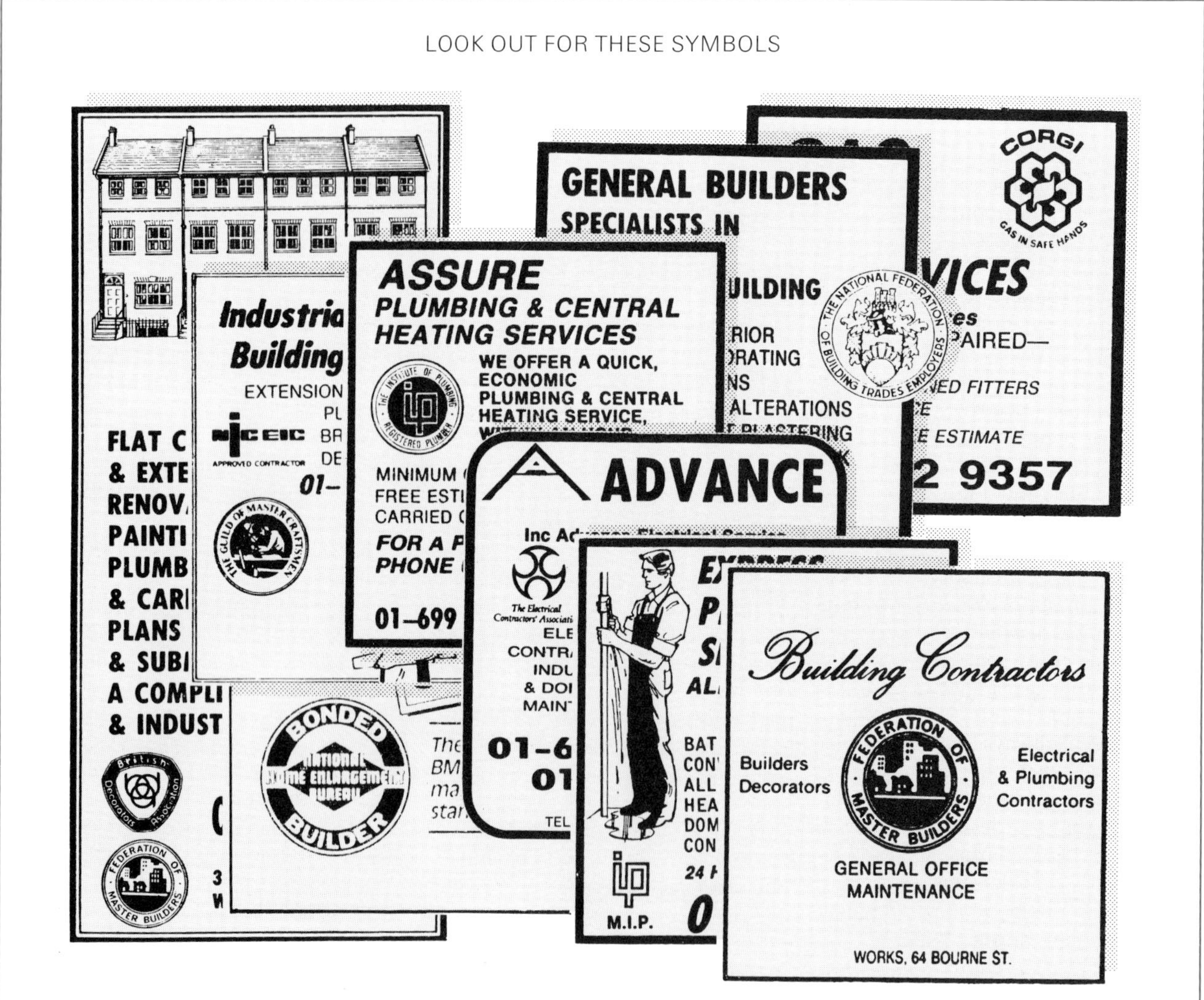

# Obtaining materials and equipment

If you employ a builder or other tradesman to do the work, most of the building materials will be provided as part of the contract price. Builders are able to claim back the VAT on materials used for 'alterations' (see page 38) and can usually buy at trade prices so even if, as is likely, a builder makes some profit on the materials it's probably cheapest to buy basic materials through him. For d-i-y projects, the way to buy cheap is to look and behave like a builder, to shop at places a builder would go and to know what you are talking about when you ask for materials. Under the current tax laws, you won't be able to claim back the VAT unless you're building an entire house.

## Places to shop

Apart from small quantities of things and Saturday afternoon panic buys, which you might as well get at the nearest d-i-y shop, the cheapest places to shop are generally large d-i-y superstores with building material departments and builders' merchants.

### Large d-i-y superstores

These are a relatively new development. The best stock most items that you would need including a range of building supplies that you wouldn't normally find except at a builders' merchant or specialist shop – bricks, aggregates, plasterboard and flooring-grade chipboard, for example. Some have a glass cutting service. Timber may be sold shrink-wrapped in bundles.

You nearly always have to serve yourself: the staff may not be very knowledgeable. Some larger stores have information desks and some have information charts, or sell their own leaflets or booklets fairly cheaply.

### Builders' merchants

These may be a warehouse, or a yard, or something resembling a shop, and you may find building supplies stacked without prices and without any indication as to what they are – you have to ask. A builders' merchant may be the only place in your immediate area to buy bricks or plasterboard, or the more unusual items connected with building – concrete additives, for example. The size of the merchant, and the choice and range of items available, vary enormously. The larger ones have showrooms where they sell 'clean' items like baths and central heating equipment.

Although builders' merchants are principally suppliers to the trade, many are trying to encourage the d-i-y public to use them so they'll welcome your custom. If you're buying large quantities or collecting goods yourself from a builders' merchant, it's usually worth asking for a discount – though some shops won't give discounts on principle to customers who ask. You may be able to open an account, and get trade discount that way.

The people who serve you in builders' merchants can be very knowledgeable about building, and able to answer fairly technical questions. However, they are used to dealing with the trade and you will be able to make better use of their time – and your own – if you have a grasp of the basics.

There are three things you must look out for when buying in a builders' merchant's or other specialist merchant's:

- whether the prices quoted include VAT – a few do, but the majority don't
- whether the prices include delivery – many builders' merchants quote two prices – one including delivery (or a delivery surcharge), and one for goods collected. In some cases, prices from the 'public' counter, or the high street branches, may be lower because they don't include delivery
- how you can pay – few builders' merchants accept credit cards and most are wary of accepting cheques for more than £50 unless they know you.

### Other places

There are a number of specialist suppliers for building materials:

- timber merchants
- quarries and pits
- ready-mixed concrete firms – see page 38
- plumbers' merchants
- concrete works
- brick works.

## Special materials

If you need or want an unusual building material – a special brick or roof tile, perhaps, to match your existing house – then you'll have to do some detective work. It's best if you do this yourself, since you're likely to be more tenacious than a builder. Manufacturers of things like roof tiles are aware of this matching problem and can be helpful when it comes to tracking down small stocks. The Brick Development Association who have displays at all the Building Centres (see page 314) are helpful when it comes to matching and finding bricks.

When making an enquiry for the purpose of matching it's best to produce a sample of the real thing – a brick cut away from a corner of the wall, a tile removed from the roof.

### Buying second-hand

Demolition contractors' yards, more elegantly called 'architectural salvage firms', are good sources of sound, recycled materials and sometimes the only source for 'sympathetic' or matching materials for older houses. But note that second-hand materials may not always meet the requirements of the Building Regulations. You also need to allow for wastage.

## GETTING MATERIALS AND EQUIPMENT HOME

If you're buying a large quantity of building materials, you can have problems getting it home.

Some d-i-y shops will loan or hire you a roof rack – or you may be able to hire a trailer. However you carry it, you must make sure that your load is safe and that you are within the law. You are required to load your car (or van) so that it doesn't interfere with your driving – and this includes driving in emergencies. So, for example, you must make sure that if you had to stop quickly, the load would stay put – you need to be particularly careful when transporting sheets of chipboard or plasterboard for this reason. Ensure that you haven't overloaded your car's suspension so that it doesn't function properly – the maximum load should be in your car driver's manual. Many building materials are very heavy – for example, bricks weigh about 2½kg each, so 100 bricks weigh as much as three sturdy people. Don't forget to pump up the tyres, and load the car evenly. The lights and the number plates must not be obscured, and you should have one usable rear-view mirror.

If your load projects beyond the car, it's a good idea to mark the overhanging parts clearly – you're obliged to by law if they project more than 1.83m beyond the front or 1.07m to the rear (you must have another person in the car if the load projects more than 1.83m to the front). Use a special triangle at the front or rear if over 1.83m, which must be illuminated at night. If you want to carry a load which will project any further than 3.05m to the rear, you must give prior notice to the police.

Most suppliers of building materials offer a delivery service. The way shops charge for delivery varies a great deal and some shops might be open to negotiation.

- no charge, but you may have to wait until the delivery van or lorry is in your area, or you may have to spend a minimum amount
- a fixed charge, provided you're within a reasonable distance
- a charge which varies according to how much is being delivered and/or what distance the delivery vehicle has to travel. This sort of charge can be applied in a number of ways. You can be charged a basic price plus a handling charge per quantity of whatever it is you want delivered
- you can be charged one of two prices for the same item, depending on whether it's delivered or collected, and this may be in addition to other delivery charges
- you may be charged for unloading, or for moving the goods from the roadside to where you want them (private driveways are not usually constructed to bear the weight of a lorry) or, at least, be expected to help the driver do these things. You may have to accept some items – such as aggregates – delivered to the kerbside.

### Insurance

There are some points to watch with regard to your car insurance policy:

- you can collect things for friends, but any form of payment will invalidate the usual insurance policy for private cars (returning a favour would not be a problem, but if a friend bought you some petrol it might be regarded as payment)
- if you knowingly overload your car, and this then contributes to an accident, you may find your claim is turned down
- you should inform your insurance company if you're using your car for transporting building materials in the course of business.

### Hiring a van

If you hire a van for this purpose it's sensible to check the insurance and courtesy to tell the owner what you intend to use the van for. Remember that a van may be considerably taller than the vehicle that you are used to driving.

---

If you're considering second-hand materials, it's worth looking for:

- **bricks** – you can expect to pay half to two-thirds of the new cost – but they are a good source for small quantities (1,000 or less) or special bricks. Treat bricks that aren't clean with some circumspection: check that any residue will clean off easily – cement-based mortars don't
- **timber** – especially beams, floorboards, staircases, doors and window frames. Old timbers will be seasoned, so should not warp when used. Avoid timbers that show any signs of rot or insect damage and treat with preservative, if necessary woodworm fluid, before installing.

  Superficial damage to the surface of planed wood can usually be sanded out. Rough sawn structural timbers can be planed and sanded if you intend to expose them, but working the timber like this may then cause it to move in use
- **rolled steel joists** – these deteriorate very little, any rust is usually superficial
- **roofing materials** – slates are usually available for about half the new price. Old clay tiles may occasionally be found but are expensive.

Consider also radiators, quarry tiles, fireplaces, ironmongery, stained glass windows, mirrors, Victorian or Edwardian sanitary ware. Even old taps can be salvaged – there are firms who will rechrome them for you.

## Hardcore

Good hardcore is composed of material which is free from large lumps, rubbish (especially plaster, timber, plastics and metal) and chemical contamination. Hoggin (clayey gravel) is suitable and is obtainable from sand and gravel suppliers or builders' merchants in many parts of the country. If hoggin is unobtainable, crushed stone is a good substitute. *True* hardcore – clean, well-broken concrete – is also an excellent sub-base material but is almost impossible to get: what is now usually advertised and sold as 'hardcore' is actually unsorted 'as-is' builder's rubble and is unsuitable except as fill material. Avoid clinker, which is likely to contain sulphates.

## Hiring equipment

A large and ambitious project like an extension will usually need tools and equipment that you wouldn't normally use or have room to store and for these jobs hiring is one answer. You can hire almost anything – even a bucket. Any job is easier with the right tools and it's usually worth the saving in time and effort and the quality of the finished job to hire special tools for small jobs as well as the big ones when you couldn't cope without the proper equipment. The top ten list of hire items includes things like cement mixers and ladders. Some others worth considering are a carpet stretcher, pipe freezing kit, creosote spray unit, pipe bender, drain rods, steel props.

### Where to hire

Hire shops are listed under Hire Contractors in local directories and these days some d-i-y superstores have hire counters. Hire shops are usually helpful, if they don't have what you want, they'll often get it from somewhere else or recommend another shop. In past surveys *Which?* has found that hire rates in one shop could be as much as three times those in another so it's well worth shopping around. On the whole, larger companies with several branches have tended to be more expensive than average. Note: hire departments in superstores are often branches of larger companies.

EQUIPMENT YOU MIGHT HIRE

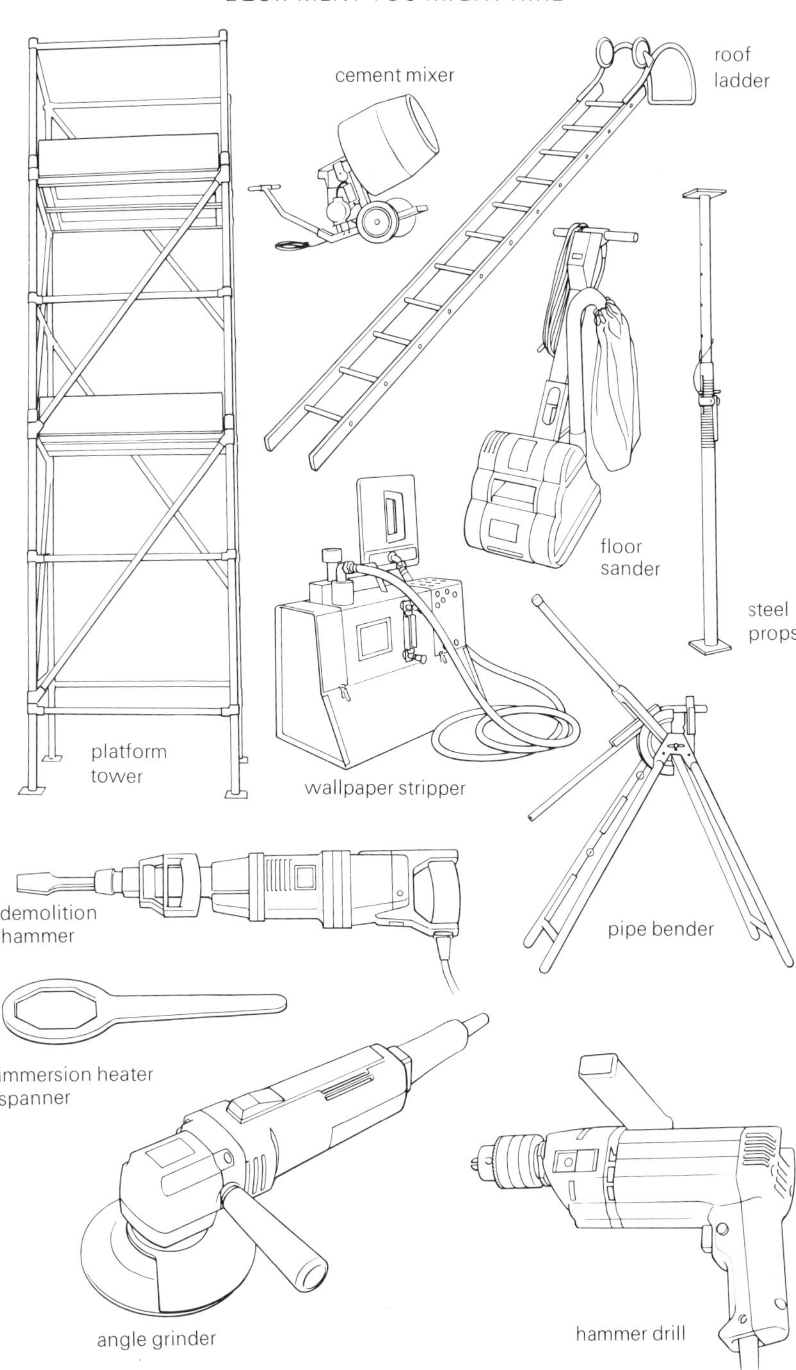


Almost anything can be hired. The proper tools and equipment make d-i-y much easier.

### Length of hire

The shortest hire can be from 4 hours – a morning, an afternoon, or overnight if you collect after 5pm – but some firms have an eight-hour minimum hire period; others a 24-hour minimum. Some larger pieces of equipment and some very small pieces are hired only on a weekly rate. It makes sense to plan your work efficiently around a piece of hired equipment.

**Deposits**
Most firms will ask for a largish deposit when you hire, this may be a cheque which they return when you return their equipment clean and undamaged. Sometimes they also want positive identification such as a driving licence. Some shops go as far as taking your photograph which they develop only if you don't return.

**An alternative to hiring**
With any large d-i-y project, the chances are that you will take longer over it than a professional would, and if you slot the work around your normal working day, it can take months (or years) rather than weeks. Hiring equipment for such extended periods would be very expensive and an alternative is to buy with the intention of selling later on. If you buy second-hand, it may even be possible to make a profit, or at least break even on the costs of the equipment. *Which?* members have done this successfully in the past with things like scaffolding and cement mixers.

## Ready-mixed concrete

For large amounts of concrete, ready-mixed is much easier than making your own and may well cost less than just the materials for mixing your own. You *should* also be able to depend on high and consistent quality. The minimum load is usually one cubic metre, most lorries carry about 6 cubic metres.

When phoning suppliers for prices you may find that the cost depends on how long the lorry has to stay on site – so discuss this with the firm, agree the time the lorry will stay and muster enough help to deal with the concrete in that time – you'll have four hours at most to lay and compact the whole load. Check with the supplier on how much notice they need for the firm delivery date and find out what arrangements they have for stopping the delivery if the weather is bad.

For small loads some firms now offer a mini-mix scheme, where the concrete is mixed on site in a special vehicle at a speed to suit you.

**Concrete mixes**
The strength and durability of concrete which has been properly mixed and laid depends to a large extent on its cement content: the richer the mix, the stronger and more durable it is. The three basic mixes which cover the majority of jobs are C7P, C20P and C30P. When ordering ready-mix, all you have to do with some depots is to quote the mix number – together with the type of cement (ordinary Portland), maximum aggregate size (normally 20mm), workability (high) and any special requirements.

Of the three basic mixes, you're most likely to use C20P, it's a good all-round mix, especially for ground slabs and floors and paths of 75mm or greater thickness. The *BS specification* (kg per cu m approx) for this mix is cement 300, fine aggregate 700, coarse aggregate 1170. Or if *batching by bucketful* 1 bucket loose cement, $1\frac{2}{3}$ buckets damp sand, $2\frac{2}{3}$ buckets coarse aggregate *or* 1 bucket cement, $3\frac{3}{4}$ buckets all-in aggregate. If possible, use separate aggregates. The *Yield per bag of cement* is approximately 170 litres; approximately 6 bags of cement per cubic metre of concrete.

**Estimating materials**
The yields given for C20P is for finished concrete. When calculating the volume of concrete required, remember that excavations for foundations, ground slabs and so on are rarely accurate, so err on the generous side.

For foundations and other fairly deep work, multiply width by depth by length to get the volume. Irregular areas can sometimes be dealt with by dividing into rectangles and triangles. Really irregular areas are best handled by sketching them out to scale.

### VALUE ADDED TAX

Whether VAT is payable on building work is uncertain following a series of legal decisions which cast doubt on the criteria adopted by the Customs & Excise. The following was the situation in early 1983, but it is worth checking with the Customs & Excise office. Don't take a builder's word, we've found they sometimes get it wrong.

**Zero-rated (no VAT to pay)**
Many services, materials and fittings used in building work are currently zero-rated for VAT purposes. There is no VAT to pay on the supply of services used in the cause of *construction, alteration or demolition of a building*, and if you have the work done for you there is no VAT to pay on the materials used in these cases. So if you have an extension or a conversion built, have two rooms knocked into one or have a bathroom built in an existing room – you don't have to pay VAT.

To qualify for zero-rating, the work must in its own right be an alteration to the existing building.

**VAT is due**
There is VAT to pay on any job which comes under *repair or maintenance* of a building and the *hire* of tools or equipment used in any building work.

Some work is neither alteration nor repair or maintenance and VAT is charged. This could be jobs like converting a fixed window into an opening window or bricking-in or unbricking a fireplace.

If you do the building work yourself, you have to pay VAT on the materials, and you *can't* claim it back.

## REMOVING RUBBLE

When a builder carries out work in your house, it should be part of his contract to remove the debris and leave everything neat and tidy. But if you do it yourself, or you've hung on to rubble intending to use it for hardcore for another job and then decide you don't want it after all, you'll have the bother and expense of getting rid of the debris yourself.

Before doing anything assess what your rubble consists of and roughly estimate how much you've got so that costs are realistically estimated. Then consider:

**Private contractors** A very convenient but possibly most costly way of disposing of rubbish. The contractor will provide the labour and means of removal. If the convenience suits you, its worth getting as many quotes as possible as they will vary. Many firms won't consider small jobs.

**Local authority service** Some local authorities will collect excess rubbish for an agreed fee, usually an inspector will come round to estimate how much it will cost. It is worth checking whether they will tackle hardcore and general rubble: some require it to be in bags.

**Free to collector** You may be able to give your rubble away. It's worth trying an advertisement offering hardcore free to collectors.

**Do-it-yourself** If you've got an old banger or other suitable vehicle, there's usually nothing to stop you carting rubbish off to the local authority refuse tip. There's normally no charge for taking smallish loads to a tip; large loads may be considered as trade, which tips don't officially accept. Refuse tips open early – about 7.30am and often close early too – few are open after 4.00pm; some shut at mid-day. Most are open at weekends.

**Hiring a skip** Skips are hired out by waste disposal service firms and by some local authorities. As the skip hirer's name and telephone number must be listed on the side of a skip, looking at skips other people have hired is one way to find a hirer. As well as the ordinary-sized skips there are mini-skips.

Think carefully about where you site a skip: if it's on the road other people may take advantage of it and it may be a long way to cart your rubbish; if it's on your own land the collecting truck might damage your trees or drain pipes.

If you're going to leave a skip on the road, there are legal requirements under section 31 of the Highways Act 1971. You need a permit from your local authority before you can park a skip and it is *your* responsibility to make sure its conditions are complied with. The conditions relate to the siting of your skip, its size, visibility, lighting and removal. Your local authority usually need 5 working days to issue a permit and notify the local police. Some hire firms won't take a firm booking without a permit number.

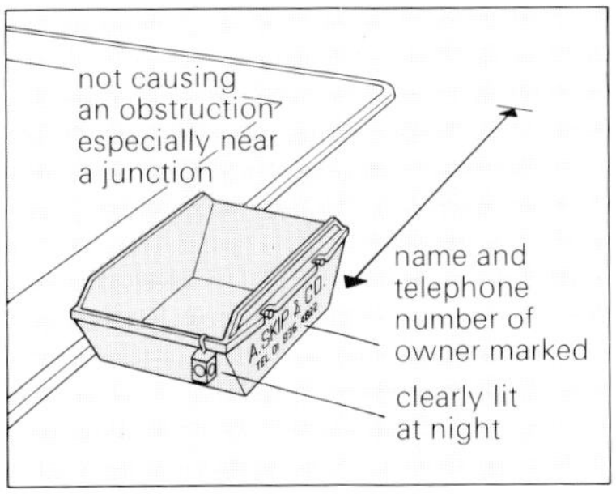

A skip in the road must be correctly parked and removed as soon as practicable. A permit is required.

Before deciding on a particular hire firm, make sure they fulfil your requirements. Check that they will supply lights. Make sure your skip is large enough for your requirements. Bits left over can be awkward to dispose of.

**Loading a skip**
When you've got your permit and your skip is booked to arrive on a particular day, get organised.

You'll need at least one wheelbarrow, a plank of wood for getting the load into the skip and shovels. Hiring these can add to the costs so try to borrow them. Old clothes and particularly protective gloves and shoes will save damage to hands and feet.

Chain gangs are quick and efficient – it's worth bartering your services with friends. If this isn't possible and you don't want to do the job alone, you might consider hiring one or two experienced labourers for half a day – try the local job centre.

Make sure access to the skip is clear and sort your pile into obvious types. Wood should be separated from hardcore for instance – if there are wooden doors you can use them to line the sides and they won't take up so much space.

Skip hire firms can provide advice on how much a skip will hold and how to load it properly. For example don't put loose rubbish on the bottom or you won't fit so much rubble in. Loads shouldn't come above the skip sides and need to be flat so they can be removed safely.

Work out a simple system with your team. For example, one (or two) filling the wheelbarrow, one runner and one dumper. Swap jobs to alleviate fatigue. For the quickest turn round, you need three wheelbarrows.

# Planning improvements

Deciding where to start work in a house which needs an overhaul isn't easy, especially if you have to live in the house while you're working on it and if, as is likely after moving, money is in short supply.

## Surveyor's report

If you've had a building survey done, you should know about the main problems of the new house. Among other things, the surveyor should have told you:

- whether there are any major structural faults – such as settlement or subsidence
- whether the roof is faulty
- whether there's wet rot, dry rot or woodworm in the structural timbers.
- whether there's a damp problem with a damp-proof course perhaps penetrating damp or condensation.

A surveyor will normally comment briefly on the electrical system, plumbing and central heating. He doesn't usually carry out a full examination of these and usually isn't qualified to, but if he finds something wrong with a part of the property on which he's not expert, he should advise a specialist survey.

## Further surveys

If the property you've bought was previously occupied and furnished, it's likely that the surveyor was hampered in his inspection. Once you're the owner, it's often possible to inspect more thoroughly and to find out more about how the house works. For instance the departing owner may have removed carpets, so you'll be able to get at (and under) floorboards that were previously covered up. You'll be able to run the heating (which is worth doing immediately even in summer) and, after living there a week or so, you'll discover any dodgy fittings.

Now's the time to sort out how all the services work: to find the stopcocks, to label the house fuses if they are not already, and to work out where the cables and pipes run – see Chapter 2. This is probably also the time to obtain further advice from experts, if necessary. Take advantage of free surveys and quotations offered by firms carrying out remedial damp and rot work; if you're doubtful about the wiring, pay to have it properly inspected.

**Priorities**
These are jobs that will deteriorate if left or that involve major upheaval, including lifting of floorboards and cutting into plaster.

**Damp-proof course** (dpc) – *seen as* peeling wallpaper or damp stains on downstairs walls, starting near skirting boards which may themselves be suffering from damp. There may also be a damp smell.
*work* – repair or install dpc, may involve lifting ground floor and stripping inside plaster up to 1m high. Could mean remaking a solid floor altogether.

**Penetrating damp** – *seen as* damp stains on inside walls, or soft loose mortar between bricks.
*work* – outer walls often need repointing, inside walls on both floors may need replastering and redecorating.

**Faulty roof** – *seen as* missing or broken tiles, bumpy top to flat roof, in bad cases damp stains on upstairs walls (inside or out) and ceilings. Flashings around chimneys may be defective.
*work* – replace or repair, roof covering and perhaps upstairs ceilings.

**Installing central heating**
*work* – plumbing, lifting floorboards, fitting, boxing and chasing pipes, fixing radiators.

**Old plumbing** – *seen as* old lead pipes which may have been repaired with copper. Tell-tale stains on ceiling or walls.
*work* – major replumbing, some floorboards have to be lifted, boxing in surface pipes and possibly chasing some.

**Woodworm (or beetle)** – *seen as* lots of tiny holes in timber; thrives in the same conditions as dry rot.
*work* – if timbers haven't weakened, affected areas can be treated. Floorboards will be lifted. If serious, structural timbers in the floors and roof may need replacing.

**Old wiring** – *seen as* old-fashioned round-pin sockets or fuse boxes; damaged sockets, lights and sockets that don't work or are loose on the wall; untidy wiring.
*work* – new wiring; some floorboards have to be lifted; for the neatest concealed wiring, plaster on walls may have to be chased to take cables and mounting boxes.

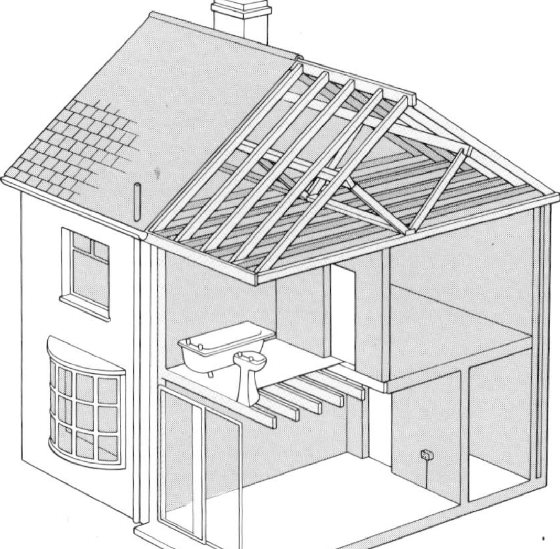

**Settlement, subsidence** – *seen as* cracks, which can be both inside and out, in the brickwork and plaster, particularly around window and door frames. Gaps between floor and skirting board. Doors that stick.
*work* – underpinning the foundations, probably refitting frames out of true, filling cracks in plaster and masonry, floors may need to be lifted.

## Where to start

Armed with all this information it should be possible to plan a sensible order of work. Obviously major structural faults come first, they will need immediate attention before there's any more deterioration.

Many of the priority jobs – see below – involve lifting floorboards and sometimes stripping plaster off the walls. While a property is in this state of upheaval, it's worth considering which of the other improvements that you intend to make will involve similar disruption to the floors and walls. Rewiring and installing central heating usually will. Work on the floor above can often have a jarring effect on the ceiling below so any ceiling repairs that might be needed should generally be delayed until the floorboards are back in place.

## Redecorating

In any practical order, redecorating is the last thing you should do in a new home, but you may decide that you need at least one habitable and presentable living room as well as use of bedrooms, bathroom and kitchen. Which rooms you choose to live in will depend on the work which needs doing. If you need a new damp-proof course and that's going to involve stripping off the plaster up to 1m high round all the ground-floor walls, then you'd probably do best to choose to live upstairs for a while. If it's the roof that needs attention you might vacate the upper floor.

D-i-y improvements usually have to fit around your normal daytime activities and therefore they often take longer than employing a tradesman. So if you do the work yourself, it's possible that you'll end up 'squatting' in your own house for a period of months, even years. In this case, if the existing decoration is dreadful, it can be worth brightening the rooms you're occupying with a cheerful coat of emulsion. Unless you're painting over a wallcovering which will be removed, buy a paint of reasonable quality or you could have problems with later decorations.

## Other considerations

Try to plan your improvements so that some rooms are finished sooner than others. Rewiring is the best example of a major task that can be tackled in stages. It's simple enough to plan your new circuits so that they can be installed in stages, completing one and getting it operational before you tackle the next.

It's also worth bearing in mind (and making provision for) improvements that you plan to do at a later date. For instance, if you plan a loft conversion, you might install the electricity cable up to the loft while rewiring the rest of the house. Or while installing central heating you might keep the pipes well away from a wall you intend to demolish later.

**Wet rot in wood** – *seen as* flaking paint and soft fibres which will break apart easily (test with something like a pen knife) – particularly floorboards, skirting boards and around door and window frames.
*work* – if not extensive, bits of timber can be treated or replaced, otherwise whole timbers or frames may need replacing and plastered walls making good around; floors can be affected in kitchens and bathrooms.

**Dry rot** – *seen as* dry, cracked, powdery wood and visible fungal growth. There is often a musty smell; thrives in damp, unventilated conditions particularly look at floorboards, and in cellar and loft.
*work* – extensive repair and replacement of timbers and plaster. Floorboards up, plaster off.

### Intermediate jobs

These may affect the plaster and decoration in the immediate area but usually have no great effect on other parts of the property.

**building partition walls**

**knocking down walls**

**removing chimney breast**

**patio doors**

**replacing bathroom fittings**

**installing extra power points on existing circuit**

**replacement window frames**

**installing loft insulation and draughtproofing**

**built-in storage**

### Jobs to leave until last

The finishing touches cover the work that has been done underneath. You won't want to undo them so make sure all that is necessary has been done.

**final decorating**

**laying floorcoverings**

**secondary double glazing**

**shelving**

# Timing an extension

## FIRST THOUGHTS

| Early stages | Week 1 | Week 2 | Week 3 | Week 4 | Week 5 |
|---|---|---|---|---|---|
| Gather information, discuss ideas with all and sundry. Having decided to proceed approach: ■ possible designers ■ possible builders ■ the local authority – get the necessary forms and have an informal chat with the local officials ■ possible lenders. | First discussion with chosen designer. If d-i-y start tracking down materials, costing local firms and so on. If builder to do, shop for any special fittings – a bath perhaps or particular windows. | | | Drawings and specification finalised with designer. | |

## PREPARING THE SITE / DRAINS / FOUNDATIONS

| Week 13 | Week 14 | Week 15 | Week 16 | Week 17 | Week 18 | Week 1 |
|---|---|---|---|---|---|---|
| Work begins, site cleared, adjacent house wall is prepared, bricks knocked out for bonding windows removed etc., storage for materials is organised. Some materials collected or delivered . Trenches for foundations and any drain runs set out and dug, shored if necessary *BCO in. | | New drains laid and connected to existing drains – tested and left unburied for BCO inspection. Concrete order finalised. Bricks, blocks or timber arrive for walls. | | Drains, backfilled, concrete arrives. Strip foundation and walls constructed up to damp-proof course *BC Orders for doors and window frames finalised. | | |

ORDER
DOORS AND WINDOWS

## ROOFING

| Week 27 | Week 28 | Week 29 | Week 30 | Week 31 | Week 32 | Week 3 |
|---|---|---|---|---|---|---|
| Roofing timbers arrive. Roof construction begins, timbers are installed. | | Roof covering fixed, gutters are installed. Windows are glazed. Doors are hung. Building is now watertight (storm clouds can gather). | | | Materials for services arrive; wiring, plumbing and heating installed. | |

From first thought to finish, the average single-storey extension takes about 10 months, though some people clearly mull things over for much longer. The Chart gives the average times when things could happen.

The organising stage will take around 12 weeks whether you go it alone or call in professionals. Thereafter a builder would be faster through the building stages with a single-storey building complete in 10 to 15 weeks on average compared to the average of 26 weeks for the d-i-y project outlined below. A d-i-y project involving some hired help seems to take longer than an all d-i-y job – clearly there is some waiting time.

**PROVAL**

| ek 6 | Week 7 | Week 8 | Week 9 | Week 10 | Week 11 | Week 12 |
|---|---|---|---|---|---|---|
| wings and specification submitted for necessary roval. Likely builders approached for costings. i-y continue shopping around for best prices. | | | Any necessary modifications to drawings agreed between you, designer, and local authority. Builder's quotations received and compared. | | Receive official approval. | Builder appointed. If d-i-y, firm orders placed for materials and equipment allowing flexible delivery dates. |

FIND UILDER

ORDER MATERIALS

**NCRETING** / **BUILDING WALLS**

| k 20 | Week 21 | Week 22 | Week 23 | Week 24 | Week 25 | Week 26 |
|---|---|---|---|---|---|---|
| rete arrives, ds are rallied, elbarrows nised, solid is laid, or if be a timber ended the over- s laid. red with hene and cure. | Windows and door frames, lintels and so on arrive. Materials are organised for convenient working | Walls are constructed and frames set in as work proceeds. If the extension is to be two-storey, scaffolding is based out when walls are about 1.2m high. Otherwise a bandstand is used. *BCO in. | | | | |

ORDER ROOFING

**ISHING**

| ek 34 | Week 35 | Week 36 | Week 37 | Week 38 |
|---|---|---|---|---|
| material oor arrives floor is pleted – er timber eeper s or the layer of rete (the ed) O in. | Exterior is finished, painting, rendering, pebble-dashing etc. | Building is lined with plaster, plasterboard, cladding or whatever. Roof is insulated. | | Final fixings are made indoors – skirtings, cornices and so on. If the walls are dry-lined the walls can be papered otherwise painted for the time being. |

# Chapter 2

# FACTS ON HOUSEHOLD SERVICES

The three main household services are water, gas and electricity. Almost all houses have water and electricity and most town houses also have access to a gas supply. Many of the improvements you might consider making to a house will involve one or other of these services, so it's useful to understand the way they are supplied and organised in a home. Knowing how things work in your own house also pays dividends in emergencies.

Although there is nothing in the UK to stop anyone from carrying out a gas, electricity or water installation of any kind, regulations and checks by the authorities legally preclude installations by incompetent people. Anyone considering do-it-yourself must therefore be certain of the correct methods and procedures and anyone employing a tradesman should make sure that he is suitably qualified to do the work.

The results of incompetent plumbing may never be fatal, but incorrect wiring or gas plumbing could and jobs involving electricity and gas should always be treated with caution.

# Gas

The transmission, distribution, and supply of natural gas is under the control of the British Gas Corporation, the administrative headquarters of which are situated in London. There are 12 Regions of British Gas, covering the whole area of England, Scotland and Wales.

The Regions are responsible for carrying out all practical aspects of the Corporation's operational duties. Among other things, these duties include:

- distribution of gas within each regional boundary, including laying and repairing of mains and service pipes
- selling of gas supplies and equipment
- installation of pipework systems on industrial, commercial and domestic premises including repair of such systems
- installation and maintenance of gas appliances.

All telephone directories contain detailed information on the local offices, including emergency numbers, under the heading 'Gas', the number is also on the back of your latest bill.

## Bringing gas to your home

From the numerous gasfields in the North Sea gas is piped ashore and taken to all parts of the country through the large diameter trunk mains which comprise the National grid. In rural areas the normal operating pressure of this grid system is about 70 bars (1000 lbs per square inch). Within urban areas this pressure is reduced for safety by regulators to about 7 bars in trunk mains and again to a maximum of 2 bars in street mains.

This is still too high to operate gas appliances, so a regulator fitted to each domestic gas meter reduces the pressure in the installation pipework to 20 millibars – the pressure at which most gas appliances operate. Those which operate at a lower pressure incorporate a further pressure regulating device.

## The installation

The gas supply into a domestic dwelling can be conveniently divided into four sections:

- **the service pipe** – being the pipe which conveys gas from the street main to the gas meter and terminates with an isolating valve
- **the meter installation** – incorporating the meter, the short length of pipe connecting the meter inlet to the isolating valve on the service pipe and the first 600mm of pipe leading from the meter outlet to the installation pipework
- **the installation pipework** – the network of pipes carrying gas from the meter outlet to the appliances,

■ **the appliances** – including their installation.

The service pipe and the meter installation is the property of British Gas, who is responsible for its upkeep. Any work carried out on this part of the installation may only be carried out by British Gas or its nominated contractor.

The installation pipework and appliances are the responsibility of the house occupier (or landlord) and this involves ensuring that the system is kept in good condition so that it remains gastight. Appliances must also be kept in good working order so that they are safe in operation.

## Gas Safety Regulations

The work of installing gas pipework and appliances in the home is not always straightforward and is, in many instances, beyond the capability of untrained people. A high percentage of incidents involving gas explosions and fatalities result from the effects of incorrectly installed pipework or gas appliances and can be directly attributed to work carried out by persons having little knowledge of what is involved. It is all too easy to unknowingly produce conditions which are potentially dangerous.

For many years, methods of good practice to be followed when installing gas pipework systems and appliances have been available as British Standard Codes of Practice. Towards the end of the 1960's however successive Governments became alarmed at the number of gas explosions and fatalities occuring and so in 1972 a comprehensive set of Regulations were introduced which, by law, impose specific responsibilities on those persons who install gas systems and appliances and also on those who use them.

These regulations, known as the *Gas Safety Regulations* are published by HMSO. Their emphasis is upon the safe installation and use of gas and concerns both the individual's safety and that of the general public. Under the Regulations you must:

■ have only competent persons to install or service gas systems or appliances. You must not do it yourself if you are not competent

■ not use, or let anyone else use any gas appliance you know or suspect to be dangerous

■ turn off your gas supply at the isolating valve adjacent to the meter inlet if you suspect an escape of gas on the system and not turn the gas on again until the escape has been properly repaired

■ inform your local gas service centre immediately if the smell of gas continues after the isolating tap at the meter has been turned off.

A fine of up to £400 can be imposed on any person found contravening any part of the Regulations.

In addition to the Gas Safety Regulations and the relevant Codes of Practice reference must also be made to the Building Regulations.

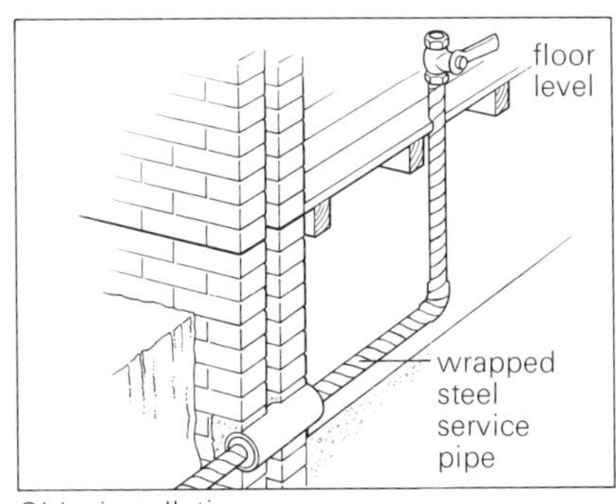


Older installation.

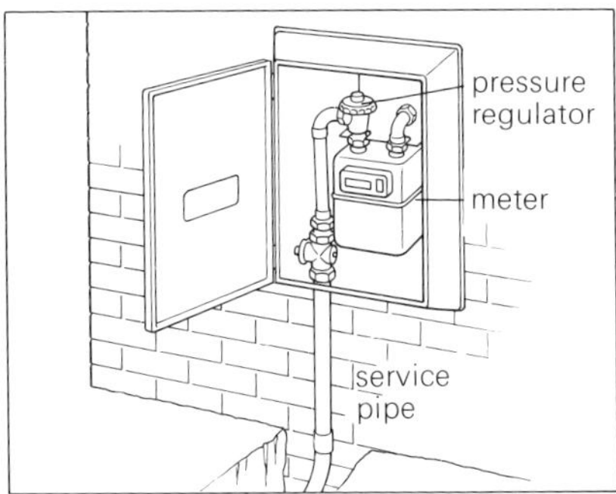


Meter installations are now installed where the isolating valve is readily accessible from outside.

THE GAS SUPPLY

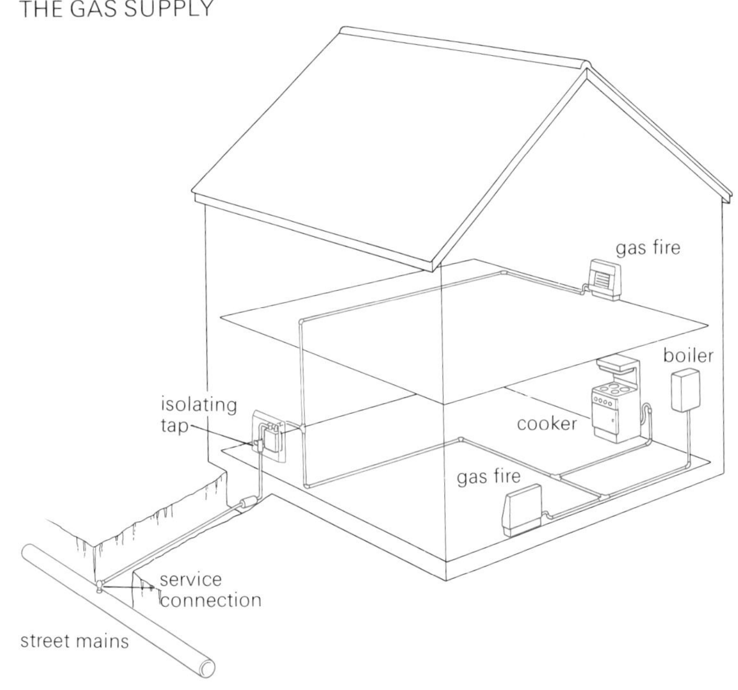


The installation from street main to appliances, the householder's responsibility starts beyond the meter.

## Gas plumbing

Much of the work involved in gas plumbing is similar to water plumbing, but there are some important differences. When gas is flowing through any pipe, a certain amount of resistance to the flow is caused by friction between the moving gas and the internal surface of the pipe through which it is passing. This friction is increased by sharp changes in direction where bends, elbows, tee-pieces and so on are used. Consequently the internal diameter (bore) of each pipe used in the installation must be adequate to allow the gas to flow without undue restriction.

When installing a gas pipework system (or extending an existing one), it is vital to ensure that sufficient gas pressure is available at each appliance – ie 20 millibars. This pressure must be checked with *all other appliances operating* in order to ensure that they will operate properly. Any loss of pressure between the regulator on the meter inlet and the appliance inlet (with the appliance working) should not be more than 1 to 2 millibars.

Materials for pipework systems have in the past included thin wall lead composition pipes, iron pipes and more recently copper pipe. The first two have fallen into disuse and now, as for water plumbing, copper pipe is mainly used. When using copper pipe for conveying water, it is possible to use either compression or capillary soldered fittings for jointing the pipes. When the system contains gas however, it is vital that leakage cannot occur because of slight movement of the pipework and for this reason only capillary soldered fittings should be used. Plastic and stainless steel pipe and fittings are not suitable for gas.

When installing pipework the requirements of the Gas Safety Regulations have to be observed. There are a number of Regulations to satisfy and it is not feasible to list them all here. A selection is however listed below.

- no pipe may be installed in a cavity wall other than to go directly through at right angles (90°) to the cavity
- where a pipe is passed through a wall or floor of solid construction – including a cavity wall – the pipe must be enclosed in a sleeve cemented into the wall. The space between the pipe and the sleeve must be filled with a non-setting mastic
- whenever a pipe is in contact with or likely to be exposed to any material likely to cause corrosion it must be fully protected – eg by using pipe with a factory-bonded PVC coating or by wrapping with PVC tape
- an installation pipe must not be laid in such a manner likely to impair the structure of the building
- all pipework must be properly supported.

Recommendations for installing pipework are contained in British Standard Code of Practice CP 331 Part 3 1974 and this Code of Practice and the Gas Safety Regulations must always be consulted before any gas pipework is carried out.

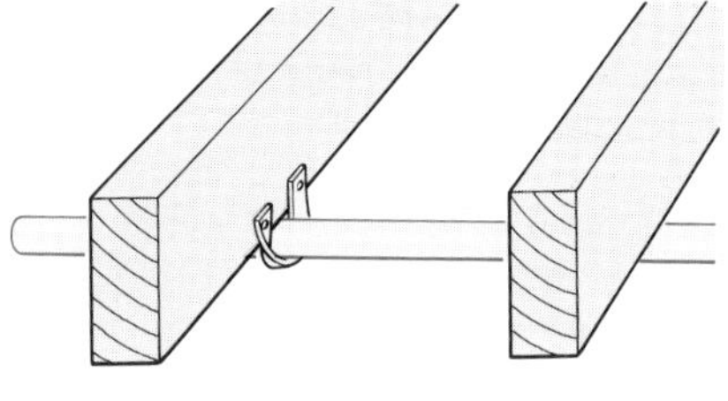

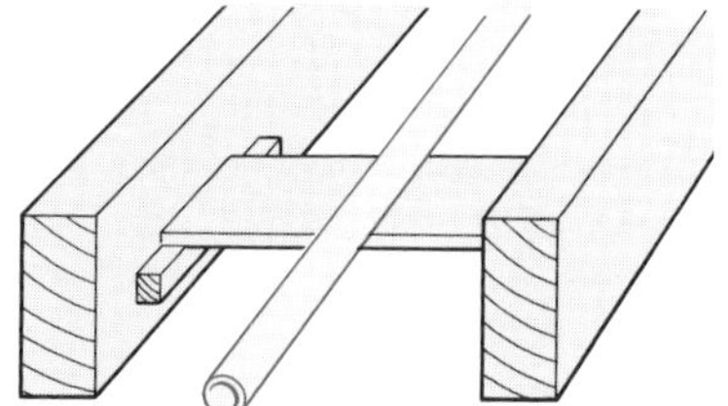

All pipes must be properly supported.

## Testing

The most essential requirement – after ensuring that the pipework is correctly installed in all respects – is that the system is gastight. This is checked by filling the system with gas or, if no gas is available with air, and testing for any leakage with a special gauge called a water or 'U' gauge. A completed installation containing gas is tested before connecting an appliance. An extension to an existing system can be tested before it is connected to the system – in this case the test is done with air. Then after the extension has been connected up and the gas turned on, the joint connecting the extension to the system must be tested by means of a leak detection solution. **NEVER USE A LIGHTED MATCH FOR TESTING.**

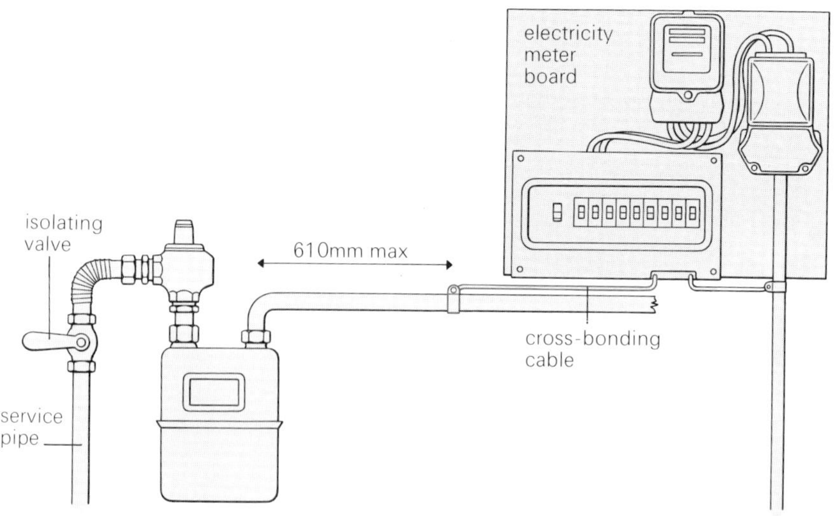


Gas pipework may have to be bonded to the electrical earth on the meter board. Only a competent electrician should do this work.

The technique of soundness testing using a 'U' gauge requires specialist knowledge and is best left to British Gas or other qualified installers. If however the joints contained in a small extension to an existing installation pipework system are all accessible each joint may be tested by applying leak detecting solution with a small paint brush after the gas has been introduced into the extension. Any leaking joint will be seen by bubbling of the solution on the surface of the joint.

**'U' Gauge**

Gauges used for measuring gas pressures are called 'manometers'. The simplest form is the 'U' tube manometer, commonly called the 'U' gauge. This consists of a glass or transparent plastic tube usually about 300mm long which, when containing water, will measure pressure up to 30 millibars. The tube is bent into the form of a U and has a scale fitted between the two 'limbs' or upright parts of the tube. One limb is connected to the gas supply and the other remains open to the atmosphere.

The scale is usually capable of adjustment so that the zero can be lined up with the water levels equal. When the gas pressure is applied, the water will be displaced downwards in the limb connected to the gas supply and upwards in the limb open to the atmosphere. The total height of the column of water supported indicates the gas pressure.

## Other considerations

As well as requiring a gas supply at the correct pressure, many gas appliances also need flueing to vent gases and all appliances need an adequate combustion air supply. Depending on the house wiring earthing system it may also be necessary to cross-bond the supply pipes.

**Combustion air supply**

*All* gas appliances need a freely available air supply in order that the gas being used can be burnt completely. Failure to provide this could affect the burning of the gas and may result in carbon monoxide being produced. It is essential therefore in order to comply with the Gas Safety Regulations to make arrangements for combustion air in accordance with the requirements of British Standard Code of Practice 5440 Part 2 1976.

**Flueing of gas appliances**

It is necessary to vent burnt gases from certain gas appliances. Requirements for all types of appliance are given in British Standard Code of Practice 5440 Part 1 1976.

**Electrical Cross Bonding**

In premises supplied with electricity using the system of 'protective multiple earthing' it is necessary by law to ensure that the gas installation pipework is bonded to the electrical earth on the consumer's electrictiy meter board. Not connected to the earth wire in the house system.

On all such installations a permanently fitted continuity bonding wire should be attached (by means of a proper earthing clip) to the installation pipework not more than 600mm from the meter outlet connection and connected to the terminal on the electricity meter board. The water installation is connected in the same way.

This work must be carried out by a competent electrician.

The purpose of the continuity bond is to avoid any hazard of electric shock, cross-arcing, etc, should a fault occur on the electrical installation. For this reason, wherever the gas pipework is cross-bonded, any work involving the cutting of a pipe – to insert an extension for example – requires a temporary bond.

This temporary bond is a short length of wire – say 2 metres – fitted at each end with crocodile clips that enable the wire to be clipped to the installation pipe at each side of the intended cut.

Once the cut has been made and the branch fitted, the bonding is re-established and the temporary bond can be removed.

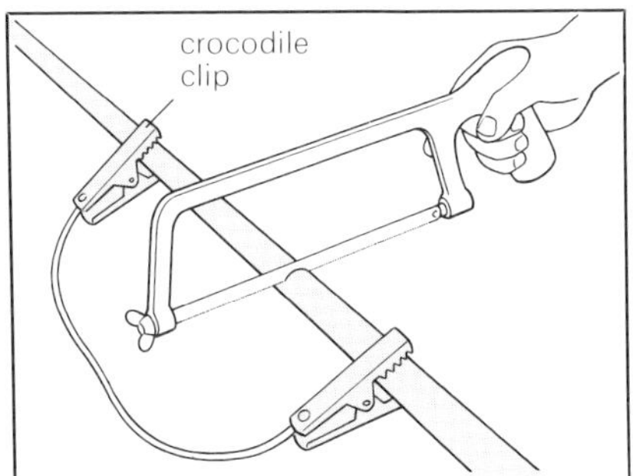


To maintain a temporary bond a wire is clipped to the pipe either side of the intended cut.

### CAN YOU D-I-Y?

The potential hazards, and the existence of the Gas Safety Regulations (and the associated penalties) are such that any handyman contemplating work on gas installations should obtain a copy of the Regulations and study them in detail. There are some 20 Regulations covering the installation of gas pipework systems and a further 16 covering the actual use of gas. If having read them you do not understand what they mean you should not under any circumstances undertake the work – leave it to a qualified installer.

Any d-i-y work must be confined to installation pipework between the meter outlet and the appliance or installing the appliance itself. Even so some appliances require specialist knowledge and their installation is best left to professional installers.

Gas plumbing is not a job for a novice plumber. The making of sound capillary joints requires practice and it is essential to gain this on water plumbing before even contemplating gas. Water is a much more forgiving fluid and faults in water plumbing are easy to detect.

# Electricity

In England and Wales, the Central Electricity Generating Board is responsible for the power stations and the national grid. Twelve Area Electricity Boards are responsible for the distribution networks and the supply and sale of electricity. In Scotland, there are two Boards each responsible for generation, transmission and distribution within their areas; Northern Ireland also has a separate service.

The standard voltage for the domestic supply of electricity in Britain is 240V. (In Northern Ireland the supply is 230/240V.) Under normal conditions the voltage is constant – the permitted variation is plus or minus 6 per cent. Although exceptionally heavy demand in cold weather may cause a regional drop, a drop is usually only of brief duration seen as dimming lights or a failure of the TV picture.

## The supply

Electricity is supplied to most homes through an underground cable. In country districts, electricity is often distributed by overhead line on wooden poles – the live, neutral and earth conductors entering the house through a porcelain tube under the eaves.

The main supply cable goes to a sealed unit that holds the service fuse. The fuse is usually rated 60 or 100 amps, depending on the total household load and is designed to blow if a serious fault occurs in a particular house, thus preventing the neighbourhood being affected. If this fuse fails, you have to call the emergency service of the Electricity Board (it is in the telephone directory, but it is a good idea to write the telephone number on the wall close to the meter – keep a torch there too). Check all the other fuses in the house first as it is rare for this fuse to 'blow' and check with neighbours that it is not a temporary power failure.

There is usually another terminal on the outside of the sealed unit to which the household earth connection is made. Adequate earthing is vital for the safety of any electrical installation and inside the consumer unit there is an earth connector block to which all the circuits in the house are connected. This block can usually be connected to the household earth terminal using 6·0mm$^2$ conductor wire protected by a green-and-yellow striped sheath. The main earth connection is provided either by the outer metal sheath of the Electricity Board's incoming cable or, where the system known as protective multiple earthing (PME) is used, by the neutral conductor in a special mineral-insulated PME-type cable. Where the PME system is used, it is essential that all metal water pipes, gas pipes, central heating pipes and radiators and large metal objects, such as baths, are bonded to the main earth terminals.

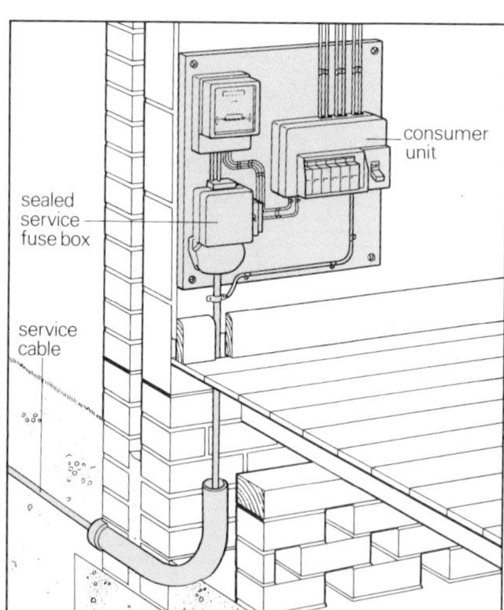


Electricity is supplied to most homes through underground service cables and goes through the Board's service fuse and meter before it gets to the consumer unit (or fuse box) where the house circuits begin.

## The meter

Two cables are taken from the service fuse to the meter which records the quantity of electricity used. Both the sealed fuse unit and the meter are the property of the Electricity Board and must never be tampered with. From the meter onwards, the electrical installation is your property and your responsibility.

For homes using off-peak electricity, the meter works on two rates with the energy taken at a cheaper rate during the specified night hours.

## The house fuses

The meter is connected to the household installation by meter tails – hefty lengths of single-core cable. These belong to the householder but can be connected to, or disconnected from, the meter only by the Board. The meter tails run to one or more switches – the mains switches.

In houses thirty or more years old it is still common to find two or more fuse boxes each with its own switch – sometimes in a separate box alongside. In modern homes the mains switch and the fuses are contained in a box called a consumer unit. This has rewirable fuses, cartridge fuses or miniature circuit breakers.

Rewirable fuses consist of plastic fuse holders with a length of fuse wire held in position by brass screws. New consumer units rarely have rewirable fuses and they are not allowed as the protection for some types of circuits – see page 51.

Cartridge fuses are also in a plastic holder but can be replaced like the cartridge fuse in the 13 amp plug – you must keep spares handy. Cartridge fuses are better than rewirable ones. One of the advantages is that the fuse is made more precisely than a length of fuse wire and therefore blows at currents which can be predicted more accurately. Also cartridge fuses of different ratings are different

MODERN WIRING

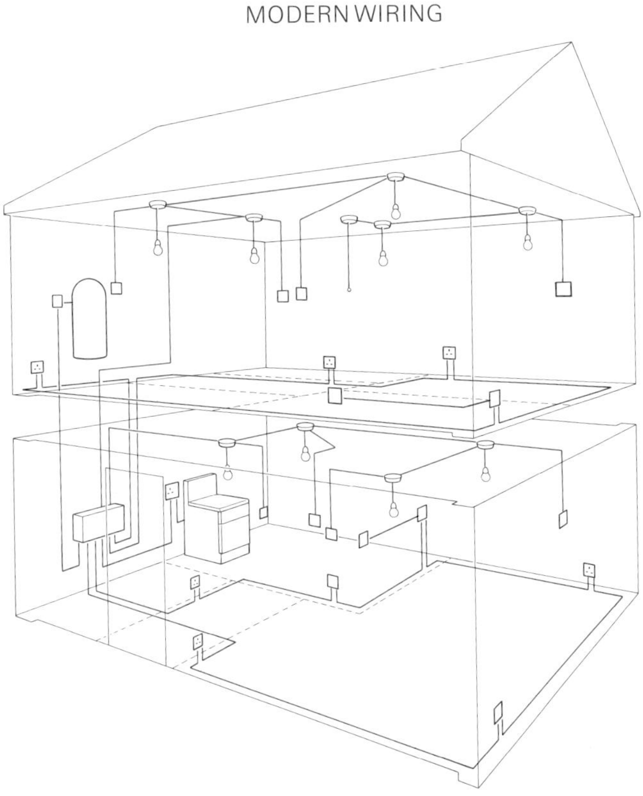

Modern wiring in pvc-sheathed cable has ring circuits supplying 13A rectangular-pin sockets. Lights are often on loop-in circuits.

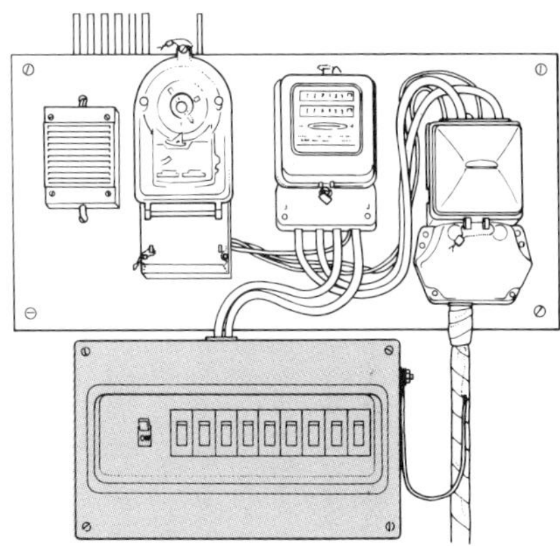

Modern consumer unit contains the fuseways and mains switch in one neat box.

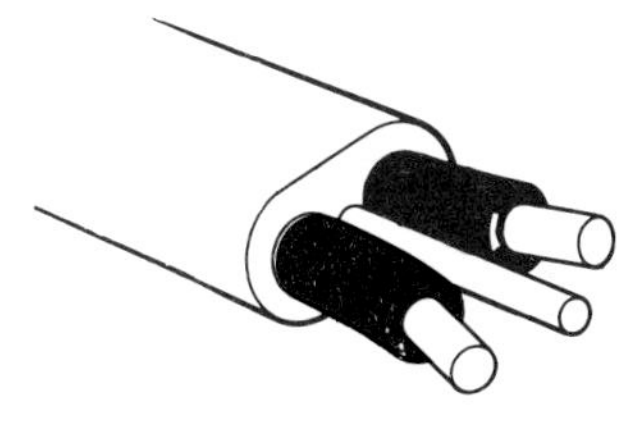

2·5mm² flat twin and earth pvc-sheathed cable.

sizes so it isn't possible to mend a fuse with one of the wrong rating.

Miniature circuit breakers look like ordinary switches or push buttons but they automatically flick themselves off if any circuit is overloaded, or if a fault in a piece of electrical equipment fails to blow the fuse in the plug. The circuit is brought back into use by resetting the switch. MCB's give even more precise protection than cartridge fuses. The ease of resetting is also a considerable advantage and means that an MCB can be used as a switch to turn off an individual circuit. In some consumer units, MCB's are interchangeable with cartridge fuse holders and you can opt for one or other or a mixture of both.

Modern fuse carriers are colour coded: 5A is white, 15A is blue, 20A is yellow, 30A is red, 45A is green. The job of fuse finding is easier if each fuse in the box is labelled with the circuit, rooms or equipment it serves.

**The circuits**

From the fuseways in the consumer unit, cables form separate circuits supplying socket outlets, lights and fixed appliances. Flat twin and earth cable is used for most circuits. It contains two supply conductors, live and neutral, and an earth conductor inside a pvc outer sheath. The live is sleeved with red insulation and the neutral with black. The earth conductor is not insulated separately but should be protected by a green/yellow striped pvc sleeving wherever the cable sheath is stripped to make a connection – at a socket outlet for instance. Cables sometimes run in steel, aluminium or plastic tubes (called conduits) but modern practice is simply to bed cable in the walls with a protective plastic capping.

The last link to electric equipment is usually made in pvc-sheathed flexible cable. Flex must be sized to suit the current it will carry.

## THE REGULATIONS

There are strict rules for electrical wiring. These – the *Regulations for Electrical Installations* – are laid down by the Institution of Electrical Engineers. Known popularly as the *Wiring Regs*, they are not legally binding (except in Scotland where they are mandatory under the Building Regulations) but are followed by all responsible electricians

Reference libraries generally keep a copy of the Wiring Regs. They are not easy reading for the layperson. The latest edition – the Fifteenth – was brought out in 1982; for a while it runs concurrently with the Fourteenth Edition which is gradually being phased out.

## Wiring improvements

The sorts of improvements you might want to make to an existing system include adding sockets, installing fixed equipment and re-organising lighting – but before you do any of this it's important to assess the state of the existing wiring. If the system is old, untidy or badly-organised, it will be safer, and probably easier, to rewire throughout. Rewiring means replacing all the cables, socket outlets, switches and ceiling roses and probably the old fuse boxes and main switch, too. As this is a major home improvement involving redecoration and some structural work, it is advisable to do the complete job. In the end this could be cheaper than a piecemeal approach. You must rewire if an old system in rubber-insulated cable is no longer sound.

### Assessing the wiring

You can learn a lot about your wiring by looking at it yourself. Look for cables that are old and perished. Look first at the socket outlet circuits, which tend to deteriorate more quickly. Old fashioned sockets with round holes are usually an indication that the wiring predates the 13 amp ring system introduced in the 1950's. Old fashioned round light switches are not necessarily indicative of old wiring so look in the loft at how the lighting points have been wired. Modern 13A sockets and square light switches, don't necessarily mean new wiring.

Wiring in old metal conduit is suspect: the cable inside is possibly rubber-covered and may have perished if it has been exposed to the air. You'll probably find that the cable inside conduit is just two conductors (live and neutral). The metal conduit would also have served as the earth conductor and if any joints have parted then there is no effective earth now operating.

Switch off at the mains and open switches and sockets. Look for signs of overheating which is seen as perishing or charring of the cable insulation or the fitting. Outlets which get hot in use are suspect.

### Testing

Thorough testing of an electrical circuit is best carried out by an electrical contractor who is qualified to carry out the test procedure laid out in the Wiring Regs. The Wiring Regs set out a recommended form for the report. The form gives a standard list of the items inspected or tested and these are deleted if they don't come up to the standard. There is also space for comment about departures from the Wiring Regs. When testing is complete, the contractor will sign the form which tells you that the inspection has been carried out to standards laid down in the Regs and also gives his recommendation for when the wiring should be next inspected. For modern wiring in pvc-insulated cable, this is usually five years, for old wiring in rubber-insulated, which passes the tests, it may be less – one or two years.

It's most unlikely that you'd be able to tell from the form whether your wiring is safe or not – you'll probably have to ask the contractor. But it helps to have some idea of what the main test results mean. The inspection report form should tell you:

- the type of *earthing system*
- whether the electrical resistance (called *impedance*) of the connection to earth in each of the sockets and switches is low enough. If there were a poor connection to earth, the resistance would be high and would not prevent you getting a shock or blow the circuit fuse.
- whether the *total resistance* (called earth loop impedance) of the earth circuit is satisfactory. This applies to conventional earths such as that provided by the Electricity Board on the supply cable, which must have a resistance below a specified value
- whether *residual current devices* operate effectively. Once again, as these are your protection against electric shocks any faults should be rectified immediately
- whether the *polarity* throughout the wiring is correct. It can be corrected easily
- whether single-pole *switches* interrupt the current in the live conductors as they should
- whether the electrical resistance of the *insulation* separating the three wires of the wiring cables is adequate. Old wiring often fails on this account
- whether the electrical resistance of the insulation on *fixed appliances* – immersion heater or electric cooker, say – is adequate
- whether *switches and connections* are in good order
- whether any circuits are *overloaded* – too many lights on a lighting circuit for example.

POLARITY

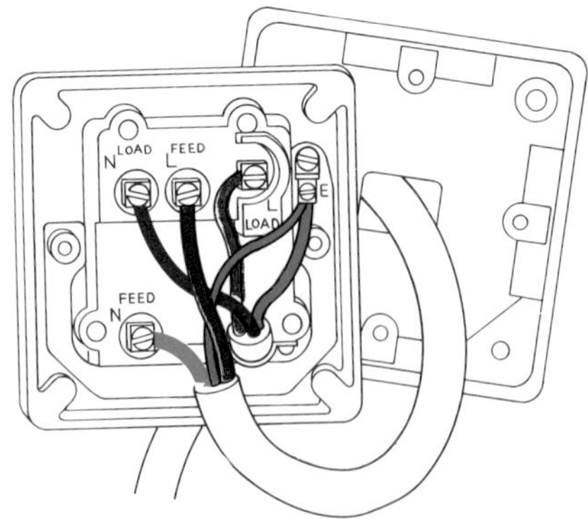


Correct polarity is important: which means that fuses are in the live conductors and all connections are the right way round. If wrong it can be corrected easily.

The form also gives space for general comments about the state of the wiring and departures from the Wiring Regs. These may be things like whether the consumer unit is positioned so that it is easily accessible.

### Tests on new circuits

To conform with the Wiring Regs any major new wiring has to be inspected and tested before it is used. If a new consumer unit has been fitted, the Electricity Board will have to connect (or reconnect) the supply. Their own tests carried out at the time of reconnection are for their own satisfaction and not an indication that the Regs have been met in detail.

## Socket circuits

In new installations, socket outlets are generally installed on ring circuits. But radial circuits are useful in some circumstances, particularly for fixed high-rated equipment.

### Ring circuits

The ring circuit is a loop of cable from a 30 amp fuse at the consumer unit and back. It has one size of socket – the 13 amp distinguished by its three rectangular holes. This socket will supply up to 3kW and has safety shutters which automatically close when the plug is withdrawn.

There is no set limit for the number of socket outlets that can be installed on a ring, but it is important to assess the likely load on a ring and limit the numbers of sockets to avoid overloading. The total load that can be taken from a ring protected by a 30 amp fuse is 7200 watts. Although a ring wired with 2·5mm$^2$ cable can serve a maximum floor area of 100 sq m (provided the total length of cable does not exceed 60 metres), it is usual to have a ring circuit for each floor of the house. If the kitchen has a large number of appliances it may need its own ring to avoid overloading.

An advantage of the ring circuit is that you can easily extend it or add spurs to the ring.

**Unfused spurs** are run in the same size cable as for the ring circuit (see *Extra sockets*). Each unfused spur is normally limited to a single or a double 13 amp socket outlet or one fixed appliance and the total number of unfused spurs should not exceed the number of socket outlets on the ring circuit. Unfused spurs can be connected to the ring at socket outlets or at junction boxes but no more than two spurs can be connected from each outlet – it's better to stick to one.

**Fused spurs** are connected to the ring at fused connection units. The capacity of the fuse must not exceed 13 amp and the cable rating must be at least that of the fuse.

Either sort of spur can be used *within* the area served by the ring.

### Radial circuits

These used to be allowed to serve only individual rooms but now (under the 15th Edition of the Wiring Regs) are limited only by area – provided, of course, that the load is unlikely to be exceeded. A radial circuit run in 2·5mm$^2$ cable, and protected by a 20A fuse (any type) can supply an area of up to 20 square metres; a circuit wired in 4mm$^2$ cable and protected by a 30 amp cartridge fuse or MCB can supply an area of up to 50 square metres.

These cable sizes will be satisfactory for most purposes; but cables that run through insulation or run next to one another for a considerable distance should be bigger.

### Special circuits

Powerful water heaters and cookers draw a lot of current when in use and so are supplied with their own circuit which terminates in a switched outlet to which the equipment is permanently connected. Special circuits are dealt with under the appropriate jobs in Part II.

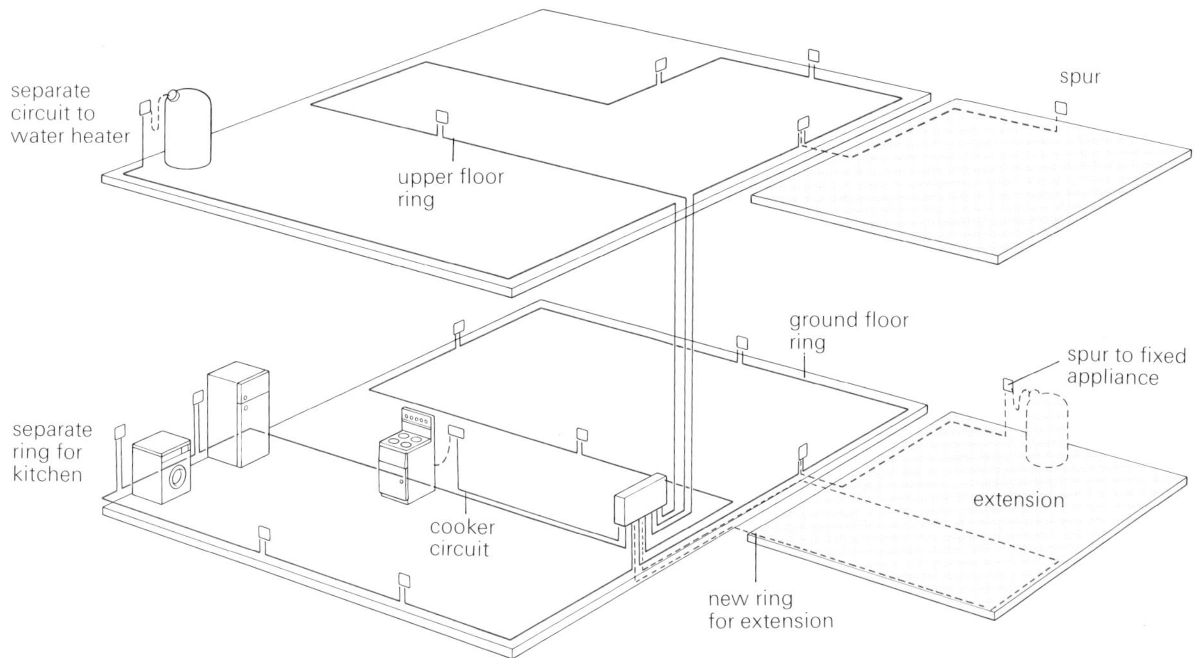


Sockets are usually wired on ring circuits, but special radial circuits are used for supplies to high-rated equipment.

Sockets in an extension to a building can be on a new ring or an extension to an existing ring.

## Lighting circuits

There is nothing to prevent lights being taken from the ring circuit – via a fused connection unit – and this is often a practical method for adding new lights. But it's normal and much better practice to have the lighting circuits completely separate from the socket circuits. This makes the most economical use of cable and simplifies the circuit plans. Lighting circuits are a little more complicated than socket circuits, because the lighting points are normally controlled by a separate wall switch and so extra connections are required.

There are two methods of wiring lights – by the junction box system or by the loop-in system.

With the **junction box** system, the circuit cable is taken to a series of junction boxes sited between ceiling joists close to where a cable is run to the switch. A further cable runs out to the ceiling rose.

In the **loop-in system**, which is more widely used, the junction box and the ceiling rose are combined. This method may use more cable than the junction box system – because ceiling roses are further apart than junction boxes – but it reduces the number of connections needed.

### Cable and fuses

Lighting circuits are normally run in $1mm^2$ cable and protected by a 5A fuse. The maximum number of lighting points on such a circuit is usually ten. This allows for 100W light bulbs at each lighting point with 200W to spare. A circuit in $1{\cdot}0mm^2$ cable can be protected by a 10A fuse and can then supply more lighting points, but the length of $1{\cdot}0mm^2$ cable from the 10A fuse to the furthest lamp must not be more than 15m. For larger circuits you can use $1{\cdot}5mm^2$ cable, but it's usually better to install two small circuits instead.

Extra lighting points can be added to an existing circuit by connecting cable (of the same size as the existing circuit), usually via a junction box, provided the total number of lights on the circuit does not then exceed the total loading.

### Two-way switching

Lights are often controlled by more than one switch. This is achieved by connecting further switches in the supply cable. Two-way switching is common and most switch plates are now supplied with the necessary extra terminal (if two-way switching isn't needed this terminal simply isn't used). The theory behind two-way switching is illustrated below – the live supply goes to the common terminals on the switches – the remaining terminals L1 and L2 are connected by strapping wires.

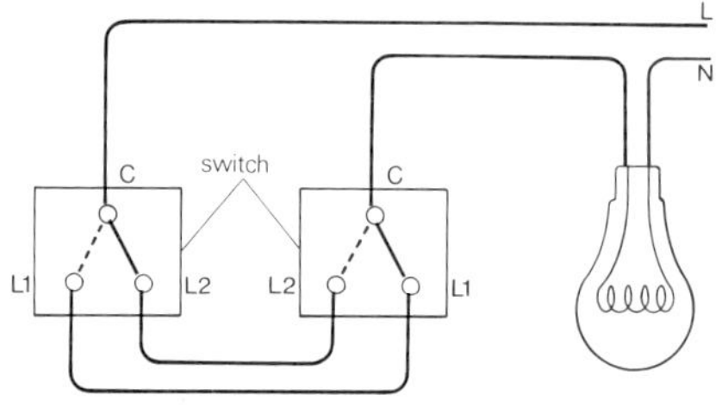


In practice the wiring is rather more complicated as the switch cable from the lighting point goes only to the first switch and three-core and earth sheathed cable is used to connect the two switches. The method is described on page 176.

For switching from more than two points, special intermediate switches (available as single switches only) are installed between the two-way switches, but this is rarely necessary for domestic installations.

LIGHTING CIRCUITS

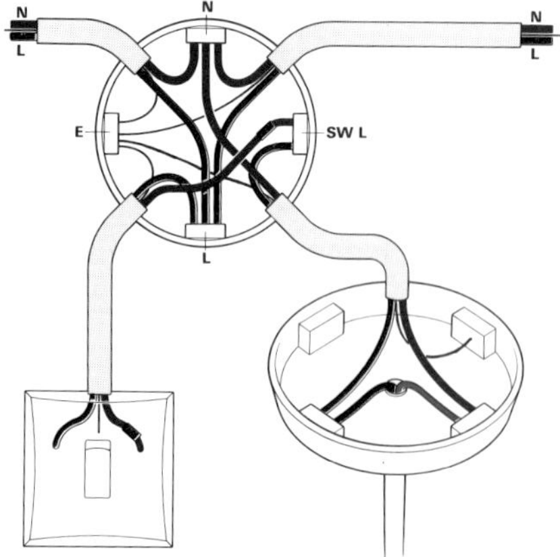


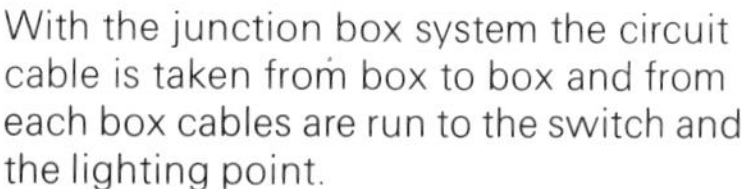

With the junction box system the circuit cable is taken from box to box and from each box cables are run to the switch and the lighting point.

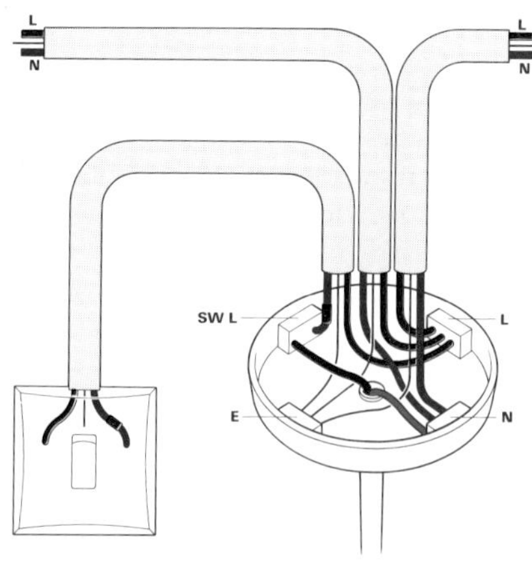


With the loop-in system the circuit cable is taken (or looped) from rose to rose and the switch cable is run from the rose to the wall switch.

## Getting down to work

Much of the work in installing house wiring is structural, lifting floorboards, drilling holes in joists, cutting into walls – for cable routes and for mounting boxes – and whoever does the work must be prepared for the upheaval.

### Cable routes

In many homes it will be possible to run cable under the floor. Where there is a solid ground floor, the cable has to run in the plasterwork, in hollow metal or plastic skirting (to replace the old skirting) or along the existing skirting protected by plastic conduit. Cables up and down walls are usually recessed into the plaster and covered up.

All cables should run in straight lines vertically up and down – it's then easier to work out where a cable might be hidden in a wall or under a floor.

**Under the floor** In floor spaces, there must be sufficient slack in the cable to make sure it is not strained. Under a suspended ground floor the cable should ideally be clipped to the joists. In the space under upper floors, cable that runs parallel to the joists should rest on the ceiling of the lower floor; cable that runs at right angles to the joists should loop from one joist to the next. Where cable has to pass through joists the holes should be drilled at least 50mm down from the top surface. This avoids the risk that nails will go through the cable when the floorboards are put back and does relatively little harm to the strength of the joists. However, if well-placed holes are not possible, cables can be run in notches cut in the joists, protected by conduit or sheets of metal nailed over each notch.

**In walls** Cutting plaster is not difficult. Using a sharp knife score two lines 25mm apart along the proposed route. Use a club hammer and a brick bolster to chip out enough plaster to allow the cable to fit comfortably. (Another method is to use a plaster router bit fitted to the electric drill. It must be run at a slow speed and first you should cut a series of holes along the cable route.)

CABLES UNDER FLOORS

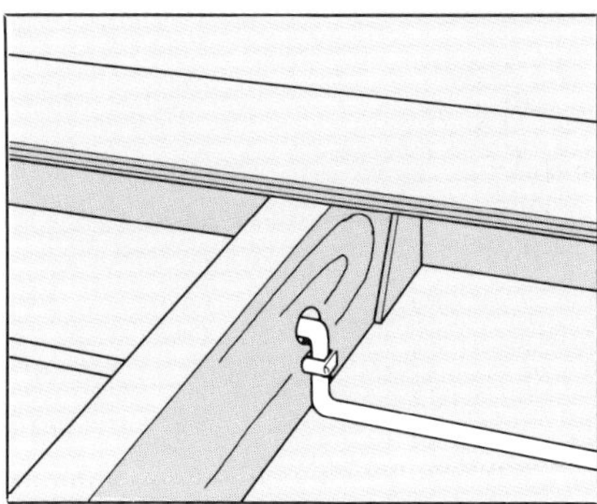

Cable through joists should pass through a hole 50mm down from the top, but this can be difficult.

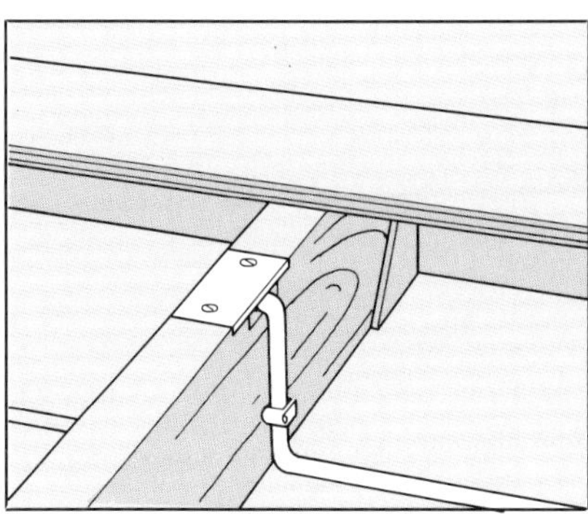

The alternative is to cut a notch and protect the cable from damage by a metal plate (or conduit).

### Fixing accessories

Flush fitting metal or plastic boxes are the neatest way of mounting accessories to a wall – but surface-mounting boxes are also available. To cut the hole use a masonry drill, marked to the correct depth, to cut a series of holes along the sides of the marked square and at intervals over the whole area. With a bolster chisel cut a hole about 8mm bigger all round than the box.

Check that the mounting box fits; knock out the required holes for access for the cable and fit a grommet (a rubber ring) into each hole to protect the cable. Drill and plug the holes for the box mounting screws. Check the box sits level. Feed the cable into the box, fix the cable in the wall with cable grips and replaster.

Fixing a wall-mounted box is easier as you need channel out only enough of the wall for the cable. The plastic box is then screwed to the surface using wall plugs.

Hollow internal walls covered in plasterboard need more care. Cable access is easy in the hollow space (use flexible wire to pull cable through), but some scrap timber may be needed to form a mounting surface behind the plasterboard to take the box. The easiest method is to locate one of the timber uprights and mount the box against it – though it may be necessary to chisel away some wood to accommodate the box.

If you think ahead, mounting blocks can be incorporated as the plasterboard is fixed.

### Making connections

Before connections can be made, the sheath and insulation of the cable have to be stripped back. The sheath is removed only from the length of cable which is within the steel box or the accessory itself: carefully slit the plastic lengthways with a sharp knife, keeping the cut away from the live and neutral conductors. Peel the sheath back and cut off the waste.

Insulation is best removed with special strippers. The amount to remove will depend on the type of terminal being dealt with, aim to leave virtually no bare conductor exposed once the connection has been made, but allow plenty of conductor for the terminal screw to grip. Where there is only one thin conductor to go in a hefty terminal, bend it double. When two or more conductors go in one terminal twist them together with pliers.

When installing any kind of circuit in which the conductors go on from one accessory to another, it is better to remove the sheath and insulation without breaking the continuity of the conductors. The conductors may have to be squeezed into a tight loop with pliers before they will fit into the terminals. In this way, however bad the connection made at one point, there is still a good, low-resistance path on to the next point.

The earth continuity conductor has no insulation, but wherever the sheath is removed it should be covered in green and yellow sleeving (previously green) which can be bought for the purpose. This prevents accidental contact with the live or neutral terminals as well as indicating that it's the earth.

Before an accessory is screwed in place, check that the terminal screws are tight and that all the conductors are firmly gripped. As the accessory is offered up to its box or pattress, help the conductors to bend into a shape which fits comfortably into the box – they should not be bent too sharply or trapped or pushed up hard against the metal surface of the box.

## PROTECTION AGAINST SHOCK

The job of the earth conductor – the *protective conductor* to give it its proper name – is to provide an easy path for the current so that if a fault develops the fuse will blow.

The electric current flows along the live conductor to its point of use and returns along the neutral conductor. Most of the current passes where there is least resistance: the lower the resistance, the greater the current that passes. If an appliance such as a washing machine develops an electrical fault where the live conductor suffers damage, the exposed metal of the casing could become live – carry electric current – and there would then be a serious risk of electrical shock to anyone who came in contact with it. The convenient path of low resistance provided by the earth conductor causes a large current to flow which blows the fuse and disconnects the appliance.

At one time the fault current left the house through the mains water pipe to which all the earth wires were connected. Now that so much plastic pipe is being used which will not conduct electric current, it is obligatory to have an effective alternative. The metal sheath of the Electricity Board's own supply cable is one system which provides a continuous path for the fault current back to the sub-station.

### PME

The Electricity Board often offers another safety system known as protective multiple earthing (PME). With PME all the house circuits earths are connected to the electricity board *neutral/earth conductor* wire which is then connected to earth at multiple points on its way back to the sub-station. When this system is used service pipes, supply pipes and other fixed metal work – a metal bath – for instance must be cross-bonded to earth. This is done by 2·5mm$^2$ earth conductors sleeved in green/yellow striped insulation running from the metal to be bonded back to the main earth terminal. Incoming service gas and water pipes are bonded as near as possible to their entry point into the house. In some houses, reliance for the bonding of things like metal baths is placed on the connecting metal pipework (which is bonded at source). This is against both the IEE Regs and the water bye-laws and is inadequate. For one thing, it is all too easy for such an earth path to be broken by the insertion of a plastic pipe of fittings into the pipe run.

If your electricity supply is earthed by PME, there is probably a notice posted by the meter or consumer unit. When the system was installed the Electricity Board would have specified the extra metalwork which needed bonding. If you're doubtful, pay to have it inspected.

### Residual current devices

Modern wiring practice, as urged by the IEE Wiring Regulations, is to install a residual current device (RCD) – also known as a current-operated earth-leakage circuit-breaker (ELCB) – to protect all circuits or sockets designated for supplies to equipment for outdoor use (for an electric lawn-mower, for instance). The RCD keeps a constant check on the live and neutral circuits which normally operate in equal balance. If it senses a sudden change in the current the RCD cuts off the current almost instantly.

An RCD can be fitted as a separate unit between the meter and main switch to protect the whole house. If you are renewing a consumer unit another option is to fit a consumer unit with an RCD in place of the main switch. The disadvantage of both these arrangements is that a fault that activates the RCD will cut the electricity supply to all the circuits including the lights and any freezer. There is a consumer unit in which an RCD protects only selected socket circuits – so if the supply is broken not all the electricity goes off and, in particular, the lighting is retained. Alternatively a separate RCD can be installed to protect selected circuits. For individual protection there are socket outlets which contain an individual RCD; portable RCD socket outlets and RCD plugs are also available.

### Safety precautions

The first and most fundamental precaution to take before beginning any wiring work is never to start anything you are unsure about. There are also some procedures which should become part of your routine way of working.

Any circuit that is to be worked on must be dead. This means that it should not simply be switched off, but also isolated from the supply by the removal of the fuse which links the two. Put the fuse in your pocket.

If there is any doubt about which circuit is which (and therefore about whether the one to be worked on has been made dead) the circuit should be tested with some device which reliably indicates the presence of mains voltage – a meter or a purpose-made test lamp.

If there remains any doubt that the circuit is dead and will remain so then switch off the whole installation by the master switch at the meter and check again. **Never work on a live circuit**.

Before any circuit is made live, check all the connections.

# Water

There are two main parts to a household plumbing system – the water supply system and the waste system. The water supply system carries clean water to baths, basins, sinks, WCs and so on: it is under the control of the local water undertaking (variously called water authority or company). The waste system is a completely separate set of pipes which carries used water away to drains and sewers. They come under the control of the Building Regulations.

## Water Supply

A household plumbing system starts at the water authority's stopvalve. This is usually situated outside the boundary of the property about 750mm below ground, under a small metal cover, probably in the pavement. Most water authority's stopvalves need a special key to turn them on and off. The stopvalve controls the flow of water between the water authority's water main and the household water supply. The responsibility for maintaining the service pipe which carries water from the stopvalve to the house lies with the householder. Before 1939, service pipes were usually lead or steel, nowadays they are often copper, or plastic. The service pipe may slope upward slightly from the stopvalve to the house but should always be at least 750mm below ground. Once inside the house, the pipe can be protected against freezing by running it along an inside wall. In houses with suspended floors it may be necessary to give the pipe additional frost protection. The supply pipe terminates at the householder's main stopvalve where it is connected to the rising main.

There are two ways of arranging the supply from the rising main to places where it is wanted. These are called indirect or direct, depending on whether there is a cold water cistern supplying most cold taps.

### Indirect plumbing systems

In an indirect system, the primary purpose of the rising main is to feed water into a cold water cistern (sometimes, wrongly, called a tank) which is usually situated in the loft. Most of the taps and other plumbing fittings in the house get their water supply from this cistern, which is kept topped up from the rising main through a ball-valve. However, at least one tap – usually the cold water tap in the kitchen – has to be supplied direct from the rising main to provide a supply of pure (potable) water for drinking and cooking.

Depending on the local water byelaws, one, two or more fittings may be made direct to the rising main – one for an outside water tap, and one for a cold water supply to a washing machine or dishwasher, say.

Most indirect plumbing systems have two pipes (often called draw-off pipes) taking water out of the cistern. One draw-off pipe feeds WCs and cold water taps in bathrooms and any other rooms where there are basins.

INDIRECT PLUMBING SYSTEM

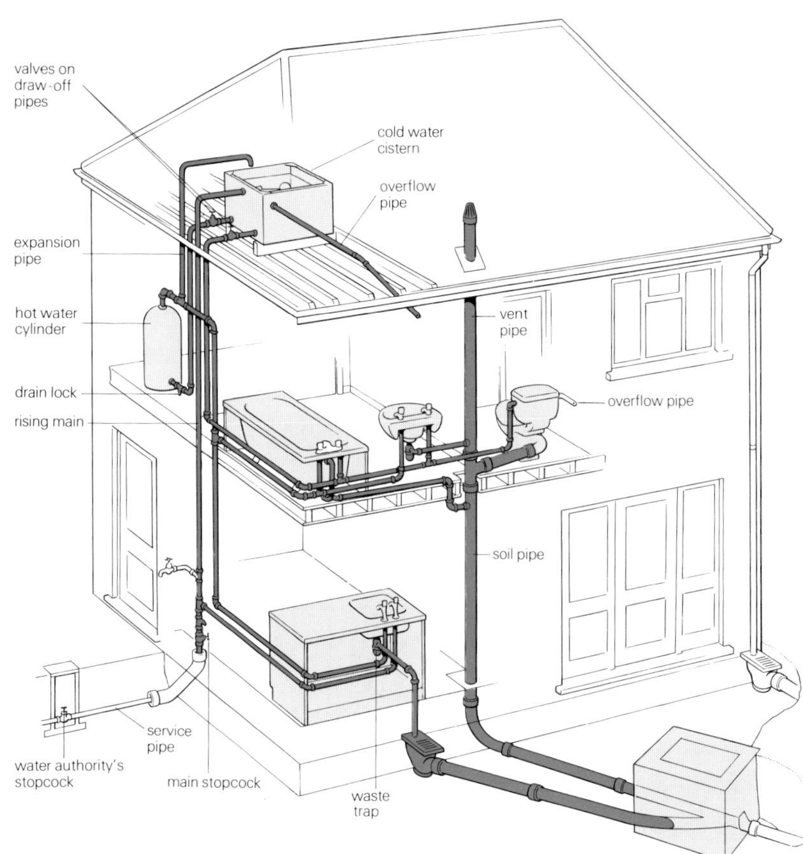


An indirect system is generally preferred. The house supply is isolated from the mains by the cold water storage cistern. Only taps supplying drinking water (usually just the one over the kitchen sink) are taken directly from the rising main.

The other feeds a hot water cylinder where the water is stored and heated – for example, by an electric immersion heater. Indirect systems may have extra draw-off pipes for some types of bidet or shower or to make pipe runs to some fittings more convenient.

Hot water taps draw their water from a pipe connected to the top of the hot water cylinder – again, most bidet and shower installations need their own, individual connections. The hot water cylinder will also have an expansion pipe (leading back to the cold water cistern) to allow for expansion of the water as it heats up, and to provide a safety vent if the water should start boiling.

The system needs a stopvalve as near as possible to the point where the service pipe enters the house. Drain cocks are also needed: one just above the main stopvalve to drain the rising main and any branch pipes connected to it and a second, as low down as possible on the pipe feeding the hot water cylinder, to drain the cylinder are essential. All other parts of the system can be drained by turning on the taps.

It can be useful to fit more valves so that parts of the plumbing system can be isolated from the rest – on each draw-off from the cistern, or individual fittings, for instance. This is useful for maintenance; for draining down during cold spells when the house will be unheated and for removing fittings. There should be a valve on the pipe feeding the hot water cylinder but not on the outlet pipe from it.

An indirect plumbing system has four main advantages. First, and possibly most importantly, because most of the system is isolated from the mains by the cistern, water is less likely to be drawn back into the mains so there is much less risk of contamination of the water supply. Secondly, the system operates at constant water pressure so you do not need to worry about variations in the mains water pressure – this is particularly important for some types of shower which need roughly equal pressures of hot and cold water. Thirdly, the water pressure is relatively low which helps to reduce noise and, finally, the cistern provides a reserve supply of water if the mains fails or is temporarily cut off.

DIRECT PLUMBING SYSTEM

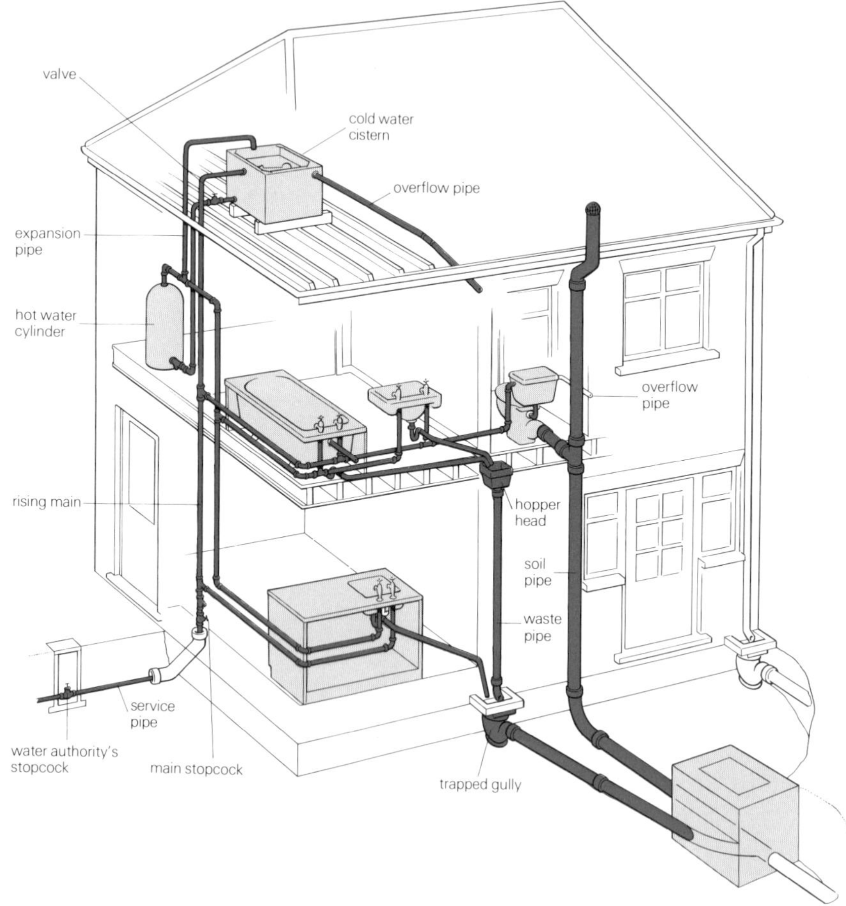


A direct system may have a small cold water storage system to supply the hot water cylinder, but the cold water taps and most other fittings are connected to the rising main.

**Direct plumbing systems**

In a direct plumbing system, all the cold taps, WCs and so on are fed directly from the rising main and so turning on one tap may cut the supply to another. There must be a stopvalve as near as possible to the point where the service pipe enters the house. Although there is no large cold water storage cistern, there will be a small feed-and-expansion cistern if the hot water is heated by a storage hot water cylinder rather than by instantaneous heaters.

A direct plumbing system is a little less complicated and can be cheaper to install than an indirect one. But some of the fittings used may have to be specially designed to lessen the risk of contamination of the mains. Most water authorities prefer an indirect system and in most cases it is also the best sort of system for a householder to have. Changing from a direct system to an indirect one isn't difficult, it's a job that could be done all in one go. Or, if you plan to replace all the plumbing fittings eventually, it can be done in stages. But if you've a direct supply in lead piping, replace and convert all at once.

## WATER BYE-LAWS

The water bye-laws operated by regional water authorities control what you can do to the plumbing system in your house. Although the regulations can vary from region to region, they're all based on the *Model Water Bye-laws*.

The aims of water bye-laws are to reduce water wastage and undue consumption, to prevent the water supply from being contaminated and to prevent reverberation in pipes. If you are contemplating doing some d-i-y plumbing, you should get hold of a copy of your region's bye-laws. The list below details the main regulations with which you must comply and a few other rules which any good plumber would be sure to stick to to ensure a good job.

All pipes drawing water from a cold water cistern should be fitted with a stopvalve so that you can do maintenance and improvement work without having to drain the whole cistern. You should fit a stopvalve between the cold cistern and the hot water cylinder and also to pipes serving ballvalves.

Plumbing has to be arranged so that there's no chance of stored water (from a cistern, for example) or dirty water (from a bath, for example) coming into contact with fresh water in the mains. The concern here is that fluctuations in mains pressure may cause contaminated water to be syphoned back into the mains. In effect, the regulations mean that a mains tap discharging into a sink has to be at least 13mm above the top edge of the sink; if you want to install a shower or tap mixer and connect it so that one is taken from the mains and the other from stored water, then you must make sure the mixer has a non-return valve incorporated into it. When installing a mains-fed, instantaneously-heated shower without a non-return valve but with a handspray and flexible hose, this be positioned so that, if it's allowed to hang down, the handspray is at least 13mm above the top edge of the bath or shower tray.

Cisterns must be sited where they can be conveniently inspected and cleaned (with at least 350mm clearance above the top). Each home must have a cistern capacity of at least 200 litres and there are regulations covering the size and position of overflows.

There are limits to the length of hot water pipes.

Pipes should be reasonably accessible for maintenance. Pipes may be boxed in as long as the boxing is fairly easy to open.

Pipes must be supported. Use pipe clips to prevent rattling.

Fittings have to made to the appropriate British Standard, if there is one, or be as good.

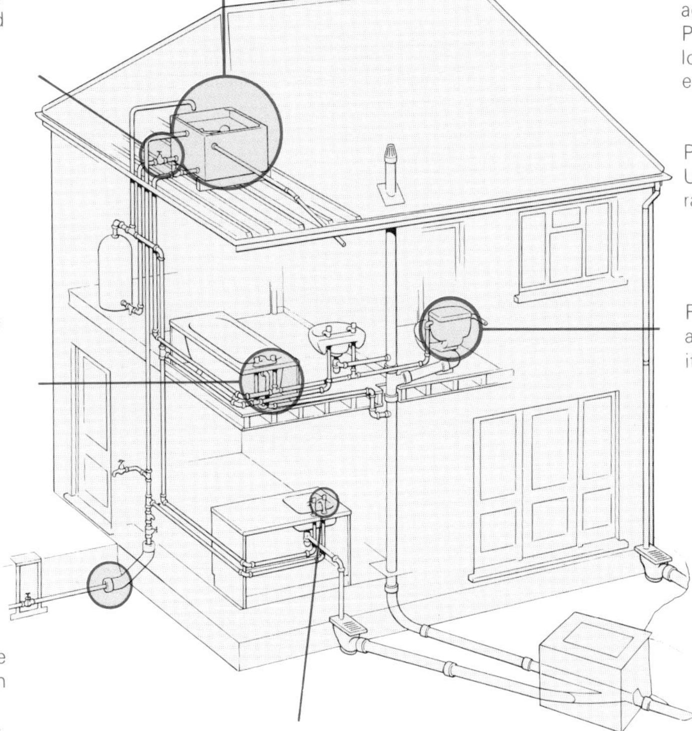

Every home must have a drinking water tap supplied directly from the rising main.

Pipes laid underground must be corrosion-resistant or protected from corrosion and must be buried at a depth of 750mm to 1350mm.

Plumbing installations have to be protected from frost, and they have to be drainable. So if your plumbing scheme involves a U-shaped run, especially outdoors, the lowest part should be fitted with a drain-cock so the pipe can be emptied.

In some areas of the country the water may cause dezincification of pipe fittings. In these regions you must use fittings made of an alloy resistant to dezincification, such as gunmetal. Your local plumbers' merchant should be able to help.

The Water Bye-laws vary a little from region to region, but are essentially similar.

## Pipes and fittings

Nowadays, most plumbing pipes are copper, though plastic pipes are often used for waste and plastic pipe is becoming common for supply too.

### Copper pipe

Copper pipe is sized by its *outside* diameter – 15mm, 22mm and 28mm are the most common sizes (equivalent to ½in, ¾in, and 1in *inside* diameter). Main runs and pipes feeding bath taps are usually 15mm.

Copper pipe can be cut with a fine-toothed hacksaw, or with a special pipe-cutting tool. Care must be taken to cut exactly square and the cut must be filed smooth both inside and out. A pipe cutter tends to leave a burr inside the pipe – this should be filed off.

Copper pipe can be bent by hand but it must be supported by bending springs or it will kink. These are stiff metal coils of the appropriate diameter pushed into the pipe where the bend is to be made.

For small plumbing jobs, using pipes up to 22mm, bending springs are probably all that you need. For large plumbing jobs and larger pipes a bending machine is worth hiring, though it requires practice to get the bend in the right place in the pipe.

Bends are better than fittings for altering the direction of a run – bends are cheaper and allow a smoother flow. Special bendable copper pipe is useful for the odd bend, at taps for instance, but very expensive to buy.

### Joining copper pipes

The main methods of joining copper lengths of copper pipe are to use compression joints which are fitted to the pipes using spanners –an *olive* makes the watertight seal – or capillary joints which are soldered on to the pipes.

There are two types of capillary fitting. The solder-ring fitting is most suitable for d-i-y, this has its own, built-in, supply of solder which when heated flows to fill the gap between the fitting and the pipe ends. End feed fittings are similar but with these a length of solder wire is melted at the mouth of the fitting and allowed to creep into the gap.

For plumbing water pipes either capillary or compression fittings can be used. Compression fittings are usually first choice for a novice, they're fairly easy to make, can usually be undone and reconnected and if they leak, the leak can often be stopped by slightly tightening the fitting. (They're also useful if you have to joint into stainless steel pipes.) Capillary fittings are neater and cheaper, but require a little practice to become expert. A leaking capillary joint often means that the solder hasn't flowed properly and in this situation the joint generally has to be sawn apart and replaced. Capillary fittings are required for gas plumbing.

Push-fit plastic connectors are a third choice for water plumbing with

MAKING JOINTS

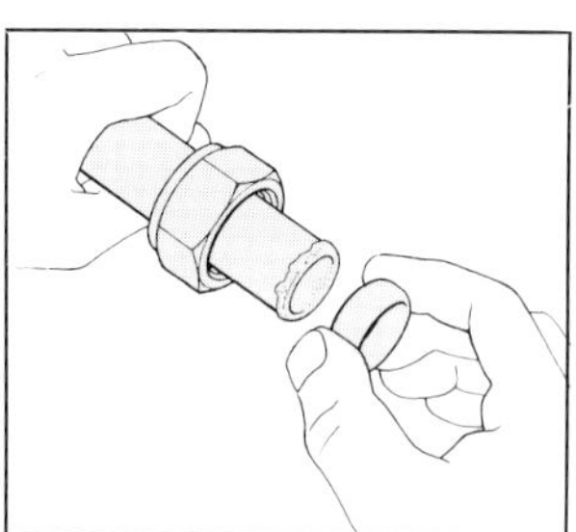

**A compression joint** File the end of one piece of pipe smooth, pass the cap nut from the fitting over it, smear the end

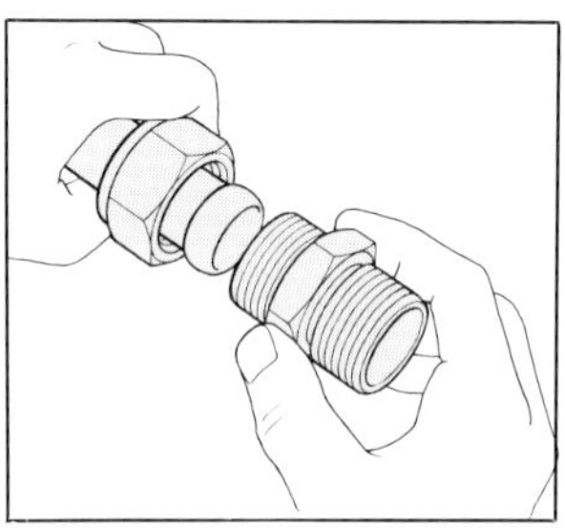

with an approved jointing paste and push the olive on to the pipe. Then push the fitting over the end of the pipe.

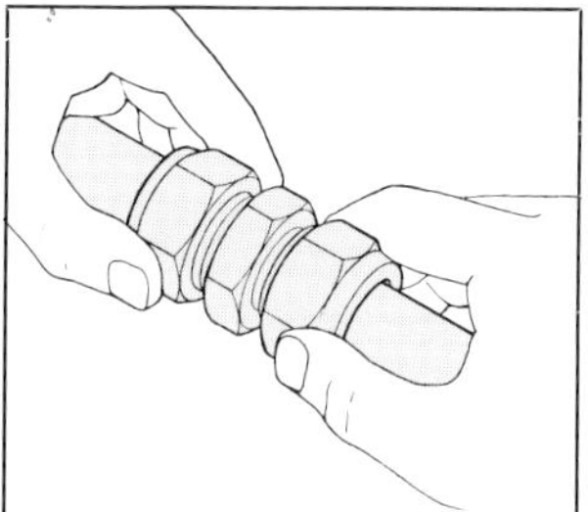

Prepare the end of the other piece of pipe in the same way – with jointing paste and an olive – and push this into the fitting.

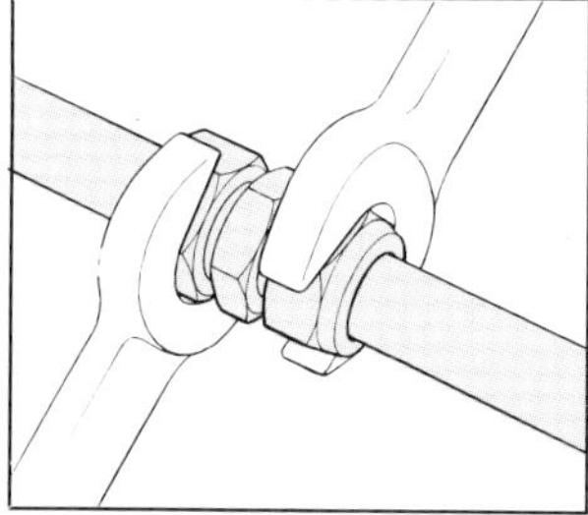

Tighten the fitting with spanners. Do not overtighten: if there's a small leak, tighten a little more.

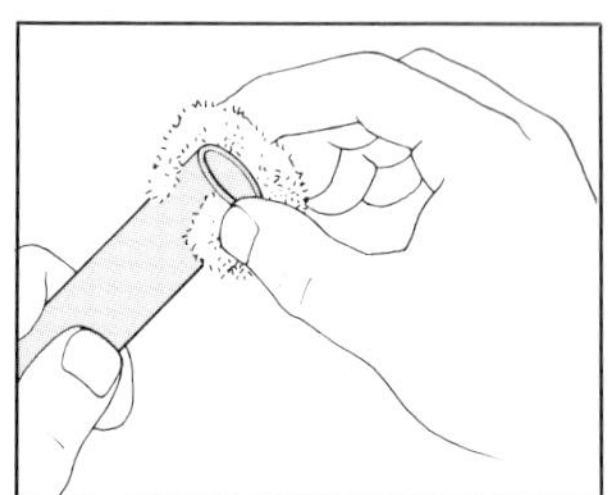

**A capillary joint (solder-ring type)** Thoroughly clean the outside ends of the pipes, and the inside of the fittings

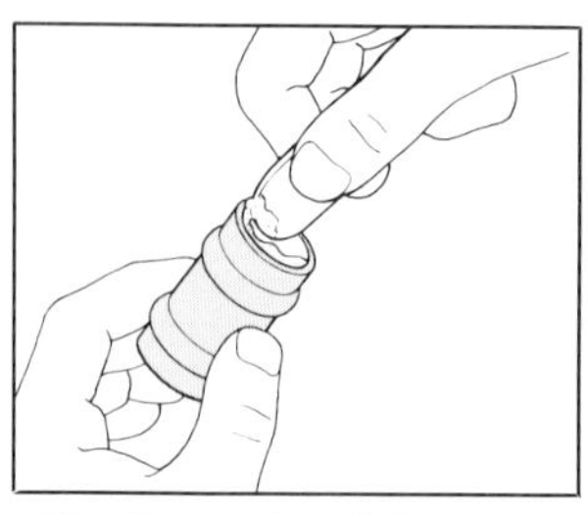

with wire wool until they are bright and shiny. Using a brush or spatula, smear a small amount of solder flux all round

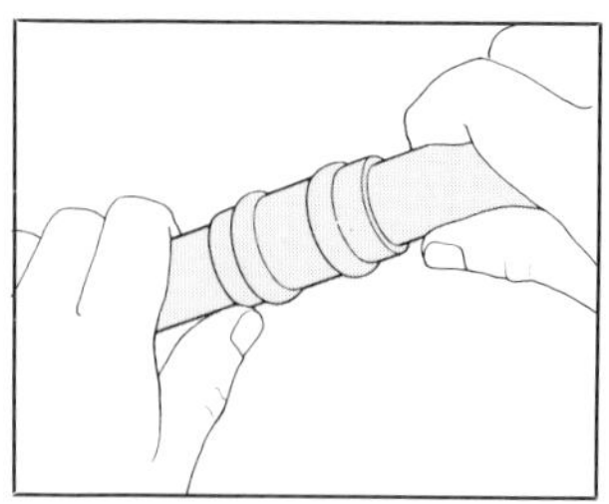

the inside of the fitting and push the fitting and pipes together so that they overlap.

Carefully heat the joint with a

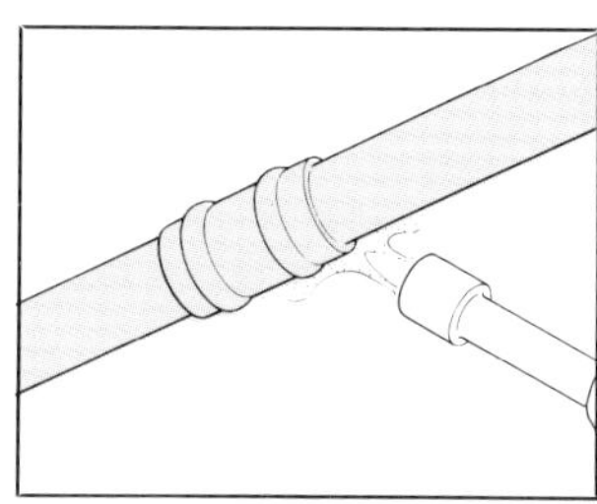

blow-lamp until a ring of solder appears at each end. Do not disturb the joint until cooled. If the joint leaks, reheat.

15mm and 22mm pipes. These plastic connectors are very easy to fit and can easily be undone and refitted, but they are more expensive than the other types of fittings. To make the joint smear the pipe end with lubricant and push it into the connector – a plastic ring makes the watertight seal and a grab-ring holds the pipe firm.

There are many different types of fitting with either capillary or compression joint ends: **straight couplings** for joining two lengths of pipe together in a straight line; **elbows** and **bends** for joining two lengths together at an angle (usually a right angle); **tees** for joining a branch pipe; and **adaptors** for joining pipes to taps. Merchants often stock only the most common ones.

Some fittings, such as taps for garden hoses and washing machines, have a *screwed* end. These fittings can have different sizes of screw thread – $\frac{1}{2}$in BSP (British Standard Pipe) is the most common. There are a number of ways of making a watertight joint with these fittings. The simplest is to wrap PTFE tape around the male thread before screwing it into the female part of the fitting. But PTFE tape will not seal large threads. For these, smear a small amount of jointing paste on to the threads followed by a few strands of hemp (which looks like unravelled string) before screwing the joints together. Screwed fittings which may need to be undone have a washer to make the watertight joints.

### Adding to copper pipes

Joining a new pipe to existing old pipework usually means forming a branch – often by making a tee joint. If the existing pipes are copper and metric sizes there's no problem, but if the existing copper pipes are the old *imperial* sizes a special adaptor may be needed to connect the new piece of metric pipe to the old imperial one. Capillary fittings almost always need adaptors; with compression fittings only 22mm pipes (joined to $\frac{3}{4}$in) do.

As the actual sizes are only slightly different it is difficult to tell whether old pipework is imperial or metric just by looking so it's worth having some adaptors in stock. Joining to pipes of other materials can be tricky, especially copper to lead joints – these are best left to a professional. If your house contains much lead piping it may be better to have it stripped out.

### Plastic supply pipes

Plastic pipes in 15mm, 22mm and 28mm sizes are now available for both hot and cold water supplies and are also approved for use in central heating systems. *Which?* has not tested these yet, but they look set to be the d-i-y plumbing material of the future.

The pipes are made of rigid plastics and joined to fittings by the solvent-weld method as described for waste pipes, except that the ends do not need to be chamfered and you push the pipe into the fitting with a slight twisting motion. Pipes are not bendable and fittings are required at all changes of direction.

Although the pipes can carry hot water, a length of copper pipe is required at the outlet of a boiler (or other heat source). Adaptors are available to join plastic to metal pipes and fittings. The pipes must be well supported along their length at a minimum of 500mm for horizontal runs; 1m for vertical runs. Thought must be given to the expansion that will occur as the pipes heat up. At each end of short runs (under 3m) leave an expansion gap in the joint of about 3mm. In longer runs exceeding 10m, an expansion loop must be turned somewhere in the length.

### Plastic waste pipes

Plastic pipe is easily cut with a knife or a fine-toothed hacksaw. There are two methods of joining. All pipes can be joined with *push-fit connections* which have rubber sealing rings ('O' rings) to make the seal. To make a joint, smooth off the pipe ends and chamfer the outer surfaces to about 15 degrees. Smear with lubricant, push into connector and then withdraw slightly to allow for thermal expansion – consult the brand instructions.

Solvent-weld joints are the alternative (though not all pipes are suitable for this). To make a solvent-weld joint wipe the chamfered ends and the inside of the connector with a degreasing cleaner. Coat with solvent cement, push together and leave undisturbed for a few minutes. Surplus cement is not removed.

A TEE JOINT

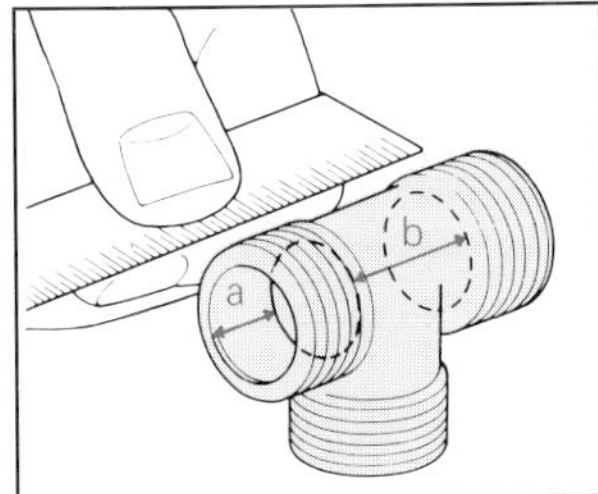


Measure, by pushing in a pipe or with a ruler, the distances 'a' at each end – it's the length of pipe which can be pushed into the fitting. Subtract 2 × 'a' from

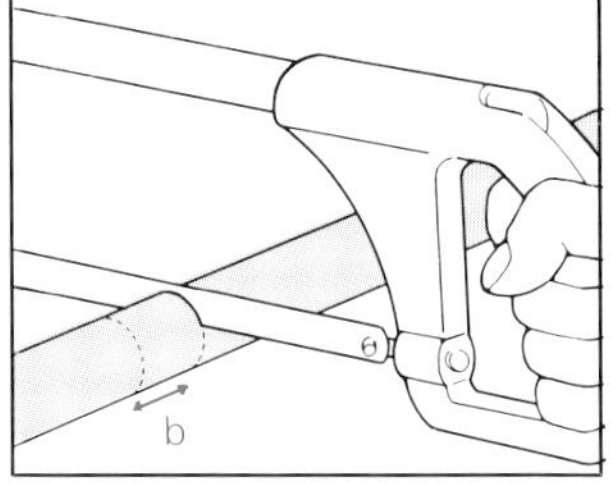


the overall length to get 'b'.

Carefully cut the length 'b' from the pipe at the point where you want the branch to start. To fit the tee connector, it will

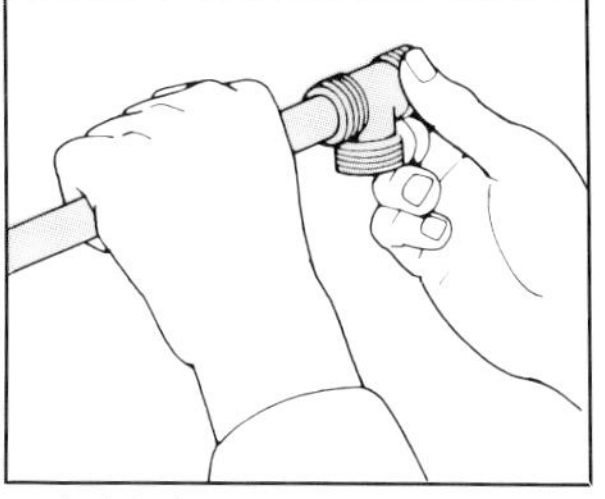

probably be necessary to remove some pipe clips, so that the pipes can be pulled slightly out from the wall.

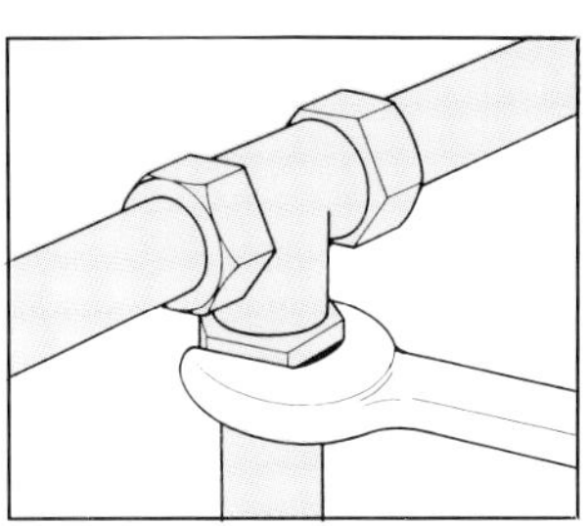

Fix the connector, as any other joint. Fit the branch pipe into place: with a capillary fitting, do this before any soldering.

## Wastes and drains

In modern plumbing systems, the pipes which carry used water away from baths, basins, WCs, bidets and showers have traps – often called U-bends – full of water. The water in these traps prevents smells from the sewers getting into the house. On a WC, the water trap is part of the fitting, in other cases, it is part of the outlet pipe.

### Single-stack systems

Most houses built since about 1960 have a single-stack waste system. The branch pipes from the U-bend traps, attached to baths, basins, WCs and so on in the upper storeys of the house, connect into a single pipe (usually 100mm in diameter) – called a discharge pipe, soil pipe or soil-stack – which runs vertically down to the drains. This pipe may be on the outside of the house, but Building Regulations now require that it runs inside the house. The top of this pipe should terminate outside the building, not less than 900mm above the top of any opening windows. The bottom is connected directly into the house drainage system – there is no trap at this point.

When designing a waste system, care has to be taken to ensure that the water in traps cannot be sucked out so breaking the seal against smells. This can happen if waste water rushes through the branch pipe leading from the trap (or through other pipes connected to this branch) quickly enough to create sufficient suction to pull the water out of the trap. To guard against unsealing, the top of the soil stack is left open. It should, however, be fitted with a cage to stop birds nesting in it and stopping up the open end. (Technically, the length of the pipe above the highest branch connection to it is called a vent pipe.) In the single-stack waste system, there need to be other design constraints – the slope, length and diameter of branch pipes, the position of their connections to the soil-stack, and the radius of the bend at the foot of the soil-stack all have to be worked out carefully. Despite all this, the single-stack system is widely used, because it is economical and neat.

WCs at ground-floor level may also be connected to the soil-stack but are more usually connected directly to the drain. Other ground-floor waste pipes will probably discharge through a gully. This is a water trap with the top open to the air at ground level and an

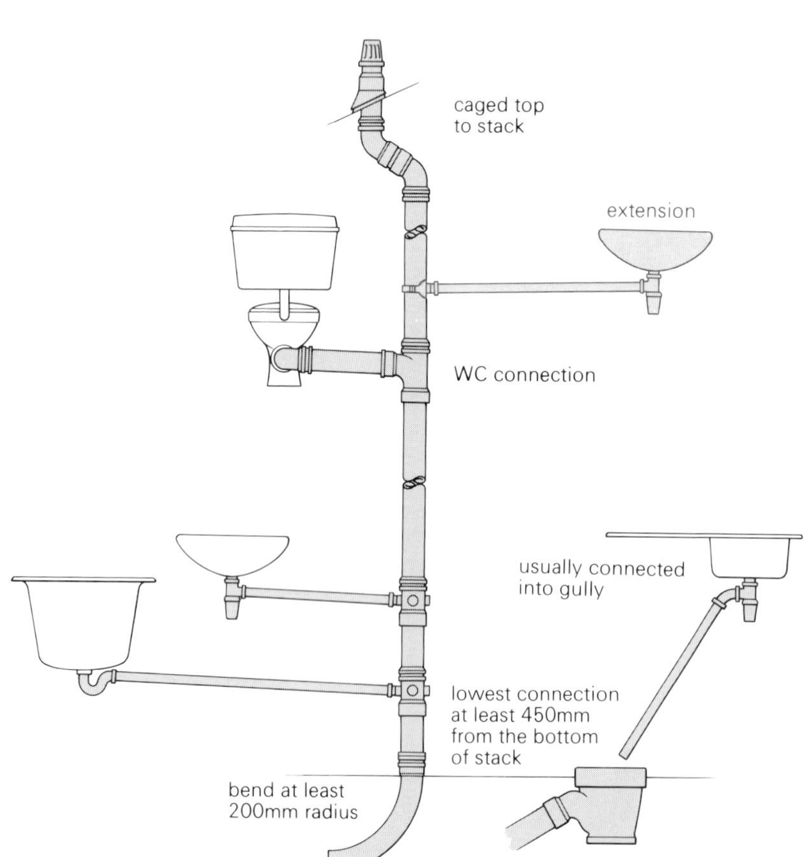


A single-stack waste system is economical and neat, but needs careful design.

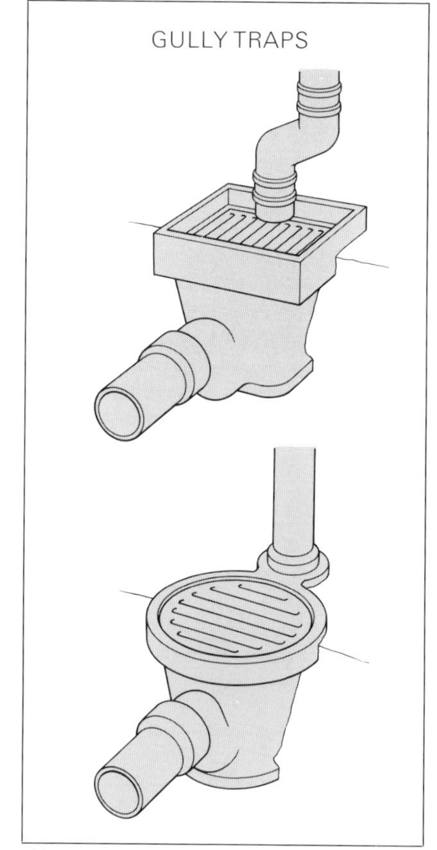


*Above:* an older system with waste pipe discharging above the grid.
*Below:* a back-inlet gully to comply with Building Regulations.

outlet connected underground to the house drains. Pipes to gullies used to discharge above the level of the grid fitted to prevent leaves and other things blocking it. But this can give rise to problems with overflowing drains, so now waste pipes must enter the gully below the level of the grid but above the level of the water in the gully trap. This can be achieved either by simply passing the pipe through a hole cut in the top of the grid, or by connecting it to an inlet forming part of the gully. When this inlet is at the back of the gully (the front of the grid is where the outlet is) it is called a back-inlet gully, when the inlet is at the side, it is called, not surprisingly, a side-inlet gully. The different forms are simply to make installation easier and there is no practical difference.

**Two-pipe systems**

Many older houses have a two-pipe waste system with WCs connected into one vertical soil pipe, and other wastes (baths, basins, and bidets) connected into a second separate vertical waste pipe. This system calls for less careful designs of slopes and connections, but the vertical pipes still need to be vented to the air. In the drawing, the soil pipe is vented by having its open end above the eaves – as in the single-stack system. But the waste pipe is open to the air at first floor level, and the branch pipes discharge into a funnel – called a hopper – fixed to this open end.

A two-pipe system like this can be extended by allowing extra waste pipes to discharge into the hopper. But in new two-pipe systems installed nowadays, all branch waste pipes have to be connected into the side of the vertical waste pipe and hoppers are not permitted.

In the two-pipe system, the soil pipe is connected directly to the drains, and the waste pipe is connected via a trapped gully.

## Building Regulations

The design of the pipes and fittings used to carry waste away from baths, basins, showers and WCs is controlled by the *Building Regulations*. The aim of the section that covers drainage is to protect public health and make sure that domestic waste is carried effectively to a public sewer. You must comply with the Regulations below when connecting waste pipes from newly-installed kitchen or bathroom equipment including any fittings in a new extension.

- wastes should be fitted with traps. The waste pipe must be arranged and the trap installed so that it's always full of water, so sealing the waste and preventing air coming up from the drains into the house.
- waste pipes must be at least 32mm in diameter. They must be adequately supported, properly jointed and be reasonably accessible for maintenance.
- waste pipes should connect directly with the stack pipe and not discharge into hoppers unless a hopper is already there (which pre-dates the current Building Regulations). Ground-floor waste pipes can be discharged into a gully with a grating cover above the level of discharge.

TWO-PIPE SYSTEM

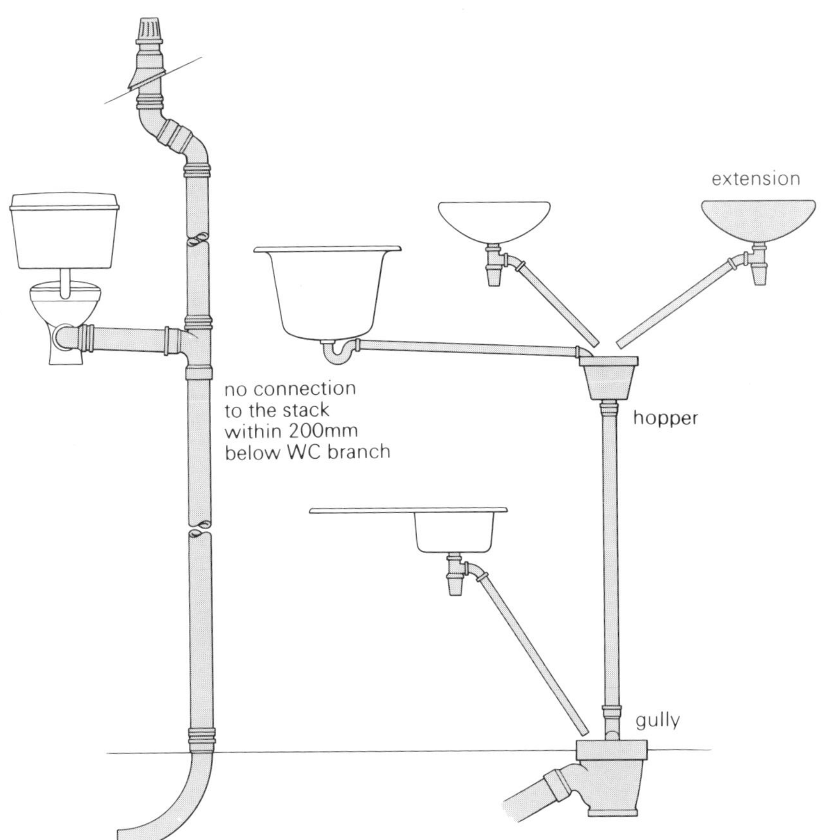


An existing two-pipe system can be extended by running more pipes into the hopper. In a modern two-pipe system branch pipes have to be connected as for a soil pipe.

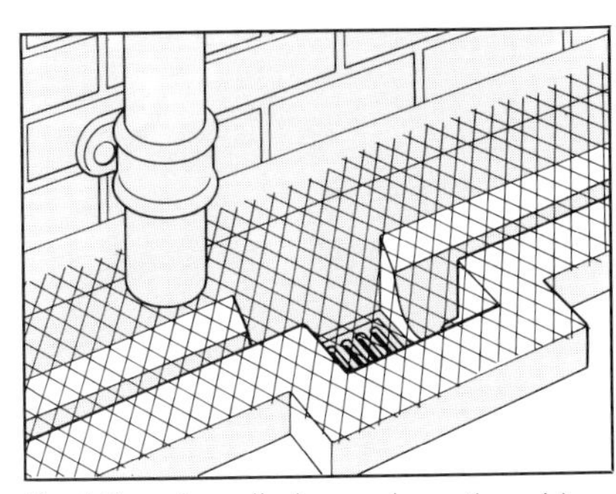

If existing pipes discharge above the grid the drain can easily be blocked, so fit an extra grille to catch leaves.

# Drains

The underground drain system of a house takes the waste from soil pipes and gullies to the public sewer or, if the house is not on mains drainage, to a septic tank or cesspool. In most cases these drains do not also carry rain-water, which is generally disposed of through a separate set of drains either to a public surface-water drain or to a *soakaway* in the grounds of the house. Combined (or partly-combined) foul waste and rain-water drainage systems are increasingly rare these days.

The layout of underground drains can usually be traced by the position of the inspection chambers. These or some other form of access – such as a rodding eye – are required within 12.5m of junctions between drains; at any change of direction or gradient of the drain; at the beginning of the drain (near the entrance of the soil stack) and at intervals of not more than 90m on long straight runs. A single house often has a fairly simple layout connected directly to the public sewer. But where houses are more tightly packed – terraced houses and high density housing estates – the individual house drains usually join a private sewer which takes the waste to the public sewer.

Drains laid for the use of one house are the sole responsibility of the householder. If they run through neighbouring property there should

SEWERS

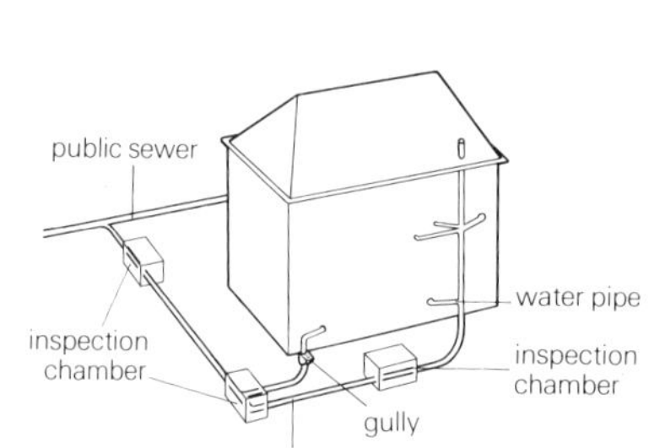


A single house usually has a simple layout as illustrated.

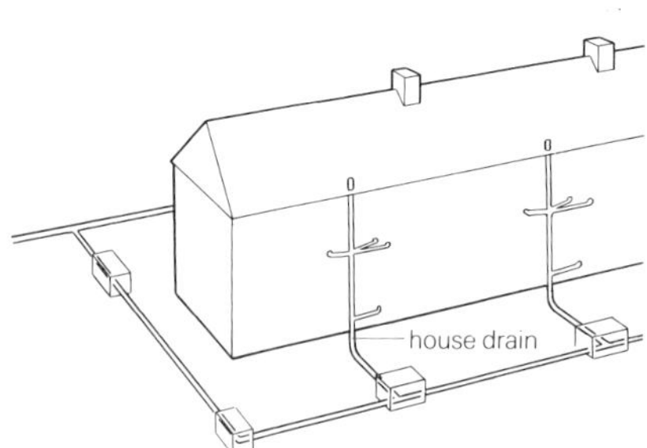


Private sewers carrying communal waste are used where houses are tightly packed on estates and in terraces.

be provision in the deeds of the house allowing access for maintenance and repair. Private sewers are the shared responsibility of the houseowners concerned, except where the private sewer was constructed before 1937, when the responsibility rests with the water authority. But they can pass on the cost of maintenance and repair of any section of the private sewer to *all* the individual households connected to it. The public sewer, and the job of connecting any private drain or sewer to it, is the responsibility of the water authority.

**Tracing drains**

By pouring water down the WC, sink and so on, it should be possible to look in the inspection chambers and to tell which waste pipe connects to which branch drain and where the branch drains meet the main drain. If water from a fitting doesn't appear in the chamber it may be connected to a branch drain which connects to a neighbour's drainage system. Fluorescent dyes can be helpful.

A plan with the deeds of the house may show the drains or they may have been mapped on a plan prepared for previous building work and held by the local building control office. Most local authorities keep plans which show the drains on properties in the district.

Land drains to a soakaway are much harder to trace as there are no access points to mark their way and normally no indication of where the soakaway might be. When building an extension, excavations may uncover land drains and then it is usually necessary to reconstruct the drain run.

DRAIN JUNCTIONS

benching

half channel

An inspection chamber is required close to where drains meet; two branch drains flow in here.

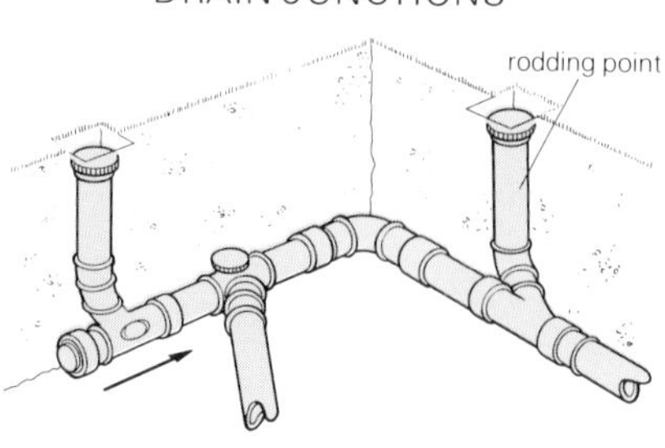


Rodding points are used here at a junction and a bend; elsewhere in the drain run, an inspection chamber gives better access.

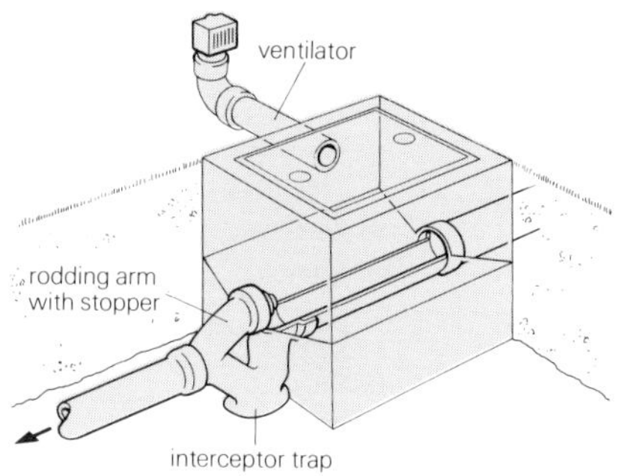


The inspection chamber at the boundary of a property may have an interceptor trap.

# PART 2
# IMPROVEMENTS ROOM BY ROOM

# Chapter 3 KITCHEN IMPROVEMENTS

Not surprisingly, installing a new well-designed kitchen in a room previously ill-equipped is one of the best improvements you can do to make a house more saleable. Provided you keep the cost within sensible bounds new kitchens generally add much of their initial cost to the value of the house. But, if you spend the earth on fitted units, it's unlikely to turn out to be a worthwhile investment. One of the best improvements you can do is to make a poky kitchen into a room large enough to take other activities – mainly family dining. You might be able to do this by stealing some space from an adjacent room or perhaps demolishing a walk-in larder, but in most houses it's much more likely that the extra space will be part of an extension or will take over existing space released by a new extension.

Although moving activities *into* the kitchen is the commonest rearrangement there are two quite different choices: one is to take the kitchen activities into the living space, the other is to make the kitchen much smaller, either by decreasing the size of the existing room or by creating a new compact room somewhere else. Taking the kitchen into the living space means going open-plan and to make it work you need an efficient air extraction system – to take grease, smells and moist air away at source.

A small kitchen becomes an essentially functional room and may mean moving out some activities – laundering for instance (this isn't a big disadvantage, where possible it's best to keep laundering away from food preparation areas anyway). Small kitchens are unlikely to be popular with most people, but the restraints of a tight space can be used to advantage in designing an efficient, even dramatic, kitchen and because it's small there's more scope for resiting the room. This is particularly true if you're prepared to create (and work in) an internal room with artificial lighting (note that this wouldn't be allowed in Scotland or Inner London where a kitchen must have daylight). Like an open-plan kitchen an internal one will need an efficient ventilation system which vents directly to the outside.

Arranging the plumbing is often the biggest constraint on where you can site and how you can organise a kitchen. Moving these can be difficult, as well as expensive if you employ a professional to do the installation. Plenty of people will be prepared to plan your kitchen for you – interior designers, unit retailers and manufacturers. Make sure they design to *your* requirements.

## Initial planning

The planning decision and choices are closely linked to each other and you'll probably do most of the early planning almost subconsciously, thinking and talking over several weeks or months about what you want to do in your new kitchen and consequently the *type* of kitchen you'll choose. In the early stages you also need to think about the *style* of kitchen you want, which equipment and fittings you want to replace and can afford to replace, whether you're prepared to move the services about – the position of plumbing will be all important. This is the time to do some window shopping, to pick up ideas from catalogues, books and magazines and, if necessary, to talk to the Building Control Officer.

During the initial planning stages you should also think hard about how the members of the household interact with the present kitchen – the ergonomics. It might be interesting to carry out an ergonomic study – which simply means observing and recording people's actions in the kitchen – to identify the good and bad points. The main kitchen user can do this alone, but it's easier to have an observer who notes down the individual tasks and movements that add up to a job – cooking a meal, for instance. Then you can isolate the unnecessary movements and ones which involve over-reaching, stooping etc and aim to eliminate these in your new design.

Use the opportunity to rethink your storage requirements and to sort out your kitchen equipment. If you find things you haven't used in the past year consider now throwing them out.

An internal kitchen may be the answer if space is tight; it wouldn't be allowed in Scotland or Inner London. ▶

A kitchen/dining room is a common combination which works well. ▼

This kitchen is open-plan in a corner of the main room. ▶

## The kitchen planning rules

The main function of a kitchen is for the preparation of food and all the associated tasks like washing up. The planning rules are intended to allow the easiest and safest progression from task to task around the kitchen. This sequence can be designed as a straight line, but more often it's some sort of triangle. The idea is to have a natural work sequence on the lines: work surface/cooker/work surface/sink/work surface. This order is for a right-handed user, it's reversed for a left-handed one. The cooker and sink should be in fairly close proximity to minimise the distance you carry heavy pans for draining and in moving from sink to cooker you shouldn't cross a traffic route through the kitchen – see drawing – or climb up or down a step.

Food and equipment should be stored close to the work surface or appliance where they'll *first* be needed – vegetables, and perhaps vegetable saucepans, near to the sink, baking tins close to a work surface, frying pan and seasonings within reach of the cooker.

### The layout

Kitchens which are U-shaped or L-shaped are easiest to work in and if you study designs of large kitchens which look more complicated (a kitchen with an island unit for instance) you'll see that they are often combinations of U-shaped and L-shaped banks of fittings. A straight bank of units with a separate table doubles as a sort of L and a narrow galley kitchen with banks of units on opposite walls comes close to a U.

If possible try to avoid a narrow galley kitchen which is also a thoroughfare. You should have at least a metre space between opposite banks of units. If people will have to pass down the centre leave at least a metre and a half between opposite banks of units or a bank of units and a table – more if an oven opens into a gap. For this sort of kitchen where space is tight, you'd do best to choose kitchen units with doors that open through 180°.

KITCHEN TRAFFIC ROUTES

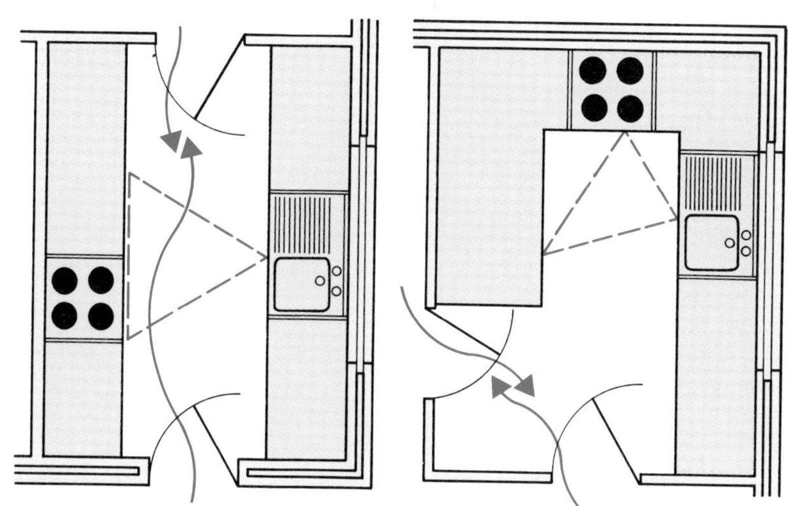

Avoid traffic routes which cross the main working triangle of the kitchen. If a route has to be allowed for, leave sufficient space between the units on either side.

LAYOUT IDEAS

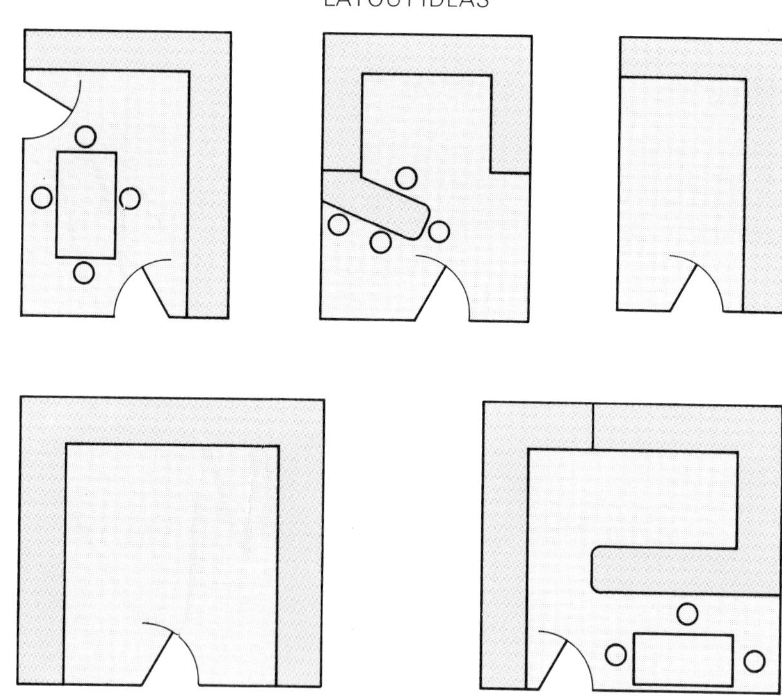

L-shaped and U-shaped kitchen are usually easiest to work in. Most designs are based on these shapes.

## THE SCALE PLANS

If you've thought hard enough in the initial stages, the detailed planning becomes a jigsaw – juggling the space and the components to get the best possible layout within the limitations you've decided (or had) to accept.

In addition to a scale plan you'll need wall elevations (best on graph paper) outlining the available wall areas – a scale of 1 to 20 is a good one to use. If you're re-fitting an existing kitchen, mark in, as accurately as possible, the position of doors and windows (including their frames), water and gas pipes and any socket outlets that you're intending not to move.

### Modules

Like most building components, kitchen equipment – cookers, fridges, sinks etc – and cabinets are built on a module. Nowadays most are designed on a metric module, and even if you're re-using some old equipment built on an imperial module it's best to use metric measurements for making your drawings.

There are modular sizes for the depth (front to back); width (side to side) – sometimes called length – and height (top to bottom) of units and equipment. Width and height vary from one type of unit to the next; but depth is consistent through a range – with the wall-mounted units typically half the width of the base units. Before you start fitting the furniture it's important to decide whether you'll use 600mm deep units or 500mm ones intended for narrow kitchens. Ranges of units 500mm deep are cheaper than 600mm ones, but where possible 600mm ones are better because the extra 100mm is useful space. Most kitchen equipment is 600mm deep.

### Heights

The module height for floorstanding units is about 900mm. This is designed to be 75mm lower than the elbow of the average person, so, if the person who's going to use the kitchen most is especially tall or short, it's worth considering altering the heights by cutting down the plinth or buying or building an extra plinth. Usually no more than 100mm or so is involved and this small amount won't upset the balance of the units. (Check that it won't upset the fit of any built-under equipment you have.) Wall units are usually set about 1350mm above the worktop.

Having all the surfaces in a kitchen at the same height lends continuity to the design but different surfaces really need to be at different heights. It's often possible to achieve say a higher sink or lower worktop without upsetting the main line of the units by making use of a natural break such as a corner. Changes in the height of the working surface should never be abrupt and surfaces adjacent to equipment – such as a hob – should be at the same height as that equipment.

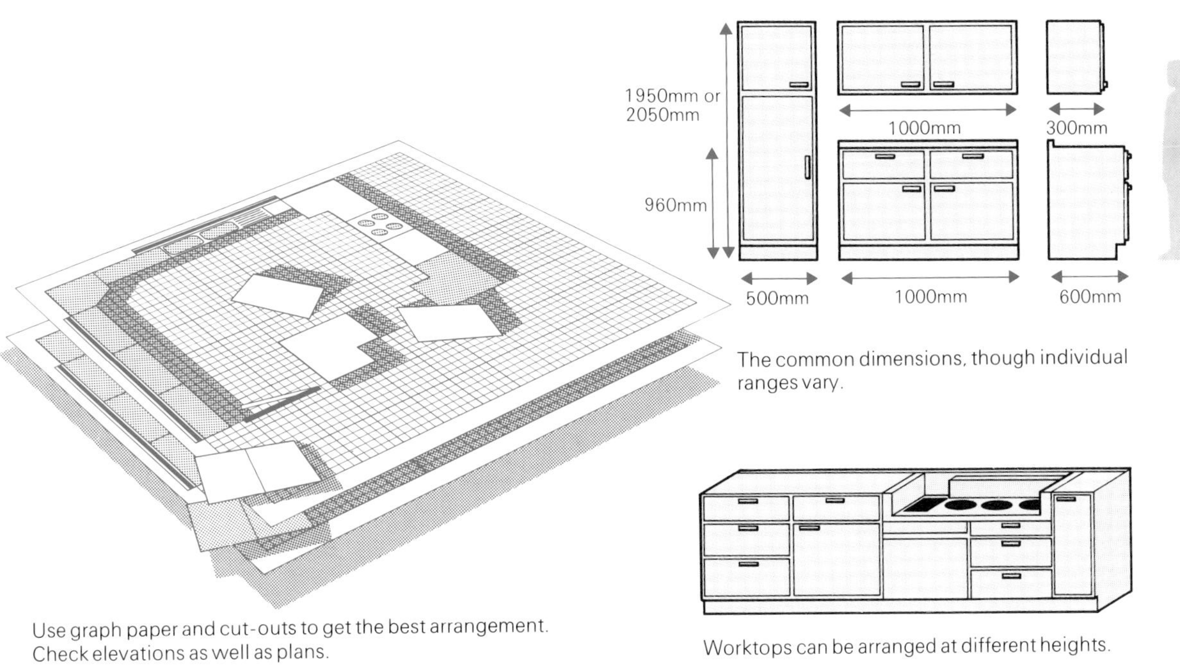


The common dimensions, though individual ranges vary.

Use graph paper and cut-outs to get the best arrangement. Check elevations as well as plans.

Worktops can be arranged at different heights.

## Equipping a kitchen

A new or refurbished kitchen usually means new storage units, often a new sink and taps and frequently new pieces of kitchen equipment – cooker, fridge and so on. Sinks and storage units are dealt with in this chapter. *Which?* regularly publishes up-to-date reports on the important pieces of kitchen equipment and the latest report is the best source of information. Nowadays most kitchen equipment can be freestanding or built-in. Built-in cookers can be split-levels with the oven set in a housing unit and raised to an easier working height, but such installations decrease the available space for worktops and built-under ovens are now becoming more popular. Freestanding cookers are also being designed to integrate more successfully with a bank of units. An advantage is that they can be moved if the house is sold.

## Sinks and taps

The linked rectangular sink and drainer that fitted over a base unit instead of a worktop is still common, but these days you can opt instead for units inset into the worktop. Stainless steel units are pressed from sheets of metal. The simplest and cheapest are rectangular with one square bowl and an integral drainer to the left or right of the bowl; two bowl, one drainer sink units are widely available, but one bowl, two drainer sinks are less common. The more expensive stainless steel sinks are formed from thicker gauges of metal; often have deeper bowls and may have small shallow bowls for food preparation. Shiny stainless steel can lose its lustre when water dries on, satin and matt versions shouldn't.

Enamelled steel sinks are less durable than steel ones, they're easy to chip with a heavy object and can be scratched, but they are available in many colours – typically brown, red and blue – and some manufacturers make hobs and other equipment to match. Enamel bowls and drainers are

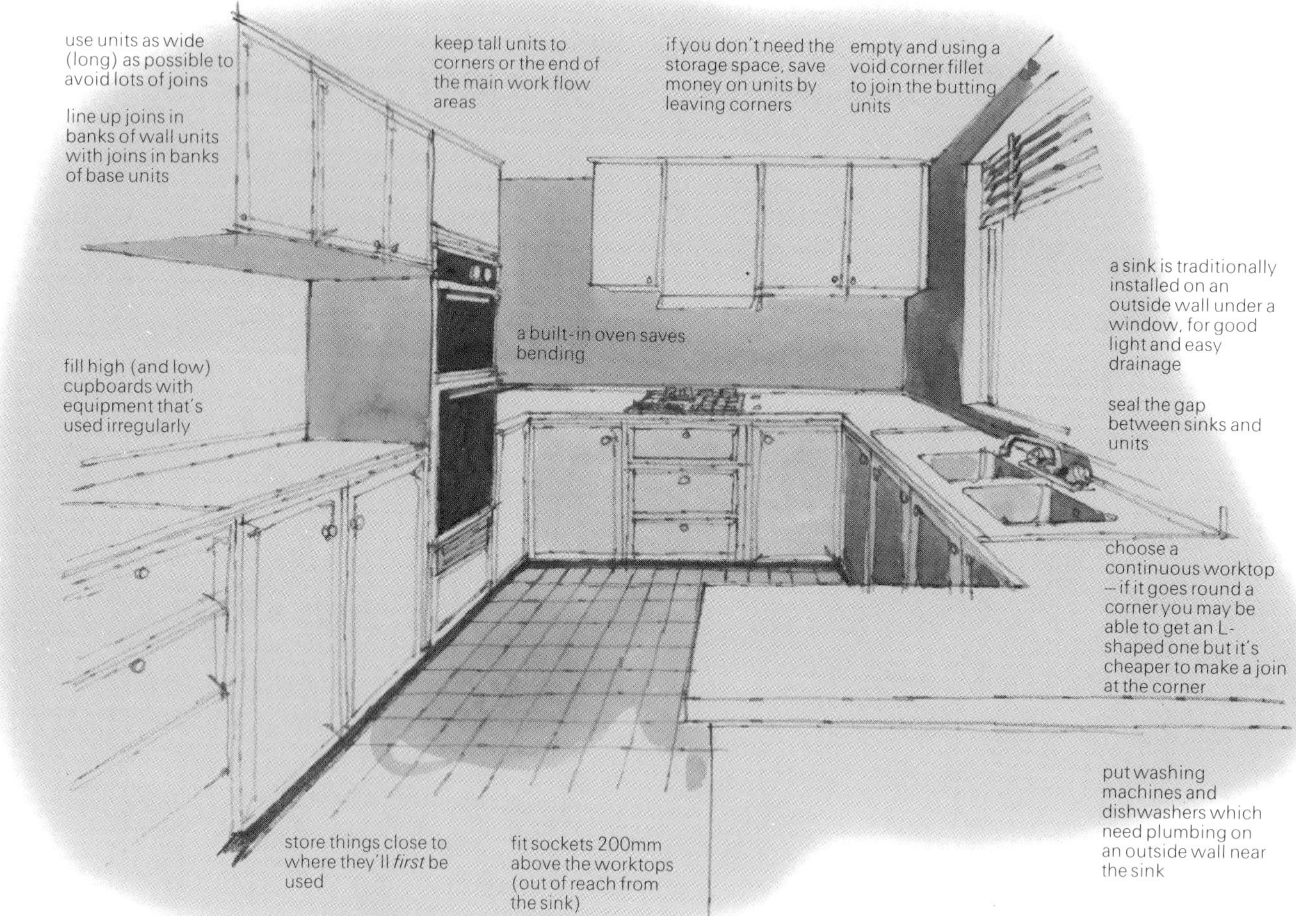
use units as wide (long) as possible to avoid lots of joins
line up joins in banks of wall units with joins in banks of base units
keep tall units to corners or the end of the main work flow areas
if you don't need the storage space, save money on units by leaving corners
empty and using a void corner fillet to join the butting units
a sink is traditionally installed on an outside wall under a window, for good light and easy drainage
seal the gap between sinks and units
a built-in oven saves bending
fill high (and low) cupboards with equipment that's used irregularly
choose a continuous worktop – if it goes round a corner you may be able to get an L-shaped one but it's cheaper to make a join at the corner
put washing machines and dishwashers which need plumbing on an outside wall near the sink
store things close to where they'll *first* be used
fit sockets 200mm above the worktops (out of reach from the sink)

When putting a kitchen together think about the practicalities, such as drainage.

often circular and may be sold individually for insetting separately into a worktop or as an oval unit with one bowl linked to a drainer. These are the commonest materials, but you can also get plastic sinks, the most recent in a material called Sylac, made from silica (sand) and resin.

If you go for separate units, it's worth considering having two bowls, using one of the bowls as a drainer or bowl as required.

However a sink is installed, it (and the taps) should be well sealed all round to stop water getting to the chipboard core of the worktop.

Use an acrylic or silicone sealant to fill the gaps.

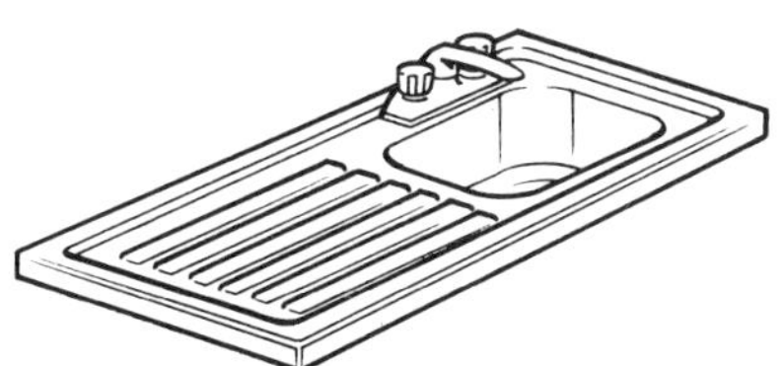

single bowl, single drainer

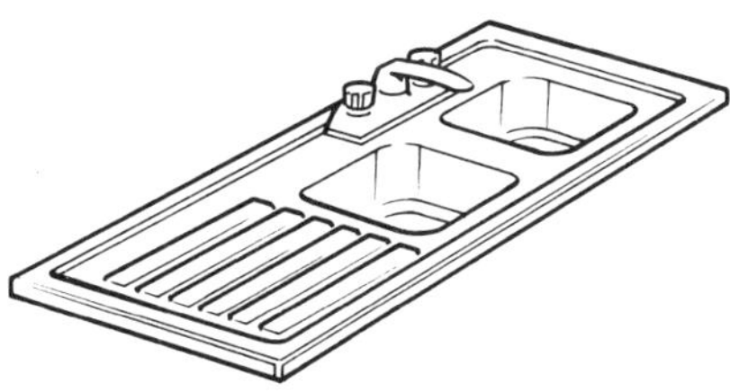

two bowl, single drainer

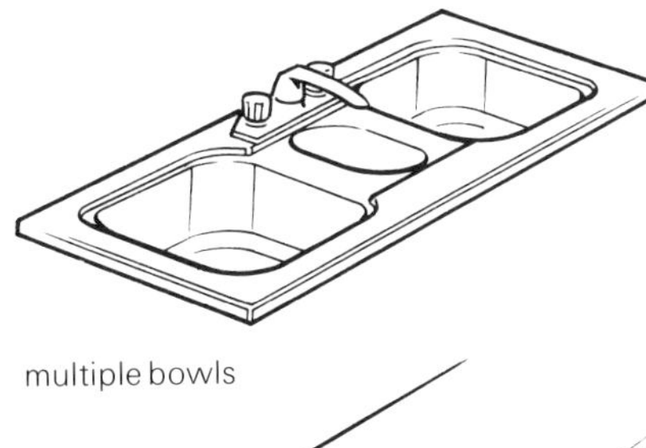

multiple bowls

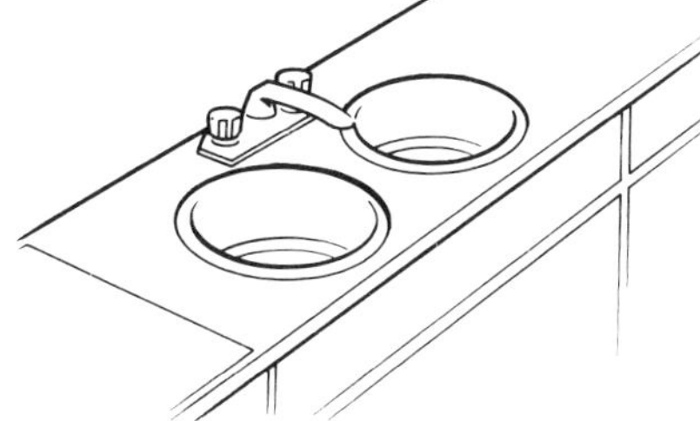

bowls let into worktop.

**Single taps**

Most have a chromium finish. There is a vertical inlet and a back-nut is used to bolt the tap to the deck of a sink. A sink tap will be tall enough to allow buckets to be filled but, before you buy, check that the distance from the bottom of the sink to the bottom of spout will be enough. The inlet has $\frac{1}{2}$in BSP male thread – usual pipe fitting is a tap adaptor.

Single taps are available as Supataps designed so that the washer can be changed without turning off the water supply.

**Mixers**

Most mixers have separate hot and cold inlets, but a single outlet. There are also one-hole mixers which fit into a single standard tap hole. On both sorts the spout outlet swivels. The spouts are often shorter on one-hole mixers. Most kitchen sinks are fed with cold water direct from the mains and hot water via the cold water cistern. Water bye-laws do not allow stored hot water to mix with mains cold water inside a fitting, so sink mixers should have divided flow (also known as dual flow) which stops the water mixing in the tap. Mixers without divided-flow can be used only when the hot and cold supplies both come from the cold water cistern (unlikely in a kitchen).

Tap holes in sinks, and inlets on two-hole sink mixers, are usually a standard distance of 7in apart. Tap holes at non-standard distances can be accommodated by mixers having adjustable inlets. Inlets are $\frac{1}{2}$in BSP male threads – other sizes indicate the mixer is probably a continental type, which may not be suitable. One-hole mixers are often continental taps. They are usually designed to work on direct (high-pressure) systems and are therefore usually not divided-flow. The pressure of water from an indirect supply may not be high enough to give an adequate flow rate. Inlets are usually plain-ended 10mm bendable copper and adaptor fittings are needed to attach them to the usual 15mm pipe supplies.

## ALTERNATIVE UNITS

Most people have fitted kitchens with manufactured units and plastic-laminated worktops, but there are alternatives if you want to cut the costs or create a more original kitchen.

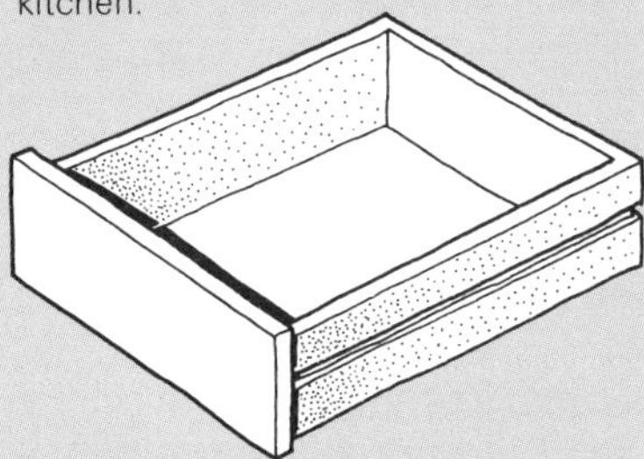

**Home-made chipboard units.** These can easily be constructed using manufactured doors and drawer fronts and plastic drawer boxes.

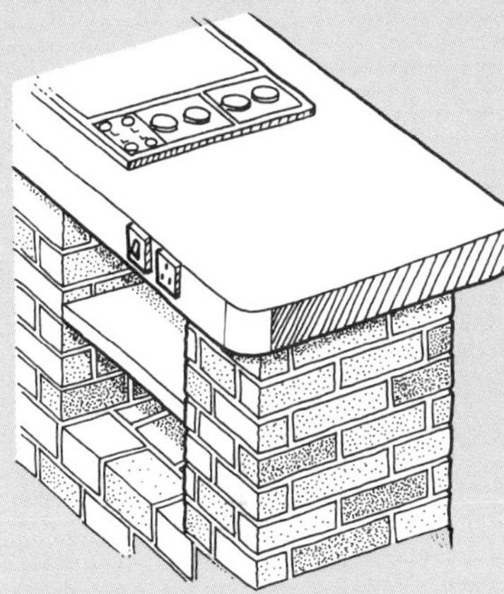

**Brick units.** Walls of brick can be used to construct open-fronted storage units. The brick walls must be supported by a solid floor and should be sealed with PVA adhesive. Fronts can be provided by roller blinds.

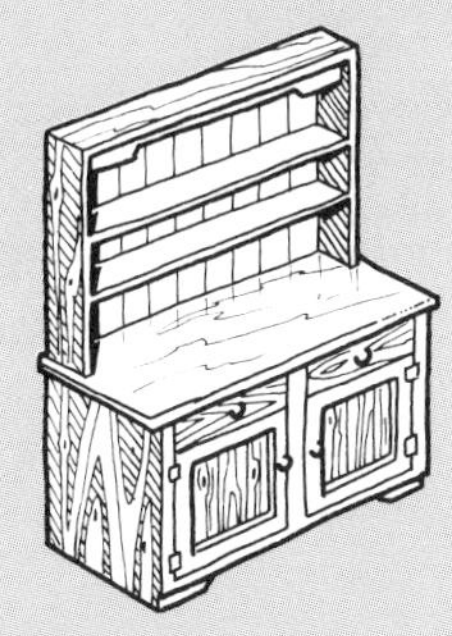

**Pine furnishings.** A dresser, table, butcher's block and so on can be used to create a country style kitchen.

# Kitchen units

If you wanted to, it would be possible to build a kitchen with floor-to-ceiling cupboards and a home for everything from the teaspoons to the ironing. There are manufactured units to suit almost every storage requirement and d-i-y fittings and fixings make it possible to build home-made furniture with few traditional carpentry skills.

## Manufactured units

Manufactured units can be sold ready-assembled or flat-packed for self-assembly at home. Flat packing is popular with manufacturers and retailers because it means the furniture is easier and cheaper to transport and store and less likely to be damaged in transit. For these reasons even quite expensive furniture ranges are now sold in flat-packs.

Self-assembly kitchen unit prices start extremely low – the cheapest units compare favourably for price (although not always for quality) with d-i-y ones – and because self-assembly furniture is easy to store, many shops sell cash and carry or, if they keep stock in a central warehouse, quote short delivery times of around 7 to 10 days – you'd rarely have to wait longer than 4 weeks. Ready-assembled furniture can take several months to arrive.

You don't have to assemble flat-packed furniture yourself, some shops quote a ready-assembled price and you can always employ a tradesman to assemble and install it for you. The more expensive flat-packed ranges are generally sold through kitchen specialists who will plan your kitchen, order the units and appliances and arrange for the installation as well. Ready-assembled furniture is usually sold by specialist retailers and many of the large manufacturers have their own showrooms.

## Choosing a range

You'll choose a kitchen that you like the look of, but that shouldn't be your only criterion. The quality of the carcase (the frame of the unit) is important and you should also consider the selection of units available in a range. Some of the cheapest self-assembly ranges include only a limited number of units. Ready-assembled ranges usually have the widest choice and include more unusual units such as trolley units on castors or pull-out ironing board cupboards. You could adapt ordinary units yourself to get these special features at a lower cost.

Although most manufacturers offer several ranges of kitchen unit with different drawer and door fronts, the basic carcase of the units in each range is usually standardised. The material used for the fronts is reflected in the price – within a range melamine-faced chipboard is invariably cheapest, followed by chipboard faced with thicker laminates or veneer, wood-frames with a faced panel of some sort or slatted pine and finally solid, often carved, wood – such as oak. The difference between these materials is mainly aesthetic, although melamine can be scratched fairly easily, door and drawer fronts aren't generally at risk.

Whatever the front material, most

A carousel unit gives better access to the corner but allows less to be stored.

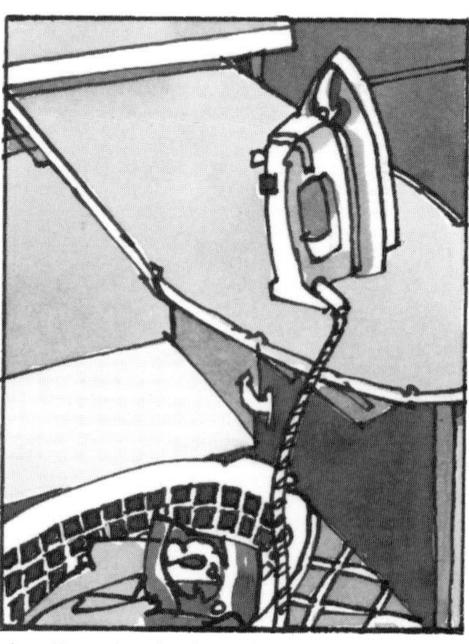
A pull-out ironing board.

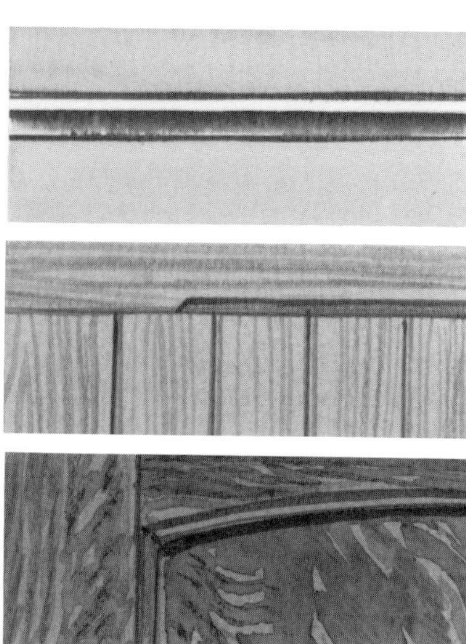
The same carcase can have different doors.

carcases are made of white, or more recently beige melamine-faced chipboard and drawers are often factory-made plastic units which slot easily together. Before you buy a range of furniture you should have a good look at some made-up units from that range. Take a tape measure when you go shopping and run through our Checklist.

Don't worry too much if the display units seem a bit wobbly. Often they've been put together quickly and aren't bolted together or to the wall. When they're fitted in a kitchen they'll probably be satisfactory. The only exceptions are peninsular units. If you're intending to use ordinary base units as peninsular units you should check that they'll be stable enough.

**Styles and sizes**

Some styles and sizes of unit are illustrated on the following pages with a note on how common they are in self-assembly and ready-made ranges. See page 67 for a note on the modules used for kitchen furniture. These days most are metric sizes, but imperial-sized (feet and inch) units are still available and useful if you want to re-

## THINGS TO CHECK ON A CARCASE

☑ **the general level of workmanship** – are the door, drawer fronts well finished, do the doors hang square? Can you see the hinges?

☑ **backs** – do the wall units and base units have backs?

☑ **the drawers** – do they run smoothly and have a stop to prevent you pulling them out accidentally? Can you re-fit them easily? Are the fronts securely attached? Are the sides full or only part depth?

☑ **door hinges** – do they open to 180° so that they won't project into the room? This could be essential in a narrow or galley kitchen. Are hinges adjustable so that doors can be lined up, even if the unit has to be fitted slightly out of plumb?

☑ **shelves** – are they the full depth of the cupboard or do they stop short of the front? Are they well supported at the centre as well as the ends in a double unit? Are they adjustable? What's the tallest object you can store in the cupboard? In some units you may find the maximum height is about 300mm.

☑ **worktop height** – this doesn't vary much between units, but some are slightly higher than others and this could be important for someone other than average height.

☑ **the materials** – you can't tell much just by looking at these, most units are made of chipboard. Find out whether the bottom edges of the carcase are sealed against moisture which will destroy chipboard otherwise.

**Storage**

The most efficient store cupboards:

- have pull-out shelves or drawers so that you can easily get right to the back
- are narrow enough for the contents to be only one row deep
- are filled with regularly-used things at the front and objects used less often at the back.

Be flexible about what you keep in the kitchen. Utilise storage in other rooms where possible.

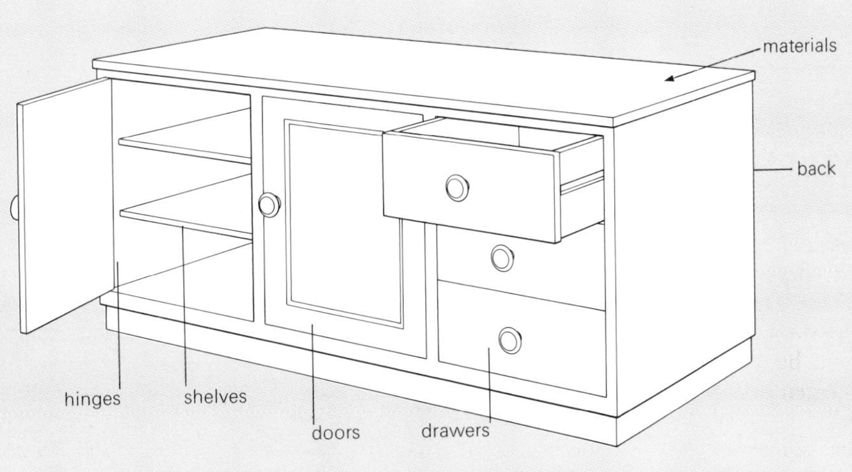

use imperial-sized fittings – a sink for instance.

### Getting fully-fitted

If a range doesn't include all the units you want, there are some tricks to make units double as others. For instance, wall units can be installed below a worktop to make a breakfast bar with room for your knees. Spare door fronts can be used instead of decorative end (or back panels) or as cooker hood panels. Also most of the internal fittings such as carousel shelf units and pull-out baskets are available separately.

### Re-using existing units

If your existing units are basically sound it is possible to replace just the door and drawer fronts and worktops. You can buy made-to-measure fronts or find a standard-size front that will do. If you're intending to extend your kitchen at the same time, this is your best solution because you'll be able to buy complete units to match. Old fronts in good condition can be repainted. A comparable finish to the original can be achieved by spraying – a local car sprayer may be willing to do this work.

### Worktops

The worktops sold with most kitchen ranges are plastic-laminated chipboard. Plastic-laminates – like Formica and Warerite – have proved themselves over the years in kitchens and are hard-wearing and easy-to-clean. Other alternatives are cork tiles – with many thin coats of a polyurethane varnish – ceramic tiles (though the grouting can cause problems), or solid wood. The first two are favourably priced, but wood is usually very expensive.

Worktops are usually fitted by screwing up into the chipboard core from underneath. There's usually no reason why you have to buy the worktop for the units you buy, and by shopping around it's often possible to buy at a better price.

Worktops can be square-edged, postformed on just the top edge or postformed on both the top and bottom edges. Some units are designed to take worktops with a deep front which comes down several inches at the front – see drawing. Wood-framed (or lipped) worktops are also in vogue and there are worktops with a raised front edge meant to stop water spilling over the front. Square-edged worktops are usually cheapest. No edge has any significant advantage over the others, but check that you'll be able to wipe off easily. Another suggestion is to have a slot in the worktop through which crumbs could be wiped. It would need to have a flush-fitting lid and some method for attaching disposal bags below. A slot in a chipboard top would need to be well sealed.

The chipboard core of a worktop should be at least 30mm thick and many of the double-postformed ones are 40mm. The thicker the laminate the more resistance it will have to knocks, but it's total thickness has little influence on the surface wear which gradually rubs away any pattern. A worktop should be flat along its length – reject any that are bowed by more than a few mm deflection across a metre span.

Often, the presence of pipes, wiring or a skirting board behind the kitchen units, means that units can't be built in absolutely flush against the wall. In this situation you need to cover the gap that's left between the worktop and the wall. Some worktops incorporate an upstand, with others you fit a plastic or aluminium upstand. If the wall units fit flush you can tile down on to the worktop or fit an upstand to hide the narrow gap that will be left.

WORKTOPS

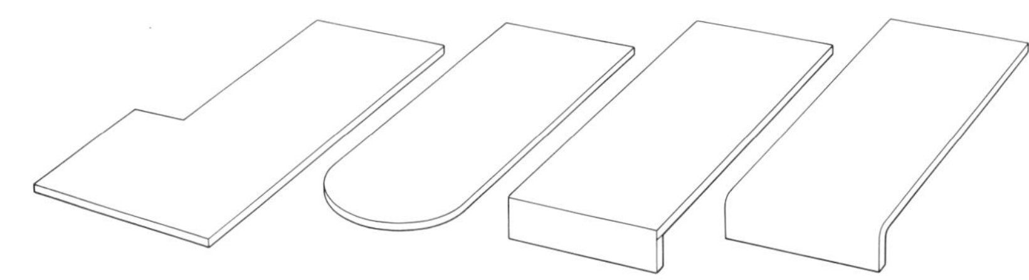

Straight tops are most widely available, but there are often many forms.

In the Table of Kitchen units – RA is ready-assembled furniture, SA is self-assembly furniture.

**Kitchen units**

| | d-i-y | flat-packed | ready-assembled |
|---|---|---|---|
| carcase cost | £ | £ to £££ | £££ to £££££ |
| delivery times | — | usually 7 to 10 days | often several months |
| where to buy | parts from d-i-y shops and timber merchants | mainly specialist furniture retailers, d-i-y stores and builders' merchants | usually specialist kitchen installers who will design and fit too. Manufacturer's own showrooms |
| advantages | no limitations on design, size, cost or materials | rarely damaged in transit, low-priced, cash and carry | wide choice of unusual and special units, high quality components, assembled for you |

## Kitchen units

**Full door double base units**
Common SA and RA, single and double – 300, 500, 600, 1000, 1200.

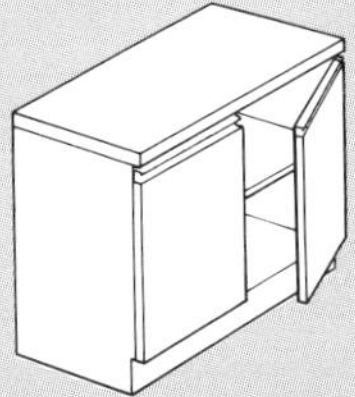

**Triple base units**
Rarely available – you can get the same effect with single and double units side-by-side. SA only in 1500mm, RA in 1500mm and 1800mm wide.

**Drawerline double base units**
Common SA and RA, single and double, 300, 500, 600, 1000, 1200 (less common SA). For sinks or hobs you need a special unit with a dummy drawer.

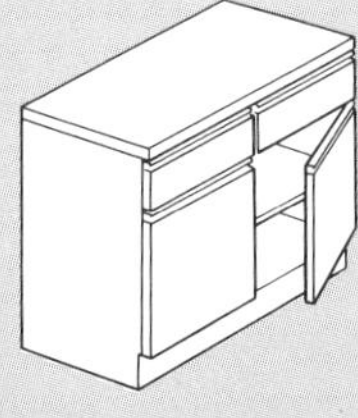

**Drawer packs**
SA and RA most common single width (500, 600) with 3 or 4 drawers: RA also widely available with 2 drawers.

**Pull-out with internal drawers**
These single units are fairly common in RA ranges, rare SA.

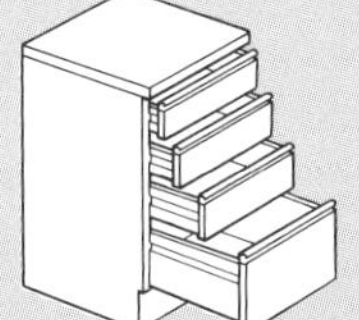

**Radius end unit**
An open ended shelf unit for end of run. Rare RA and SA.

**Chefs trolley**
Only found RA – 800. Unit is on castors.

**Tea towel unit**
Unusual RA or SA, but can be made from tray plinth fitted with holder.

**Peninsular units**
Widely available RA, they are rarely found SA but you can use an ordinary base unit with a backing board. Peninsular corner units are only available RA.

**Oven/Fridge housing**
Common SA and RA. Make sure though that your choice of oven (fridge) will fit and will operate safely without over-heating. Give the appliance supplier and the unit supplier (or the manufacturer) the exact details and ask for confirmation.

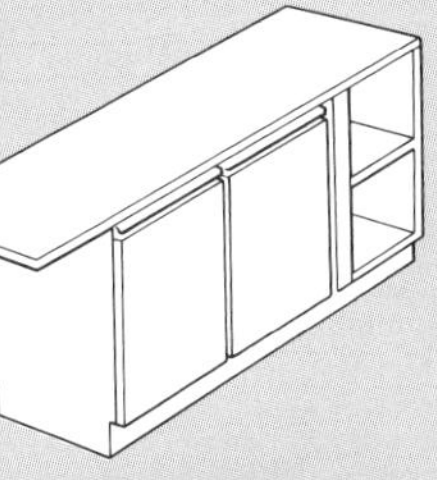

**A combined unit**
With drawers one side, shelves the other. A few RA ranges include a mixed triple unit like this.

**Larder**
With shelves removed becomes broom cupboard. May be sold as this without shelves commonly available SA and RA.

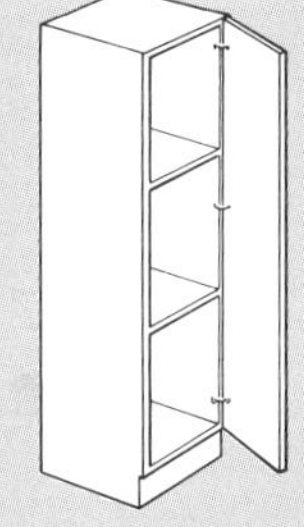

**Under-the-worktop oven housing**
Commonly available RA (600). SA are fairly easy to find and should become more widely available.

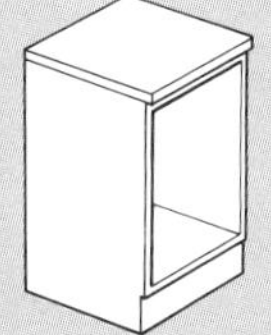

**Pull-out wine basket**
Most common RA but found in some SA ranges.

**Unusual units**
Special storage units – for instance an automatic food mixer shelf, an ironing board storage unit or a swing bin unit. Usually only available RA.

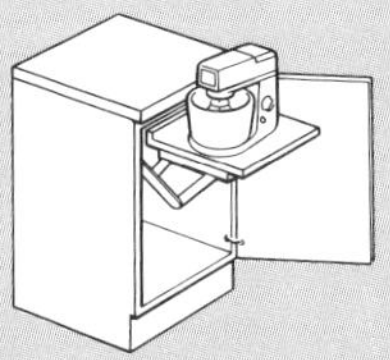

**Drawer packs**
With two deep drawers for storing pans and large pots, these are commonly available RA, and much rarer SA, but very useful.

**Corner units**
RA and SA commonly available 1000 (with units 600 deep this means you lose 100mm of corner space). SA also 800, 1200, RA, 1200, 1500 (even 1800) come with a set of carousel shelves.

**Wall units**
SA and RA are most common 300, 500, 600, 1000, 1200. Others sizes are less widely available.

**Corner wall units**
Open-ended ones butt against the units on the adjacent wall and are common in SA. L-shaped units with a hinged door are commonly available RA and now fairly common SA.

**Midway units**
These units for storing small bits and pieces are common to both RA and SA.

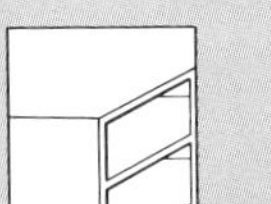

**Upper wall unit**
For installation above housings or short wall units. These are common RA and SA.

**Display wall cupboards**
Open fronted units are commonly available as straight radius end or corner units but rarely available SA. Units with glass doors are common RA, rarer SA.

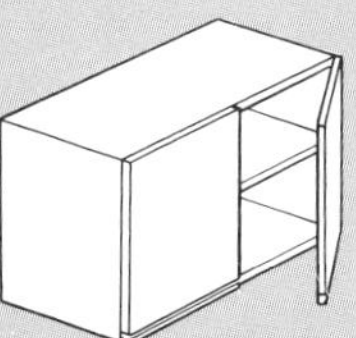

**Peninsular wall units**
Fairly common as straight or corner units RA but rarely available SA.

**Other bits**
These help to get a fully fitted kitchen **Cooker-hood panel**. Fairly common RA and SA. **Decorative end and back panels** are commonly available RA and fairly common SA. They're intended to match exposed ends and backs of units to the fronts. **Tray plinth**. Common SA and RA. Can be cut down to size. **End support panel.** To support a worktop. **Front filler panel.** To mask a void in a run of units – perhaps to conceal plumbing or to save money on an unnecessary unit. Commonly available RA, rarely SA, but door fronts could be adapted to suit. **Void corner fillet.** This is fairly common SA and RA. It's used to blank a corner where two units meet but the corner isn't utilised. **Housing for cooker hood.** Sometimes available RA or SA. Also Corner housing.

## Installing units

Achieving a 'good fit' is important for how your kitchen looks in the end. If things fit well gaps are easy to seal properly and that's important for kitchen hygiene and to protect the units from damp.

Plan to install the wall units before most of the floor-standing units. This makes life easier because you don't have to stretch across the base units. If you have any tall units – a broom cupboard for instance – install them first as your reference height.

### Fitting wall units

Strong fixings are important for a wall unit. For a solid wall consider using screw-fixed wall anchors – most of these provide fixings a lot stronger than ordinary wall plugs. Most require a large – 10mm – hole, but once the hole is drilled they are easy to use. Most have a machine screw and are tightened with a spanner.

If the walls are timber frame or dry-lined, you'll need to find the uprights and screw into these, if the stud spacing doesn't suit the unit layout fit a standard horizontal batten between the wall studs and secure the units to this top and bottom. For fixings between studs you need special cavity fixings.

Most wall units are fixed at the four corners; some are screwed through the carcase frame; others have wall brackets. Use large screws – at least no 10 $1\frac{1}{2}$in long. Wall units are bolted together through the sides. To get a tight fit cramp the units together while the bolts are tightened.

A batten fitted along the wall under the units is useful to give extra support to the wall units and help line them up correctly. It can be temporary or installed permanently.

### Fitting base units

Most base units are screwed to the wall for extra rigidity. The strength of fixing isn't so important here though the same principles apply. Getting the units level and square is essential – they will usually need packing underneath and possibly also between the unit and the wall. Some units come with levelling strips or wedges for this purpose. Plastic wedges can be bought separately, but strips of wood are as good. Decide whether you will fit the floor covering before or after the base units.

Skirting boards can be an obstruction. Either remove them and make-good or trim the side panels to fit.

Start by finding the high spot on the floor. You can do this with a set of long battens and a spirit level on the floor or by assembling a few units and standing them around the kitchen. Then it's usually best to start with the sink unit. This will usually need some pipe holes in the side of the units. Butt the units together for a good fit. Check each unit horizontally and vertically before screwing it back.

### Fitting the worktop

When the units are finally installed the worktops and any sink top can be installed. Worktops are usually fitted by screwing up through brackets fitted to the unit walls. Sinks have brackets which hook over the lip of the sink and are screwed to the side walls. It's important to seal the gap between the worktop and the wall. Some worktops have integral upstands – such as a wood finish or laminated batten, but most now have a plastic fixing strip which locates over a metal fixing strip screwed along the back of the worktop.

### Fitting the doors

The doors are fitted last and will usually need adjusting to get an even hang. Although it can be fiddly take plenty of time over this. Getting the doors right is crucial to the final appearance of the whole kitchen.

Most kitchen units have the doors fitted flat on the front of the carcase. This lay-on design is more tolerant of small inaccuracies than a door that's flush with a frame. There are dozens of different hinges that can be used to hang doors; for a d-i-y project *Which?* tests have found the *lay-on hinge* (sometimes called easy-on) is strong, easy to fit, adjustable and can't be seen when the doors are closed. Most bought kitchen units use this or a *concealed hinge* which is readily adjustable. It's easy to fit on bought units, which always have the necessary holes pre-drilled, but isn't so easy d-i-y because the part that attaches to the door needs a large circular recess – to drill this you require a tool called an end mill and for good results a drill stand.

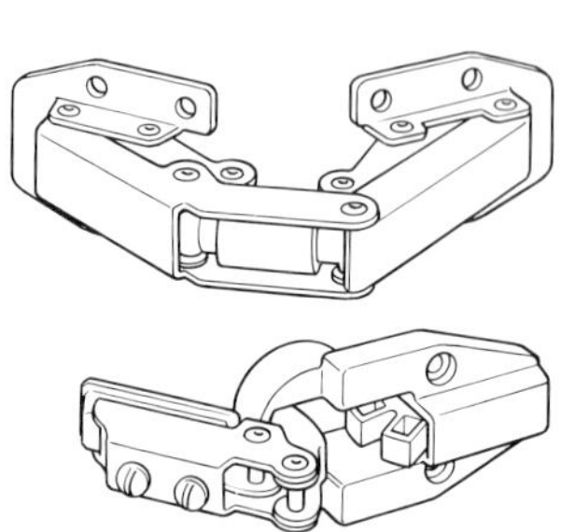
Fitting the doors is the last job, it's easy to do with adjustable hinges such as these.

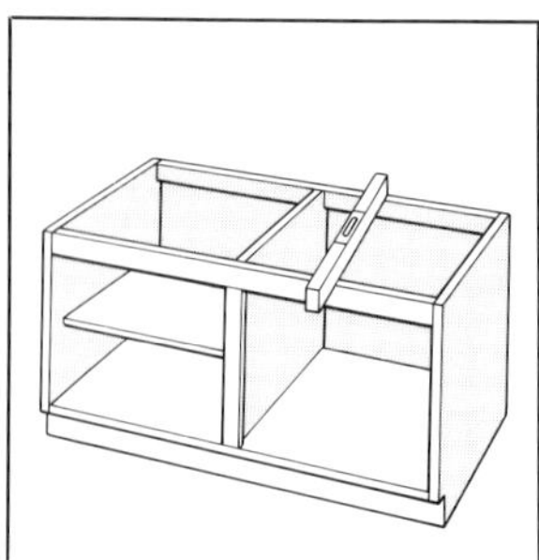
The base units may need packing underneath to achieve a level top. Use plastic or wooden wedges.

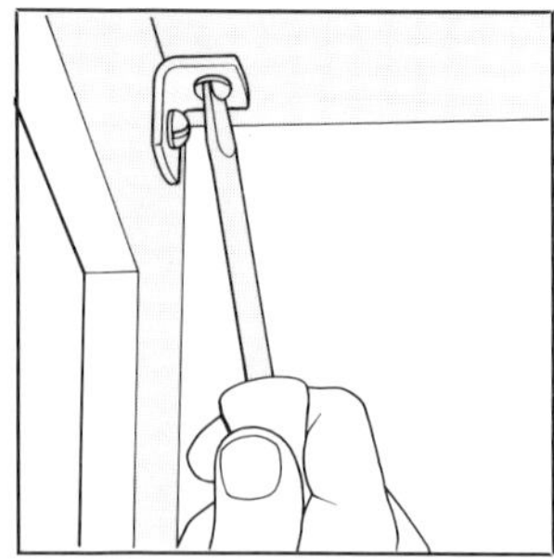
The worktop is attached from beneath by screwing up through brackets attached to the unit walls.

The gap between the worktop and the wall must be covered; normally an upstand such as this is used.

# Electricity in the kitchen

The minimum number of double sockets recommended for a kitchen is four, but considering the number of different pieces of electric equipment used in most kitchens, and the fact that many sockets in kitchens are almost permanently in use for things like kettles and toasters, this number of sockets is likely to be inadequate.

Add up the permanently-fixed electrical appliances you have in the kitchen and count one socket outlet for each. For safety choose switched sockets. Each stretch of worktop should have at least one double socket for use with smaller equipment such as a food mixer or liquidiser. If there's an area of lower wall unoccupied by cupboards, add a socket at a lower height for a vacuum cleaner. If you have a breakfast bar then consider having a double socket there.

In a medium-sized kitchen ten sockets wouldn't be too many. Fixed equipment, such as refrigerators, automatic washing machines, cooker hoods and fans can be wired through a plug and a socket, but it's better to connect them permanently to the ring circuit through a switched fused connection unit. An electric cooker must be permanently connected to its own separate circuit of appropriate capacity.

Kitchen sockets and fixed equipment, other than a cooker, are often installed on the ring circuit which serves the ground floor of a house, but it's recommended that a separate kitchen circuit is provided to allow for the heavy loads which are likely.

## Installing sockets

For more sockets in a kitchen you can:

- make single sockets into doubles – page 147
- install a spur to an existing ring circuit – page 148
- install a new circuit from a spare way in the consumer unit – page 257.

An existing socket can be repositioned by use of a junction box – page 148.

Avoid fitting sockets directly behind pieces of equipment. If cupboards are to be fitted in front of sockets carefully work out the spacing, check that the side panels, base support or shelves of the cupboard will not interfere with the access to sockets. Switching is easier if sockets are installed above worktop level. As an alternative unswitched sockets can be installed with remote switches (suitable for 13 amp supply) above the worktop.

Have sockets high enough so that they cannot be splashed – about 200mm above the worktop is one recommendation.

## Installing fixed appliances

A lot of electric kitchen equipment is left in a fixed position. Such equipment is usually wired through switched fused connection units.

### Extractor fan or cooker hood

Extractor fans fitted in windows will always need an external flex to supply power; those fitted in walls *can* be supplied directly by cable buried in the wall. Either sort can be supplied through a fused connection unit.

For a simple one-speed extractor, the supply can be taken direct to the fan. If it does not have a switch built-in there will have to be a switch in the connection unit or between the unit and the fan.

Some fans can be used with special control units so that the user can switch the fan to supply or extract air and can choose different speeds. With these, the fused supply goes to the control unit, and separate wiring goes from the control unit to the fan. The instructions should show you what is needed.

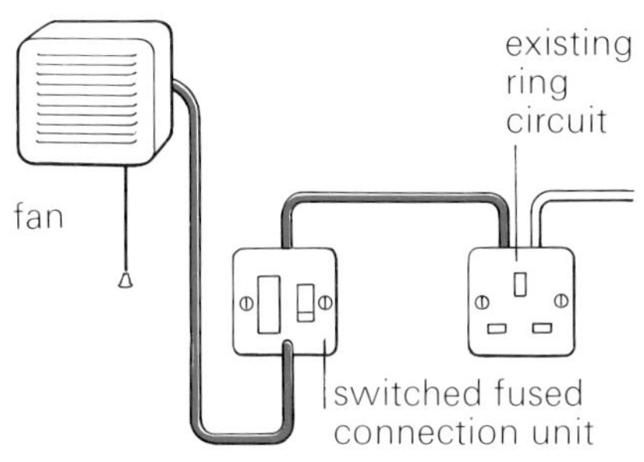


### Washing machine or drier

Although a washing machine will usually be movable for servicing, it can be wired via a fused connection unit provided enough slack is left to allow it to be drawn out when necessary. Often the switched connection unit is installed behind the machine under the worktop. More accessible switching is desirable and this can be achieved by installing the switched fused connection unit above the worktop, and running a cable vertically down to a flex outlet plate where the final connection to the washing machine flex can be made. Otherwise a separate control switch can be installed between the connection unit and the machine – normally a 20 amp double-pole switch. The cable down from the switch would terminate at a flex outlet plate.

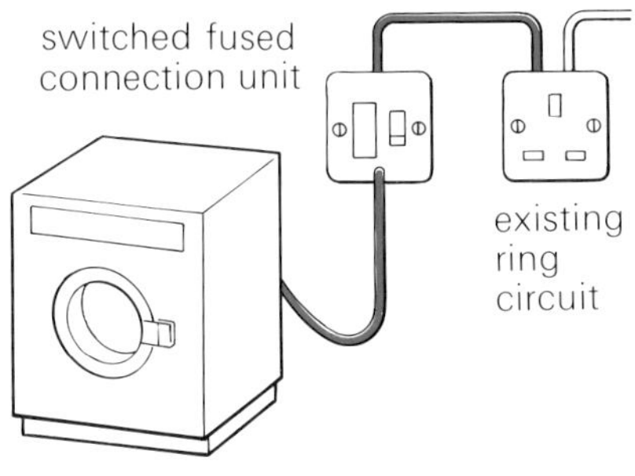

# Installing an electric cooker

A cooker requires its own circuit – 30 amps for cookers up to 18 kW (provided there is no socket outlet on the cooker switch unit); 45 amps for those above that loading – such as large split level ovens and hobs operated from the same circuit.

These fuse ratings assume that it is unlikely that everything – grill, oven and all the hotplates – will be in use at full load at the same time. If they were the fuse would blow, for a 18 kW cooker has a total current rating of 75 amps on a 240V supply. An electrician works to a formula which counts the first 10 amps then assesses the rest at 30 per cent, with 5 amps added if a cooker switch unit which incorporates a socket will be used. The sum is thus 10 amps plus 30 per cent of 75 amps (19·5), total 29·5 amps so 30 amps is enough for the circuit.

A 30 amp circuit is usually satisfactory in 6mm$^2$ cable (max length 28m). For cookers with a higher loading which require a circuit of more than 30 amps the circuit should be run in 10mm$^2$ cable (max length 31m) and supplied with a 45 amp fuse. Normally twin and earth cable is used.

The circuit begins at the consumer unit. The cable is run to a *cooker switch unit* mounted on the wall to one side but within reach of the cooker. With a free-standing cooker it is usual to run a cable from the cooker switch unit to a terminal outlet box fitted to the wall about 600mm from the floor. A final length of trailing cable (6mm or 10mm to match the circuit) joins the terminal box to the cooker. The Wiring Regulations make an exception of cookers in allowing this final connection, to an appliance which is strictly speaking movable, to be made in cable rather than flex – it allows the cooker to be drawn away from the wall for cleaning.

The two parts of a split level cooker can be on the same circuit controlled from one switch provided neither the hob nor the oven is more than 2m from the switch. From the cooker switch unit cables can be run separately to each part of the cooker or taken first to one part of the cooker and then the other. When the two parts of the cooker are more than 4m apart a second switch unit is required.

A cooker switch unit has a double-pole switch that will disconnect both the live and neutral conductors. Units are available with or without a neon indicator and can be flush or surface mounted. Although cooker switch units with a socket outlet on the same plate are also available, they're not the best choice for a kitchen that has plenty of sockets elsewhere.

METHODS OF CONNECTING COOKERS

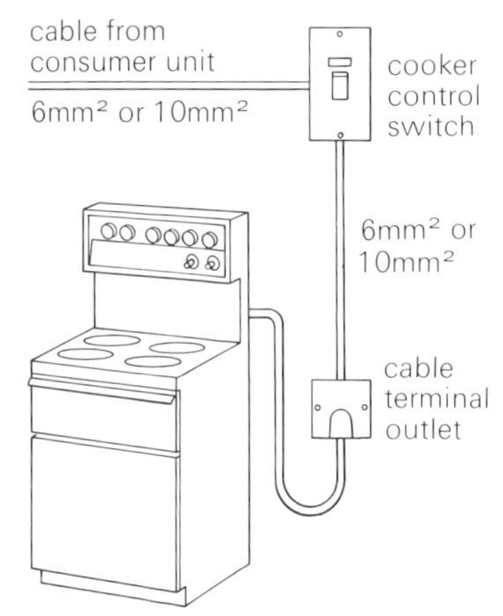


A freestanding cooker.

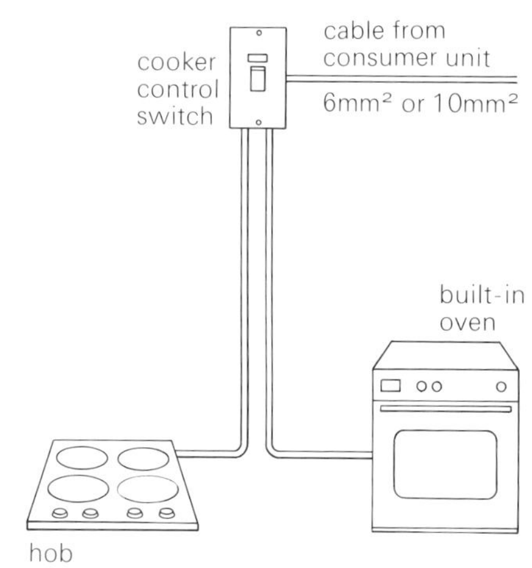


Split-level wired separately from cooker control unit.

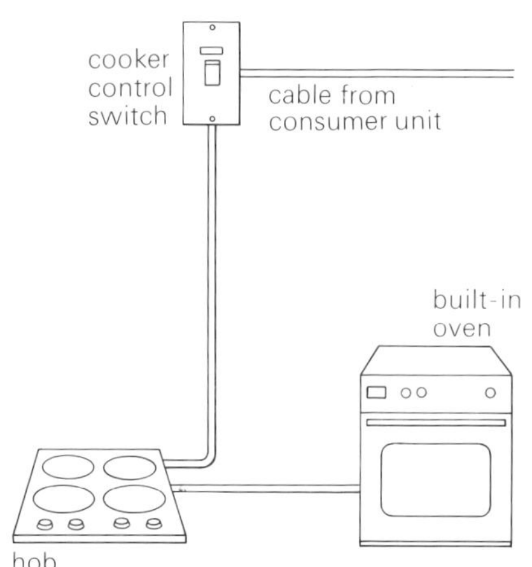


Split-level cable from cooker control unit taken first to one point then the next.

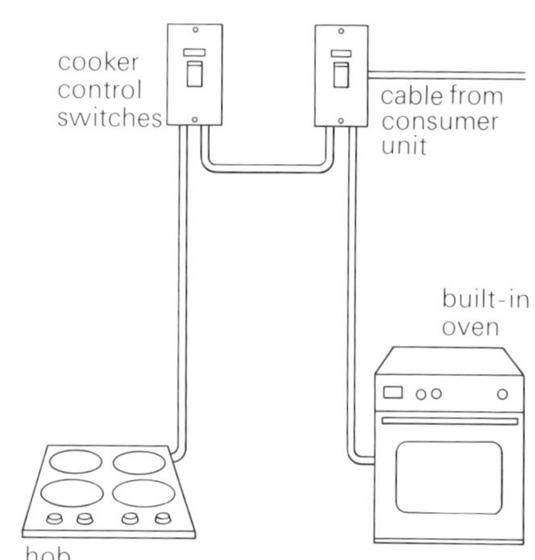


Split-level each with cooker control unit.

## CONNECTIONS CHECKLIST

These details should be checked each time you connect a socket, switch or anything at all. Full details of Electrical work are given on pages 48 *et seq*. You should:

- SWITCH OFF AT THE MAINS
- always fit grommets in the knocked-out holes in boxes
- remove the sheath from cable within a box or fitting
- aim to leave virtually no bare exposed conductor once the connection has been made
- protect bare *earth* conductors with green and yellow sleeving and connect to *earth* terminal
- connect *red* (live) conductors to *live* terminals
- connect *black* (neutral) conductors to *neutral* terminals
- double-check each connection
- shape the connected conductors to fit comfortably inside the box.

**If in doubt don't meddle.**

### Getting down to work

As the cable is heavier and thicker than the cables used for ring or lighting circuits a deeper channel will be needed and holes in joists will need to be bigger. Bending and connecting the conductors will be more difficult.

If the cooker is free standing, there will be a cable connection point at the rear of the cooker – (usually located behind a metal plate with a cable clamp). Prepare the cable for connection leaving more bare conductor than usual at the cooker end, as it normally has to be wound around a screw and clamped down with brass washers and screws. If the cable is run through thermal insulation, the cable size must be increased.

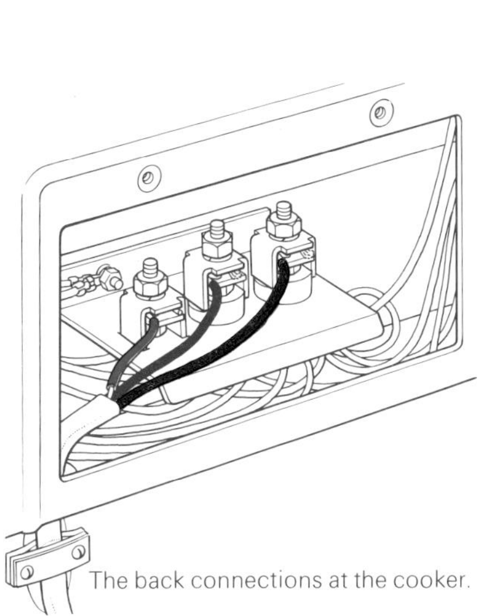

The back connections at the cooker.

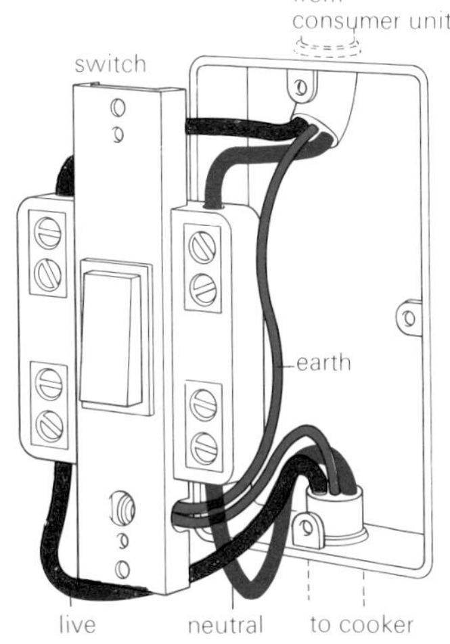


Wiring for cooker control unit with supply to all-in-cooker or just one part of split-level.

WIRING THE OUTLET

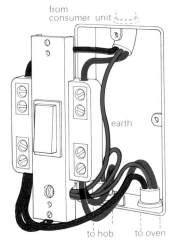

Wiring for cooker control unit with separate supplies to split-level hob and oven.

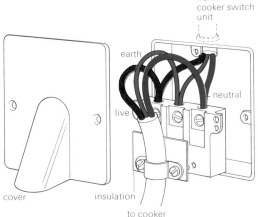

Wiring for terminal outlet.

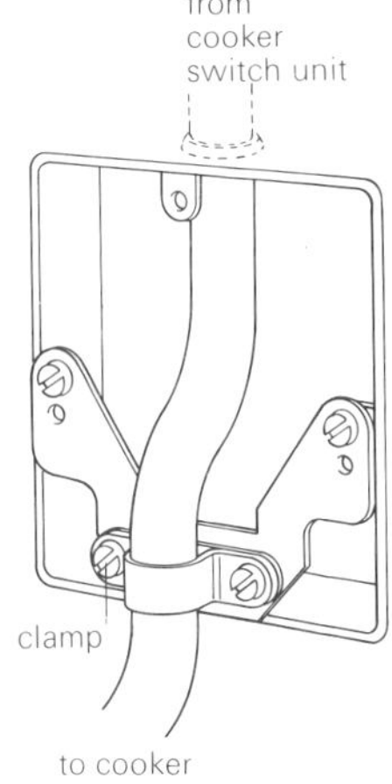


Outlet for split-level oven or hob.

# Plumbing in a kitchen sink

Select the site for a new sink with care, giving special attention to the plumbing requirements – both the supply and the waste need to be considered. The cold supply must come from the rising main; the hot supply will usually be taken from the nearest branch pipe off the hot water cylinder – if it's a dead leg it must not be longer than 12m for a 15mm pipe; 7·5m for a 22mm pipe. Longer runs will have excessive heat loss.

## Step-by-step

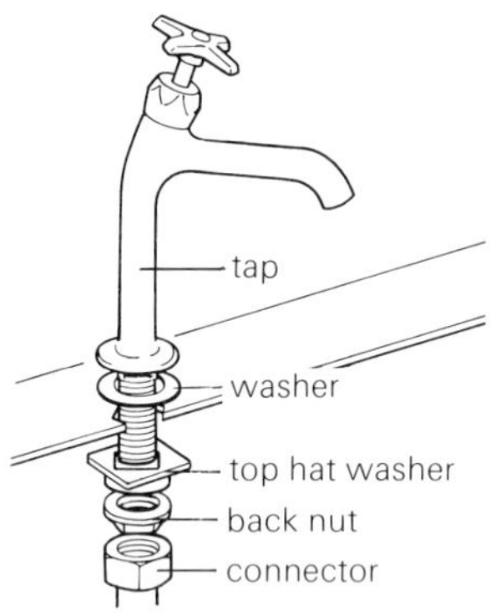


The rising main stopvalve is likely to be located near the site of the old sink. When re-arranging your kitchen make sure the stopvalve is easily accessible.

The drawing shows the parts you will need to install the taps.

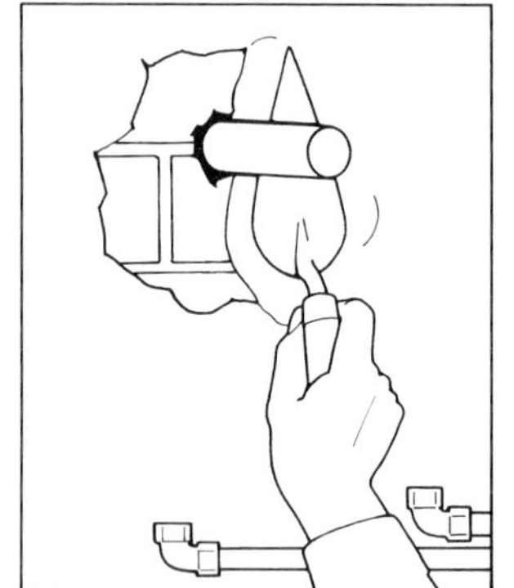

**Step 1** Knock the hole through the wall for the waste pipe, insert a short length of 38mm plastic waste pipe. Outside, a further piece of pipe is connected, this can be run to a gully or connected to the stack pipe by a boss or collar fitted higher than 450mm from the ground.

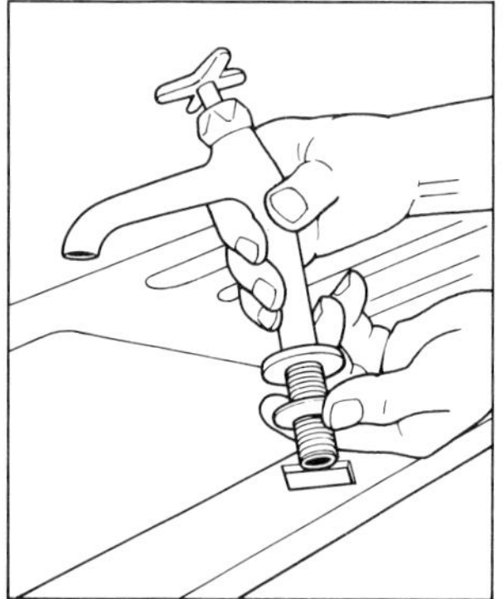

**Step 2** Install the kitchen sink base unit – securing it firmly to the wall. Attach the taps or sink mixer to the sink before you fix it in place. Slip plastic washers over the tap tails and push the tails through the tap holes at the back of the sink.

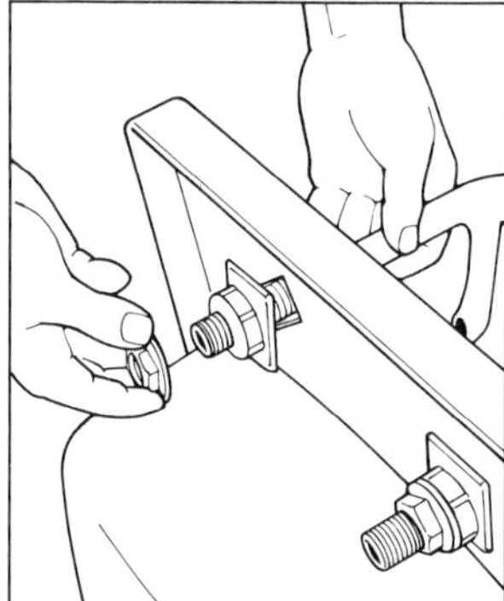

**Step 3** Stainless steel sinks are made of such thin material that part of the tap itself will protrude through the hole. Thread top-hat washers over the tails to overcome this, then screw on and tighten the tap back nuts. Fit tap connectors to the tails.

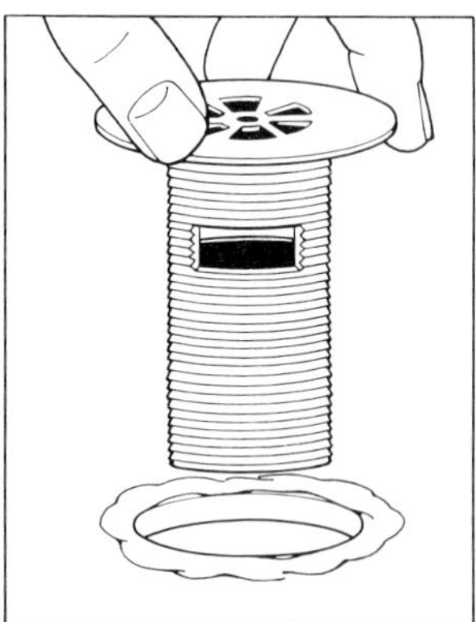

**Step 4** A combined waste and overflow system allows the main wastehole and overflow to be conveniently connected to the waste. Make a bed of plumber's mastic around the sink waste hole and push the slotted waste outlet through, embedding the flange in the mastic.

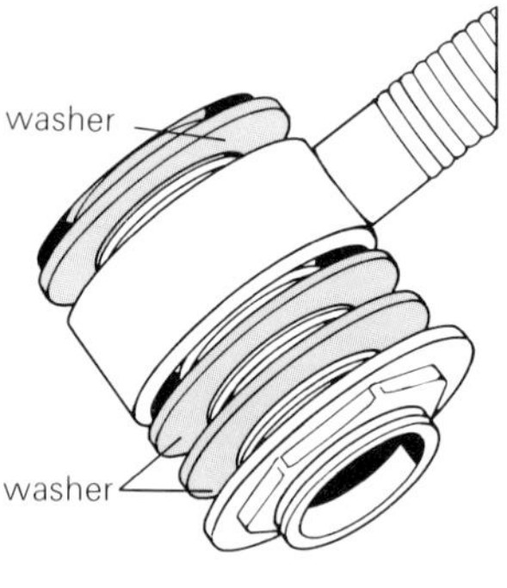


**Step 5** Under the sink, thread the following, in order, over the waste tail: rubber washer, overflow sleeve, rubber washer, plastic washer and backnut. Then tighten the backnut, gripping the waste outlet, with pliers for instance, from inside the bowl to prevent it turning.

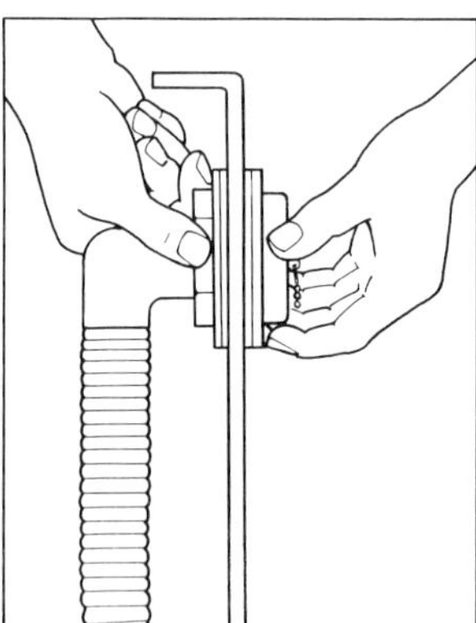

**Step 6** Fit the end of the flexible hose and the overflow rose to the back of the sink, using washers to ensure a watertight joint. Position the sink top on the base unit and fix from below.

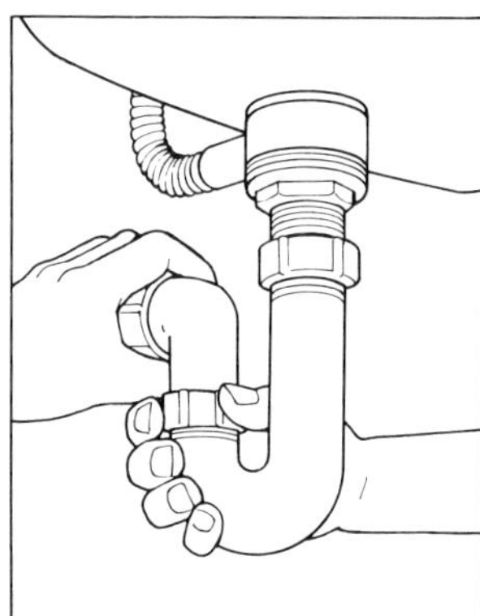

**Step 7** Finish by plumbing the tap connectors back to their supply. Fit a 38mm tubular or bottle trap to the waste tail and connect its outlet to the pipe you set in the wall. Make good the hole in the wall. Note it might be easier to make good the hole before the sink unit is installed.

# ...waste disposal unit/garden tap

A waste disposal unit is a motorised device to reduce soft kitchen waste into a slurry that can be washed away.

Although waste disposal units can be adapted to fit sinks with a standard 38mm outlet, most require an opening of 89mm diameter. The outlet of your existing sink (as long as it's stainless steel) can be enlarged to this diameter using a hole cutter, but it's probably better to buy a sink which has a waste opening of the right size. So the ideal time to consider installing a unit is when you're replacing your old kitchen sink.

## Step-by-step

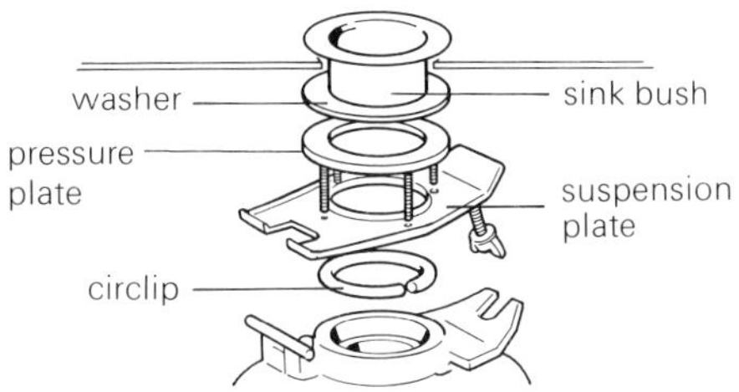


**Step 1** Push the waste outlet through the sink opening and bed the flange on a ring of plumber's putty. Under the sink, thread a washer over the outlet tail, followed by a pressure plate, suspension plate and circlip. The suspension plate is tightened against the pressure plate by four screws; the disposal unit is then clamped on to the suspension plate.

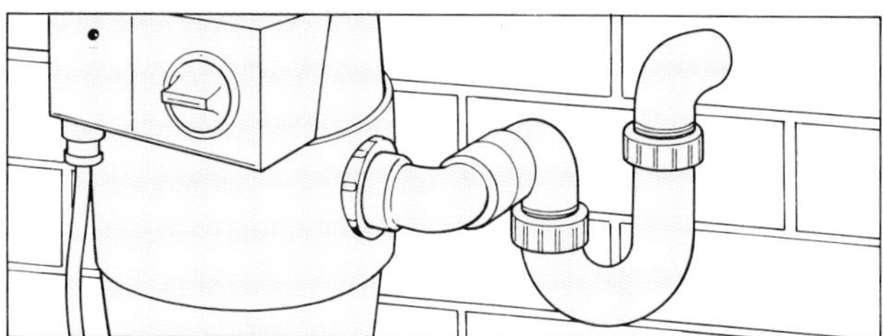

**Step 2** A 38mm tubular P trap is screwed on to the waste disposal unit outflow and connected to 38mm waste pipe. The waste pipe is joined to the drains as for ordering a sink outlet. If it is discharged in to a gully, it must discharge below the grid.
**Step 3** Wire the waste disposal unit permanently via a switched fused connection unit.

## Plumbing in an outside tap

Fitting an outside tap can also be done at the same time as installing a sink. You should tell your local water authority as having a garden tap will affect your water rates. Plan to have the shortest possible run of pipe outside the house.

Most outdoor taps are brass bib taps, though you can get them in plastic. Most have a ribbed parallel-sided nozzle that takes a hose securely. Bib taps and stopvalves usually have compression fittings for connecting to pipe.

## Step-by-step

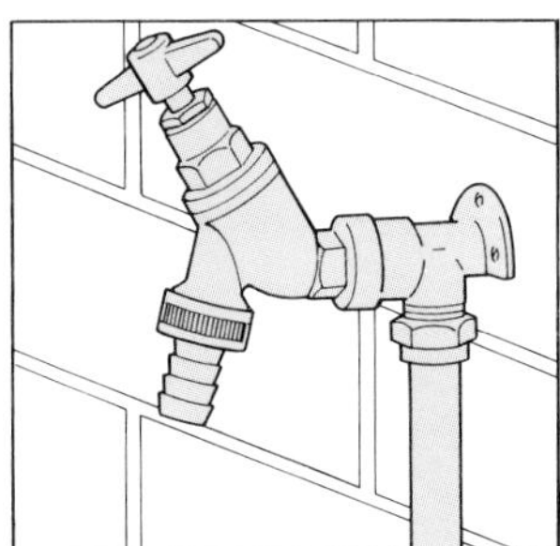

**Step 1** Drill and plug the wall and fix a wallplate elbow. Insert a fibre washer and screw the bib tap into the elbow, using extra washers to make the tap upright.

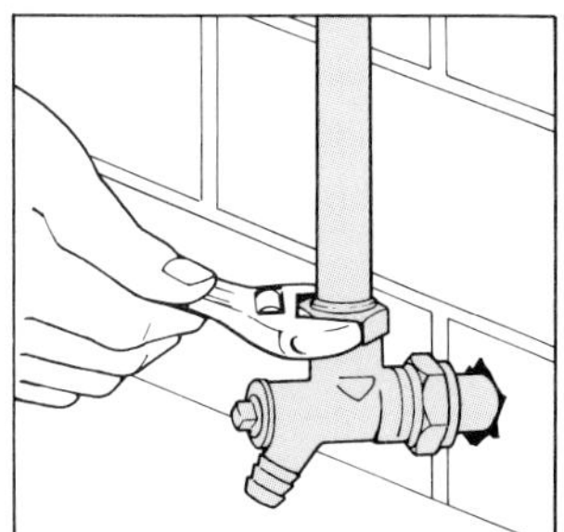

**Step 2** Make a hole through the wall at a point convenient for connecting to the rising main inside. (Do not disturb the damp-proof course.)
**Step 3** Turn off the rising main stopvalve and drain the water.

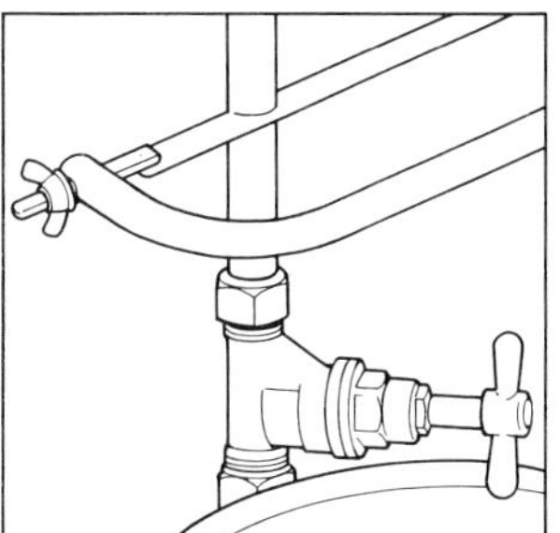

Cut through the rising main pipe downstream of the stopvalve–have cloths and a bowl handy to catch residual water in the pipe. Fit an equal tee.
**Step 4** Fit the branch pipe with a stopvalve. Plumb from the stopvalve to the bib tap using 15mm

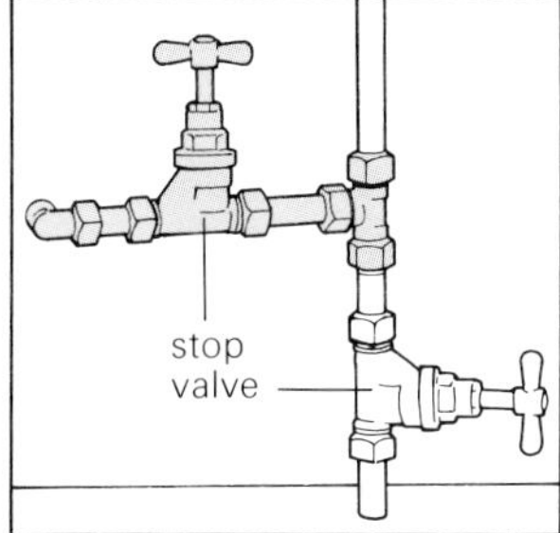


pipe. Avoid pipe loops that can't be drained in winter – if the tap itself isn't at the lowest point in the circuit, fit a draincock elbow on the pipe. Turn on both stopvalves. Check for leaks. Protect any pipes outside with waterproof lagging.

# ...washing machine/dishwasher

The Guides cover three methods of installing a washing machine that takes hot and cold water. The principles for machines (or a dishwasher), that heat their own water and so need only a cold supply are much the same.

Once you've chosen a site for the machine, locate the nearest hot and cold supply pipes. If you intend to keep the washing machine in the kitchen, these are likely to be the pipes supplying the sink taps. Cut off and drain the water in each of these pipes (the most likely cut-off points are the mains stopvalve for the cold supply and the stopvalve between the cold cistern and hot cylinder for the hot supply).

The method you adopt for arranging the supply plumbing will mostly depend on where the supply pipes are relative to the washing machine. The waste plumbing is common to all three methods.

## Step-by-step

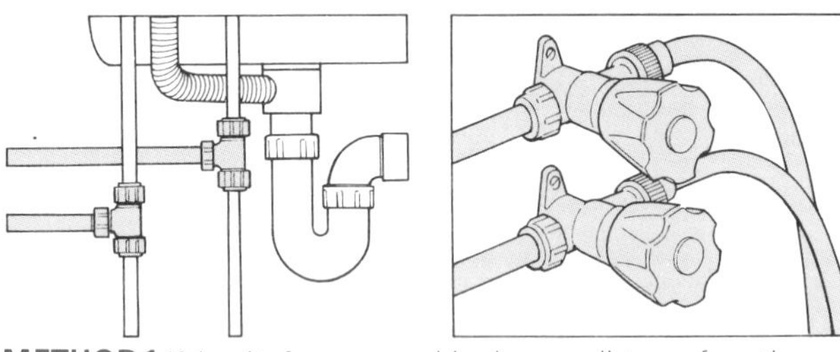

**METHOD 1** If the site for your machine is some distance from the nearest supply pipes, you'll have to bridge the gap with pipes.

**Step 1** To provide a permanent hot and cold supply fit tees into the hot and cold pipes and plumb to the washing machine with 15mm copper pipe.

**Step 2** Fix a pair of wall-mounted stopvalves in a convenient position. These are often colour-coded for hot and cold. Join up to the washing machine with rubber hoses, leaving enough slack to allow the machine to be pulled away from the wall for servicing.

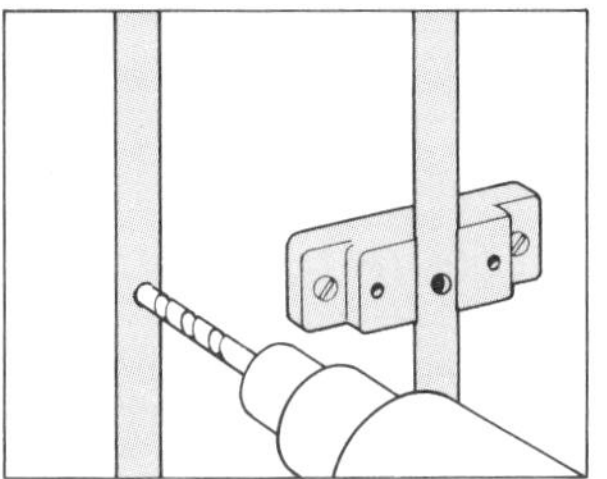

**METHOD 2** For washing machines close to supply pipes, saddle valves can be fitted to the pipes without cutting them.

**Step 1** Mark each pipe with a centre punch and drill into the mark with the drill bit diameter recommended. A depth-stop on the drill will help prevent damage to the back wall of the pipe.

**Step 2** Base plates are fixed to the wall behind the drilled pipes and the valves are screwed to these. Inside, a small pipe penetrates the hole and a rubber washer seals the connection. Make sure the pipe is clean and smooth (remove paint and rub with steel wool) to get a good join. The washing machine hoses are connected directly to the valve outflows allowing some slack as method 1.

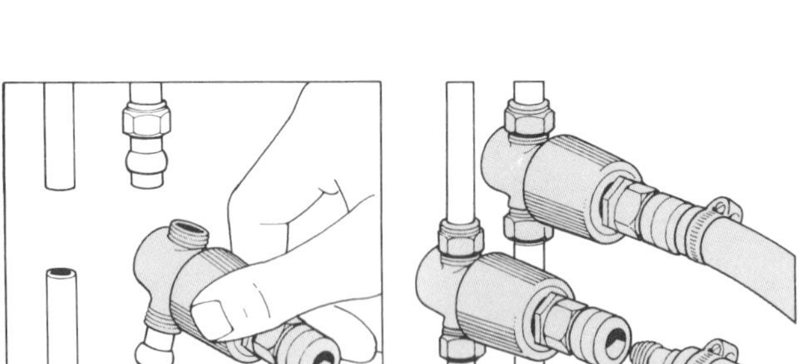

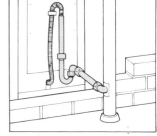

**METHOD 3** When hot and cold pipes are nearby a thru-flow valve can be fitted in exactly the same way as a tee-joint to provide direct connection to the washing machine hoses. The valves are controlled by milled cylinders that are turned to cut off the water supply. The machine hoses can then be released and the valves used to supply a garden hose or a dishwasher.

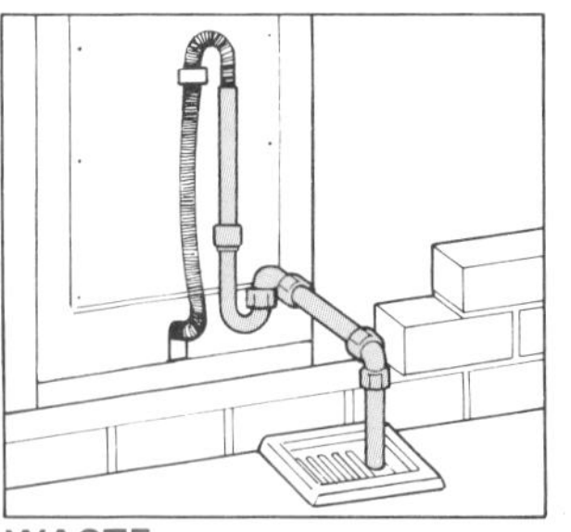

**WASTE**

**Step 1** Fix a waste standpipe to the wall with brackets and make sure it's as long as recommended for the washing machine (about 610mm) – the machine outlet hose hooks into this. The waste pipe can be run through the wall end below the grating of a gully.

**Step 2** An alternative discharge point is the waste trap of the kitchen sink (in which case you need a special sink trap), or direct to the soil pipe via a pipe boss. See page 60 for details of wastes.

# Kitchen ventilation

Opening a window is one way to rid a kitchen of cooking smells and moisture-laden air. This often works very well, but may not be the best solution if the window is small or badly-placed – if it's on the windward side of the house air may come in instead of out. Keeping internal doors closed helps to contain kitchen air, but this won't work in an open-plan kitchen. In any kitchen it's better to remove the steamy air at source through an extractor fan or a cooker hood. At least 10 to 15 air changes an hour are required for a kitchen.

**Extractor fans** take air to the outside of the house. They can change air fairly quickly and may be cheaper than a cooker hood with the equivalent extraction rate. One disadvantage is that they are usually positioned away from the cooker and therefore don't trap much of the greasy vapour rising from the cooker.

Generally, you choose the type of fan to suit where it will be fitted – window, wall or duct to a wall.

A *centrifugal* fan, which has an impeller like a paddle wheel is usually better at opposing high pressures than a similarly-sized *axial-flow* fan which has the more familiar vaned impeller. Centrifugal fans are deeper than axial-flow ones and can't be fitted in windows but they are the best choice for ducts.

Most manufacturers of fans quote the volume of air that a fan can move when there is no opposition to the air flow. In practice a fan may have to work against the wind or has to develop a suction to draw air from a well-draughtproofed house, so it's sensible to buy a larger fan than a first glance at the extraction rates would suggest. This is especially important if the fan is installed in a duct which will cause considerable resistance or if the fan will extract through a wall that is exposed to the wind.

To prevent air from having free access, extractor fans have louvres on the outside. These open automatically when the fan is switched on. It is also possible to make the fan automatic by fitting a thermostat or a humidistat. Then a rise in temperature or humidity will turn on the fan.

Fitting a fan in the right place is as important as choosing a fan of the right size and type. The fans should be as close as possible to the main source of water vapour. Try to install a fan opposite its air source and beware of short-circuiting air paths which will make it less efficient. A window fan is often cheaper than a similar wall fan and easier to install, but you have more choice about where to install a wall fan. Making a hole in a wall for a fan is much like a larger hole – see page 116.

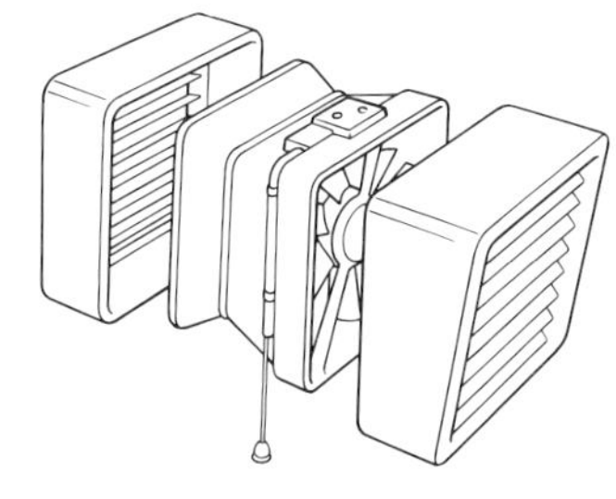

An axial-flow type extractor fan.

**Cooker hoods** have a much better chance of catching the cooking vapour, as they are installed above the cooker. There are two types of cooker hood – recirculation and extraction. The recirculation type passes fumes from the hob through grease and charcoal filters and returns the cleaned air to the kitchen. The extraction type passes fumes through a grease filter and then to the outside through the wall directly or via ducting. The advantage of an extraction cooker hood is that it will also expel greasy moisture-laden air. It is also more efficient than the recirculation type which needs to have the charcoal replaced at regular invervals. (A few hoods combine both functions – though they can work only in one way at once.)

Most hoods can be wall mounted or fitted beneath a kitchen wall unit. The hood should be wider than the cooker or the hob to trap the rising steam. They are available in four common widths, 550mm, 600mm, 700mm, 900mm. Many hoods have a flap at the front of the hood which may be pulled forwards to increase its effective capture area Some slimline modern ones have a vapour screen to pull out when the cooker's in use. There are also cooker hoods that will fit in a 600mm wall unit. Most operate at different speeds for varying cooking conditions and include a light to illuminate the cooking area.

**Safety note**

If the room contains a fuel burning appliance which is not the 'balanced flue' type, make sure that there is an adequate air inlet at all times so that fumes are not drawn down the flue when the fan is in use.

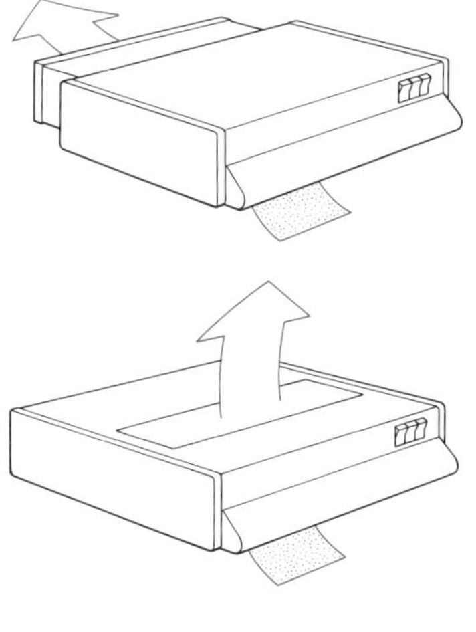

The two types of cooker hood.

# Gas cookers

**Installation must always be carried out strictly in accordance with the instructions issued by the manufacturer**. These are normally very comprehensive and take into account all the relevant requirements such as the Building Regulations, the Building Standards (Scotland) Regulations, the Gas Safety Regulations and British Standard Codes of Practice. Read page 44 *et seq* for notes on the rules, practice and testing of gas plumbing.

## Gas supply

Generally speaking the size of the supply pipe (its internal bore) must not be smaller than that of the inlet connection on the appliance. In any case it must be large enough to provide a pressure at the inlet of the appliance of 20 mbars. This must be checked with the cooker and all other gas appliances in use simultaneously.

## Electrical supply

If the appliance requires an electricity supply – for a light for instance – it will have to be connected to the nearest circuit. A flexible cable – already wired to the cooker – is provided by the manufacturer and this must not be extended. The flex will require attaching to a 3 pin plug (with 3 amp fuse) for connection to an adjacent socket outlet.

## Ventilation

To comply with the Gas Safety Regulations and Building Regulations, the room containing the cooker must have an adequate air supply. (It must also contain an opening window or some equivalent – such as a louvred window.)

A gas cooker may not be installed in any room which has a volume of less than six cubic metres.

Rooms of volume between $6m^3$ and $11m^2$ with no door direct to the outside air require an area of permanent ventilation in addition to the opening window. The vent area must be at least $6450mm^2$ for a room $6m^3$ to $9m^2$; at least $3225mm^2$ for a room $9m^3$ to $11m^3$ in volume.

## Position

Ideally the cooker should be placed in a good light and freedom from draughts is essential. It should be levelled both side to side and back to front using a spirit level on the centre oven shelf and adjusting the levelling feet. Some cookers are fitted with wheels at the front to assist moving forwards for cleaning. These are also fitted with levelling screws.

## Fire precautions

Cookers are heat producing appliances and it is necessary to provide clearance between the appliance and any combustible materials adjacent. The manufacturer's installation instructions give details.

LEVELLING A COOKER

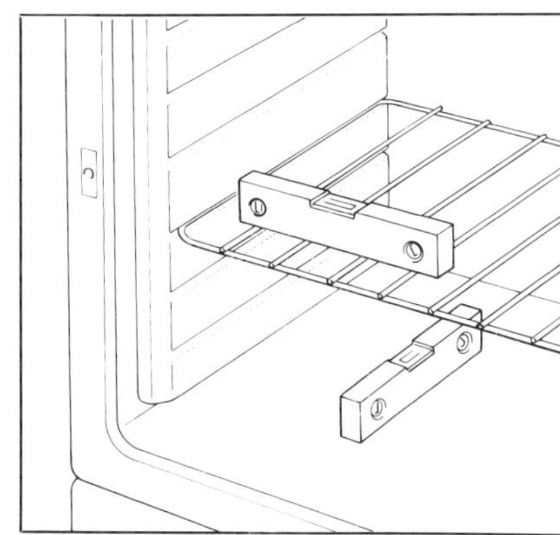

The cooker must be properly levelled using a spirit level on the middle oven shelf.

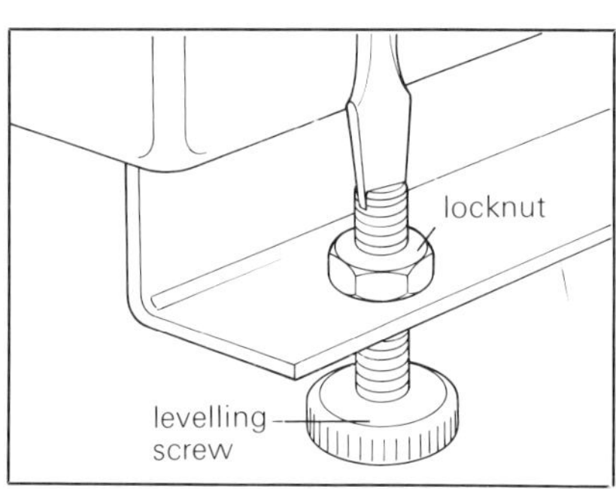


A freestanding cooker has adjustable feet for levelling.

CHECKING GAS PRESSURE AT THE COOKER

It is essential that the gas pipework is gastight and that the pressure at the gas appliance is the necessary 20 millibars.
A do-it-yourselfer is unlikely to have the proper equipment to make the tests so anyone who decides to d-i-y install a cooker should ask a qualified gas installer to check the installation for correct pressure and gastightness.

## A freestanding cooker

The preferred method uses a flexible 'plug-in' connection where a specially prepared length (normally 900mm) of reinforced hose with a 'bayonet' fitting on one end is screwed into the inlet pipe on the cooker and plugged into a self-sealing socket connector fitted to the cooker end of the gas supply pipe. The socket connector must face downwards so that the flexible hose falls in a natural loop.

When this method of connection is used the possibility of the cooker tipping forwards if downward pressure is placed upon the oven door, when open, must be prevented. This is done by fixing a stability bracket on the wall behind the cooker – this fitting is supplied by the manufacturer of the cooker.

The alternative method of fixing is to use a 'rigid' connection where the gas supply pipe is attached direct to the cooker inlet pipe as for a built-in cooker.

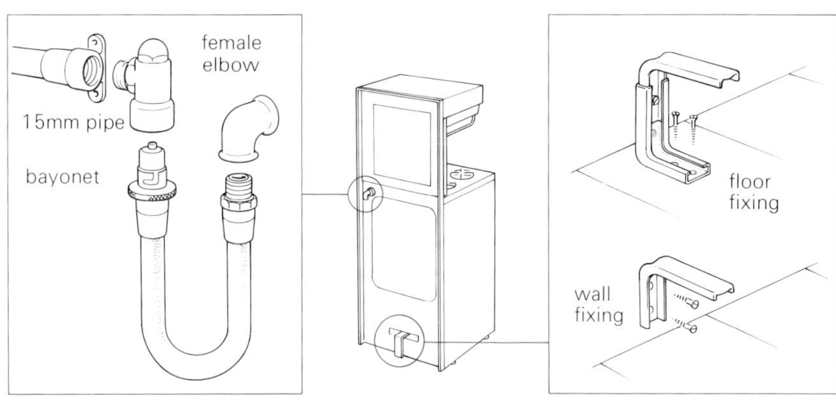


A freestanding cooker is usually connected by a flexible hose which falls in a natural loop.

## A built-in cooker

Hob (hotplate) and oven units are designed to be incorporated into the kitchen furniture; grill units are normally fixed on the wall adjacent to the hob unit. For all sizings and clearances it is essential to follow the manufacturer's instructions.

The hob is designed to be set into a worktop through a hole cut to an exact size specified. The unit is normally held in place by clamps or screws. Clearance must be left below the hotplate to give access to gas and electrical connections.

### The oven unit

The oven unit is designed for fitting into a correctly-sized cupboard housing strong enough to support the weight of the unit. The housing must be securely fastened to a wall. Again space must be left below the oven unit for gas and electrical connections.

### The grill unit

The grill unit is normally fitted on the wall in a convenient position above the worktop – usually adjacent to the hotplate unit. Because of the heat generated by the grill, space must be provided above and at each side of the unit in accordance with the manufacturer's instructions. Around the grill and it may not touch any combustible material.

### The gas supply

The gas supply to individual built-in units normally runs to a point from which branch points are taken to each unit. As the units are built-in, the connections are always rigid with the gas supply pipe attached direct to the unit inlet connection. However the gas supply pipes are run, they must be sized to provide a pressure of 20 mbar at the inlet of the unit and this must be checked. Each unit must have a separate isolating or service tap fitted into the supply pipe to that unit.

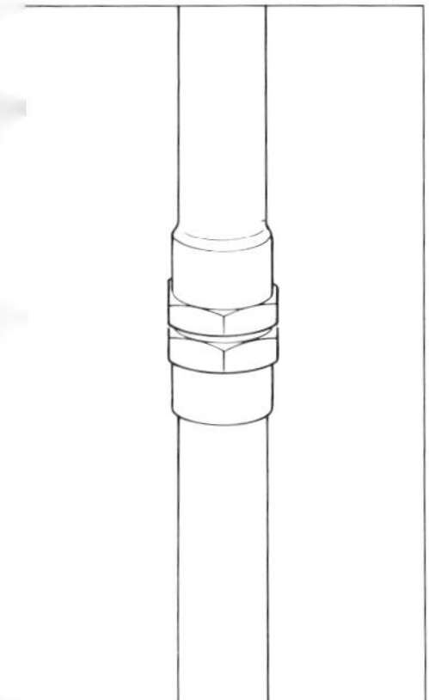

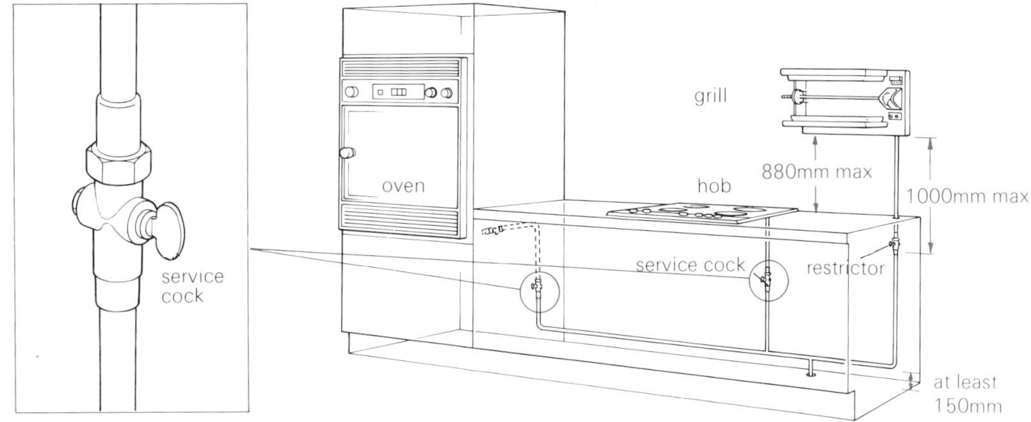


Built-in cookers on split-levels are always connected by a rigid coupling.

# Practical floor coverings

A practical floor covering is essential in a kitchen where spills and food debris, and mud traipsed in through the back door will quickly ruin anything more luxurious. Sanded and sealed floorboards (with any gaps between or around the boards filled to stop food getting trapped) are one choice, but you're more likely to buy and lay a proper covering. There's a wide choice. Most floor coverings that would be suitable for a kitchen floor will also do for a utility room, bathroom or a conservatory.

■ **linoleum** Although many people still call almost any sheet flooring lino, most are vinyl.

■ **vinyl floor covering** The most widely available is *cushioned vinyl* (a sandwich of pvc and a centre strengthening layer). This nearly always comes in sheets, not tiles. There are simpler cushioned vinyls (thinner) available in both sheets and tiles.

Most tiles (and some sheet vinyls) are solid vinyl all the way through.

Vinyls can be patterned, plain coloured or veined. Patterned vinyls have the design printed underneath a thin, transparent PVC layer; coloured and veined vinyls usually have the colouring mixed into the top PVC layer.

■ **cork tiles** Dense tiles are best for floors as they are likely to wear less quickly. Vinyl-layered cork tiles have a surface layer of transparent vinyl.

■ **clay/ceramic tiles** There are two basic sorts – *clay floor quarries* and *ceramic floor tiles*. In general, ceramic tiles are manufactured to closer tolerances than floor quarries and have a smoother finish, they absorb less water than quarry tiles. Tiles can be glazed – but glazed tiles are usually ceramic.

■ **carpet** A carpet for a kitchen must be hardwearing, so go for heavy domestic polypropylene, polyester or low-loop nylon carpet. Or try a bonded or needlefelt carpet made from non-absorbent fibres – these have been used successfully in industrial working environments. Most are heavily patterned which helps to hide the bits which inevitably fall on a kitchen floor. Using carpet tiles means a spoilt patch can easily be lifted and replaced.

## The choices compared

The Table on page 86 sums up the first four floor coverings. For carpets see page 157.

■ **durability** Practical floor coverings are by definition durable. *Wear* is often not as important as people think. Laid on a good floor, most materials are good. Thin, solid printed vinyls can't really be expected to last for more than about four years in the most hard-worked areas. If there are small unevennesses in your floor, it would make sense to go for the thicker types.

clear

coloured chips

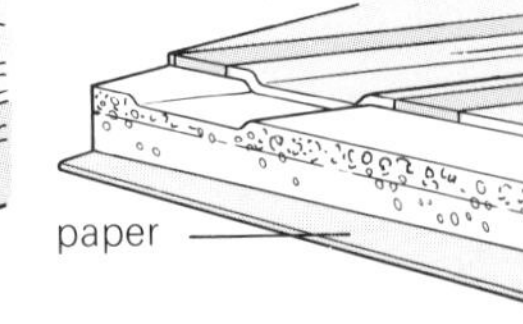


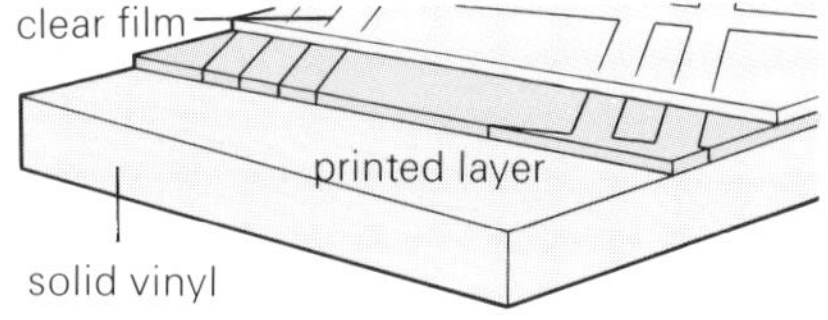


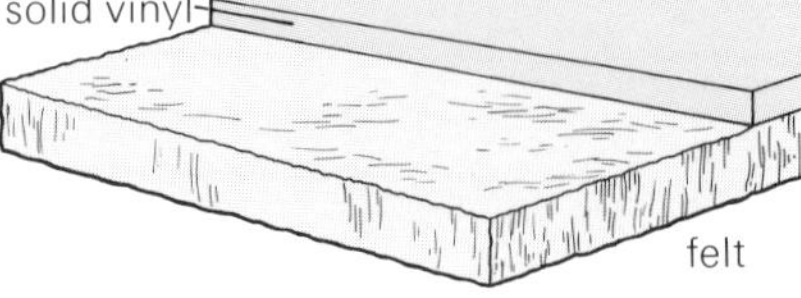

Cross-section through the four main types of flooring.

Hot things, household chemicals and grease can all cause permanent damage to all floor coverings and are common spills in a working area. Water that sits on the surface does little harm, but can present problems if it gets to the underside. Mop any spills. Dropping heavy things on the floor won't damage most practical coverings, but could crack ceramic tiles.

■ **flexibility** A material good for flexibility should be easier to lay, especially in sheet form. It should also be more tolerant of movements in the floor itself – timber shrinking, for example – but rather less tolerant of bumps, which would show through. If you've prepared the surface properly for laying, flexibility won't matter much.

■ **comfort** The type of floor covering you use won't make a great deal of difference to the actual temperature of a room, but different types will give a different feeling of *warmth* to your feet.

Different types of floor covering vary in the amount of *noise* they make when walked on, and the amount of that noise that's transmitted to the room below.

A floor covering that has good slip resistance is safest. Most are all right when dry, but they can be much more slippery when they're wet, or if waxed highly.

*Resilience* is a measure of how 'bouncy' the flooring is to walk on.

## Preparing the floor

Whichever practical floor covering you choose, it will be only as good as the floor beneath – any defect there will cause wear on the floor covering – so it's important to prepare the subfloor properly.

## Solid concrete floors

A sound floor needs little more than brushing clean. Slight dampness can be held at bay by an epoxy pitch waterproof coating. Slight unevenness can be levelled with a self-levelling compound.

A bumpy, badly cracked or damp concrete floor is cause for concern, usually sign of a failed floor screed (a screed is the top concrete layer of the floor applied when the main slab is dry to give a smooth level surface). Failures are all too common even in quite modern houses.

A failed screed will have to be removed. You may need to hire an electric hammer, but a very badly-laid screed may be removed with little more than a shovel.

If the underlying floor is sound, fine cracks can be ignored – unless obviously recent in which case obtain the advice of a building surveyor or structural engineer.

Unfortunately, inadequate screed thickness is a common cause of failure and replacement with a proper 60mm screed may well mean raising the floor level – and skirting boards, door sills, etc – by 25mm to 40mm. If this is unacceptable you may be able to get by with a thinner screed, but with a greater risk of repeating the failure.

### A CONCRETE FLOOR IN AN EXISTING HOUSE

Concreting of the slab differs from that for a new floor – see page 235 – in that there are no side forms for level control. Instead, lay and level the concrete in strips in a manner similar to that used for laying a screed. Cure under polythene unless you can lay the screed immediately.

The screed is laid as normal, but unless a lot of other work needs doing in the same room lay it as soon as possible – preferably the next day, as soon as the slab concrete is hard enough to walk on (a few surface scruffs won't matter). Cure for three days and if necessary to pass through the room lay planks or sheets of board as protective walkways when the screed has hardened enough not to be marked.

If you're living in the house at the time, getting back into the room is a major priority. A well-laid screed should be hard enough for near-normal use after a couple of weeks, but furniture with small feet or casters should be placed in rubber caster-cups, and anything that is flush on the floor should be raised on blocks of wood to let air circulate while the concrete is drying out.

Open-textured rugs of matting can be used during the drying-out period, but not material with an impervious or foam backing. Keeping the room heated with some ventilation will reduce drying-out time but don't use paraffin heaters which produce moisture vapour. Even so it is likely to be getting on for six months before a 100mm thick slab with a 40mm screed is thoroughly dry.

If it is important to lay permanent floor covering quickly, use high alumina cement (HAC) in place of ordinary Portland cement (OPC) – see page 38 – in the screed mix. It should not be laid, however, until slab concrete made with OPC has cured thoroughly, and the screed should be kept *wet* – not merely damp – for at least 24 hours, by regular spraying.

A HAC screed will be hard enough to use within 24 hours, and permanent floor covering can be laid after four or five days. (Although high alumina cement gains strength very rapidly, the workability of a HAC mix is about the same as OPC – about 2 hours in normal conditions.)

## Wooden floor

If a wooden floor is basically sound – go over the surface nailing and screwing down loose boards and removing any upstanding nails or tacks. Smooth any uneven areas – if the floor is badly uneven through excessive shrinkage, hire a floor sander. Cover the floor with sheets of hardboard laid rough side up (unless the floor supplier specifies otherwise) and nailed all over at 150mm intervals. (Allow these boards to condition for a few days in the room where they will be used.) If any of the floorboards give access to wiring below, make an access hole in the board above and arrange the top floorcovering for access too. Ceramic tiles need more rigidity, so use 9mm plywood or chipboard – a moisture-resistant grade – as the cover.

More serious problems with a suspended timber floor may mean that some or all of the supporting timbers or the floorboards have to be replaced. An upper floor will have to be rebuilt in timber but a suspended timber ground floor could be replaced by a solid concrete floor and provided less than about 600mm of fill is required a concrete floor is usually cheaper.

Whichever sort of floor is installed design and construction are exactly the same as for a new floor (pages 235 to 239) except that all the work must be done between constructed walls – and as quickly as possible if the house is occupied, especially if it is necessary to get across the floor to reach another part of the house. This is most important for a concrete floor or new screed – see Box.

## Brick-on-earth floors

These are very common in older cottages, especially in kitchens and sculleries, and are frequently damp, uneven or both. They are best dealt with by removal and replacement with a new floor, usually in concrete.

In low-ceilinged houses additional headroom can often be gained at the same time, but take advice on this first as the foundations can be disturbed by the necessary excavations.

## FLOOR COVERINGS

| | Linoleum | Cushioned vinyl |
|---|---|---|
| **Material** | Natural oils, cork and wood powders and pigments mixed together, pressed into shape and matured in ovens for up to two months. Special hardened grades available. | Multi-layered PVC containing at least one cushioned layer – usually foamed plastic. Usually printed but some plain coloured or veined. |
| **How it comes** | Sheets and tiles, fair range of colours. Reasonably priced. | Mostly sheets, large range of colours and printed patterns. Reasonably priced. |
| **Durability:** wear | very good | good |
| very hot things | good | fair |
| household chemicals | good | good |
| water | poor (better if waxed) | very good if it can't get down joints; otherwise fair to poor |
| grease | good | good |
| **Flexibility** | Fair | Very good |
| **Comfort:** warmth | very good | good |
| noise | good | very good |
| slip resistance | dry – good, wet – fair | dry – good, wet – nearly as good |
| resilience | fair to good | very good |
| **Underfloor heating** | Only for types where floor temperature doesn't exceed 80°F | Usually unsuitable |
| **Maintenance** | Polish at first, then wash and buff | Wash with dilute detergent or polish (not necessary for printed) at first, then wash and buff |
| **Good for** | Hallways, playrooms, well-used areas | Bathrooms and kitchens (but make sure water can't get down seams), halls, playrooms, bedrooms |
| **Don't use in** | Wet areas | Can be used anywhere if properly sealed |

| Solid vinyl | Clay or ceramic tile | Cork tile |
|---|---|---|
| Plastics with fillers and pigments. The whole thickness of material can be one layer with the colouring going right through, or it can be laminated with only top layer having the colouring. Printed solid vinyls often have a very thin top layer of transparent vinyl with the printed pattern | Clays and other materials are mixed with water and pressed into shape and fired. Floor quarries are usually rougher in finish than floor tiles. All tiles can have a printed pattern and glazed surface. | Cork granules compressed and stuck together under heat. Surfaces other than prefinished and vinyl-layered should be sealed with wax or polyurethane. |
| Sheets and tiles, large range of colours, some patterns in solid, unlimited colours and patterns in printed. Can be cheap. | Floor quarries; in range of sizes, very limited range of colours. Floor tiles: wider range of sizes, shapes and colours, patterned. Expensive. | Tiles only, in limited range of natural colours. Can be cheap. |
| very good, except for thin printed when usually poor. | very good (patterned types perhaps good) ceramic tiles can crack | fair |
| fair, poor for thin printed | very good | fair |
| good | very good | good to acids, but only fair to alkalis |
| very good if it can't get down joints; otherwise fair | very good | fair if sealed |
| fair | fair to very good | good if sealed |
| Very good | Non-existent | Poor |
| good | poor | very good |
| good | poor | very good |
| dry – good, wet – fair to good | dry – good, wet – quarries good, glazed tiles poor to good depending on finish | dry – very good, wet – very good |
| fair to good | non-existent | very good |
| OK | OK | Unsuitable |
| Wash with dilute detergent or polish (not necessary with printed) at first, then wash and buff | Seal unsealed quarries. Wash with neutral detergent. Can be waxed. | Seal unsealed types, then apply polish and buff, vinyl layered types don't need polishing |
| Bathrooms and kitchens (but make sure water can't get down seams), halls, playrooms, bedrooms | Heavy use areas, wet areas (but use tiles with slip resistant finishes) | Bathrooms and kitchens (but make sure water can't get down seams), bedrooms, playrooms |
| Most thin printed vinyls shouldn't be used in heavy traffic areas | Difficult to lay in areas with suspended floors, bedrooms | Heavy use areas (especially if tiles are not pre-sealed) |

# Laying floors

## Step-by-step guide to laying vinyl, cork and rubber tiles

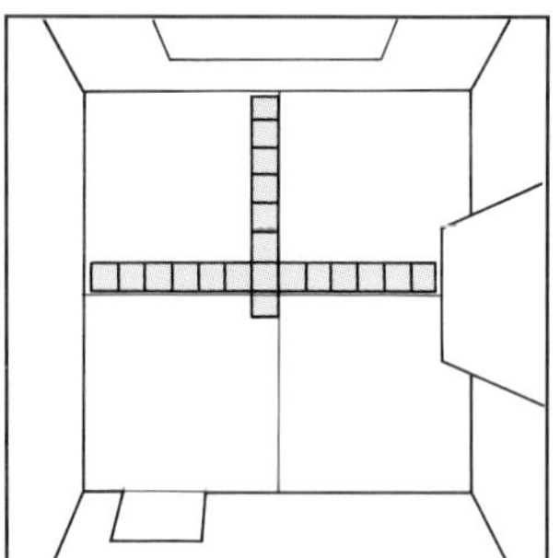

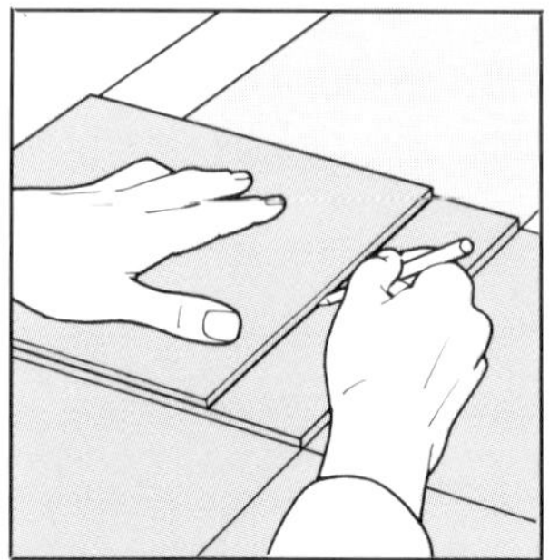

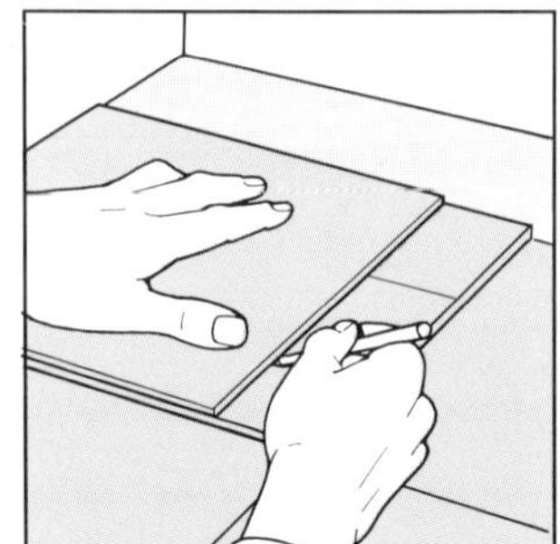

These floor coverings are marked out and laid in much the same way, using an adhesive recommended by the manufacturers (some vinyl and cork tiles are self-adhesive). Vinyl tiles are easier to lay if they are kept in a warm room for a day before laying.

**Step 1** To get an even border laying should start from the centre. Stretch a string across the room between pins knocked into the floor at the centres of two opposite walls. Stretch another string across the centre of the room the other way exactly at right angles to the first.

Dry-lay a run of tiles along each string, starting where they cross, and butting them tightly. When you come to the last tile in each direction, aim to have an even space at each end, as near to a full-size tile as possible. Slide the tiles along the string if necessary to achieve this. When you are satisfied with the arrangement, realign the string guides with the tile positions and mark lines on the floor.

**Step 2** Start gluing the tiles in place, working outwards from the centre following the lines. With self-adhesive tiles, remove the backing and press into place. Otherwise, use the adhesive as directed, over a slightly larger area than the tiles. Take account of any pattern direction. Arrows marked on the back of the tiles should all point the same way. Continue working out from the centre in all directions until only the borders are left.

Where a border tile must be cut to fit, overlay it exactly on top of the tile last laid. Hold a spare tile on top, flush against the wall, and use its edge to mark a cutting line on the border tile below. The same technique can be used at corners, by marking the tile first against one wall, then, without turning it, against the other. For awkward shapes such as architraves, use a profile tracer or tear a paper pattern. In all cases, take care that any pattern on the tile is matched to its neighbours.

When all the tiles are laid, clean off any surplus adhesive—a plastic pan scourer used gently is best. Do not use solvents. With unsealed cork tiles, sand lightly, then seal with at least three coats of a suitable floor sealer.

## Step-by-step guide to laying sheet vinyl.

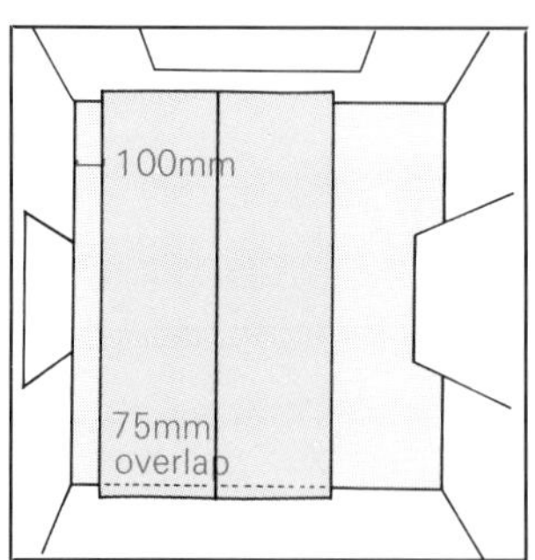


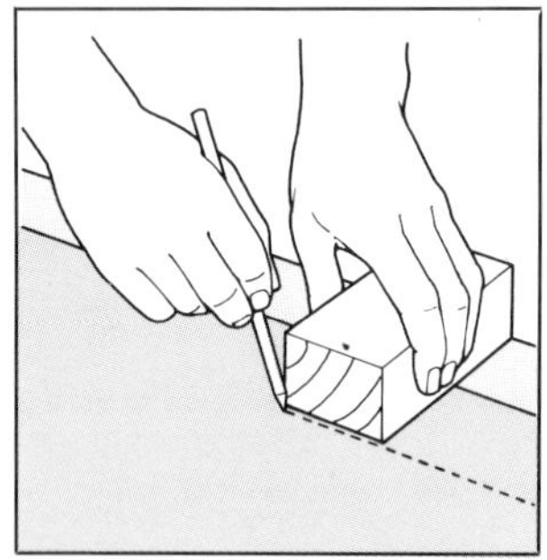

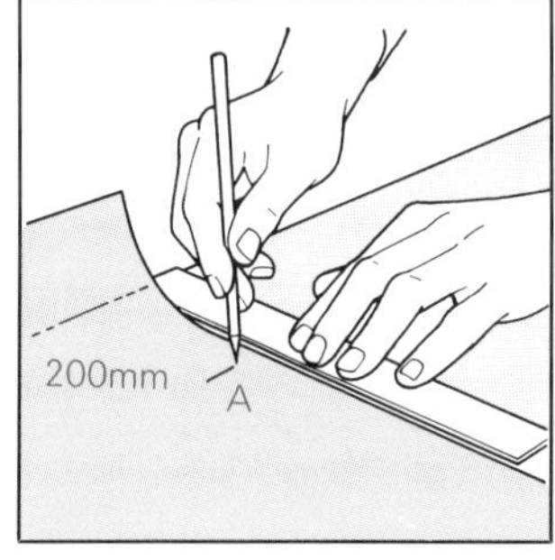


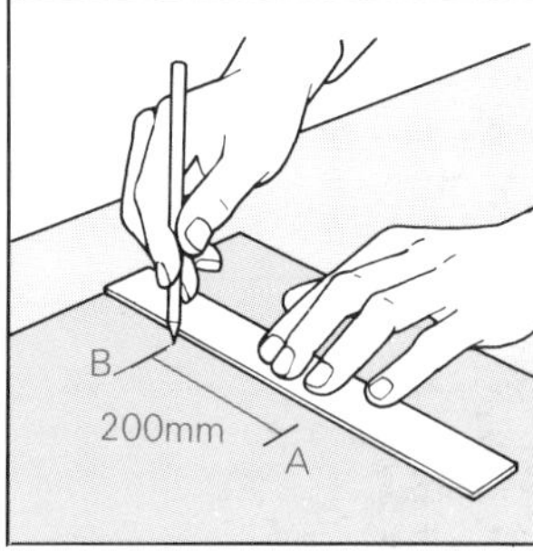


Most vinyl sheet is sold in up to 4m widths, so it is generally possible to cover a whole room. Vinyl and rubber sheet in narrower widths may need to be laid in strips.

When you buy, choose the most economical width, but allow at least 75mm overlap all round. If there are to be joins, avoid having them across a doorway. In general, patterns should align with the doorway, the longest wall, or the most visually prominent feature.

Before laying, reverse-roll the sheet loosely, and leave it in a warm room for a day or so. Then trim it roughly to fit leaving the 75mm overlap. At corners, make diagonal cuts to allow the overlap on both sides to bend up. Use a soft broom to smooth the sheet out flat.

Though not the simplest method for trimming the sheet the most accurate method for a beginner is to use a scribing technique.

**Step 1** Lay the sheet along the straightest side wall, parallel to it, but about 100mm away. Use a block of wood about 150mm long as a scriber, running one end along the wall and marking the sheet at the other end. This outlines the shape of the wall: cut with a sharp knife and slide the sheet to the wall.

**Step 2** To trim the ends, measure 200mm back from the wall and mark the edge of the

## Step-by-step guide to laying ceramic tiles

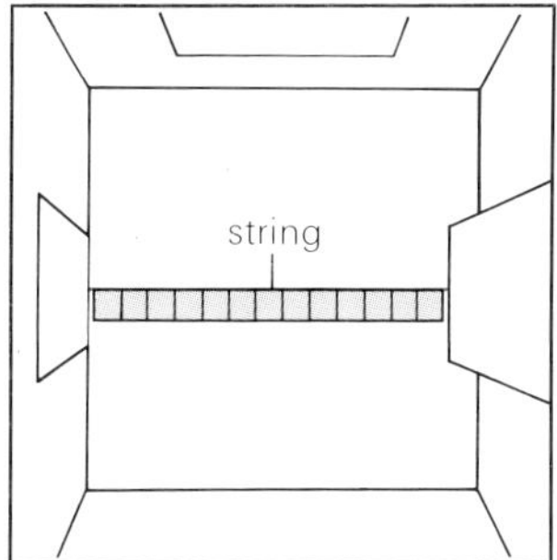


Ceramic tiles are laid with tile adhesive – as recommended by the manufacturer. Floor tiles rarely have spacers for grouting joints, so you need a supply of 3mm thick spacer slips – strips of wood or card are suitable. The method described is for square or rectangular tiles. Interlocking tiles are more complicated to mark out and cut.

**Step 1** Work from the furthest corner back towards the doorway. Stretch a string out at right-angles to the doorway across to the opposite wall. Dry-lay a row of tiles out from the line of the door along the string, butting them tightly together but with spacers between.

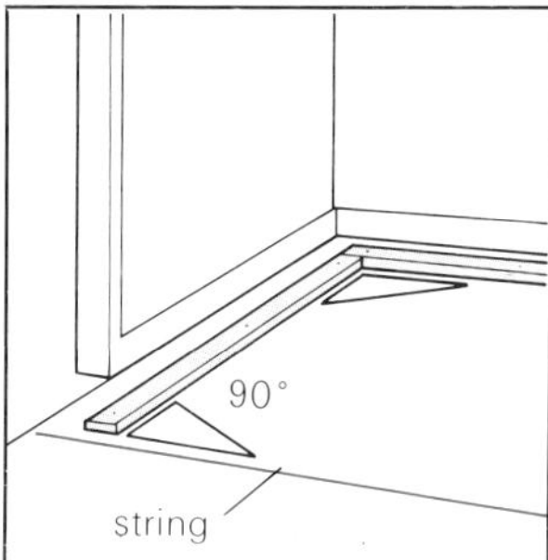


**Step 2** Mark the position of the last full tile, then remove the row. Nail a long batten to the floor, against the mark and at right-angles to the string line. At the furthest corner, fix a second batten rather less than a tile width from the wall, and at an accurate right angle to the first.

Start in the corner formed by the battens. With a notched spreader lay a thin, even bed of adhesive across an area of about one square metre at a time. Press the tiles firmly into the adhesive and interposing spacers and scraping off any excess adhesive as you go. Continue working back to the door along both battens and the area between until the whole floor except the borders is covered. Leave to harden for 24 hours before walking on the tiles.

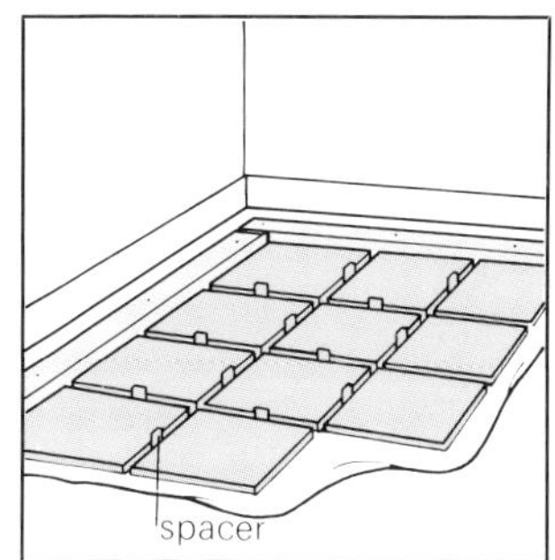


**Step 3** Remove the spacers. Finish the borders by removing the battens, then marking the border tiles, (as for vinyl ones) leaving 3mm for the grouting joints. Cut by scoring with a tile cutter, then breaking over an edge, or with a disc cutter or angle grinder. Spread adhesive on the cut tiles and press into position, levelling them against their neighbours.

After 24 hours, grout the joints with a sponge or plastic scraper, making sure the joints are well filled. Buff stains off when dry with a clean, dry cloth.

## . . . quarry tiles

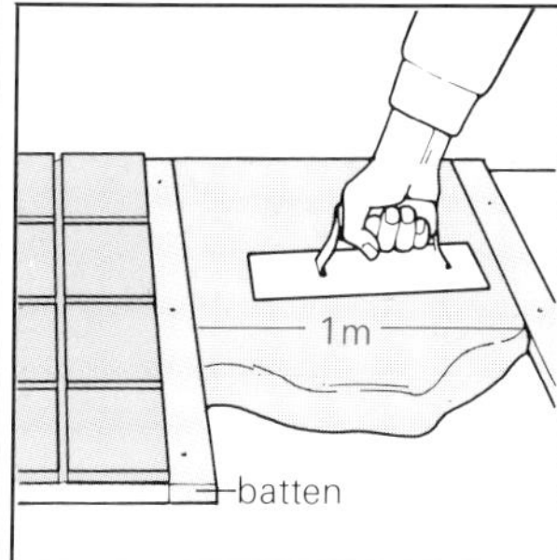


Often quarry tiles can be cut and laid like ceramic tiles but irregular hand-made tiles need setting in a wet cement screed laid 15mm deep in small bays with the guide battens about a metre apart. See page 236 for details of screeding – use a fairly dry, 1:3 mortar mix.

Lay the tiles damp and set them in the wet screed with 6mm spacers between. Press the tiles down with a wooden straight-edge – checking that they remain level. Repeat in subsequent bays. Awkward areas may be best left until the rest of the floor has hardened.

Grouting can be applied wet or the dry powder can be brushed in and sprinkled with water. Remove any surplus before it hardens. Finally buff and polish with linseed oil.

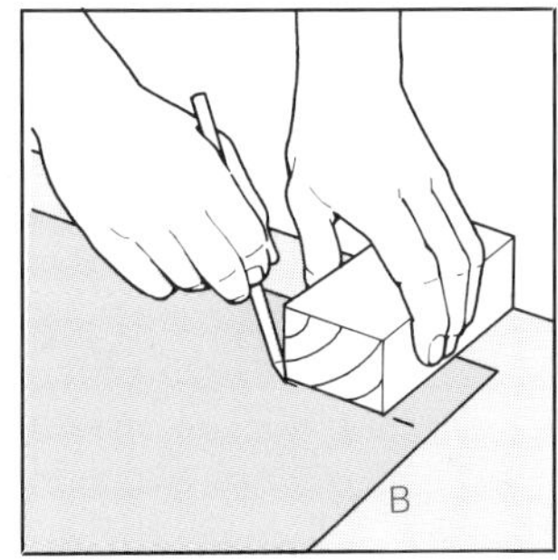


sheet. Then form a fold and pull the end back, keeping it straight, so that it lies flat on the floor. Make a further mark on the edge, 200mm forward of the first. Adjust the position of the sheet so that when the scriber is held against the wall, its end lies against the *second* mark, and scribe across the sheet. When cut, the sheet will then fit back

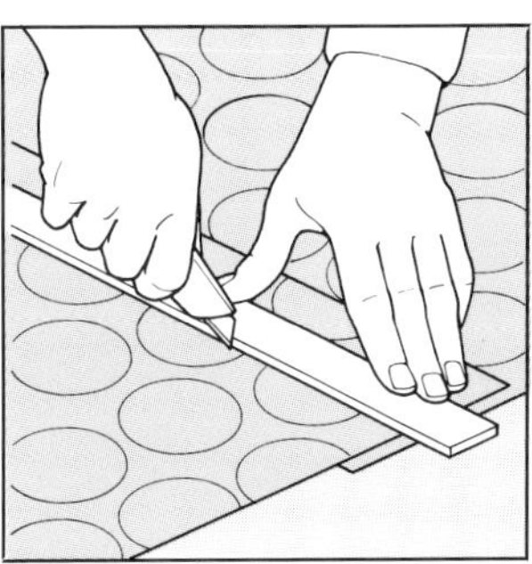

against the wall. Repeat other end.

**Step 3** If you have to join widths, you can normally just butt them, but if the design allows an overtrim you will need to overlay the sheets, matching the pattern, and cut through both together. Secure the joins and any edges that might

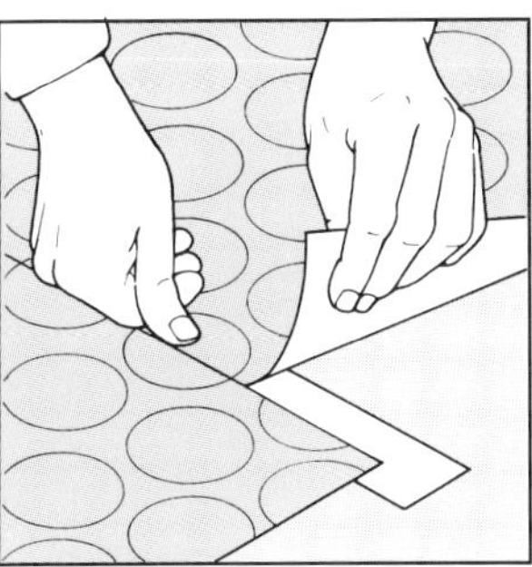

otherwise lift with heavy-duty double-sided adhesive tape. If adhesive is recommended, use as directed by the manufacturer.

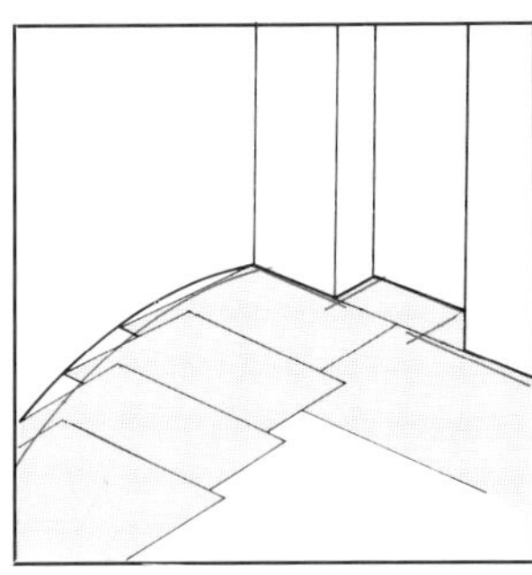

**Step 4** Complicated shapes, especially in small rooms, are easiest to deal with if a paper pattern is made. Tape sheets of paper together to fill the room roughly, and use a scriber to mark the outline of the room on the paper. To mark the design on the floor sheet reverse the process, using the scriber to mark outwards from the line.

# Ceilings and lighting

A kitchen ceiling is one of the most vulnerable ceilings in a house: it's attacked from below by dirt, steam and grease from cooking and as it's often under a bathroom floor it can be damaged by water from above. Consequently in an older house it may be the first ceiling to show serious signs of wear.

When choosing a new kitchen ceiling it makes sense also to consider the lighting. A kitchen is essentially a working area so a high level of illumination is required and it's important to position the lights correctly. A suspended kitchen ceiling can incorporate a fairly sophisticated lighting system using fluorescent fittings or downlighters or both.

## Types of kitchen ceiling

Most houses are built with a simple plaster kitchen ceiling. In older houses a plaster ceiling would have been lath and plaster, but nowadays most are constructed from plasterboard nailed to the joists. A bumpy or badly damaged lath and plaster ceiling is best replaced – see Guide page 262. A plaster ceiling is a reasonable choice for a new ceiling – painted with a washable emulsion paint it's easy to keep clean and it's easy enough to repaint the surface at regular intervals.

Cladding is a common choice for kitchen ceilings. Tongued and grooved boards are relatively easy to install either directly to the joists or to battens screwed to the underside of the ceiling. Softwood boards are most common. Once installed they can be varnished or painted. Boards are usually 85mm wide when fitted (they're about 100mm including the tongue) and come in lengths up to 3m. They can have square or chamfered edges – sometimes called vee edges. They can be installed as full width pieces or in a regular or random pattern of short pieces. Setting the boards on the diagonal can be effective.

Tiling is another choice. There are two main types of ceiling tile: the type made of expanded polystyrene is inexpensive and very common in the shops; the other type made of wood fibres or mineral fibres may need seeking out. Tiles are usually stuck to the ceiling with a pva adhesive and for safe sticking of polystyrene tiles it's important to apply a continuous coat of adhesive, not just spots at the corners. If they're stuck incorrectly polystyrene tiles can be a serious fire risk. For the same reason they should be painted only with water-based paints such as emulsion – gloss must not be used. Most experts dislike their use in kitchens (or anywhere that there is a potential for fire). Square-edged fibre tiles are stuck up, but tongued and grooved fibre tiles are also available and these can be fixed by secret nailing or stapling through the tongue into battens screwed or nailed to the ceiling joists.

## Suspended ceilings

Any of the ceilings above could also be installed on a structure of new joists suspended by hangers from the joists of the existing ceiling. The new joists should also bear on loadbearing perimeter walls. A much lighter suspended ceiling can be constructed using a suspended metal grid supporting lightweight panels.

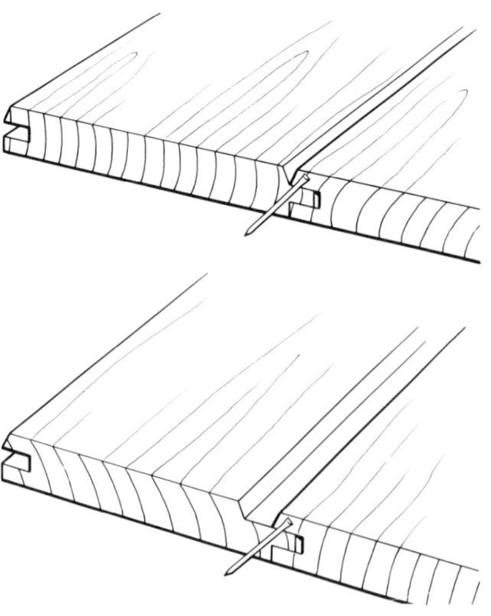

Tongued and grooved cladding with vee-joint and, below, wide joint.

### Grids

There are 3 main types of grid. A concealed grid – sometimes called a C-system – which is used with grooved fibre panels which conceal the grid section and two visible grids. Both types of visible grid support the panel all round on small ledges: they differ in the way they're put together – with one, a thin steel section, normally faced with aluminium, interlocks to give a rigid grid which could be used for a sloping ceiling, with the other, a slightly wider aluminium section is used to form continuous supports across the width of the room and shorter sections to complete each panel opening are simply laid across the main sections, supported by the same ledge that holds the panels up.

### Panels

Plastic panels for suspended ceilings are usually made of either pvc or polystyrene. Most pvc panels are white and appear opalescent when lighted from behind. Polystyrene panels are often described as 'crushed or cracked ice' and made in various colours. Colour can be introduced to colourless panels of either material by using coloured lights behind, normally fluorescent tubes in red (which appears pink), yellow, blue, green. An important difference between the two types of plastic is their behaviour in a fire – see Fire Risks. There are also plastic louvre (or eggcrate) panels.

Fibre panels are the same as those used for tiling directly on to the ceiling – they're often called acoustic panels.

Those used in visible grids have straight edges and simply lie on the grid. Panels for concealed systems have grooved edges. Acoustic panels can usually support lights.

A third type of panel is a wad of glass fibre 20mm or 25mm thick faced with a thin washable vinyl coating. These simply rest on the grid and are not strong enough to support lights.

## General considerations

When you're thinking of a new ceiling there are a number of things which can affect your choice of ceiling and the way you set about its installation.

### Headroom

A suspended ceiling shouldn't reduce the headroom below the minimum 2·3m height generally required. Even in a small kitchen which is exempt from this Building Regulation in England and Wales, it's sensible to allow headroom of about 2·3m.

### Condensation

Water vapour rising up through an insulated suspended ceiling below an uninsulated loft space (a bungalow kitchen for instance) may cause condensation. It's almost impossible to stop the vapour rising and the best preventive means is to provide some ventilation either by stopping the ceiling slightly short of the walls or, if the ceiling is tight to the walls, by installing air bricks to allow a flow of air behind the ceiling. Insulating the roof will also help. This is desirable to save heat anyway – see page 190 – but then the roof space itself will usually need improved ventilation to reduce the risk of condensation there.

### Fire risks

Whenever you do work on a ceiling it's worth considering the implications for fire. A ceiling in a new house or extension will have to meet the requirements of the Building Regulations. There are two things to consider: the fire resistance and the ceiling's contribution to the rate of growth of the fire.

The Building Regulations require all floors (except ground floors which are not above basement rooms) to have $\frac{1}{2}$ hour fire resistance, but as in practice a ceiling (particularly a plaster ceiling below a boarded floor on joists) often contributes much of the resistance, it's worth ensuring that a replacement or repaired ceiling maintains the standard. Provided a suspended ceiling is installed beneath a sound floor and ceiling (which already meets the requirements for fire resistance) there's no need to worry.

The rate of growth of a fire can be determined by the materials used to face the ceiling. Materials used for the purpose are therefore tested to establish a class of performance for the surface spread of flame. There are four classes of performance based on tests set out in BS 476: Part 7 – 1 being safest, 4 being least safe. A fifth class, 0, is attributed to a lining that is non-combustible or has a surface Class 1 and also does well in a test measuring fire propagation. In a house all ceilings must be Class 3 or better.

A plasterboard ceiling or a suspended ceiling with mineral fibre or glass fibre panels is usually Class 1. Wood fibre panels can be Class 1 if they've been treated with flame retardant. Timber cladding is usually Class 3 or better.

Panels of thermoplastic, such as those used to transmit light in suspended ceilings, cannot meet Class 3 in the tests for surface spread of flame. Different test methods (set out in BS 2782) are used on plastics for which the Building Regulations specify five types which can be used for new ceilings subject to various provisos. Panels of pvc are usually classed as Type 4 and are a safer choice than panels of polystyrene which are usually Type 2. Type 2 panels are best avoided altogether for kitchen ceilings, and in other rooms you should limit their use to half the ceiling. Surface spread of flame is also important for wall linings.

A suspended ceiling can be fixed to a framework of battens and hangers.

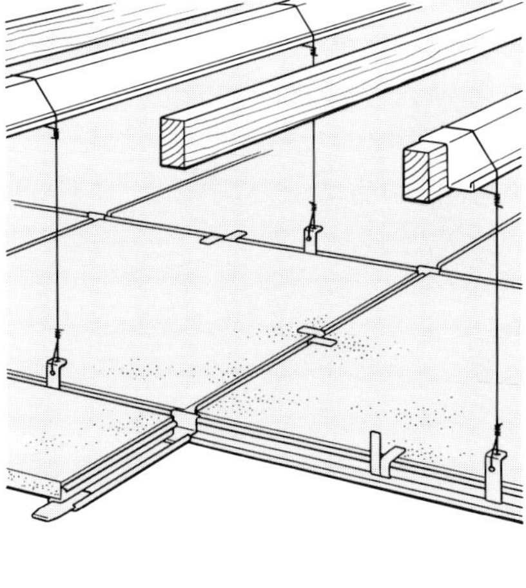

Visible steel interlocking grid with fibre panels.

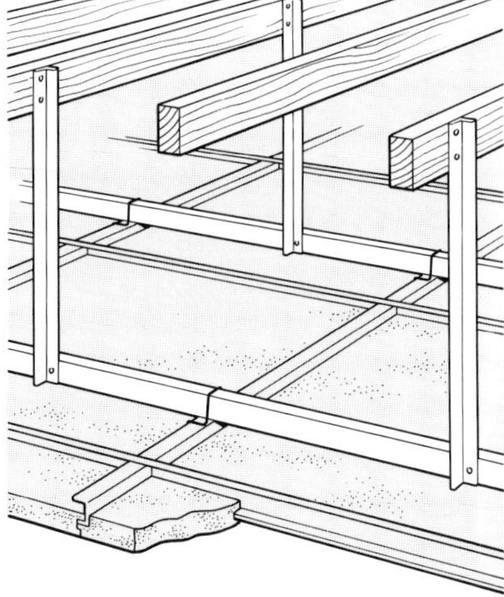

Concealed grid with fibre panels.

# Kitchen lighting

To provide good, overall general lighting ceiling-mounted fluorescent fittings are ideal as they give a 'line of light' spread over a large area. Two – or more – tubes can be mounted side by side in a fitting. There are circular tubes for circular fittings, but the straight batten version is normally best for the kitchen as the usual recommendation is to fit the light so that it is above the sink unit – slightly over the front edge and parallel to it. Another suggestion is to fit the tube diagonally on the ceiling with one end above the sink.

Allow between 8 to 10 W of fluorescent lighting per square metre of well-lit surface. Most kitchens need only one tube – the 65W (1500mm); small kitchens may manage with a 40W (1200mm) tube but would usually need some supplementary light. New fittings are likely to be supplied with 'energy saving' fittings of 58W and 36W.

A fluorescent tube should be fitted with a diffuser to prevent glare.

## Illuminated ceilings

Another way to disguise fluorescent lights is to put them behind a suspended ceiling supporting translucent or louvre panels of plastic – but see the note on Fire Risks.

Installing fluorescent lights to illuminate a suspended ceiling means you need to supply more light to achieve the same light levels on the surfaces below. Most ceiling suppliers recommend a minimum of 60W a panel – since most panels are 600mm square – this is about 15W a metre – roughly half as much again as you need for direct fluorescent lighting on the ceiling.

Ordinary batten fittings can be used above a translucent ceiling provided there's sufficient depth, but compact fittings, which have the controls housed in a unit separate from the tube are useful if there is little room above the ceiling and in other tight spaces – such as behind cornices.

## Recessed lighting

In a kitchen downlighters are often inlet into timber cladding. They can also be fitted in plasterboard or used in conjunction with lightweight suspended ceiling grids fitted with mineral-fibre or wood-fibre panels. A critical factor is the gap behind the ceiling which is determined by the joist depth, usually 225mm. With a suspended ceiling choose the downlighter first. Most downlighters are about 175mm deep. The depth figure is usually given in lighting catalogues, or on the downlighter packaging. As the lights can get hot it's sensible to make sure they are not touching or close to any combustible material in the void.

Downlighters are usually round, but there are also square ones. They can be fully-recessed or semi-recessed. There are fixed and swivel (eyeball) versions. Most lamps are 60W or 100W and they take GLS or reflector lamps.

Downlighters can be used for specific lighting, above a worktop (in which case allow about 25W per square metre of surface). The beam is emitted as a cone of light widening downwards – typically to about 1·8m at floor level; around 1m at worktop height – so for even light levels arrange lamps at spaces to take account of this. They can also be used where fluorescent lights might be too harsh, as general lighting above an eating area for instance.

### LIGHTING WORK SURFACES

Preparing food at a work surface often involves having your back to the main light source and therefore creating a shadow. Lights above the worktop are one answer and where there are wall cupboards, miniature fluorescent tubes can be mounted beneath them. The tubes can be concealed behind a wood baffle fitted to the edge of the cupboard. Smaller versions of the ceiling batten and compact types of fitting are available. Compact fittings can be set with the tubes fitted beneath the cupboard with spring clips and the controls concealed elsewhere – inside the cupboard for instance.

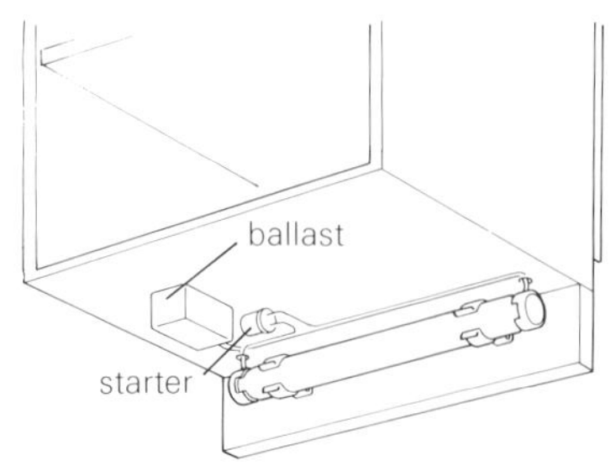


Some cupboards have a bar to disguise the lights; on others it has to be fitted.

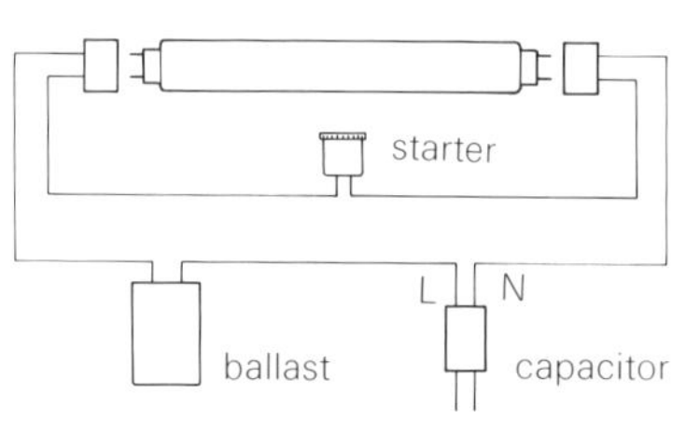


A fluorescent light's circuit.

## Installing the lights

Organise the wiring as for any other lighting – see page 50 for theory; page 152 for practice. Remember that all connections should be made in an enclosed box. Some downlighters do not have proper provision for this.

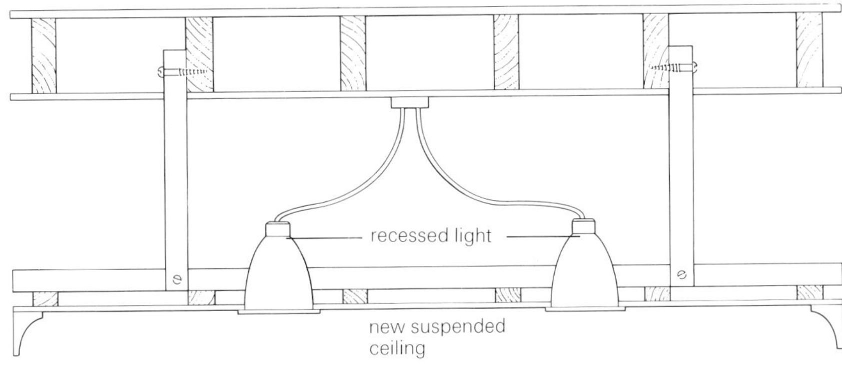


A series of downlighters installed in a suspended ceiling can be wired from the same lighting point. The lights can get hot and must not touch anything combustible.

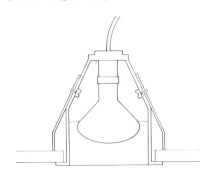

### A downlighter

Although most fittings can be fitted from below without removing any floorboards above, for an existing ceiling access from above is best. From there you can see where the joists are and it is easier to cut the hole. Plan and measure before cutting. Cut the hole carefully, even though the rough edge will be hidden by the trim on the fitting. Some light fittings clip to the trim, others are a complete unit. Cable can be run between the joists and it is easiest if the fittings can be placed in a line parallel with the joists.

When a downlighter is fitted into cladding it will usually straddle two planks of wood and it's best if the light is centred on these planks. Fit the appropriate planks tightly together on the ground and mark the hole. The planks can be separated for cutting.

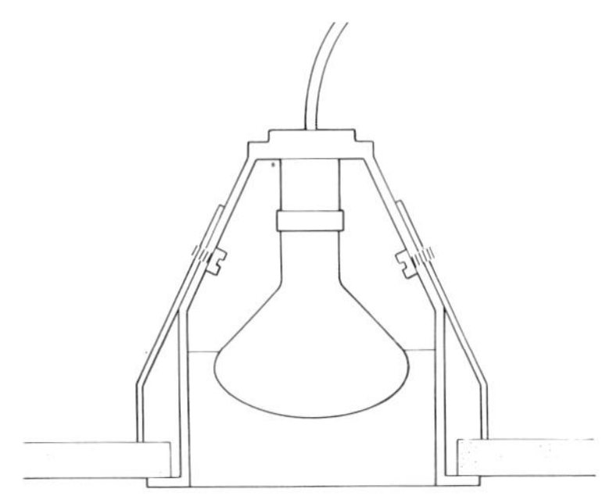

A flush downlighter which needs a space of about 185mm height.

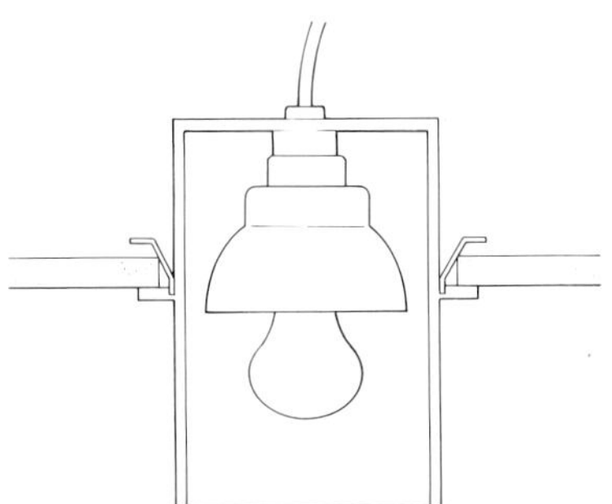

A semi-recessed downlighter which can be fitted into a ceiling with a shallower void behind.

### A fluorescent light fitting

Remove the tube and dismantle the fitting. Take the cover off the metal batten and you see the mounting holes and the terminal block, to which the lighting cable through the ceiling (or cupboard) has to be connected.

Hold the fitting to the ceiling and check where the cable will enter the fitting. Mark the position of the mounting holes. Feed the cable through its hole (using a grommet if one isn't already fitted), then attach the fitting to the ceiling with the mounting screws.

Connect up the cable to the live, earth and neutral connections on the terminal block. Replace the metal cover and fit the tube. Switch on at the mains and test.

If nothing happens, check the starter is in place and try reversing the tube, before checking the wiring.

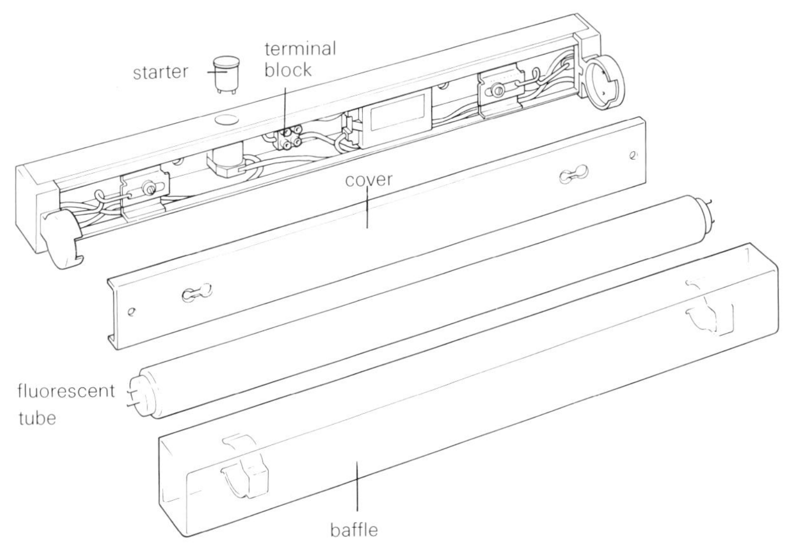


Fluorescent straight batten fitting exploded to show parts.

# Cladding a ceiling

Store the timber – both cladding and frame battens – in the room in which it will be used for up to three weeks to allow the wood to adjust to the atmosphere (and avoid pulling apart later on). Stack it carefully with piling sticks between bundles to allow air to circulate. Weight the top of the pile to reduce the chances of bowing. If you intend to varnish the cladding, a first coat can be applied before you start fixing it up.

## Step-by-step

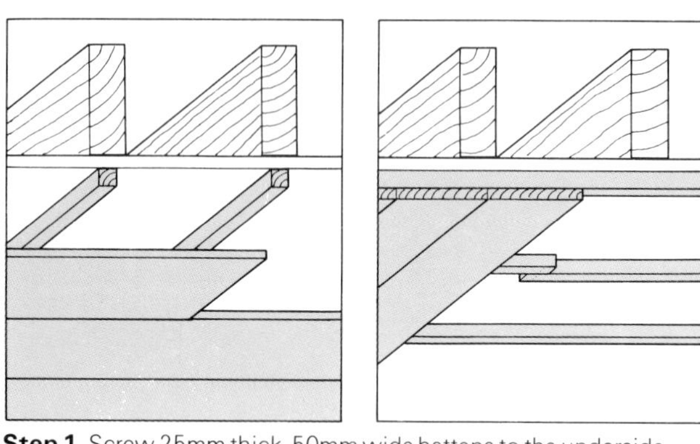

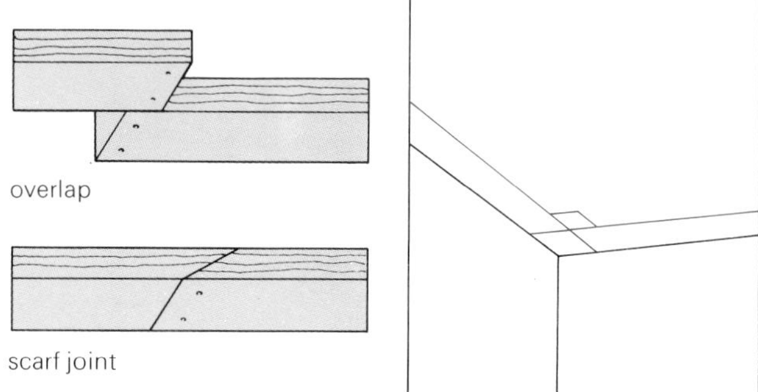


**Step 1** Screw 25mm thick, 50mm wide battens to the underside of the ceiling joists in the opposite direction to that which you intend for the boards. The battens may correspond with the lie of the joists, in which case fix a batten to each joist, or may cross the joists, in which case set the battens at any convenient spacing between 450mm and 600mm.

**Step 2** Where battens need to be joined to make a long length avoid a butt joint – either overlap the battens or use a halving joint or a scarf joint.

**Step 3** Check that the wall from which you'll work is truly at right-angles to the side walls. Use two string lines fixed across the ceiling a set distance – say 150mm from each of the two adjacent walls. Adjust these until the angle at which they cross is exactly 90°.

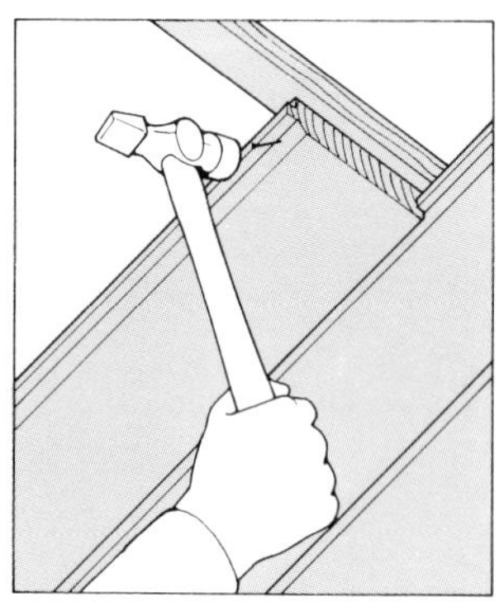

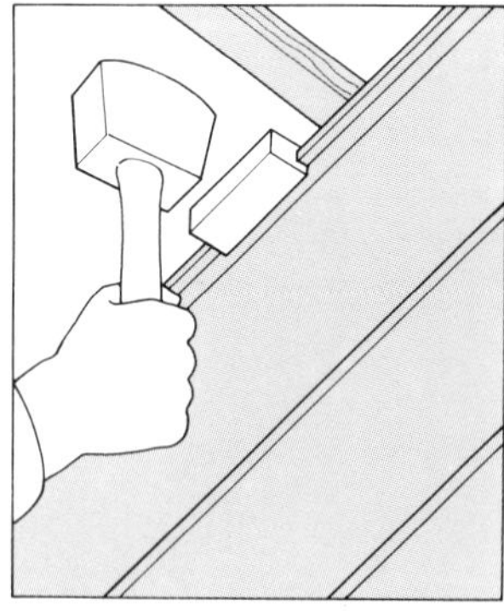

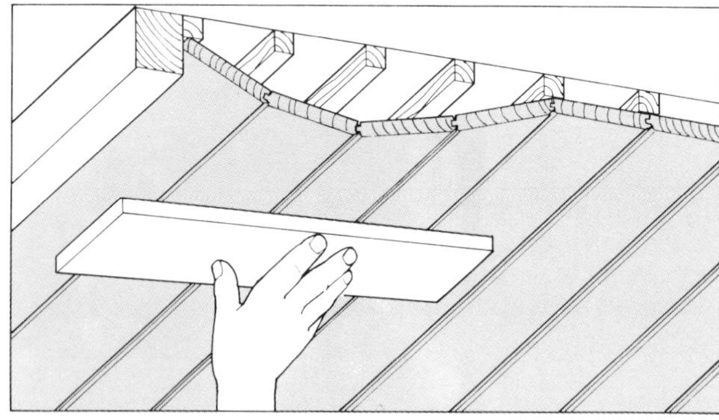

**Step 4** Secure the cladding by skew-nailing through the tongue into each batten. Use 32mm oval brad nails with lost heads and punch below the surface. Fix the boards from alternate ends – one row from the right end and the next from the left.

**Step 5** Push each board firmly home and if possible nail while under compression. You can do this with a mallet and spare piece of wood at each nailing point.

**Step 6** With the last board you have a choice. You can cut the last board slightly undersize and disguise the gap with a piece of wood coving – you'll need to do this anyway if the walls are out of true. You can trim off the tongues and secure the last two boards by nails through the centre of the plank punched home and filled. Or you can fit the last three boards together, spring them into place and nail through the centre of each board.

# A suspended ceiling

Whether the ceiling will be fitted with translucent panels and fluorescent lighting or acoustic or insulating panels, the method of fixing a visible grid is the same and the panels are installed last.

If you're fitting fluorescent lighting it's easier to do the wiring and fix the light fittings before installing the grid. Use a compact fluorescent fitting when the gap between the suspended ceiling and the existing ceiling is less than 150mm which is the minimum required for a batten fitting. Compact lights will need at least 100mm.

For wiring the light – see page 152. Position each tube directly above a grid section and allow at least one 1500mm (60W) tube for 4 square metres (approximately eleven 600mm panels).

## Step-by-step

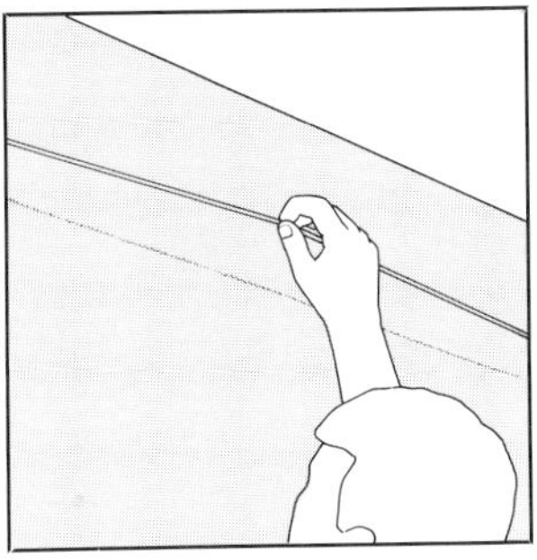

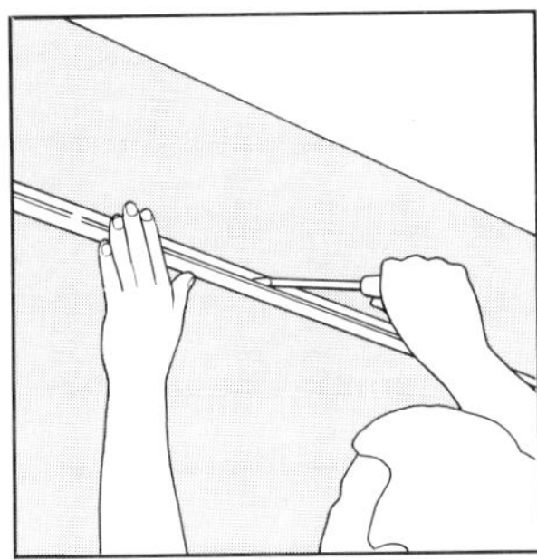

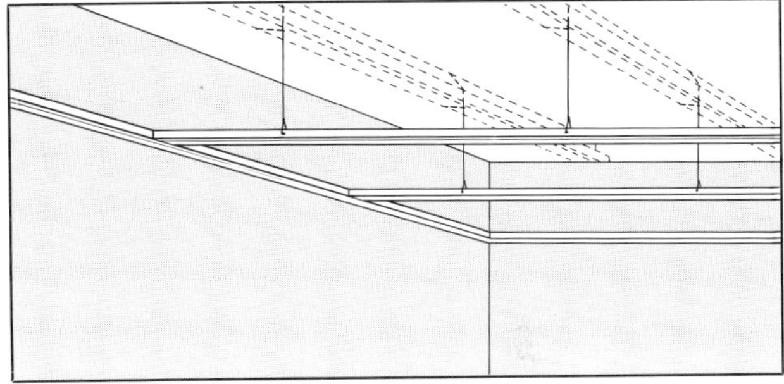

**Step 1** Stretch and snap a horizontal chalked line around the perimeter walls at the height for the new ceiling. Screw the wall angles into place along this line – you'll probably need a twist drill to make holes in the angle at the end of each piece and at about 500mm spacings.

The wall angles will be visible from below so joints between lengths must be neat. Butt joints will suffice, but it's worth mitring at corners. Screw the wall angles tight to the wall, but keep the angle straight and if there are any high spots on the wall ease the screws and leave a small gap which can be filled later.

**Step 2** The main sections of the grid are installed across the room. These may just drop into place or be slotted together and to the wall angle. The sections are spaced a panel's width apart. If suspension wires are necessary for extra support on large spans, fit the main sections at right angles to the ceiling joists.

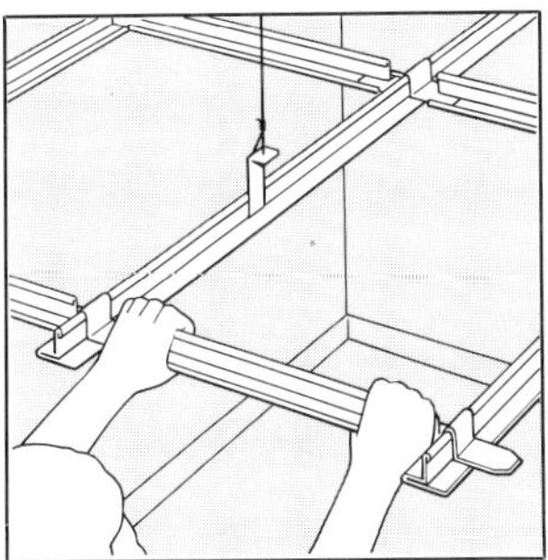

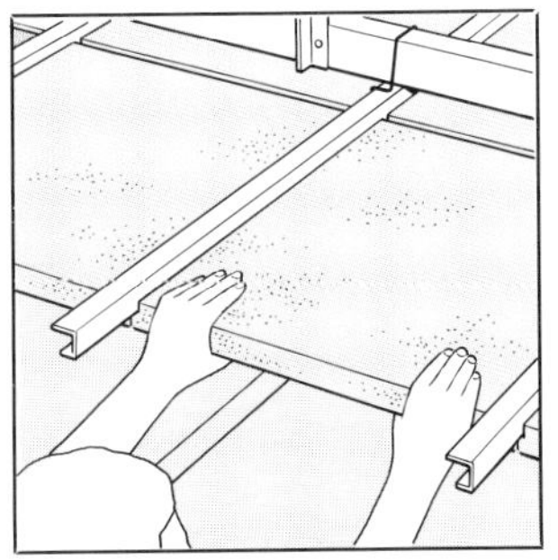

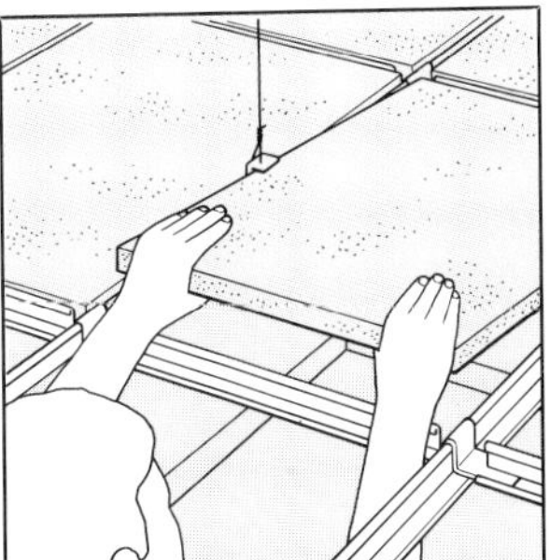

**Step 3** Using a panel as a template, fit the cross sections at the appropriate distance. With visible grids these are short sections which either just lie on the ledge or clip into place. Concealed grids have full width sections which are clipped to the main section with special clips – the sections and panels for a concealed grid are then put up together.

**Step 4** The positioning of all the grid sections should take account of the need to cut panels at the borders. Generally it's best to centre the ceiling so that the amount of cutting required is the same on opposite borders. This means more cutting, but looks a lot better (but be careful if you use moulded panels which cannot be cut to size). Panels for visible grids simply drop into place, panels for concealed grids are installed a row at a time, fixing the next cross section as each row is completed so that the frame is concealed in the grooves of the panels.

# Chapter 4

# BATHROOM IMPROVEMENTS

The way you go about adding or improving a bathroom can be vitally important as far as selling your house goes, it's very easy to make decisions that you find acceptable but other people (potential buyers) won't. For instance if the existing bathroom is cramped with room just for a bath, basin and WC you might decide to swop the bath for a shower cabinet and make room for a bidet – this could be very unpopular with many people. Enlarging a bathroom by stealing part of a bedroom is usually acceptable, but if a whole bedroom is lost, the value and saleability of the house is probably decreased – this is especially true if you turn a 3-bedroom house into a 2-bedroom house.

Knocking a bathroom through into an adjoining loo is another way of creating extra bathroom space but this can be inconvenient unless you have, or can install, an extra WC somewhere else in the house. Although a couple can often cope with a combined bathroom and loo, it's not so convenient for a family house.

Many terraced houses built at the turn of the century have had bathrooms added in a single-storey extension (often with access through a kitchen and lobby) or upstairs with access through a bedroom. Neither of these is very satisfactory, but usually they're the cheapest solutions and common enough in this sort of house not to affect the price adversely. Nevertheless it would often be worth the extra money and effort to add a bathroom which makes more imaginative use of space – a room above the stairwell for instance. A bathroom is classed in the Building Regulations as a non-habitable room, so it's possible to build one internally without a window and with mechanical ventilation.

When a bathroom is installed in a house for the first time a grant should be available from the local authority.

Adding a second bathroom is often a good investment. En-suite bathrooms are particularly popular (again provided that you don't steal a whole bedroom). And bathrooms that help to make part of a large house effectively self-contained are usually successful improvements.

Even if all your bathroom needs is refurbishing with modern equipment, there are still pitfalls for the unwary because strong or currently fashionable colours may suit you but could alienate some potential buyers – white or subtle pastels would be safer.

## Initial planning

During the early stages you'll need to decide which pieces of equipment you must fit in your bathroom and which you'd like but will do without if necessary. This doesn't just mean sanitary-ware; with careful planning a washing machine and tumble drier could be installed in a bathroom or you could have built-in seating or a chair – see *Prompt list*. Decide whether the existing space is satisfactory or too large, too small or just inconvenient for some reason. To help with this decision the Table gives minimum floor areas for various combinations of equipment.

**Area required for:**

| | area in sq m |
|---|---|
| bath and basin | 3 |
| bath, basin and WC | 4 |
| bath, basin, WC and bidet | $4\frac{1}{2}$ |
| shower, bidet and basin | $4\frac{1}{2}$ |
| corner bath, basin and WC | $4\frac{1}{2}$ |
| shower, basin, WC and bath | $5\frac{1}{2}$ |
| shower, basin, WC, bath and bidet | 7 |
| bath, twin basins and seating | 6 |

The areas in the Table allow for a door that opens into the room, if some other arrangement is made space can be saved.

A small bathroom is perhaps the most difficult to plan effectively. Usually the shape of the room and the position of the door fixes the position of the equipment. One solution is obviously to move the door. Plan the room initially without reference to the door and see how that affects things. A small bathroom usually won't have much spare floor space. Little is gained by retaining this and the room may even look better if the floor is encroached upon further, by installing storage units for instance. Modular furniture – see page 103 – can be very effective in a small space. Mirrors, necessary in a bathroom anyway, can help to give the illusion of extra space.

**Prompt list of equipment**

| | |
|---|---|
| Shower | Bath |
| Basin | WC |
| Linen Basket | Bidet |
| Seating | Cabinet |
| Towel Rail (possibly heated) | Radiator |
| Shelving | Cupboard |
| Washing machine | Drier |
| Grab rails beside bath | |
| Full length mirror | |

## The bathroom situation

It's cheaper, neater and easier if all the plumbing in a house is kept together and so most houses are arranged with the bathroom over the kitchen and any other plumbing on the same side of the house. Installing baths, basins or showers away from the main 'water' area of a house is fairly simple but expensive. The biggest problem is often disguising the long pipe runs though these may usually be taken through the loft or ceiling space.

Moving a WC is much more difficult. One way to get round the inherent problems is to fit a shredding device to break down the waste so that it can flow through an ordinary 38mm waste pipe – see WCs, page 101. Otherwise you may need a new soil pipe. The cost of this and its link to the drains would be very expensive.

## Stepped floors

On page 154 we describe how to go about building raised or platform floors. If a bathroom's large enough, this can be a very effective way of dividing up the room into small zones – something that may be worth doing for practical reasons, to hide the WC from someone taking a bath perhaps.

Building a platform around a bath can simulate a sunken structure: the platform can be used for seating; the space beneath for storage; the walls as supports for a basin, WC or bidet and as ducts to hide the plumbing. If steps are provided they can make it easier for children and elderly or disabled people to climb in and out of a bath. But remember that a sunken bath can be awkward for bathing small children.

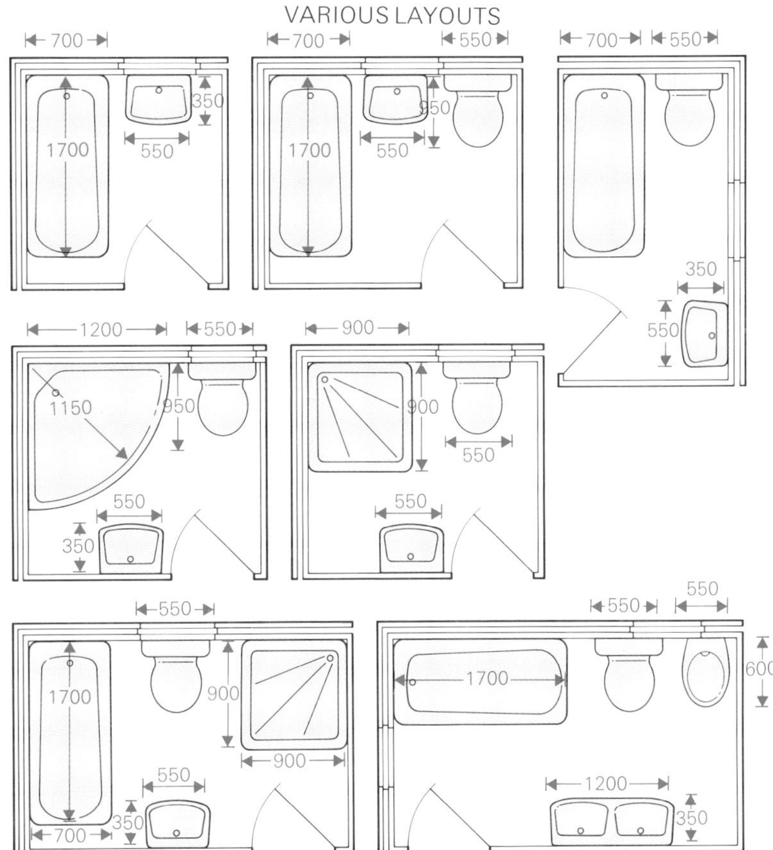

Fitting the equipment in bathrooms of various sizes.

A platform floor around a bath creates the illusion of a sunken bath; the wall of the raised area can be used for a basin or WC.

## DETAILED PLANNING

When you get round to the detailed planning, you'll need to start thinking about the individual space required around each piece of equipment. It's called the activity space. The drawings show recommended minimum dimensions. These are rather generous and you might well get away with less. If necessary, the activity spaces for pieces of equipment that aren't going to be used at the same time can overlap – a WC and a bidet perhaps.

There are sometimes good reasons for putting pieces of equipment next to each other. A WC can double as a seat or a small table if it's placed next to the bath; a WC and a bidet obviously pair up. If a basin is positioned next to the bath, a bath mixer shower spray on a flexible pipe can be used with both. When thinking about where to place a WC, consider also where the toilet paper holder will go – when a WC is midway between a basin and a bath, there's often no suitable place – except the floor. Similarly with a basin think about where the mirror will go, if a basin is installed under a window, as is common, it may mean hanging the mirror on an adjacent wall and craning your neck to shave (or whatever).

Planning a bathroom also means thinking hard about the plumbing. If you're refitting an existing bathroom the cheapest plumbing arrangement will usually be to put new equipment where the old equipment used to be, but if you decide to change things, remember that good plumbing design means keeping the pipe runs as short as possible with few bends. The usual way to achieve this is to have everything on an outside wall, but another solution worth considering is a peninsular dummy wall between say a bath and a basin so that the taps are effectively back-to-back and the branch supply pipes can be kept to a minimum. In some circumstances it may be easier to get a cold supply direct from the rising main, but check that the water authority don't object. A peninsular wall will also hide the pipes. Most modern bathrooms have concealed pipework which looks much neater. Concealing pipes can mean channelling the wall to bury the pipes in the plaster, but more often they are simply boxed in behind some sort of panel.

### Plans

Scale drawings are useful to help with the details. Draw the equipment to scale and cut it out with an extra tab scaled to the size of the necessary activity space.

### Help with design

Some bathroom equipment manufacturers will design your bathroom if you buy their equipment. Interior designers and architects deal with bathroom design. A plumber should be willing and able to help with the practical design as well as the installation. Manufacturers' catalogues may give you inspiration.

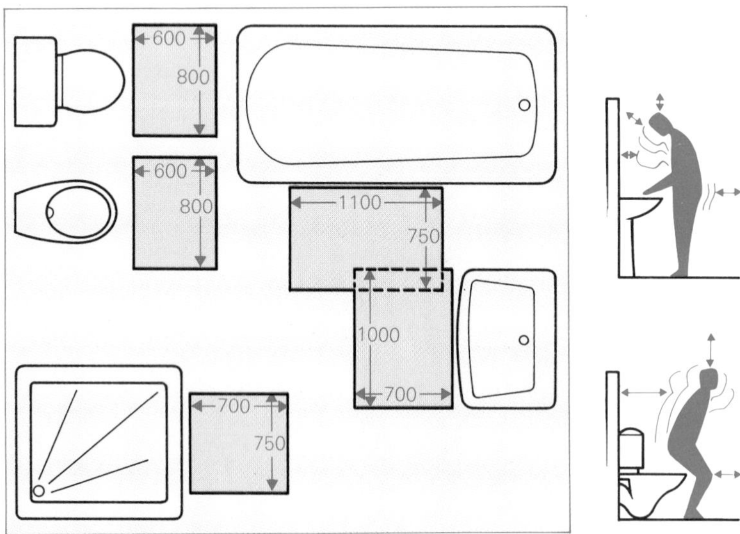


Activity space is necessary for easy and convenient use of each piece of equipment.

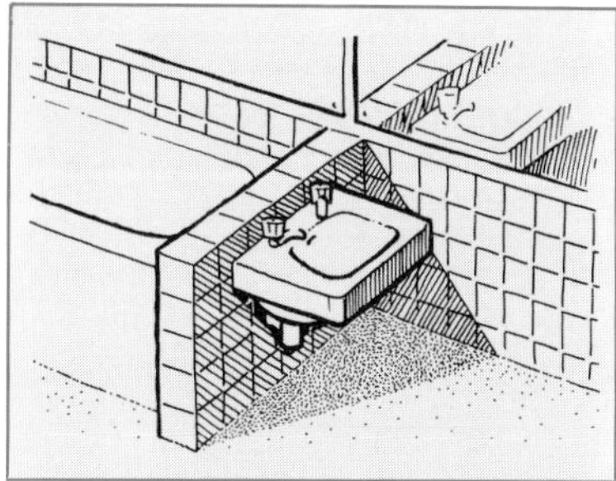

Plumbing back to back on a common wall.

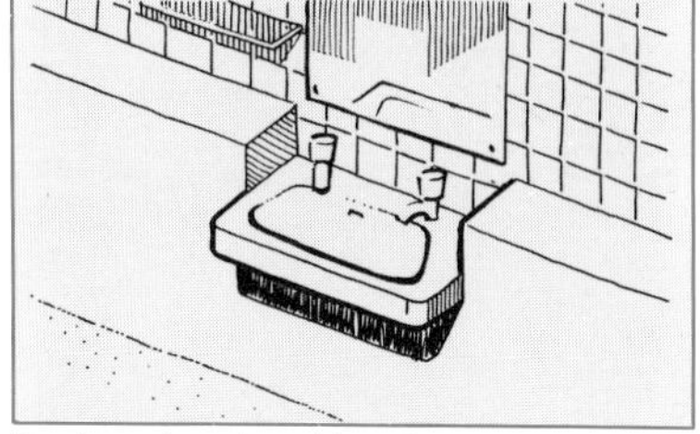

Boxing pipes in with a duct.

# Choosing bathroom equipment

The main pieces of equipment to fit in any bathroom are bath, basin, bidet, WC and shower.

## Buying

Some manufacturers have a range of prices depending on colour. White is always at the bottom of the range and pastel shades, or group 1 colours, may cost the same as or around 15 per cent more than white. Deep shades cost a little more.

You can buy components separately or as a suite. Many shops will give you a discount of between 10 per cent and 20 per cent if you buy a suite – at least bath, basin and WC. Some offer low-price suites including taps. These suites fall into two definite types. One typically consists of a mixture of brands, a plain bath (often pressed steel or acrylic), a pedestal basin and a low-level WC, often with plastic cistern, plus acrylic-headed taps.

The other is usually a combination of 8mm acrylic bath, pedestal basin and close-coupled WC all in a group 1 colour plus taps with chromium-plated heads.

For all equipment there are large variations in price and it's worth shopping around to see if you can find cheaper prices.

Bathroom equipment is sold mostly in builders' merchants and special bathroom centres (which may be kitchen-and-bathroom centres combined), although some d-i-y superstores also carry stock.

Most places that sell bathroom equipment have showrooms where they usually set out mock-ups of bathrooms or show individual pieces of equipment in working positions. As well as showing what the equipment will look like, these displays indicate how much room the equipment takes up and also show things like the amount of space there's going to be around the taps for cleaning.

## Baths

Baths are mostly made of acrylic, enamelled cast iron or enamelled pressed steel. Cast iron is usually the most expensive, although it gives a solid rigid bath, it is heavy and has poor resistance to chipping. Enamelled pressed steel is cheaper and lighter but more flexible. It also has poor resistance to chipping. Acrylic baths are usually 3mm, 5mm or 8mm thick – thin acrylic is often reinforced for strength. Acrylic is light and comes in many shapes and styles. The bath does flex beneath weight, but this isn't usually a problem. Acrylic cannot be cleaned with normal bathroom cleaners, but washing-up liquid can be used. Acrylic won't chip or crack, and although it can be scratched, scratches polish out. It costs much the same as steel.

The commonest shape for a bath is rectangular, usually 1700mm long by 700mm wide and about 500mm high. Shorter and longer baths are also available and many models are wider – around 800mm. You can still get baths made in Imperial sizes if you need to fit one into a space exactly 5ft 6in long.

You can get lots of additional features on a rectangular bath and nowadays even the cheapest baths may have handle grips, a slip resistant base and reclining backs.

Tap holes are usually at one end above the plug but they can also be at a corner, half-way down one side or even plumbed into the wall leaving the bath rim clear. For this you'll need a bath without tap holes, most manufacturers will supply one to order, but they're not common in shops. Taps should be easy to reach, but it's better not to site them on or near the part of the rim you climb over to get in and out of the bath. If you don't want your taps in the traditional place, close to a corner on the near side is one of the best solutions – it keeps the plumbing to one end and the taps out of the way. Above the bath on a long wall is also worth considering.

More expensive baths are available in unusual designs. The commonest of these is the *corner bath*, designed to fit into the corner of a room. The bathing area in corner baths is often oval, set across the corner with the spare space in the corner used as a shelf or recessed to make a bathing seat. You can also get: corner baths with bathing areas that go into the corner, *round* baths with round, heart or clover-leaf shaped bathing areas, *square* baths with a large round normal-depth bathing tub or a small deep tub for bathing in a sitting position, *rectangular* with oval, double or offset rectangular bathing areas.

Many luxury baths have seats built into the design as well as the additional features available with rec-

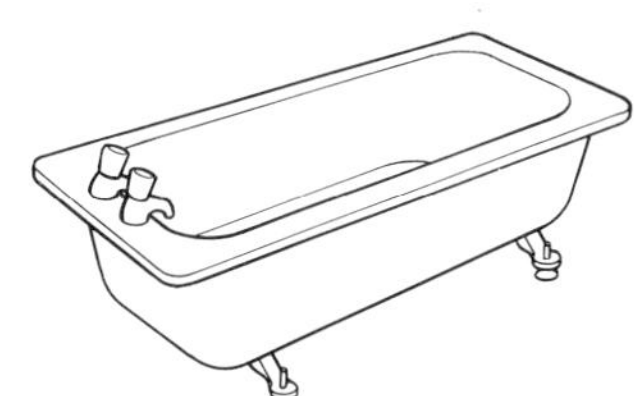

Conventional bath.

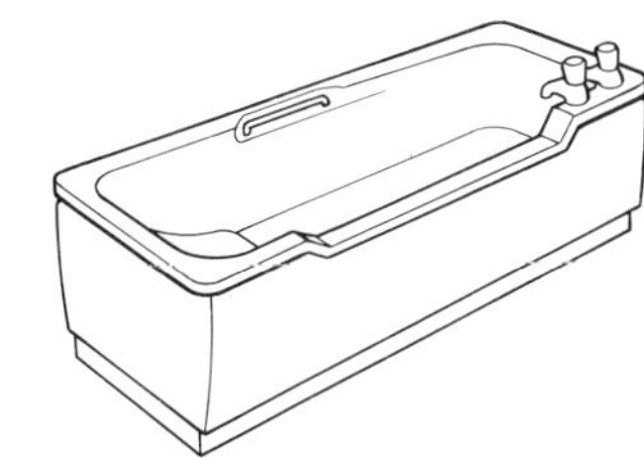

Dropped front bath.

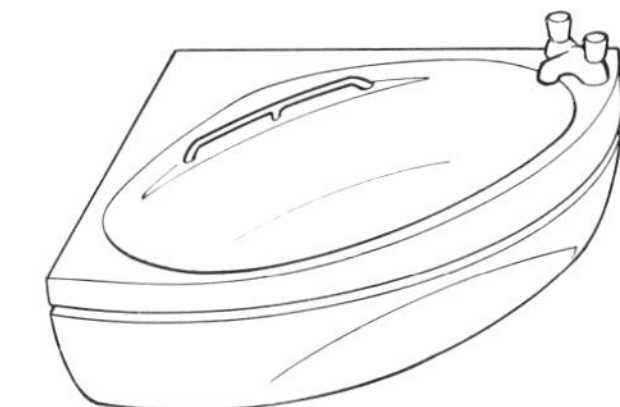

Corner bath.

Baths come in all shapes and sizes.

tangular baths. Shaped baths are usually acrylic or GRP because they're easy to mould and also light. Shaped baths are usually quite big: they take a lot of water, so are more expensive to fill and heavy once full. Getting a big bath into the bathroom could be difficult, so measure doors and tight corners carefully – people have been known to get stuck. Also remember that some baths are 'handed' – you don't get a choice about which end the taps and waste are. This may be important for a corner bath.

**Bath panels**
Most manufacturers make side and end panels (usually in polystyrene) to go round their baths. With shaped baths, the panels may be part of the price package, but panels for rectangular baths often cost extra. Rectangular panels are usually 'universal' and can be adjusted in height or cut to fit a particular bath. The panel should be easy to remove. For d-i-y panels see page 113.

## Basins

Basins are made of vitreous china, enamelled cast iron, enamelled pressed steel, acrylic, GRP or other plastics. There are pedestal basins, wall-hung basins and 'vanity' basins for setting into a dressing-table type surface.

**Pedestal** basins are at a fixed height, usually with the rim at a height of 800mm. This is too high for small children and too low for many adults. It may be better to position a basin higher and provide a steady box for children to stand on. The pedestal can hide pipes if the basin is always looked at from the front, but if it's seen from the side, pipes may still show unless you use a fillet between the pedestal and the wall to hide them. A pedestal isn't designed to support the whole weight of the basin – it still has support brackets. A pedestal can make cleaning the floor difficult.

**Wall-hung** basins overcome the problem of floor cleaning, but you need a strong wall to support them and unless boxed their pipes will be on show. Some small wall-hung basins can be recessed into the wall (useful in a cloakroom). Others fit into a corner.

**Vanity basins** may be set into the top of a storage unit or the top of any piece of furniture like an old washstand – they can be let into a hole cut into the top or be apron-fronted and let into a recess in the front part.

The basin can be flush with the surface or have its rim a little higher. You can also get basins moulded all-in-one with the top. The height of a vanity basin is limited by the unit on which it sits: if you make this yourself, you can choose the height, but with ready made (or self-assembly) units, the basin is usually 800mm high. If you're having a hole cut for a vanity basin, make sure that the dimensions are taken off the basin itself, as ceramic basins especially can vary a few millimetres in size and these millimetres can be crucial.

Basins have additional features, like anti-splash rims and a choice of tap positions. You'll want to choose a basin that you like the look of, but try to choose one that'll be easy to clean (no awkward bits behind taps) and is spacious enough to allow for all the activities you want – washing your hair for instance.

BASINS

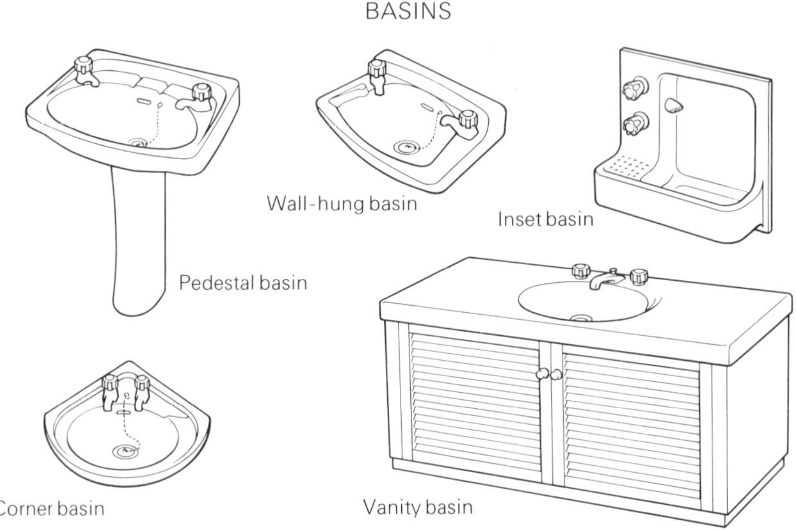


BIDETS

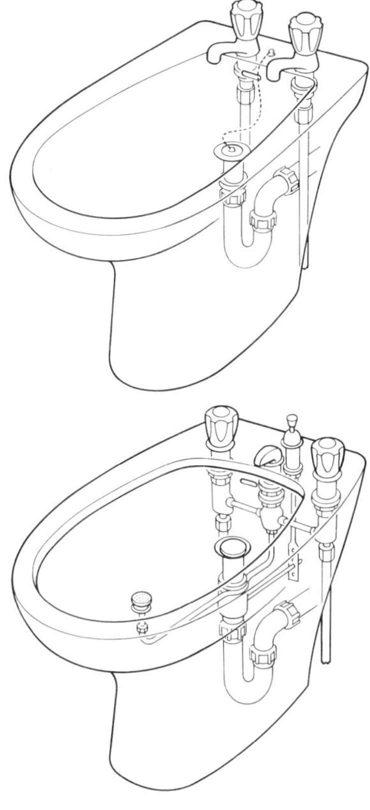

Top: over-rim bidet.
Bottom: through-rim bidet.

## Bidets

Besides its main purpose for washing the genitals, a bidet, which is usually 400mm high, can be used by small children as a basin or play tub and also for bathing babies, washing feet and soaking clothes.

If you want a bidet, you have a choice of one with *over-rim* supply or one with *through-rim* supply, sometimes with a spray too. Both kinds can be floor-standing or wall-hung and they are usually made of vitreous china. The over-rim ones are similar to a basin with taps and a plug; the through-rim type is more complicated and if it's got a spray, requires controls with a pop-up waste. Hot water running through the rim warms it up, making it more comfortable to sit on.

Through-rim bidets are banned by some water authorities. This is because of possible back-siphonage which can occur if water (often dirty water) travels back along the supply pipes and mixes with incoming fresh water. A through-rim supply bidet with a spray may suffer from back-siphonage and, because of this, is usually required to have its own cold water supply pipe which must be taken from a cold-water cistern. The hot water pipe must be the highest pipe taken off the hot water cylinder. These pipes must not have any branch pipes to other pieces of equipment.

This means that an over-rim supply bidet is the simpler to plumb as well as cheaper. If you have a bath mixer tap with an integral hand spray, you could put an over-rim supply bidet near enough to the bath taps to be able to use the spray with both pieces of equipment.

## WCs

These consist of two parts: a vitreous china pan and a cistern, which may be vitreous china or plastic. Nowadays, most cisterns are *low-level*. An ordinary low-level cistern is connected to the pan by a short pipe (called a flush bend), but you can also get *close-coupled* WCs, where the cistern is linked directly to the pan. For converting a high-level cistern to a low-level one without replacing the existing pan, you need a special narrow cistern which will fit in the gap between the pan and the wall.

TWO KINDS OF WC

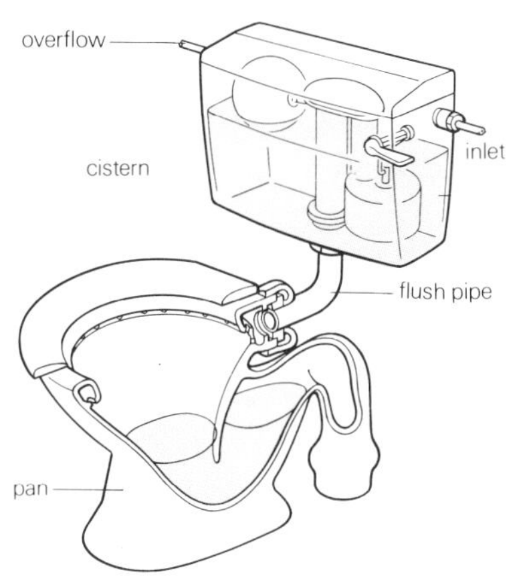

Washdown WC with standard cistern.

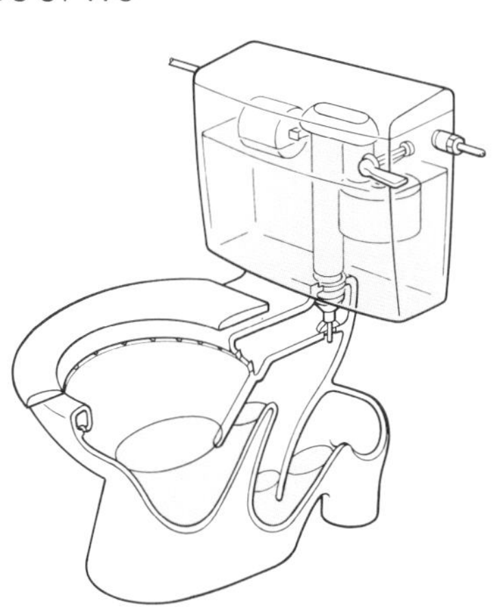

Syphonic WC with close-coupled cistern.

When you buy a WC, you get a choice of flushing system. You can have either a *washdown* closet, like the majority of old WCs (low-level and high-level), or a *syphonic* one. A syphonic flush works by sucking air out of the waste pipe and creating a pressure differential which draws the waste out of the pan. Water from the cistern then replaces the water in the pan. Syphonic WCs may be single-trap or double-trap; double-trap is more efficient and more common, but can get blocked more easily than the single type.

Syphonic WCs are quieter than wash down ones and the pan is less likely to get soiled because it has a larger surface area of water and water covers more of the sides of the pan. But they cost more.

You can get washdown and syphonic WCs which hang on the wall clear of the floor. The brackets, and often the cistern too, are usually concealed behind a false wall.

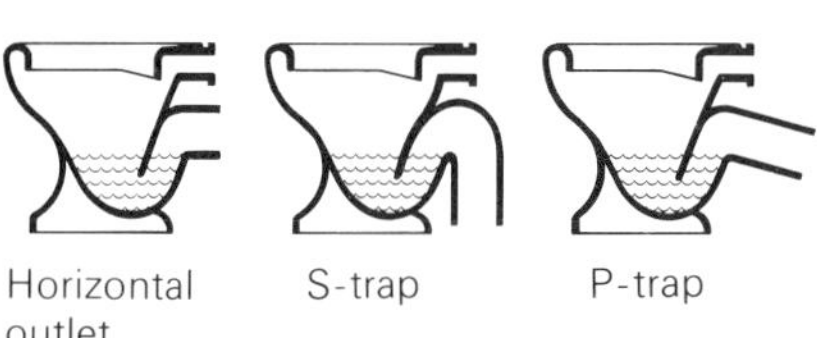

Horizontal outlet S-trap P-trap

Cisterns with a dual flush are becoming more common, these give the choice of a full or a half flush to save water.

When you buy a WC, it's essential to get a pan with the right sort of trap. The trap is the outlet pipe which joins up to the soil pipe taking the waste to the drains. It holds a water seal and stops smells from the drains coming into the house. The trap will be *S-shaped* if the soil pipe in your bathroom disappears vertically into the floor, or *P-shaped* if the soil pipe discharges into a stack. Most WCs have a connector (ceramic or plastic) to make the leg of the S or P which joins to the soil pipe. This makes things easier if you need a trap to go round a corner.

Shredder loos are useful WCs that are installed at some distance from the soil pipe. They have an electric-powered shredding unit which breaks the waste down small enough to pass along a normal-size waste pipe of 38mm diameter.

## Showers

You may be attracted by the convenience and economy of a shower and plan to improve your bathroom by fitting one yourself. There are a number of different shower systems in the shops. Which suits you best depends to a large extent on the layout of the plumbing in your house.

The route map opposite gives details on choosing a shower.

Whatever the type of shower, the valve part can be connected to the outlet (the rose) by a rigid pipe or flexible hose. A rigid pipe may look neater, but a flexible hose allows the rose to be positioned at different heights to suit different members of the family and to be used for hair washing over a basin or bath.

**Push-on rubber hoses** These push on to the existing bath or basin taps. They're cheap and no installation is required. They are widely sold and used, but can cause back-siphonage.

**Bath/shower mixers** These mixers, installed instead of separate bath taps are relatively inexpensive. They can be used only when hot and cold water comes from a storage cistern or with certain instantaneous gas water heaters. A few have temperature control.

**Shower mixers** These are usually mounted over a separate shower tray, but could be used above a bath. Cheaper ones have only flow controls. Expensive versions have *temperature and flow* controls.

**Electric shower heaters** These can be mounted over a bath or a separate shower tray. The water must come from the mains cold water supply, so plumbing may be extensive. Water is heated instantaneously as it passes through the heater – the spray may not be as forceful as with a conventional shower. Special electric wiring is needed as well as plumbing but an electric shower can be used where a conventional type is impractical.

## Shower pumps

A shower pump could be the answer if your water supply hasn't got enough head to produce an invigorating shower. Some shower booster pumps are fitted to both hot and cold water pipes and pump the supplies separately to a bath/shower or shower-only mixer. Others are fitted between the mixer and the shower rose and boost the mixed water.

## Showering areas

Shower trays are normally square or rectangular, but you can also get triangular or circular trays. Trays are usually plastic. Some trays are extra deep and double as a shallow tub. There is a shower tray with raised sides which can be tiled over to overcome the water seepage problem. Once fitted it's difficult to remove so the floor is removable for access to the plumbing below. Shower trays usually have a slip-resistant finish.

A shower cubicle should be large enough for you to move comfortably about in and have enough space for bending over. You should be able to reach the controls without getting wet and be able to step out of the shower stream without stepping out of the cubicle. It's useful to have a seat, too. All this means a cubicle is ideally about 1100mm square. Unfortunately, many manufactured cubicles are smaller than this, typically 900mm by 900mm.

A cheap alternative to a separate shower area is to have the shower fitted at one end of the bath although this may be rather cramped.

Another possibility is to turn part of your bathroom into a shower area where the floor and the walls are tiled and the floor is drained (as in sports centres). You'll need a raised thres-

SHOWERS AND SHOWER ATTACHMENTS

Shower cubicle

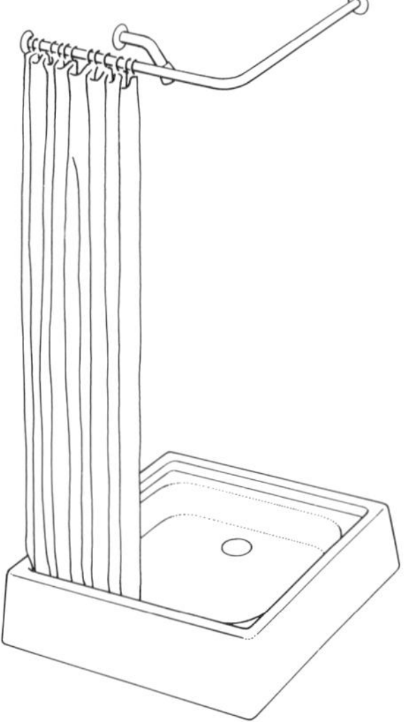

Shower tray

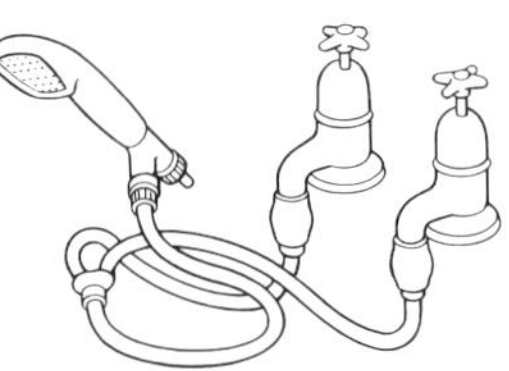

Push-on hose.

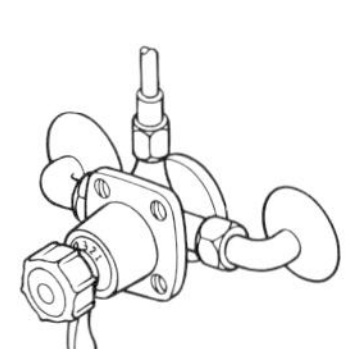

Shower only mixer

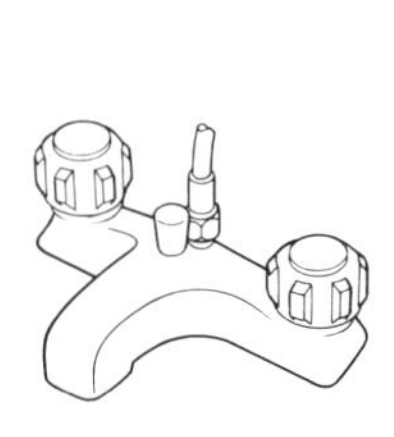

Bath/shower mixer

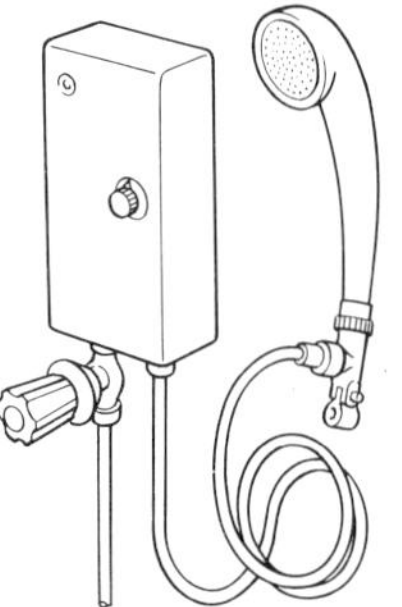

Instantaneous electric shower

hold to keep water off the floor and you must make sure the base is adequately sealed.

## Modular furniture

Co-ordinated ranges of storage units and bathroom equipment are stylish, but expensive. Most are built on a metric module. The units are usually either plastic or melamine-faced chipboard. They are often cantilevered to allow easy cleaning of the floor, ducts for pipes are incorporated to conceal the plumbing.

A FORM OF MODULAR UNIT

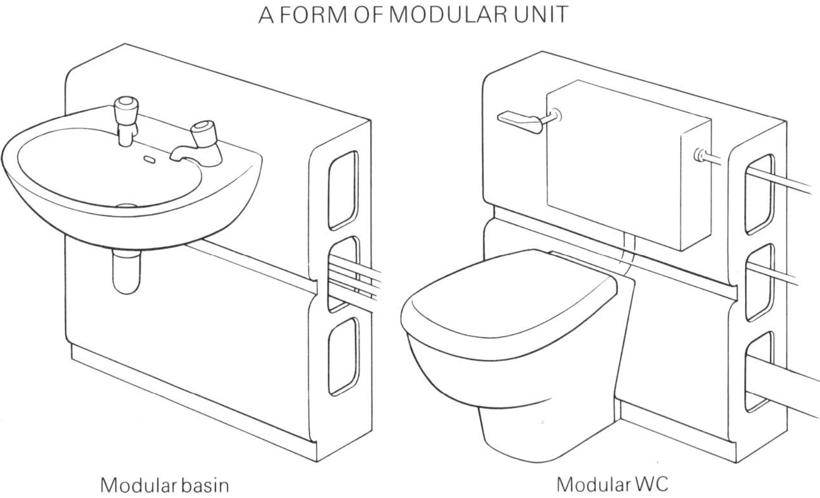

Modular basin

Modular WC

Use the route map to establish which type of shower will suit you.

▼

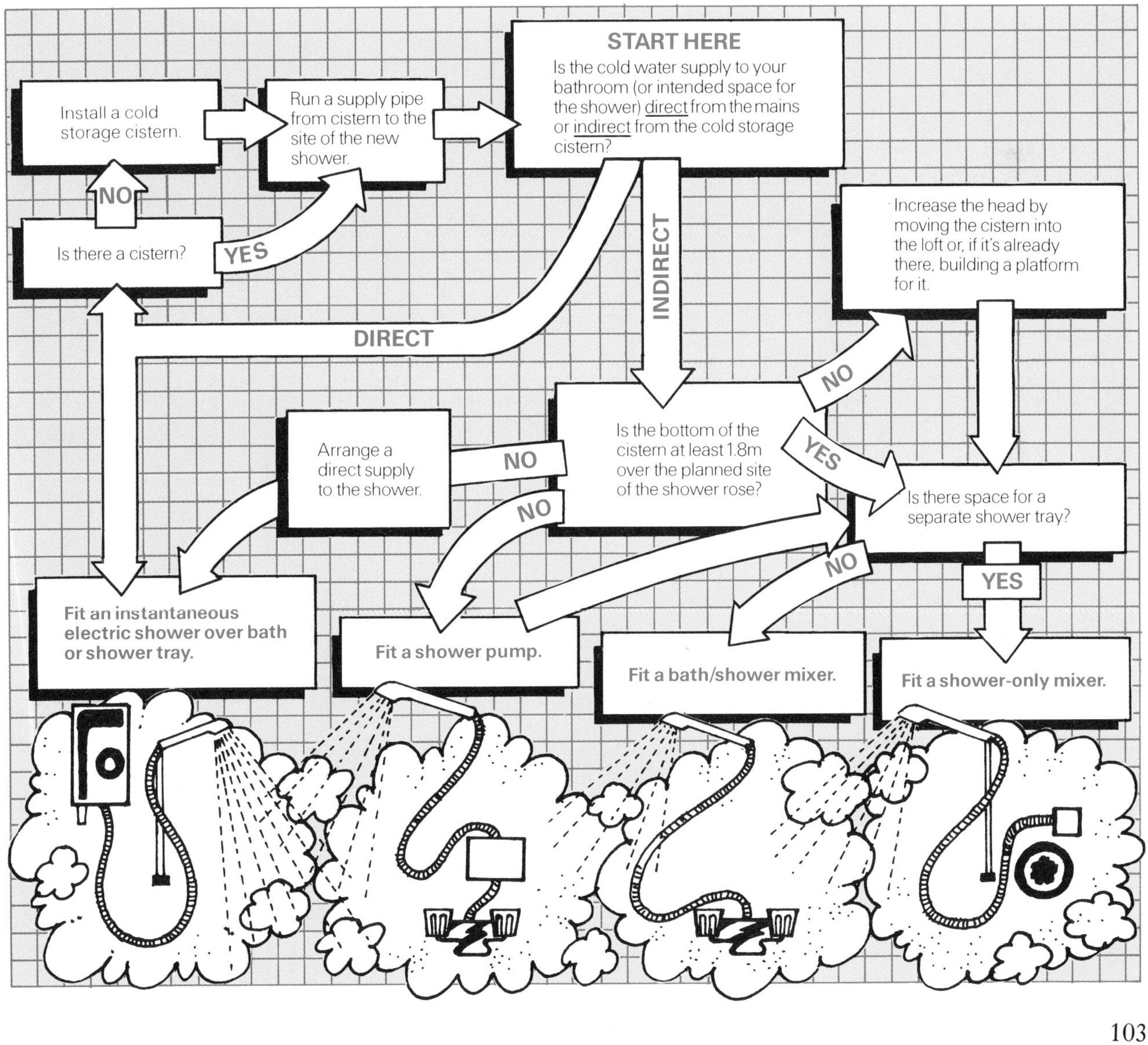

**START HERE**

Is the cold water supply to your bathroom (or intended space for the shower) direct from the mains or indirect from the cold storage cistern?

DIRECT

Is there a cistern?

YES

NO

Install a cold storage cistern.

Run a supply pipe from cistern to the site of the new shower.

INDIRECT

Is the bottom of the cistern at least 1.8m over the planned site of the shower rose?

NO

Arrange a direct supply to the shower.

NO

YES

NO

Increase the head by moving the cistern into the loft or, if it's already there, building a platform for it.

Is there space for a separate shower tray?

NO

YES

**Fit an instantaneous electric shower over bath or shower tray.**

**Fit a shower pump.**

**Fit a bath/shower mixer.**

**Fit a shower-only mixer.**

# Plumbing a hand basin

Before starting any plumbing work, make sure the new basin fits properly and that there is sufficient activity space around the basin.

Check that the wall can take the weight if necessary. Prepare the basin mountings – fix the wall brackets, check the position of any pedestal and drill fixing holes.

## Step-by-step

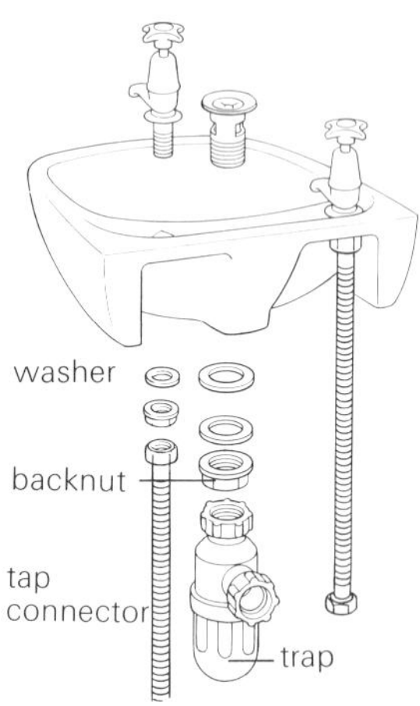


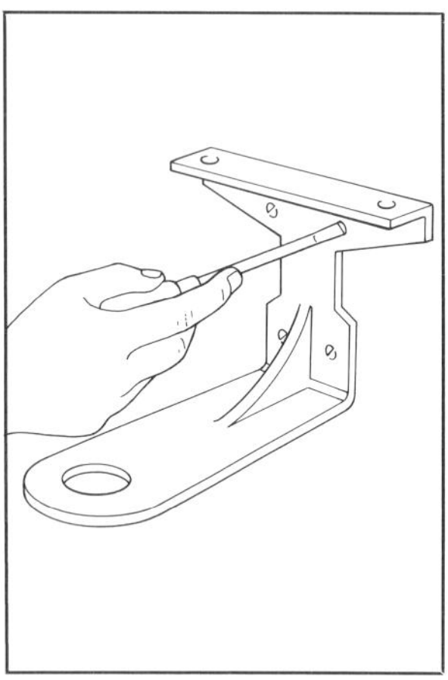

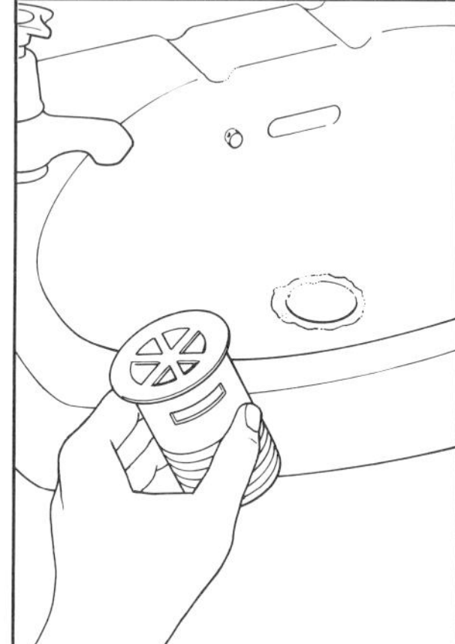

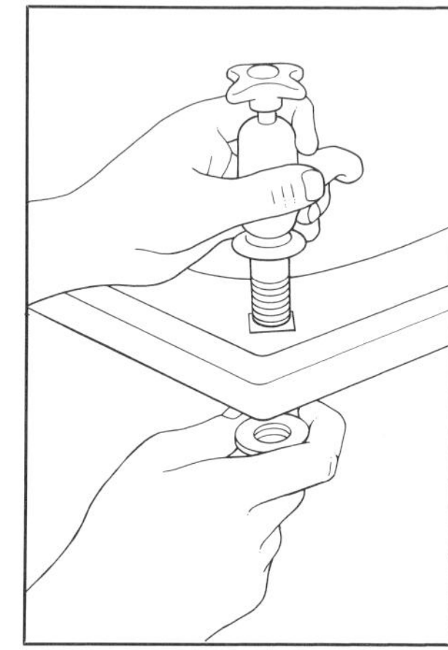

**Step 1** If the basin has an integral overflow, fit a 32mm slotted waste outlet on a bed of sealing compound, with the slot aligned with the lower end of the overflow. (Overflows are becoming less common in modern basins so this may not be necessary.)

**Step 2** Fit the taps to the basin next. If the shape of the basin makes it awkward to screw up the tap back-nuts with an ordinary spanner, a basin spanner which can be turned in a smaller space can be useful.

**Step 3** Next screw tap connectors on to the tap tails. Flexible tap connectors are easiest to work with, but cost more than straight or elbow connectors. Conceal the supply pipes behind the pedestal if there is one.

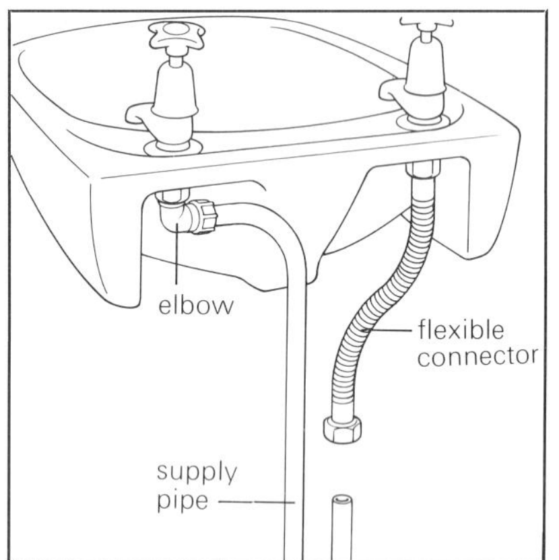


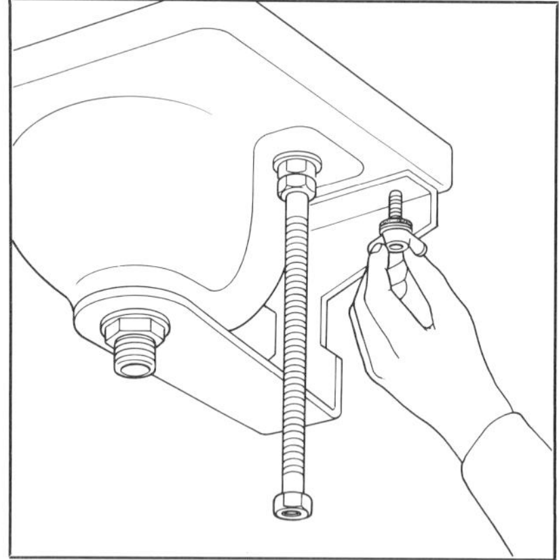

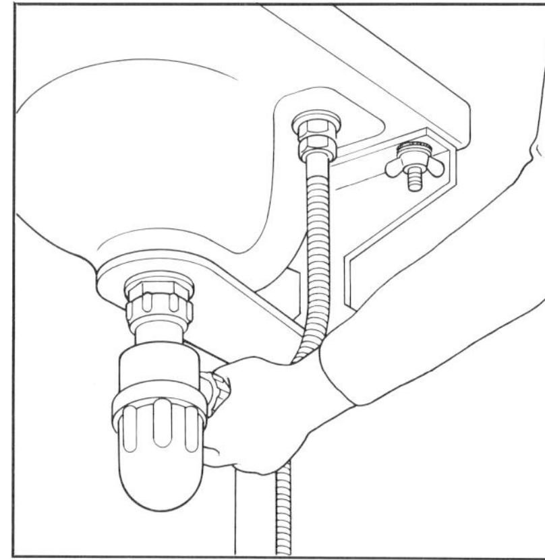

**Step 4** Before mounting a wall-hung basin on its bracket push rubber sleeves over the fixing bolts, followed by washers and a nut. Tighten the nut before locating the bolts in the bracket. Secure the basin with wing nuts on the bolts and a locking nut on the waste outlet. A vanity basin is simply let into its surface surround and sealed with flexible sealant (acrylic sealants are easier to use than silicone ones).

**Step 5** Finally, connect the tap connectors to the supply pipes and check that there is no strain on the pipes or any joints. Clip the pipes to the wall – every 2·4m for vertical copper pipes 15mm diameter; every 1·2m for vertical plastic pipes; 1·8m and 0·5m respectively for horizontal pipes.

**Step 6** Fit a plastic bottle trap to the waste outlet, completing the drainage system with 32mm plastic pipe to the stack pipe or hopper. The basin waste should slope downwards slightly (no more than 40mm drop per metre run) and should not be longer than 1·68m. For a longer run, use 40mm diameter pipe. Check the overflow, if any, is properly installed.

# ...a bath

Plumbing in a new bath usually means removing an old one first. If the bath is made of cast iron, you have no use for it and its second-hand value is low, consider breaking it up on the spot. Disconnect the pipes – sawing is easiest – cover the surface, with sacking say, and protect any nearby ceramic ware. Put on goggles and gloves and smash the bath to pieces with a heavy hammer.

If a gentler approach is required, undo the tap connectors and waste trap nut or, if these refuse to budge, cut through the pipes with a hacksaw. If the old bath has adjustable feet, lower it a little to prevent damaging any tiles as you pull it away.

## Step-by-step

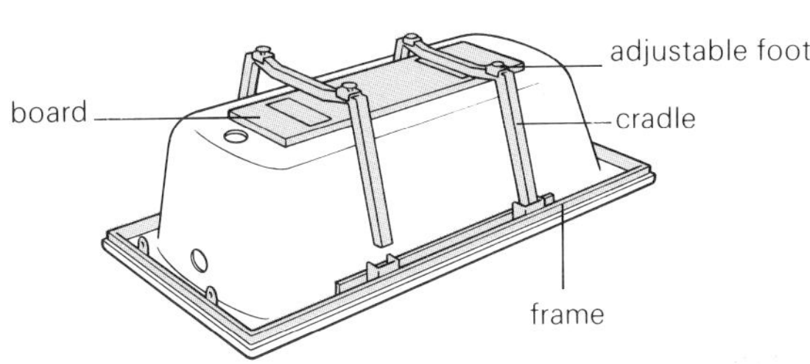


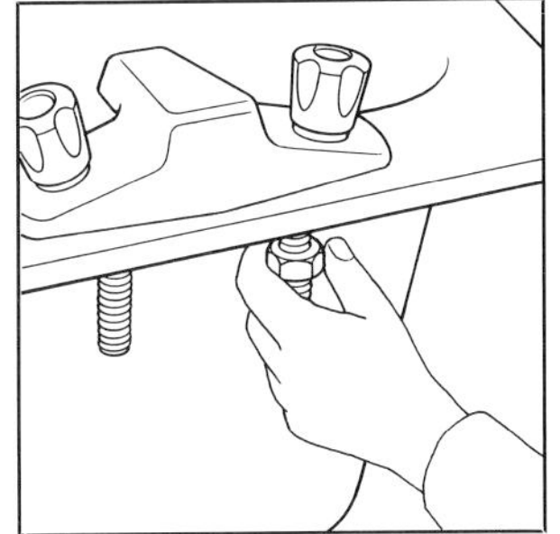

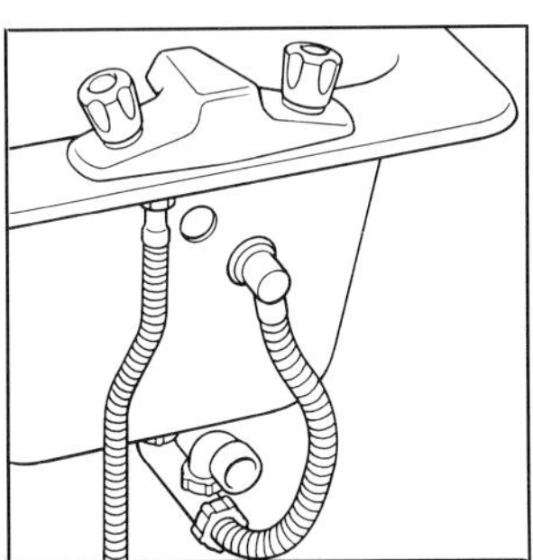

**Step 1** Plastic baths need a proper supporting cradle to ensure that they don't creak or sag in use. Make sure you get the right cradle for the bath. You put the cradle together by attaching legs to the board fixed to the bottom of the bath and also to the frame that runs around the bath rim.

A steel bath usually has two brackets which you fit to the bottom. These have adjustable feet to ensure that the bath can be positioned so that the bottom slopes slightly down towards the waste outlet. Cast iron baths also have adjustable feet. If you're installing a cast iron bath, check the floor can take the weight and get help with lifting.

**Step 2** You may wish to fit separate hot and cold taps. If your cold water comes from the storage cistern rather than direct from the mains you also have the choice of a bath mixer or a bath/shower mixer. Fit the taps, tap connectors and waste trap before moving the bath into position.

For work in inaccessible places, flexible tap connectors are the most convenient to use. They can be bought plain ended or with an integral compression fitting for connection to 22mm copper pipe. (When fitting a plastic bath, avoid the use of capillary joints – the blowlamp flame could damage the bath.) A combined waste trap and overflow system is the most convenient – some have specially shallow tubular traps to fit under the bath.

Fit the trap end before installing the bath, bedding the waste outlet in a ring of mastic before tightening the backnut.

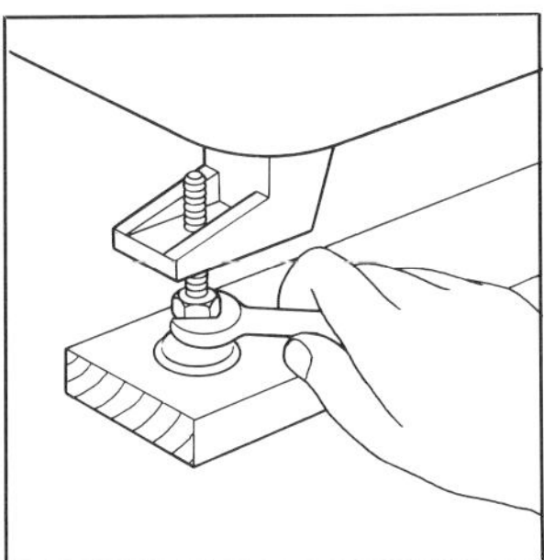

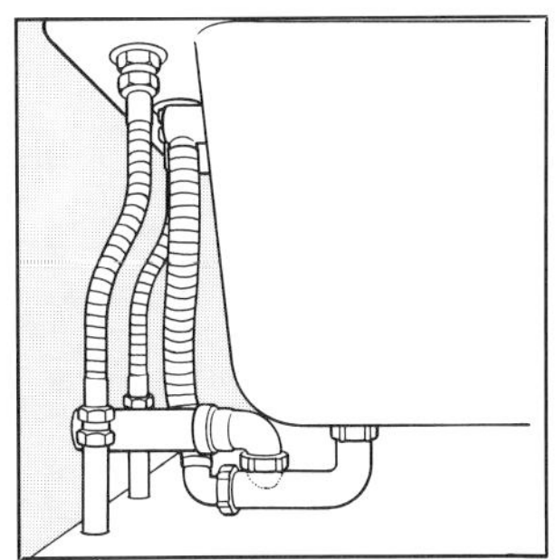

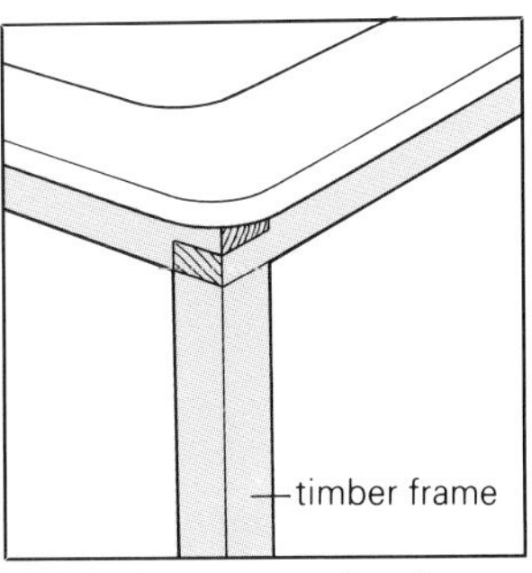


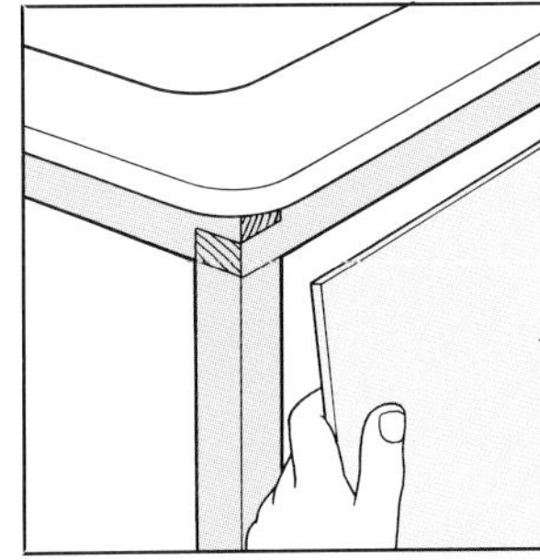

**Step 3** Lift the bath on to battens to spread the load evenly over the floorboards and adjust the feet to make it level – with the rim horizontal the base will slope slightly down towards the waste outlet.

**Step 4** Make the pipe connections underneath the bath in this order: join the tap connector further from you to its supply; fix the overflow outlet to the bath; connect the waste trap, by means of 40mm plastic waste pipe, to the stack pipe or (in an older house with a two-pipe drainage system) to the hopper, and finally join up the tap connector nearer to you.

**Step 5** Before boxing the bath in, run some water and check the bath is level and the plumbing doesn't leak. For details of boxing see page 113.

# ...a WC

Often the most difficult part of fitting a new WC in place of an old existing one is connecting the new pan outlet to the existing soil-pipe opening. Unless the new pan is an exact replica of the old one, the outlet and the opening probably will not coincide. Furthermore if a low-level cistern is being fitted in place of an old high-level one, the pan will have to be sited further out from the wall to allow the seat to stay up once lifted – slimline cisterns are available to get round this. A variety of connectors is available – probably the most useful is the range of *Multikwik* connectors: these can cope with any offset between the WC outlet and the soil pipe.

When plumbing a new WC, organise alternative facilities or do the work when the family are out.

## Step-by-step

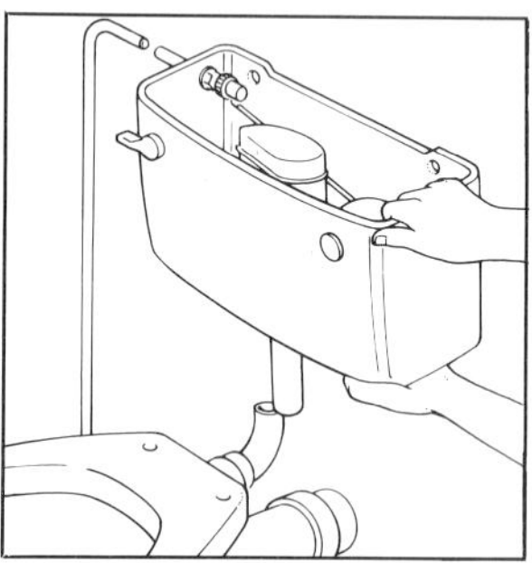

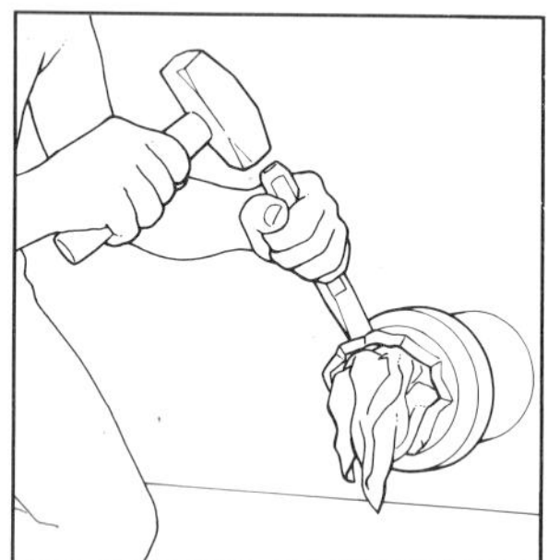

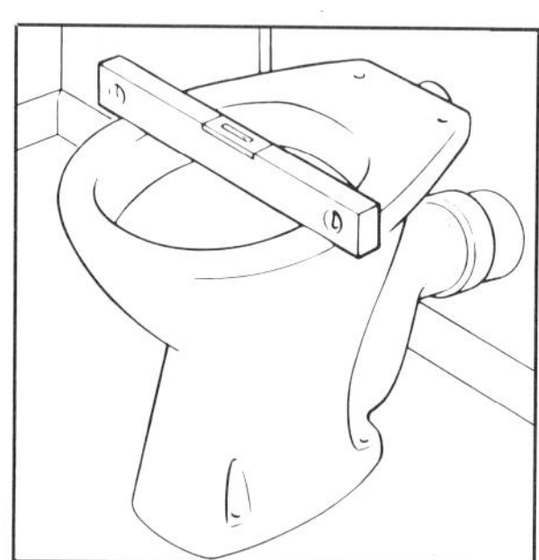

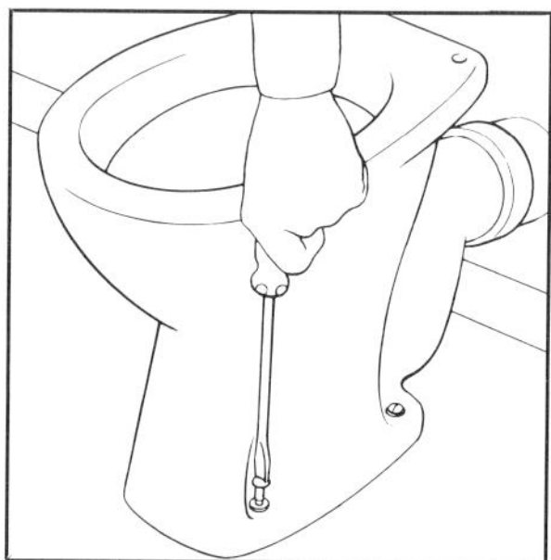

**Step 1** Once the connecting problem has been solved, start removing the old WC. Cut off the water supply, flush the cistern and empty the water in the pan.
**Step 2** Unless the joints undo easily, saw off the supply pipe to the cistern and the flush pipe to the pan. Remove the cistern and its wall brackets – they may also need sawing through. Undo the floor screws for the pan.
**Step 3** If the soil pipe is plastic (or connected with a rubber connector) you should be able to just pull the WC away, otherwise to remove the pan, break the top bend of the WC trap (not the soil pipe) then unscrew or lever the pan from the floor.

If necessary tuck a cloth in the outlet to stop falling debris and rising smells, and *carefully* chip away the rest of the pipe outlet.
**Step 4** Try the new pan in place, and ensure that the connector you have is suitable. (It's worth doing the job while the shops are open.) Check that the pan is level.

Mark screw positions on the floor with a bradawl through the hole in the WC base, then remove and make the holes.
**Step 5** Remove the cloth, align the WC outlet, the connector and the drain socket as you return the pan to its position. Then screw the pan to the floor using non-corroding screws with washers and tighten them gently to avoid cracking the pan.

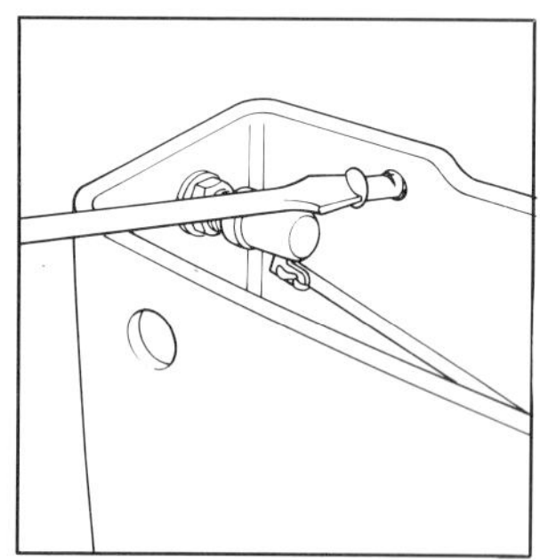

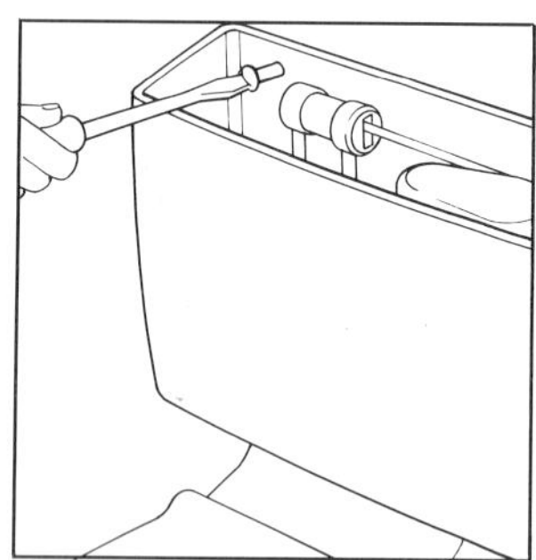

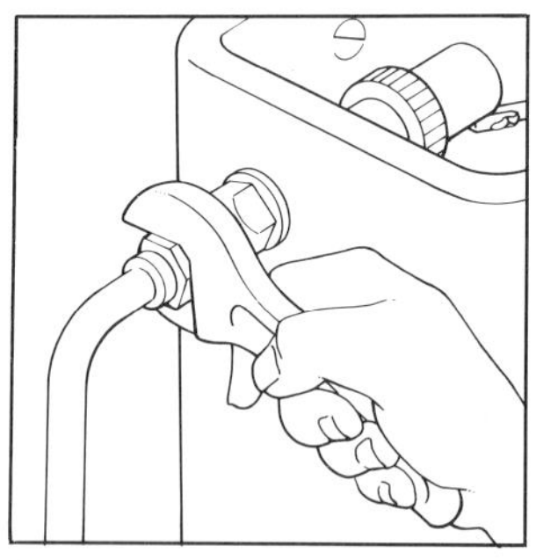

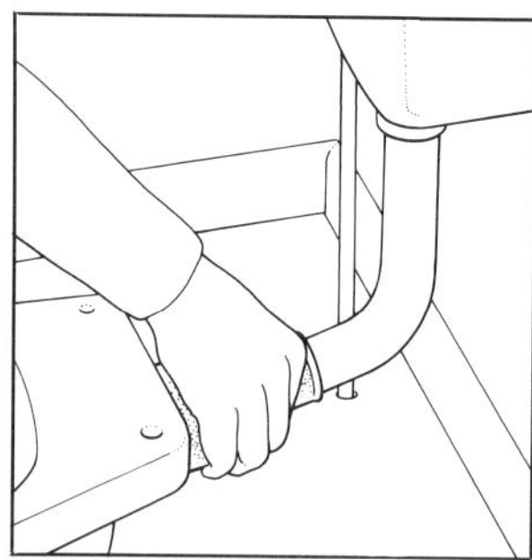

**Step 6** Level the cistern and screw to the wall and connect it to the pan. With a close-coupled WC there is an in-built connector, with a separate pan and cistern a flush bend is connected to the underside of the cistern with a union joint and to the pan with a rubber cone connector or O-ring seal. With some WCs it is easier to connect the flush pipe to the pan before the cistern. The connector is pushed about 100mm on to the flush bend and the outer collar is turned back on itself. Then when the flush bend is fitted into the spigot in the back of the pan, the collar is pushed back to seal around the spigot.
**Step 7** Connect the water supply pipe to the ball valve inlet with a tap connector. The ball valve should be the right sort for the supply – a high-pressure valve if supplied from the mains, a low-pressure valve if supplied from a cistern. Use plastic piping and fittings for the overflow. A hole drilled through the wall with a masonry bit is needed for the overflow which should slope outwards. Organise the outlet so that any fault will be noticed.
**Step 8** Turn on water and test the WC. Look at the cistern, the water level must be below the overflow. It may be necessary to bend the arm – up to raise the level, down to lower it.

# ...a bidet

## Plumbing a bidet

There are two types of bidet: those with *over-rim* supply which are plumbed like a basin and those with *through-rim* supply which have their supplies plumbed slightly differently.

### Over-rim supply

The water is supplied to the bowl of the bidet from taps, in exactly the same manner as a wash basin. This type is easier to plumb but the rim can feel cold when sitting on it.

### Through-rim supply

Special water valves are needed instead of taps and the water flows round the rim and warms it before filling the bowl. This type often has a spray fitted to the base of the bowl, which is used for douching. Both the bidet and the taps are more expensive than the over-rim type and special plumbing regulations have to be observed. Some local authorities don't allow this sort of bidet because of the back-siphonage problem.

**Step-by-step**

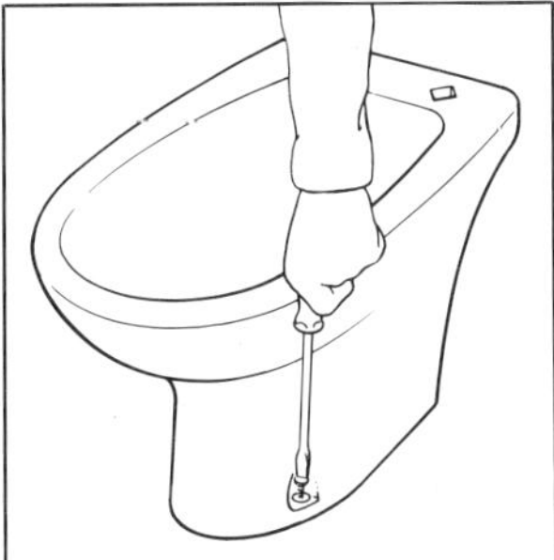

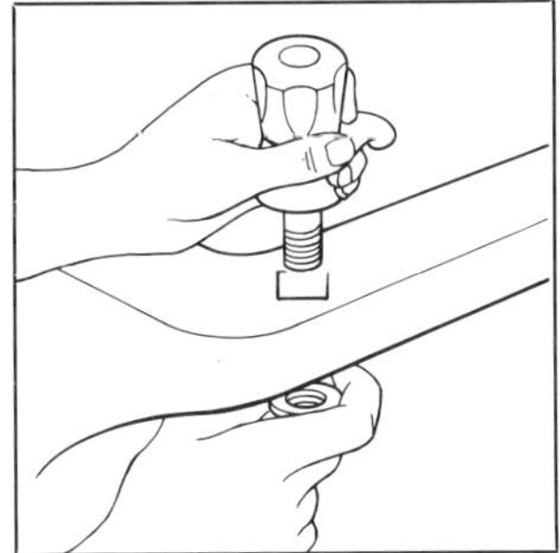

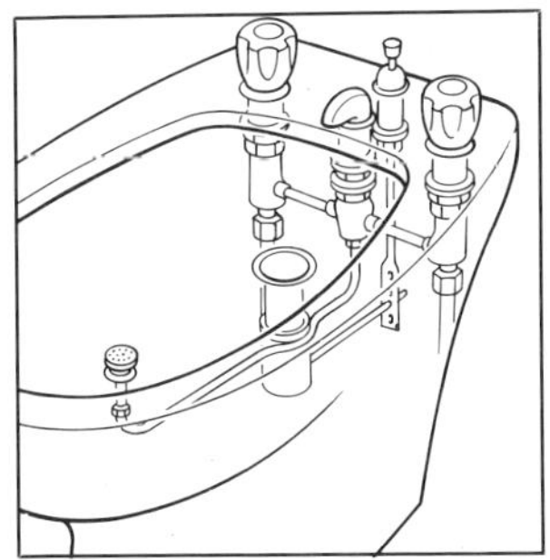

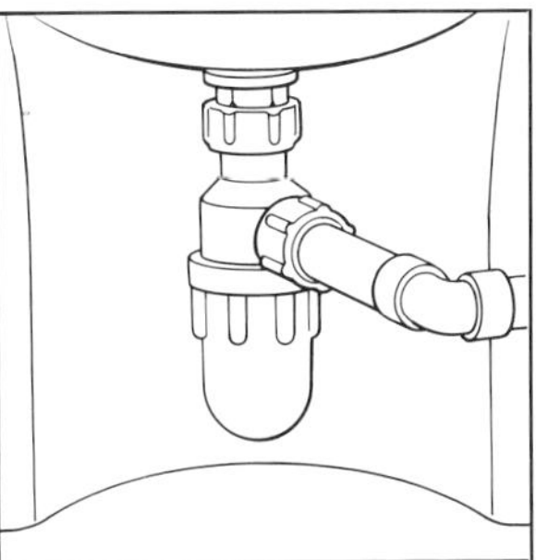

**Step 1** Screw the bidet to the floor using brass screws – special ones that take a covering cap which conceals the screw can be bought. Use washers and tighten gently to ensure the bidet is not cracked.

**Step 2** For an over-rim supply organise the taps as for a basin. If a basin mixer is used instead of separate taps, then both hot and cold supplies must come from the cold water cistern, or a divided-flow mixer must be used – see Taps page 69.

**Step 3** Through-rim bidets without a spray can be plumbed in as a branch to the existing bathroom supply pipes in the same way as an over-rim bidet. The taps which supply the water to the rim form a bidet set – this should come with instructions on fitting and with sealing washers. Through-rim supply bidets that incorporate a spray must have their own separate supply pipes run directly from the hot water cylinder and the cold water cistern.

**Step 4** As with a basin, a bottle trap is fitted and the waste piping run in 32mm plastic pipe to the hopper or soil pipe – see page 60.

## CONNECTORS AND TRAPS

**WC connectors** The easiest joint to make to a WC is with a plain-ended connector. This should be dry-jointed to the WC outlet, using a rubber gasket. Various patterns of connector are available with different angles and lengths of plain-ended spigot (depending on the position of the WC pan and the soil pipe to be connected). For particularly awkward joints, a *Multikwik* connector can be used.

**Traps** P-traps have a horizontal outlet; S-traps have a vertical outlet. Trap inlets usually have BSP threads for connecting directly to waste outlets. Shallow seal traps can be used on wastes discharging into gullies or hopper heads; on single-stack systems deep-seal (3in) traps must be used. Deep-seal traps take up more room, and to install one beneath a bath you may need to cut away the floorboards. *Bottle traps* are neater than tubular ones and may be easier to use in tight spaces.

Special *adjustable* traps are available for repair work to mate with existing pipes. *Bath traps* often come complete with overflow system attached. *Washing machine traps* have an inlet at the side for taking a washing machine outlet hose. In some situations, *automatic resealing traps* may be necessary – for example, for extra long basin wastes to single-stack systems.

# Fitting an electric shower

## Step-by-step

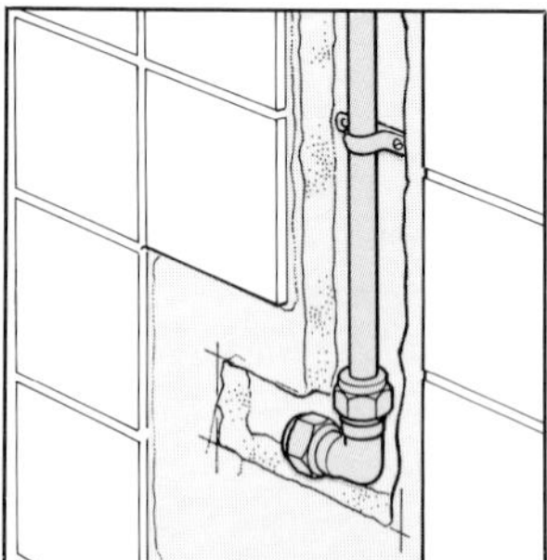

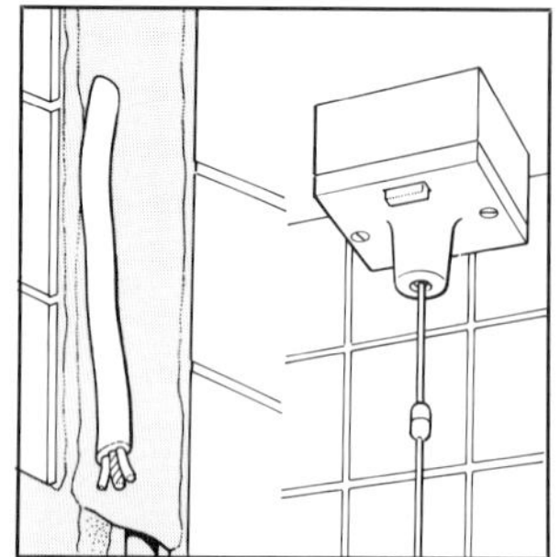

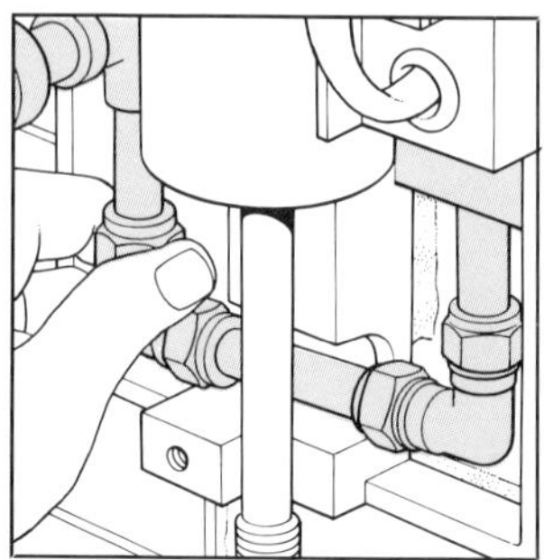

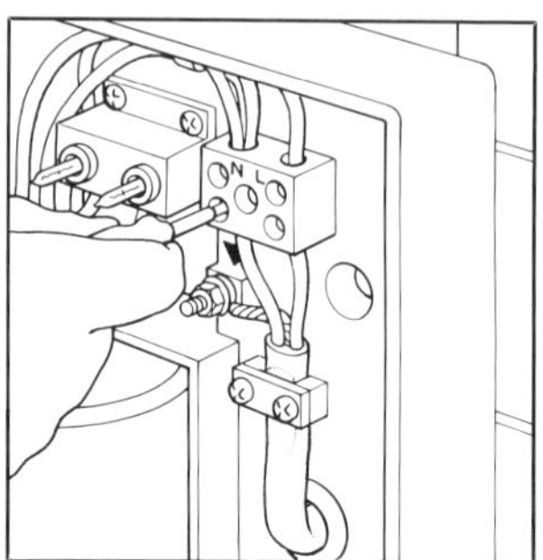

**Step 1** Turn off the mains stopvalve and drain. Tee into the nearest convenient mains pipe. Plumb from the tee to the site of the shower. If the control valve is part of the heater unit, the whole unit will have to be mounted inside the showering area. Incorporate a stopvalve into the supply pipe run and conceal the pipe in the bathroom in a channel in the wall.

**Step 2** Arrange the electric wiring. The heater will need its own special circuit from a fuseway in the consumer unit. The shower rating will dictate the size of fuse and cable needed. Most are 7kW which draws a current of 29.1A and so a 30A fuse is required and $6mm^2$ cable. Earthing is essential. See also Electricity page 48 *et seq.*

Fix the shower heater to the wall and connect up the water input pipe and the shower outlet hose.

**Step 3** Connect the wires to the terminal block and clamp the cable. Be careful to follow the wiring diagram supplied with the shower.

**Step 4** Replace the shower cover. It is important to do this properly to maintain the integrity of the waterproof seal.

Arrange for the circuit to be tested *before* the shower is used.

Water and electricity are a potentially lethal mixture and unless you're competent, you should leave the wiring to a qualified electrician. If you do-it-yourself get the circuit tested before connecting to the consumer unit.

### Fitting a bath/shower mixer

If you're installing a new bath, fitting it with a bath/shower mixer shouldn't be any more difficult than fitting two separate bath taps. It's important that a shower should have an easily controllable temperature so make sure that hot and cold supplies do not branch off from pipes from the cylinder and cistern downstream of any other taps. If you're replacing existing taps with a bath/shower mixer your greatest difficulty could be undoing the backnuts on the old taps. See if they will give before buying the mixer or you may be committed to removing the whole bath to get them free.

### Fitting a shower-only mixer

The water supply for a shower mixer should be taken from as far upstream as possible – ideally as a direct connection with the cold cistern (with a stopvalve in the pipe run) and as the first branch from the hot pipe after it emerges from the cylinder (fit a stopvalve here, too). Mixers are secured to the wall using screws and wallplugs and their inlet connections are usually made via elbows which come directly out of the wall.

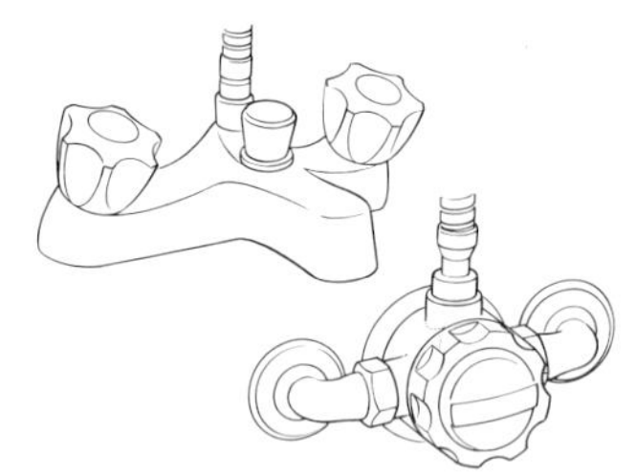

### Fitting a shower pump

A shower pump for pumping the hot and cold separately is housed most conveniently in an airing cupboard next to the bathroom where it is wired via a fused connection unit (with a fuse of the correct rating) which should have a double-pole switch to isolate the pump. At least one brand of pump has a low voltage (12V) switch circuit which allows it to be operated from a switch inside the bathroom, close to the shower – any other switch is not allowed in this position.

The second type of shower pump which pumps mixed hot and cold water is mounted on the wall below the shower rose. These pumps are usually operated by a cord pull switch. Some work on a low voltage supply from a transformer situated outside the bathroom.

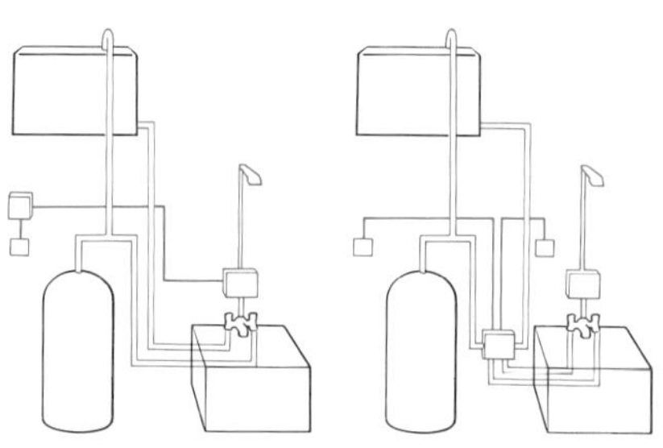

Shower pump circuits.

# Installing a gas water heater

There are two types of gas water-heater other than a central heating boiler:

**gas circulator** This is the equivalent of the electric immersion heater and can be used either as the sole means of heating water or as a supplementary system to an existing solid fuel appliance. It can also be used to provide summer hot water where the water – in winter – is normally heated by a central heating boiler.

**a multipoint** This is intended to be the sole means of supplying hot water to any number of taps in the dwelling. It cannot be connected into an existing hot water system.

This type of water heater heats water 'instantly'. That is, cold water flowing through the appliance is heated as it passes through. Gas is burned only when a hot water tap is opened.

## Installing a circulator

A circulator is connected to the hot water storage cylinder by flow and return pipes separate from any existing pipes. The pipes must be sized and connected in accordance with manufacturer's instructions. If fitted to the domestic hot water side of a central heating system the connections must be made direct to the storage cylinder and not to the central heating circuit.

The flow and return pipes from the circulator to the storage cylinder must rise continuously. The rise on horizontal pipes need not be much – normally 25mm in 3 metres is sufficient. If this is not done circulation of hot water may be prevented. Long runs of horizontal pipe work should be avoided and the manufacturer will state a maximum length.

Flow and return pipes should not be buried in walls and floors. It is sensible to insulate them and the cylinder.

The 'circulating head' which is the distance measured vertically between the position of the return connection on the circulator and the flow connection into the storage cylinder is important. The minimum and maximum will be stated by the manufacturer but generally the minimum is approximately 300mm and the maximum about 15 metres. If the circulating head is more than about 1·5 metres it will be necessary to restrict the speed of water circulation, by means of a restrictor washer in the return pipe at the circulator.

Running costs can be reduced by fitting a two-way valve (economy valve) on the return pipe from the storage cylinder. This enables only a part of the water in the storage cylinder to be heated at a time. Two return pipes are connected to the cylinder – one near the base and another about quarter of the distance from the top. These two pipes are connected to the two inlets of the valve and the outlet from the valve is connected to a common return pipe to the circulator.

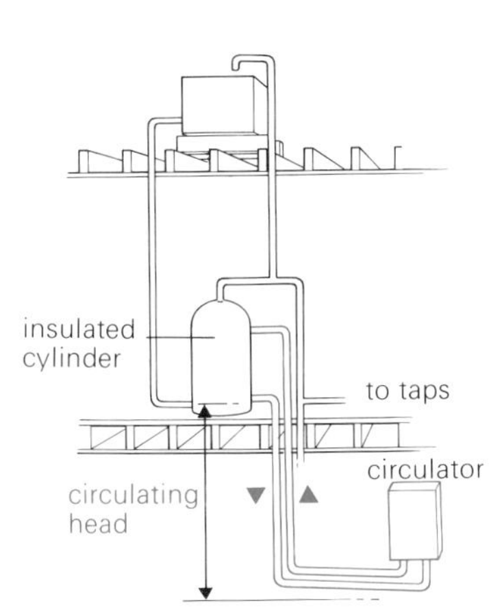


**Circulator:** The flow and return pipes must rise continuously. A drain-off plug should be fitted on the return pipe.

**Gas plumbing**

Circulators can be obtained as 'balanced-flue' (room-sealed) or 'open-flued' types. Room-sealed appliances are to be preferred for d-i-y installations as open-flued appliances are more complicated to install. They require a flue pipe which may need to be taken above the eaves of the roof and a supply of combustion air will be needed. See page 45 for the Regulations with which a flue must conform.

The amount of gas used by circulators is relatively low being about 15,000 Btu/hr (15 cubic feet). A gas supply pipe of 12mm bore is normally sufficient. The pressure of gas at the inlet of the appliance whilst in use must be 20mbar – it must be tested – see page 46. An isolating valve should be fitted on the gas supply at the inlet to the appliance to facilitate servicing.

## Installing a multipoint

As with other gas appliances there is no general method of fixing – it will vary between models and manufac-

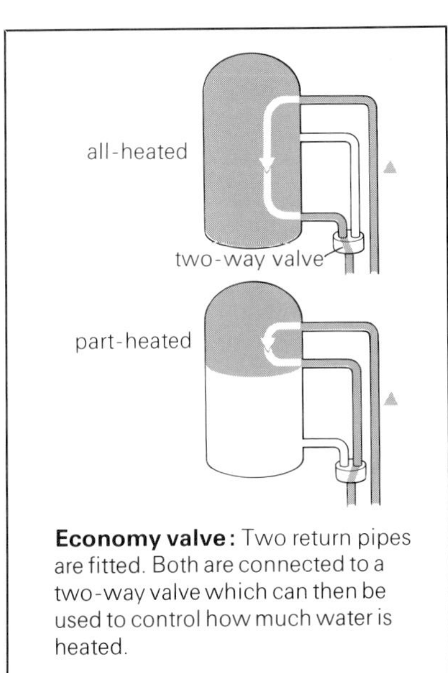


**Economy valve:** Two return pipes are fitted. Both are connected to a two-way valve which can then be used to control how much water is heated.

turers. In every case the manufacturer's installation instructions for the particular appliance being fitted must be followed.

If hot water is required for a shower, washing machine or dishwasher, a number of extra conditions may apply and it will be necessary to determine in advance whether the water heater is suitable.

The cold water supply to a multipoint heater may be taken either direct from the cold water mains supply of the dwelling or from a cold water storage cistern. The method to be adopted will depend upon local water bye-laws. In either case permission to install a multipoint water heater may be required.

If the heater is to be connected direct to the mains water supply, the water pressure available must be determined. A minimum pressure is required to operate the automatic gas valve in the heater. There is also a maximum pressure to which the appliance can be subjected. These pressures are quoted by each manufacturer in the appliance literature.

In addition to maximum and minimum pressures, any fluctuating pressure can affect the operation of the appliance and the fixing of a water pressure governor to the supply may be necessary.

When the cold water supply is taken from a cold water feed tank, the pressure required to operate the heater is quoted as 'head of water'. This is the distance measured vertically between the level of water in the feed tank *and the level of the highest draw-off tap*. It is NOT the distance between the level of water in the feed tank and the water heater.

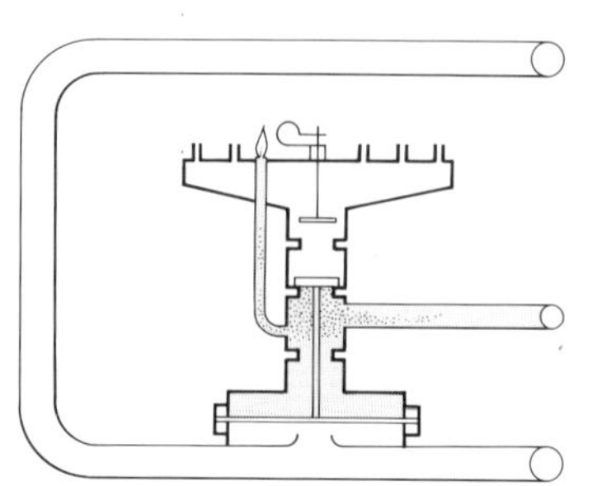

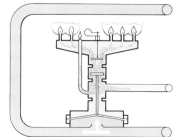

Gas is supplied to a multipoint heater only when a hot water tap is opened. The flow of water opens a special valve which allows a supply of gas to be ignited by the pilot light.

## Gas plumbing

To heat the water as it passes through the water heater a relatively large volume of gas is required – about 100,000 Btu/hr (100 cubic feet). For this a gas supply pipe not less than 22mm bore will be needed, taken directly from the gas meter outlet to the heater. It is not possible to take the supply from an existing installation 15mm pipe supplying another appliance.

In common with other appliances a gas pressure of 20mbars at the appliance – tested whilst all other appliances are in use – is essential.

Nearly all multipoint water heaters are now room-sealed appliances and these are to be preferred for d-i-y installations as they are easier to install. This means that the flue system is incorporated within the appliance with the flue outlet at the back. Fixing must be always on an outside wall of the dwelling (wall thicknesses of between 100mm and about 500mm can be accommodated). The method used to install the flue system depends upon the brand of heater and the instructions must be followed.

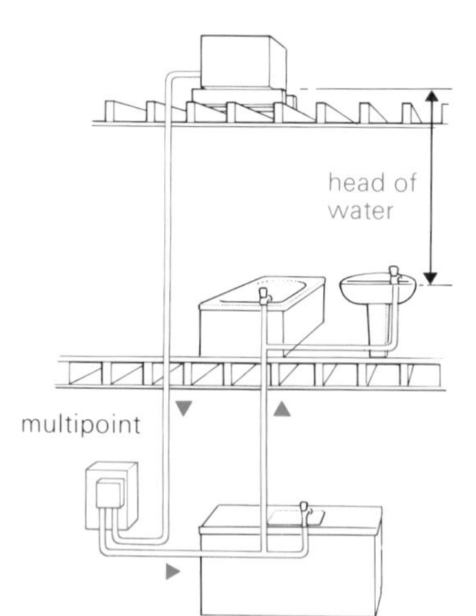


**Multipoint:** The cold water supply may be from a storage cistern as here or, if the water bye-laws permit it, from the mains.

There are certain restrictions regarding the placing of the flue terminal from a room-sealed appliance and this can affect the position of the appliance inside the house – see page 196.

The water heater may be fitted in any room of a dwelling, but obviously the best position is one near to the most frequently used tap – otherwise long lengths of pipe will result in loss of heat between the heater and the taps. There are water regulations regarding maximum lengths of draw-off pipes – see page 57. If long lengths of pipe cannot be avoided the pipe should be insulated.

The wall to which the appliance is fixed must be sound, and any combustible material adjacent to the appliance may need to be insulated in accordance with the instructions.

Isolating controls should be fitted to both water and gas supply pipes at the appliance for servicing purposes. Some appliances incorporate these.

## Hard water

With either sort of gas water heater if the water supply is 'hard' water it may be necessary to incorporate some form of water treatment to prevent formation of scale in the heat exchanger.

# Electricity in the bathroom

Water and electricity do not mix, so there are strict regulations listed in the Wiring Regulations of the Institution of Electrical Engineers about the electrical appliances you can and cannot use in the bathroom or in a room containing a shower.

The reason for complying with the Regulations is to avoid the risk of electric shock should a fault occur, and the metal casing of a piece of electrical equipment becomes 'live'. In the bath or shower the damp human body is usually in direct contact with earth via the waste pipe and water supply pipes to the taps.

## Switches

The Wiring Regs state that a switch or any other electric control must be sited so that it cannot be reached by anyone using the bath or shower. Ceiling-mounted, pullcord switches are allowed, but the switch body must be positioned out of reach. In an average-sized bathroom the light switch and the switch for any other electric equipment must either be a ceiling-mounting pull-switch or installed immediately outside the bathroom door.

## Electric equipment

Electric heaters (and electric-heated towel rails) are allowed in the bathroom provided they are not placed within reach of anyone using the bath or shower, and are permanently fixed to the floor, wall or ceiling. Under this regulation heaters can be mounted above a bath, but must be well out of reach of anyone standing in the bath.

Combined heat and light units for wall or ceiling mounting are useful for a bathroom, but they must be the type that has been designed specially for bathroom use, capable of withstanding damp conditions. They are not suitable for use on a lighting circuit as this cannot supply the higher power consumption.

All electrical equipment installed in a bathroom must be wired through a fused connection unit which is itself out of reach. The Wiring Regs. exclude the use of socket outlets in bathrooms because these would allow what the Regulations call 'the indiscriminate use of apparatus, particularly portable appliances' such as hair driers and heaters. Any other room containing a shower cubicle can have socket outlets but these must be sited at least 2·5m from the cubicle.

A special socket is allowed for shavers. This must be of the type for use in bathrooms, either on its own or with a light. The type for the bathroom – made to BS 3052 – has an isolating transformer with an earthed metal screen so that the output winding is isolated from the mains. It is unsuitable for use with other equipment. The transformer has two sets of windings and most of these sockets will switch to give either the standard mains voltage or 115 volts. The socket is also usually made to take both round and flat pin razor plugs.

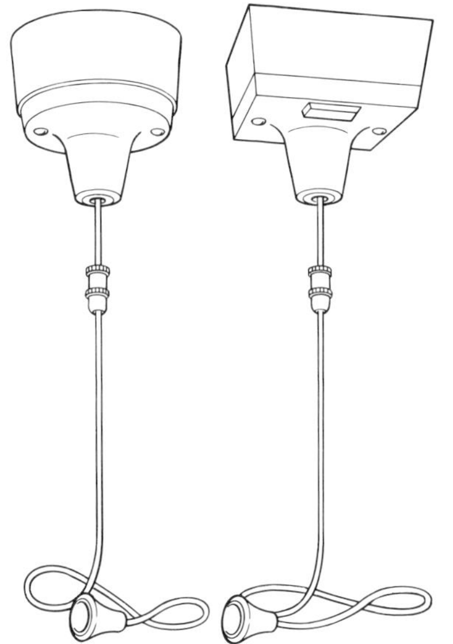

Ceiling mounted cord switches

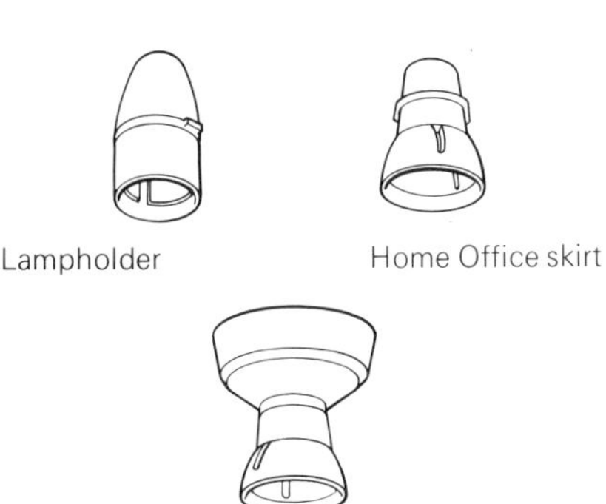

Lampholder

Home Office skirt

Batten holder

## Washing machines

Washing machines which are properly and permanently installed and tumble driers can be fitted in bathrooms but their controls must be out of reach of anyone using a bath or shower. In most bathrooms this prevents the installation of these machines unless the room is very large or the machines can be isolated behind permanent screening, such as louvred panels, so that effectively they are in a room of their own. As a washing machine has to have a supply of water and empty through a waste pipe which will usually be on the bath side of the room, conforming to the Regulations may make plumbing both expensive and inconvenient.

## Lighting

The Regulations on lighting say 'parts of a lampholder likely to be touched by a person replacing a lamp shall be constructed of, or shrouded in, insulating material and, for bayonet-type lampholders, be fitted with a protective shield'. So for bathroom lights either a special sort of lampholder with an extended skirt (sometimes called a Home Office or HO skirt) is required or a totally enclosed ceiling fitting should be used – this can be lights behind a suspended ceiling.

If you want wall or downlights in a bathroom, they also must be totally enclosed, with no exposed metal parts, and of a type resistant to damp.

# Installing an electric...

## Step-by-step

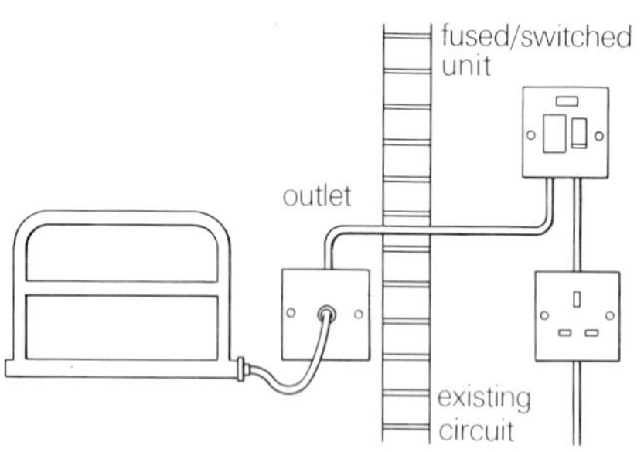

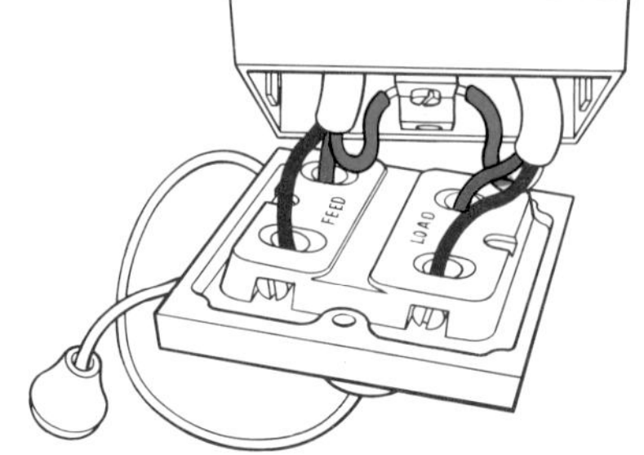

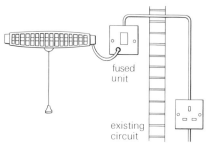

**. . . heated towel rail**

Take a spur from the ring circuit to a switched fused connection unit. Site the connection unit outside the bathroom where it will be seen as you pass. Choose one with a red pilot light to show when it is in use.

From the connection unit carry a cable through the bathroom wall to a flex outlet plate fitted next to the towel rail. Pass the flex from the towel rail through the hole in the surface plate of a flex outlet plate and join flex and cable (live, neutral and earth conductors) to the terminals. Another way to wire a towel rail is to use an unswitched fused connection unit outside with a ceiling-mounted switch inside the bathroom.

**. . . wall-mounted heater**

Take a spur from the ring circuit to an unswitched fused connection unit mounted high on the bathroom wall close to the heater (in other words well out of reach). If the heater has its own pull-cord switch and complies with BS 3456, the cable can run direct, otherwise a double-pole ceiling-mounted switch is required. A cable from the switch is passed down the wall and connected to the heater itself. The heater is then mounted onto its brackets previously screwed and plugged to the wall.

**. . . ceiling-mounted switch**

Pass the cable through the ceiling hole and remove the outer insulation and insulation on the live and neutral conductors.

Fit the base section of the switch over the cable and then screw the base to the ceiling. This fixing must withstand the downward pull on the cord. A wood mounting block (with a hole in the wood for the two cables to pass) should be placed in the ceiling and jointed to the joist to form a firm mounting platform. Sometimes a joist can be used for fixing, in which case a small hole for the cable is cut into the joist close to the ceiling.

Connect the live and neutral wires. Screw the switch section on the mount.

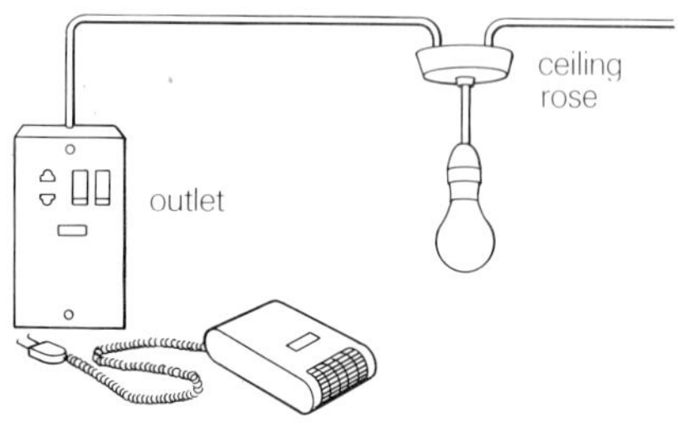


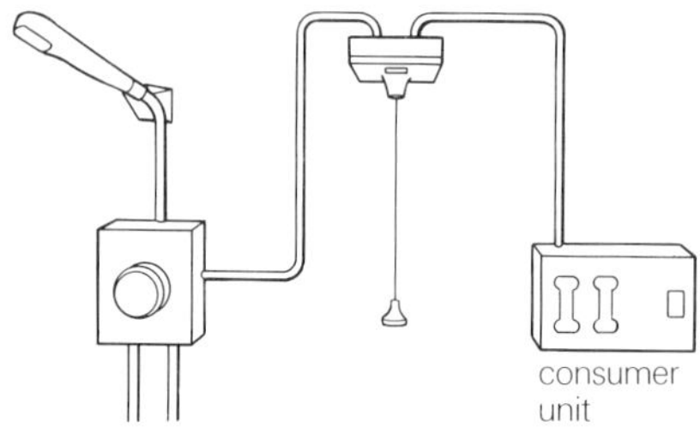


**. . . shaver outlet**

The only type of socket outlet allowed in bathrooms is a shaver supply unit with a transformer conforming to BS 3052.

The shaver supply unit or outlet imposes very little load, and may be connected to any convenient circuit—either a socket circuit or a lighting circuit. Using a bathroom lighting circuit has the attraction that it's likely to be close at hand—there will be no socket circuit in the room—and that the unit is always switched off when the light is off. There are combined shaving lights/shaver outlets available; these too need to conform to the relevant British Standard.

**. . . shower**

An electric shower unit is basically a water heater which heats the water rapidly as it flows over the heating elements. When the water inlet valve is opened the pressure of water closes a switch which operates the heating element. The temperature of the water varies with the rate of flow: the slower the flow the higher the temperature.

As the water is only briefly in contact with the element, the electric loading has to be 6kW or more and this high loading means that an electric shower must have its own circuit of at least 30 amp (showers more than 7kW need 45 amp).

A 6·0mm² cable is normally used although, if a cartridge fuse or a miniature circuit breaker is used (instead of a rewirable fuse) and the cable run is less than 18 metres, the cable can be 4·0mm² which is cheaper and easier to connect.

The switch must be the ceiling-mounted pullcord type—double-pole 30 amp rating. It's useful if it has a pilot light. The cable to the shower can sometimes go direct from the switch, but a few showers have a flex which needs to be connected to the cable inside a flexible cable connection unit similar to that used for the towel rail—30 amp rating.

If the bathroom is already tiled the cable from the switch to the shower unit can be enclosed in plastic trunking otherwise it should be concealed in the wall.

**. . . shower pump**

This will usually operate from a 13 amp supply and can often be wired up in the same manner as a bathroom wall heater. A good place for a pump is beneath the bath, as this makes the plumbing fairly simple, but note that some pumps are not waterproof and have to be installed outside the bathroom.

# Hiding the pipes

For easy cleaning and simple uncluttered lines in a bathroom or kitchen, pipes should be boxed in, but this can cause problems with regard to the access, should it become necessary.

In older properties, there may be no option, but in a new design, a major consideration should be to minimise the number of pipes that need boxing and to run those that do close enough together to minimise the size of the box.

Box frameworks (or ducts) usually look better if they are built across the whole wall or to match the width of an appliance rather than making them just wide enough to enclose the pipes. A half height duct that stops 150mm or so higher than the basin forms a useful shelf, though some people would argue that providing a shelf above a basin creates an unnecessary hazard. Arrange the pipework and box frame-work so that there is access for maintenance and room to manoeuvre in the critical areas, behind taps for instance – try not to fit these tight against a wall. Plan any ducts to be tiled, so that they are an exact number of tiles wide and long (most tiles are 100mm or 150mm square or 150mm by 75mm).

**Vertical boxing**

The simplest vertical boxing consists of wooden batten of about 18mm wide and the necessary depth to clear the pipes, screwed on with masonry fixings either side of the pipes, covered by plywood sheeting screwed on with brass cup washers and brass screws. The plywood should slightly overlap the battens. The sides of the box can then be painted, papered or tiled to match the wall. In order to be able to remove them, paper round the edges and tuck it back on itself.

It is worth insulating the pipes before boxing them in. This cuts down on condensation especially on the mains cold supply; it also reduces heat transfer between hot and cold supply pipes; helps to avoid frozen pipes and reduces heat loss.

## BOXING-IN THE BATH

Unless you buy a panel with the bath you will normally need to surround a new bath with a frame. Softwood battens 50mm by 25mm or 38mm by 38mm are suitable for a simple frame just to enclose the bath and not take any weight, for a more substantial frame intended to provide a ledge around the bath use larger battens 50mm by 50mm.

It's useful to have a plinth at the bottom of the panel. Build this from softwood or 12mm thick exterior-grade plywood screwed to the frame or nailed with panel pins punched below the surface.

Bath panels can be made from a sheet material such as hardboard or tongued and grooved softwood – allow for the thickness of these boards when you make the frame. With hardboard, the corners can be conveniently concealed with metal angle strip, fixed with domed-head screws. Magnetic tape fixings and adhesive touch-and-close fasteners (like Velcro) meant for d-i-y double-glazing can be used to attach a lightweight panel and allow access when necessary.

A hardboard panel can be finished off in almost any way – by painting, carpeting (continuous from the floor), or tiling – with ceramic or cork tiles. A vinyl-coated wallpaper may be successful.

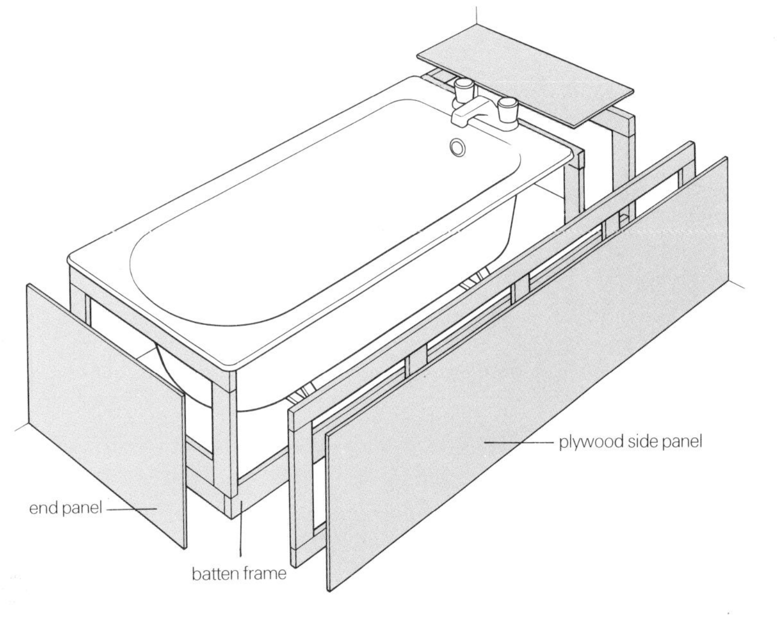

# Chapter 5

# LIVING SPACE

Living space means rooms like sitting rooms, bedrooms, dining rooms, studies and playrooms. The sorts of improvements carried out in these rooms are usually to make things more comfortable and convenient.

A fair proportion of the money spent on improving living space will go on furniture, curtains, flooring and decorations – all things which can be considered room by room. Other improvements you might make, such as heating, new and better provision of electricity power points and lighting can also be dealt with room by room, but it's usually better to think of these services as part of a plan for the whole house, and it's only a whole house improvement that would add any significant value to your house or have any significant effect on its saleability.

Space (or at least the impression of space) can be created or altered by moving doorways or making new ones; putting in new windows or replacing existing windows with larger ones. Installing patio doors instead of french casement doors is a common improvement and one that nowadays many people expect.

Fireplaces are important in main living rooms. In many houses the existing fireplace was blocked off when central heating was installed. The current vogue is to re-establish a focal point and this usually means some sort of fire.

You might think about television aerial points. The advent of breakfast TV makes a point in the dining room or kitchen a possibility. A portable television could be used with points all over the house.

Further improvements to living space include things like knocking walls down to improve the arrangement of space and, the converse, building partitions to separate or enclose parts of the house. When you carry out these sorts of structural improvements it is usually worth bearing in mind that the decisions you take might be significant when you come to sell the house. The general rules set out on page 216 give an idea of the things to consider.

▲ Knocking down a wall between rooms is a very common way of re-arranging living space. A supporting beam is usually required for the floor above.
The original cornice has been retained in this conversion of one room into two. ▶

◀ Raising the level of the floor in one part of a room creates the impression of a well in another part.
◀ Pets need living space too.

# Knocking rooms through

Unless it's a change of use (or your house is a special case – see page 22), planning permission is not necessary to knock two or more rooms into one. However, you should obtain Building Regulations approval (see page 24). Apart from the structural implications, approval may be needed because, for instance, the removal of a wall means the existing window is no longer large enough. If in doubt consult your local authority.

When planning to remove a wall separating rooms, the first thing is to determine whether the wall is a loadbearing structural one which supports parts of the building above.

In many cases loadbearing internal walls are constructed of masonry, but they can be timber frame. Non-loadbearing walls are often referred to as internal partitions – they're usually lightweight materials.

### Loadbearing walls

If the wall which is to be removed is found to be loadbearing, a beam or lintel which is adequate in strength to carry the weight of the building above must be installed in place of the wall. This beam must be properly supported on sound bearings at either end – usually masonry piers – and adequate temporary supports must be provided to ensure that no settlement occurs as the wall is removed.

### Non-loadbearing walls

When it is established that the wall which is to be taken down is a non-loadbearing partition – because it is not supporting a floor, floors, roof or wall above – then it can probably be taken down without risk of disturbing or weakening any part of the building above. A beam or lintel is usually needed only if some masonry is to be left or some new masonry will be constructed at the top of the opening – perhaps to reduce the height.

The fact that a wall is not loadbearing doesn't mean that it isn't an important part of the structure. Often each room forms a box which provides strength to the other boxes around it, and the removal of a wall forming part of such a box could take away the stiffness of walls at right angles. The stiffness can usually be maintained by leaving adequately-sized piers at either end, but take advice.

### Professional help

If in the slightest doubt about the structure, it is essential that you engage an architect, structural engineer or building surveyor. Once structural settlement has occurred, it is difficult and costly to restore a building.

## TEMPORARY SUPPORT

Temporary support is usually provided by adjustable props, on a firm base, which support temporary beams placed immediately under the floor (or roof) parallel to the wall to be disturbed. The load should be spread by standing the props on lengths of timber about 150mm wide by around 50mm thick. When dealing with an external wall firm ground will suffice. Indoors, solid floors are best; with hollow timber floors it is often necessary to remove the floorboards and position the props between the floor joists. In upstairs rooms the load should be spread by laying the timber across a number of floor joists – it will usually also be necessary to support the floor from below with extra props.

The adjustable props should be about 900mm apart on both sides of the wall and placed about 600mm from the wall. Once the props are in position they are, in turn, gradually tightened until the whole weight of the floor or roof is taken up.

Any part of the wall to be removed which is to be left above the opening also needs supporting. For this cut out a few bricks about 600mm apart above the position for the beam and insert needles (timbers about 150mm deep by 100mm wide will suffice where only one wall or floor above needs support) through the holes. The needles are supported by more adjustable props, which are placed inside the line of the main props and not more than 600mm from either side of the wall.

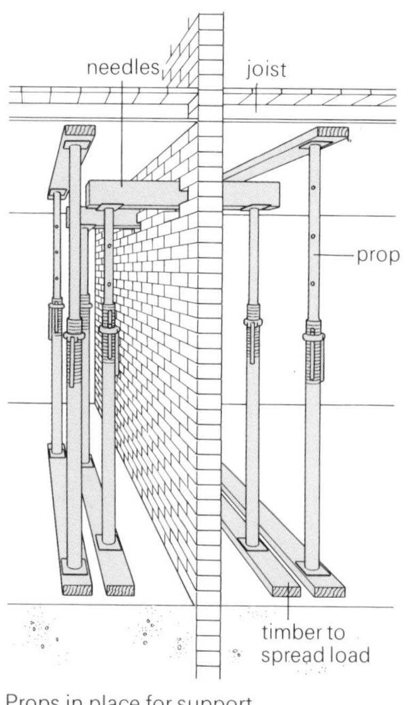


Props in place for support.

## TO DETERMINE IF AN INTERNAL WALL IS LOADBEARING OR NOT

It is useful to know at the outset, the thickness and material used to construct the wall which is to be taken down. The material can be determined by inspecting from above with the floorboards up or by removing a piece of skirting or a door frame that is to be removed anyway.

At the same time check that the ceiling and floors on either side of the wall are aligned. If they are not the resulting step when the wall is removed will have to be disguised in some way.

**The roof** To determine whether the wall carries directly (or indirectly) some of the weight of the roof inspect inside the roof space, establish whether any of the roof timbers take a bearing on the wall – see page 279 for roof construction.

Joists carrying the ceiling may also rely upon an internal loadbearing wall for support.

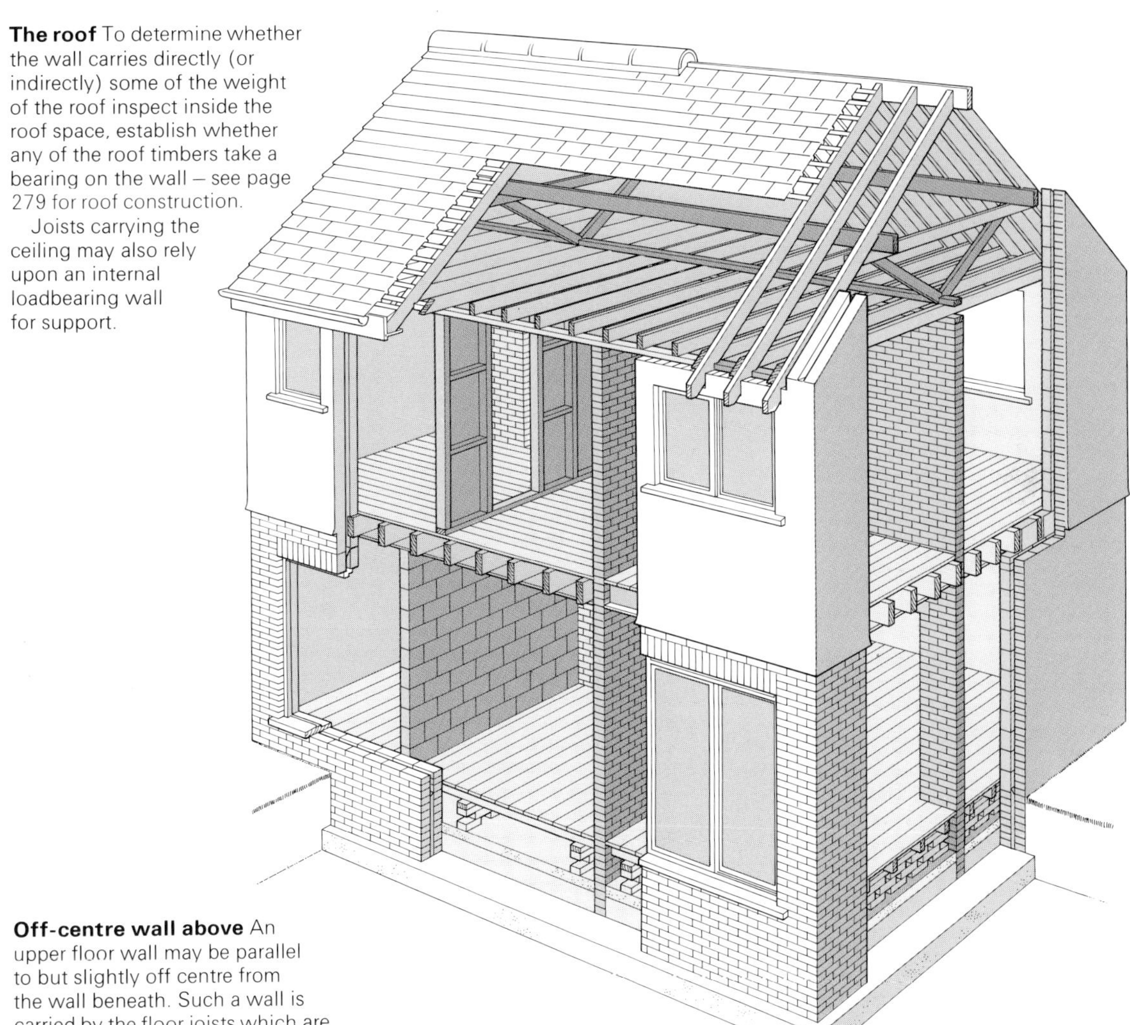

**Off-centre wall above** An upper floor wall may be parallel to but slightly off centre from the wall beneath. Such a wall is carried by the floor joists which are supported by the wall beneath.

**The floor above** Whether the wall carries directly (or indirectly) some of the weight of a floor above can be checked by finding the direction of span of the floor joists. This will be at right-angles to the span of the floor boards of the floor above. Joists that cross the wall are usually supported by it; joists that run parallel generally are not.

**The wall directly above** Whether the wall supports the continuation of the same wall or the floor above can be checked by taking dimensions between the wall to be removed and a fixed point which is common to the floor on which the wall stands and the floor (or floors) above. This common point must be directly above the point below. External walls may provide a common point, but beware of external walls which bow away from vertical.

**External walls** As these all carry their own weight and that of the roof, they are invariably load-bearing.

# Removing a stud partition

## Step-by-step

**Step 1** This Guide is for a non-loadbearing wall. Measure and mark out the size of the opening. Switch off the electricity supply to any cables contained in the partition. Remove the skirtings and architraves and any simple coving. If there is an ornate plaster coving, which you want to retain, the job becomes more difficult. One way to get round it is to install a beam across the opening and leave the coving intact above – such a beam wouldn't have to be very strong a timber rail might suffice.

**Step 2** Remove the plasterboard (or plaster on lath if an older house) from one side by cutting a hole between stud frames and pulling away the boards. To avoid damaging the ceiling, cut through the partition/ceiling joint with a trimming knife. With the stud framework exposed on one face, deal with any electric cables (or other services) carried in the partition – see page 48 *et seq*. Remove the facing from the opposite side of the partition – again slicing through the partition/ceiling joint first.

**Step 3** Once the timber stud framework is fully exposed the vertical studs can be cut through near the top rail and pulled away. Carefully pull or lever the top rail away from the ceiling and the bottom rail from the floor. The bottom rail is usually fixed with masonry nails, but may in some cases be fixed with screwed metal brackets.

When there is a concrete floor you may find two bottom rails with the lower one set into the concrete. If this is the case, this piece of timber should also be removed – to cover it over could subsequently cause problems.

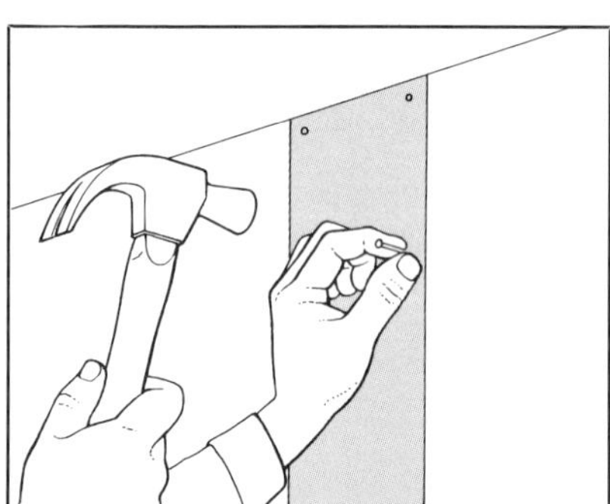

**Step 4** Once the partition has been removed the opening can be made good. The edge wall gaps can be filled with a piece of plasterboard and skimmed with plaster filler or filled with wet plaster to a smooth finish (see page 260).

A timber lining can be fixed to form a surround. To get the best finish under a clear timber finish, countersink the screws and cover the hole with a pellet of similar wood. There is a special drill bit that will cut both the countersink hole and the pellet.

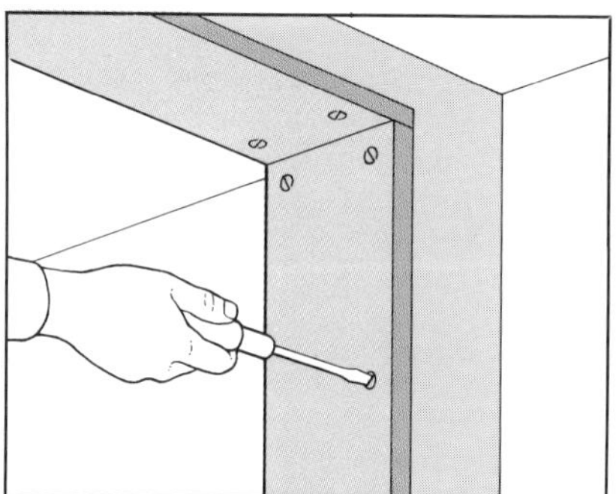

**Step 5** The ceiling plasterboard may run across the top of the existing partition leaving only the original fixing holes to fill or there may be a gap in the plasterboard. If so, this should be filled with a narrow piece of plasterboard of the same thickness, fixed at approximately 150mm centres. There should already be noggings across the slot – a rail of 75mm by 50mm or 50mm by 50mm timber can be nailed between these to provide support for the plasterboard. If the plasterboard piece to be fixed is not wider than approximately 120mm, one timber member should be enough, otherwise two are needed. The surface may be made good with a thin coat of filler.

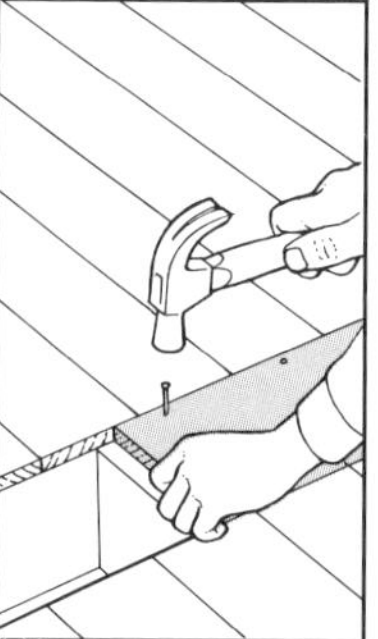

**Step 6** A concrete floor finish should be made good with sand and cement screed; a timber floor with plywood or chipboard of the appropriate thickness to match the existing finish on a timber floor – this will often not be necessary as it is common to find that the floor boarding is continuous under timber partitions. With concrete floors you may find that the surface of the screed is not at the same level on either side.

Make as good a job as possible of finishing the floor smooth. Any undulations will show through and cause rapid wear of carpets and other floor coverings.

# ...when loadbearing

When a timber stud partition is found to be loadbearing, under no circumstances should it be altered without making provision to support the floor and roof above – temporarily and permanently. It is possible to remove a section of the wall provided that a suitable timber beam is inserted to carry the loads.

The information given in the Guide is adequate under normal conditions to make finished openings up to 1·8m wide. Where larger openings are desired (or there are other complications) professional advice should be obtained before starting work. Structural alterations must have Building Regulations approval before work is commenced and the Building Control Officer will require a drawing showing what is intended.

## Step-by-step

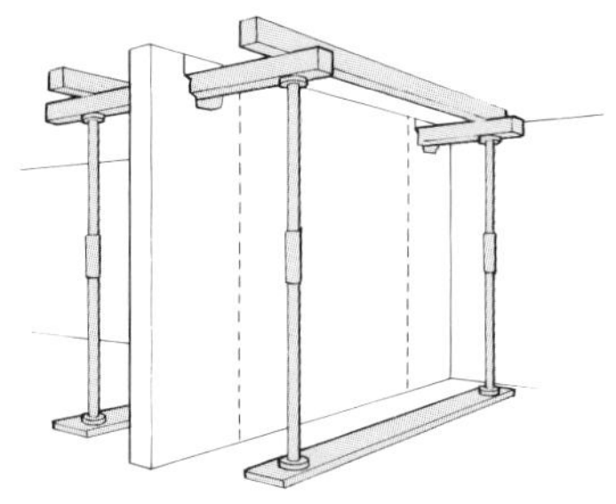

**Step 1** To temporarily support the floor or roof whilst work is carried out use adjustable props – see page 116. Once the temporary support is in place an opening can be made in the same way as described for non-loadbearing partitions, except that the top rail of the partition should be left in place and the edge of the plasterboard should be kept as neat as possible.

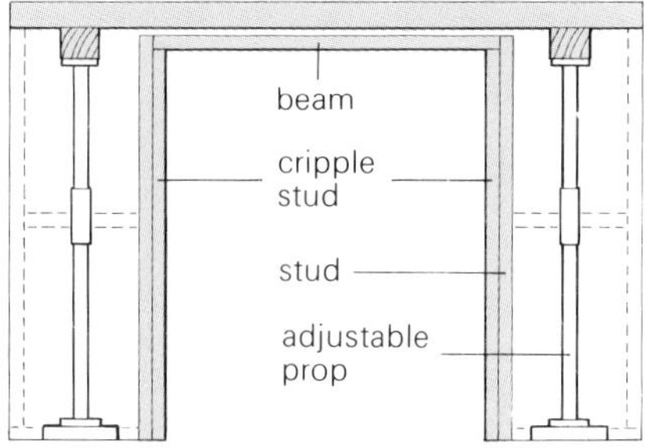


**Step 2** To allow for the new support frame and subsequent lining the opening should be cut the depth of the beam taller and 125mm wider than required. Plasterboard can be cut with a coarse-toothed saw or cut through with a trimming knife. Special saws are available but a key hole saw (or a saw blade for a trimming knife) will usually be satisfactory. Plasterboard will rapidly blunt woodworking tools.

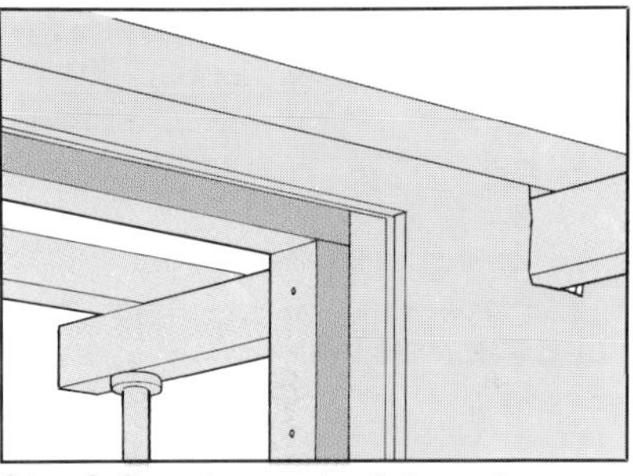

**Step 3** Once the opening is formed, a timber beam should be accurately cut to length to fit between the vertical studs on either side of the opening. Place the beam tightly beneath the existing top rail and hold it temporarily in place by skew-nailing it to the studs on either side. Additional cripple studs of timber 50mm thick, are required between the beam and the floor. Cut them accurately to length and fix them to the outer stud with 100mm long nails at 200mm centres. The cripple studs will carry all the load and must be a tight fit.

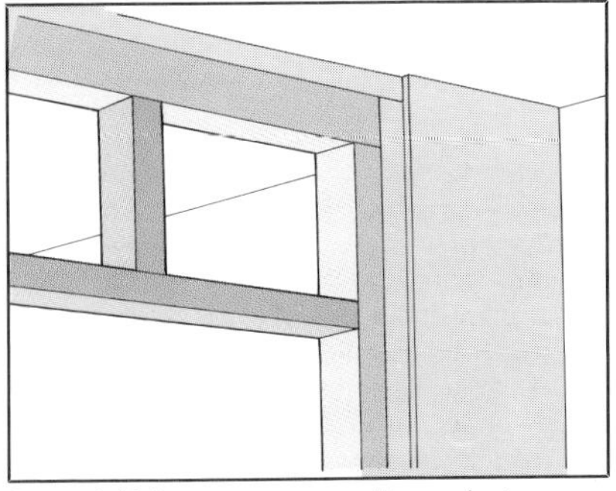

**Step 4** If there are any small gaps between the top of the beam and the top rail of the partition, pack them out with thin pieces of timber or plywood. If the top of the finished opening is to be lower than the bottom of the beam, a horizontal rail can be fitted across at the appropriate height and packed down from the beam. This will support the head member of the surround and the section of wall above it.

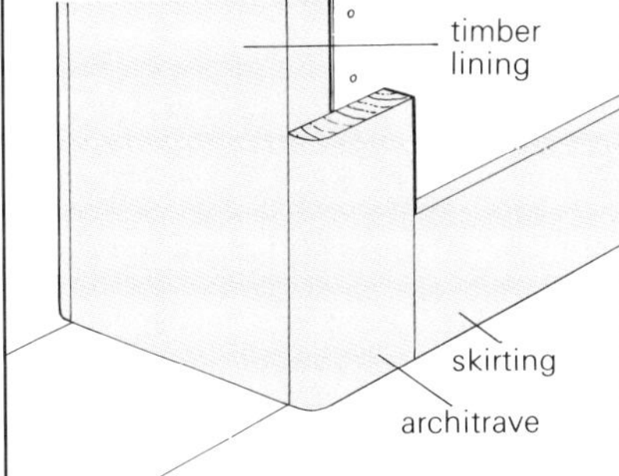


**Step 5** Once the supporting structure is fully nailed in place, the temporary supports can be carefully removed and the opening finished off with its lining and architraves.

### Lintel sizes

FOR SPANS UP TO 1.2m
2 x 200mm by 38mm or
2 x 20mm by 50mm or
1 x 200mm by 75mm

FOR SPANS UP TO 1.8m
2 x 225mm by 38mm or
2 x 225mm by 50mm or
1 x 225mm by 75mm

Use softwood to general structural grade.

# Masonry walls

A loadbearing masonry wall needs a beam (or lintel) to carry the load above. Both the beam and it's bearing need careful design for a safe construction.

## Bearings for the beam

The bearing is best provided as a pier at each end of the opening. As all the load from above will find its way into these piers they must be large enough – 450mm (ie two bricks length) at either end should be adequate. If you made piers in a 100mm wide wall any shorter than this, they could be overstressed. The pier would then have to be widened to at least 225mm, and taken right down to the foundations – a complicated job, needing expert bricklaying.

Piers are of course often a nuisance – they jut out into the room making it difficult to disguise the fact that a through-room used to be two rooms and often making it difficult to arrange furniture effectively. It is not easy to avoid this, since, in addition to being the best way to support the lintel, piers may be essential to maintain the walls at right angles to the one you're demolishing.

If you don't want piers at each end, take expert advice on what to do and make certain anyone you are employing to do the job has good advice.

The beam itself requires a bearing on each pier of at least 150mm at each end – so the beam should be at least 300mm longer than the opening.

If the load that the beam or lintel is to carry is large or the area of brickwork or blockwork on which it is to bear is weak, the bearing surface must be replaced with something stronger – a concrete block for instance. Beams and lintels should be bedded on mortar to provide an even and level bed. They can be placed on pieces of slate or similar hard strong material and packed afterwards with mortar. In extreme cases a pier may need rebuilding.

## Access for the beam

It isn't always possible to carry a long beam through the house to where it will be installed and it may be necessary to cut a temporary hole in an external wall through which to feed the beam. Any such hole should be as small as possible and cut where the beam will meet the wall, but above the line of the beam so that the bearing masonry is not disturbed.

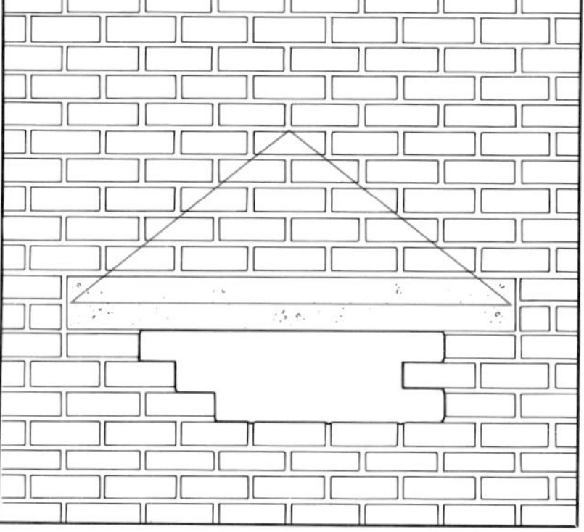

**Making the opening**
When the building is properly supported make the opening for the lintel. Start by removing a brick near the centre of the opening – chip away the mortar using a plugging chisel (the narrow type of masonry chisel) and knock the brick out, with the hammer if necessary. Lever out the bricks around it – using a bolster on horizontal joints and continuing to use the plugging chisel on vertical joints. Angle the chisel into the wall rather than holding it at right angles. This will help to prevent cracks spreading outside the area you're demolishing. Work steadily, enlarging the opening gradually, taking care not to disturb the construction above the beam position.

If you're using an RSJ, its depth may not be an exact multiple of a brick course: this means you'll have to cut bricks. It's better to do this above the lintel.

Examine the masonry the lintel will bear on and check that it is sufficient. If it is crumbly, or if the wall is built of hollow blocks, it's best to use either a concrete 'padstone' or two or three courses of engineering bricks. If the piers are at all loose it will be necessary to rebuild.

**Installing the beam** Place the beam and bed in position. A light-to-medium weight beam can be lifted in position fairly easily by two or three people capable of handling the loads. Secure trestles are necessary for the lifters to stand on and to support the beam which should be lifted, carefully, in stages one end at a time. For heavy beams such as RSJ's and pre-cast concrete lintels, lifting gear and secure scaffolding is required.

Place the beam on a bed of mortar. When it is in place pack the gap between lintel and masonry with thin pieces of slate and press relatively dry mortar well into the joints. Ensure that the beam is level.

Once the beam is in place continue to remove the rest of the wall, trimming the piers to a true vertical line – an angle grinder can be useful for this.

After a couple of days when the new brickwork is dry, remove the props and make good the holes. Rake out any masonry units that have been loosened and fill in with cleaned salvaged units jointed with mortar.

Enclose the lintel, make good the floor and walls with matching materials. Fix any frames and doors.

## Beams and lintels

The means of providing support across a large, clear opening is a beam. When the support carries masonry over a door or window frame, it is called a lintel. In essence both beam and lintel perform the same function.

The weight, the look, the need for boxing or plastering, the ability to take screw fixings are all things to consider when choosing a beam.

**Lightweight steel** Lightweight, pressed-steel beams or lintels are the most popular type because they are easy to handle. They can carry quite heavy loads over large spans – typically up to 3 tons over 4·5 metres. There is little likelihood of any corrosion problems when using these lintels internally. However, they do need to be plastered or enclosed in plasterboard for fire protection. They can be obtained with expanded metal mesh attached to provide a key for plastering. Don't drill holes in this lintel.

**Concrete** Pre-cast reinforced and pre-stressed concrete lintels are generally available for spans up to around 3·5m. Some manufacturers make them longer than this, but their load-carrying capacity begins to fall off, compared with steel.

A concrete beam could be specially designed, but casting it – either on the ground or in-situ – is not a d-i-y job.

Pre-cast lintels which are made from aerated concrete weigh about the same as lightweight steel ones, but ordinary concrete beams are heavier.

It's important to install concrete beams the right way up. The top may be marked, or the ends of the pre-stressing wires or strands may be visible – these should go at the bottom. Don't attempt to install a concrete lintel if you're not sure.

In their favour, concrete lintels will usually be cheaper than steel, and can be plastered directly.

**RSJs** Rolled Steel Joists are made in standard I-sections in a wide range of sizes suitable for almost any load – although the larger ones can be considerably heavier than pressed steel lintels. One disadvantage is that, unlike pressed steel and pre-cast concrete lintels, the sizes in which they're made don't necessarily fit in with the height of the brick courses.

You may be able to buy new RSJs at steel stockholders (see local telephone directories) or builders' yards. Secondhand ones are marginally cheaper. An RSJ has to be protected against fire, by a wooden framework covered with plasterboard or a fire resistant board, or using wet plaster on expanded metal. RSJs cost about the same as pressed steel lintels.

## The beam or lintel design

The size and strength of the lintel required will depend on the load it has to support. You won't be able to calculate this yourself but if you provide enough detail about the existing structure – preferably an accurate drawing to scale – a building surveyor or structural engineer should be able to advise. A specialist manufacturer can usually recommend a suitable standard unit. If you obtain a beam or lintel from a builder's merchant or the manufacturer's agent, make certain that the unit they offer you is suitable for your need. If necessary check with the manufacturer direct – most offer a free design service. Your builders' merchant should be able to put you in touch. When *Which?* contacted a number of manufacturers to ask what size lintel was required for a particular job, the manufacturers generally asked the right questions and suggested the correct size.

The Building Control Officer will require that the beam you are proposing to insert is adequate in its structural design and this is itself a further safeguard. He will normally expect the calculations to be put forward for his comment.

TYPES OF LINTEL

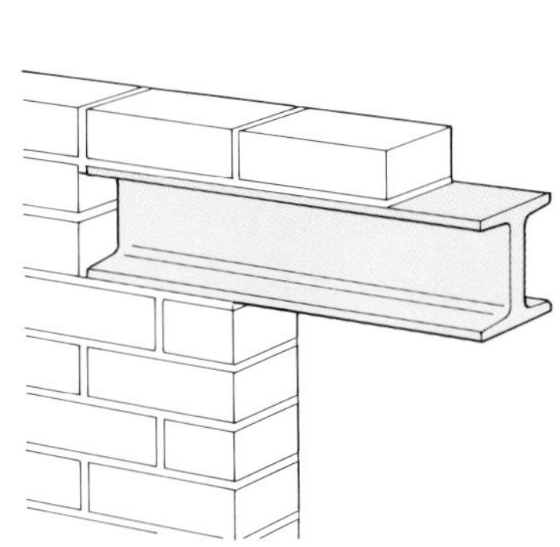

RSJ-rolled steel joist.

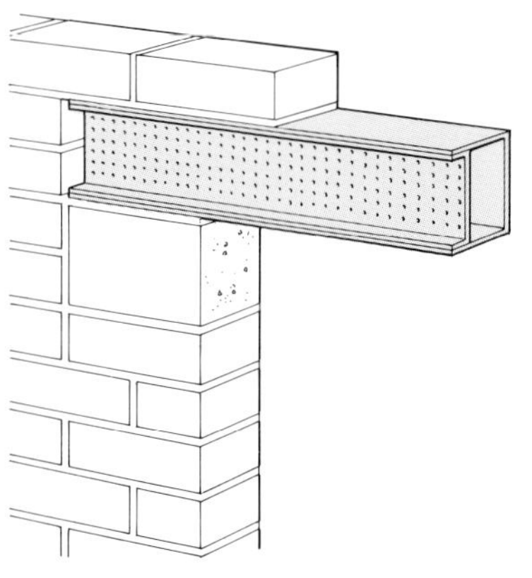

Lightweight pressed steel lintel.

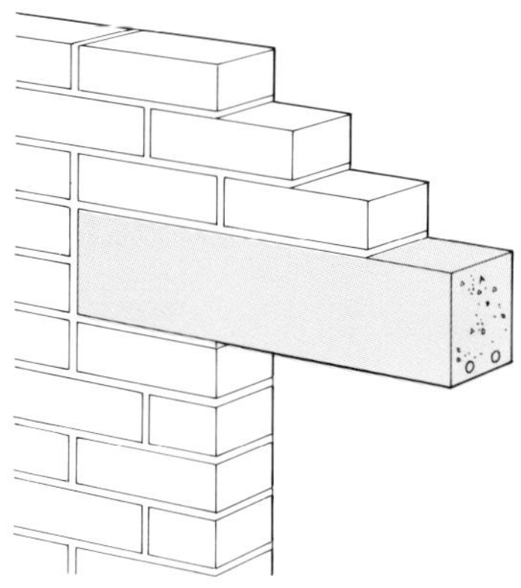

Pre-stressed concrete lintel.

# Forming an arch

You may choose to have a more decorative opening in the form of an arch, possibly with doors and screens. An arch can be structural, to support the construction above, or simply decorative with a hidden beam. There are complex reasons why the design of a structural arch is difficult and hardly justified when a decorative arch is similar in appearance and suitable in all other respects.

**Decorative arch**
One way to create a decorative arch below a beam is to build a brick arch from fair-faced bricks to be left unplastered. A plastered arch can be made by installing a hardboard and batten framework or by using a prefabricated metal unit which forms the frame and is keyed to take the plaster.

**A brick arch** Such an arch needs adequate support from below on piers built up from the ground or supports built into the wall. The arch can be constructed with wedge-shaped bricks, which are soft bricks cut or rubbed to shape and jointed with parallel mortar joints – this is known as a *gauged arch*. Or it can be a *rough arch* constructed with rectangular bricks with wedge-shaped mortar joints. The first method is the superior, but obviously more difficult, form of construction.

For either arch a shaped formwork frame of wood needs to be constructed and temporarily propped in position to support the arch until the mortar has set. The frame and props should be left in position for 14 days.

**A plastered arch** can be formed within a structural opening with, say, a 38mm by 19mm softwood framework fixed to the opening with masonry nails and lined with expanded metal lathing or thin wooden laths as a key for the plaster. Alternatively, the curved face of the framework can be lined with hardboard and the edges with plasterboard.

The advantage of using hardboard is that there is little plastering to be done but there will be a joint to fill (or cover) between the boards and the wall. Plaster on metal or lath is likely to produce the better quality finish. For Plastering see page 260. A simple plastered arch can be made more ornate by incorporating fibrous plaster features – like columns and corbels – around the opening.

**Prefabricated arches** Preformed expanded metal arch frameworks are available in various styles, including semi-circular, gothic and spanish, for spans up to about 3m. Corner pieces are also available to form a wide and spanning arch with the structural beam forming the centre section of the arch. The frameworks are manufactured in two halves which are inserted from either side of the rectangular structural opening formed by the beam. The two halves overlap to allow for a variation in wall thickness of up to 225mm (that is one brick end to end). An infill (soffit) strip is available for thicker arches – up to 450mm (two brick lengths).

The arch framework is fixed into position with galvanised nails or dabs of plaster and then plastered over.

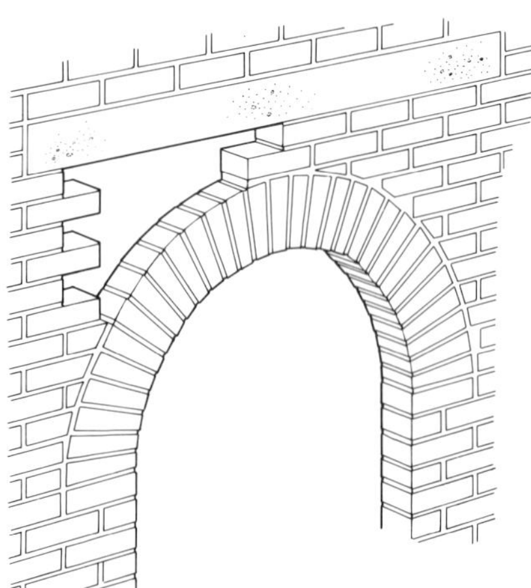
For a gauged arch the bricks are cut to shape against a template and the joints are all regular.

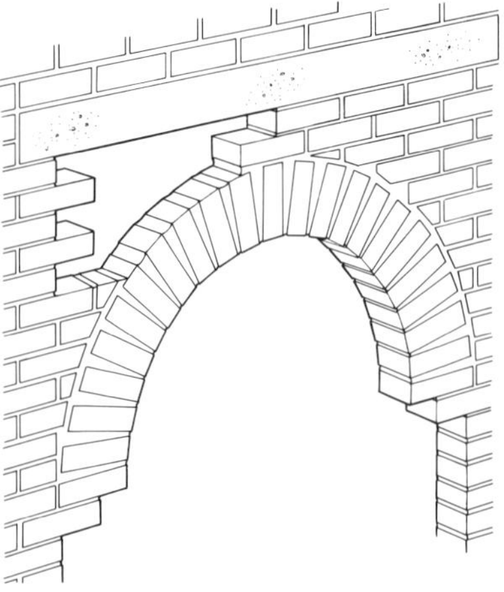
For a rough arch the bricks are uncut and the variation is taken up in the joints.

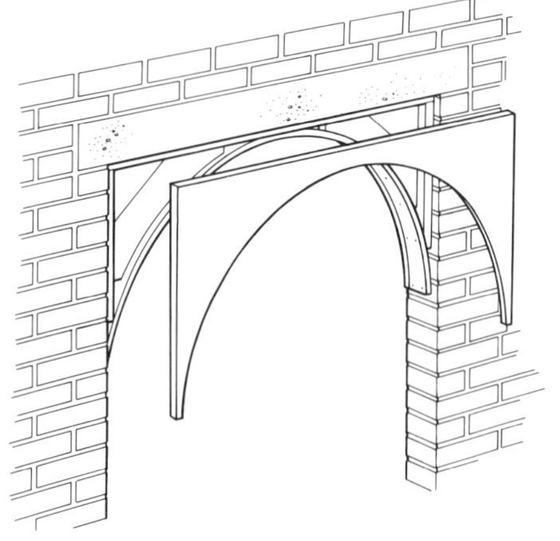
A plastered arch can be built on a batten frame lined with hardboard as shown or with metal lath for plastering.

# Partitions

There are many reasons why you might want to partition a room and there are almost as many types of partition – permanent and fixed or temporary and movable.

## Permanent partitions

The most obvious reason for building a partition is to split a large room into two (or more) smaller rooms. If you do this to provide space for a new bathroom or to create an extra bedroom, the partition will have to be permanent and you'll probably want it to have some degree of sound insulation to give privacy to each of the new rooms. Permanent partitions should also meet the requirements of the Building Regulations.

If both the new rooms are intended to be habitable rooms then each room should have window openings (in Scotland and Inner London the Building Regulations demand this – see page 220; in England and Wales there is only a requirement for ventilation, but daylight is always desirable). Non-habitable space, such as a bathroom, can be an inner room, but must then have mechanical ventilation of some sort.

## Design

The simplest way to split a room in two is to divide it straight across the width. It's also most economical on material for the partition, but it isn't the most imaginative way. Partitions that bend in the vertical plane and or the horizontal plane give more interesting rooms. It's often possible to construct a recess in one room with a corresponding bulkhead in the other.

## Doors

It's worth thinking about where to put the doors. You may keep the door to the original room and provide a door in the partition for access to the new room, but this won't always be satisfactory. The simplest way to get sep-

DIVIDING A ROOM

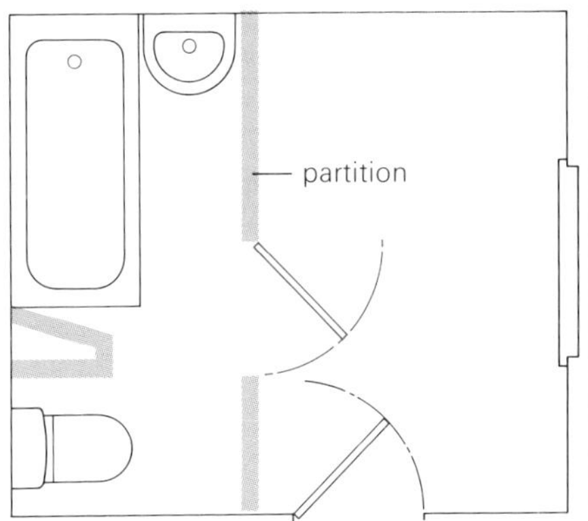

A bathroom can be created as an internal room with mechanical ventilation.

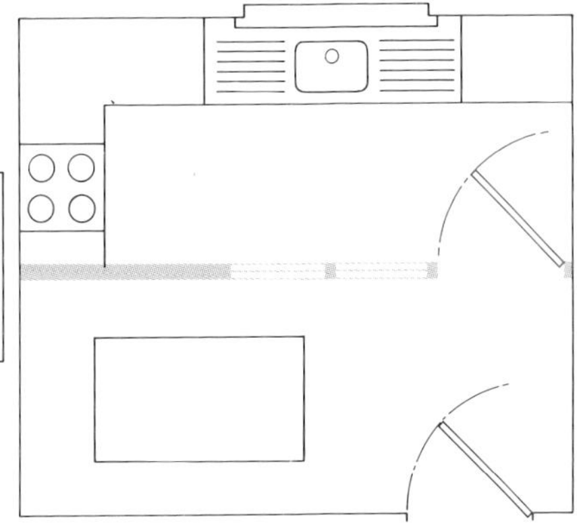

An open or glazed partition can separate the dining area from a kitchen.

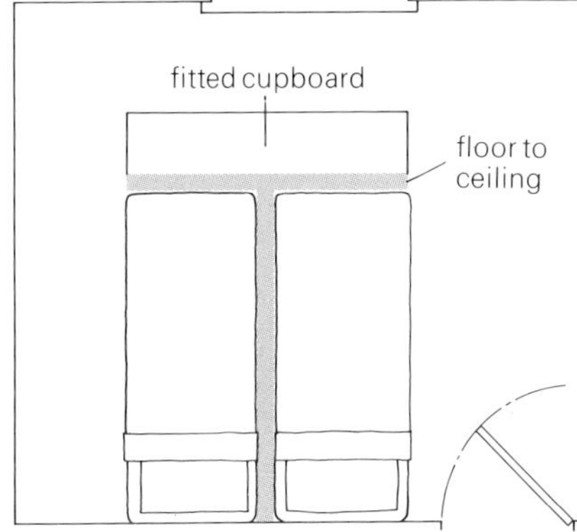


A short floor-to-ceiling partition can give privacy in a children's room.

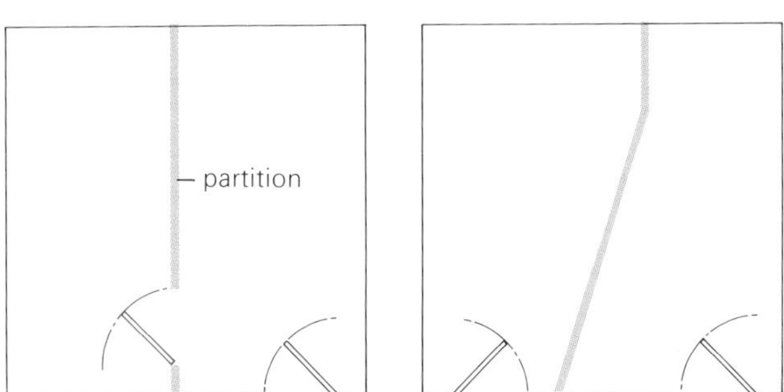


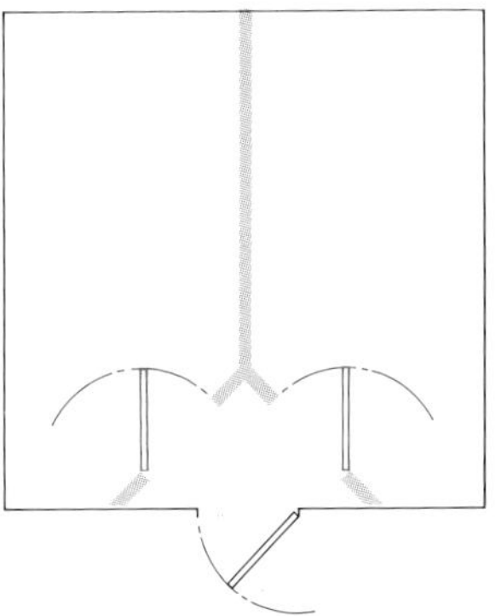

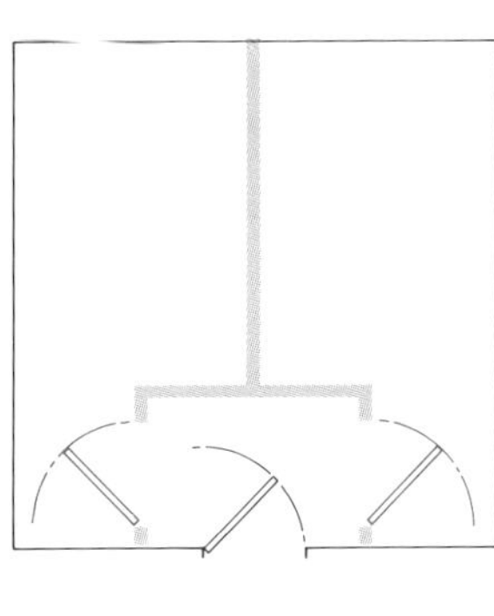

The position of the doors needs careful thought, separate entrances are better in most instances. A new door can open to the corridor or open off a lobby created inside the existing door for more privacy and better soundproofing.

ONE ROOM INTO TWO

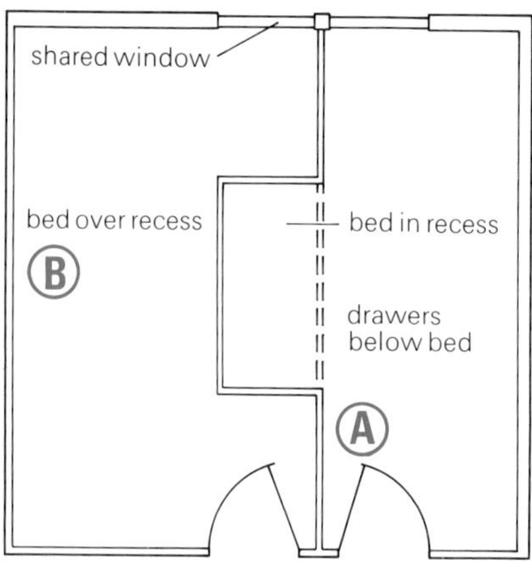


A stud partition between rooms can incorporate recesses (A) and corresponding bulkheads (B) to house furniture and provide storage space.

arate doors may be to partition off a lobby round the existing door and create two new doors – least space is lost if the doors are arranged to create a triangular lobby. Less space still is lost if a second door is made from the corridor to the new room, but this may not always be possible. Note: that a lobby is necessary between a WC and a habitable room unless the WC is 'en suite' with a bedroom and there's another WC in the house.

**Part-partitions**

Partitions that reach part of the way out from a wall or just a metre or so from the floor need careful construction (because there's no end wall for support), but they're useful to separate areas of the room that have different functions and they provide additional wall space for shelves and so on. In a bathroom or a kitchen they're useful, in a bedroom you might use a part-partition to separate a dressing room from the part of the room containing the bed or to give two children sharing a room a little privacy.

**Construction**

When a new partition is required light timber framing faced to match the existing walls usually provides the simplest solution. Plasterboard is often used to face the frame – plasterboard 12·7mm thick gives any necessary fire resistance. A Guide to timber stud wall construction is given on pages 126 and 127.

There are many other materials that can be used to face a timber stud framework. Any of the man-made boards such as hardboard, plywood and chipboard can be used. Timber cladding is another choice.

Permanent partitions can also be built as single-leaf partitions. There are several types of these of which the commonest is probably the box-section plasterboard sandwich panel (which is manufactured by British Gypsum under the brand name Paramount) – see Guide page 128.

**Sound insulation**

Good sound insulation isn't easy to achieve with a stud partition. Increasing the thickness and therefore the density of the partition will help and one way to do this is to use a double layer of plasterboard on one side. Filling the cavity with insulating materials such as glass fibre or mineral wool blanket insulation may also help.

Sound will often still be transmitted by the wall, ceilings and floor around the partition and through any holes around the partition. Sealing these is important, use glass fibre insulating material to fill any crevices, under and between the floorboards, behind the skirting boards and in the roof above. Fill even the smallest cracks with a flexible filler. A door in the partition will reduce the sound insulation between the two rooms.

## MOVABLE PARTITIONS

Movable partitions are useful for when you want to change the shape of a room temporarily or to shut part of it off for some of the time – to save on heating bills, or to make a large room more cosy.

**Doors** Hinged, sliding or folding doors are one possibility – see page 129. You might even consider a patio door (with safety glazing) as the partition between say a kitchen and a dining room. It could be used in conjunction with blinds.

**Blinds** Vertical louvre blinds are particularly versatile and they can be altered to give a closed screen, an open screen or drawn aside completely. Roller blinds are more useful for hiding things behind – to tidy away laundry equipment in a utility room which doubles as a passageway for instance. A firm bottom fixing on both ends of the pole is needed to hold them taut when rolled down. Festoon blinds which fall in folds can be used in bedrooms for a prettier effect.

**Concertina screens** These are like folding doors, but with many more leaves. Depending on the number of leaves they can be used for openings from 350mm to 9·2m wide and up to about 3m high. The leaves are usually chipboard faced with a plastic laminate such as melamine or veneer. They hang from metal ceiling tracks, so the floor is clear. Folded back they fill around one-tenth of the opening and they can be arranged to open from the end, both ends or from the centre.

Vertical blinds.

Concertina screen.

**Freestanding screens** Hinged screens used to be used around chairs in Victorian rooms to cut out draughts. They could be useful around a front door which opens straight into a living room for instance. More substantial taller screens hinged together can be used to create a room within a room, the space behind the temporary walls can be used for storing things, the walls can be moved when the shape loses interest.

Folding doors.

Freestanding screen. ▶

# Constructing a stud partition

It is usually necessary to obtain Building Regulations approval for a timber stud partition. The Building Control Officer will expect to see plans with details of the materials to be used and dimensions of the room, means of ventilation and so on. D-i-y plans should usually be adequate for such a relatively simple project. Plans are worth drawing anyway to use as a shopping list for materials and fixings.

The timber used for non-structural stud partitions can be 75mm by 50mm section for partitions up to approximately 2·4m high and 100mm by 50mm for partitions higher than 2·4m. The timbers adjacent to the existing walls and the floor and ceiling can be 38mm thick and this makes fixing them slightly easier. It is not necessary to have planed timber for partition framing. The timber can be rough sawn, or *regularised*, which means that a small amount of machining has been done to smooth off the surface on two faces.

A partition will normally consist of a top rail, a bottom rail and verticals (studs) at 600mm centres to which the plasterboard or other sheet material lining is fixed.

Most partitions are built in place. As an alternative, it may be more convenient to make the partition laying flat on the floor and then to lift it vertical for fixing to the walls. In this case the partition is made approximately 15mm smaller in height (and length where appropriate) to give a fitting tolerance. The resulting gaps are packed with timber spacers and then covered over by the facing boards.

Attention to the skirting and any ceiling detail of the new wall gives the job a professional finish.

## Step-by-step

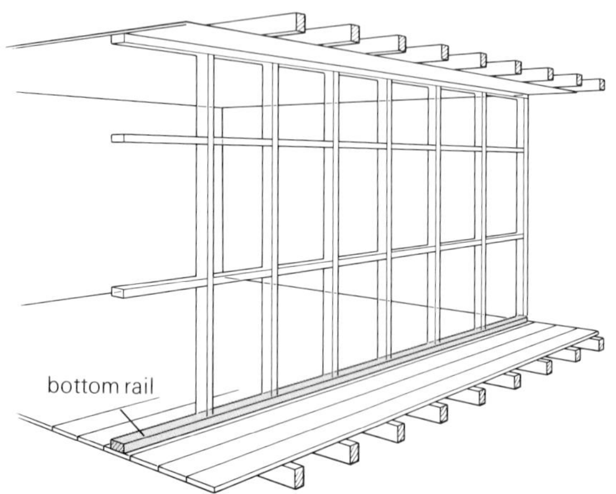


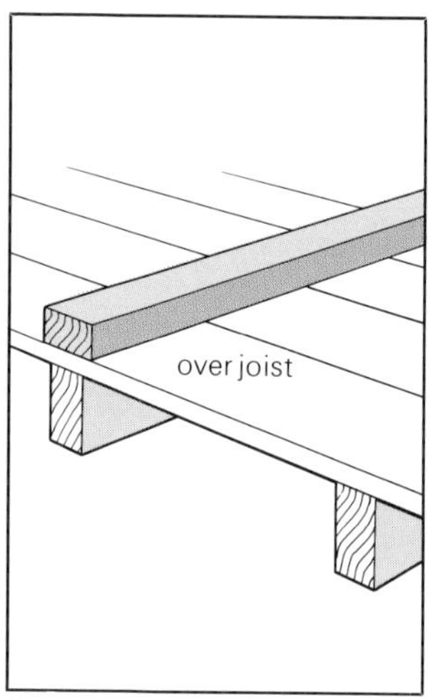


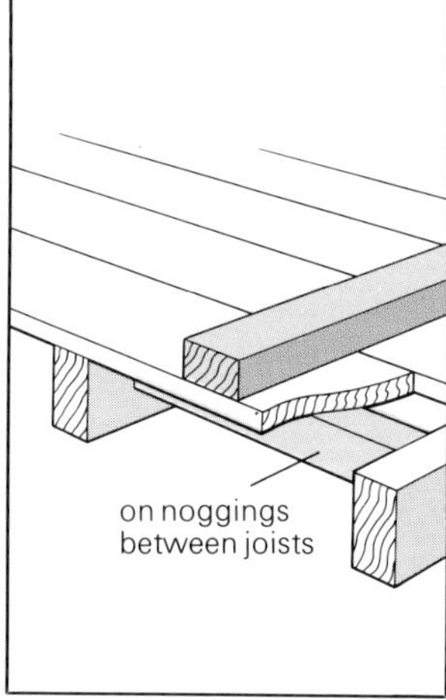


**Step 1** Carefully cut away the adjacent skirtings and any other mouldings, or temporarily remove them from the wall where the new partition adjoins. Then cut and fix the bottom rail of the partition to the floor. Even if the partition is to include a door opening fit a full width rail and cut away the unwanted piece later. If the floor is concrete use 75mm masonry nails (or drill, plug and screw) at approximately 600mm centres. (On a concrete floor, if there's any doubt as to whether a damp-proof membrane is present install a damp-proof course under the bottom rail.)

If the new partition is at right angles to the floor joists the fixings should be into these. If the partition is parallel to the floor joists (and the joists are strong enough) it's easiest to align the partition above a joist. Otherwise take up the floor boarding above and insert supporting cross members (noggings) of at least 100mm by 50mm timber, nailed between the joists so that they fit tight to the floorboard at approximately 1m centres. When short lengths of new partition (up to approximately 2m) are to be constructed, and these will not be required to carry heavy loads, such as wall cupboards in a kitchen, it is acceptable to support the partitions directly from the floor boarding.

Whenever fixings are made into the floor, take care not to puncture any cables or pipes that may be located in it. Also check whether the partition will cross any floorboards which might need to be lifted for access – to a junction box for instance – and if so cut the board and provide a nogging to support the cut ends. Fill any crevices if you want a reasonably soundproof partition.

**Step 2** Fit the bottom rail with screws but before tightening use the plumb line to check that the head and sole plates are vertically aligned. Once the bottom rail is fixed, measure and cut the vertical timbers at the ends of the partition (do them separately, they may be slightly different lengths). Plug and screw the end studs to the walls with 75mm screws at approximately 600mm centres, use packing pieces if necessary. It is important to ensure that these timbers are vertical. When cutting the end timbers to length, leave them sufficiently short to allow for the top rail.

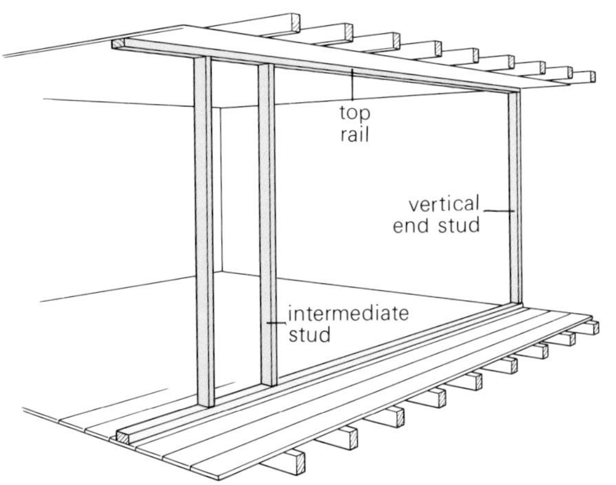


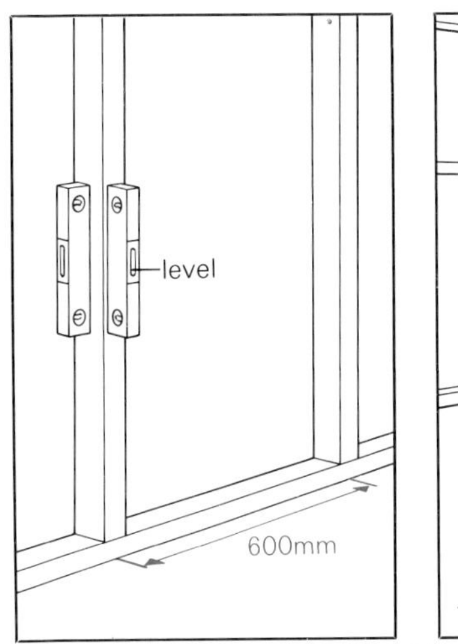


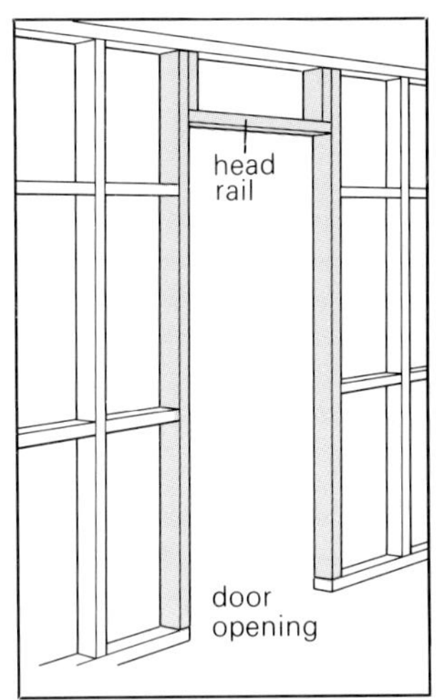


**Step 3** Fix the top rail by nailing through the ceiling plaster into the ceiling joists. These can be found by tapping with a hammer or by drilling small pilot holes along the line of the partition until you locate the timber member or by checking the floor decking nails and measuring from an adjacent wall in the room above.

If the partition is running parallel to the ceiling joists, and is not aligned with a joist insert, noggings between the ceiling joists to provide support.

**Step 4** Measure and cut the intermediate studs, one by one, fitting them by skew-nailing top and bottom at 600mm centres (or whatever is required to suit the lining you intend to use). It is best to work from one end so that any odd dimension for cutting plasterboards is at the other end. Check each stud is vertical in both upright planes. If any openings are required in the partition the necessary dimension should be left between studs. A door head rail must be fitted across the top of the opening between the studs. This rail is nailed through the studs into the end grain of the rail with two nails at each end and extra pieces of timber are inserted above as fixing points for the lining.

A head rail is not fitted if the door is to be installed with a fan-light above. For a door the soleplate will need to be cut away later to clear the threshold.

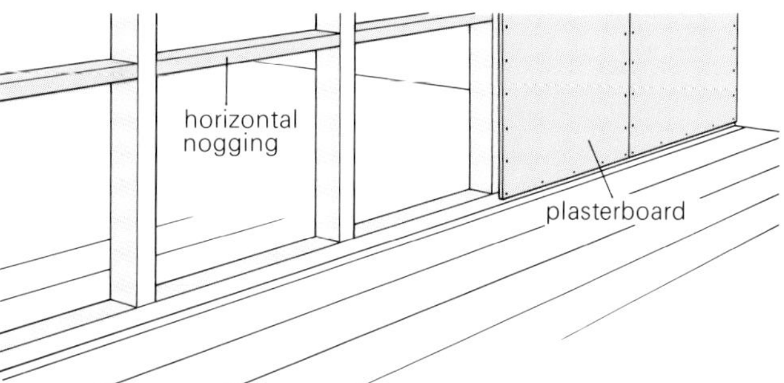


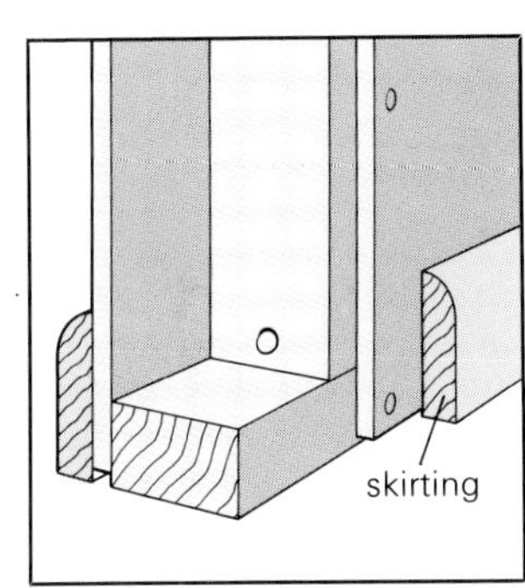


**Step 5** The partition is now ready for lining on both sides. Plasterboard is generally used and for a wall that will be decorated tapered-edge boards are the best choice – see page 260. It may be convenient to fix horizontal noggings, at approximately the mid-height of the partition, in order to stiffen the construction and keep the studs straight. If the partition is taller than one plasterboard length then a nogging is necessary to support the joint between. Fit the full board to the top so that any joint is low down.

Extra noggings should be included at this stage to give fixing points for light switches and any other fittings such as radiators. Fix these noggings by nailing through into the end grain with two nails at each end.

Any electrical services required in the studs can be run within the wall thickness by drilling small holes on the centre line of the studs to take the cable. Centre holes are much better than notches which will weaken the stud structure.

The edge plasterboards should butt to the wall to hide any packing pieces used to keep the end studs vertical. Hold a wide board against the wall and use a long straight edge to mark the centre line of the last stud on the face of the plasterboard, this is your cutting line – it is unlikely to be quite parallel with the edge of the board as most house walls are slightly out of true.

**Step 6** Finish the wall off with skirting board which matches the existing skirting board, nailed through the studs with nails punched low below the surface and filled to give a smooth unmarked line. If matching skirting board is difficult to find you could remove all the skirting board from one of the new rooms and use this to make one matching room, buying new boards for the other room. Otherwise choose a plain skirting the same height as the existing one.

# A single leaf partition

These partitions, sold by British Gypsum under the name Paramount dry partitioning, are prefabricated panels constructed of two leaves of plasterboard separated by, and bonded to, a cellular core. The panels are available (normally to special order) with all three typical plasterboard finishes – ivory-faced with square edges for featured joints or with tapered edges for decorating and grey-faced for plastering with square edges.

There are three sizes of panel. For partitions up to 2.4m high a 50mm thick panel is used; for partitions up to 2·7m high a 57mm thick panel is used; for taller partitions up to 3·6m a 63mm thick panel is used.

Panels are secured to the walls and ceiling and jointed with vertical battens, which should be a good press fit. There is no soleplate, but on the floor the joint between panels is bridged with a 300mm length of batten. This batten is pushed halfway into the panel which has just been fitted and has its leading edge bevelled to make it easier to slide the next panel on.

The panels are installed one at a time by engaging the top of the panel over the ceiling batten and then lifting the panel to bring the bottom into line. Once plumb on the centre line each panel is pushed sideways to engage the battens and butt the preceding panel. (The first panel butts the wall.) Once in place each panel is nailed from both sides to the vertical battens on either side and to the ceiling batten.

If there is an opening in the partition the installation is fairly simple and you work from either side towards the opening fitting any panel which has to be cut to the wall so that the opening is framed by whole panels. If there is no opening you still work in from either end but things are more difficult as the last joint batten has to be introduced between two abutting panels. There is a clever way to do this – see right.

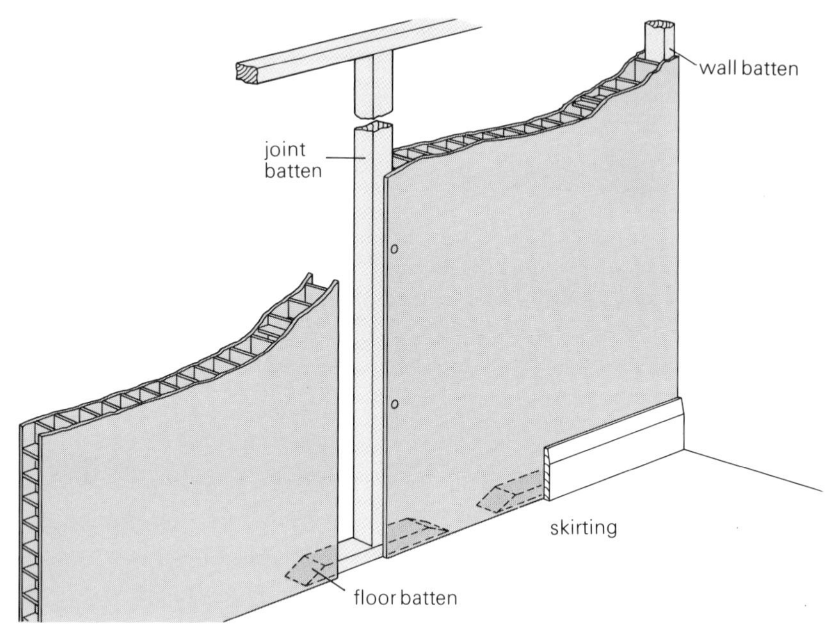


For 50mm or 57 mm thick panels, which are made from 9.7mm thick plasterboard, use 30mm nails; for 63 mm thick panels, which are made from 12·5mm thick plasterboard, use 40mm nails.

Nail at 230mm centres, not less than 10mm from the edge of the board.

For 50mm partitions floor, wall and ceiling battens are 30mm by 19mm and joint battens are 30mm by 37mm; for 57mm and 63mm partitions floor, wall and ceiling battens are 37mm by 19mm and joint battens are 37mm by 37mm.

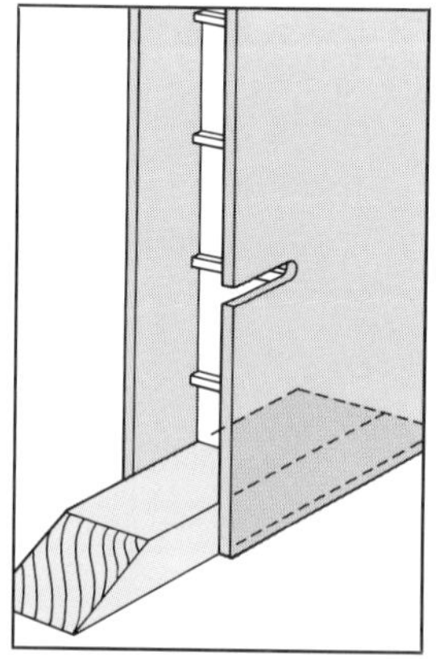

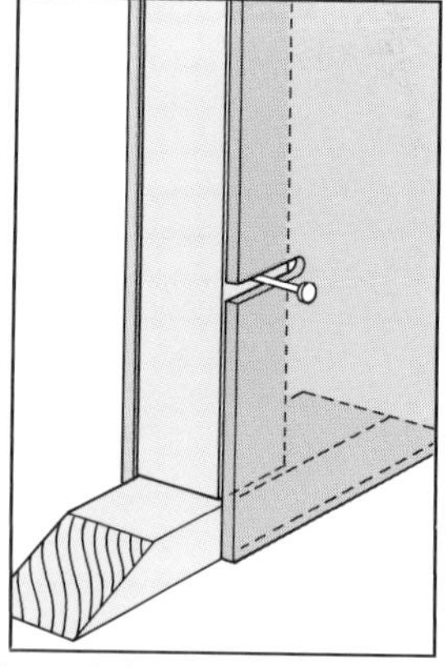

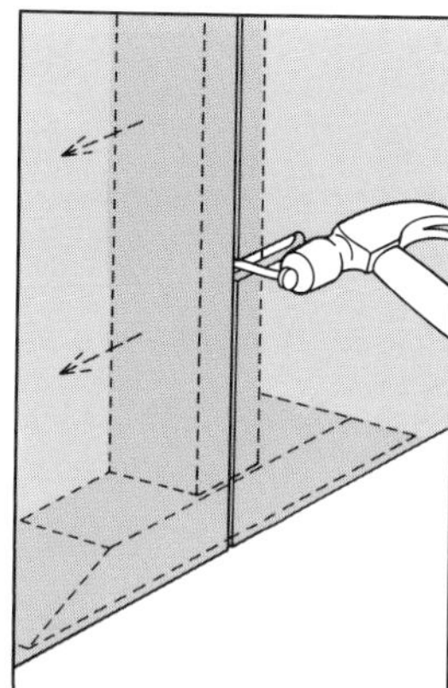

**To fit last panel** Cut three horizontal slots about 20mm long (equally spaced between floor and ceiling) into the vertical edges of each of the panels which sit either side of the space for the last panel. Fit a joint batten into each edge and push this home so that it is flush with the edge of the plasterboard. Insert a 75mm wire nail through each slot, so that it passes through the centre of the joint batten but is left protruding from the slot. Position the last panel over the ceiling batten and lift the bottom edge into place. Then tap the protruding nails sideways, progressing each nail a little at a time until the joint batten bridges the joint. Remove the nails and make good.

# Doors

Doors provide privacy by filling entrance holes in walls. At the same time an external door has to keep out rain, draughts, noise and intruders, an internal door also provides a degree of soundproofing and may need to control the spread of fire.

Internal and external doors are usually made of wood or are part wood, part glass, but there are also all-glass doors and glazed doors with aluminium or plastic (uPVC) frames – see page 134. Although most doors are hinged, there are sliding, folding and tilt-and-turn doors too.

## Types of door

Even in new houses, doors are still mainly imperial sizes, though you find them quoted in mm. The most common size for an internal door is 6ft 6in high by 2ft 6in wide (1981mm by 762mm). External doors can be taller and wider – 6ft 8in (2032mm) by 2ft 8in (813mm) or 2ft 9in (836mm). External doors are usually 1¾in thick (44m), internal doors are normally 1⅜in (35mm).

If your door frame isn't one of the common sizes, you will have to buy the nearest size door above the one you need and cut it to fit – the door should be ⅜in (9·5mm) less than the frame in height and ¼in (6mm) less in width. Whether or not you can trim a door depends on the type. With most panel doors, you can safely saw off up to ¾in (18mm) all round. With most flush doors, unless you buy a special one intended for trimming, you can cut hardly any.

You may be able to buy very cheap second-hand doors from demolition merchants – but you'll need to check them carefully for damage, warping or rot. In an old house a second-hand door may be the only way to get one which matches your other doors. For new doors, builders' merchant or joinery stockists are the best places to shop.

The cheapest sort of door is usually an internal flush door with hardboard facings. Unfinished plywood-faced doors are a bit more expensive, softwood and hardwood doors more expensive still.

It's important to make sure that any softwood door you buy is treated with preservative to prevent rotting. Flush doors are less likely to rot than panel ones and are therefore better for exterior doors.

Hardboard flush doors are less likely to twist than plywood ones and hemlock is probably the best material for panel doors. Neither hardboard nor hemlock is a good material for an external door.

### Flush hinged wooden doors

Flush doors consist of a light wooden framework of horizontal rails and vertical stiles, faced side. The hollow centre (core) of the door is filled to help support the facings. The cheapest flush doors have only small amounts of core material – a strong paper honeycomb, for example. Most expensive is a solid core of chipboard or strips of wood laminated together. A flush door that doesn't have a solid core generally won't be able to hold screws, so a piece of wood – called a lock block – is fixed to the stile to cope with locks, latches and handles. You can't see where the lock block is, because the facing covers it up and it isn't always marked. An external door will also need a letter plate block or centre rail.

To make a neat edge covering up the stiles and the edges of the facings, flush doors have a lipping. Lipping is essential on external doors, to help stop water seeping in under the facings.

There are many different sorts of facing for flush doors – from cheap hardboard to expensive hand-cut veneers on carefully-selected plywood. There's not a lot to choose between plywood and hardboard facings of a given thickness. If you want a door to stand up to a rough treatment, pick one with a thick facing – at least 4mm, say. Weight is quite a good guide to how well a flush door will stand up to rough treatment – the heavier the better.

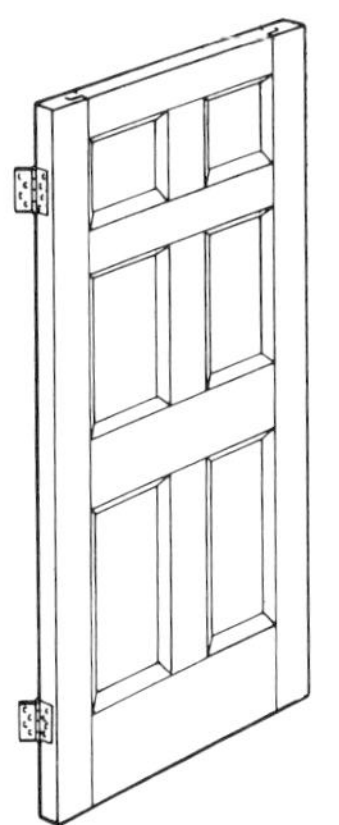

Panel door.

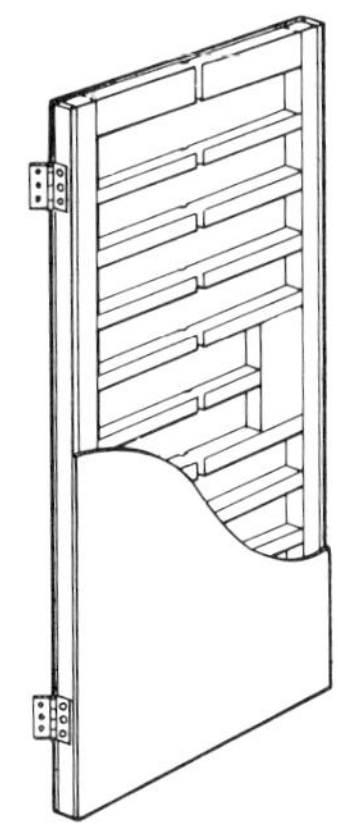

Flush door.

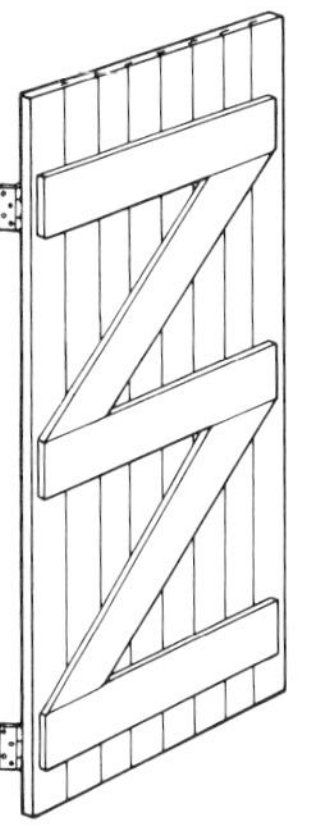

Ledged and braced door.

### Panel doors

Panel doors have a framework of substantial rails and stiles, fixed together by woodworking joints. There are many combinations of part-glass and part-wood panel doors as well as all-wood and all-glass.

Traditionally, panel doors have had mortice-and-tenon joints, but you're now more likely to find dowelled joints. A centre rail provides extra strength to the door and is also convenient for mounting a letter-box. It also gives a sort of lock block for extra-deep locks, though using the centre rail for this isn't a good idea because you can weaken its joint with the stile.

Wooden panels are often plywood – you need to make sure this is an exterior grade of plywood for external doors.

Doors for glazing are usually sold unglazed. Some door suppliers stock safety glass in standard sizes to fit their doors. Although expensive safety glass (laminated or toughened) is the best choice for low level glass and any other glass which is in a hazardous position.

### Boarded doors

Boarded doors are made of tongued-and-grooved vertical boards, about 100mm wide, held together with horizontal ledgers. The simplest sort of boarded door has only ledgers but, to help prevent sagging, doors should also have diagonal braces. These types (also available as stable doors) aren't really suitable for front or back doors. More substantial boarded doors have a frame.

### Panel-look flush doors

There are flush doors which look like panel doors. Door makers do this in two ways. One is by fixing raised wooden moulding, in panel-like patterns, to the facing of the door – out of doors this might cause problems if water can seep behind the moulding. The other way is to mould hardboard facings into panel shapes before fixing them to the framework.

### Aluminium doors

Aluminium external doors are sold complete with aluminium frames. These could be a useful way of replacing a badly-rotted door and frame, but they are *very* expensive.

### Fire-resisting doors

To satisfy the Building Regulations, you may sometimes need to fit a door that will give half an hour's resistance to fire – for example, doors that open on to the hall and landings if you've put a room in your loft, or between the house and an attached garage. Fire-resisting doors are flush ones – usually with a plasterboard or asbestos core.

To comply fully with the regulations, you usually also have to modify the door frame and make the door self-closing.

### All-glass doors

For safety, all-glass doors are made of toughened glass. This can't be cut once it's made, so you need to measure your door frame carefully, and make sure it's square.

### Sliding doors

If you haven't got room to allow an ordinary hinged door to open properly, you might think of installing a sliding door between rooms. You generally buy the gear and use this with an existing door. If you want to use your existing door and it's slightly narrow you can fix wooden battens (liners) to the door frame.

Patio doors are a type of sliding door with a large expanse of glass (which must be safety glass). They bear more resemblance to windows than doors – see page 138.

### Folding doors

There are two sorts of folding door. The bi-fold door which has two (or four) leaves, each half a doorway wide – typically 1ft to 1ft 6in per door – and the concertina-type door which has many narrower (around 13½in) leaves hinged together, to fold up, like a concertina, within the door frame. This type of folding door never lies completely flat and takes up a fair amount of the doorway width – about a tenth – when folded back, but it can be installed curved as well as straight. (To get round the width of the folded door it is possible to form a recess in the door jamb into which the door can fold.)

You normally buy a folding door complete with panels and track. Bi-folded doors are sold as complete sets, but you can also buy the doors and gear separately. As well as flush and louvre wooden bi-fold doors, there are mirrored bi-folds – made from mirrored glass mounted on steel panels.

### Tilt-and-turn doors

These are a fairly new innovation which have developed alongside uPVC windows. They are exterior doors with a frame and picture glass, which should be safety glass, which can be operated normally on side hinges or, by moving a handle; be tilted inwards from the top to provide controlled ventilation which is secure against intruders. They're available only in uPVC, which is usually white, and are expensive.

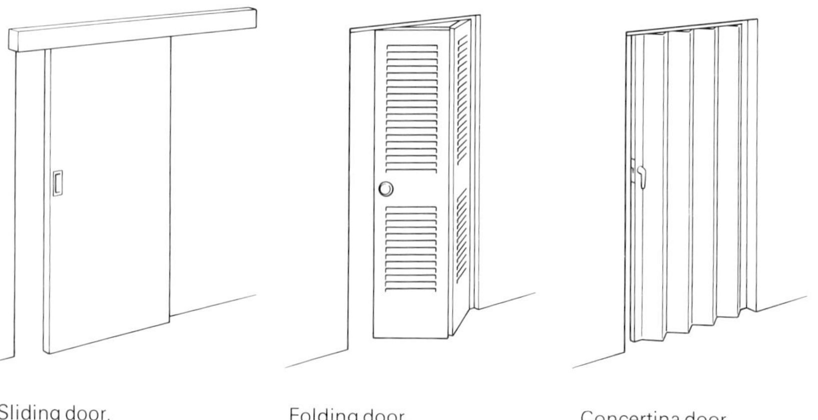

Sliding door. Folding door. Concertina door.

# Moving a door

Moving a doorway or closing up an unnecessary one is a fairly simple job which can have a significant effect on the way you utilise space – amongst other things it can help to make a room feel larger and make it easier to position furnishings. There are two parts to the job: removing the existing door and door frame and blocking up the opening, and then creating a new hole, lining it and fitting a new door.

Very often a light switch will have to be moved to a new position – see page 48 *et seq*.

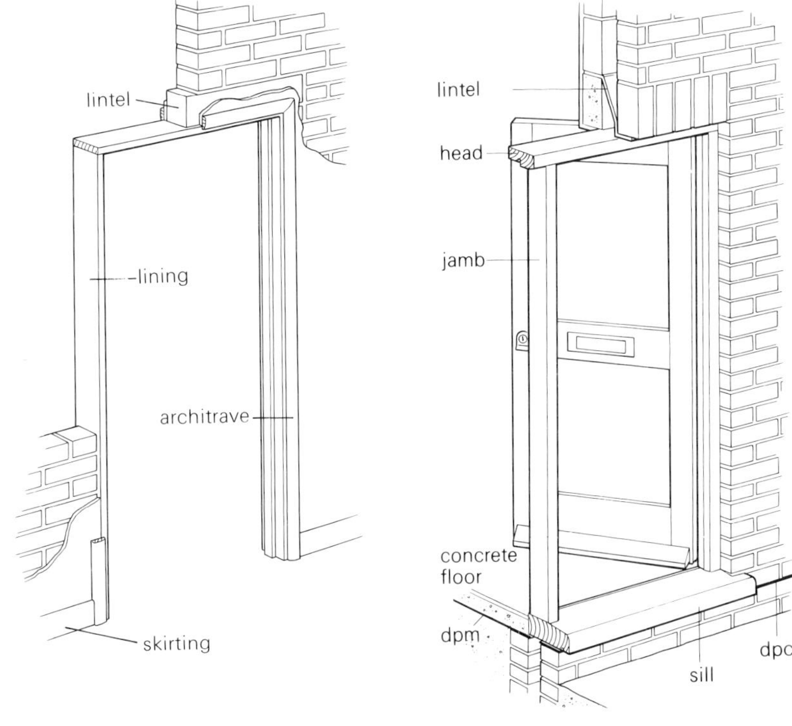


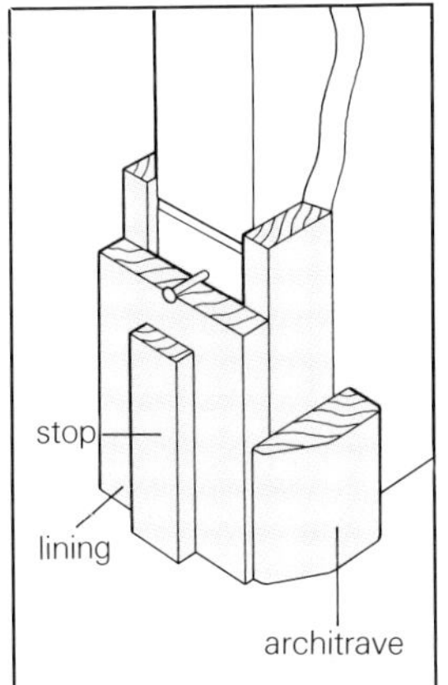


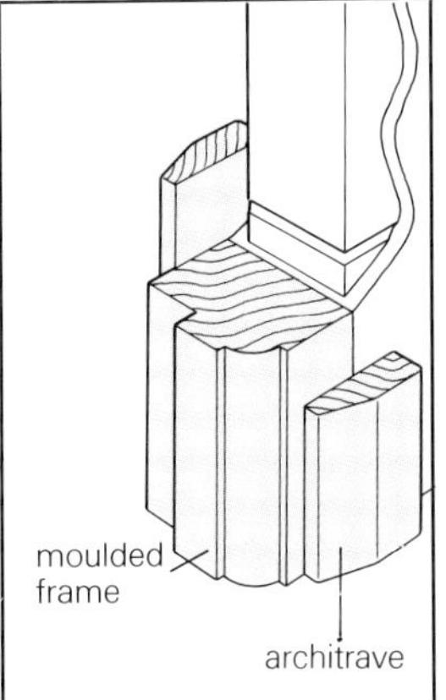


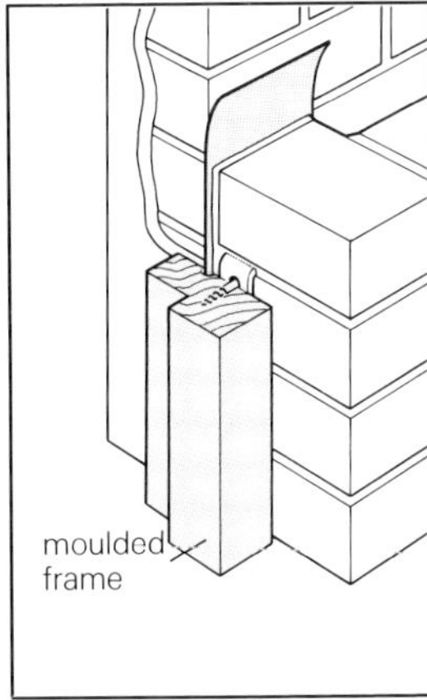


Internal doorways have a lining the thickness of the wall and joints are covered with an architrave. External doorways have a frame narrower than the wall.

## Removing the door frame

When the door is to be reused, remove it from the frame or lining to avoid damage. It is usually most convenient to disconnect the hinges first. Sometimes, the securing screws are difficult to loosen in which case, clean out the paint from the screw head slots, place an old screwdriver in position and hit it with a hammer (or try heating the screws with a blowlamp). When the door is to be scrapped or if it is not excessively heavy, it can be left closed and removed together with its lining or frame.

### What you'll find

Internal doorways usually have a wooden lining which is equal to the thickness of the masonry wall plus the plaster thickness. The joint between the faces of the lining and adjoining plaster is covered with a wooden moulding called an architrave. There is also a piece of wood to stop the door. This planted door stop may look as if it is integral with the lining, but close inspection will usually show that it is nailed on.

For all external doors and for internal doors which are installed in fair-faced brickwork a frame is provided. The dimensions of a door frame are less than the thickness of the wall. Often cover moulds are provided to cover the joint between masonry or plaster and door frame and, usually, the skirting overlaps the joint.

Architraves, cover moulds, skirtings, dado rails and picture rails are usually nailed to the frame or lining and before work can start on the frame (or lining) itself, these fixings need to be removed. Normally they can be gently prised off with an old wood chisel using some gentle persuasion with a hammer or mallet.

When the frame or lining is taken out the lintel carrying the masonry above the opening remains – it's

REMOVING THE FRAME

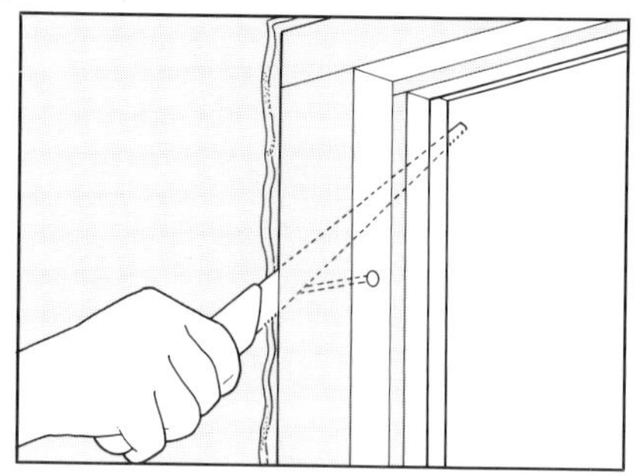

Depending upon the age of the building, the frame or lining will be packed with wood packing pieces and either plugged and screwed or nailed to the wall and often the lintel. Often, it is possible to remove the screws, but it is virtually impossible to remove nails. Planted door stops may have to be prised away to get at screwheads. Usually, the easiest and quickest method of taking out the door frame or lining is to cut the fixings from behind. Scrape out the joint between wall and frame with a hammer and chisel – and then ease a hacksaw into the gap and saw through the fixings.

Sometimes, the jambs have steel dowel rods set into a concrete floor – these dowels may also have to be cut with a hack-saw.

Having released the fixings, often the frame or lining is still secure and you will need to ease the frame or lining backwards and forwards until it works loose.

easiest to leave this in place and fill the space below.

## Blocking up the opening

If the wall is fairfaced the filling must match the existing. When the wall is to be plastered, the choice of materials, is not so important, timber frame is often easiest.

### Timber-frame fill

This may be a better choice for a first floor opening to be blocked but it will have less good sound reducing properties. Install a frame of timber the width of the opening less the depth of the plasterboard to be used for facing. If appropriate a hardwood fill could be used and the opening framed as an alcove to be fitted with a mirror or shelving perhaps. Or the existing lining and the architrave on one side could be left in place to achieve a similar effect.

### Masonry infill

With a masonry infill, the ideal form of construction is to tooth every course. This is necessary for good appearance when the wall is fairfaced but block bonding where three or four courses are toothed together is usually satisfactory when the wall is to be plastered or plasterboarded.

A straight vertical joint is easier to make. Although it is likely to result in an identifying crack in the plaster caused by movement of the new masonry, any crack that develops after plastering can usually be made good with filler.

## Making a new opening

Cutting through a wall to make a new door opening isn't nearly as drastic as knocking down a whole wall and most handymen should be able to tackle it. The procedure for making the hole is much the same, you start from the centre and work downwards and outwards leaving the top brickwork until last. A lintel is usually required across the top of the opening to support the masonry above which should be propped while the opening is made – see page 116. The lintel should bear on at least 110mm of masonry on either side.

Unless the door position is absolutely crucial, it should be possible to cut your opening so that at least one side lines up with the edge of alternate bricks so that as few bricks as possible need to be cut. Neat square sides to an opening can be achieved using an angle grinder.

A masonry fill can be toothed at alternate courses (as shown) or in blocks. Or simply be built with a vertical joint.

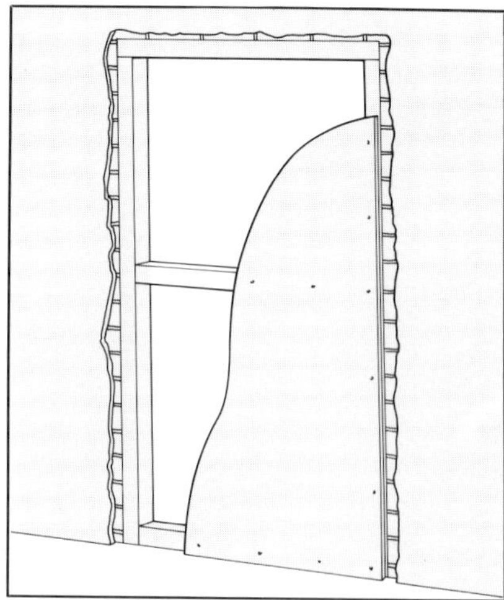

A timber frame can be constructed inside the opening and lined with plasterboard.

# Fitting a door

## Step-by-step

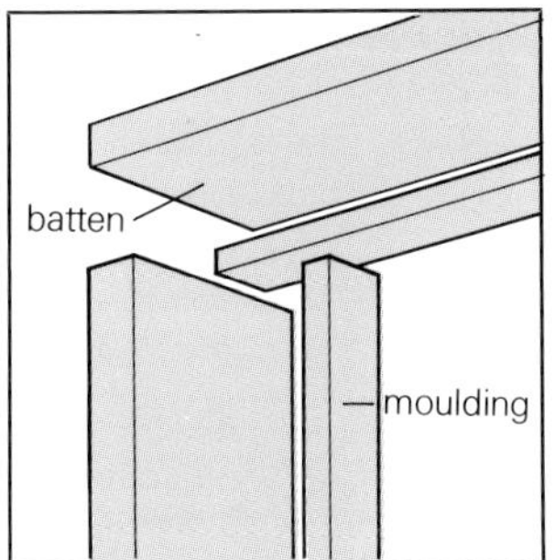


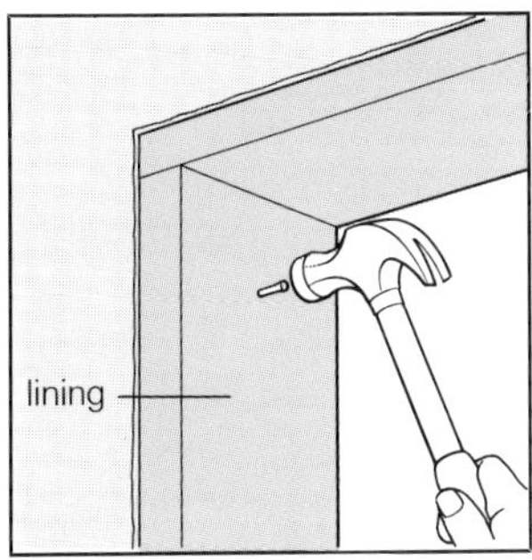


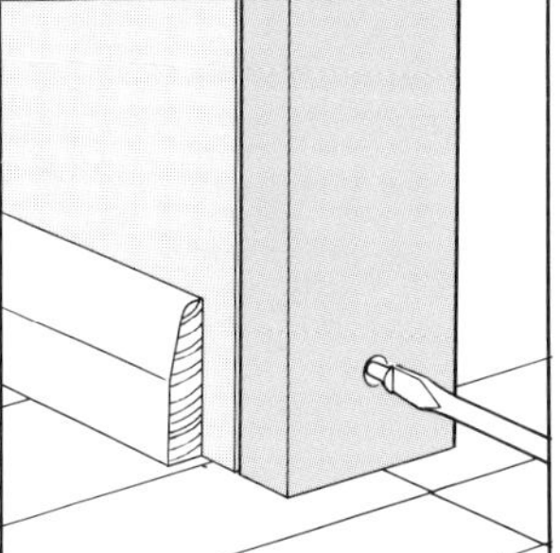

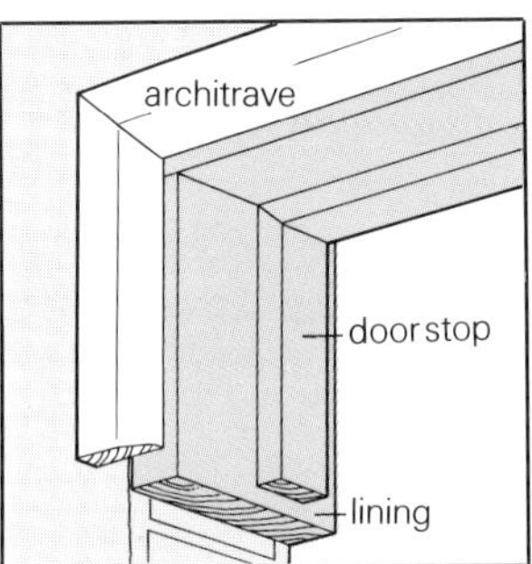


**To fit a new door in an existing lining start the Guide at step 1. A completely new opening will need a new lining and architrave.**

A new lining can be constructed from simple planed-all-round timber batten – the depth of the wall (100mm) deep and 50mm wide – with a moulding (called a doorstop) – nailed on the batten in the right position to stop the door. Otherwise a recessed door jamb – 63mm deep and 100mm wide – can be used.

In a newly-formed opening in an existing masonry wall it may be possible to build in fixing pellets of wood slotted into joints raked out in the bricks or blocks. Alternatively, the lining can be fixed with masonry nails punched below the surface or with screws countersunk into plugged holes drilled into the brick. Use fixings long enough to penetrate through the lining and extend about 50mm or 60mm into the wall. If the wall is a stud partition of timber frame, the lining can be screwed into the studs surrounding the opening.

The lining itself can be butt jointed at the top corners but the doorstop mouldings and door jambs need to be mitred for a good appearance. Before fixing the frame check that it is plumb down the sides and that the top is level. The lining may need packing to achieve this.

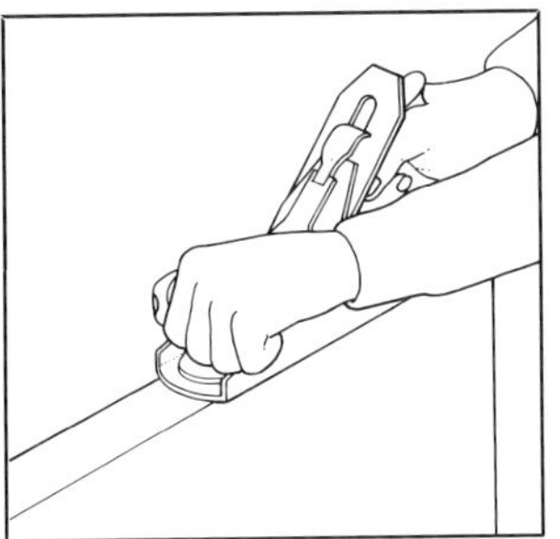

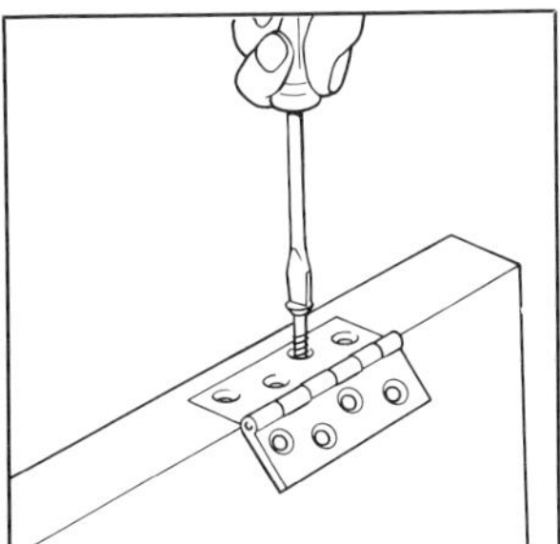

**Hanging the door**

**Step 1** Many new panel doors have horns – bits of the stiles that project beyond the top and bottom of the door. These protect the corners of the door until it's ready to be hung. Saw off the horns – preferably with a tenon saw. For an external door coat cut edges and new wood with preservative.

**Step 2** Put the door against the frame with the side to be hinged firmly up against it. Stand the door on a piece of packing or use wedges to raise it about 6mm off the ground. Allow for floor coverings and for any slope in the floor). Mark the position of the door on the frame. If the door is much smaller than the frame at any point, fit battens of wood to the door frame, and start again.

**Step 3** Transfer the measurements of any overlap from the door frame to the door, then subtract about 6mm from the side and 3mm from the top – to allow clearance all round the door. If you have to cut off a lot, divide the amount between the top and the bottom of both sides. If you cut anything off the hinge side make sure it's still vertical – see page 129 for how much you can safely trim.

**Step 4** Carefully plane off the door. When planing the top and bottom rails, work from the ends inwards, so that you don't splinter the edges. (A door can fit more snugly if its non-hinged side is very slightly angled – to clear the frame as it closes. Doors rarely come with angled edges, with care, you could plane the angle yourself.)

**Step 5** Check that the door fits properly in the frame and that it leaves the correct clearance. Mark the position of the hinges on the door and, if necessary, on the frame. It's a good idea to paint the bottom of the door at this stage.

**Step 6** The knuckle of the hinge should be just clear of the edge. Chop out the recess with a sharp chisel to about as deep as the thickness of the flap part of the hinge. Screw the hinges to the door making sure to use the right size of screws – they should fit neatly into the countersunk holes provided. Cut recesses in the door frame if necessary. Check the hinge position first. With wedges taking the weight of the door, fix the hinges to the door frame with one screw in each – start with the top hinge. Check that the door opens and closes properly. If it doesn't and there is sufficient clearance all round you probably recessed the hinges too much or too little. Too much is tricky – you'll have to pack the recess with bits of cardboard. When the door fits, put the other screws in.

# Windows

Windows are an important feature of every house, their main functions are to let light in and allow the occupants to see out. But they also reflect a house's architectural character (and can make or mar it). In some parts of the country, particularly in conservation areas, the planning authorities have strict rules about what you can and cannot do to the existing windows. Basically the planning authorities require that whatever you do doesn't destroy the balance or character of the dwelling. For instance you are sometimes not allowed to replace timber windows with metal-framed ones. Even if your house has no great architectural or historical importance, it is important to get the window proportions right.

## Window choices

Replacement windows and patio doors can be timber (softwood or hardwood), aluminium or plastic (unplasticised polyvinyl chloride – uPVC). All are available made-to-measure to fit exactly into an existing opening, but wooden made-to-measure windows are less easy to come by than aluminium and uPVC ones, which are supplied and fitted by many small local firms and a dozen or so large national ones who advertise widely. There are only one or two large manufacturers making made-to-measure timber windows, most are made locally by small joinery firms who may make from scratch or from stocks of timber sections. They are usually able to match existing windows.

Of the three materials timber is the cheapest *even when made-to-measure*. It's cheaper still if you are able to use an off-the-shelf wooden window in one of the standard sizes. It's always worth checking whether a standard-size one will fit (or could be adapted to fit). The simplest way to check is to measure the wall opening inside and out. Add about 40mm to the internal width to allow for plaster and then compare the two measurements – if one is greatly different from the other the opening probably has some sort of rebate and you'll probably need a window, without an integral sill, which can be fitted from the inside. Ask at a builders' merchants, timber merchants or joinery depot whether there's a standard window to fit – it will need about 6mm tolerance all round.

Off-the-shelf wooden windows vary from relatively cheap softwood-framed side-hung or top-hung windows without weatherstripping and with narrow rebates for single glazing to high-performance double-glazed windows in hardwood – prices go up accordingly. In between there's a new Energy Saving window (in softwood or hardwood) with weatherstripping and a rebate suitable for double glazing.

Aluminium and uPVC windows are also available off-the-shelf, but they are not much cheaper than made-to-measure ones and unlike the standard wooden window, they're not easy to adapt to fit a slightly smaller or larger opening.

### Material facts

The Table gives details of the main materials.

**Price** Softwood is by far the cheapest, closely followed by hardwood, then aluminium and uPVC.

**Glazing** Aluminium and uPVC windows are dry glazed in the factory with a gasket: reglazing is not usually a do-it-yourself job. Timber windows may be double glazed in the factory, but many are glazed on site using a non-setting glazing compound which provides a flexible seal around the double glazing unit. Linseed oil putty can be used for single glazing wooden windows provided the window will be painted. If it is stained, beads and mastic are used for glazing.

**Shape and style** With timber windows, it's possible to have curves and arches; aluminium and uPVC windows usually have to be square or rectangular. Timber can also be made to match the existing which is useful for an extension or if only a few of the windows have deteriorated beyond repair. Aluminium has the advantage of slim sections, so will cut out the minimum of light. UPVC windows can have 'slimline' sections similar in size to wood and will match in quite well with wooden windows. With tilt-and-turn styles, the uPVC sections are usually more bulky.

Aluminium windows and patio doors usually require a timber subframe in the window opening and this is often hardwood. You can also have the windows fitted to an existing sound timber subframe. Subframes are always needed (for uPVC as well as aluminium frames) if the opening is not completely square or if the old window provided any support for the brickwork above and you're not intending to have a supporting lintel fitted.

**Insulation** We give the *U-value* of a double-glazed window (the lower the U-value the less heat is lost – see Chapter 7). Aluminium has a fairly high U-value and manufacturers have sought to overcome the heat loss through the frame, by making the window from two pieces joined by a material with a lower U-value (usually a plastic resin or foam) called a 'thermal break'. These solutions may also help prevent condensation on aluminium frames, though a thermal break may not be successful if the aluminium is badly jointed at the corners and air can get into the frame and cool the metal surface. The energy performance of any window is of little value if it is necessary to open a large sash to obtain ventilation. Many window manufacturers offer small hit-and-miss ventilators which allow a small trickle of ventilation. These are recommended, especially for the main rooms (including the bedrooms) of the house, since without some small amount of ventilation condensation is inevitable. All but the cheapest off-the-shelf softwood frames have weather seals to ensure a good fit.

**Finish** Both treated softwood and hardwood window frames can be decorated externally with paint or with the more recently introduced decorative stains. Paint and stains are available in a large range of colours. In certain localities stains can require more frequent maintenance than paintwork, but the task is much simpler, simply brushing or washing down and redecorating. Aluminium and plastic are usually white or silver.

**Maintenance** Timber needs regular attention. Aluminium and uPVC frames are fundamentally maintenance free, but aluminium requires regular washing to avoid corrosion and, of course, any timber sub-frame will need attention.

**Durability** It's difficult to predict how long windows will last and there's probably not a lot to choose between the materials. Provided they're properly maintained, a life of 50 years or more wouldn't be unreasonable. In the past it was common for badly-maintained softwood windows to deteriorate, but modern windows of preservative-treated softwood or hardwood can, given sensible maintenance, be expected to last as long as the building in which they are installed. If you buy a softwood made-to-measure window, ask for it to be preservative-treated – as all off-the-shelf ones are.

**Window frame materials**

| | aluminium alloy | timber | uPVC (unplasticised polyvinyl chloride) |
|---|---|---|---|
| shape and style | square or rectangular only. Slim sections | any shape or style; bulky sections | usually square or rectangular slim or bulky sections |
| typical insulation (U-value) | 4.3W/m²°C (3·7W/m²°C with 'thermal break') | *hardwood* 2·7W/m²°C *softwood* 2·5W/m²°C | 2·5W/m²°C |
| finish | satin anodising (matt silvery grey) or factory applied white paint are the most common. Other colours are occasionally available | *hardwood*– usually treated with a preservative stain in natural wood colour. Sometimes clear varnished which can give a more glossy finish. Can be painted if required *softwood*– usually supplied primed and requires painting. Unprimed windows can be stained instead | white is most common, grey and brown may be offered |
| maintenance | require washing with a mild (non-alkaline) washing-up liquid at least once every three months in towns or by the sea, once every six months in the country. Painted finishes need less frequent cleaning. Wooden subframes also need attention | *hardwood*– stains need re-applying every three years or so but if a low-build stain is used almost no surface preparation is required; varnish needs rubbing down and re-applying every three years or so *softwood*– if painted rub down and repaint every five years at least. Stain as above | requires occasional cleaning with a mild non-abrasive washing-up liquid solution – not bleach or washing powder. No decorating needed A wooden subframe if used will need attention |
| durability | alkaline or abrasive cleaners will damage anodised surfaces – slight damage can be polished out with sandpaper. After 20 years or so if the window hasn't been washed often enough, an anodised finish may need painting. Wooden subframes may rot | *hardwood*– mahogany-like hardwoods are moderately durable. *softwood*– must be preservative treated. Rot is main problem if protective finishes are allowed to deteriorate. Hardeners and fillers are available to repair rotten timber | uPVC is unlikely to deteriorate. Main problem is due to broken joints if badly fitted. Can be scratched or affected by naked flame; polish out slight damage with fine sandpaper. Could need painting after 20 years or so |

# Installing a window

Installing a window in an existing wall may mean removing the old one and fitting a replacement of the same size or may mean adapting an existing opening to take a new size of window (larger or smaller) or cutting a completely new opening. As the structure will be altered you'll need Building Regulations approval for the last two.

## A new opening

The principles of cutting holes are outlined on page 116 *et seq.* A window opening no more than 900mm wide can often be cut safely without temporary supports, but if in any doubt take advice. No opening should be too close to a corner, other opening or end of a wall or it will weaken the structure – this is the sort of thing the building control authority will look for.

Start by cutting out the joints of a masonry unit, in the centre of the opening and about 450mm below the lintel. Cut the joints with a plugging chisel and club hammer or drill them out with a masonry drill. Tap the masonry unit out with the hammer, then, gently tap out the masonry units on either side. Work carefully upwards tapping along each horizontal joint in turn until you are at a level one or two courses above the top of the lintel. If you are careful, the masonry above the opening may not fall, if the units become loose or fall out, they will need to be replaced.

Form the bearing recess for the lintel. The lintel can be any of those described on page 242. If the lintel used is not a combination type, a dpc tray must be provided to catch rainwater which penetrates the external leaf.

The dpc tray is bedded in the mortar joint immediately above the lintel in the outer leaf and bedded into a masonry joint about 150mm higher on the inner leaf. If the inner leaf is timber frame the tray is fixed with galvanised nails. (To get access to the inner leaf it may be necessary to remove another course of masonry from the outer leaf.)

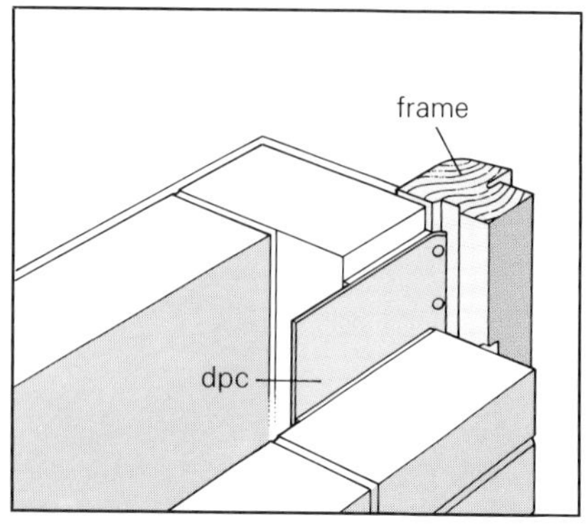


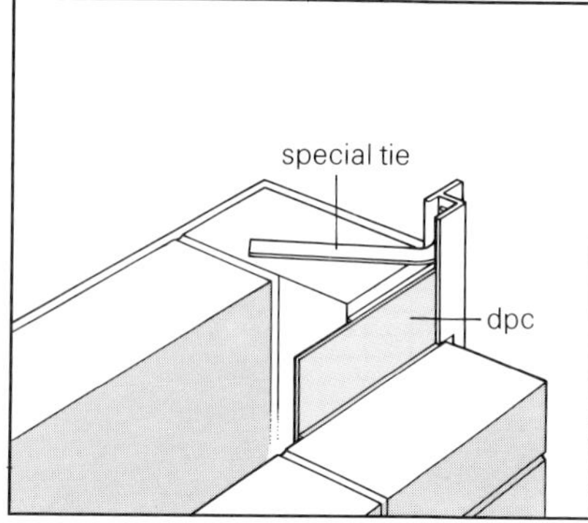


A dpc is needed around all openings. The vertical piece is nailed in the groove in the frame and tucked into the cavity.

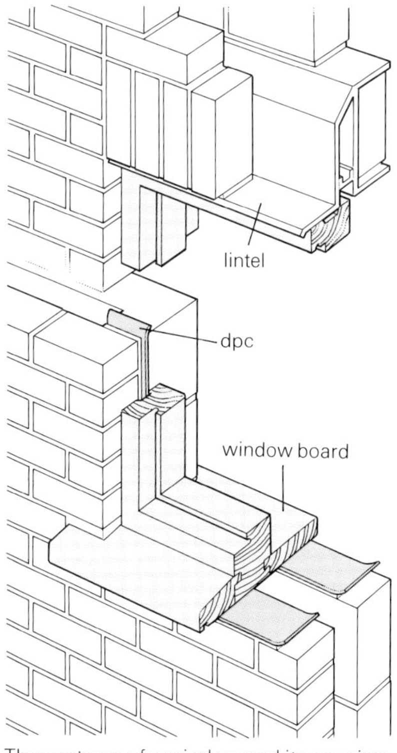


The anatomy of a window and its opening.

Bed the lintel in mortar and cover the opening with polythene sheet. After two or three days, when the lintel bedding has set, any loosened or missing masonry units above can be replaced and made good.

Except in exposed positions weep holes are provided above the lintel in the outer leaf of a cavity wall. These are formed by cutting the mortar out of every other vertical joint in the course immediately above the joint containing the dpc tray.

After about seven days, work can continue with creating the opening below the lintel to receive the door or window frame and any temporary props can be removed. When the opening is being trimmed to size, that is, about 6mm bigger all round than the frame the cavity is normally closed by cut-bricks incorporated in the one leaf of the wall. A vertical dpc is installed at the junction of the cavity closing masonry and the face of the other leaf of the wall. The other end of the dpc is tucked into the groove in the back of the window frame. If it is wide enough, this dpc can be carried forward to protect the side of the window frame from the ingress of water.

If both leaves of the wall are masonry, hardwood plugs can be provided for fixing the window. These are tapped into raked out horizontal bed joints at about 450mm centres. Otherwise the window can be screwed and plugged directly to the masonry – see opposite.

# Replacing a window

## Step-by-step

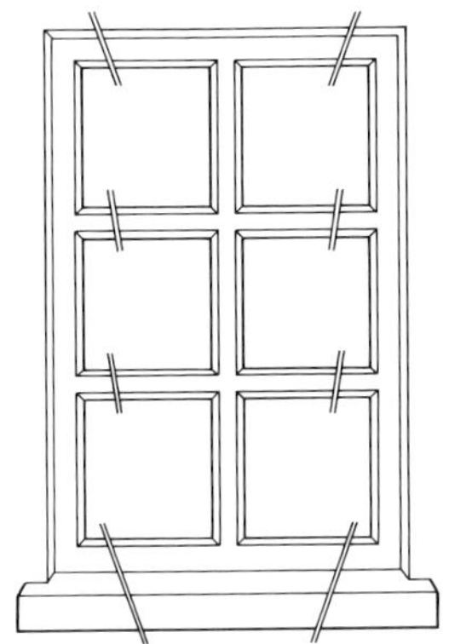

First remove any glass. Make the angled saw cuts shown and remove the centre pieces of the frame. The frame will be fixed by any of the methods shown left. It may be possible to loosen screws, but it's more likely that you'll need to lever out the rest of the frame. Work carefully using something like a crowbar. Clear any loose mortar, and projecting nails, plugs or whatever. Decide what to do with the inside window sill (the board) you may need to remove it for safekeeping.

On modern buildings a damp-proof course will be found when the window is removed. Do not remove a sound dpc. It should be refixed around the window frame when the new window is placed. If there is no dpc one will be required as in a new opening.

**The new frame** When buying a new frame or having one specially made, make sure it is slightly smaller than the size of the opening – about 6mm all round. This tolerance makes it easier to locate the window and to adjust it so that it is straight and vertical.

Check the fit of the frame in the opening. If the frame is just a little smaller than the opening, insert packing pieces of timber between the frame and the brickwork. If the resulting gap is too big to be filled by a strip of mastic, a piece of timber moulding can be fitted around the edge of the frame to cover the gap.

When the fit is tight shave off bits of the frame with a trimming tool or a plane.

Before a new timber window frame is fixed any areas of bare woodwork should be brushed with a preservative and primed with two coats.

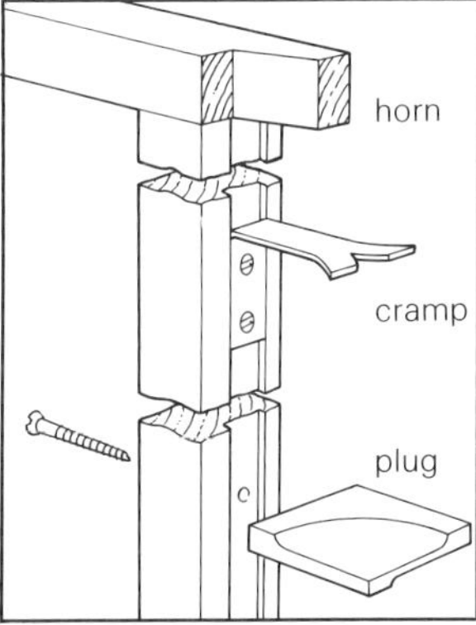


**Fixing the frame** If the previous window was fixed to hardwood pellets in the joints of the brickwork round the window it may be possible to re-use these for attaching the new frame. New pellets can be set by using a plugging chisel to rake out joints at appropriate places, otherwise the new window can be secured by screwing through the frame into plugged holes in a brick or block wall or straight into the studs of a timber frame.

Fix the dpc. Hold the frame in position making sure that it is square, and mark the positions of the fixing points. The holes in the frame can then be pre-drilled with the frame on the ground. Lift the frame into position again and screw into the plugs, wedges or studs. If the window has horns at the top corners, make good the holes with cut bricks, cladding or whatever.

Point the mortar bed under the sill striking off the mortar so that it drains away from the frame. Point the gap between the frame and the brickwork. When the mortar sets it may shrink back and the joint can then be finished with a non-setting mastic.

Glaze fixed lights and glaze and hang opening lights. Paint, stain or varnish as necessary.

# Patio doors

Sliding doors with aluminium, plastic or hardwood frames are available off-the-shelf in all sizes, commonly with two panels (only one of which slides), but also with three, four and more panels. Patio doors are also available made-to-measure, but since the opening can usually be made to fit the door, you rarely need to go to the expense of a door made to fit the opening.

When a door is fitted in place of french doors there is usually an existing lintel to support the wall above and the job is little more difficult than installing a replacement window. A patio door that replaces a smaller door or a window or needs a completely new opening in a wall is another matter. Temporary supports will be needed while the hole is made and a lintel must be fitted to support the wall above – see pages 116 and 242. Building Regulations approval will be needed for the structural alterations and sometimes planning permission too.

Patio doors are normally used to give access to the garden from a living room, but they can also be used effectively in other places, to enclose a porch for instance. They can also be used indoors as a glazed partition between rooms. New patio doors should be double-glazed and must be fitted with safety glass – either toughened or laminated. This is now almost standard practice, but some firms still offer the option of ordinary float glass – don't be tempted by the cheaper price.

## Measuring up

It's vital to get the measurements right. Take the width at several places – top, bottom and centre – and measure top to bottom at both sides and the centre. Start by taking rough measurements across the planned opening and then take final measurements, and prepare the opening, when you've found the standard-sized door that fits most closely to the estimate. For a door to be installed beneath an existing opening the maximum possible width will be limited to the width of the opening already there. You cannot trim back the sides without weakening the structure supporting the lintel over. The height will also be limited by the height of the existing lintel – if a large gap will result above a standard door a skylight or night ventilator could be fitted to fill the gap.

# Installing a patio door

## Step-by-step

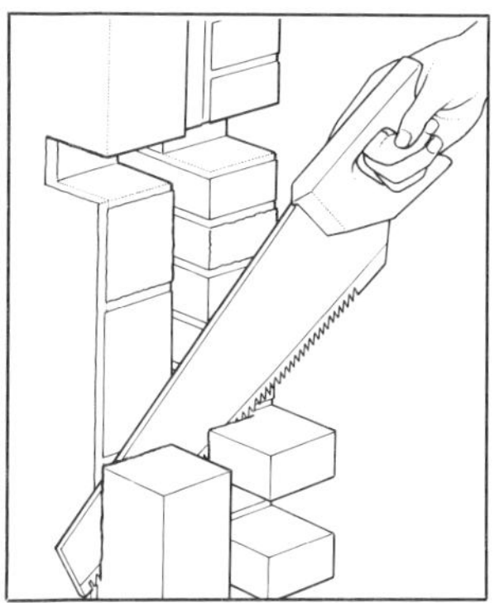

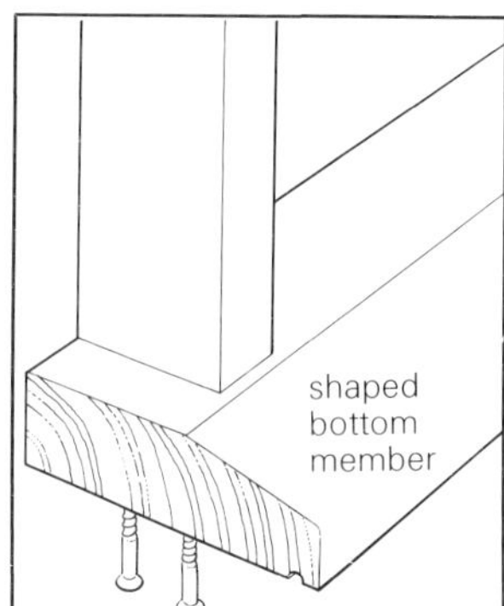


**Step 1** If the door is to go in a new opening or an enlarged opening, see page 121; if the opening already exists check whether there is a suitable lintel. Usually there will be, but occasionally window openings were constructed without lintels, relying on the sturdy timbers of the window frame to support the structure above. Provided there's a satisfactory lintel the existing window or doors can be removed and any short wall below can be demolished. Do this neatly cutting half bricks where necessary. If the horns of a window extended into the brickwork it may be necessary to set new bricks at the top corners of the opening.

**Step 2** An aluminium door will need a timber sub-frame of preservative-treated softwood or, hardwood. This will usually have to be fabricated on site from lengths of planed timber. The bottom member of the frame should be a proper sill bevelled to shed water and with a drip groove underneath – the side members can be shaped timbers or simply planed rectangles, the frame is put together with screwed butt joints – brush the timbers ends with preservative before joining. The subframe should fit closely to the patio door frame but a small tolerance is needed both to fit the subframe in the opening and the door frame in the subframe.

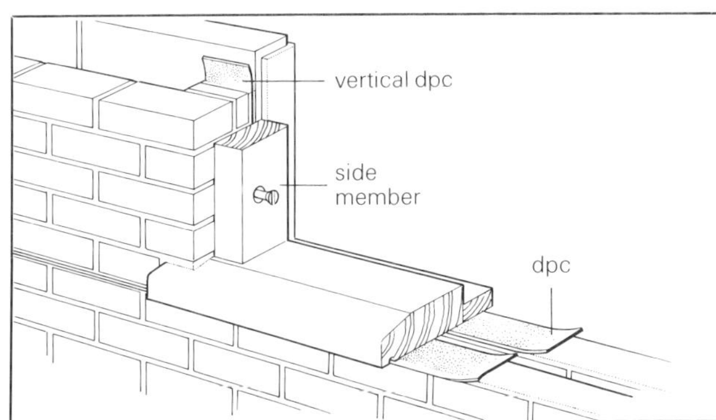


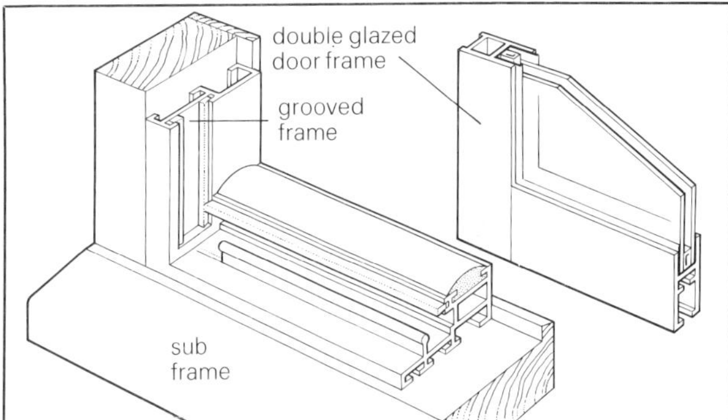


**Step 3** Under and around any external door frame there should be a damp-proof course. Patio doors are often installed without them using a mastic seal to keep water out, but a good installation will include a dpc. The sides of the opening in a cavity wall should also be closed by bricks cut to size and fitted end on.

Lay a 10 mm strip of mortar, bed the new strip of dpc on this mortar so that its tail extends beyond the face of the wall and top with 10mm of mortar. (If it's in line with the main dpc – overlap the old and new by at least 100mm.) Bed the subframe on the mortar and check that it is level, plumb and square. Fit the side dpc's to overlap with the bottom one and screw the frame to the wall with no 10 or no 12 screws which are long enough to penetrate 60mm or so into the wall. If the wall is masonry, mark and plug the holes first. Fit the screws every 300mm or so, staggering them not to coincide with the frame to sub-frame screws – the holes for these screws are normally pre-drilled in the metal. Check again that all parts of the frame are square and that the diagonals are equal.

The aluminium frame is usually bedded on mastic. It is lifted into position inside the timber sub-frame and screwed in place. Again double check that all is square.

**Step 4** The doors will usually be supplied glazed. Fit the fixed door panels first, sliding the panel into the top track and then lifting the bottom into the bottom track. Slide to the appropriate side and screw in place through the fixing brackets.

The sliding panel will have rollers – take care not to damage them during storage and fitting of the panel and do not let the rollers take the weight of the door until it is in the bottom track – until the door is in place use wooden blocks to raise the panel off the ground. The rollers may need to be adjusted to get the door to slide easily.

With the door installed finish off by pointing the outside window/wall joints or by running a strip of mastic round the frame. Inside strips of moulding pinned over the joins give a neat finish.

# Fireplaces

When solid fuel open fires went out of vogue, lots of working fireplaces and chimneys were closed up or removed and many new houses were built without chimneys. Now the cycle has gone full turn and there's no doubt that fires are popular again – usually in the main living room as a cheerful supplement to full-house central heating.

If you have a serviceable chimney and flue in the right position, reinstating it is not usually a difficult or expensive job. Installing a new chimney however is more daunting: the materials aren't cheap and it's complex work strictly controlled by the Building Regulations. For most people do-it-yourself would be out of the question.

## Selecting a new fireplace

The most suitable fire for d-i-y installation is an open fire inset into a standard type of fireplace surround. If a boiler is required for domestic hot water and, possibly, some radiators, the installation becomes more complicated and expert assistance is often advisable. It is possible to leave the brick opening as a bare structure (or for neater appearance to mortar the opening) with a basket or dog grate, but an open fire on these lines is less likely to draw properly.

The components required are a fireplace surround and hearth, a fireback and lintel, and an inset open fire. The two popular sizes are for 16 inch fires or 18 inch fires. Where there is no background central heating in the room the 16 inch size is adequate for a room of 50 cubic metres volume and the 18 inch can heat a room up to a volume of 56 cubic metres. Although larger sizes of 20, 22 and 25 inch fires are available they should be avoided if possible because they may not be suitable for the size of the chimney flue and could be prone to cause smoke to escape into the room. Most of the most attractive fireplaces available are in any case based on a 16 inch or 18 inch fire.

To help you to form some idea of the type of fireplace which would suit you there are two publications available from the National Fireplace Council – address page 314. The first is a free leaflet giving the locations of Approved Fireplace Showrooms where a range of fireplaces can be seen and prices obtained (also advice on where to obtain the fireback and lintel and help in installation if required). The second is a brochure which contains over 90 pages of coloured illustrations of fireplaces of all styles.

An alternative to a prefabricated fireplace surround and hearth is a stone or briquette surround built from a d-i-y kit. You will still require a fireback, lintel and inset open fire. When choosing, take care to ensure that the kit is for the correct size of fire opening.

## A new chimney

Until recently, your only choice if you wanted a new chimney was a very expensive construction of bricks and mortar, which would have taken several days to build and caused considerable upheaval. Now you can have a sectional chimney made from factory-made units put together on site in just a few hours, although preparation and finishing-off time will probably mean that the whole job takes a builder two or three days to

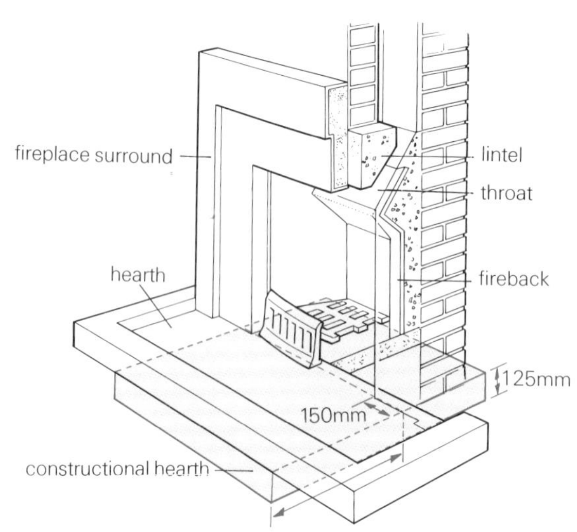

Cross-section of an open fire with hearth dimensions.

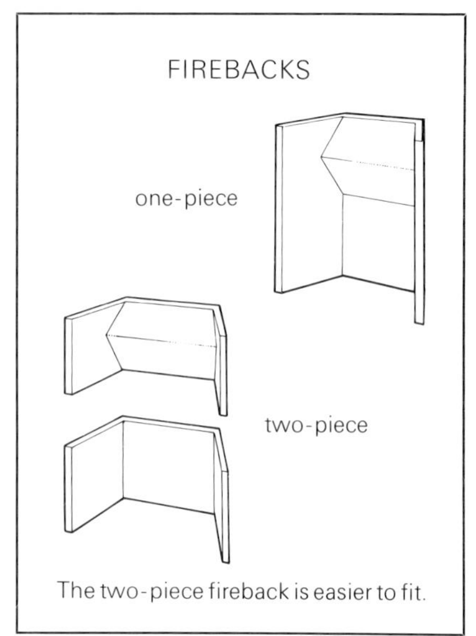

The two-piece fireback is easier to fit.

complete. Sectional chimneys are cheaper than brick ones and take up less space. They can be boxed in to give a more traditional chimney breast appearance, but any combustible material must be at least 50mm from the chimney wall.

There are two sorts of sectional chimney:

- insulated twin wall metal sections which interlock
- insulated concrete flue blocks which are built up with mortar courses. Some have integral ceramic liners; others have to be lined.

Both types of chimney can be used inside of or outside the house, but where there is a choice it is always better to have a flue on an inner wall. The chimney will retain more heat there and will be more efficient. (Straight chimneys are also more efficient.) If you have to have an outside chimney a concrete block type is a better choice. Indoors a metal one is usually easier to install.

# Opening up an old fireplace

The drawing (left) shows what is likely to exist in the chimney breast. Usually the old fireplace opening will have been covered with some kind of board or have been bricked up. There should be a ventilator and this can be a starting point – remove the grille and feel inside to find out if it is mounted on board or brick. Where there is no ventilator you should be able to tell by tapping the surface – board will sound hollow, but masonry will sound solid.

## Step-by-step

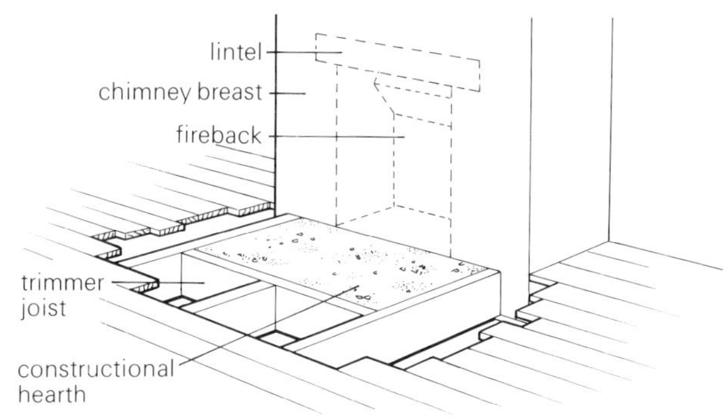


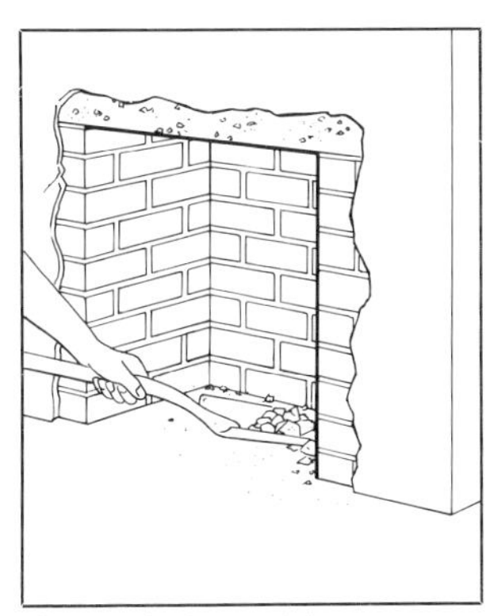

**Step 1** If it is board find the outer edges and chip away the plaster to disclose the screws or nails. If it is brickwork choose a position in the centre of the chimney breast and about 300mm above floor level and chip away the plaster to expose an area of brickwork. Using a heavy hammer drive a whole brick into the hollow space of the recess behind and then work outwards to open up the whole fireplace recess.

**Step 2** The exposed recess may be just a rectangular space with a brick wall at the back or it may contain the old fireback. Before proceeding further check the chimney flue. Push a piece of crumpled newspaper up into the flue at the top of the opening and light it. If it burns away with the flames pulled up the chimney it can be assumed that the flue is reasonably clear. If the paper smoulders and smoke billows back out of the opening it is likely that the flue is blocked up. This may be caused by a capped chimney – see page 143, *Checks for flues*.

**Step 3** Remove all loose material to clear the recess. If there is a fireback in position, it is probable that it will not be in good condition or at the correct height for any new fireplace surround. In which case it should be removed along with all the loose rubble behind. Be careful not to disturb any lintel or iron bar which may form the top of the opening. Finally, check the floor at the base of the opening. This is called the constructional hearth and the Building Regulations require this to be concrete 125mm thick and to extend not less than 500mm beyond the front of the chimney breast and a minimum of 150mm beyond each side of the recess opening.

If you are planning to install a new fireplace surround and hearth with an inset open fire this constructional hearth should be checked and if it does not conform to the required measurements it will be necessary to break up the floor and put in new concrete.

If you intend to install a fire with an underfloor air supply or a hole-in-the-wall fire which uses the same type of grate and ashbox it will not be necessary to reinstate the constructional hearth. Instead the area will have to be excavated to provide a sunken ashpit and the underfloor air supply. However, both these types of fire involve other, complicated, considerations and expert assistance is advisable before attempting such installations. For example, the recess in the chimney breast may not be deep enough for some hole-in-the-wall fires, there may be complications concerning the air supply under the floor, and the construction of the front of the chimney breast may not be suitable to receive some types of metal fire openings.

# Installing a new fireplace

## Step-by-step

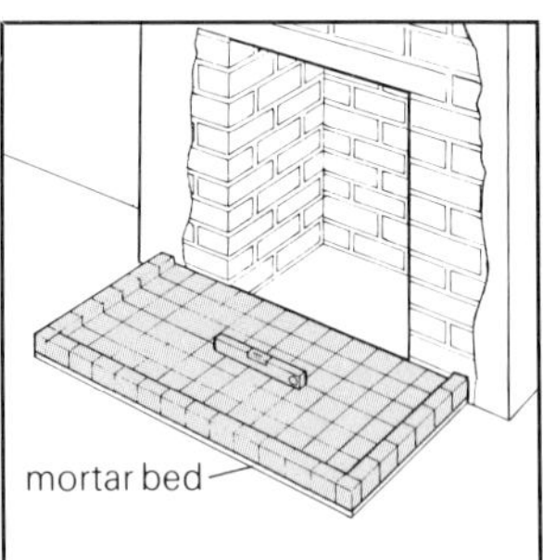

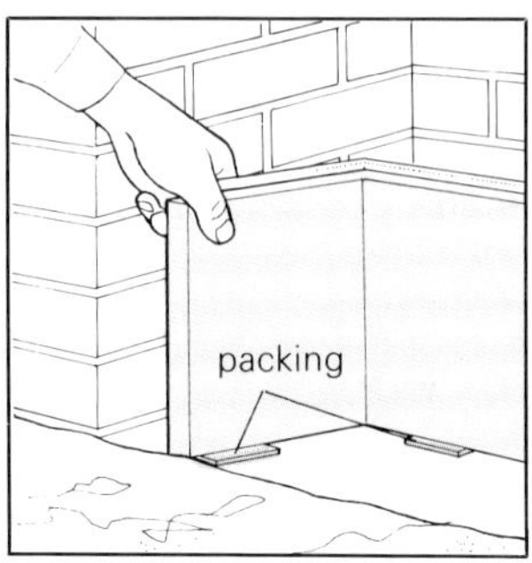


Installation can be made in several different ways and the following order of doing the job is just one of them. Allow several days to do the work as at several stages you will have to halt to allow mortar to set.

**Step 1** Bed the decorative hearth on the floor in a position central on the chimney breast and the opening. The hearth should be fixed with its back edge against the face of the chimney breast using a weak bedding mortar of 6 parts sand 1 part lime and 1 part cement mixed to a fairly sloppy consistency. Only a thin bed of cement, say 8mm, is necessary but it must be sufficient to allow the hearth to be bedded level in both directions (using a spirit level) and to ensure that if is not resting on any lumps or high spots on the constructional hearth. Leave for 24 hours for the cement bed to become firm.

**Step 2** Cover the hearth with a quilt of several layers of dust sheet to thoroughly protect it while the rest of the work is carried out. Place a layer of strawboard, or two thicknesses of corrugated cardboard, against the wall at the back to allow the concrete to expand when it becomes hot. Float the space behind the hearth within the recess level with the top of the hearth using a concrete mix of 4 parts finely crushed brick or special aggregates (sold under the brand names, Lytag or Aglite, or Leca) to 1 part cement. Leave this also to harden for at least 24 hours.

**Step 3** Position the fireback on the new concrete within the recess. The fireback may consist of just one piece or two pieces – the latter is easier to install and can be expected to last longer. Before positioning the fireback again put a layer of corrugated cardboard or strawboard over the back of the lower half. This can be made to hold in place during handling if it is attached to the fireback with a few dabs of fire cement, or it can be soaked in water and draped on to the back. It is most important that the front face of the fireback should be vertical in all directions and level with the face of the chimney breast. Also, the fireback must be exactly central on the hearth. Use pieces of thin card or paper, if necessary, to pack the base of the fireback until it is perfectly positioned.

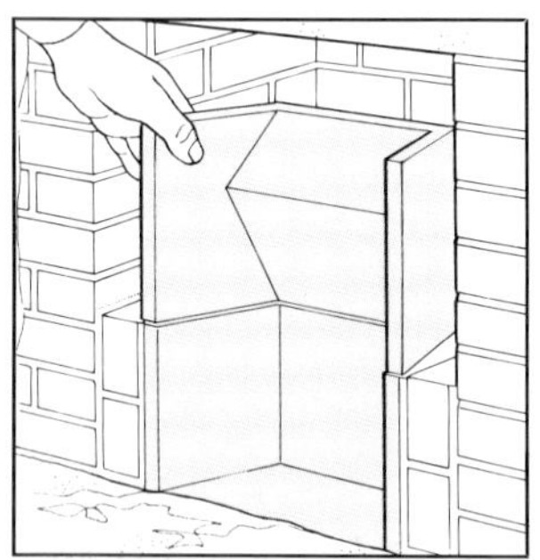

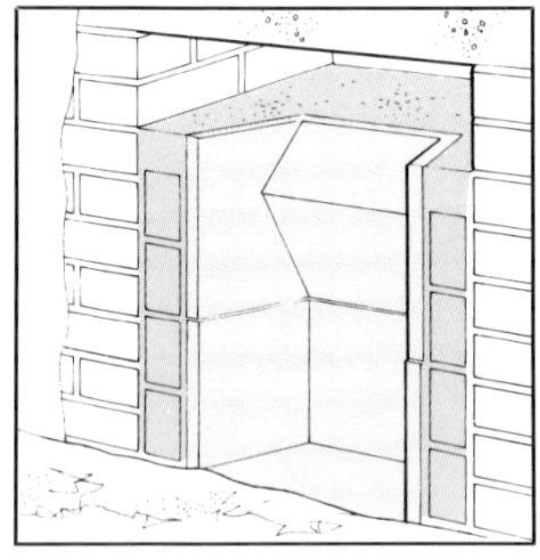

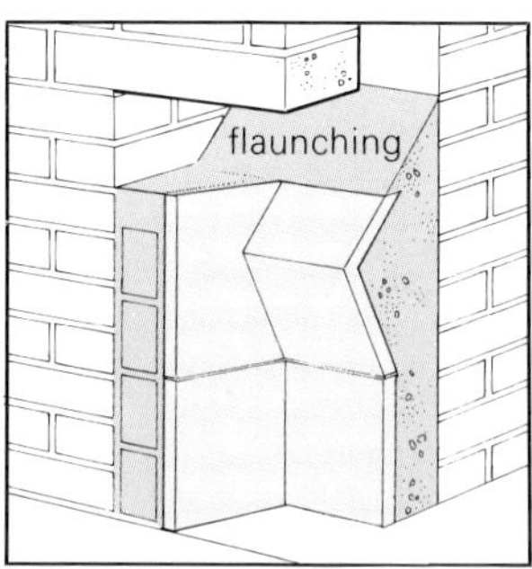


**Step 4** The space behind the fireback has to be filled in. Where there is a wide space between the outer edges of the fireback and the chimney breast brickwork, it can first be closed with bricks used flat or on edge. If this space is too small for brickwork it can be shuttered by holding a strip of wood over the gap while packing the infill behind. The ideal mixtures for filling behind the fireback are damp mixed of 4 parts vermiculite to 1 part hydrated lime or 6 parts of vermiculite to 1 part cement, mixed dry and moistened just enough to hold together when squeezed in the hand. After filling behind the lower section, the upper section is positioned with a very thin joint of fire cement and then a second layer filling is installed behind this upper section.

If there is not room to reach over the fireback to insert the second layer of back-filling it is necessary to remove any existing lintel or bar and two or three courses of brickwork to provide access. The vermiculite mix should be packed down into the space behind the fireback and finished level with the top. Then, using a fairly stiff mix of concrete, continue filling above the level of the vermiculite filling. At the sides the cement walls are vertical. At the back the concrete surface is sloped off in line with the fireback until it reaches the recess brickwork. It is important that this concrete, known as flaunching, provides a smooth slope to meet the back wall, as a smooth passage here will assist the draw of the flue.

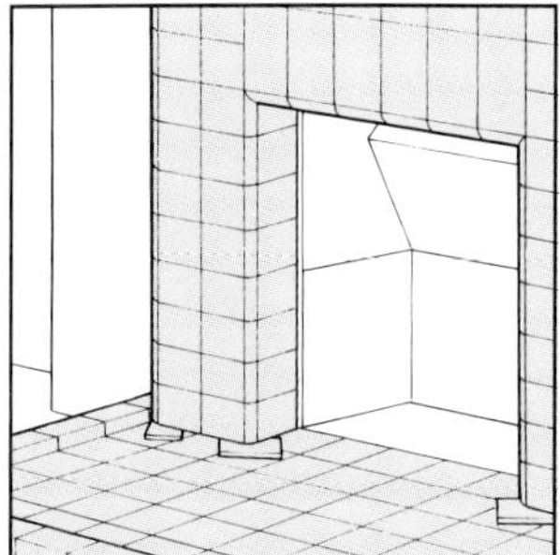

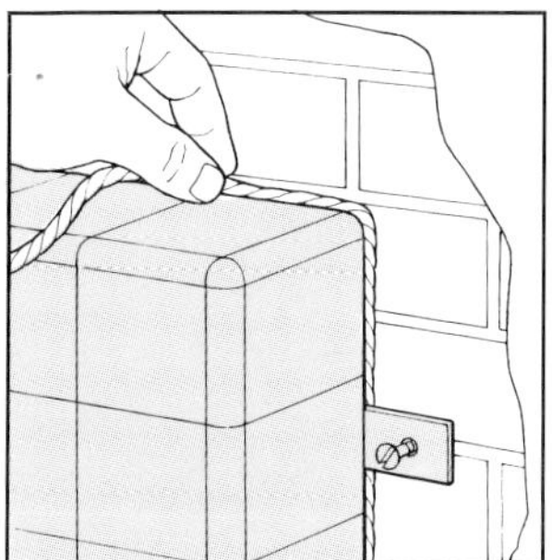

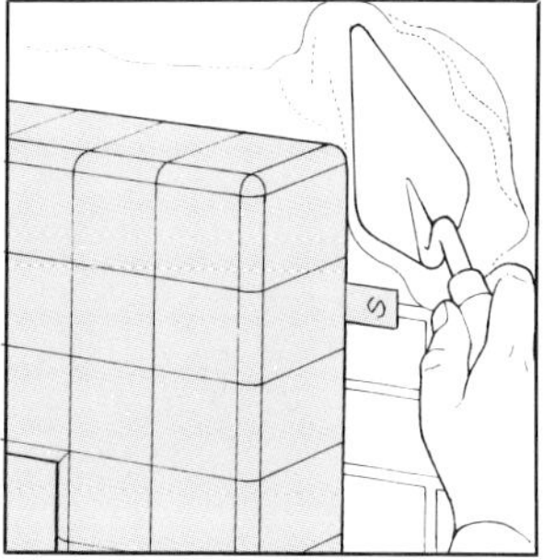

**Step 5** Install the chamfered lintel which forms the front slope of the chimney throat in the front of the chimney breast, using ordinary sand/cement mortar, and closing up the hole above it to leave a smooth front face to the chimney breast. The lintel should be carefully positioned to just clear the top of the fireback so that it can expand slightly when heated.

**Step 6** The final stage is the fixing of the fireplace surround to the face of the chimney breast. The base of the surround should not rest heavily on the hearth and there must be a slight gap to allow the part round the fire to expand with heat.

The surround should be positioned carefully on the face of the chimney breast with several pieces of thin packing (about 3mm) between the bottom of the surround and the hearth. (These will be removed after fixing.) The positions of the holes in the fixing brackets on each side of the fireplace are marked on the brickwork and the fireplace removed while these holes are drilled and plugged. There should be a length of asbestos rope on the back of the surround round the fire opening which provides a seal between the front edge of the fireback and lintel and the back of the frame round the fire. If this is missing it will be necessary to obtain a length of 19mm asbestos rope which can be pushed into position before the surround is screwed to the wall. If there are any blocks or pieces of wood fixed to the bottom edge of the surround to protect it during handling they should, of course, be removed before fixing.

Remove the packing between the hearth and the surround and plaster the surface of the brickwork round the fireplace to cover the fixing clips and provide a smooth wall surface up to the surround.

The whole installation should be left for at least two days before the fire grate is fitted following the fixing instructions provided.

It is vitally important to dry out and warm up the fireplace very slowly and carefully commencing with a very small fire which should be lit and allowed to die out, in the first instance, followed by a slightly larger fire and building up to full service only gradually.

## Checks for flues

If the fireplace seems to be ready to use, you'll need to check that the chimney is in working order.

Strictly speaking, there are two parts to a chimney: the *flue* is the passage through which the gases pass to the outside; the *chimney* is any part of the building structure which forms the flue including the fireplace walls and hearth.

Provided that your chimney was capped off to stop the rain getting in and the flue was ventilated at the bottom, there should be no problems and, once opened up, the chimney should work as well as ever. If the chimney is slightly damp inside, it will soon dry out once in use. If you think there are no major problems, have the chimney swept. You can do this job yourself with hired brushes or a set of brushes you've bought, but a sweep's services are usually very reasonable and he will be equipped to do the job with very little mess.

The capping – probably a slate or concrete slab – will need removing. A sweep may be prepared to do this for you. It means getting up on the roof to remove the capping and possibly some making good to the pot.

Most sweeps use a brush to sweep the flue and a vacuum cleaner to collect the debris and to do the job in 15 to 30 minutes.

It's also important to check the external chimney walls for damage: brick pointing may have deteriorated, the flashing between the chimney and the roof may be ineffective, the chimney pot may be broken or insecurely fitted or the mortar flaunching around the pot may have cracked. If any of these things are obvious, or the chimney stack is leaning to one side, the chimney will need some additional attention before it is used – see *Repairing chimneys*, page 145.

Sometimes a flue may need to be relined before it can be used safely, and occasionally it may be necessary to re-line for other reasons – to improve flue efficiency by decreasing the cross-sectional area for a particularly large flue, for example. If after sweeping and lighting a fire a chimney appears to have problems that you can't solve, the SFAS (address page 314) may be willing to advise.

### Re-lining a flue

There are several ways to re-line an existing flue above a solid fuel fire. Some involve breaking into the chimney all the way up and are not usually practicable propositions. An easier, though expensive, method involves employing specialists to line the flue with insulating concrete which is poured around an inflatable tube blown up in the flue. This forms a new circular flue. It is called the Supaflue chimney lining system.

A Supaflue lining reduces the diameter of a typical brick 215mm flue to about 180mm which is smaller than preferred for a fire on which coal or wood is burned, though fine if only smokeless fuel is burned.

The flexible stainless steel flue liners sometimes used above gas fires are not suitable for use above a solid fuel fire.

# Removing an old fireplace

Before starting to remove a fireplace make sure that it is not an integral part of the chimney breast structure. If it is, you will probably have to seek professional advice, however, most fireplaces are simply fixed on to the chimney breast and can be removed without creating any structural problems.

The job needs some brute force and is messy – have the chimney swept, remove carpets and furniture (or cover it up), keep the door shut, wear old clothes, tie a handkerchief over your mouth and nose and wear goggles, particularly when you are chipping at brickwork or plaster. If there used to be a gas fire in the fireplace, the gas pipe will need sealing off. Copper pipe can be cut back and sealed with a blanking-off fitting; with mild steel you unscrew the last length of pipe and screw on a cap – to make a good seal wrap the male thread with PTFE tape wound in the direction of the thread.

## Step-by-step

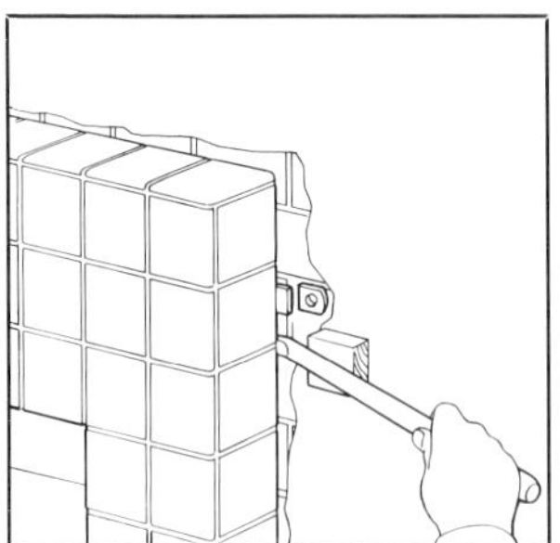

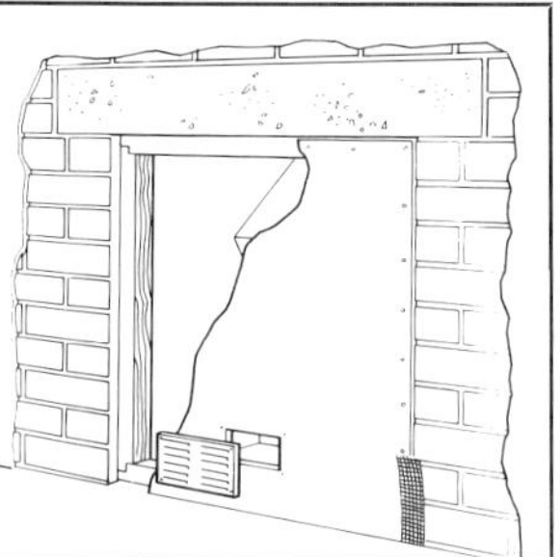

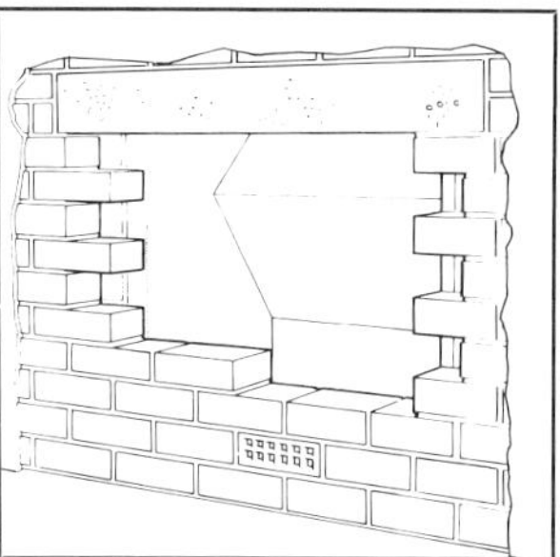

**Step 1** Remove the grate from the fireplace. In most cases the surround stands directly on the hearth – so it will have to be removed first. If it is fixed in, use a hammer and cold chisel to chip it out from the sides.

Fireplace surrounds are generally nailed or screwed to the brickwork with four or six fixing lugs (two down either side and sometimes two at the top). These lugs are usually metal plates cast into the surround, fixed to the brickwork structure and plastered over.

If there is a separate mantelshelf, this may also be attached to the wall with lugs, but marble and stone shelves may be cemented in. Remove any mantelshelf before the surround. If the shelf is cemented in, loosen it carefully using a hammer and cold chisel until you can lever it out. If the mantelshelf is fixed by lugs, treat them in the same way as the lugs on the surround.

**Step 2** Remove the surround by chipping away all the plaster around the perimeter to expose the fixing lugs. Try to unscrew any screws or yank out nails. If they won't budge, knock the fixings sideways until they are loosened. Have a helper to prevent the surround toppling over while you do this. It may also be necessary to use a crowbar to lever the surround from the wall. Any separate metal frame covering the gap between the surround and the opening may need releasing separately – the fixing lugs for this are usually inside the fireplace.

The hearth slab will probably be fixed in place on a bed of mortar. To remove it, break the mortar joint by cutting into the bed with a hammer and plugging chisel and then prise up the slab.

**Closing up the opening** The builder's opening can be blocked off to leave the chimney breast flat or recessed for shelves or an electric fire perhaps. Blocking off can be done simply with a covering board or, more permanently, by filling with bricks or blocks. For a neat job you could remove the fireback before blocking up the opening, but if it's not in the way just leave it in place.

When an existing fireplace chimney is sealed the chimney flue must always be permanently ventilated. The chimney should be left open at the top (it may need a hood to prevent rain getting in) and a permanent ventilator fitted at the bottom of the flue – either inside or outside the building.

**Boarding up** Construct a softwood frame screwed or nailed to the inside of the opening set back the depth of the board to be used. Plywood or hardboard will do unless the chimney is shared with a fireplace still in use, in which case use an incombustible board of plasterboard. Cut a hole for a small ventilator and fit this before nailing the board to the frame, aim to fit the board *exactly* flush with the surrounding plaster. Make good the edge gaps.

**Bricking the opening** Bricking a fireplace opening is much like any other opening apart from the need for a ventilator. Your choice is whether to key in the bricks (or blocks) or simply build an infill wall with straight sides. Take care that the wall is flat and doesn't bulge outwards. When the mortar has set, plaster over the brickwork, feathering the new plaster neatly into the existing – any hollow or bumps will show under wallpaper. Finish the infill wall (of board or bricks) with skirting board to match the existing.

**Leaving a recess** There are many ways of finishing off and leaving a recess, including leaving the bricks bare. Whatever you do make sure that you do not disturb the lintel and, if you share the chimney with the house next door, make sure that you do not remove too much from the back of the fireplace. Fit an insulated roof to the recess, this should be ventilated and strong enough to hold anything that might fall down the chimney. Another way to ventilate is to provide a false back with the ventilator in that.

**Covering the hearth** If necessary smooth over the floor where the hearth was using a 3:1 sand and cement screed.

## Removing a chimney breast

A fireplace chimney breast extends from its foundations all the way up to the flue pot. It is often an integral part of the house and sometimes the house next door as well – so you cannot simply cut it out without taking precautions to ensure that the remaining part of the house is structurally stable. Seek professional advice before starting this sort of job. The following notes do not tell you how to do it – they simply state what the problem is.

The most satisfactory approach from a structural point of view is to take down the entire chimney breast from the ground floor all the way up to the chimney pot and make good the brickwork, walls, floors, roof and so on. Obviously, if the chimney is shared this cannot be done, without the consent of your neighbours.

The alternative is to take half the chimney breast away but this immediately raises the problem of structural instability. When taking a fireplace and chimney breast away at ground floor level, you have to think about how you can support the chimney structure above. It is sometimes possible to do this satisfactorily, but each house has to be considered on its individual merits. It is usually quite safe to take down the upper part of a chimney – removing it down to roof level for instance (however even this cannot easily be done if the chimney is shared).

### REPAIRING CHIMNEYS

Minor repairs to a chimney can often be carried out using a conventional ladder with roof ladders for access. Place sacks of rags or straw under the roof ladder to prevent damage to the roof covering.

Never attempt to carry out major repairs working off ladders. Erect a proper scaffold.

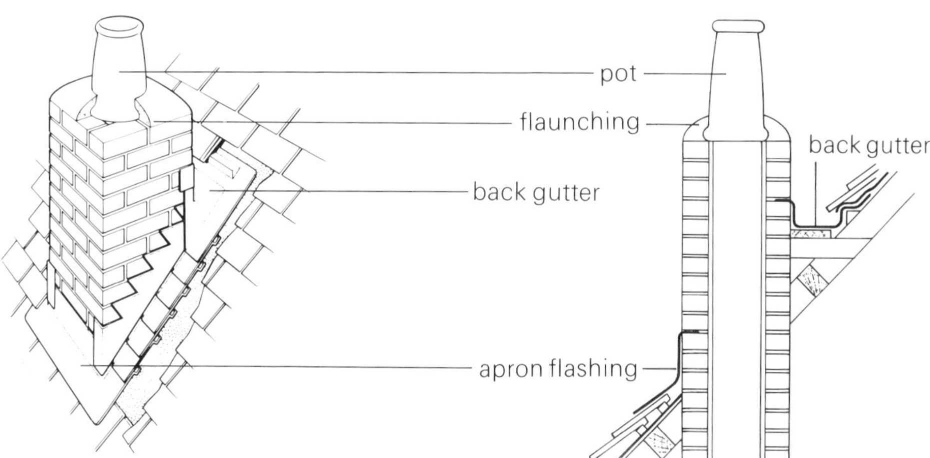


**Insecure or damaged pots**
Pots are secured to the stack by a cement flaunching. If the flaunching has cracked or broken away it should be removed and replaced. Use a club hammer and bolster to break the flaunching. Lower the old pot to the ground on a rope. Clean away the top of the stack with a wire brush and, if necessary, repoint the top course of brickwork.

Wet the brickwork on top of the stack and the bottom of the new pot, place the pot in position then build up the new flaunching, one part cement to three parts sharp sand, to about 75mm deep around the pot. Trowel it smooth so that it slopes away from the pot in all directions.

**Defective pointing**
Defective joints should be raked out to a depth of about 20mm and all powdery material brushed away. Damp the brickwork before repointing with a mixture (just moist enough to be plastic) of one part cement to three or four parts soft sand with a plasticiser added to the water. Repointing is done by putting the mortar into a flat cake, cutting a slice the same width as the joint and then sliding this into the joint.

**Defective flashing**
There are two major defects which occur with traditional lead flashing. The joint withthe masonry may be loose, allowing water to run down the back. To remedy this rake out the masonry joint, rewedge the lead flashing using strips of lead driven into the joint with something like a blunt chisel, then repoint. The flashing may need replacing. This can be done with sheets of lead, zinc, aluminium alloy, a rigid bitumin-based material or with a purpose-made self-adhesive foil-backed flashing strip. Remove the lower layers of roof covering to expose the edges of the flashing. Remove this with a cold chisel and rake out the mortar from the flashing joint to a depth of about 20mm or 25mm. Shape the new flashing to match the old – use a sliding bevel to measure the angles. Wet the brickwork, place the new flashing in position and wedge it in the flashing joint. Replace the roof covering and repoint. Take the old lead to a scrap merchant.

# Power points

Since the ring circuit can carry as many socket outlets and fixed appliances as you like, within the restraints of total possible loading, it's usually possible to have sockets wherever you need them at relatively little extra cost. And, if you plan your sockets effectively, they can all be installed at a height to suit the piece of equipment with which they will usually be used – 150mm from the floor (or any other surface – such as the top of a sideboard) is the minimum height; maximum height should be within reach of all the adults in a household.

There is a danger that a scheme, tailored in this way, to particular pieces of equipment, will work with only one arrangement of furniture. So it's worth thinking about alternative positions too, perhaps installing sockets where they'll be concealed by the present position of a piece of furniture (and will therefore remained unused), but are likely to be accessible, if the furniture is rearranged. All sockets should be easily accessible when they are in use so that equipment can be switched off and unplugged without trouble.

Apart from a whole new circuit (which might be the best solution if your wiring is old or if you want to install equipment which draws a heavy current – see page 50), it's possible to get extra sockets by changing single socket outlets to doubles, by installing more sockets on the ring or by adding a spur to the ring.

Before adding additional sockets you must make a careful examination of the wiring. There are limitations on adding sockets to spurs from the ring circuit or to a radial circuit (see page 51). To ignore these restrictions is to risk overloading the circuit.

You can tell whether a socket is on a spur by inspecting the connections. Turn off the power at the mains and ease the selected socket from the wall by undoing the screws in its face plate. Behind it is the mounting box containing up to three cables.

One-cable sockets are either on a

THE SOCKETS YOU MIGHT NEED

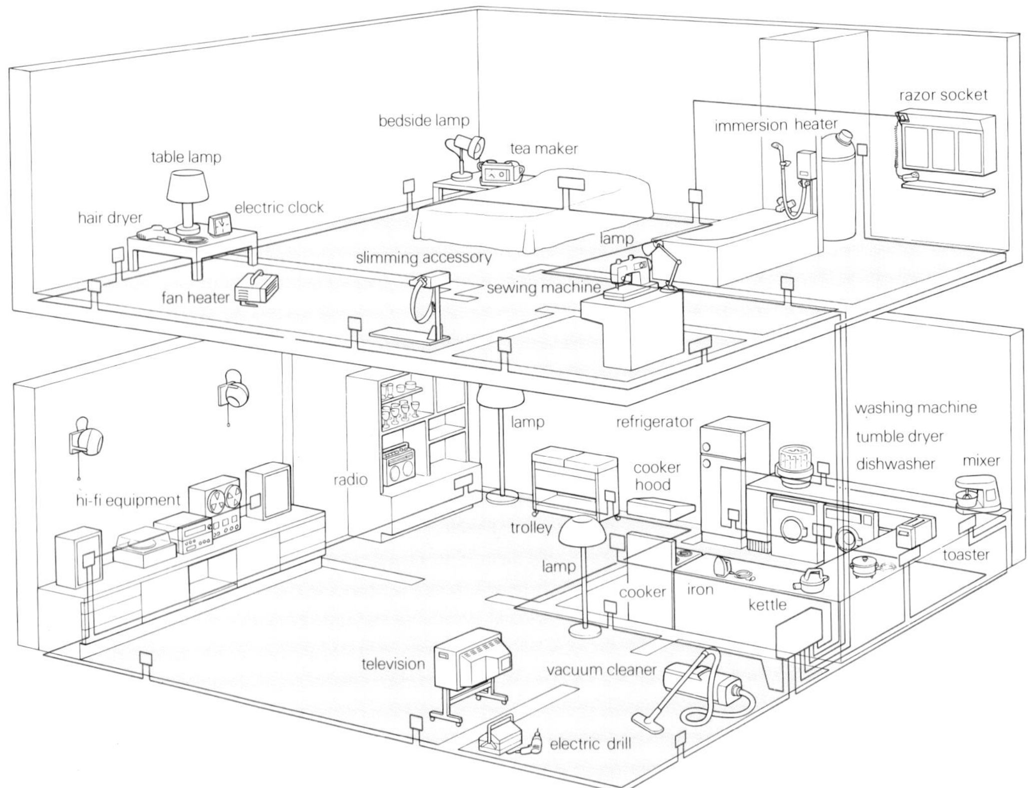


You may be surprised to realise how many pieces of electrical equipment you have. Many things will need to occupy a socket more-or-less fulltime, other pieces of equipment are portable or can 'borrow' a socket when they need an electricity supply.

spur or on the end of a radial circuit. Two-cable sockets can either be on a ring or be an intermediate socket on a spur or radial circuit. Three-cable sockets usually indicate a spur has already been taken from the ring at that point but they may also be a sign of incorrect wiring. Either way three-cable sockets should be avoided.

It may be necessary to check the layout of a circuit further. The best way to do this is with a circuit continuity tester. With the mains *off*, disconnect all appliances from the circuits and the two live conductors from the socket terminals. Use the tester to link these two conductors; if the tester indicates continuity, the socket is on a ring circuit. If it does not, the socket is probably on a spur or radial circuit (though it may be a broken ring or, of course, a damaged testing device and both these will need investigating.

## A double for a single

Like single sockets, double sockets have their terminal connections for the cable ends in the middle of the back of the plate. So provided there is sufficient cable all that needs to be done to exchange a single socket for a double is to replace the single box with a double one and install the new double socket.

Whether the existing box is recessed into the wall or surface-mounted, the easiest way to make the change is to install a new surface-mounted double box – there are special boxes 20mm deep sold for this purpose. Any existing surface-mounted box would of course have to be removed, but a recessed one could be left in place.

Mount the new box so that it is plugged into the wall each side of the old box–beware of buried cables.

If there isn't sufficient slack cable, or if you want the new double socket to be flush with the wall, the job will involve removing the existing box; making or enlarging the hole in the wall to take the new double box; fitting the new box and making good. It's best to do this when you're redecorating anyway.

## More sockets on the ring

Sockets can be added to a ring circuit at any convenient point by turning off the supply, finding and cutting the cable, installing the socket and connecting as usual. The difficulty with this method is that there is rarely enough slack in the cable to allow it to be drawn into a new mounting box and the cable must never be stretched or pulled. For this reason a spur from a junction box inserted into the ring or an existing socket is best.

EXTRA POWER POINTS

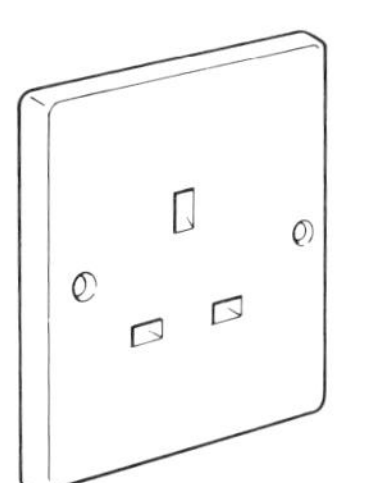

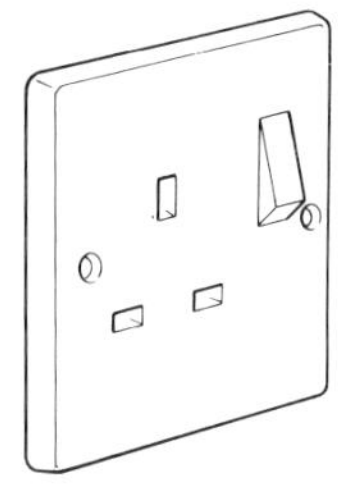

Single socket outlets – switched and unswitched.

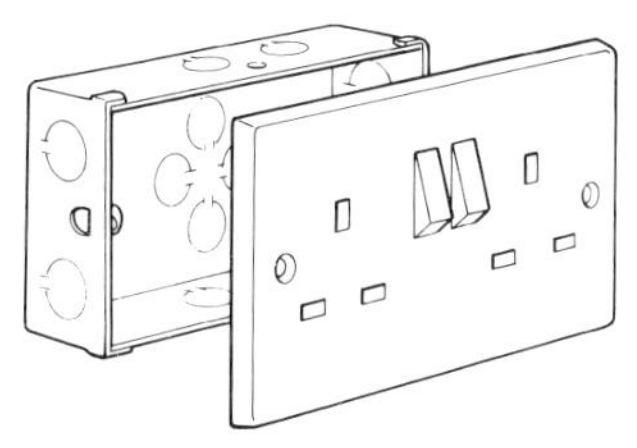

Double socket outlet and metal box for recessing.

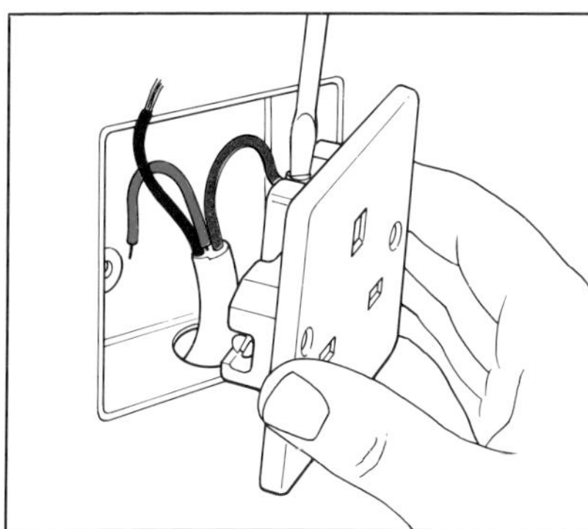

With the electricity off, disconnect the cables to the single socket which you have established as suitable for replacement with a double.

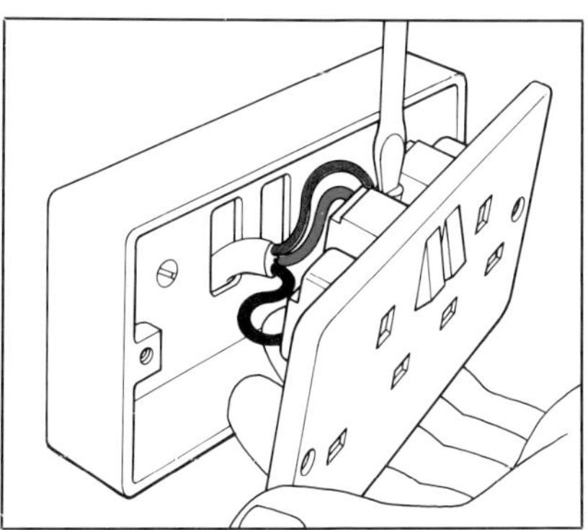

Leaving the old single box in position install a new surface-mounting double box centrally over the existing and remake the connections.

### CONNECTIONS CHECKLIST

These details should be checked each time you connect a socket, switch or anything at all. Full details of Electrical work are given on page 48 *et seq*.

- **switch off at the mains**
- always fit grommets in the knocked-out holes in mounting boxes.
- remove the sheath from cable within a box or fitting only
- aim to leave virtually no bare conductor exposed once the connection has been made
- protect the bare earth conductors with green and yellow sleeving and connect to earth terminal
- connect *red* conductors to *live* terminals
- connect *black* conductors to the *neutral* terminal
- double-check connections
- shape the connected conductors to fit comfortably inside the box

**If in doubt don't meddle**

# Installing a spur

This is usually the simplest way of extending the number of sockets and providing a supply to additional pieces of equipment. A spur is simply a branch off a ring circuit. Within the restraints of total possible loading, you can have as many spurs from a ring as there are sockets and fixed pieces of equipment connected directly to the ring, and each spur may feed one double socket or one single outlet – either a single socket or a piece of fixed equipment connected via a fused connection unit. A spur to supply a socket outlet or fused connection unit need not itself be fused but it must be run in the same size cable as the ring circuit. The spur can run from a socket on the ring or from a 30 amp junction box inserted into the ring.

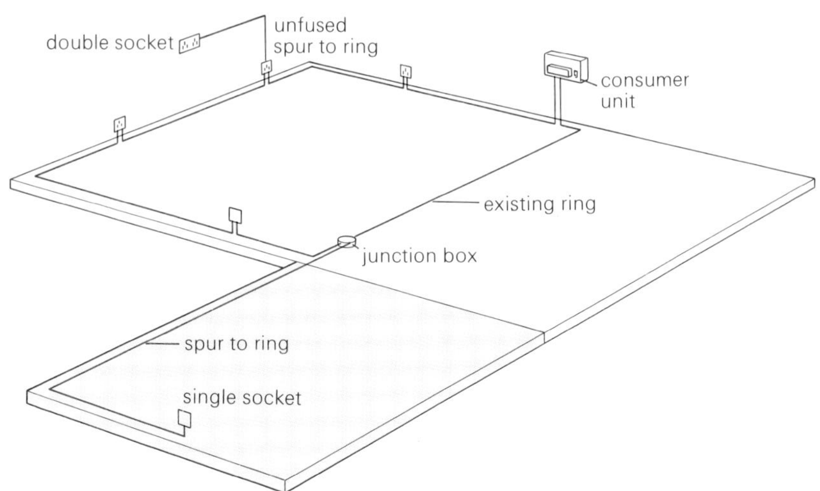


Before adding a spur think about the likely load the circuit must supply at any time, it should not exceed 7200 watts.

## Step-by-step

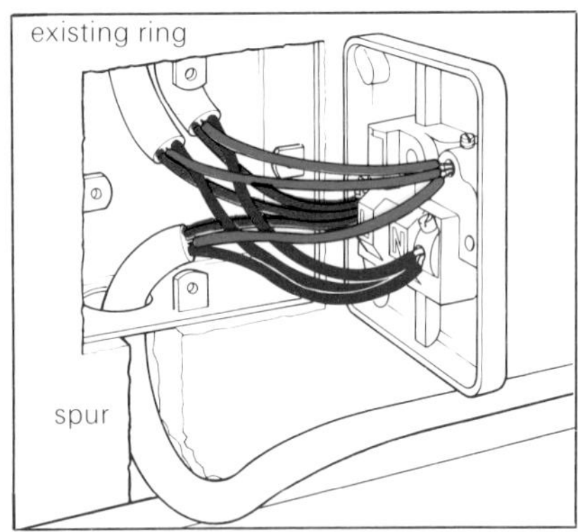


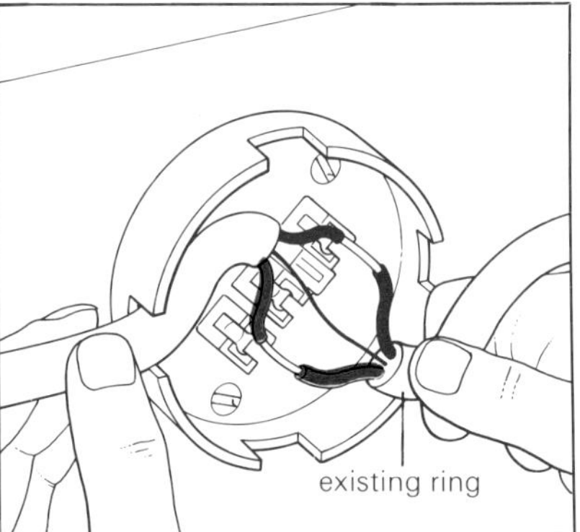


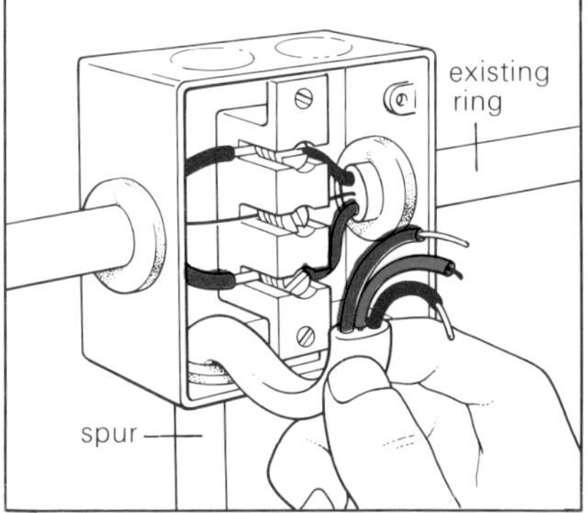


**From a socket** Select a convenient socket and check whether this socket is on a ring, or on a spur.

When you have located a suitable socket on a ring, connect a length of 2·5mm² twin and earth and run it to the position of the first point on the spur.

At the new socket (or fused connection unit) position, fit a plastic surface mounting box or a recessed metal box. Feed in the cable and connect up.

**From a junction box** It is possible and preferable to insert a junction box without having to cut through the live and neutral conductors of the ring circuit. Mount the junction box base to a secure surface on the route of the ring circuit–such as a wall or the face of a joist–whatever its position it should be accessible for inspection. Then mark a section of the ring circuit cable slightly less than the diameter of the junction box and carefully strip the sheath off this marked length. Divide the live and neutral conductors and strip away just a short section of insulation at the centre. You will have to cut the earth conductor so that you can fit its sleeving. Insert the conductors into the terminals with the earth in the middle. Prepare the end of the 2·5mm² spur cable and connect that into the correct junction box terminals.

An alternative to a junction box is to use a terminal block inside a standard mounting box fitted with a blank plate. This system can also be used where you want to move a socket on the end of a spur. Use the box with a blank plate to connect the extra cable and fit the old socket in a new box further along.

# Lighting

Most houses are built with a minimum of thought given to the proper provision of lighting and, often rooms have just one central ceiling light fitting. A more sensible arrangement – for most rooms in the house – is to provide at least two sorts of light – *general light* for seeing across and around the room and *specific light* directed at particular places or provided to illuminate particular tasks. You can also have *effects light* for decoration – to light pictures, curtains or prized objects, for example.

**Lamps and fittings**
All lights consist of two parts – the bulb or tube (more properly called the lamp) and the fitting into which the lamp goes. They both have an effect on how much light is given out and the sort of light given out. The light given out can be *directional* – a well-defined (and usually powerful) beam – or *diffusing* – spreading light over a wide area, sometimes in all directions, but often more in one direction than any other. Lamps and fittings are often classified as directional or diffusing.

## How much light?

Illuminating engineers describe light levels in lux (the amount of light – in lumens – falling on a square metre of surface). The more lux, the higher the light level. The general light level recommended for most rooms (living rooms, studies, bedrooms and so on) is about 50 lux; as a general guide, in order to achieve this you need to allow at least 16W of a GLS lamp for each square metre of surface to be lit.

Ordinary pendant ceiling lights can provide some or all of your general light. How many you need depends on how reflective the room's decorations are and how transparent the shades are. To provide 50 lux in a living room about 5m by 4m, you'd need a total of around 300W of tungsten light in two or more fittings.

If you use directional fittings aimed at walls and ceilings, you'll need quite a high wattage – up to four times the amount you need for pendant ceiling fittings – especially if the walls are decorated in dark colours. Fittings with large beam angles will help to give an even light – so PAR 38 floods, ISL lamps, or GLS lamps with wide reflectors would be best. You could use fluorescent tubes in this way too. Concealed fluorescent tubes behind cornices or pelmets, for instance, give a good flood of even light.

Specific light is necessary for watching TV, operating hi-fi, reading in armchairs, working at a desk and for close work like sewing or darning.

For watching TV, the position of the light is more important than how powerful it is – you need only enough light to prevent the picture from being too glaring (which is tiring on the eyes) – you should position it to light the area around the screen without producing any reflections in it.

The recommended level for casual reading and things like operating hi-fi is 150 lux; for prolonged reading and working at a desk it is 300 lux.

These levels can be achieved with standard or table lamps with ordinary shades using 100W bulbs provided they're close enough to the work (and the shade can take the load). But it's probably best to use directional fittings, spotlights or desk-type lamps.

The amount of light you need on close work depends a lot on how much the work reflects light – needlework on dark material may need twice as much as light-coloured material.

A separate fitting isn't necessary for each of these jobs, if you use movable fittings and position them carefully you can use them to light different areas. If you use adjustable directional fittings for your general lighting, you might be able to re-direct them for occasional specific lighting.

### LAMPS

There are five main kinds of lamp used in the home: four are filament lamps, the fifth is fluorescent. The lamps are described overleaf, the main things you need to know are:

- *the type of cap* – most are the familiar bayonet type, but many now have Edison screw caps. The cap affects the sorts of fitting in which you can use a lamp
- how long it will last. This really depends on how often you switch the light on and off. *Lamp life* is a guide – an average of tests on many samples
- the sizes available. Lamps are sold in *wattages* as a measure of the power they consume (a 100W lamp uses 1 unit of electricity in 10 hours)
- the amount of light. Wattages can be used to indicate light levels, but there's no simple formula as the amount of light per watt also depends on the type of lamp and the fitting. The amount of light actually arriving at a surface varies with the distance of that surface from the light and will vary depending on whether the surface itself is centre beam or off beam. *Light levels at 2m* are a guide.

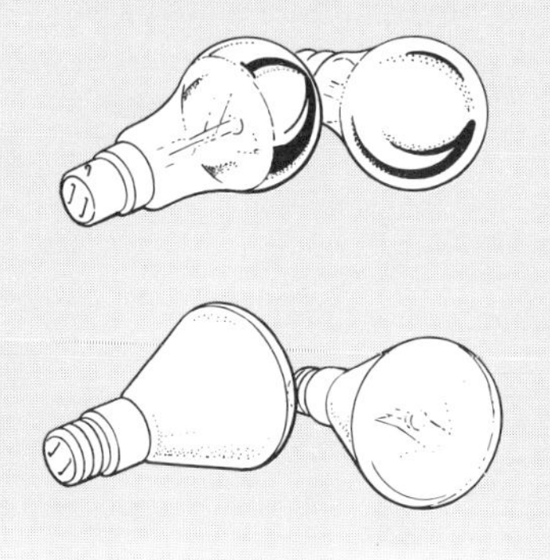

## Types of lamp

### General lighting service (GLS)

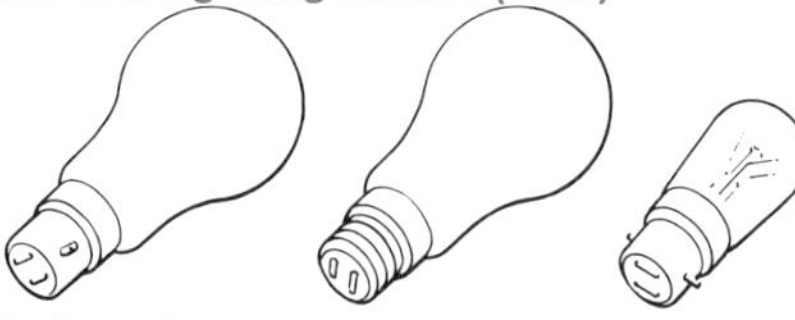

Ordinary filament light bulbs can be used in all sorts of fittings.
**Lamp life** 1,000 hours (long life last 2000h or more, but cost more)

**Wattages** 25W, 40W, 60W, 100W, 150W
**Light levels at 2m** Depend on how light is reflected or diffused. With reflector fittings producing narrow beams of 12° to 25°, a 100W lamp could give 300 to 1,700 lux. With fittings that don't reflect light, levels might be as low as 30 lux. A 60W lamp gives about half the output; a 40W lamp about a quarter.

### Fluorescent tube (MCF)

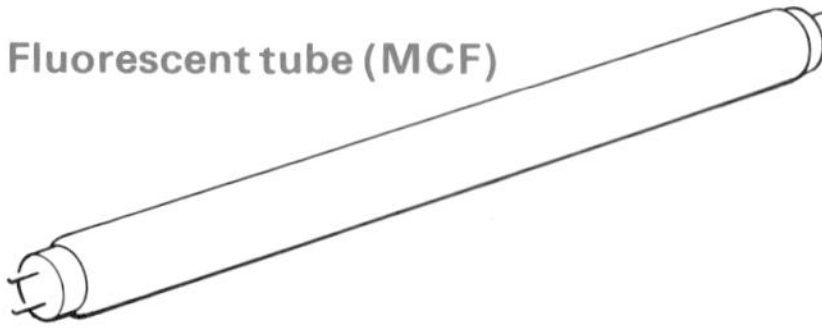

Lamps are mostly tubular and come in a number of lengths and two main diameters– 25mm and 38mm. But there are now also special (expensive) fluorescent bulbs which will fit in fittings which take GLS lamps. Light is produced by the electrical discharge in the tube, and by the fluorescent coating on the inside. Different coatings on the tube produce different sorts of white light. Must be used in special fitting.

**Lamp life** About 7,500 hours for lamps 1200mm or more long
**Wattages** Generally depends on length– 1200mm is 40W (or 36W in energy-saving version)
**Light levels at 2m** Much of light will be reflected, so depends on size of room, and how reflective ceilings and walls are. A 1200mm 40W *warm white* tube should give about 50 lux in a room 4m x 3m. Most other tubes have roughly the same efficiency (a 65W one produces about 90 lux) but a 600mm 40W tube produces only about 34 lux. *De-luxe warm white* will give about two-thirds of these levels but gives a warmer light with better colour rendering closer to a GLS lamp

### Crown-silvered (CS)

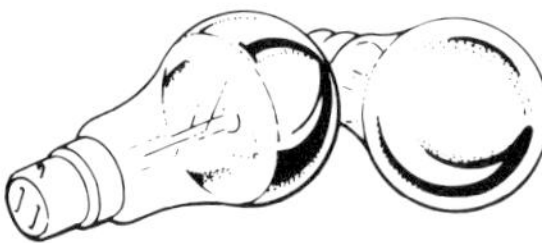

Looks much like an ordinary light bulb, but front is silvered so that all the light is projected back. Used with fittings having a special parabolic reflector to reflect light forward again in a narrow beam. Very little glare from side. Coloured reflectors available
**Lamp life** About 1,000 hours
**Wattages** Usually 60W, 100W. Also 40W miniature version
**Light levels at 2m** Depend mainly on reflector used: 100W typically between 600 lux and 2,000 lux, 60W about half that of 100W

### Internally-silvered lamp (ISL)

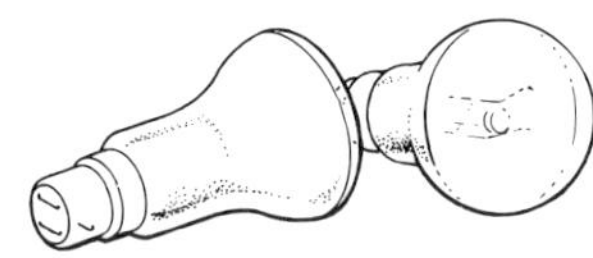

Available in 'flood' or 'spot' versions, although the spot beam is considerably wider than a CS spot beam. Has an internal reflective coating, so light comes out only at the front. Long neck; front can be coloured
**Lamp life** About 1,000 hours
**Wattages** Usually 75W, 100W, also available in 60W and in miniature 40W versions.

### Parabolic aluminised reflector (PAR 38)

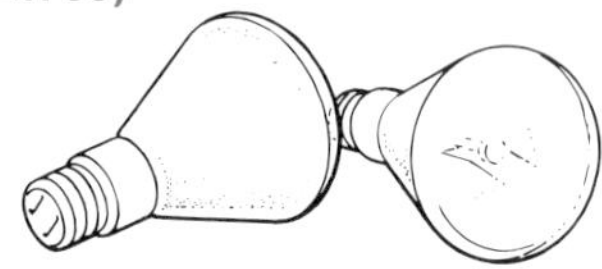

Bulb is pressed from toughened glass which can withstand thermal shock–sudden cooling due to rain for instance. Can be used outdoors in waterproof lampholders. Has an internal reflecting coating so light comes out only at the front. Available in both spot and flood versions. High-wattage PAR lamps are also available–eg PAR 56 (300W)–which have an elliptical beam and produce very high lighting levels.
**Lamp life** About 1,500 hours
**Wattages** 100W and 150W, spot and flood. Can be coloured
**Light levels at 2m** 100W spot gives about 1,000 lux, 150W spot about 1,800 lux: 100W flood gives 400 lux, 150W about 700 lux.

In living rooms you've a very wide choice of light fittings and the ways you can arrange them are also wide ranging.

**1 Pendant lighting** Pendant shades hide the lamp and spread the light. They're good for general diffused illumination, but can be lacking in interest and decorative quality. Long pendants can provide a semi-directional light in a corner or over a table. Single pendants can be on a rise-and-fall suspension. Pendants can be grouped from a multi-outlet ceiling rose – a good arrangement for a stairwell where the lamps can be hung at different heights.

**2 Down lighting** Downlighters mounted in matching pairs give a directional light which can be a wide or narrow beam. A variety of different types and shapes including fully-recessed, partially-recessed and ceiling-mounted (concealed) fittings are available. They take GLS or reflector lamps. Eyeball spotlights are among the most versatile as the angle of light can be varied (though you have to climb up to alter them).

**3 Spot lighting** Spotlight fittings with reflector lamps mounted on or in the ceiling give directional light. The angle of spot and choice of beam – wide, narrow or shaped – can alter the appearance of objects. Care is needed in angling to avoid casting glare into the eyes.

**4 Diffused wall lighting** A fluorescent lamp and fitting mounted behind a pelmet or baffle give an even spread of wall light. Wall-mounted lights are best shaded from the eyes and should use low-powered lamps.

**5 Local lighting** Standard and table lamps provide good local light – for reading, for instance. The light can be diffused or directional. For a table lamp, the height to the bottom of the shade should be about 300mm; for standard lamps 1·2m. If the light source is visible use pearl rather than clear lamps.

**6 Picture lights** Any sort of directional light can be used for pictures. Linear filament lamps can be used in suitable fittings for lighting pictures. Make sure you cannot look directly at the bulb from a standing or sitting position and that there's no glare off the glass.

SOME KINDS OF LIGHT

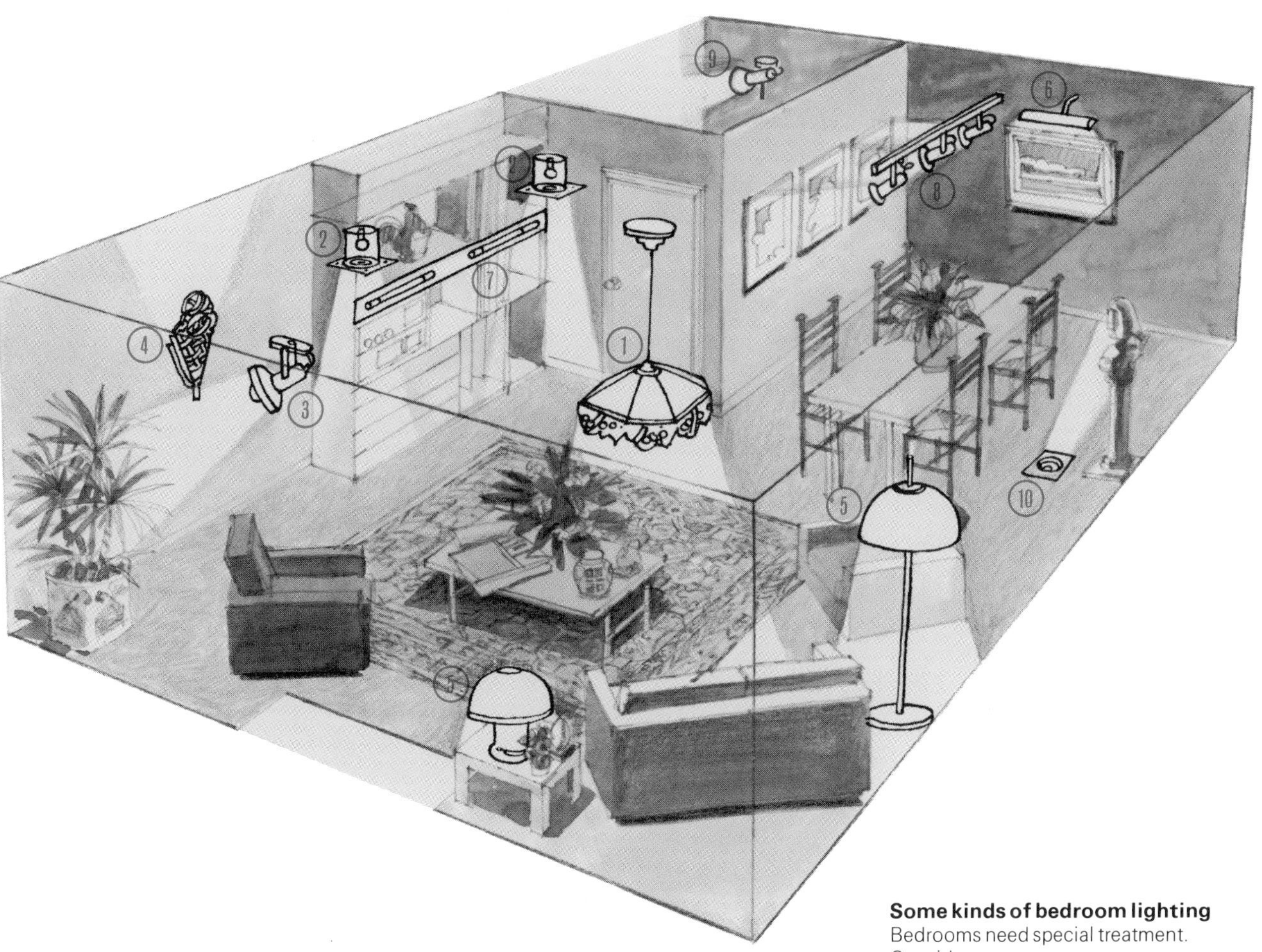


**7 Shelf and cupboard lighting**
Miniature fluorescent or linear filament lamps can be fitted to the back edge of a cupboard or below or above shelves, anywhere in fact where the lamp can be concealed and the light will be useful.

**8 Track lighting** A metal or plastic channel carrying concealed electrical conductor allows lights with special adaptors to be clipped along its length. Lengths of track can be clipped together. Although normally ceiling-mounted, the track can also be fitted on a wall. It can be connected via a ceiling rose or directly to the lighting cable (it isn't suitable for bathrooms).

**9 Flood lighting** Although they're normally used outdoors, large rooms can use high-wattage PAR lamps in special fittings. They should be dimmer controlled and fixed high on the ceiling as they give off a lot of heat.

**10 Up lighting** An interesting effect can be achieved by installing a lamp on the floor – there are cylindrical fittings for this purpose. A lamp could be installed in a recess in the floor, but then it must be sealed with a strong, well-supported cover – a glass brick for instance.

**Some kinds of bedroom lighting**
Bedrooms need special treatment. Consider:

- two-way switching at the door and bed for the main light fitting
- lighting for reading – 150 lux is recommended. Lamps can be placed at the side of the bed as standards supporting spot lamps, or wall-fixed in the centre, or over each pillow. Ordinary pendant ceiling lights (or wall lights) over the bed with 100W bulbs can give you enough light provided they're close enough and have fairly transparent shades. Choose a fitting with a very sharp beam for reading without disturbing a partner
- dressing table mirrors need lights either side at head height when sitting down. The light should shine on *you* – not on the mirror – and it's helpful if it doesn't shine directly in your eyes. Don't use bare bulbs – they can explode in your face.

# Wiring new lights

If you intend to make dramatic changes to an existing lighting system with lots of new lighting points and new switch positions, it's probably better to install a whole new circuit than to try to adapt or extend an old circuit. This is also true if the existing lighting circuits are not earthed, although it is possible to install a single earth to a new lighting point – see below.

The theory and background of lighting circuits is outlined on page 52.

For an additional light on an existing circuit, it is usually best to organise the new wiring on the junction box system, the advantages being that only one twin and earth cable has to be run to the new light and that a shorter switch cable is required.

**Linking into the circuit**

There are three possible methods and the method which will suit will depend on the position of the new light relative to the existing circuit. Trace this circuit by lifting floor boards on the floor above (or by going up into the loft space). Look for boards above existing lighting points which have obviously been lifted before – there should be a trap fixed with screws for easy access. Having found the circuit work out how many lights are already supplied and check that the new light (or lights) will not overload it.

Remember to turn off the mains before interfering with the existing wiring even when removing ceiling rose covers or junction box covers just to look at the wiring within.

**Connecting to a loop-in ceiling rose** Remove the cover of the selected ceiling rose and check whether it is the loop-in type. A loop-in ceiling rose will contain three (or if it's last in the line two) cables with the conductors (nine in total) connected to a centre bank of terminals. Although the loop-in type of ceiling rose fitting is now often used whether or not the circuit is wired on the loop-in system, it is simple to detect the difference, a rose which is wired on the junction system will have just one incoming cable and several empty terminals.

By far the easiest loop-in rose to connect into is the last one in the circuit – the one with just two cables coming into it. In roses already containing three cables there is little room in the terminals for the conductors of a further cable.

**Connecting to an existing junction box** Where the lighting circuit has no loop-in ceiling roses, the circuit will be wired on the junction box system. The first task is therefore to locate a junction box. If the new light is to be on the first floor of a two-storey house or the ground floor of a bungalow, all the junction boxes will be in the loft space and it will be easy to locate one suitable for connecting new cables – again the emptiest and therefore easiest one is the last one.

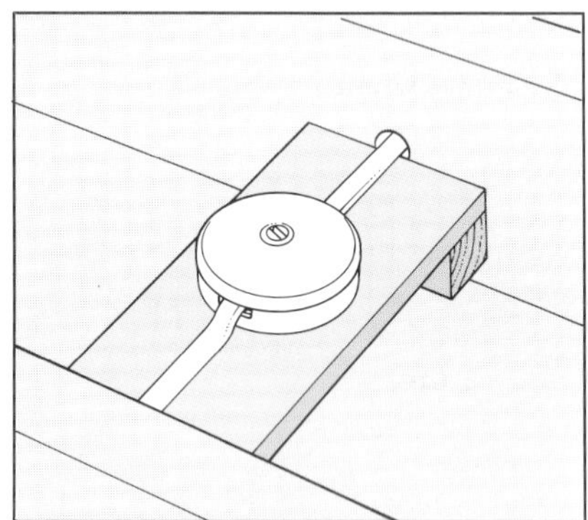

A junction box must be securely fitted to a batten placed between joists. An inserted box needs to be close to the circuit cable run. For the most economic use of cable, a box for a new light is best placed about midway between the new light and the switch.

If the new cable is to be taken from a loop-in ceiling rose, it is easiest if the rose is the last in the line. This will have spare terminals for connecting the live, neutral and earth conductors of the new cable, as shown.

If the new cable is taken from a junction box, the wiring may look more complicated, but the connections are essentially the same as in a rose, with all the live (red) conductors to one terminal, all the neutrals (blacks) to another and the earths (often bare but preferably insulated with green/yellow sheathing) to a third. The fourth terminal usually contains one black and one red insulated conductor, these being the return from the switch and the supply to the rose respectively. (The return from the switch is live and should be marked with red insulation.)

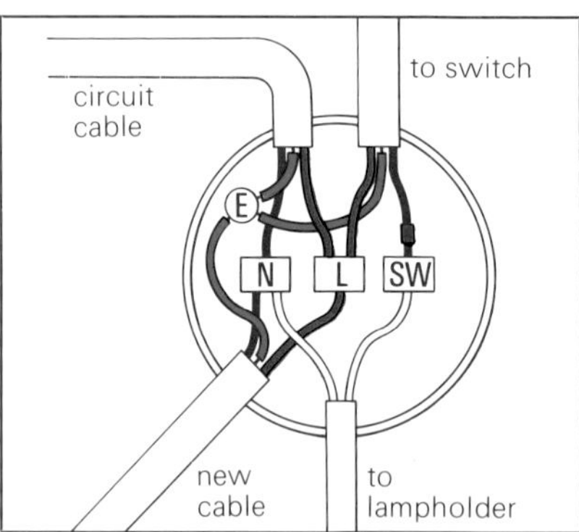


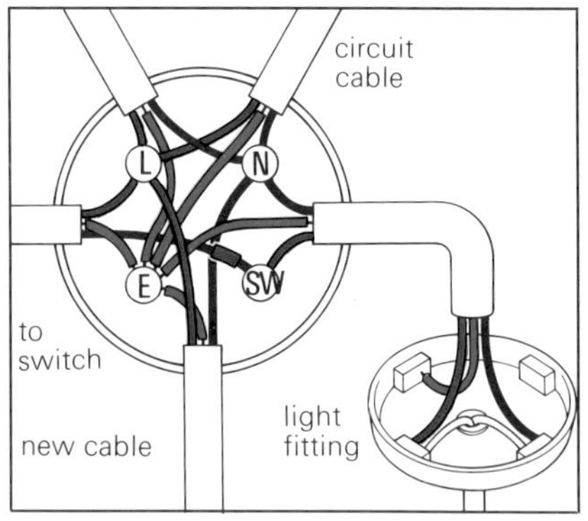


The new junction box is wired so that the three conductors of the incoming circuit cable each go to their respective terminals. The cable is sized to match the rest of the circuit—usually 1 $mm^2$. The cable to the switch has its red conductor connected to the live terminal; its black conductor sleeved with red and connected to the fourth terminal. The cable to the light fitting has its red conductor connected to the fourth terminal and its black conductor to the neutral. All earth conductors are connected to earth.

## LIGHT FITTINGS

The method of attaching the light fitting depends on its type but all connections should be made in a non-combustible enclosure.

**Simple ceiling fittings** These are either a *ceiling rose* with a pendant flex or a *batten lampholder*. Both these fittings have an integral backplate which contains the terminals and a screw-on cover.

**Multi-outlet pendant fittings** These are larger than the standard ceiling rose sometimes with a separate terminal block mounted on the inside. All connections must be completed before the plate can be screwed to the ceiling.

**Close-mounted fittings** These are fixed direct to the ceiling with the circuit cable connected to a lampholder or terminal block in the light fitting. All these fittings should be supplied with an integral backing plate or be designed to fit directly on to a purpose-made pattress or a round conduit box – sometimes called a BESA box. In practice, a lot of close-mounted light fittings are sold without a backing plate and won't easily fit on a box or pattress. For these the easiest solution is often a home-made backing plate–cut from a hardwood such as beech or mahogany with a neatly-cut cable hole.

**Wall lights** Most wall fittings are mounted on a recessed mounting box or an architrave box.

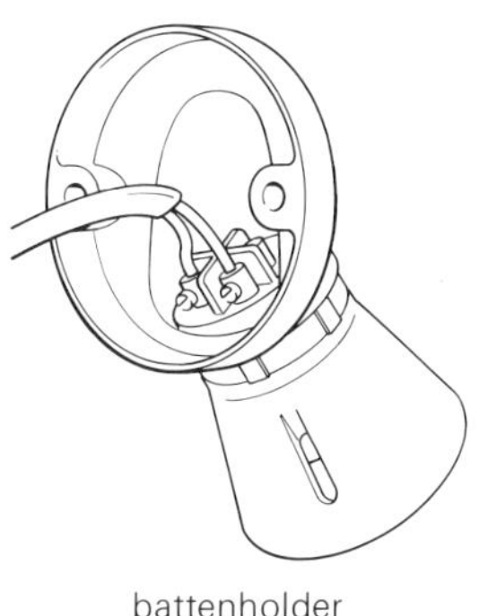

battenholder

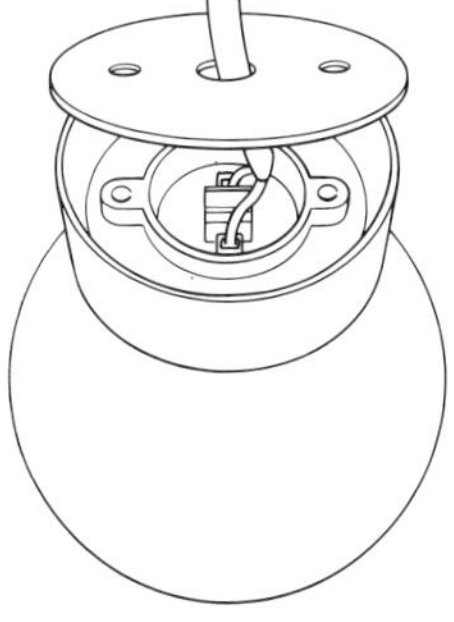

close-mounted globe

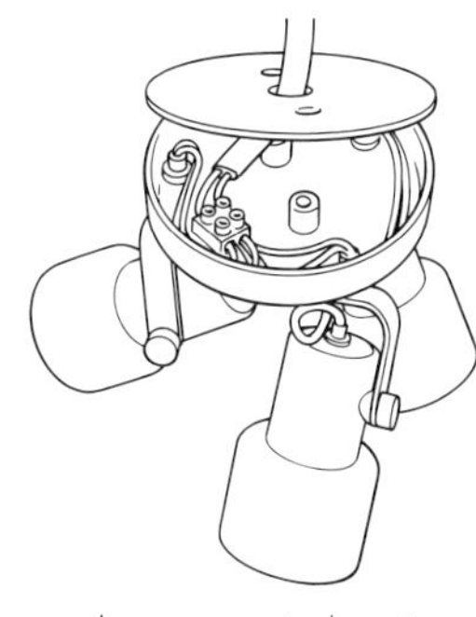

close-mounted spots

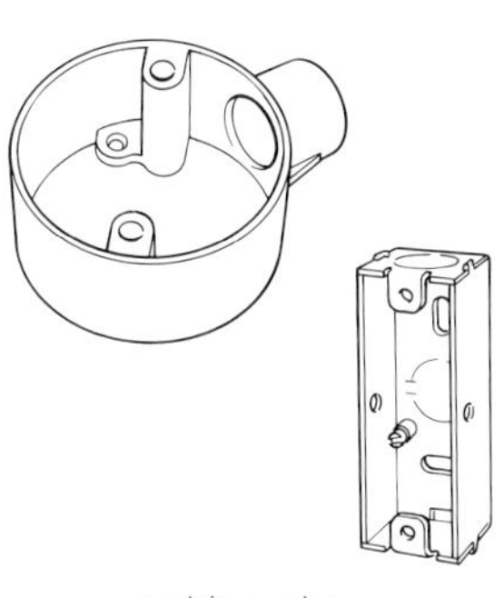

architrave box

Where junction boxes are situated in the space between floors the search can be a thankless task as it isn't always easy to guess where the boxes are. There are, however, two possible clues: first look immediately above the wall switches in the floor below; second look under the board running continuously along the landing.

When you locate a convenient junction box check that it is on the lighting circuit and not a 3-terminal 30 amp ring circuit junction box – the size of cables is a good clue.

**Connecting to an inserted junction box** If the terminals of existing nearby junction boxes cannot accept an extra cable, the answer is to insert a new junction box into the circuit. This could then be the box for the new light or be an intermediate box.

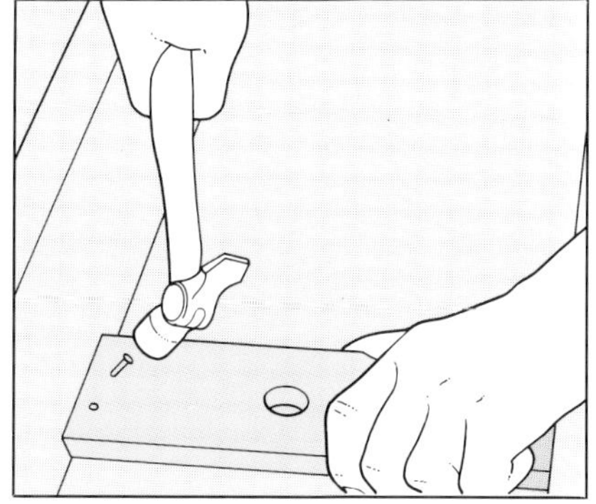

**Installing a light fitting**
All ceiling light fittings should be screwed through the ceiling to a proper support—a batten securely fixed between joists for instance. A hole is cut in the batten for the cables to pass through. Nailing the batten as shown will do for a fitting that isn't too heavy, but a heavy pendant would need its batten supported on brackets screwed to the joists (see left). A ceiling-mounted pull-cord switch also needs a secure fixing.

## EARTHING LIGHTS

If there is no existing earth conductor, one should be installed for the new light at least. Run a length of 1·5mm² single core green/yellow pvc insulated cable from the junction box earth terminal back to the earth terminal in the consumer unit. This cable will not earth the rest of the existing lighting circuit, but it will provide an earth connection for the new light and switch. This is really only a contingency plan, if your lighting circuit is not earthed, consider renewing the whole circuit in twin and earth cable. Metal light fittings must always be earthed.

# Floors: ideas for platforms

Changing the level of a floor can be an effective way of demarcating an area for a specific purpose, a dining area in an open plan living room for instance. Changing levels usually means a platform of some sort, but the area singled out doesn't have to be higher than the rest of the room. By raising the floor in the one part you can create the impression of a well elsewhere which is actually at normal floor level.

Whenever floor levels are altered, you'll need to give some thought to the skirting boards and also door thresholds and remember to retain sufficient headroom. If you create a gallery floor you'll probably need enough headroom to stand above and below the new floor.

There are various ways to construct a raised floor. The method to choose mostly depends on the area and height of the platform and on the type of sub-floor which you might find below.

The spacing for the supports is decided by the floor decking. Flooring-grade chipboard 18mm thick is used most often. For this the supports should not be more than 600mm apart – for other deckings see page 239. As a rule of thumb the depth of timber should not be less than one tenth of the span between supports. To avoid damp or damaged timbers, air should be able to circulate beneath the raised floor. When using solid supports, such as joints laid directly on the existing floor or a chipboard box or eggcrate, drill holes with a diameter of 25mm or so for ventilation.

Most platforms will need wall-plates for edge support – use timbers 75mm by 50mm firmly plugged to the wall. Don't hang a raised floor on a wall lined with plasterboard. Build an edge support instead. On a solid floor this can be a small brick or block wall.

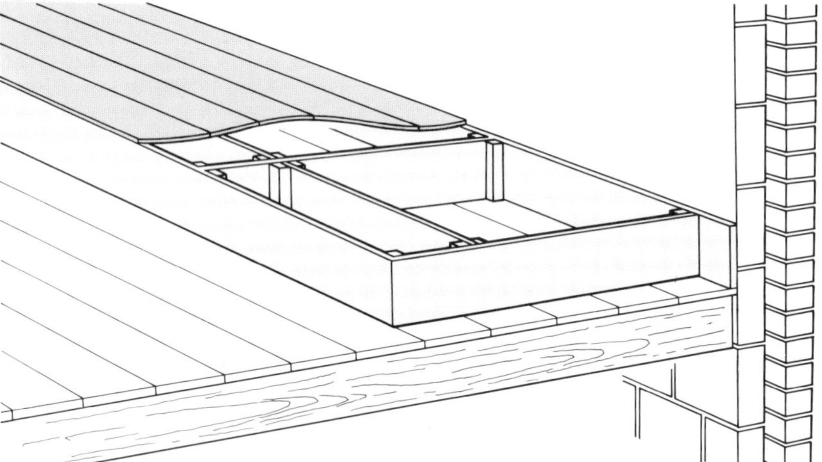

Chipboard box.

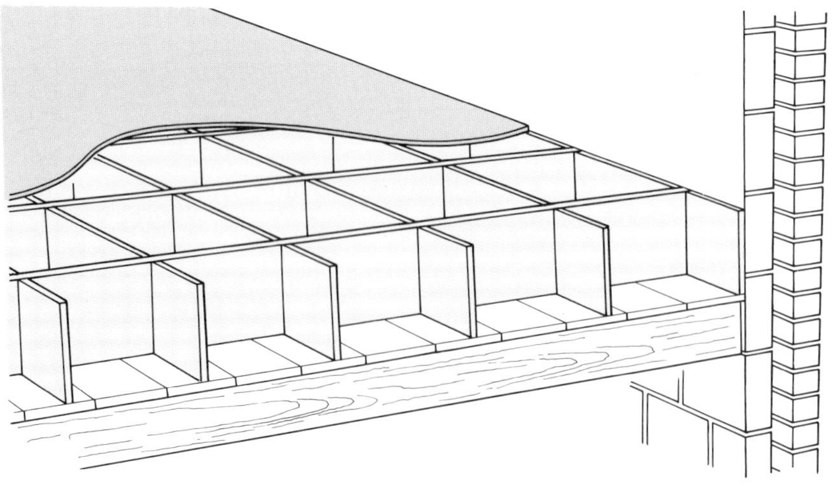

Eggcrate.

### Chipboard box

Separate boxes of 18mm chipboard are particularly useful for steps, but can be used for a low platform over wider areas. The corners are butt-jointed and strengthened with 25mm square battens glued and screwed into place. Use on solid or suspended floors. Can be freestanding.

### Eggcrate

A very sturdy platform can be created from lengths of 18mm chipboard or softwood planks joined together with half-lap joints – see drawing. The joints are usually glued for extra strength. Useful for low platforms over small or large areas. Use on solid or suspended floors. Can be freestanding.

### New joists

Joists (new or perhaps sound second-hand ones) can be suspended from hangers fixed into the masonry joints of opposite load-bearing walls. In this situation they will take the full load that was on the existing floor and must be sized to suit this purpose – see page 238. This method is useful for a fairly high-level platform in a room which is not too wide. One of the other platform construction methods – such as the chipboard box can be used to create steps up if required. Joists can also be laid directly on the existing floor. In which case smaller timbers can be used though this obviously creates a lower platform. The joists could be held in place by skew-nailing into wallplates.

### Timber stud

Lengths of softwood 75mm by 50mm can be used to create short timber stud walls – see page 126. Timbers can be joined with glued and nailed half-joints, or simply skew-nailed. The bottom plate is fixed to the existing floor. Can be used on suspended or solid floor, but on a solid floor the brick honeycomb wall method is probably easier.

### Brick honeycomb walls

On a solid ground floor the support for a new floor can be provided by sleeper walls constructed of bricks bonded in an open honeycomb – like the sleeper walls for a suspended timber ground floor. To provide a fixing for the floor covering, a framework of 50mm by 50mm sawn softwood is bedded in mortar on the brick walls. For walls which are a little cheaper to build, one or two courses of bricks can be built on edge, but for platforms higher than 250mm the walls are more stable if they are constructed with the bricks the correct way up.

### A gallery floor

A gallery in a high-ceilinged room can be constructed: as a new floor on joist hangers; as a timber framework taking its support from posts to the floor and the adjacent walls or as a freestanding structure of scaffold tubes. The design is peculiar to each situation and as you'll be adding to the load on the existing floor and walls professional advice is useful, if not essential.

New joists.

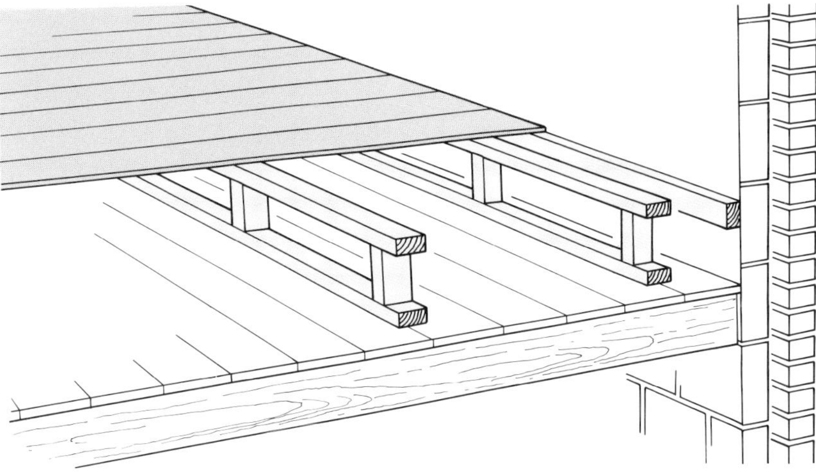

Timber stud.

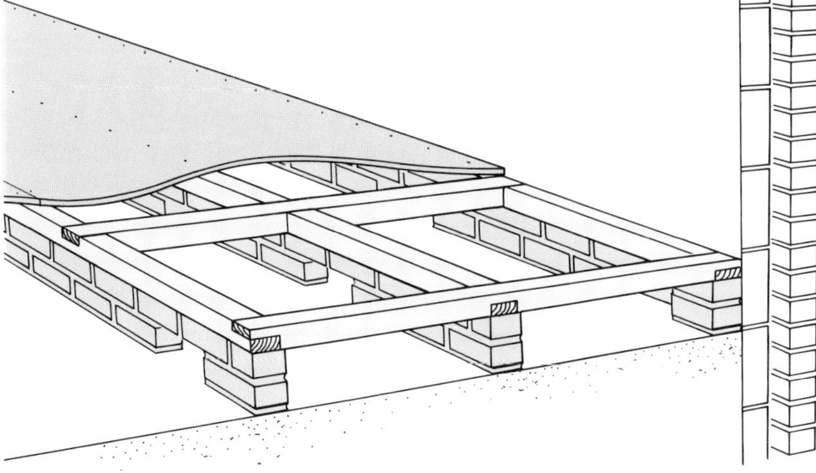

Brick honeycomb walls.

# Luxury flooring

For living rooms, bedrooms and halls, any room in fact which isn't a kitchen, bathroom or utility room, carpet is the commonest floor covering, but wood flooring is another choice.

## Wood flooring

There are various types of timber flooring, which are intended to be the finished surface of the floor. Most are made of hardwood. They can be subdivided into two basic groups: those intended to be fixed directly on to the floor joists – solid strip – and those which require a sub-floor – mosaic, block and thinner strip. With the exception of block, floors intended for laying on a sub-floor are thinner and are proportionately cheaper.

Laying some types of hardwood flooring and achieving a good finish is a skilled operation and this should be borne in mind when a flooring is selected. If it is intended as a do-it-yourself project, or if a tradesman without the specialist skills will do the work, it would be sensible to choose one of the simpler types of floor. Some types of wood flooring (especially wood mosaic and the pre-finished types of thin strip flooring) can be obtained in the larger do-it-yourself stores, or from some timber merchants. The other types of wood strip and wood block floors may have to be obtained from specialist sources or from the manufacturer direct. Retail outlets tend to stock only the more popular timber species.

When all types of wood flooring are purchased they should be at an appropriate moisture content (dryness) to be laid. They should be stored in an equivalent situation to where they will be used (not in a damp shed or garage) and they must not be laid on a new concrete screed floor until it is really dry (5 per cent max moisture content). This can be measured with a moisture meter if one is available; failing this, wait six to eight weeks after the screed is laid and keep the room warm and well ventilated.

### Floors laid on joists

A solid strip floor is the only type which can be laid on joists. In normal circumstances the joists would need to be no further apart than 400mm. Strip flooring will normally be tongued and grooved on the long edges and end matched (that is tongued and grooved on the ends). The strip should not be less than 19mm in thickness (before sanding). Different types will vary in width, but 75mm (including the tongue) is average.

When a large (room-sized) area is to be laid, strip flooring looks best if random lengths are used so that the end joints are staggered across the room.

Most of strip flooring is plane finished and requires sanding after it is laid. Strip flooring can be obtained in a variety of hardwoods, including Afzelia, Ash, Beech, Gurjun, Keruing, Mahogany, Maple, Oak and Opepe.

### Floor laid on subfloor

When the decorative flooring is laid on to a floor of tongued and grooved softwood boarding, chipboard, plywood or a screeded concrete slab, any wood flooring can be used.

When fixing over a softwood boarded sub-floor a layer of 3·2mm hardboard or plywood is recommended (see page 85).

**Mosaic flooring** Mosaic panels are made up from fingers of wood arranged in a series of squares and glued to a felt base. The normal panel size is approx 450mm by 450mm and is 6mm to 8mm thick.

Wood mosaics generally require sanding prior to the application of the surface treatment, although it may be possible to obtain pre-finished panels. Wood mosaic flooring is the most tolerant finish for any situation where there is slight spring or bounce in the sub-floor construction. The panels can be laid square or diagonally to the

WOOD FLOORING

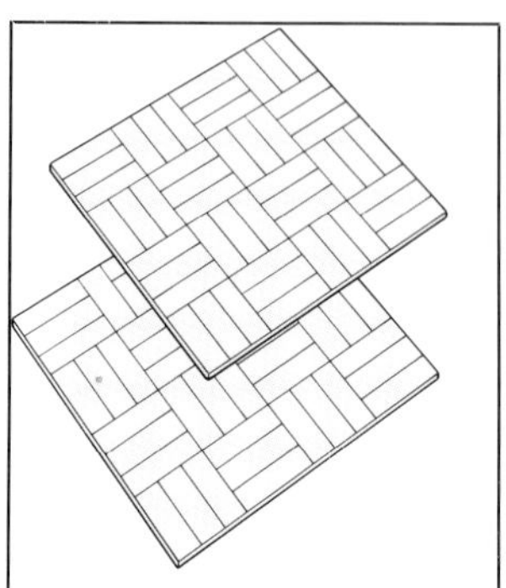
Mosaic panels.

Solid strip to lay on joists.

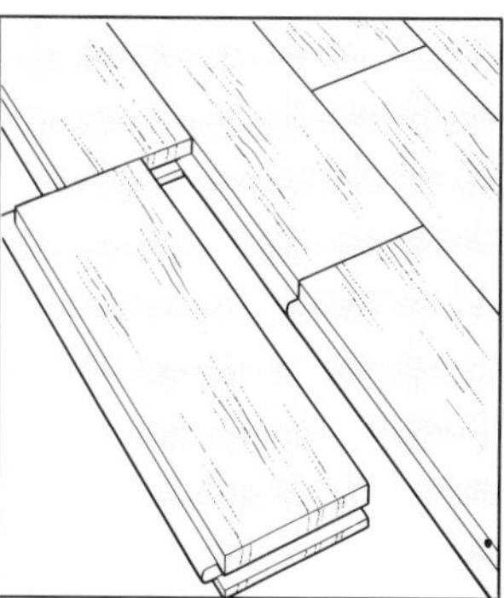
Blocks (parquet).

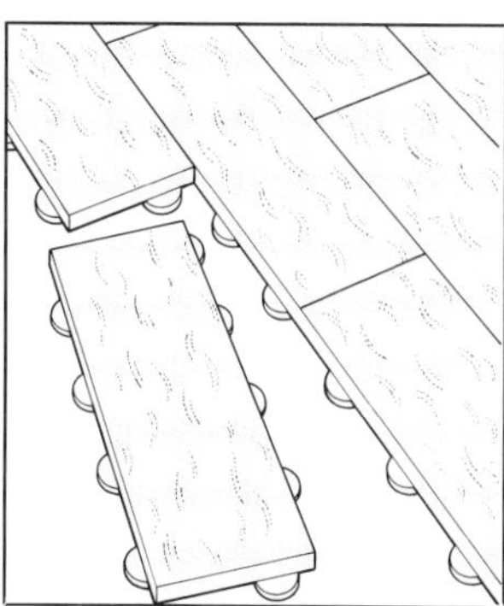
Laminated strip.

walls of the room. The panels are available in a range of hardwoods, including Afzelia, Teak, Iroko, Oak, Saple, Walnut, Eucalyptus, Meranti, Mahogany and Agba.

**Block (parquet) flooring** This is made up from individual blocks of timber interlocked with tongues and grooves of all four edges. The blocks are usually 18mm or 20mm thick (before sanding) and have a surface area of approximately 225mm by 75mm. Herringbone, basket and brick are common patterns for laying and to achieve a good fit it is very important that individual blocks are identical in size and thickness. The blocks are fixed down with appropriate adhesive and sanded before finishing. Laying paraquet flooring is usually considered a job for experts. Blocks are available in Afzelia, Mahogany, Maple, Oak, Iroko, Opepe and Sapele.

**Strip flooring** Strips for laying on to a sub-floor can be much thinner than those laid on to joists, thicknesses of approximately 10mm to 12mm are typical. They can be laid on any prepared timber floor, but not on concrete. The strips have tongued and grooved edges with matched ends.

Solid strip floors are usually plane finished and require sanding before the surface treatment is applied. They are available in a range of hardwoods, including Oak, Mahogany, Maple, Beech, Ash, Keruing and Karri.

**Laminated strip** This is another type of thin strip flooring. The strip is made up from glued laminations of hardwood (like plywood) or hardwood faces on softwood or chipboard backings. The strips vary in thickness from 6mm for the thinnest to approx 20mm. Panel sizes also vary greatly, some being individual strips – nominally 75mm in width – others made up into sheets 200mm or 300mm wide.

Laminated strips are generally prefinished and require no further treatment for normal use. They are available in a range of hardwoods, including Afzelia, Oak, Birch, Iroko, Mahogany and, in addition, selected Pine boards. It is arguable whether they offer the same feel of quality that a well laid and finished solid strip floor has, but they are less work to lay.

## Carpet

You may decide to fit carpet primarily for its look and feel, but when buying a carpet you'll be equally interested in how long it will last.

Two of the most important factors that determines how long any particular carpet will last are *where you put it and how much abuse it gets* – the same carpet would survive much better in a spare bedroom than in a living room.

Although there are many different *types* of carpet – the factors that will have most bearing on a carpet's life once it's installed are the density of the pile and the pile material.

CARPET TYPES

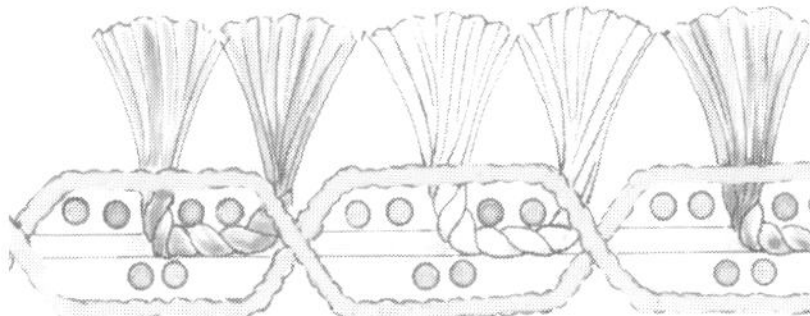

Axminster cut pile

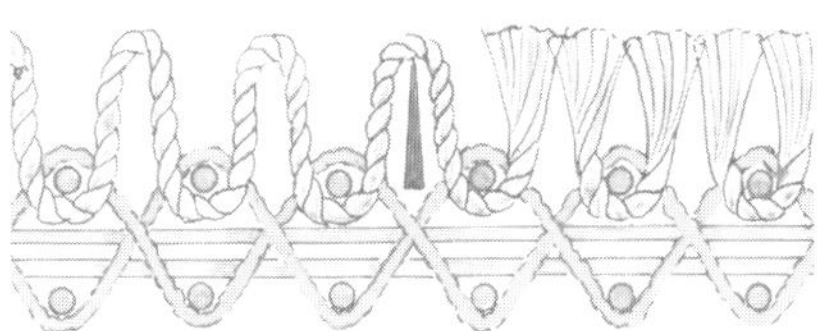

Wilton loop and cut pile.

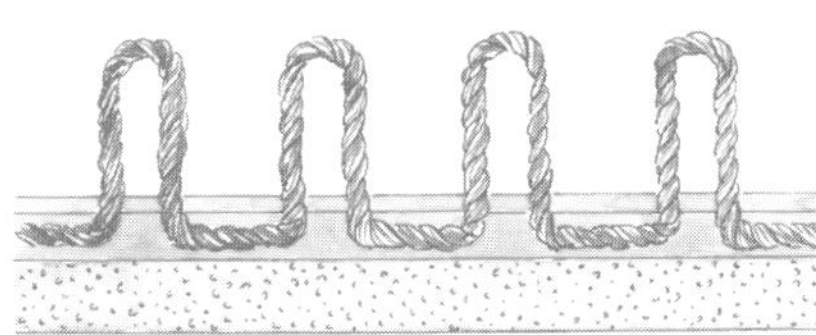

Tufted – loop pile.

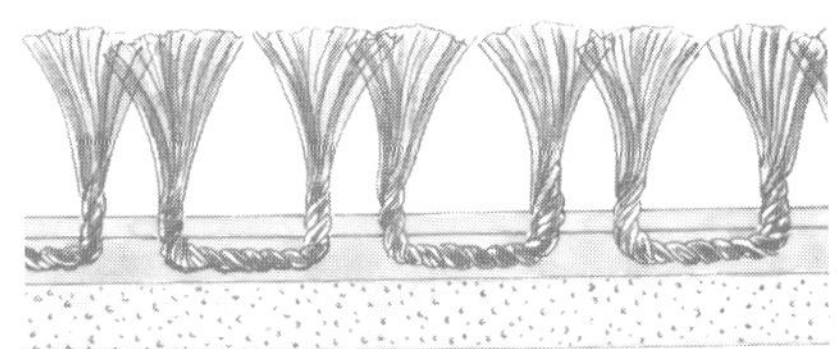

Tufted carpet – cut pile.

**Density** is important, particularly in traditional pile carpets, because fibres wear more rapidly if you tread on the sides rather than on the ends. The more tightly the fibres are packed, the more likely they are to stay upright so that the carpet will wear better.

To get some idea of how dense and thick the pile is, bend the carpet back on itself. If it 'grins' – showing the backing easily – it isn't very dense. Turn the carpet backing, count the number of rows per inch (it probably varies between 4 and 10 down the carpet's length). The more the better. How securely the tufts of fibre in the pile are fixed into the carpet is also very important. Poorly-secured tufts may well result in bald patches.

**The material** a carpet is made of can affect not only how long it will last, but other things, such as resistance to stains, as well – see Table. However, because, for example, acrylics are *very good* for resisting flattening, and nylon *good*, all acrylic carpets will not necessarily be better than all nylon ones.

The fibres most commonly used for carpet pile are: acrylic, nylon, polyester, polypropylene, viscose, wool (and other animal hair). Often they are blended together – for example, nylon with wool, which gives better resistance to wear. And sometimes the fibres are modified for a particular reason – for example, modacrylic is more fire-resistant than ordinary acrylic. It's quite common for carpets to be sold quoting the fibre's trade name but the generic names should also be given.

One or two other things you can check to determine a carpet's quality:

- if the carpet has a foam back, run your finger across it. If it crumbles, it is not good quality
- if the carpet has a sculptured or embossed pile, check that there are no gaps between the different levels.

- for carpet tiles and non-woven carpets, pull at the backing: it should not break away.

### Labelling
Under the Textile Products (Indications of Fibre Content) Regulations, every carpet has to be labelled to show its fibre content. This is a minimum statutory requirement, but many carpets have additional labels. One scheme established by the British Carpet Manufacturers Association (BCMA) covers a good proportion of the market. Last year the BCMA revised their existing scheme to become the British Carpet Performance Rating Scheme which grades carpets as follows:

**A Extra heavy wear** – for locations where very high standards are demanded
**B Very heavy wear** – for the heaviest domestic use and most contract areas
**C Heavy wear** – for busy domestic areas and medium contract use
**D General wear** – for most domestic areas and light contract use
**F Medium wear** – for domestic areas not subject to concentrated use
**F Light wear**

Although only members of the BCMA can label their carpets on this basis other manufacturers and retailers follow the same principle by rating their carpets as medium domestic, general domestic and so on.

### Carpet fitting
If you are going to have your **carpet fitted professionally**, ask for a written estimate and compare deals between shops and fitters. Most shops will be able to arrange fitting. Work out your own plans for how the carpet could be laid – you may come up with a cheaper solution.

If you have trouble finding a professional fitter, contact the National Institute of Carpet Fitters, for their address see page 314.

### Main pile fibres compared

| | wear and appearance retention | resistance to flattening | soil and stain resistance | ease of cleaning | other points |
|---|---|---|---|---|---|
| **ACRYLIC AND MODACRYLIC (Acrilan, Courtelle, Dralon, Teklan)** | good | very good | shows dirt easily. Good stain resistance | easy; needs to be done frequently. Doesn't soak up liquids | resembles wool in appearance and feel. Teklan (modacrylic) is flame-resistant. Ordinary acrylics burn fairly easily |
| **COTTON** | good | poor | fair for stains, poor for dirt | easy; needs to be done frequently. Colours may run | soft and smooth. Carpets often thin, so edges may curl. Burns fairly easily |
| **NYLON (Anso, Artron, Bri-nylon, Enkalon, Enkaluxe, Timbrelle)** | very good | good | shows dirt easily (but newer types claim to be better). Good stain resistance | easy; needs to be done frequently. Doesn't soak up liquids | Timbrelle is claimed to be as good as wool for resisting flattening and dirt. If exposed to flame, nylon melts, and may continue to burn slowly. May generate static unless treated. |
| **POLYESTER (Dacron, Terylene, Trevira)** | good | fairly good | shows dirt easily. Good stain resisance, except to oil | easy; needs to be done frequently. Doesn't soak up liquids | fairly soft texture. If exposed to flame, melts and may continue to burn slowly. May generate static unless treated |
| **POLYPRO-PYLENE (Meraklon)** | very good | fair | good | very easy; Doesn't soak up liquids | good for kitchens and bathrooms. Rather harsh feel. If exposed to frame, melts and may continue to burn slowly |
| **VISCOSE** | fair | poor | shows dirt fairly easily. Fair stain resistance | easy; but should not be saturated with shampoo | fairly soft and warm. Used on its own, suitable only for light traffic areas. Burns readily |
| **MODIFIED VISCOSE (Darelle, Evlan)** | fairly good | fair | shows dirt easily. Fair stain resistance | easy; but should not be saturated with shampoo | fairly soft and warm. Has better wear, resilience and soil resistance than viscose. Used on its own suitable only for light traffic areas. Burns readily (but Darelle is flame-resistant) |
| **WOOL** | good | very good | good | easy; use correct shampoo | soft, warm feel. Usually mothproofed. Doesn't burn easily |

# Laying wood flooring

The different types of wood flooring are laid in different ways – and this may depend on the sub-floor. Most types can be laid on any sub-floor which is smooth, level and dry. The major difference is whether they are laid with adhesive, nailed or loose-laid with no fixing.

Generally, adhesive is used for fixing thin, pre-fabricated panels on solid floors. Nails are used for fixing strips and blocks to timber sub-floors. Loose laying is suitable for some types of pre-fabricated panel provided there is an underlay.

The Guide methods detail how to lay mosaic panels with adhesive, how to secret-nail a strip floor and how to lay block flooring. With other types, the procedure is very similar to one or other of these. Loose-laying panels for instance follows substantially the same method as for laying mosaic panels with adhesive.

## Step-by-step

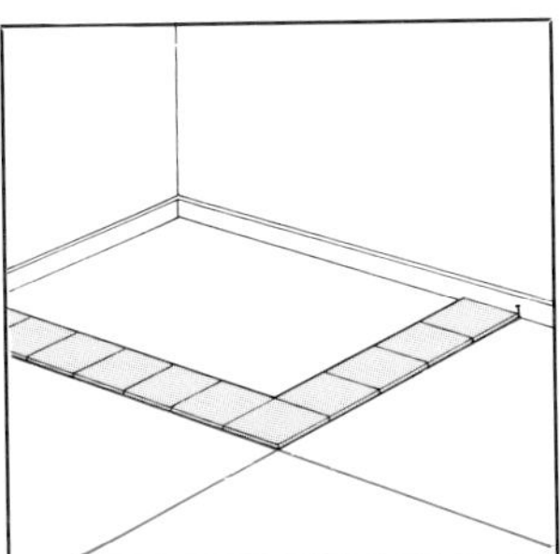

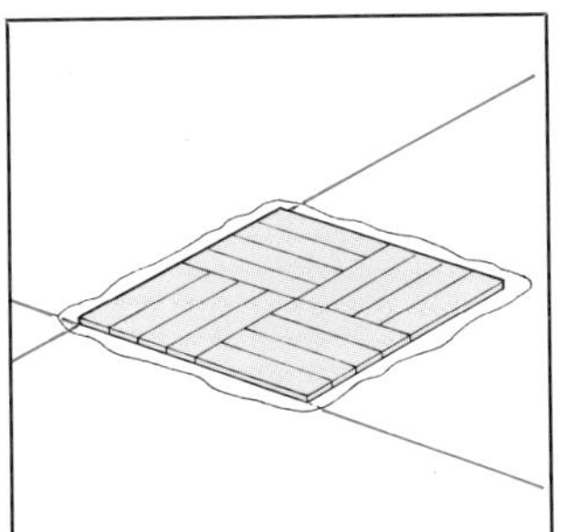

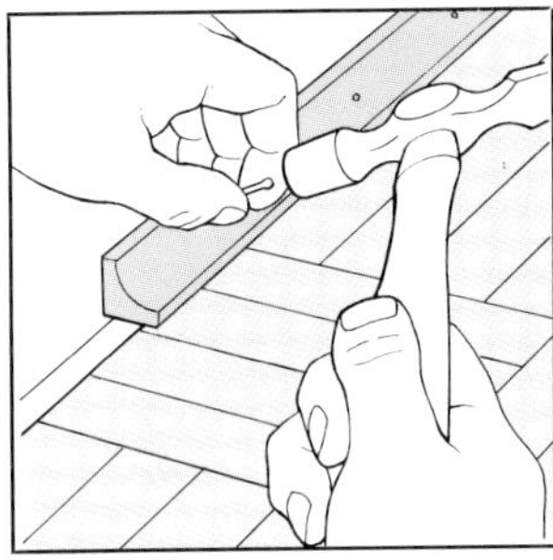

**Laying mosaic panels**
Mosaic panels are probably the easiest wooden floor to lay, and are suitable for any prepared sub-floor. They are normally laid with adhesive, although some types can be loose laid. It is also possible in some cases to use a heavy-duty double-sided adhesive tape, and this may be the best solution for individual panels which might have to be lifted for access to pipework, say.

**Step 1** Before you start to lay the panels, mark up the floor with two square lines to the centre as for cork or vinyl tiles (see page 88). If you're laying the tiles diagonally across the room these will have to go from corner to corner. Leave an expansion gap of 12mm all around the room to allow for movement, and dry-lay a run of tiles first to check the fit.

Work outwards from the centre in all direction – leaving panels around the edges which will need trimming until last. If you are gluing the panels down, use the adhesive recommended by the manufacturer – usually a bitumen-based type. Spread it evenly over a small area at a time – slightly over-lapping the panel size – and bed the panel firmly. With loose-lay panels, fit the tongued and grooved edges together.

**Step 2** At the edges, overlay the panels to mark them for cutting, as for vinyl tiles but remember to leave the expansion gap. On felt-backed panels, cuts which coincide with the gaps between the strips of wood which make the mosaic can be cut with a knife. Otherwise, use a tenon saw.

Lay the edge panels all round. Fill the expansion gap with a cork strip. Or cover it with a moulding pinned to the skirting board.

**Laying laminated panels and boards** These are laid in much the same way as mosaic panels. In most types, the edges have interlocking lugs or tongues and grooves. Some can be loose-laid over an underlay, others may be glued and secret-nailed in position – check the manufacturer's instructions. Larger laminated boards simulate strip flooring. They are usually secret nailed to a wood sub-floor, or glued to a solid one.

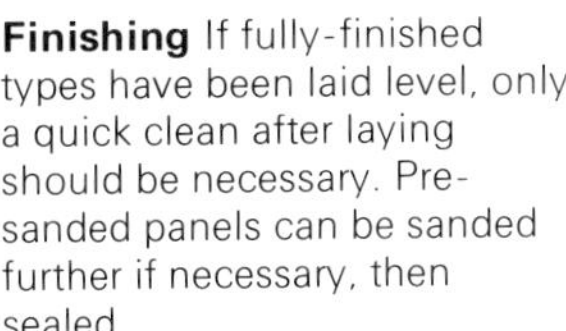

**Finishing** If fully-finished types have been laid level, only a quick clean after laying should be necessary. Pre-sanded panels can be sanded further if necessary, then sealed.

Floors supplied planed need a full finishing job. In most cases it is worth hiring a floor sander (and possibly an edge sander) to smooth the whole floor, then finishing with at least three coats of sealer. You can use a polyurethane varnish and it should wear fairly well. But for wood floors that will get heavy use, a hall perhaps, a two-pack varnish should wear better.

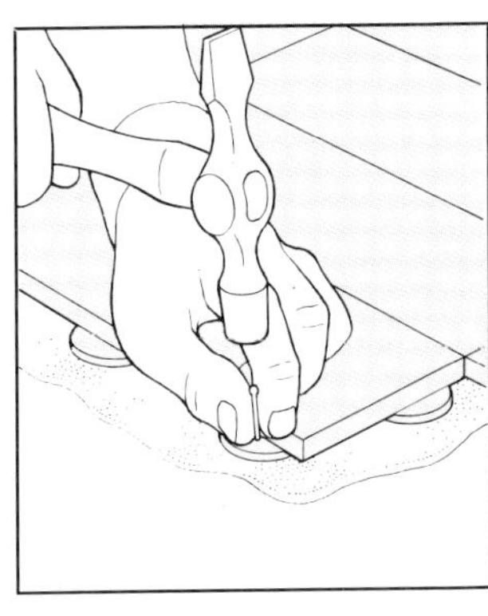

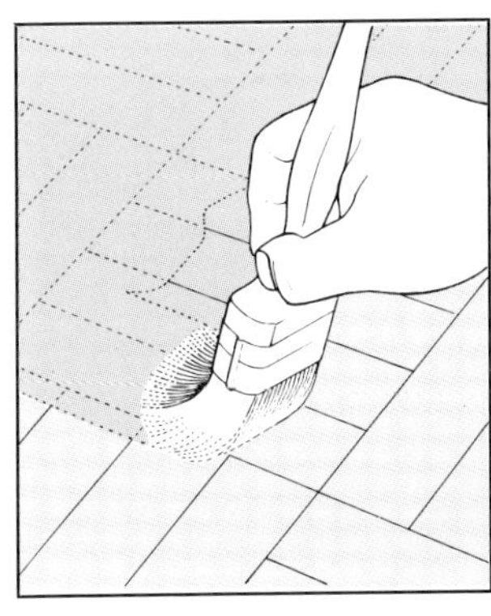

## Step-by-step

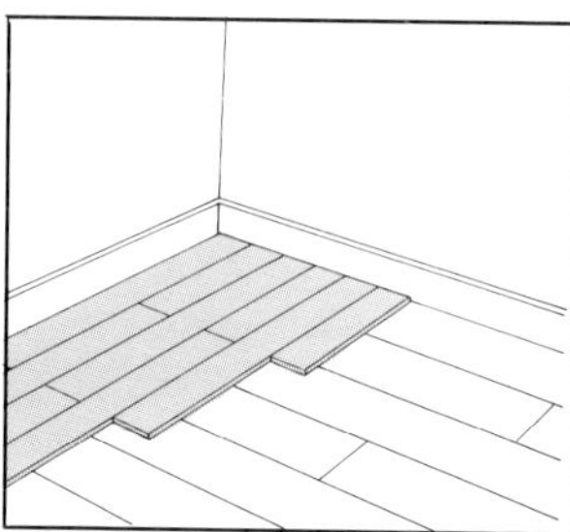
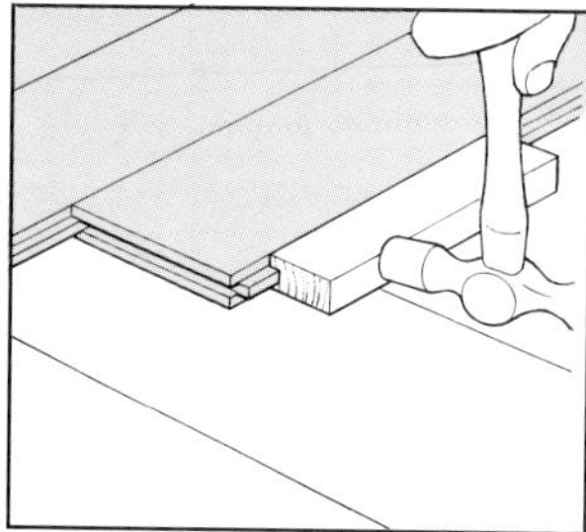
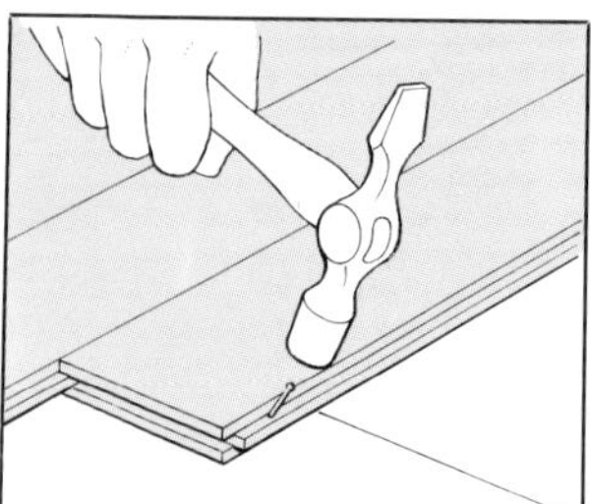
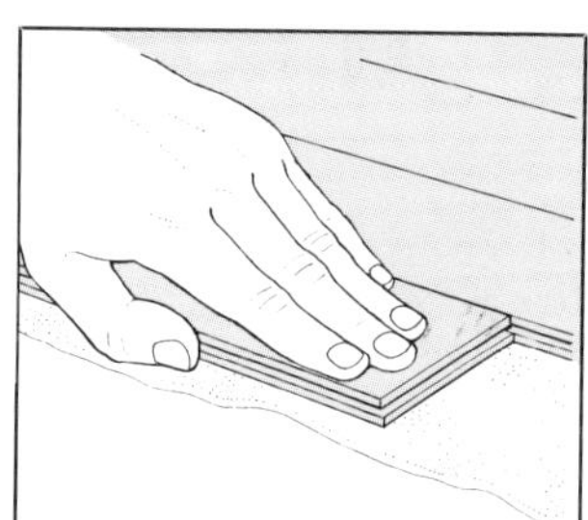

**Laying strip flooring** As all strip flooring is relatively narrow, the cutting should be minimal, and marking out is limited to establishing a square line for cutting the ends – use a try-square.

Although there is no reason why wood strip should not be laid diagonally in a room, it will look best if it is laid at right angles to the walls and it helps to disguise any imperfections of level if the strips are at right angles to the main source of window light.

*On a timber sub-floor* the thin type of strips should be laid at an angle – usually 90° or 45° – across the existing floorboards. Use a mallet or a hammer and piece of scrapwood to knock the pieces together and secret-nail through the tongue. Bitumen

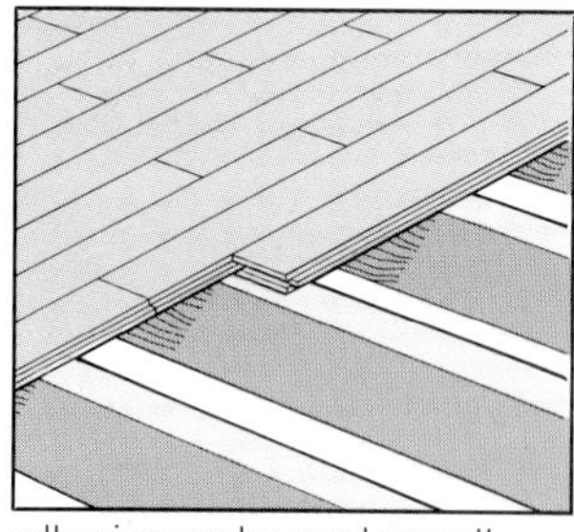

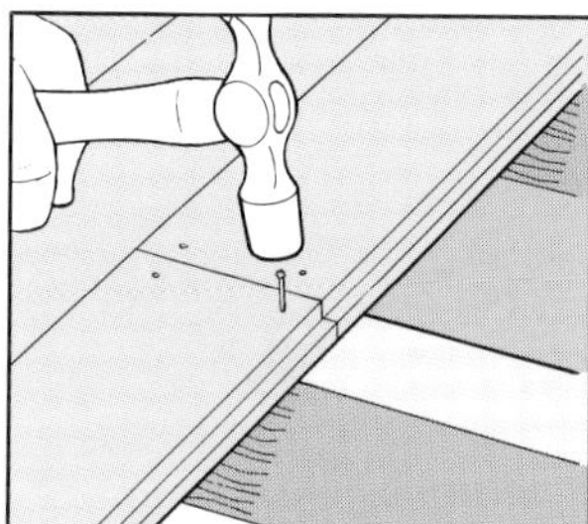
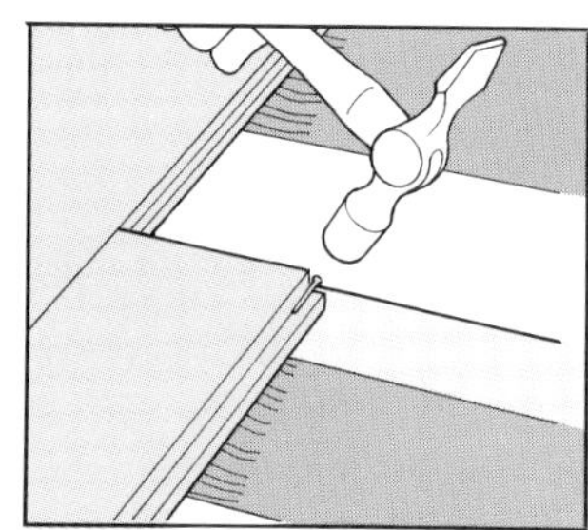

adhesive can be used as well, and may help to cut down squeaks. On a concrete floor bed the strips on suitable adhesive. The more substantial strip flooring can be laid directly over floor joists or over a concrete floor on 50mm by 50mm battens set into a 50mm sand and cement screed at 400mm centres (spaces of 450mm). If you are laying a new concrete floor, you can use a 12mm levelling screed and 50mm by 25mm battens nailed over it.

Whether it is laid over joists or embedded battens, fix the strips at right angles to the timbers by secret nailing. The alternative is to nail through the faces, punching the nails beneath the surface and filling the holes. If the strips are end-matched the joints may be made anywhere between the joists, but should be staggered. With square-ended strips, the joints must be over a supporting nogging to which both strips are nailed.

Strip floors can also be laid as a sprung floor. In which case, special cushion pads are laid between the joists and the strips.

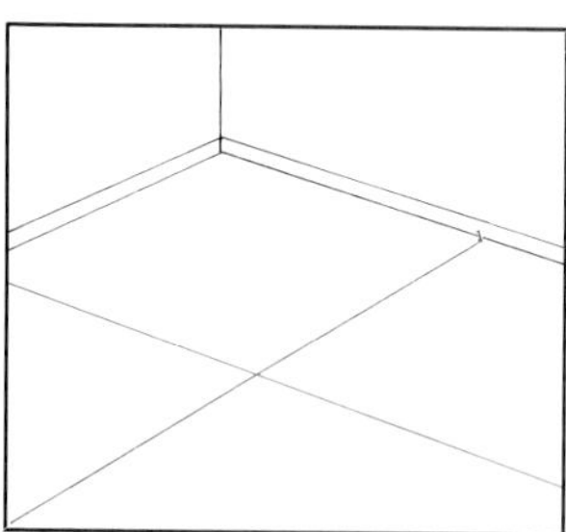
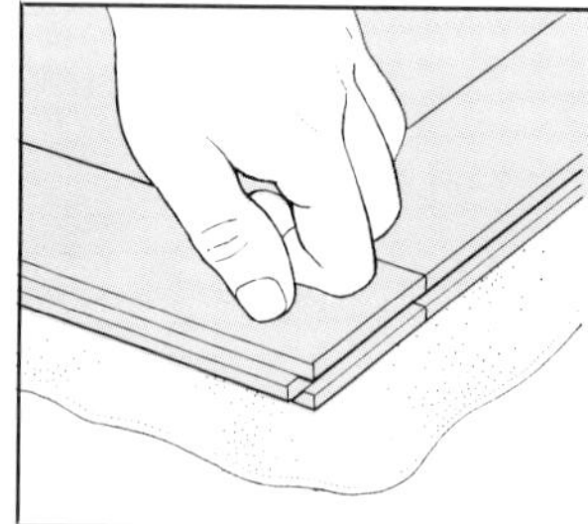
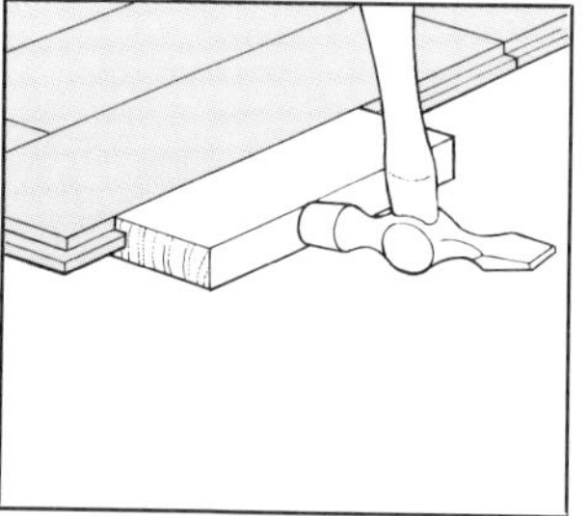
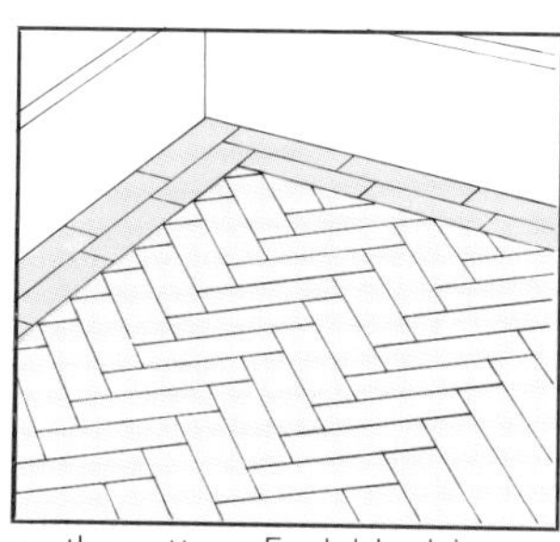

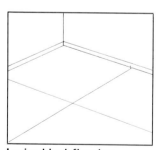

**Laying block flooring**
Individual wood blocks are tongued and grooved, and can be laid on a solid floor with a bitumen adhesive, or secret-nailed to a timber sub-floor.

They are probably the most difficult form of flooring to lay. Unlike mosaic panels, which are laid in a square grid, or strip flooring which is laid in straight lines, blocks are laid individually to form a parquet pattern. There are a number of different arrangements, and the blocks may be machined to interlock only in a particular way.

Even the simplest pattern will require a lot of cutting at the edges. As the blocks are thick, this can involve a great deal of work – especially for diagonal interlocking patterns like the herringbone. To simplify laying, most patterns leave a border one or two blocks wide, running round the room. The border incorporates the 12mm expansion gap.

The main pattern is based on guide lines starting at the centre of the room – these may be square or diagonal depending on the pattern. Each block is knocked into place against its neighbours, with the last blocks cut before fitting.

# Carpet laying

One wrong cut and a large expanse of carpet could be ruined, so if you've spent a lot of money, on a Wilton or an Axminster for instance, you might think the cost of paying a professional fitter is worth the peace of mind.

On the other hand if you work carefully and double check your measurements, an expensive carpet is no more difficult to lay than a cheap one.

## Measuring up

Before ordering the carpet you've chosen work out how it will be laid and how much you need. Make a floor plan, including the full width of door frames. Rooms are rarely true squares, so measure across the room as well as along the walls. Mark doorways and windows – where possible, the carpet pile should face *away* from natural light to avoid uneven shading and *towards* doorways to minimise wear. If seams are necessary, ensure the pile of adjoining pieces lies in the same direction and that any pattern can be matched up (allow one extra pattern repeat for this). Arrange seams in the same direction as people usually walk and try not to make them across heavily-used areas – an ideal position would be under a permanent piece of furniture. It is difficult to make seams invisible but they will be less noticeable if positioned at right angles, rather than parallel, to windows so that natural light does not fall across them.

## Preparation

Clear the room of all furniture and remove any inward-opening doors. The floor should be smooth, level and rigid – any uneven areas could eventually wear a hole in the carpet.

Carpets can be laid directly on to woodblock, cork and vinyl floorcoverings providing they are well secured. If you are laying it on a bare floor – prepare as outlined on pages 84–85.

Ensure that the floor is clean and dry – dirt and grit can work their way up into the pile and damage it. They may also prevent the carpet from being secured properly to the floor. Leave the carpet in the room for 24 hours to acclimatise.

## Laying the carpet

All carpets must be anchored to the floor to prevent movement as people walk or move furniture over them. As well as being unsightly, rucks accelerate wear and are liable to become dangerous foot traps. All carpets should also have a good quality underlay rubber, felt or polystyrene to prolong their life, improve heat and sound insulation and make them springier underfoot. Avoid the rubber type if you have underfloor heating.

Foam-backed carpets are the simplest to lay – they are pretensioned and have a built-in underlay and are simply stuck to the floor. Tensioning prevents rucking and also ensures the pile stands erect which makes for greater durability and easier cleaning. With all other carpets you need to put down a separate underlay. You also have to tension them with a knee kicker – a tool with a toothed head which hooks through the carpet pile to just penetrate the backing material – you jolt the padded end forward with your knee. Knee kickers are available from most hire shops – check that the teeth are in good condition and can be set to a suitable length for the carpet pile. (Note: carpets which have their pile glued into the backing material rather than woven or stitched must not be stretched – check with the carpet retailer if you are unsure about the type you are buying.)

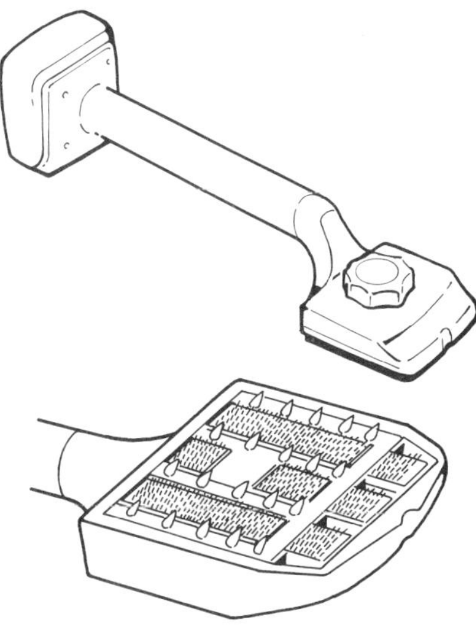

A knee kicker is used to tension a carpet laid with a separate underlay.

Traditionally carpets with separate underlay have been anchored to the floor with tacks. This method is cheap but the tacks are usually visible and the indentations they make tend to collect dirt. You are also likely to damage the carpet if you try to take it up at a future date. (Tacks should never be used with foam-backed carpets as they would damage the backing.)

Much commoner nowadays are concealed fixings – wooden strips with two staggered rows of angled pins. You nail or glue the strips around the room and stretch the carpet over the pins which hook on to the carpet backing without harming the pile. The carpet can be stretched back off the pins if it needs to be taken up at any time – this is the method described in detail on page 163.

### Turn-and-tack method

Cut the underlay to within 50mm of the skirting boards and tack it in place. Cut the carpet so that it rises 50mm up each wall. Fold the edges under so they butt the underlay. Put temporary tacks along the walls while tensioning – see page 163. Drive 19mm non-rusting tacks through the double thickness of carpet every 125mm; use longer tacks at corners to cope with the extra thicknesses.

# Laying foam backed carpet

## Step-by-step

**Step 1** Line the floor with strong brown paper or several layers of newspaper to prevent the foam backing sticking to the floor—otherwise it may disintegrate if you try to take up the carpet at a later date. Lay the paper to within 50mm of the skirting board. Join the pieces with adhesive tape and stick down the edges with double-sided tape. In large or busy rooms, use the tape across the rooms at 750mm intervals and cut the lining paper to fit between the strips. Put down double-sided adhesive carpet tape around the room without removing the upper peel-off backing paper.

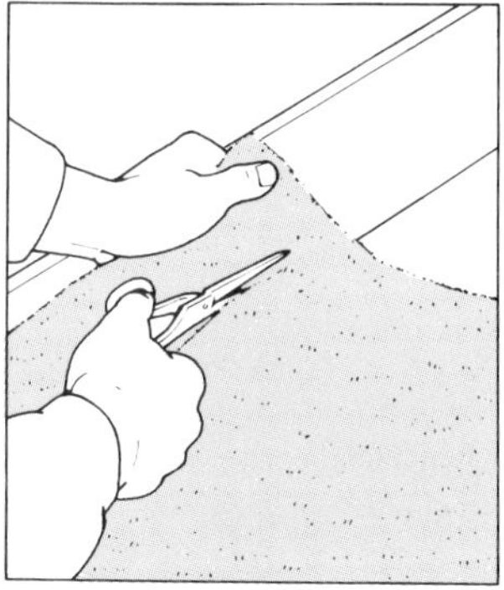

**Step 2** Unroll the carpet, check the pile direction is correct, and smooth it gently into place with your hands. Using scissors or a trimming knife, cut the carpet about 50mm oversize in each direction to allow for possible shrinkage. Make a template for awkward shapes.
**Step 3** Avoid placing seams directly over joins in the underlay. Match up the pile and pattern of the two pieces of carpet and cut one good edge using a straightedge and trimming knife. Use this edge as a template for the second piece of carpet. If there's a selvedge, use this as your edge. Butt the two edges firmly together and anchor them with weights about 75mm in from either edge.

Fold back both edges and lay double-sided carpet tape centrally under the join. To increase the strength of the seam and prevent fraying, apply latex adhesive to the primary backing of the cut edges, taking care not to get it on the carpet pile. Remove the upper backing paper and, starting at the centre of the join, press one carpet edge down. Fold down the other edge ensuring a tight butt join before pressing down. Take care not to catch down any of the pile into the seam.

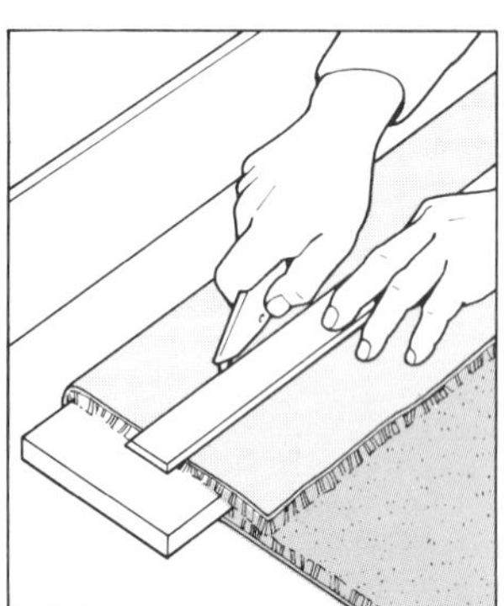

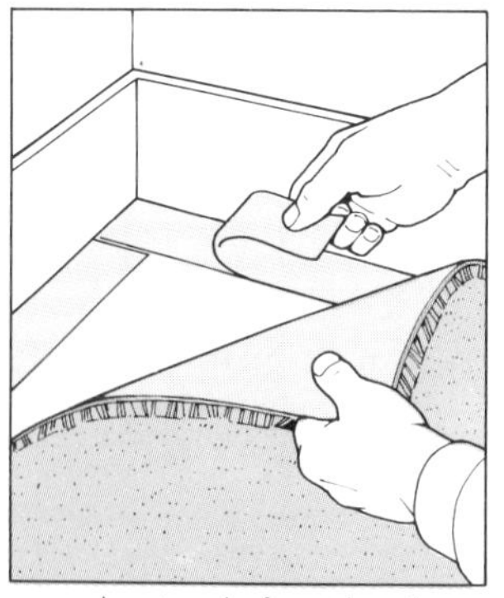

**Step 4** Leave the carpet to settle for a week or two before trimming. Avoid snipping the tips of the pile by cutting from the back through the foam and only just through the primary backing. You should use scissors only if your carpet is loop pile. Apply a line of latex adhesive to the edges of the primary backing. Remove the upper backing paper and press the carpet into position.

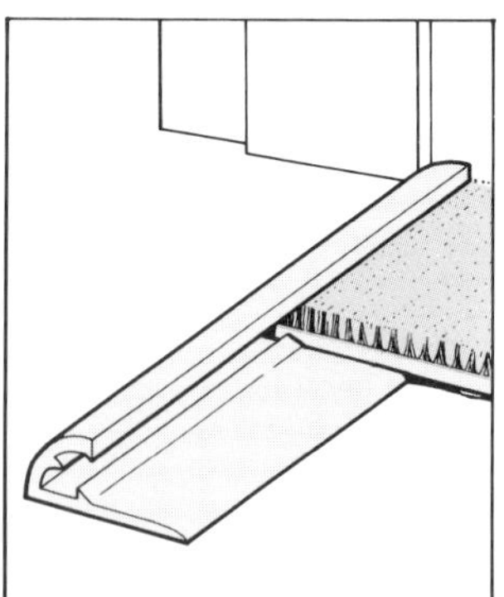

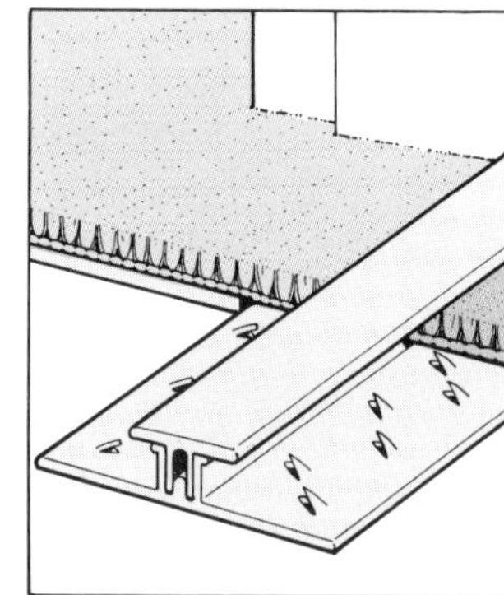

**Step 5** Fix a metal edging strip at the doorway to protect the exposed edge of the carpet and prevent it from becoming a foot trap (use a double-edging strip if there is a fitted carpet in the adjoining room). Trim the strip to size with a hacksaw and position it so that it is hidden when the door is shut. Hammer down the metal lip over the carpet edge using a wooden block between the two. If the door catches on the carpet, fit rising butt hinges or trim.

# Laying carpet with underlay

## Step-by-step

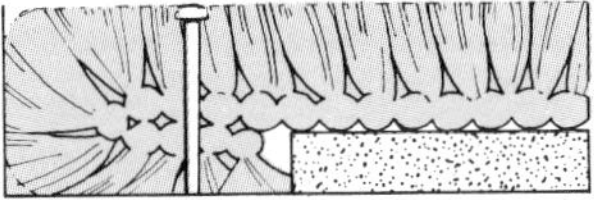

Turn-and-tack method – see page 161.

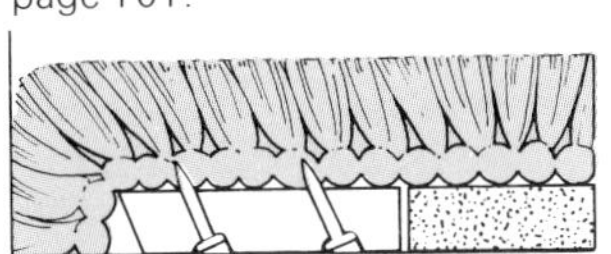

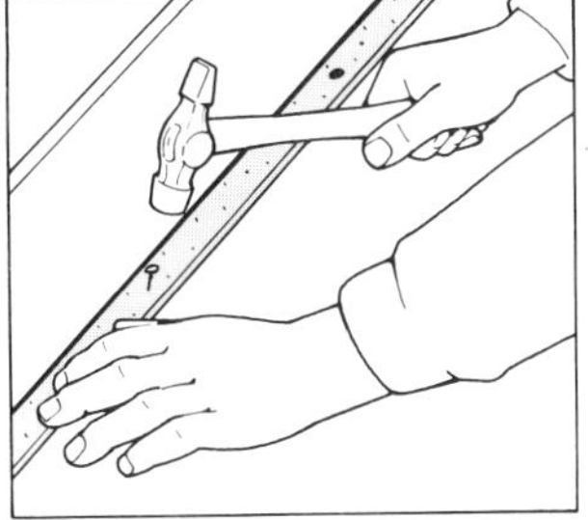

**Step 1** Nail or glue gripper strips end to end around the room with the angled pins pointing towards the wall – leave a gap equal to just less than the thickness of the carpet between the gripper strips and the skirting boards. Cut the gripper strips into short lengths to follow irregular shapes such as doorways and bay windows – use at least two nails per strip and lay them with small spaces between them. Use a small hammer or nail punch to avoid flattening the gripper pins. If you use contact adhesive, cut each gripper strip into several shorter lengths to minimise the effect of slight bumps in the floor.

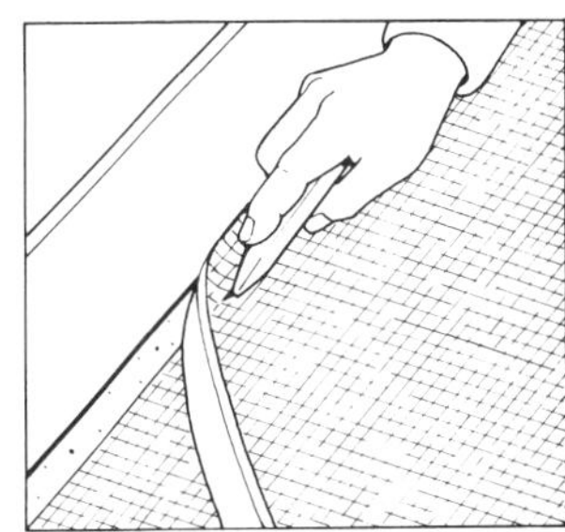

**Step 2** Put down the underlay and trim it so that it just butts the edge of the gripper strips when smoothed out. Secure it with tacks or double-sided adhesive tape. Unroll the carpet, ease it about 10mm up one wall and press it on to the grippers. Make any seams using the technique for foam-backed carpets but use tacks as temporary anchors and fix single-sided adhesive carpet tape to one edge and then to the other.

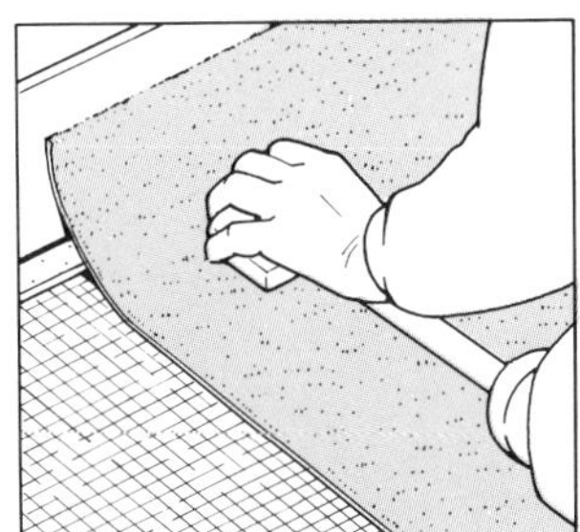

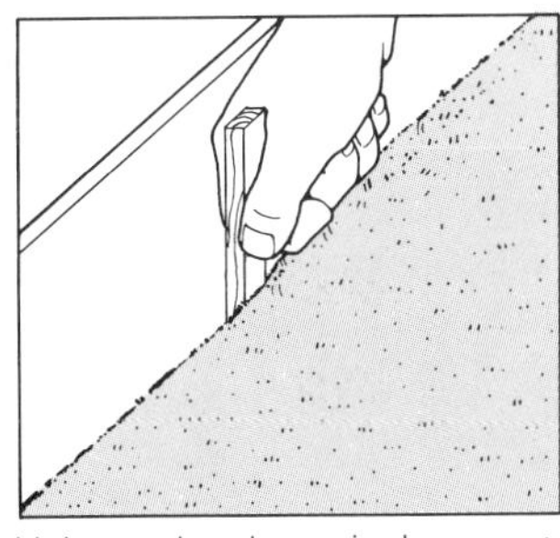

**Step 3** Adjust the teeth of the knee kicker so that they grip the carpet backing without penetrating the underlay. Kneel down and press on the head of the kicker with one hand. Using the other to steady yourself 'kick' the pad forward with your knee. Follow the stretching sequence in the drawings. The last kick in each direction should hook the carpet on to the grippers.

Once the carpet is firmly in place, check that any seams or patterns have not become distorted by over-stretching.

**Step 4** Trim the carpet oversize by 10mm in each direction. Push the edge of the carpet down into the channel between the grippers and skirting board using a thin piece of wood. Fix a carpet edging strip to the doorway as described under foam-backed carpets, but hook the carpet on to the angled pins before hammering down the lip.

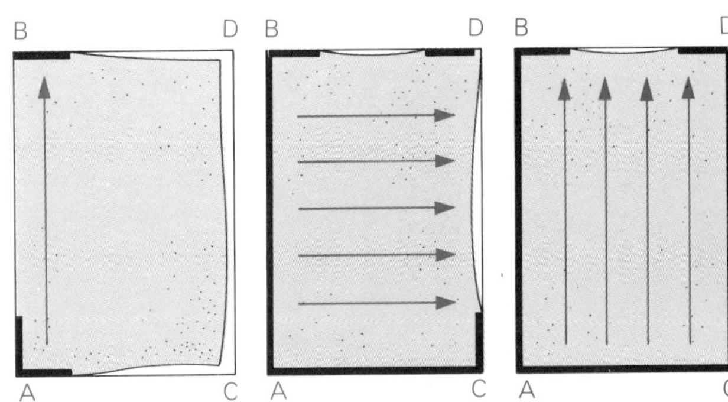


**Tensioning a carpet**

1. Start at corner A, hook carpet about 300mm along walls AB and AC. Stretch from A to B and hook on about 300mm along wall BD.
2. Hook carpet along the full length of wall AB. Repeat the procedure in direction A to C. Then stretch carpet from C to D and hook on. Stretch across the full width of the carpet as you hook on to wall CD.
3. Stretch across the full length of the carpet as you hook on to wall BD.

# TV Aerials

However good a TV set, the quality of signal it receives is all important in achieving good pictures and sound. So it's worthwhile installing the best possible aerial.

## Types of aerial

Aerials come in many shapes and sizes, the choice is dictated by the sort of signal it will receive. *Yagi* aerials are the most common, and come with different numbers of elements – 8 to 10 elements should be suitable for most viewers, but more elements would be better in areas where the signals are weak. The effect of poor signal strength is normally seen as a fuzzy indistinct picture known as snow (or a hissy radio reception).

Another design of aerial is the *log-periodic*. This covers all UHF channels and has a good *front-to-back ratio* – that is, it's good at picking up the signal from the direction in which it's pointing, and at rejecting signals from behind. So if you have a strong signal but the TV picture is spoilt by double images (a fault known as ghosting and caused by extra reflective signals) a log-periodic aerial may be worth trying. On the other hand, it may not give as strong a signal as a Yagi and, if the ghosts are caused by unwanted signals from the front, a modified Yagi may do better.

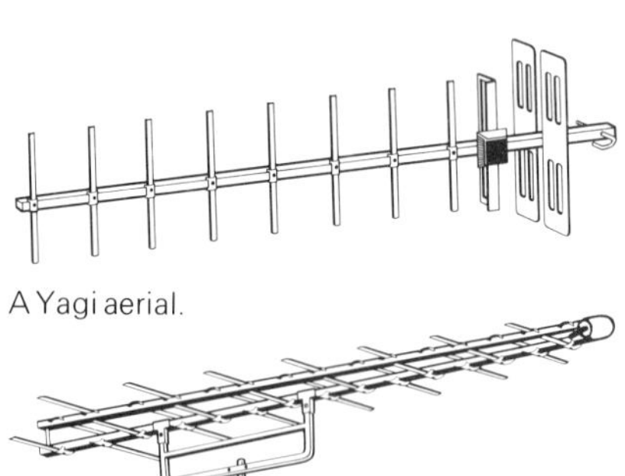

A Yagi aerial.

A log-periodic aerial.

### Where to fit them

There are three points to remember:

- signal strength is related to height – so the higher the aerial the better
- signal strength is reduced by any material or object situated between the transmitter and the aerial – a range of hills or the roofing material
- signals can be reflected by a large metal object placed in close proximity to the aerial – a cistern or old fireguard in the loft or a gasometer down the road.

The available local signal strength normally dictates where the aerial is sited. To find out about reception in your area ask local radio and TV retailers for an idea of signal strength. Check to see where your neighbours have had new aerials installed. Note how long they are – the longer they are the more signal gathering capacity they have.

In a weak signal area the aerial will almost certainly have to be mounted outside and high on the roof, but note there may be local restrictions on the use of aerials above the roof line. In a strong signal area the best place to mount the aerial will be in the loft. This is a fairly simple d-i-y job, but the risks involved and cost of equipment required for mounting a roof aerial are not usually worth the relatively small additional cost charged by a professional installer – let him do it for you.

### Obtaining a suitable aerial

Try Yellow Pages or advertisements in local newspapers or magazines, such as *Exchange & Mart*. The dipole size – aerial width – varies slightly according to the signal frequency range of the local transmitter. So you will need to tell the supplier which TV and radio transmitter you receive your signal from. A local TV retailer should be able to tell you this or you can contact the BBC or IBA engineering information departments.

## Communal aerials and cable TV

In blocks of flats it is often impracticable, or against the rules, for every flat to put up a separate aerial. There are also some areas where even an aerial on the roof is not good enough. In these cases and where roof aerials are not allowed, the usual answer is a communal aerial system. At its simplest this is a single well-placed aerial, an amplifier, and a number of outlet sockets – one in each house or flat. Town-wide cable television systems and large systems on housing estates can be more complicated, but work on the same principles. The Broadcasting authorities will give practical assistance on the setting up of self-help transmitters, but they cannot help financially.

## Tapping into or extending a cable

The effect of adding extra sockets to an existing cable will depend on signal strength as the fitting of any junctions or sockets inevitably results in signal loss. The principle for extending or tapping is the same. You need to obtain a two-way splitter. There are two types – the more expensive 'low-loss' model is better. Cut the cable at the point you wish to tap off – this should occur under cover. Fit an aerial plug to both ends of the cut cable. Plug the end of the cable attached to the aerial into the single socket end of the splitter and plug the other end of the cable into either of the two sockets remaining on the splitter – this will restore the signal (now weakened) to the original cable run, yet leave you a socket into which to plug an extension lead. An extension lead consists of no more than a further length of low-loss coaxial cable with a television plug fitted at both ends. If you want to take an additional cable from an existing wall socket then change the socket for a two-way socket and make up a suitable extension lead which can be plugged into the spare socket.

**A socket in every room?**
It is unlikely that a single aerial could provide sufficient signal strength to feed more than two sockets adequately. If you want more than this there is a choice between erecting another aerial or, for no greater outlay but a neater appearance, fitting an aerial amplifier (obtained from an aerial supplier) into the cable at a point in the loft close to the aerial. The amplifier runs off mains electricity. The signal input and output terminals of an amplifier are conventional aerial plugs and sockets. The output of the amplifier is then connected to a four-way or six-way splitter which, like the amplifier, has conventional aerial sockets on its input and outputs.

Up to that number of extension leads can then be wired from the splitter and led down to the required position by one of the routes described.

**VHF (FM) radio aerial too?**
VHF aerials, for FM radio signals, are much larger than UHF (TV) aerials and usually have to be fitted outside the loft. Given sufficient signal strength an existing cable run can be utilised by use of a suitable TV/FM two-way splitter (also called diplexers). For weaker signals one possibility would be to fit a combined TV/FM amplifier.

**Fitting a plug**
Remove the outer insulation from about 25mm of the low-loss cable and slide on the outer cap of the dismantled plug. Push back the mesh around the inner copper core and inner insulation and fit the plug clasp so that it encloses the mesh with no stray ends. Pinch the legs of the clasp over the insulation.

Trim back the inner insulation to about 7mm below the clasp and feed the bare conductor through the remaining parts of the plug. Screw the plug together. Cut the conductor flush with the plug and for the best connection solder it there.

## INSTALLING AN AERIAL IN A LOFT

An aerial should come complete with assembly instructions. A mounting kit is also required and an appropriate continuous length of 'low-loss' coaxial cable. Coaxial cable is absolutely essential for use with TV or radio signals and has been designed to reject interference signals. It's readily available in shops. When installing this cable take care not to squash or kink it.

There are three possible routes for the cable:

- through the roofing felt, under a convenient roof tile and down the roof (held by loops of soft wire with ends pushed back up under the tiles). Then down the wall to the bottom of the window frame nearest the TV. (Fasten the cable to the wall by use of plastic-headed cable clips.) Drill a hole through the frame and push the cable through. Install a socket on the window sill or run to the TV and fit a TV plug to the end. This is the simplest method
- down through the house – through the loft hatch or the bedroom ceiling and so on. This is most suitable for a TV in a room on the first floor
- down the cavity between the inner and outer leaves of an exterior wall. To drop the cable drill a small hole – about 65mm diameter – through the internal wall in a position close to the intended TV site. Attach a small, but heavy, weight to a length of string tied to the coaxial cable. Lower into the cavity wall from the loft at a point directly above the hole and hook the lowered cable out at the bottom. Obviously it is not as simple as this – the descending string can snag or become misdirected and when it reaches the right level it is unlikely to be in line with the hole. It's then necessary to fabricate a hook from bent wire and use this to fish for the string. The string and cable are then pulled down carefully and the cable attached to a wall plate.

In the loft, the aerial is fastened to a suitable mounting. The dipoles are generally horizontal, but in a few areas their orientation has to be vertical. So check.

The cable is connected and the aerial is 'swung' to align it to the direction of maximum signal strength, usually a compromise between the best pictures on different channels. The simplest way is to line it in the same direction as other local aerials. In strong signal areas it doesn't have to be too accurate. In weak signal areas swing the aerial while someone else watches the TV picture. Make sure the TV is tuned to the right channel for the local transmitter. A professional installer uses a signal strength meter – these, unfortunately, are very expensive to buy and are not easily hired.

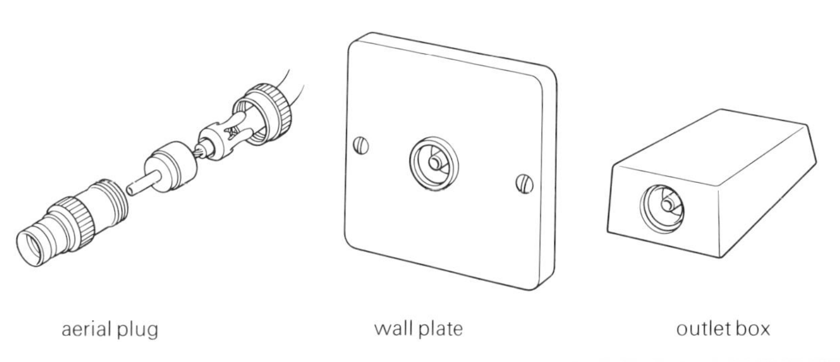

aerial plug — wall plate — outlet box

# Chapter 6

# HALLS AND STAIRS

In many houses the hall is no more than a passageway from the front door to the foot of the stairs and the doors to downstairs rooms. It's difficult to make gainful use of such a narrow space and consequently in smaller houses the wall between the hallway and the front room is often demolished to open up the space. The disadvantage of this arrangement is that the front door then opens straight into the living space and that can be inconvenient, as well as causing draughts and heat loss when the door is opened. Moreover the space gain is more illusory than real since a passageway is still required to and from the front door and this will limit the way the furnishings can be arranged in the open-plan room. In which case the answer may be to make a feature of the passageway, perhaps by raising the floor and providing steps down into the rooms.

Another way to give the illusion of space, but retain the passageway and some seclusion around the front door, is to pierce the dividing wall with narrow open strips rather than demolishing it altogether – see drawing. (This can also be an effective solution for dealing with the wall between two main rooms – a dining room and a living room perhaps.) The narrow openings could be glazed or

fitted with display shelves – of glass perhaps – or left entirely open.

An alternative treatment for a narrow uninteresting hallway is to create a lobby by installing a second door and frame partway down the corridor. If the front door is glazed or has a skylight above, a skylight can be installed above the second door to allow a shaft of light into the inner hall space, or the second door could itself be glazed.

A larger hall is of course much easier to use gainfully, if only as a place for a telephone or to hang coats and dump briefcases and other paraphernalia. It also helps to give a house a more open feeling. There are still some other improvements that might be worth considering, for instance if there is no existing porch, it may be possible to move the front door inwards to create a recessed porch. If the front doorway is narrow it may be desirable to fit a wider one or to install double doors, so that large objects, a pram for instance, can be manoeuvred through more easily.

Stairs invariably lead away from hallways and the space under the stairs is another area ripe for alteration. In most homes it isn't feasible to remove, or alter the staircase, but one idea is to build an extension to house a new staircase and use the space created in the main area as two new rooms (one upstairs and one down).

Where the hall is narrow and underused it is often knocked through into an adjacent living room. Raising the hall floor (left) or creating a partition (right) helps to maintain the passageway while opening up the space. A mirrored wall can also be effective (above right).

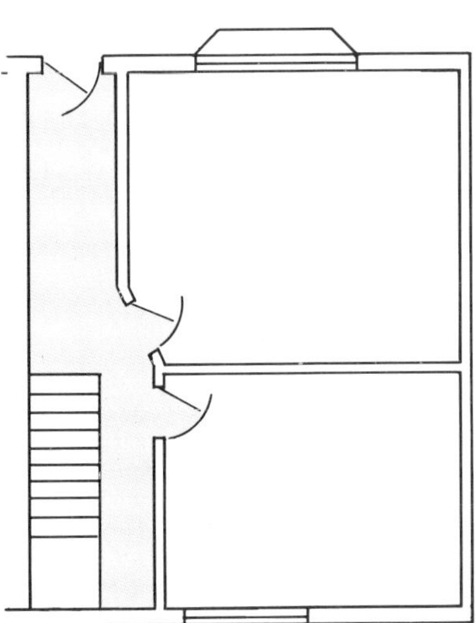

# Converting understairs

Staircases take up a surprising amount of space. The housebuilder's way to put some of this to use is to enclose the understairs area to form a cupboard. But all too often the cupboard under the stairs is an awkward shape and difficult to get into, making it of limited practical value. Knocking out the cupboard may allow a forgotten area to become part of the living space.

How much space there is to be gained, and how easy the job will be, depends on the type of stair layout and support. Timber stairs usually have at least one load-bearing timber post – called a newel – running up from the floor to the stair. This cannot be removed without providing alternative support.

## Staircase support

There are several common arrangements for supporting a staircase. The simplest is the straight-run stair, which has the most easily-used understairs space. The stair is supported by full newels at each end of the outer string, leaving a large, unobstructed triangular space underneath. The cupboard panelling will probably have extra studs to support it, particularly if the cupboard door is not hung from the newel, but these extra timbers can usually be removed without problem.

The straight-run staircase is also used when stairs are fitted into a narrow corridor, with both strings supported by the walls. Here, although the understairs space is the same, access is in the room behind the stair, with a cupboard door opening under the landing. With this type of space, opening the cupboard out to the side is rarely practical as in most cases both walls are loadbearing; as is the lintel over the door which supports the landing.

Quarter-turn stairs normally have a newel at the turn, supporting the landing and stairs. Where a cupboard is fitted, it will probably extend past this load-bearing timber to the wall under the landing. There is a variation in this type of stair, where the landing is supported on bearers set into the wall and the stairs are carried by the landing. If a cupboard has been added there may well be what appears to be a newel. However, it will not extend to the handrail or be fully jointed to the floor or string, and the bearers for the landing should be clearly visible from below. Where the newel is load-bearing, it must be left in place. This is a further restriction to the understairs space, which is of limited height.

Half-turn stairs are of similar construction. In open-well stairs, the second quarter landing may have a full newel, but it is often supported on bearers. A typical arrangement here has a low cupboard under the first flight, while the much taller space under the second flight and quarter landing forms a second cupboard, or sometimes a WC. Where the second quarter landing is supported on bearers, either or both of these areas can easily be opened up. But in some cases, the wall beneath the second flight is load-bearing, and cannot be removed without adding a newel or bearers to take its place.

Dog-leg stairs are often used to achieve a steep rise in a small space. To do this, the stair doubles back on itself with a second string fitted directly over the first. With these stairs, both strings and the half-landing are supported on a single, central newel. The top and bottom of the stairs have additional newels.

In spite of the fact that the space beneath is awkward and cramped, a cupboard is sometimes built under the upper flight. A further half newel is often added to support its panelling and door.

With any type of stair, the design may vary in detail, and there can be timbers whose purpose is not clear. A load-bearing newel will be fully fixed and jointed to the string or landing (often with a bolt and mortice). It will also be fixed and jointed to the joists or set into a solid floor. Most run to the handrail as well, although this is not a completely reliable guide. It is usually a heavy timber, around 100mm square, although it may be turned on some portions of its length.

### Removing a newel

When a staircase is supported by a newel it is possible to remove the newel and provide staircase support by some other means. But this structural conversion isn't nearly as easy as it might appear. It's a lot easier and cheaper to leave the newel in position and design the space conversion around this timber.

If you do want to remove a newel you'll have to get professional advice and the alteration will require Building Regulations approval.

### Removing the cupboard

Once you have found out which timbers, if any, can safely be removed, knocking out the panels of the cupboard is a simple enough task. You may find a partition closing off the bottom corner of the stair. Since this triangular space is difficult to clean and to use, it's often better to leave it enclosed.

If the underside of the stair is open, fit a flush panel to the strings and bearers. It is sensible to use screws to fix this so that access is easier if it ever becomes necessary to repair the stairs. If the stairs are already creaking or showing signs of wear – it makes sense to repair them first.

The service fittings – the gas and electricity meters, fuseboard or consumer unit – are often installed in the cupboard under the stairs. If these are in the way, you can pay for the appropriate service authority to reposition them – or for neatness you can box them in with an access panel.

## REPAIRS TO CREAKING STAIRS

The common causes of creaking stairs are loose or missing glue blocks, loose wedges or defective joints. Wide staircases – more than 900mm across – may creak because the centre is not well supported.

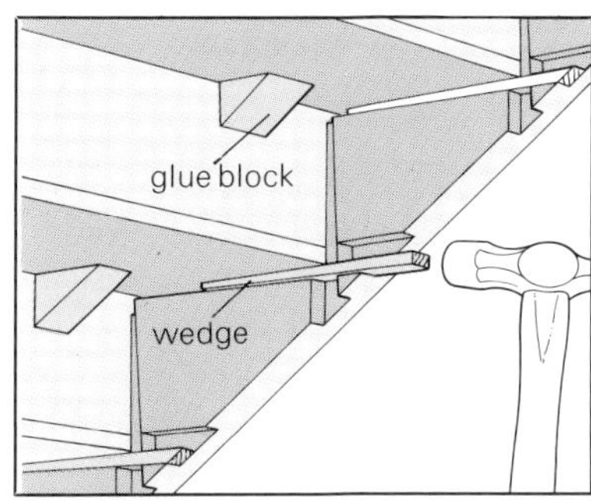


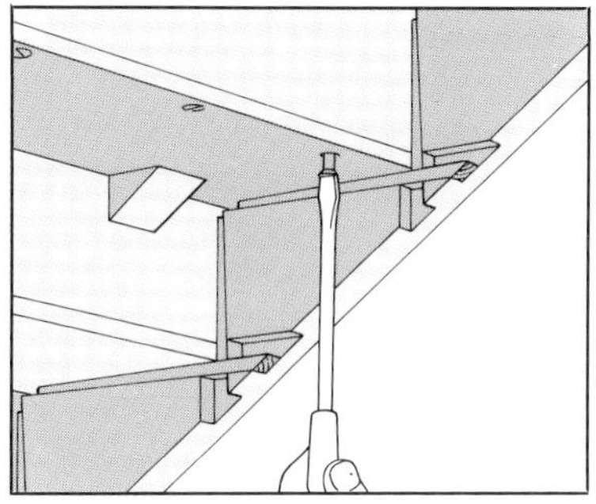

**Glue blocks** There should be at least three beneath each tread. Check that these are in position and replace any that are loose. If any blocks are actually missing, glue on new triangular blocks of softwood the same size as the existing.

**Wedges** Wedges can work loose through shrinkage, remove any that are loose, coat with glue and rewedge. If that isn't firm enough, it may be necessary to cut new wedges and knock them in place.

**Defective joints** If the joint between a tread and riser has drawn apart, screws up through the underside of the tread into the riser will pull the joint together. Be careful to position the screw in the centre of the riser or you'll risk splitting the wood. Use three screws evenly spaced across the stair width. Wax the screws before driving home and tighten them gradually in turn.

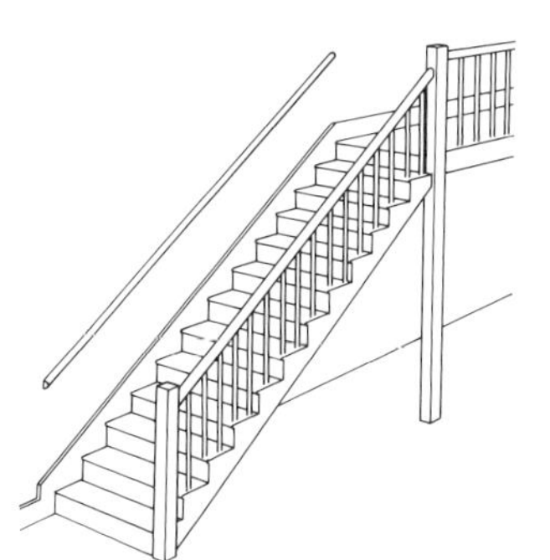

A straight staircase is the simplest type of stairs.

A quarter-turn staircase will fit into a shorter space.

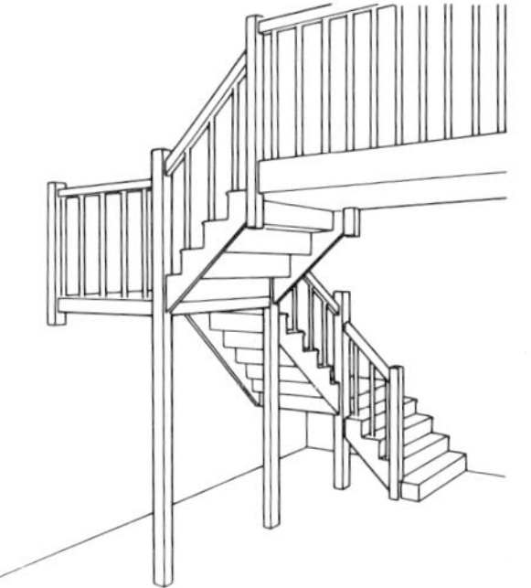

An open well half-turn staircase requires a more generous space.

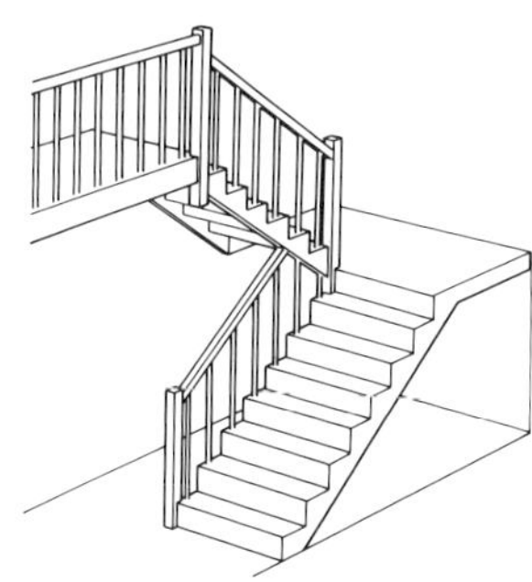

The dog-leg type of staircase turns tightly round a landing.

# A new staircase

A new staircase is normally installed as part of a major renovation to provide access to a new floor of the house or when a staircase is moved. Existing stairs rarely fall into such disrepair that they need to be replaced, so it's not an improvement many people would tackle. Installing anything other than a very simple straight-run staircase isn't a d-i-y job, if only because the job of raising the assembled stairs into position means having the right access equipment and a block and tackle, as well as strength and plenty of confidence. The other method of building a staircase, constructing it on site, is a skilled job for a professional joiner.

If you do decide to do it yourself, you'll need professional advice on the design with special reference to the provision for bearings. Any project will need Building Regulations approval.

## The Regulations

The Building Regulations in England and Wales and in Scotland are strict about staircases and give precise requirements for the headroom, width, depth of tread and so on. Winders which are often necessary to fit a staircase into a tight space are very strictly controlled – at their narrowest end the treads cannot be less than 75mm wide.

## Balustrades

All stairs which are not enclosed by walls on each side must have a balustrade to guard the outer string and landings. If the existing balustrade is old and decrepit or simply old-fashioned replacing it is an improvement that can make a dramatic difference to the hall. In some new stair systems – particularly metal and spiral staircase kits – the balustrade is incorporated in the construction. Otherwise you will have to add an appropriate balustrade.

For safety reasons, the general design is governed by Building Regulations, which set out the dimensions – see below.

The regulations are usually met by

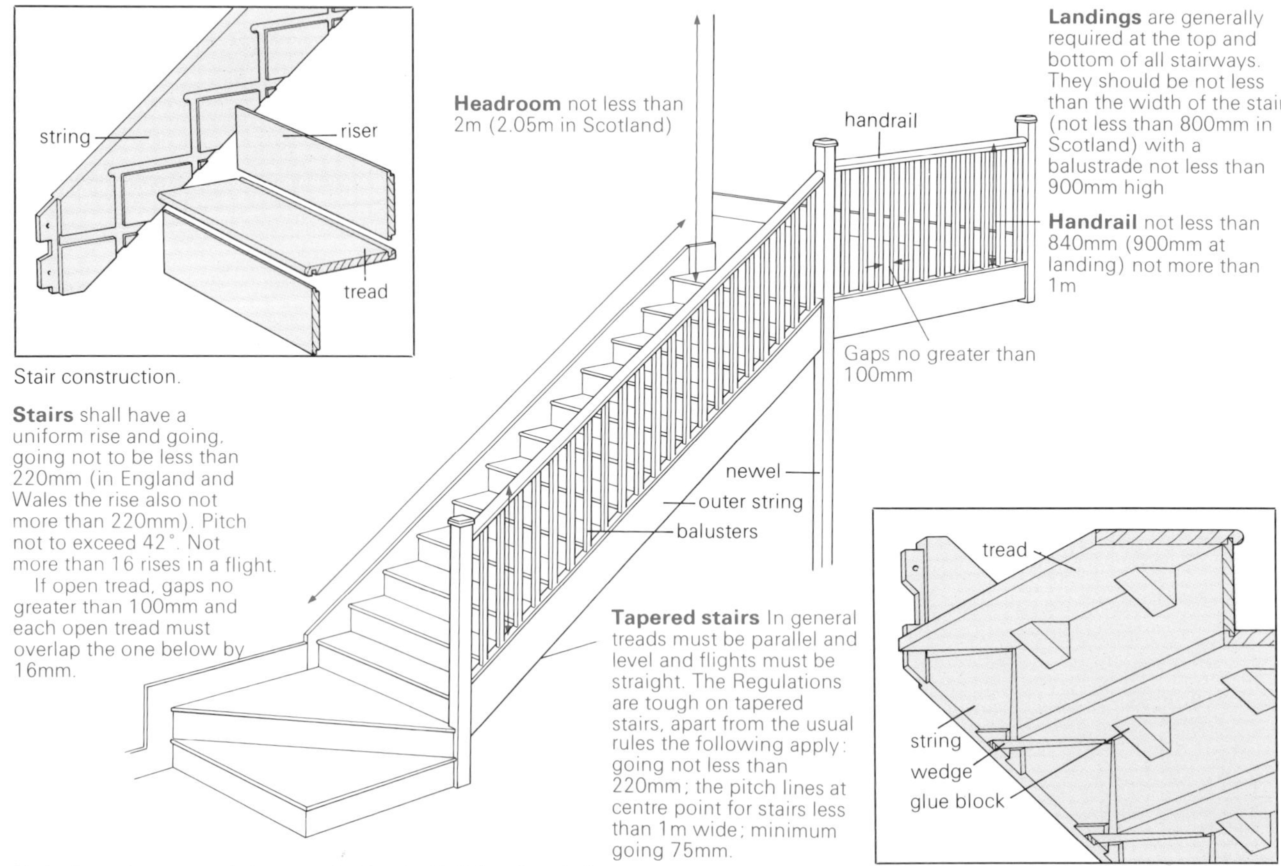
CONSTRUCTION AND REGULATIONS
string
riser
tread
Headroom not less than 2m (2.05m in Scotland)
handrail
Landings are generally required at the top and bottom of all stairways. They should be not less than the width of the stair (not less than 800mm in Scotland) with a balustrade not less than 900mm high
Handrail not less than 840mm (900mm at landing) not more than 1m
Gaps no greater than 100mm
Stairs shall have a uniform rise and going, going not to be less than 220mm (in England and Wales the rise also not more than 220mm). Pitch not to exceed 42°. Not more than 16 rises in a flight.
If open tread, gaps no greater than 100mm and each open tread must overlap the one below by 16mm.
newel
outer string
balusters
Tapered stairs In general treads must be parallel and level and flights must be straight. The Regulations are tough on tapered stairs, apart from the usual rules the following apply: going not less than 220mm; the pitch lines at centre point for stairs less than 1m wide; minimum going 75mm.
tread
string
wedge
glue block

Stair construction.

Stair dimensions are strictly controlled by the Building Regulations.

Under stair construction.

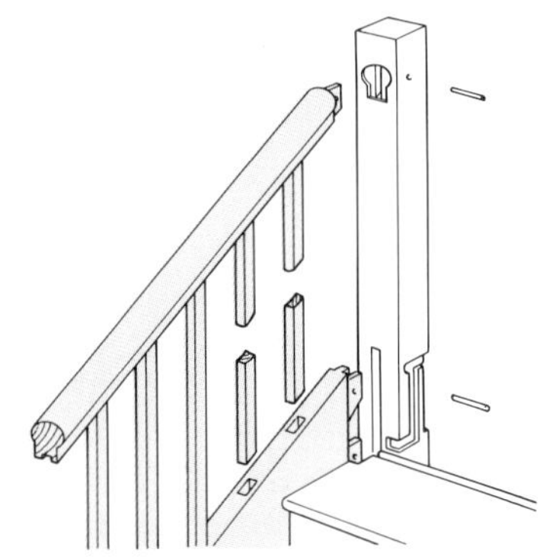

A handrail with baluster spindles not more than 100mm apart.

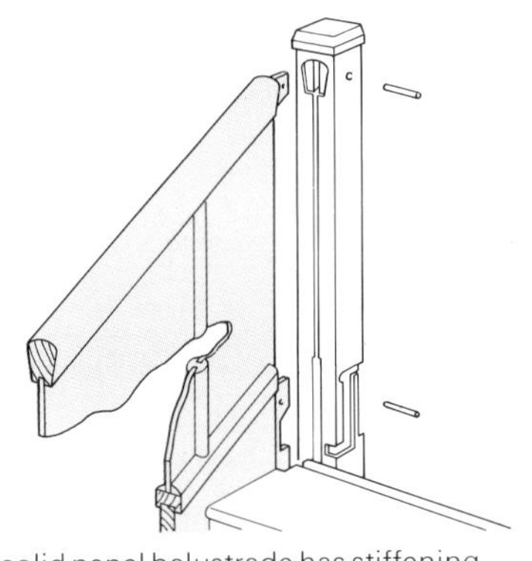

A solid panel balustrade has stiffening battens for strength.

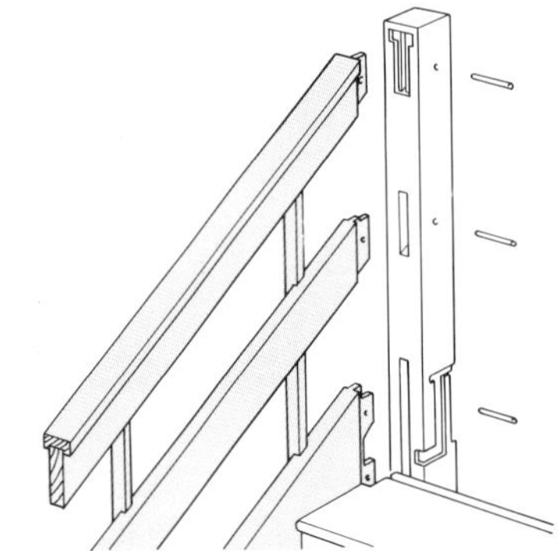

Parallel rails can be installed below a handrail – again the gaps may not exceed 100mm.

having a handrail which runs between sturdy newels (to which it is fixed with a dowelled mortise-and-tenon joint) and filling the space below by vertical balusters, horizontal rails or solid panels. Additional support for the handrail is provided by the balusters themselves, or by vertical stiffeners for rails or panels.

## Full height balustrade

Although the Building Regs require a handrail at 840mm, there is no need for the banister to stop at this height – an open staircase can be completely partitioned off with tongued and grooved boarding to create a boxed staircase, perhaps with a door at the base of the stairs. Or the banisters can be continued up to the ceiling with a handrail fixed at the appropriate height to the banister or the side wall.

### Fitting a balustrade

A cheap and simple balustrade can be made using a handrail moulding, and fitted to the newels with dowelled mortise-and-tenon joints. At the top, if there is no newel, the rail can be housed directly into the wall, or fitted into a false newel screwed to the wall. Turned balusters are often available secondhand from demolition contractors. New ones can be cut from lengths of 32mm or 25mm square softwood batten, with their tops sawn to the rake of the stair. These are then housed into the string of the stair and skew-nailed to the underside of the rail. Or, you can fit panels of 9mm plywood or rails of 19mm or 25mm softwood. (Note that as balusters are simply skew-nailed to the underside of the rail, they are remarkably easy to remove and refit – to strip off layers of paint for instance.)

The balustrade for a straight run stair is relatively simple. It becomes more complicated to arrange when the stair has landings or winders. Here, the handrail has to be fitted to two sides of the newel and incorporate a change of level.

Because of this, a kit system balustrade which consists of a range of matched, interchangeable components, is often the best solution. Although these are more expensive, they have simplified jointing and are very much easier to construct. They are also more attractive, with decoratively turned spindles and newels in hardwood or softwood.

Normally, the newels are in sections. A plain basepiece can be jointed to the string and floor joists as required, then topped with an upper section to suit the handrail. (An existing plain newel can be cut short just above the string and used as a base for a new upper section.)

The handrail in a kit may be fitted into the newels with mortise-and-tenon joints, as in the basic construction, or be continuous and dowel-jointed on top of the newels using special end and corner sections.

With a kit a new bottom rail is fitted to the top of the string. This rail and the underside of the handrail have channels to house the baluster spindles. When the spindles are cut to length and to suit the rake of the stair, they fit into these channels without the need for further jointing. The intervening spaces between spindles are trimmed with fillets to cover the open channel.

KIT BALUSTRADES

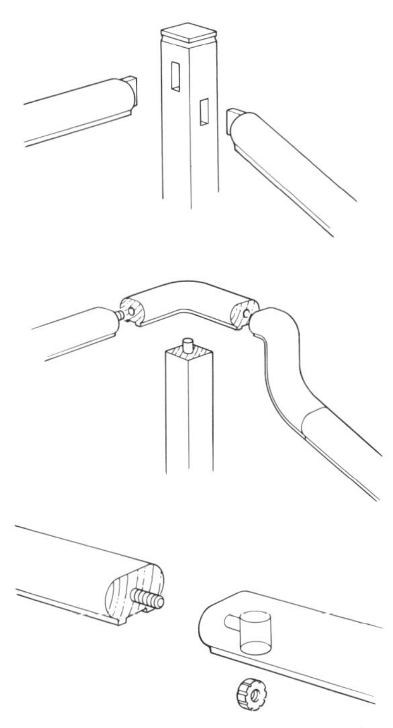

In a kit the handrail may be mortised to the newel or continuous over it.

# Stair carpet

Carpeting a staircase means that it is quieter. It is also desirable because the covering protects the treads from wear.

Stairs get much rougher treatment than rooms and are also a potential accident area so it is essential that the carpet is well secured. Most stair carpet requires a separate underlay and you should use foam-backed carpet only if it is specifically sold for stairs. If you do use foam-backed stair carpet you would need either to use stair rods or to stick it down permanently with adhesive; double-sided adhesive carpet tape doesn't have sufficient holding power for stairs and the special purpose stair grippers sold for foam-backed carpet may not be adequate for stair-grade carpet. In any case any movement of the carpet is likely to damage the backing.

**Fitted or Runner?**

Carpets for stairs can be fitted wall-to-wall or be centrally-placed runners.

Carpet runners are simpler and quicker to lay than fitted stair carpet as they are easier to manoeuvre into place and there is little, if any, cutting involved. Runners also have the advantage that they can be moved up and down to distribute the wear more evenly and as a runner is not made to measure it can be moved more easily to another house – most fitted stair carpets are sold with the house.

## Measuring up

The easiest way to measure the length of stairs is to run a piece of string over each tread and riser – following the outline of any curved nosings carefully and taking the largest dimensions of winder treads. If the stairs are to be covered by a runner, add an extra half metre so that you can reposition the carpet occasionally to distribute wear across the whole length rather than concentrate it on the treads. With fitted carpet, check the width of the stairs in several places. Plan to have any seams in the angles between the treads and the risers. If you use a seam on a runner, you won't be able to reposition it.

## Step-by-step

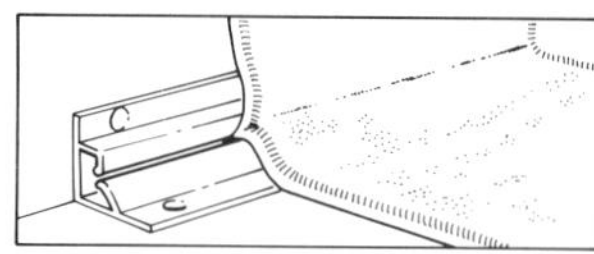

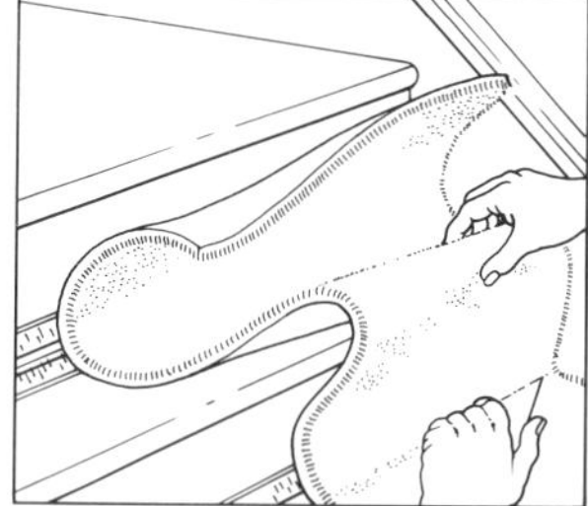

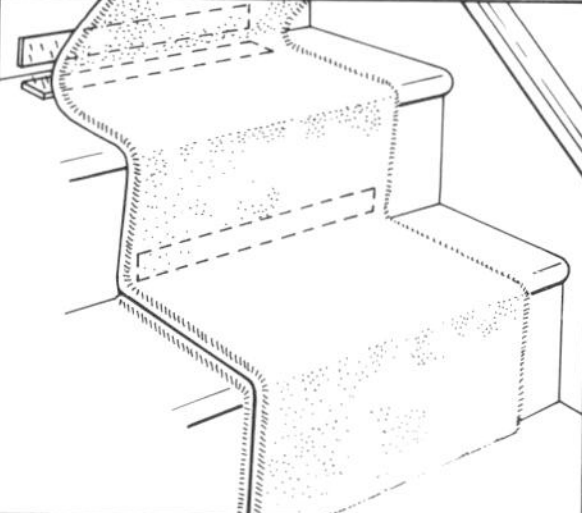

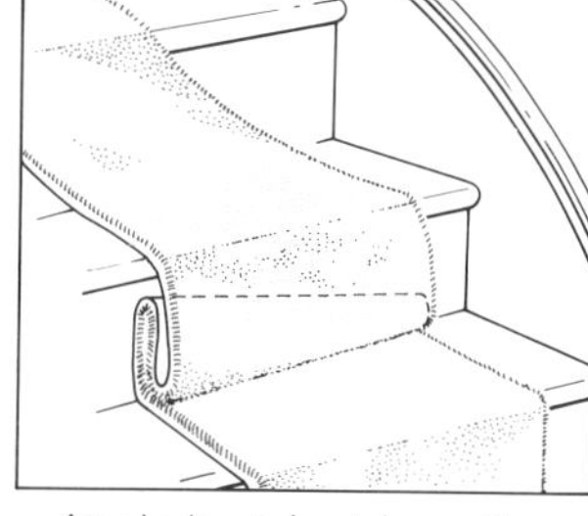

**Fitted carpet**

**Step 1** Fix gripper strips to the back of each tread and bottom of each riser so that the pins face into the stair angles. Leave a gap between each pair of grippers equal to about twice the thickness of the carpet (take the guesswork out of the spacing by using a homemade wooden spacer as a gauge). Alternatively, use special-purpose right-angled metal stair grippers. Fix additional grippers to the outside edges of winder treads. Tack a section of underlay over each tread and down the riser below. Leave the internal stair angles between grippers uncovered.

**Step 2** Leave the landing carpet with a section long enough to bring over the top stair secure to the gripper on the highest riser. Cut the carpet roughly to shape and loose lay it with the pile facing downwards to improve wearability.

Working from the bottom of the stairs, ensure the carpet is absolutely straight as you pull it taut over each tread. Use a knee kicker to stretch the carpet towards each stair angle and hook it between the grippers with a thin piece of wood. Trim the carpet as you progress up the stairs until you join up with the landing carpet at the angle of the top stair. Use separate pieces of carpet for each winding stair. Fix them between the gripper strip on the winder tread and the one on the riser below. If you have a half landing, treat it as two sets of stairs.

**Runners**

**Step 1** You can use stair rods but gripper strips give a neater finish. Cut the gripper strips 40mm shorter than the width of the carpet and use tacks top and bottom. Use your finger tips to position the carpet centrally.

**Step 2** You need to lay a runner in one piece in order to move it as it becomes worn. Fold the 0·5m wear allowance under at the bottom riser and tread and use the extra thickness as underlay. When you later move the carpet up to distribute wear you must then insert strips of underlay on the bottom stair.

At winder stairs, take up the carpet slack by making a series of folds against the riser. Instead of using a gripper strip at the base of this riser, secure the carpet with 40mm non-rusting tacks.

Carpet runners are simpler and quicker to lay than fitted stair carpet as they are easier to manoeuvre into place and there is little, if any, cutting involved.

# Telephones

Now that phones are fitted with plugs for use in wall sockets and phones can be bought as well as rented, a versatile phone system isn't too expensive to install or run. Although you can buy telephone equipment from other sources, British Telecom (BT), who run the telephone service in the UK, own the wiring and only their engineer can install a telephone system and any extension.

## Getting a phone installed

If you move into a house where the previous occupier had a telephone service, then provided that the telephone itself and the wiring is still there you can have the service transferred to you. Get in touch with the local BT Area Sales office for the area you are moving to – you'll need to tell them the telephone number you're intending to take over, and the address. They'll transfer the phone to your name and also arrange that your details are included in the next edition of the local telephone directory.

If the previous occupier did not have a telephone, provided there is a suitable cable running outside your house BT will arrange to install the telephone and connect you to the network.

Apart from some housing estates, where all the wiring is underground, houses are connected to the telephone network by means of a wire running between a pole in the street and the outside of your house. Nowadays all new internal wiring terminates on a main socket into which your telephone is plugged. You can have a socket installed in most parts of your house; discuss the position and the route of the wiring with the BT engineer when he calls. The job of installing the telephone, wiring and connecting it up takes only a few hours.

The cost of installation varies according to how much work is involved: to have an existing line transferred cost £10 in May 1983; providing a completely new line about £70 (but it could be less than this if wiring from a previous installation can be re-used).

### Extension sockets

Extension sockets can be fitted at the same time as the main socket or at a later date. As with the main socket, extension sockets can be fitted almost anywhere in the house, though not in bathrooms or other locations liable to dampness. Extension sockets can also be fitted in garages, other outbuildings although there are additional charges when external wiring is involved. Sockets can be fitted on any surface which is suitable for normal wall fittings. Wiring is normally run on the surface, around doorways and along skirting boards, and as the wire is thin and white it is hardly obtrusive. Chasing and work under floorboards is not generally undertaken.

The charge for an extension (including the main socket conversion) was £25 at May 1983, but further extension sockets installed at the same time cost only £10 extra.

### Changing to plug-in

If you buy a new phone with a plug for connection to a socket, BT will change your existing system – the main point and all existing extensions – to the new socket system for a fixed price of £10 (at May 1983). An extra extension installed at the same time costs another £15.

New phones operate on the plug and socket system.

### Extension bells

Extension bells of varying loudness and sizes are available. They can be fitted indoors or out.

## Types of telephone

With every exchange line BT provides the standard type of telephone. However they have a very large range of coloured telephones, both dial and press button.

Most BT telephones can be either rented or purchased outright. Full maintenance is included if you rent and BT will also arrange maintenance for a small extra charge if you buy a telephone from them.

You don't have to have a BT phone, phones are now available from other suppliers. But only phones approved by BT can legally be connected.

## Help for the disabled and the elderly

A telephone can be a lifeline. BT have special equipment and services which can help those who are hard of hearing, have speech problems or impaired mobility. Ask for a leaflet at the Sales Office.

Much of the equipment offered is standard commercial apparatus such as press-button phones. People with impaired vision often find these easier to use than dial phones, especially when the number five is notched in some way to aid location of the keys. Callmakers are also useful and it is possible to have a single-number callmaker, giving direct access to the operator at the press of a button. Extension bells and loudspeaking telephones are available for the hard of hearing.

Simple adaptions such as fitting the telephone sockets at waist height can also be useful.

# Ceilings

In a narrow hall or landing the ceiling, although the same height as other ceilings in the house can seem unusually high. It's partly the narrowness that gives the feeling, but the tall walls of the stairwell can add to the illusion – it's always at least a 5m drop from the ceiling above a staircase to the ground floor below. So one improvement you might make in a hall is to lower the ceiling in some way. You can do this by fitting a suspended ceiling. A lightweight suspended ceiling of grid and panels (as described on page 95) is one choice, but such ceilings tend to look better in practical environments and, in any case, the narrow width of a hall ceiling gives you the opportunity to experiment with other ideas: to use materials which would be too expensive for a larger ceiling or too heavy for a wider span.

Whatever you do consider the fire risks (see page 91), although a hall is perhaps an unlikely place for a fire to start, fires do spread rapidly through halls and up stairwells. (This is why the Building Regulations are strict about the fire resistance of the enclosure around a staircase.) You may need to use these areas as an escape route and smouldering, flaming and falling ceiling coverings will add greatly to the hazards.

### Lower by illusion

Painting a ceiling darker than the walls and floor helps to make it seem lower – carry the colour down to picture rail height to increase the illusion.

The trick of making a ceiling seem nearer can be achieved by giving the eye something lower to focus on. Stretching a grid of white string or plastic-coated wire below a dark-painted ceiling and upper walls is one way of doing this.

More substantial grids of trellis say, or square-edged boards or slats installed with narrow spaces between the boards can be used with lights behind to disguise the height of a ceiling– the open frames can be used to suspend other things. The grids can be supported by battens screwed to the walls or suspended by chains from the ceiling joists above. Fabrics such as canvas and sailcloth are sometimes suggested for suspension overhead, but both these materials are highly

flammable (mainly because of their waterproofing treatment).

A silvered ceiling to reflect light is another way to increase the feeling of space in a dark cramped hall – use silvered pvc attached with magnetic tape.

## Plaster features

In older houses hall ceilings were often given extra decorative treatment with unusual ornate plaster cornices and plaster arches on decorative brackets called corbels. If your hall has these features, they'll be worth highlighting. For a hall with a plain ceiling you might copy the idea and install an ornate plaster (or polyurethane made-to-look-like plaster) coving or cornice to give interest. Most manufacturers make panel mouldings to match, which can be used on the walls or as a border on the ceiling.

Plaster moulding is screwed, nailed or stuck to the ceiling. When it is stuck it usually needs temporary support from below to stop it slipping as the adhesive dries. A temporary batten can be nailed in place or you can tap in masonry nails.

Coving or moulding needs mitring at the corners. These cuts which angle in two directions aren't easy to cut and a gap at the corners is almost inevitable – it can be filled with plaster joint filler or finishing plaster. With a moulding that has a repeated pattern take the trouble to match the corners.

### Other borders

Timber moulding is another choice – this is available in many different cross-sections. Or, for a cheaper type of border you could use wallpaper borders on the ceiling and the walls.

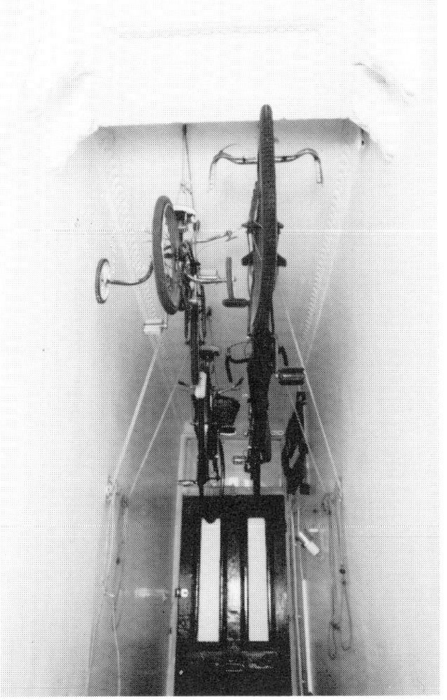

Bamboo poles are used as a high-level shelving. ▲

An ingenious pulley system lifts bikes out of the narrow passageway. Note also the ornate plasterwork common to many halls and also shown far right. ▶

◀ A grid of square-edged boards with narrow spaces between can be used with lights behind to disguise the height of a ceiling.

# Hall lighting

The most important thing about lighting hall and stairs is to ensure there's enough light to be able to move around safely. High levels of general lighting are recommended and it's particularly important that the lighting on the stairs should be right – the treads should be lit much more brightly than the risers (the vertical bits). It's also important that the light itself is well shielded so that people climbing the stairs aren't distracted by glare. A downlighter would be a good choice, because the lamp itself is well shielded. On short flights of stairs, a single fitting towards the top will probably be enough; on long flights, you may need two. For a high level of lighting in the hall or landing, you could use a couple of directional fittings placed at intervals – with perhaps 75W ISL bulbs (see page 150) in them. It's sensible, though, to have some light reflected from walls and floors or ceilings to avoid harsh shadows.

## Two-way switching

A staircase is one of the obvious places to have two-way switching. Other uses include a switch by a bed to link with the one by the bedroom door. Or two switches in a living room which has two doors. It can be reassuring to have a downstairs light or a porch light connected to a second switch next to a bed.

The theory of two-way switching is described on page 52. Basically all that is required is to wire the first switch with the switch live connected to terminal L1 and the return live connected to terminal L2 and then to link in the second switch by a strapping cable. To convert an existing switch circuit, all that is usually needed is to install a second two-way switch and run a three-core and earth pvc-sheathed and pvc-insulated cable from the existing switch to the new one. The connections are outlined below.

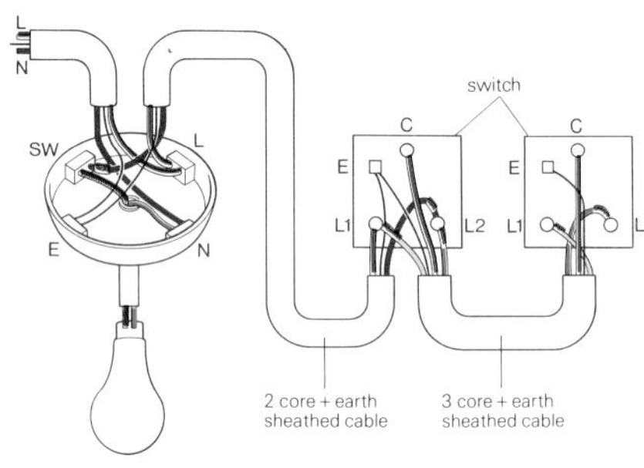

Two-way switching

### From first principles

Installing two-way switching in the first place, follows exactly the same lines. It may help to keep the wiring clear if you install the first switch together with the light, before attempting to link in the second switch.

When channelling walls and so on for the first switch cable – bear in mind that the channel will need to contain two cables comfortably. If you install an intermediate switch, it will also need a channel for two cables.

## Step-by-step

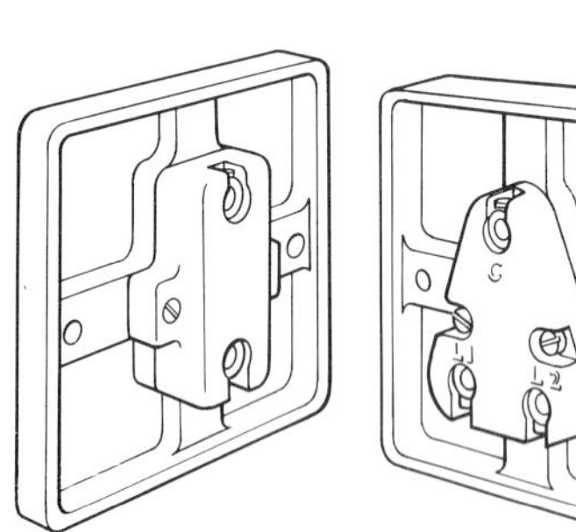
one-way switch two-way switch

The three insulated conductors (or cores) in the strapping cable are coloured red, blue and yellow; the earth is uninsulated. *Switch the power off at the mains* and remove the old switch. If this is a one-way switch with only two live terminals you will have to replace it with a two-way version, but the chances are it will be a two-way switch with three live terminals, where only two terminals are being used.

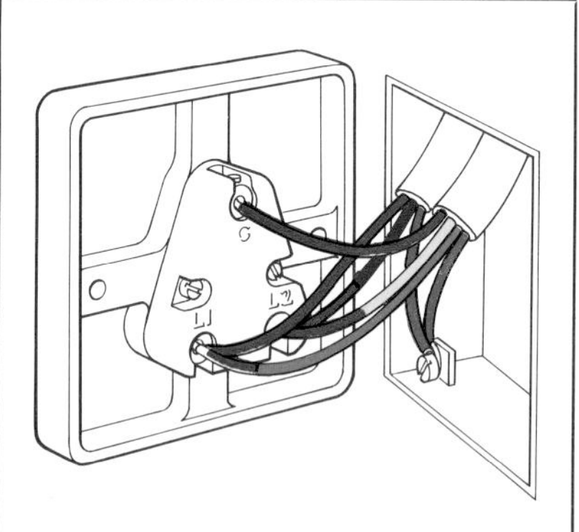

The three live terminals of a two-way switch are marked COMMON, L1 and L2. The three core cable is connected with: the red to the COMMON terminal; the blue and yellow are sleeved with red and connected to the terminals L1 and L2 respectively (it doesn't matter which provided you are consistent). The earth is sleeved with green and connected to the earth terminal of the switch box.

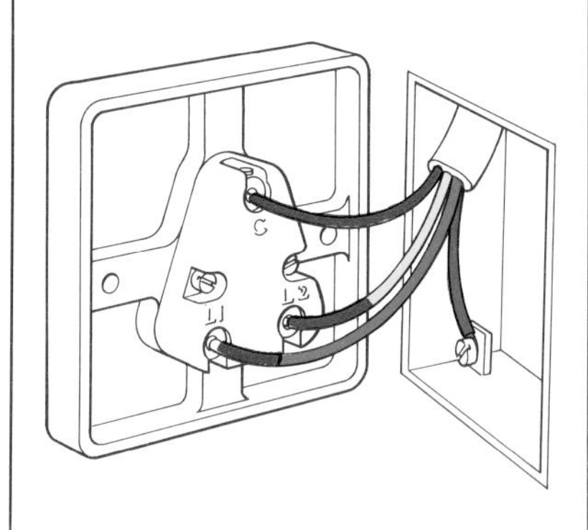

Before the yellow and blue are connected they should each be twisted together with one of the conductors in the existing switch cable (these will have been connected to C and L2, but are now rejoined to L1 and L2).

# Outdoor lighting

A light at the front door is an essential outdoor light for every home, it helps callers to identify the house and the householder to identify the caller. Where there are steps a light is important at night to prevent accidents. A porch light is also welcoming and a well-lit frontage is less attractive to opportunist housebreakers.

One justification for garden lighting can be that it deters burglars, but it also allows longer use of the garden simply for sitting out or for playing outdoor games. Garden lighting also looks attractive from indoors or out.

Then there is the safety aspect, particularly on paths and steps likely to be used at night – the route up the garden from a garage to the back door perhaps. Lights sold as porch lights can actually be used anywhere around the house – next to a patio door for instance or to light a rear entrance.

A wall-mounted carriage lantern.

## A porch light

The choice of light is important. It must be capable of providing effective illumination to the front door and its identifying street number or house name at night. Few lights take lamps of more than 100 watts. It must be weatherproof and properly installed, especially if it is mounted on an exposed wall. As well as being unsafe, a light that is likely to be affected by damp or is hung on a pendant where it can be buffeted by wind will cost a lot in regular lamp replacement, and its light output will be reduced by dirt and condensation.

**Carriage lamps** (or lanterns) These owe their design to a tradition that began with travelling gas lamps where the gas mantel was protected by a cage with glass sections. Some of the modern electric lanterns are pendant or ceiling-mounted for an overhanging porch or entryway; most are wall mounted on an arm taken from a wall plate.

A wall-mounted globe light.

A modern bulkhead fitting with plastic cover.

The best, but most expensive, have a metal casing of wrought iron with clear or amber glass inserts, but plastic, aluminium and other lighter metals often painted black are used, and are much cheaper. Many cannot be easily distinguished from the heavy metals, but they are not usually very robust and should be used only where they are not likely to be knocked or vandalised.

**Bulkhead lamps** These get their name from ships where the lamp is covered by a curved rectangular box of toughened glass screwed to a ship's bulkhead. For domestic lighting this means a fitting mounted directly by its base without brackets. Versions for the home are more decorative – rectangular, square (also called lighting bricks) and circles in opal glass, toughened glass or plastics. Be wary of the plastic type unless it is a translucent polycarbonate, as the trapped heat from the lamp can cause warping and distortion. Sunlight can cause discolouration of cheaper plastics.

Some of these bulkhead fittings can be stencilled with the house name or number using a heat resistant paint, but check with the manufacturer as the opal finish is sometimes damaged by paint.

Buy only bulkhead fittings that are clearly marked for exterior use and therefore weatherproof.

**Globe lights** These are modern bracket light fittings, similar to wall lights available for indoors, but more robust, larger and of course weather resistant. The spherical glass cover normally screws into the holder on a rubber washer and with most there is the choice of suspending the glass or sitting it in its holder. Some have covers of clear glass but there are also opal, coloured and sculptured glass covers. Most can be matched with versions to stand on a gatepost. Although a heavy gauge glass is used, very few are vandal proof.

**Wiring connections**
A porch light can be supplied from the ground floor lighting circuit (provided this does not already carry the maximum number of lighting points) – the wiring being taken from a ceiling rose or a junction box (see page 152). The hall lighting point (or its junction box) is often the nearest connection and is the first place to look. It will often be the last point on the downstairs lighting circuit.

There may be advantages in taking the supply to the light from the upstairs or downstairs ring circuit, as a fused spur from a fused connection unit inserted in the ring circuit (see page 148). The cable from the ring to the fused connection unit should be the same as the ring circuit – usually 2·5mm² – from the flex to the light it should be 1.0mm². The fused connection unit is fitted with a 3 amp fuse. In a two-storey house it is often easy to take a spur from the ring circuit in an upstairs room where a socket position shows the cable to be close to the front of the house above the porch. If there are cavity walls (and the cavity is not filled with insulation) the cable can sometimes be passed through the space under the floor and down the cavity to the light fitting.

The new wiring will normally be run in 1.0mm² twin and earth cable. Unless the lamp is double-insulated, and clearly marked as such, it is important that a metal fitting is earthed – see page 153.

**Fitting a wall-mounted light**
Begin by marking the wall where the light fitting will be sited – the position of the cable access hole and the mounting bracket and screw holes. Drill the holes for the wall plugs, then drill the cable access hole through the wall in a position such that the cable comes out of the wall straight into the light fitting. The hole should be sloped slightly down towards the outside.

When the cable is connected fill the hole with a flexible sealer. Secure the light with greased non-rusting screws. Once in place it's a good idea to seal the base of the light fitting to the wall with flexible sealer to stop the ingress of water.

## CONNECTIONS CHECKLIST

These details should be checked each time you connect a socket, switch or anything at all. Full details of Electrical work are given on pages 48 *et seq.*

- **switch off at the mains**
- always fit grommets in the knocked-out holes in mounting boxes.
- remove the sheath from cable within a box or fitting only
- aim to leave virtually no bare conductor exposed once the connection has been made
- protect the bare earth conductors with green and yellow sleeving and connect to earth terminal
- connect *red* conductors to *live* terminals
- connect *black* conductors to *neutral* terminals
- double-check connections
- shape the connected conductors to fit comfortably inside the box

**If in doubt don't meddle**

THREE WAYS TO WIRE AN OUTSIDE LIGHT

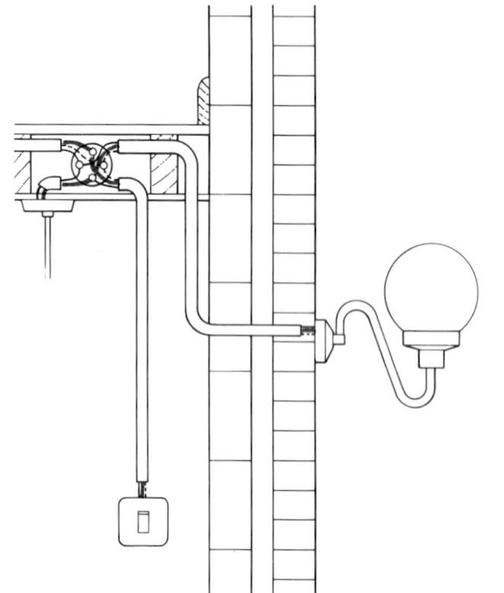
From the junction box supplying the hall light or a new junction box on the lighting circuit.

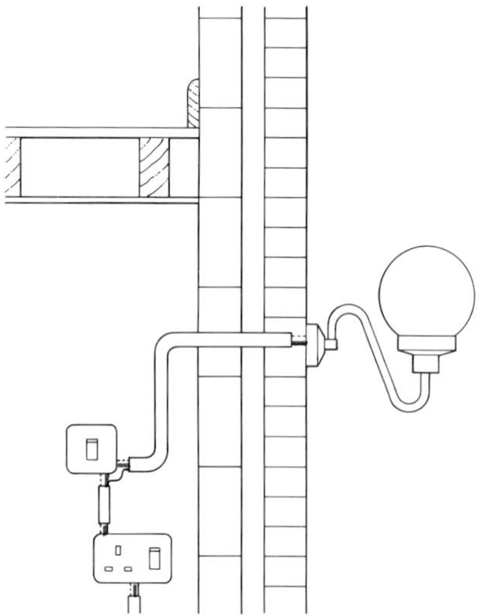
From a fused connection unit installed on the ring circuit supplying the hall.

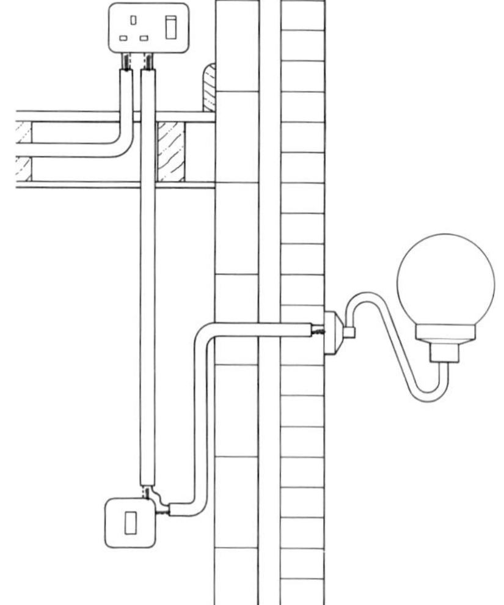
From a fused connection unit installed on the ring circuit in the room above.

**For a ceiling-mounted light** Find a suitable position where the fitting can be secured either to a joist or by suitable ceiling board or plaster fixings. Most fittings are enclosed and the cable is passed through a cable entry hole fitted with a rubber grommet. If the fitting has an open back it must be mounted on a suitable pattress or box – a plastic round conduit box can be used with a terminal block inside for instance. If the ceiling is just an open canopy it would be worth sealing around an open-backed light fitting.

## Switching

Ideally the switch for a porch light should be on the wall just inside the front door. Normally it would be next to the switch for the hall light.

Consider also the possibility of two-way switching with the second switch beside your bed or on the upstairs landing. A light switched on suddenly will discourage an intruder and enable you to investigate the cause of a night noise from a front window.

A second switch is also useful outside the house to turn on the lights when you arrive home in the dark. Such a switch should be weatherproof, but if it is protected by a porch it need only be splashproof. It could be wired as intermediate switching with two indoor switches.

### Automatic controls

A daylight sensitive photocell that will automatically switch the porch light on at dusk and off at dawn is another choice and simple to wire into the circuit. Because this control keeps the light on all through the hours of darkness, the most likely use is as an occasional alternative to hand switching and so it's best wired through a second switch. When you need to use the photocell you make sure that both the switches are in the 'on' position. If you're going to leave the light on all night, choose one that uses little energy. A small fluorescent fitting with an energy-saving lamp for instance – note this fitting could only be used in a protected dry position.

A wall-mounted timeswitch is another choice for an automatic control for a porch light. The light will then switch on and off automatically while you are away from home and the timer will take the place of the switch. Most timeswitches have two on and two off periods and a switch that allows them to be by-passed at any time.

### Remote switching

Remote switching is also possible. Small portable, battery-operated remote control units can be carried in the car or in the hand and when the trigger is pressed an invisible beam of infra-red light aimed at another cell mounted on the wall or gatepost automatically switches on the lighting. There are various types of sensor that will operate like a switch on a two-way circuit or as an intermediate switch on a three-way circuit. The maker's wiring connection must be carefully followed, but normally a three core and earth 1·0mm$^2$ cable between the sensor cell on the gatepost and the ordinary switch is all that is needed. The cable must be suitable for use outdoors and be permanently installed taking the normal precautions for outdoor wiring.

A sensor switch can also be used to open electrically operated up-and-over garage doors. One cell is mounted on the garage door post and wired into the switch circuit to the motor controlling the operation of the doors.

Splashproof switches – the switch is enclosed by a plastic membrane through which it can be operated.

Outdoor wall spot uses a 150 watt PAR lamp.

## Garden lighting

The various types of garden lights are listed opposite. Best of the outdoor lamps for most purposes is the PAR 38 made of a tough Pyrex glass (see page 150) fitted into a slim weather-proof holder which is tough enough to be used outdoors. It has a long life and gives either a narrow or a wide beam of light. Floodlights with tiny tungsten halogen lamps give the most light.

Most outdoor lighting is made to be permanently fixed temporary lighting has the merit that it can be moved when working in the garden or to suit the time of year. It is safest to use low-voltage (24V and strictly speaking called extra low-voltage) sets. Even on a temporary basis outdoor cables should be properly installed. Never run cables where they may be disturbed or tripped over. Secure overhead cables properly.

Concentrate on lighting trees and paths and patios using PAR spotlights. Conifers look best if spotlights are aimed so that the light touches the edge of the branches. Big trees should be spot-lighted or flood-lighted directly from below.

For lighting a path, lamps should be covered with reflectors that direct the light down on the pavings. Garden steps can be lighted by bulkhead fittings mounted on a side wall and there are also brick-sized fittings which can be recessed in the wall.

Water also looks attractive when lighted: swimming pools should have lighting for practical and safety reasons; ponds can have low-voltage (24V) lights set just below the surface of the water – the isolating transformer is usually concealed in a weatherproof enclosure in the rockery or under a paving slab beside the pool. Better still house the transformer inside the house so that all the garden cable is 24V. Low-voltage lights can also be used in other parts of the garden and low-voltage circuits are sometimes also used for submersible pumps for fountains – where they are a safer choice than a pump that runs on 240V.

### GARDEN LIGHTING

Permanent wiring for garden lighting must be properly installed so that it is protected from accidental damage and the weather (see page 302 *et seq*). Even temporary lighting needs special care with the installation.

Before installing garden lighting, you can test the effect on a dry night by using an extension cable and an ordinary 150W bulb in a simple reflector.

**1 Brick light**
A recessed fitting more or less the size of a brick for fitting into a wall to give low-level lighting. Around 40W or 60W.
*useful for* walkways, beside walls particularly near steps.

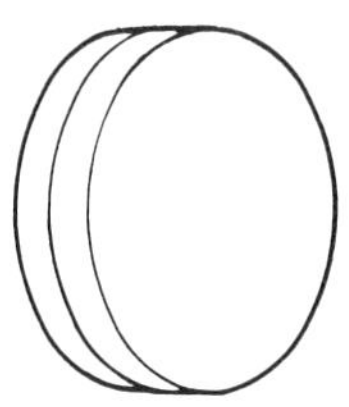

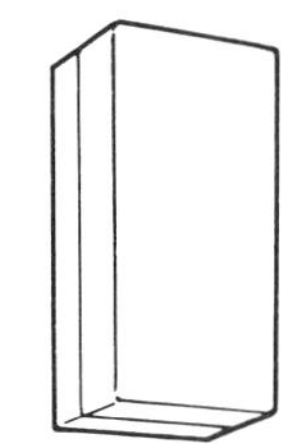

**2 Lighting brick**
A surface-mounting bulkhead-type fitting for installation on a wall. Round and square versions are available up to about 100W.
*useful for* entrance doors, patio doors.

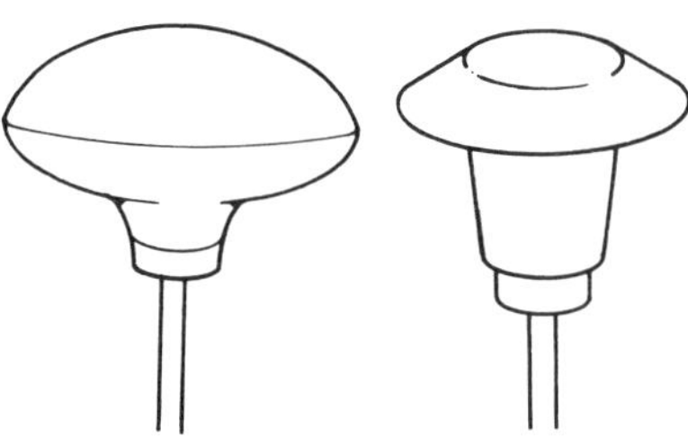

**3 Spike lamps**
Lamps in ground spike fittings available as individual lights run on mains voltage or low-voltage and also as low-voltage sets where a string of fittings is connected via a single 12V or 24V transformer (which must be installed in a dry place). Light is usually directed downwards and sideways, but not up. All are movable, so can be regarded as temporary – arrange the flexible cable so it will not be a hazard likely to trip passers by. Available 40W and 60W, *useful* for borders, shrubberies, orchards and so on. Use lights at different heights to create interesting light and shadow.

**4 Recessed, ground, floodlight**
Watertight fitting with glass cover designed to be buried in the ground. Light is thrown upwards. Often 150W.
*useful for* illuminating large patios or other parts of a garden, fit away from pedestrian traffic or in a bed of difficult-to-walk-on pebbles.

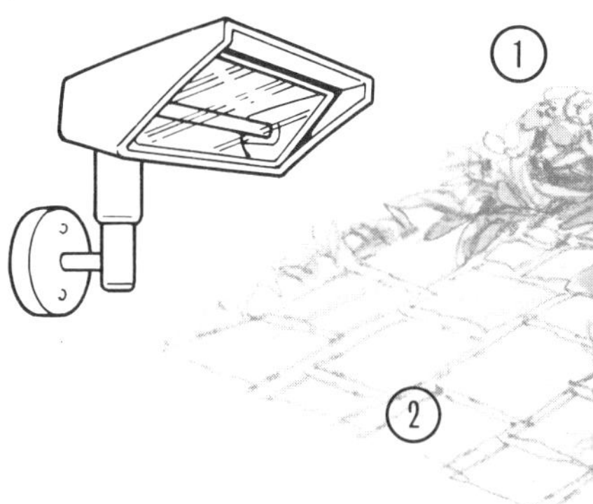


**5 Tungsten halogen floodlights**
Floodlights for installation high above an area to give a very high level of lighting.
*useful* for burglar deterrent lighting – mounted at first floor height on an outside floor, but controlled from indoors, tennis courts, swimming pools and other sports or play areas.

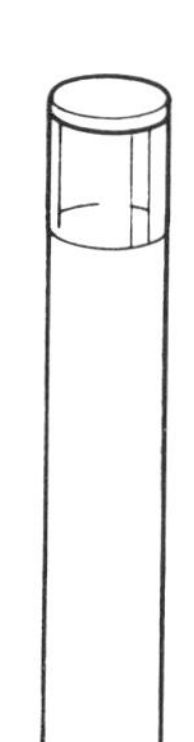

**6 Post-top lanterns**
Lamps on bollards or tall spikes directing lights down and sideways to give glare-free lighting.
Lanterns can also be set on existing pillars.
*useful for* paths, driveways – especially gateways –; swimming pool surrounds.

The types of garden light fittings are listed in the captions. The main drawing gives an idea of where each can be used.

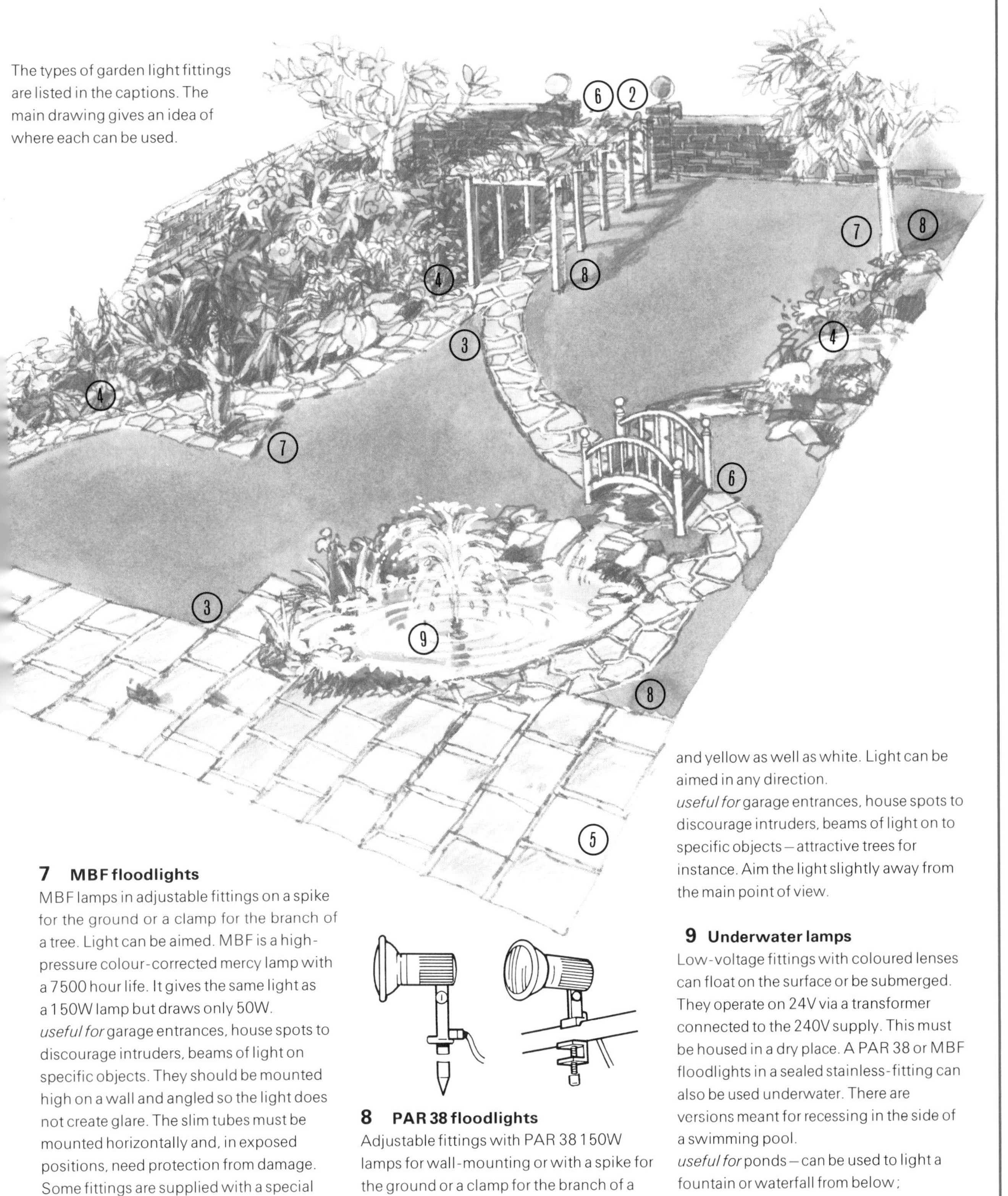


**7 MBF floodlights**
MBF lamps in adjustable fittings on a spike for the ground or a clamp for the branch of a tree. Light can be aimed. MBF is a high-pressure colour-corrected mercy lamp with a 7500 hour life. It gives the same light as a 150W lamp but draws only 50W.
*useful for* garage entrances, house spots to discourage intruders, beams of light on specific objects. They should be mounted high on a wall and angled so the light does not create glare. The slim tubes must be mounted horizontally and, in exposed positions, need protection from damage. Some fittings are supplied with a special guard.

**8 PAR 38 floodlights**
Adjustable fittings with PAR 38 150W lamps for wall-mounting or with a spike for the ground or a clamp for the branch of a tree. Lamps are available in red, green, blue and yellow as well as white. Light can be aimed in any direction.
*useful for* garage entrances, house spots to discourage intruders, beams of light on to specific objects – attractive trees for instance. Aim the light slightly away from the main point of view.

**9 Underwater lamps**
Low-voltage fittings with coloured lenses can float on the surface or be submerged. They operate on 24V via a transformer connected to the 240V supply. This must be housed in a dry place. A PAR 38 or MBF floodlights in a sealed stainless-fitting can also be used underwater. There are versions meant for recessing in the side of a swimming pool.
*useful for* ponds – can be used to light a fountain or waterfall from below; swimming pool.

# Chapter 7

# INSULATING AND HEATING THE HOME

Provided you choose a popular fuel and the installation's well done, installing a modern central heating system is perhaps the best improvement you can make. It helps to sell a house and you normally recoup a large percentage of the capital costs. An efficient heating system will also make a house more comfortable to live in and in its own way it provides extra space, by opening up parts of the house that might have been underused in the past, just because they were chilly zones.

It's a false economy to install and run a good heating system without also investing in some insulation to slow down the rate at which the heat supplied to your house flows out through the fabric of the house, as well as through cracks round doors and windows, letterboxes and so on.

All the time that the inside of a house is warmer than the outside, any heat energy that is put into it (for example, by the heating system operating) will flow out again. Eventually, *all* of the heat energy put into a house will flow out again, there is no sense in which any of it stays behind to warm you up. For the inside of a house to remain at a steady temperature, the heating system has to supply heat energy to the house at the same rate as it is flowing out.

You can reduce your fuel bills by reducing the amount of energy your heating system uses – and the only way in which you can do this and still keep the house at a steady temperature is by slowing down the rate at which the heat flows out of the house.

Of all the possible home improvements, insulation is perhaps the one in which the investment element is the most important. If you build an extension, then you get some enjoyment out of the use of the finished room, which can make up for any money that you might lose over the deal. Insulation rarely gives any actual enjoyment. Indeed, few forms of insulation are even visible – you insulate solely in the hope of having lower fuel bills. Insulation, therefore, has to pay its way: it has to be a good investment. This means that it is important to be able to calculate whether a particular energy-saving measure – such as installing an extra layer of loft insulation – is worth doing: that is, if it will save you more money than it costs you.

At the present time no insulation (even expensive double glazed replacement windows) is likely to have much effect on the selling price of your house (except perhaps in Scotland) and good insulation doesn't do much to persuade a potential buyer. So once the insulation is incorporated into the house, you can more or less write off the capital cost.

In general, energy policy in the UK is based on persuading you that it is in your own interest to save on your heating bills. But under the Home Insulation Scheme anyone who has no loft insulation can apply to their local authority for a grant to help meet the cost of installing it. The grant payable is two-thirds of the cost of the materials and labour, up to a maximum of £69. (Ninety per cent of the cost up to £95 for elderly people on a low-income.)

To qualify you have to put in the equivalent of 100mm of glass fibre blanket; insulate any water tanks and pipes in your loft and fit a British Standard 80mm thick jacket to your hot water cylinder if there is no jacket on it already. You must not start the work until your application is approved.

Grants are often available for double glazing in a house near an airport or for a house on a main road where the double glazing is installed to reduce noise.

If you already have some insulation, don't be fooled into thinking that you cannot cut your bills any further. Read this chapter and do some sums.

# The effects of insulation

One of the ways in which heat flows out of a building is by *conduction*. In conduction, heat flows through the thickness of a material as long as one end of it is colder than the other. The speed with which it flows (from the warm side to the cold side) depends on the type of material: some materials, such as metals, are very good conductors of heat, others (especially those with a lot of air trapped in them) are very bad – *bad* conductors are *good* insulators.

The rate of heat flow depends also on the thickness: the thicker the material, the slower the rate.

Adding a layer of a good insulating material – such as glass fibre blanket, or expanded polystyrene – to the comparatively poor insulating materials that most houses are built of is what is meant by insulating a house.

## The value of insulation

Insulation *saves* money year after year in the form of lower fuel bills. However it also *costs* money to install and continues to cost money year after year, because if you had not spent the money on insulation you could have invested it somewhere – in a building society for instance – where it would earn interest. In any calculation of the value of insulation the annual amount saved must therefore be reduced by the annual cost.

In a similar way, if the money to pay for the insulation is borrowed, the amount of interest to be paid on the loan has to be deducted from the savings.

Because the insulation has no resale value and adds little, if anything to the house value it's best to write off the costs. The savings on fuel bills must therefore be at least large enough to enable you to recoup the costs within the period of time that you expect to stay in the house you have insulated. On average, people stay in houses about six years.

There are many different ways of calculating whether a particular piece of insulation is worth installing – fortunately one of the simplest calculations is usually all that is necessary.

## Simple payback period

This is a very simple method of calculating roughly how many years it will take for an insulation measure to recoup its cost. Dividing the cost of the insulation by the savings in fuel bills a year gives the number of years it will take for the insulation to pay for itself. In mathematical terms:

$$\text{payback period in years} = \frac{\text{cost of insulation in £££}}{\text{savings per year in £££}}$$

When calculating the cost of an insulation measure, it is important to remember to include everything that has to be done. For example, with loft insulation, include the cost of insulating any cisterns and pipes in the loft.

This method of calculation is perfectly good for comparing one form of insulation with another – the shorter the payback period, the better. But it does have some drawbacks.

For a start, it does not tell you how an insulation measure compares with investing the money elsewhere – whether there is a better investment. It does not take into account rises in fuel prices (the calculation assumes that the savings stay the same every year). And it does not take into account the *loss of interest* on the capital cost (or the cost of borrowing).

The effect of fuel price rises is to make each year's savings bigger, and so the payback period shorter (which is a good thing). On the other hand, the effect of taking into account loss of interest (or the cost of borrowing) is to make each year's savings smaller, and so the payback period longer. The two obviously tend to cancel out and, where the payback period is short (say not more than four or six years) it is hardly worth the trouble of doing more detailed calculations; the simple payback period calculation remains accurate enough.

This leaves the problem of trying to decide whether an insulation measure is worth doing (instead of investing elsewhere). The simple answer is that if you stay in your house (and the insulation lasts) at least as long as the payback period then the insulation *is* worth installing and if you stay in your house longer, then you will, effectively, start making a profit. If you move out before the end of the payback period you are likely to be better off financially by keeping your money in the building society.

Inverting the payback period gives a simple rate of return.

### Other methods

The simple payback period is really as good and accurate a guide to the value of insulation as you will normally need. But there are other methods of doing the sums.

The easiest involves sitting down with a calculator (or home computer) and comparing, year by year, how much you gain or lose financially if you buy some form of insulation and if you do not.

If you make the right guesses about fuel price rises, interest rates and so on, this method should yield accurate answers. The sums are tedious but interesting because making different assumptions about fuel price changes and so on, it's possible to see how the answers will change.

**Fuel price changes** In 1982 the average fuel price increase was around 10%. In line with government policy gas prices rose more steeply – 23% in 1982 – but gas prices are expected to level off in 1983. In comparison off-peak electricity rises were much lower, around 4%, and this fuel is now more competitive than it used to be.

## Calculating the savings

In order to work out whether a piece of insulation is worthwhile, you need to know how much it will cost, and how much it will save.

The cost is relatively easy to find out – remember to include all the incidental expenses that may be involved.

The amount of money saving the insulation will produce requires rather more calculation. It divides into these basic parts:

- the rate of the heat loss from the part of the house (eg the loft) that is to be insulated
- the total heat loss, over the year, for this area
- the likely energy saving that insulating this area will bring
- the true cost of heating, and so the true savings to be made by insulating (which, of course, reduces the amount of heating needed).

These calculations are explained below.

### Rate of heat loss

The rate at which heat flows through the materials of a building depends on:

- the type of materials
- the thickness and area of each material
- the temperature difference between inside and outside of the building.

Different types of material lose heat at different rates – depending on whether they are good or bad insulators or conductors. The factor which describes this property of materials is called **thermal transmittance** or **U value**. The rate of heat loss, in watts, through a piece of construction is then given by the U value multiplied by the area of construction, and the temperature difference between inside and outside:

**rate of heat loss**

equals

**U × A × (Ti-To)**

where:
U = U value
A = area in square metres
Ti = inside temperature in degrees Centigrade
To = outside temperature in degrees Centigrade

The units of U value are watts per square metre per degree Centigrade – $W/m^2{}^\circ C$. But as this description is a little cumbersome, it is often omitted, and books often give U values simply as a bare number. This can lead to confusion with older publications, where the U value may be given in its old imperial unit which is an even more cumbersome $Btu/ft^2h^\circ C$. (To convert from imperial to metric units, multiply the imperial figure by 5·7.)

The rate of heat loss through a piece of construction is directly proportional to the U value: halve the U value and the rate of heat loss is also halved. (This of course means that fuel bills will be cut – though probably not by half as there are other factors to be taken into account.)

U values for the common building materials are given in the Table opposite. It is important not to regard these figures as being too precise. For one thing, there is often some disagreement about the exact figures. Secondly, the U value of a particular piece of construction can vary – a brick wall, for example, has a higher U value when it is wet. It is best to assume that quoted U values are accurate only to within about ten per cent.

U values can also vary depending on how exposed a house is – to take account of this, a correction factor can be applied to the U values given in the Table. The amount of the correction depends on the original U value – details are given beneath the U value Table.

Note also that the figures for other materials and constructions cannot be calculated directly from the U values given in the Table – for example, a brick wall twice as thick as the one quoted does not have a U value of half as much, but about two-thirds.

### Total heat loss

The calculation so far gives only the *rate* of heat loss – the amount of heat lost in each second of time. (The unit 'watts' is shorthand for heat energy per second measured in joules per second.) To calculate the total amount of heat lost from a house, the rate of heat loss must be multiplied by a period of time (which is given by the symbol **t**). So the formula becomes:

**total heat loss**

equals

**U × A × (Ti-To) × t.**

It is at this stage in the calculation that you must make some assumptions about the internal and external temperatures and the length of time that will be used in the calculation. Unless you indulge in extremely sophisticated measuring and monitoring of temperatures and so on, the figures used in these calculations can only be assumptions, and are unlikely to be highly accurate.

Deciding on the length of time is the simplest operation. It is the period during the year when the outside temperature is lower than the inside one – in effect, the winter heating season. During this time heat is being continuously lost from the house whenever the inside is warmer than the outside (whether the heating system is on or not). The length of the heating season depends on:

- how warm the house is – the warmer it is, the longer is the period during the year when the inside temperature will be above the outside temperature
- where the house is situated – in

cont. page 186

## Table 1 : U values for normal exposure

| **walls – external** | W/m²°C |
|---|---|
| solid brick, 105mm thick | 3·1 |
| with 50mm insulation | 0·60 |
| with 100mm insulation | 0·35 |
| solid brick, 220mm thick | 2·1 |
| with 50mm insulation | 0·55 |
| with 100mm insulation | 0·35 |
| cavity, brick outside and inside | 1·6 |
| with cavity wall insulation | 0·5 |
| cavity, brick outside/block inside | 1·0 |
| with cavity wall insulation | 0·4 |
| **walls – internal** | |
| brick, 135mm including plaster | 2·2 |
| block, 80mm including plaster | 2·1 |
| 105mm including plaster | 1·9 |
| 130mm including plaster | 1·7 |
| timber stud and plasterboard covered | 1·6 |
| **doors** | |
| wood, in internal walls | 2·1 |
| in external walls | 2·5 |
| fully glazed, in internal walls | 3·2 |
| in external walls | 4·0 |
| **floors – intermediate** | |
| timber, heat flow upwards | 1·6 |
| heat flow downwards | 1·4 |

| **windows** | | W/m²°C |
|---|---|---|
| single glazed metal | | 5·6 |
| single glazed wood | | 4·0[1] |
| double glazed wood (and plastic) | | 2·5 |
| double glazed metal, with thermal break or aluminium/PVC composite | | 3·7 |
| double glazed metal, without thermal break | | 4·3 |
| **roofs** | | |
| pitched, without felt | | 2·7 |
| pitched, with felt | | |
| pitched[2] | 25mm insulation | 0·9 (1·0) [2] |
| | 50mm insulation | 0.55 (0·6) [2] |
| | 80mm insulation | 0·40 |
| | 100mm insulation | 0·35 |
| | 125mm insulation | 0·30 |
| | 160mm insulation | 0·25 |
| | 200mm insulation | 0·20 |
| | 25mm topped up with 80mm | 0·35 |
| | 25mm topped up with 100mm | 0·30 |
| | 50mm topped up with 80mm | 0·30 |
| | 100mm topped up with 50mm | 0·25 |
| flat, | uninsulated | |
| | with 50mm insulation | 0·5 |
| | with 100mm insulation | 0·3 |

| | uninsulated | insulated 25mm | insulated 50mm | insulated 100mm |
|---|---|---|---|---|
| **floors – solid**[3] | W/m²°C | W/m²°C | W/m²°C | W/m²°C |
| detached house | | | | |
| square, large | 0·7 | 0·45 | 0·35 | 0·25 |
| otherwise | 1·0 | 0·6 | 0·4 | 0·25 |
| semi or end of terrace | | | | |
| very long and thin | 0·8 | 0·5 | 0·4 | 0·25 |
| otherwise | 0·9 | 0·55 | 0·4 | 0·25 |
| mid-terrace | | | | |
| very long and thin | 0·35 | 0·3 | 0·25 | 0·2 |
| 'normal' shape | 0·5 | 0·35 | 0·3 | 0·2 |
| square | 0·7 | 0·45 | 0·35 | 0·25 |
| individual rooms 3m x 3m[4] | | | | |
| 1 exposed wall | 0·6 | 0·4 | 0·3 | 0·2 |
| 2 exposed walls | 1·1 | 0·6 | 0·4 | 0·25 |
| 3 or 4 exposed walls | 1·5 | 0·8 | 0·55 | 0·35 |

**floors – suspended**
U values for suspended floors differ greatly from source to source, but what is probably more significant is the draughtiness of the floor – see page 189 for remedies. Once you have stopped draughts, it is probably reasonable to use the same U values as for solid floors. Most losses are at the edges.

[1] varies from about 3·5 for a window with a thick wooden frame to about 4·5 for a window with a slim wooden frame
[2] U values for well insulated pitched roofs are much the same whether the roof has felt or not. Where they differ, the un-felted U value is given in brackets. All values are for insulation with glass or mineral fibre, polystyrene or cellulose: vermiculite insulation gives much poorer values
[3] a thick floor covering will reduce U values by about 20 per cent
[4] for each doubling in area U values fall by very roughly half (eg the U value of an uninsulated floor 6m x 6m with two edges exposed is about 0·6)

**U Values and exposure**
Most buildings in suburbs and country areas are rated as **normal**. Buildings up to the third storey in city centres are the only ones rated as **sheltered**. All buildings, whatever their height, along the coast or on hill sites are rated as **severe**: so are buildings from the ninth storey upwards in cities, or the fifth storey upwards in suburbs and country areas.

For severe exposure, the U value is increased by a correction factor, for sheltered exposure, the U value must be decreased by the same factor.

| U value | correction |
|---|---|
| less than 1 | nil |
| 1–2 | ±5% |
| 2–3 | ±10% |
| 3–4 | ±15% |
| 4–5 | ±20% |
| 5–6 | ±25% |

general, the north of the UK has a lower outside temperature than the south.

The inside and outside temperatures are, of course, not static but vary continually – as the house cools down and warms up; and as the seasons change and day turns into night. So *average* inside and outside temperatures have to be used. These must be averages over the months of the heating season and, because the house will be losing heat 24 hours a day, they must be the average temperatures over 24 hours, irrespective of how long the heating system is on for.

Figures for heating season lengths and average outside temperatures over these seasons for various parts of the country, are given in the Table below. Note that the length is given in thousands of hours. This makes calculations simpler: the rate of heat loss in watts, multiplied by a time in thousands of hours gives a total heating loss in terms of kilowatt hours, which is a particularly useful unit of energy.

The average inside temperature is entirely dependent on how well you heat your house. The average values above are fairly typical.

With some insulation measures – double glazing a living room for instance – you would be interested in the temperature of a single room, rather than the whole house. In this case, use:

- 18°C if you heat the room all day
- 16°C if it is heated morning and evening only
- 14°C if it is heated only in the evening.

### Inside temperatures

- for a house kept comfortably warm all over for about 16 hours a day – 18°C
- for a house partly heated (eg mainly ground floor only) for about 16 hours a day – 16°C
- for a house heated morning and evening only, reduce the averages above by about 2°C
- for a house heated evening only, reduce the averages above by about 4°C.

### Likely energy saving

The total amount of energy saved over a year by insulating is the difference between the total heat loss before and after insulating – which means carrying out the total heat loss calculation twice, using different numbers for the before and after cases. The main factor that changes after insulating is, of course, the U value. But unless you can control your heating system very accurately, it is also likely that the average inside temperature will rise. Although this may make you more comfortable, it does mean that you will burn more fuel than if temperatures had not risen – and so your money savings will be lower than they might have been.

To take account of this, it is simplest first to carry out the calculations using different numbers only for the U value. Then to apply a reduction factor to the potential saving calculated to get a more realistic figure.

### Factors

- for a whole-house heating system, fitted with very good controls – see page 212 – no correction factor, assume that you can realise the whole of the potential saving
- for a house heated morning and evening only, allow about 75 per cent of the savings
- for a house heated downstairs, evenings only, allow only about 33 per cent of the savings.

### True cost of heating

Calculating the cost of heating is complicated by two factors:

- fuels are sold in a variety of units – litres, tonnes and so on – and only electricity is sold in the same units (kilowatt-hours) as those used in the energy calculations given here. So conversions are necessary to find out how much energy is provided by each portion of fuel – see *Energy content of fuels*, opposite.
- heating appliances are not one hundred per cent efficient – that is, although a heater may take in a kilowatt-hour of fuel energy, it does not deliver a kilowatt-hour of useful heat to your house.

Some of the losses are inherent in the type of heater, and are mainly concerned with heat that disappears up a chimney. Some are dependent on how the heating system is used – not all the heat given out is useful to the occupants. The *average system efficiency* (ASE) takes all these losses into account – see ASE Table for different types of heater.

To calculate the amount of fuel saved by insulation therefore, divide the energy saved by the ASE, and the energy content of the fuel used in your heating system:

$$\text{fuel saved} \quad \text{equals} \quad \frac{\text{energy saved}}{\text{ASE} \times \text{energy content}}$$

### Heating season lengths and temperatures

| | heating season from | to | thousand hours | average outside temperature |
|---|---|---|---|---|
| South west England | Oct | Mar | 4·400 | 7·5°C |
| Scotland, or exposed areas in England and Wales | Sept | April | 6·500 | 6·3°C |
| all other parts of the country | Oct | April | 5·100 | 6.5°C |

## Energy content of fuels

| | |
|---|---|
| anthracite grains | 9,100kWh/tonne |
| gas | 29·3 kWh/therm |
| house coal, group 2 | 8,300kWh/tonne |
| Housewarm (smokeless fuel) | 8,300kWh/tonne |
| LPG (bottled gas) | 205 kWh/15kg cylinder |
| oil, 28 sec[1] | 10·18kWh/litre |
| 35 sec[2] | 10·56kWh/litre |
| paraffin | 46·3 kWh/tonne |
| Sunbrite, doubles | 7,800kWh/tonne |
| Welsh steam coal, small | 9,100kWh/tonne |
| large | 9,500kWh/tonne |
| wood (20% moisture) | 4,200kWh/tonne[3] |

[1] used in wall-flame oil boilers
[2] used in pressure-jet oil boilers

## Average system efficiencies (ASE)

| Individual room heaters | ASE |
|---|---|
| electric radiant or convector | 75 |
| electric storage heater | 67 |
| gas convector heater | 46 |
| gas radiant/convector | 36 |
| coal, open fire | 20 |
| coal, open fire and back boiler | 25 |
| smokeless fuel in room heater | 40 |
| smokeless fuel in room heater with back boiler | 45 |
| **Central heating** | |
| anthracite | 52 |
| electric storage heater | 67 |
| gas | 52 |
| oil | 52 |

[3] varies, according to the moisture content of the wood

Finally, to calculate the amount of money saved, multiply the fuel saving by the cost of the fuel.

## Ventilation

Heat is lost not only *through* the structure of a house, but also because warmed air flows out of the building and is replaced by cooler air. It is impossible to stop this ventilation process entirely – in fact, it is undesirable (and could be fatal) to do so, but the cooler air coming into the building has to be heated, and particularly in a draughty house, the heat loss can represent a large proportion of the total losses.

Natural ventilation takes place as a result of wind pressure – pushing air through one side of a house and pulling it out of the other. It can also be the result of convection currents: as air is heated, it expands and so becomes less dense. It therefore tends to rise, its place being taken by cooler, denser, air. Warm air will often rise from ground floor rooms to upstairs, finding its way out through cracks and gaps in upstairs windows and ceilings, in doing so, it pulls cold air (which then has to be heated).

Though it is possible to calculate some of the heat loss savings to be made by draughtproofing, it makes little sense to do so. The calculations are not very accurate and in any case, reducing ventilation losses by draughtproofing is inexpensive and is almost without exception well worth doing.

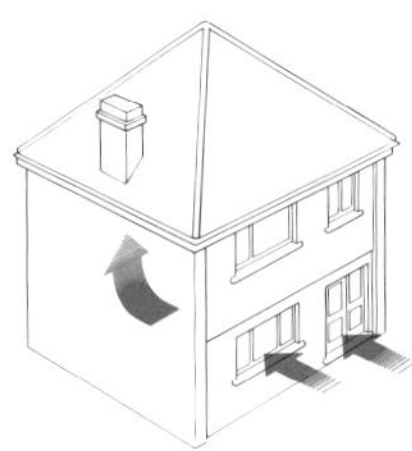

Natural ventilation can mean large heat losses

## AN EXAMPLE

How much might loft insulation save in a suburban house in the Midlands with a loft area of 35 sq m?

### The facts

**current level of insulation**
25mm
**cost of additional insulation**
£1.50 sq m (for an extra 80mm); £52.50 for whole loft
**heating pattern**
morning and evening only
**average upstairs temperature**
14°C
**type of heating**
gas central heating
**cost of gas**
33p a therm

**Stage 1** Calculate the original heat loss: U x A x (Ti-To) x t. The U value of this loft is 0·9; the heating season in the Midlands is 5·1 thousand hours and the average outside temperature over that period is about 6·5°C.

So the original heat loss (Ho) is:

**Ho = 1·0 × 35 × (14 – 6·5) × 5·1**
**= 1339kWh (kilowatt-hours)**

**Stage 2** Adding an extra 80mm of insulation will bring the U value of the loft down to about 0·35, the new heat loss (Hn) will be:

**Hn = 0·35 × 35 × (14–6·5) × 5·1**
**= 469kWh**

**Stage 3** The potential reduction in heat loss is simply Ho – Hn:

**potential saving = 1339 – 469kWh**
**= 870kWh**

**Stage 4** After insulating, the bedroom temperatures are likely to rise. The reduction for likely saving is between three-quarters and a third – say fifty per cent:

**likely saving = 870 × 50% = 435kWh.**

**Stage 5** Fuel saving equals

$$\frac{\textbf{likely saving}}{\textbf{ASE} \times \textbf{energy content of fuel}}$$

**= 435/(0·52 × 29·3)**
**= 28·6 therms a year**

**Stage 6** Multiply the fuel saving by the cost of fuel to get the £ saving.

**£ saving = 28·6 × 0·33 = 9·44**
**Roughly £9·50 a year.**

**Stage 7** Calculate the payback period – the cost of insulation divided by the saving:

$$\textbf{payback period} = \frac{52{\cdot}50}{9{\cdot}50} = 5{\cdot}5 \textbf{ years}$$

# Practical Insulating

Having calculated how much insulation you need and where your priorities lie. This section details the practicalities: what to use, where and how to install it. The plumbing, walls, roof and floors will all need your attention.

## Plumbing

The plumbing system in a house needs insulation both to conserve heat, and to reduce the chances of freezing in the winter. (But even if you've insulated you should drain the system in an unoccupied house.)

## Draughtproofing

Draughts whistling through gaps in a house are uncomfortable and cause large amounts of heat to be lost. Luckily, draughtproofing is fairly simple and cheap. It is certainly well worth doing all windows and doors.

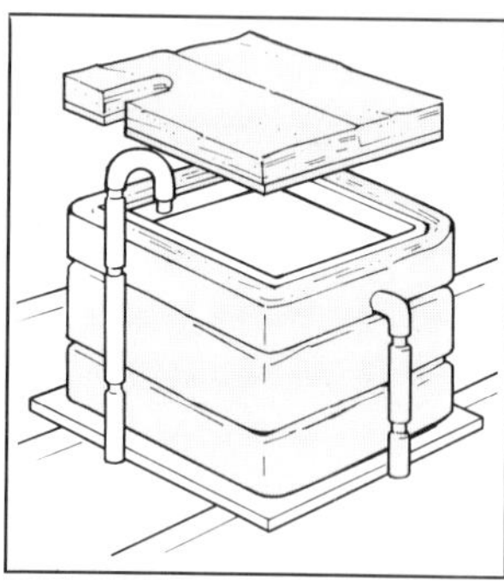

**Cold water cisterns** Cisterns in the roof space must be insulated to prevent freezing. Drape glass fibre blanket insulation round the cistern, overlapping generously. If you have not insulated the loft floor underneath the cistern then do not insulate the base of the cistern – carry the insulation down to meet that on the floor. A cistern should always be covered, put insulation over the lid – but make sure that no fibres or dust can get into the water. Sheets of expanded polystyrene are generally more expensive, but easier to fit on a rectangular cistern.

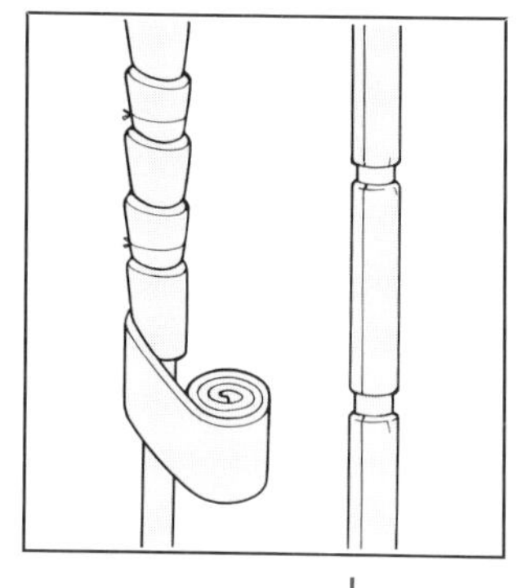

**Pipes** Both hot and cold pipes in unheated spaces should be insulated, using either glass fibre pipe insulation in strips spiralled around the pipe (or blanket torn into strips) or preformed split tubing. Long hot pipe runs will benefit from pipe insulation even if the pipe runs through a heated room.

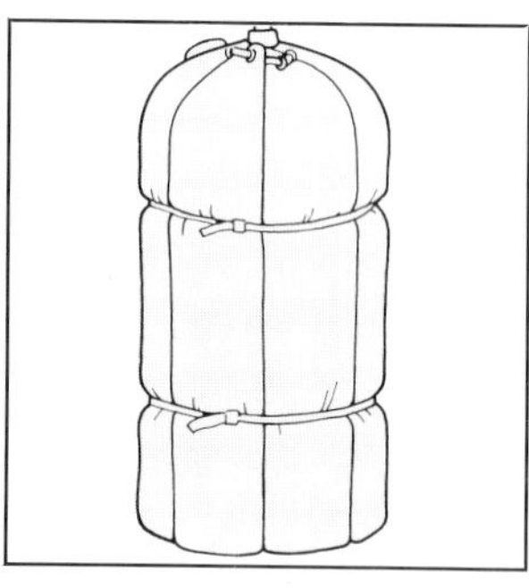

**Hot water cylinders** It is very important that these are well insulated. The easiest solution is a cylinder jacket, without gaps and *at least* 80mm thick.

A simple box around the cylinder filled with vermiculite granules is a neater but more expensive solution. Ensure that insulation is kept clear of the cap of any immersion heater, and away from any cylinder thermostat.

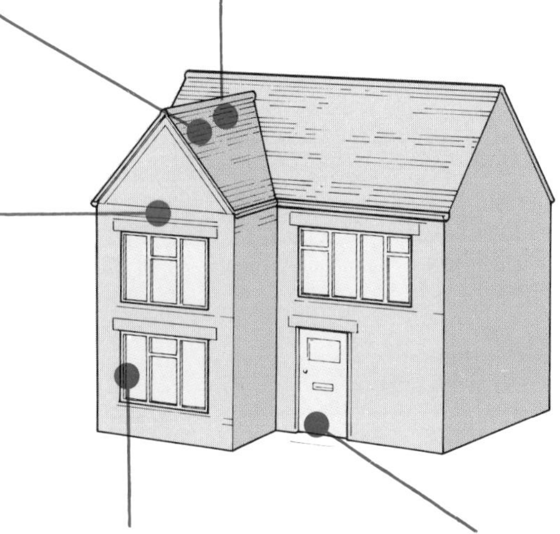

**Draughts** There are many different excluders sold to fill or cover gaps in the opening parts of doors and windows. For windows and doors that you do not open, a cheap treatment is to screw them closed, fill the gaps with crack filler, and paint. Fill between frames, and the wall on the inside with a crack filler, and on the outside with flexible mastic – check underneath the sill particularly.

Fill gaps between floorboards (not covered with carpets) with filler or *papier mâché*. Gaps between the floor and skirting board can be covered by foam strip and quadrant beading. Fill gaps between the skirting and the wall. Cover letterboxes with a letterbox sealer or a heavy curtain across the door, close fireplaces in use with a throat restrictor (or block off ones no longer used).

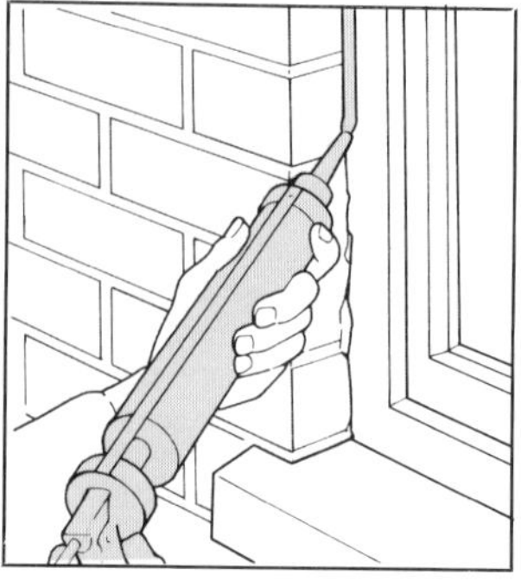

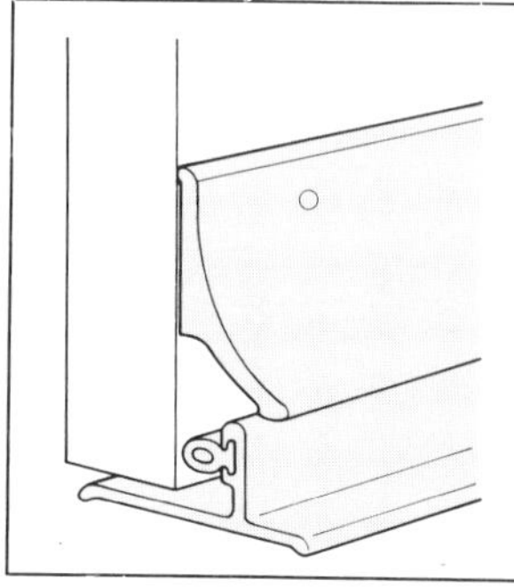

There are many other cracks and gaps in most houses, some of which are particularly important to treat. The best way to find the sources of draughts (if you cannot readily feel them) is to explore with a smoke taper.

## Walls

Insulating the cavities of cavity walls is a professional job where plastic foam, mineral fibre or polystyrene beads are pumped into the gap. It's quite expensive, but is of course out of sight and if done well should cause no problems. Solid walls can't be dealt with as easily, although there are now various types of exterior insulation on the market. Both cavity walls and solid walls can be d-i-y insulated on the inside by dry lining or by bonding rigid insulating sheets (polystyrene-backed plasterboard) directly to the wall using a special adhesive. Details of both techniques are given in Chapter 8.

## Don't overdo it

It is very important not to overdo draughtproofing in rooms where you run any sort of fire (except an electric one). If the heater is starved of air it can produce dangerous gases. A good solution is trickle ventilators placed in the top of the window frame – these can be closed when the fire is not burning. Draughtproofing can also increase the risk of condensation from moisture vapour.

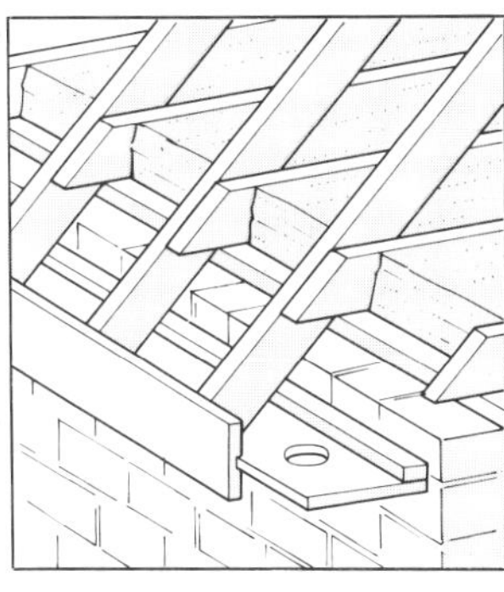

**Roofs** Provide ventilation by cutting a piece off the soffit if you have one or by making large holes in the eaves. Make sure there is a clear air passage – do not tuck the insulation down into the eaves.

For the problem sides of sloping roofs insulate on the inside of the existing wall or, if you have access to the gap between the roof tiles and the room walls, you might be able to slide in polystyrene sheets to rest on the room walls – there must be a ventilation gap of at least 50mm above.

For flat roofs slide rigid slabs between the joists or insulate on the internal side of the ceiling as for a wall. Allow gaps above so that air can flow and make ventilation holes at the eaves. A lot of heat can be drawn through cracks and gaps in the ceiling, fill with crack filler and seal the loft hatch with draughtproofing.

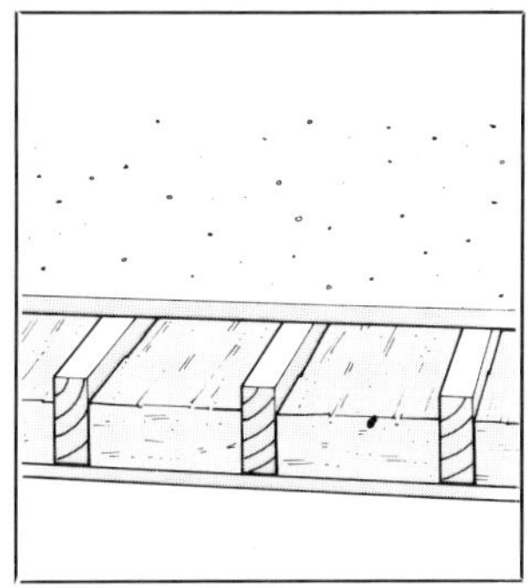

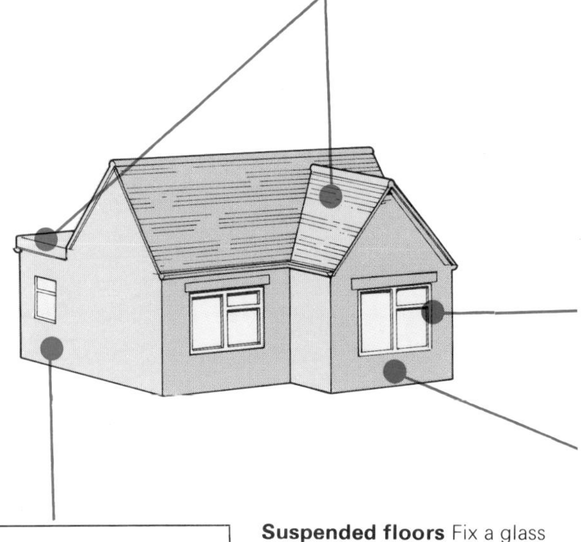

**Walls** The main problem of fitting internal wall insulation in an existing room is that everything currently fixed to the wall – light switches, architraves, skirting boards, electric sockets, central heating radiators and so on – will either have to be re-positioned or worked round. For this reason cavity fill or external insulation is often more convenient.

**Suspended floors** Fix a glass fibre blanket underneath the joists, with battens pinned to the underside of the joists to hold it in place. Or lift all the floorboards, and lay the glass fibre from above parallel to the joists, cradled by garden netting (or anything else that will not collect water) nailed to the joists. You must insulate any pipes in the space.

**Solid floors** The usual technique is to cover the existing floor with expanded polystyrene sheets or resin-bonded mineral fibre slabs, with a vapour barrier of polythene and flooring-grade chipboard laid over the top. The chipboard sheets are tongued and grooved, but otherwise the sheets are not fastened, except perhaps around the edge.

An alternative is to fix preservative-treated battens, 50mm to 100mm thick, to the floor with bitumen sealer. Lay glass fibre blanket in between and board over nailing through the chipboard tongue into the battens.

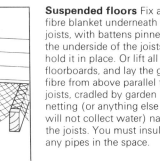

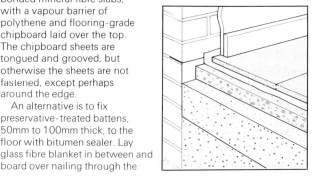

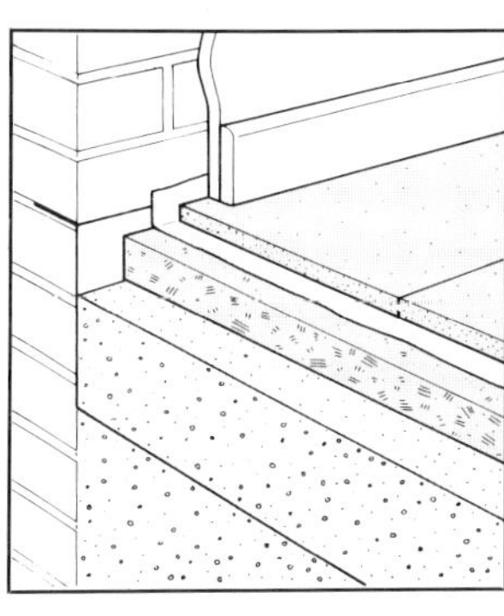

**Roofs**
The best place to lay loft insulation is on the loft floor. And usually the best material to use is glass fibre blanket. Some people find this irritates the skin when laying – so wear loose clothing, a face mask, and rinse your body well with lots of water (standing under a shower is good) when finished. It is very important to encourage ventilation in insulated lofts – because they are cold, the chance of condensation, leading to rot in the roof timbers, is high. The recommended method of ventilation is to provide a continuous gap of 10mm to 25mm wide along opposite eaves.

**Floors**
It is rarely worthwhile insulating any floors other than ground floors. Suspended floors can be dealt with fairly easily but insulating an existing solid floor is difficult and unlikely to be worthwhile. The main problem being that the floor level has to be raised significantly, resulting in a lot of extra work – re-positioning skirting boards, and so on. In low rooms, the reduction in height might be enough to rule this technique out anyway. A new solid floor should always include some insulation – see page 237.

## DOUBLE GLAZING

Double glazing is an expensive form of insulation, and rarely worthwhile installing as a money saving measure, except in the first instance – when you fit a new window or when a new house or extension is constructed. The U value of a double-glazed window is still fairly high, and so still loses quite a large amount of heat. Insulated window shutters, on the other hand, are relatively cheap (if you make your own) and the U value of a window insulated in this way is much lower than with double glazing.

Shutters have drawbacks. They are effective only when in position and this is likely to be only during the hours of darkness. However, since this is usually the time when the heat input to the house is at its greatest, the insulation benefit of shutters is still very high. You must remember to keep them closed as much as possible.

A second drawback is that, when the shutters are not closed over the windows, they take up space in the room. It is sensible to make the shutters detachable as well as hinged to the window frame, so that you can store them away for the summer.

**Making a shutter**
A simple shutter can be made from rectangular framework 50mm square, planed timber. Use simple butt-joints at the corners, glued and screwed together. Cover one side of the frame with hardboard, drop a sheet of 50mm thick polystyrene into the shallow tray created, cover with another sheet of hardboard. With small windows, or if you are hinging the shutter along the top edge, make the shutter the size of the window. For larger shutters, hinged at the side, use two shutters per window.

For large shutters use plywood instead of hardboard, and, if necessary, add 50mm by 50mm cross battens as bracing.

Hinge the shutter to the window frame, and provide catches to keep them in position both when open and closed. Ensure the shutter is reasonably airtight against the window frame – with EPDM draughtproofing for instance.

One problem is that the materials usually used for window shutters are flammable. To cut down fire risk, use fire-retardant polystyrene and hardboard, and seal the hardboard to the frame using glue all the way round. Paint with emulsion paint, not oil-based paint. And to make the shutters more attractive consider painting a mural – a mock window perhaps – or experiment with other decorative paint techniques.

As an alternative to polystyrene, you could use 80mm glass fibre compressed in the frame. Again, seal all round with glue – this time to keep in fibres from the glass fibre.

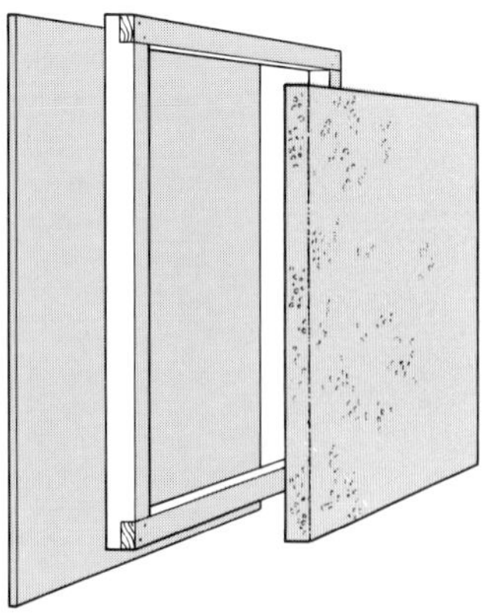
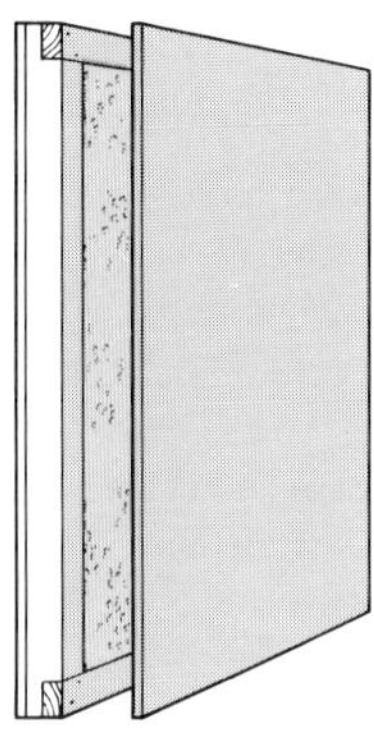

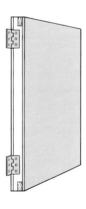

Shutters cut down heat losses through windows: they're easy and cheap to make yourself.

# Heating systems

Planning a heating system – whether for a whole house, for one or two rooms, or for a new extension – can be a complex job. An ideal heating system would be inexpensive to install and cheap to run but would keep your home as warm and cosy as you want it, it would also look acceptable and require little looking after. Needless to say, there isn't a single heating system that combines all these virtues in just the right proportions to satisfy everyone's different needs – so you have to weigh up the pros and cons of all the different types of heating and the fuels they use and select the compromise that suits your requirements best.

This section starts with the various choices.

## Types of heating

For most people, a new heating system means some form of central heating – now almost universally accepted as the most convenient method of heating. But there are advantages in having individual heaters for separate rooms; if you want to heat only a few rooms of your house, all or even just most of the time, individual heaters can cost less to install than full central heating; depending on the fuel they use, they could also be cheaper to run; and there is less temptation to waste money heating rooms you are not using. Also most individual room heaters give out direct heat which provides a room focus and is more comforting than radiators. A source of direct heat usually means that you can sit comfortably in rooms with lower air temperatures. There are some heating systems that look and behave like a cross between individual heaters and central heating.

When you are thinking about heating for a new extension, consider the existing house as well. If you have been relying on individual heaters, it could be the time to install central heating for the whole, enlarged house. If the existing house has old central heating, then replacing the old system may be better than extending the system into the extension. Extending may not be easy and in any case, depending on the way that you intend to use the extension, individual heaters may be better than central heating.

### Central heating systems

There are two main types of central heating.

**Wet central heating** This is by far the more common and most of this chapter concentrates on this type of system. A central boiler heats up water which is passed through pipes and radiators, the water gives up its heat to warm up the house, then is returned to the boiler for reheating. Wet central heating systems can be run off any fuel though in practice electricity is not often used.

**Warm air central heating** This, on the other hand, is often run from electricity (supplied on the off-peak tariff), with gas as the alternative. In a warm air system, air is drawn through a heater by a fan and the warmed air is blown along ducting to various rooms where it emerges through grilles. Warm air ducting is quite large, and is rarely installed in an existing house. It's unlikely to be a sensible choice for just an extension.

### Individual room heaters

The choice of permanently-installed room heaters largely depends on which fuel to use.

**Gas convector heaters** These are efficient, and cheap to run. But because all the heat is convected and there is no visible flame, they may not seem very comforting. They are available only with a balanced flue (see page 196) and so must be mounted on an outside wall. Most have built-in thermostatic control. Some have electric ignition – so an electricity supply must be available close by.

Gas heaters which have a flame playing through imitation coals or logs, inside a glass cover are more efficient and more pleasant to look at but cost more to buy. (They shouldn't be confused with gas log 'fires' which are not covered and are extremely costly to run.)

Gas radiant-convectors also have a visible glow. Although a little cheaper than a convector-only fire to buy, they cost a little more to run. They have either a balanced or conventional flue, and so can be fitted on to an external wall, or under a new or existing chimney.

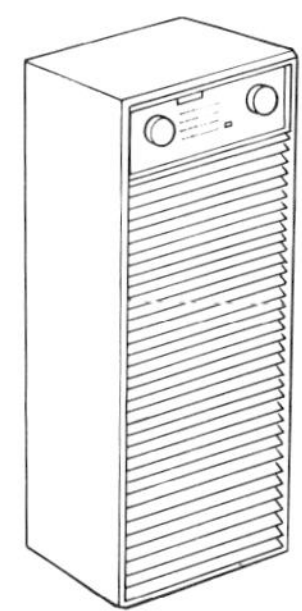
Gas convector heater for wall mounting.

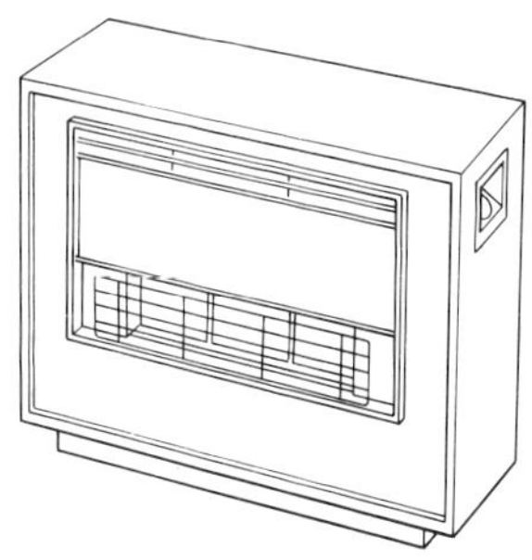
Gas radiant convector.

**Real fires (burning solid fuel or wood)** Open fires (burning solid fuel or wood) are an attractive, but very expensive, way of heating a room: closed room heaters are much more efficient and some can also be used with a back boiler to provide hot water or run a small central heating system.

All solid fuel and wood fires need a chimney which if you haven't got one already, it can be expensive to provide. An existing chimney in good condition is suitable for solid fuel but a wood burning stove may need a lined chimney – another expensive improvement.

**Other systems**
There are a number of heaters which can be classed as either room heaters or central heating. The two main ones are:

**Electric storage heaters** These can be used for whole-house heating, or just for individual rooms. They can be a good choice if you need heat all day, if gas is not available, and you think solid fuel is too inconvenient. If your existing system cannot be extended, they are a good choice for a loft conversion or extension.

**Linked gas convector heaters**
Individual room heaters can be connected to a central control, usually a timer. This makes the system more convenient.

## Fuels

One of the most important things about a heating system is the type of fuel that it burns. There are several choices.

Open fires are attractive, but expensive.

Solid fuel closed room heater.

**Gas** is clean, convenient and relatively cheap to run. But it is not available everywhere – unless a suitable gas supply runs within about 23m of your property, you are unlikely to be able to use mains gas. Gas can run both central heating and individual room heaters. All gas appliances need a chimney or flue of some kind – this can restrict positioning and increase the costs of installation (though flues for gas appliances are often not too costly).

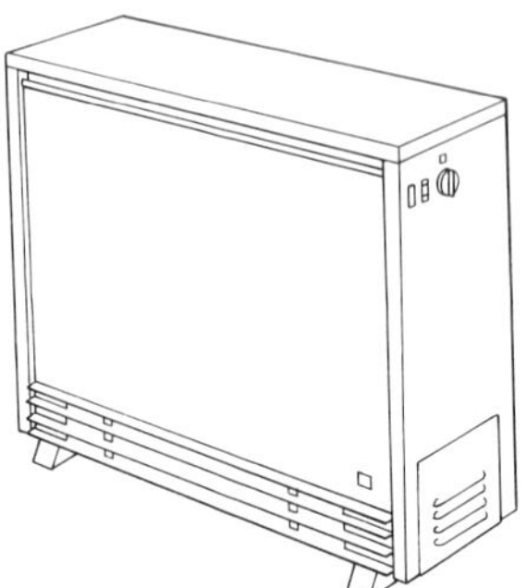
Electric storage heater.

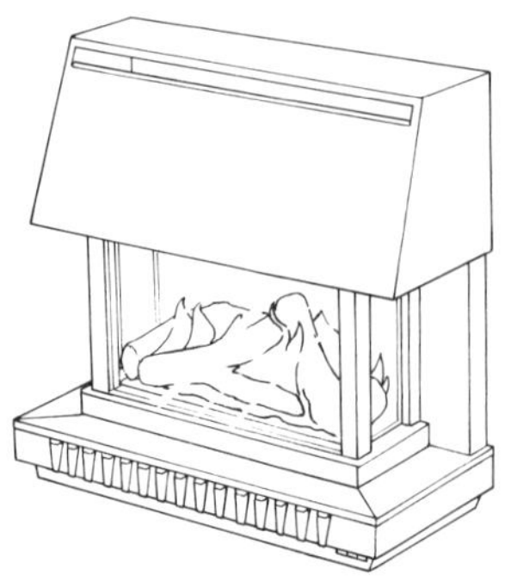
Gas heater with imitation logs.

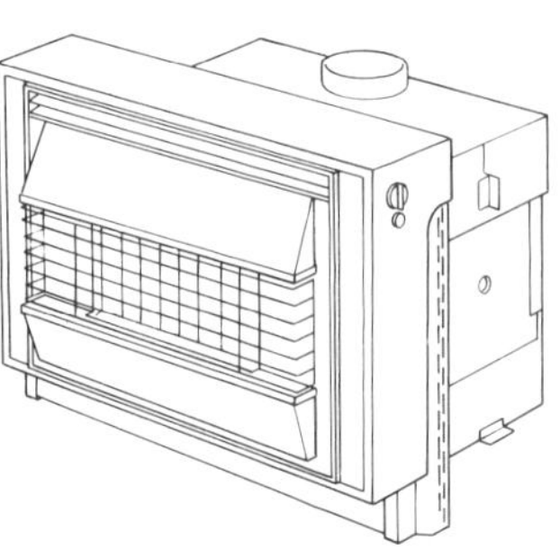
Gas room heater and boiler.

**Electricity** is very convenient and clean and is the only fuel that doesn't require a flue of some sort. Heating systems – both individual room heaters and central heating systems – can be very cheap to buy and install, but they are expensive to run. For people who use a lot of electricity the various off-peak tariffs are cheaper. These are particularly useful for storage heaters and hot water circuits which can charge at night during the off-peak hours and give out heat by day.

**Solid fuel** is not very clean nor convenient, and the fuel needs storage space. Although relatively cheap for running central heating, and closed room heaters, it is quite expensive for open fires. New (or replacement) chimneys or flues can be a considerable added expense.

**Wood** can be a good choice in rural areas, where it can work out at half the price of the equivalent solid fuel system. It has much the same pros and cons as solid fuel. Chimneys and flues over wood burning stoves need frequent attention because wood particularly green wood, which has been insufficiently dried, deposits much tar on the walls of the flue.

**Oil** Is convenient and clean, and available everywhere. But it needs storage space and a flue, and oil-fired central heating is expensive to run.

## Solar energy

Harnessing the 'free' heat from the sun sounds like a good way of heating your home cheaply. The main problem is that the times during which the house is coldest are also the times when there is very little sun. The average amount of radiant energy received by each square metre in the UK is 2·5kWh every 24 hours – from 5kWh in June to 0·4kWh in December. The main use of solar heating in existing houses is therefore to heat water for bathing, washing and so on. New houses can make use of heat from the sun if they are arranged to trap the heat.

## DOING THE WORK

Designing a complete central heating system properly is a time-consuming operation. So is installing it, and installation also causes disruption throughout the house. For most people, the least complicated way is to employ someone to design and carry out the complete installation. Usually, but not necessarily, the same firm does both jobs. This method is the most expensive, of course, but if you choose your firm carefully you should get a good system. If you decide on this course, much of the information in the rest of this section will be useful to you: it will help you to discuss your needs and choices sensibly with the designers and installers that you employ.

The alternative to having it all done for you is to do it yourself – either the whole job or just the installation following a design that has been drawn up by someone else.

Doing the installation yourself and letting someone else do the design work is a good compromise. If the design is accurate and comprehensive, the job boils down to one of reasonably simple plumbing and other do-it-yourself jobs (though on a grand scale). It's always possible to hive off the bits you don't want to tackle, so as the gas supply to a gas boiler, for instance.

### Getting a system designed

There are two main ways of getting a system designed – using a *firm selling equipment*, or employing a professional *heating engineer*.

### Firms selling equipment

Some firms specialise in selling central heating equipment, mainly by mail order. A few of these also offer a design service for a relatively nominal fee, which may be refunded if you buy the components from the firm. The firm is unlikely to see your house: instead you draw a scale plan of it, and fill in a short questionnaire. The design the firm produces cannot be better than this questionnaire and your replies. To get the best deal make sure you give the design firm any extra information you think could be relevant and tell them any special needs. Read the following section on designing a central heating system, so that you are aware of the assumptions the firm will probably make and can foresee possible pitfalls. You may find a local retailer who can produce a design.

**Heating engineers** Some specialise in designing heating systems for private homes. They will normally survey your house, and discuss your wants and likes with you. This sort of personal service is bound to cost a lot more, but the fees could be a good investment if the resulting system is well-designed – economic to buy and run.

### Other sources of design help

Do not forget manufacturers' leaflets and brochures. These are often a good, and usually a free, source of information on design and installation. Whoever sells you your components should give you the manufacturer's full instructions for the major parts – boiler, pump, controls, but as most of these instructions also contain design information, they are often worth sending off for at an early stage.

More technical help is available in literature and booklets published by the different fuel authorities – such as British Gas and the Solid Fuel Advisory Service – and trade organisations, such as the Copper Development Association – Addresses page 314.

# Wet central heating–how it works

There are various ways of connecting the radiators and boiler in a wet central heating system. The most usual method is called the *two-pipe* system. In this each radiator is connected to the boiler by two pipes – the *flow* pipe carries hot water from the boiler to the radiator, the *return* pipe takes the slightly cooler water (which has given off heat to the house as it passed through the flow pipe and the radiator) back to the boiler. To get the water to flow properly round these pipes, a *pump* is included.

It is not necessary for each pair of radiator pipes to run separately to and from the boiler, with systems using pipe of 15mm, 22mm and 28mm diameter (called *smallbore* piping) pipe runs can branch off other runs.

It is often possible to use smaller pipes – 6mm, 8mm and 10mm. These *microbore* (or *minibore*) pipes can be used in a branch system but, because they are so small, only one or two radiators can be connected to each branch and the main trunk pipes near to the boiler have to be smallbore pipes. Pairs of microbore pipes can be run separately from each radiator to the boiler (or to some other central point) and then connected together into a larger pipe: a special pipe fitting called a *manifold* is used to join many pairs of pipes in this way.

Microbore piping is much more flexible than smallbore – so it is easier to install through holes in joists and walls, especially in an existing house where pipe routes may be tricky. Because of its small size, it can also look neater when clipped to the surface of a skirting board, or in the corner of a wall.

Microbore piping comes in long rolls and this, coupled with its flexibility, may mean you need less pipe fittings. (It can also mean that you never manage to get the pipe wholly straight.) But micro-size doesn't necessarily mean micro-price – the pipe comes only a little cheaper, and you may need more of it (fittings can also be more expensive).

### Feed-and-expansion cistern

Water expands when it is heated. This means that the pipe circuits cannot form a closed loop. The most common way of overcoming this problem is to leave one pipe in the system open to the air – the open end of this pipe must form the highest point of the system. When the water is heated it will expand up this pipe, and to accommodate this expansion, a small cistern is fitted at the top. This forms a convenient point from which to fill the system – hence its name. The water is supplied direct from the rising main.

Once the system is filled and operating, there should be no need for fresh water to enter – the same water circulates all the time. This is important: 'stale' water will not cause corrosion inside the system, constant fresh water would.

### Hot water

Most heating systems will also be designed to heat the water that comes out of hot taps. In essence, the heating of water is no different from heating rooms. Instead of a radiator which warms the air, there is a coil of pipe or a ring which warms water con-

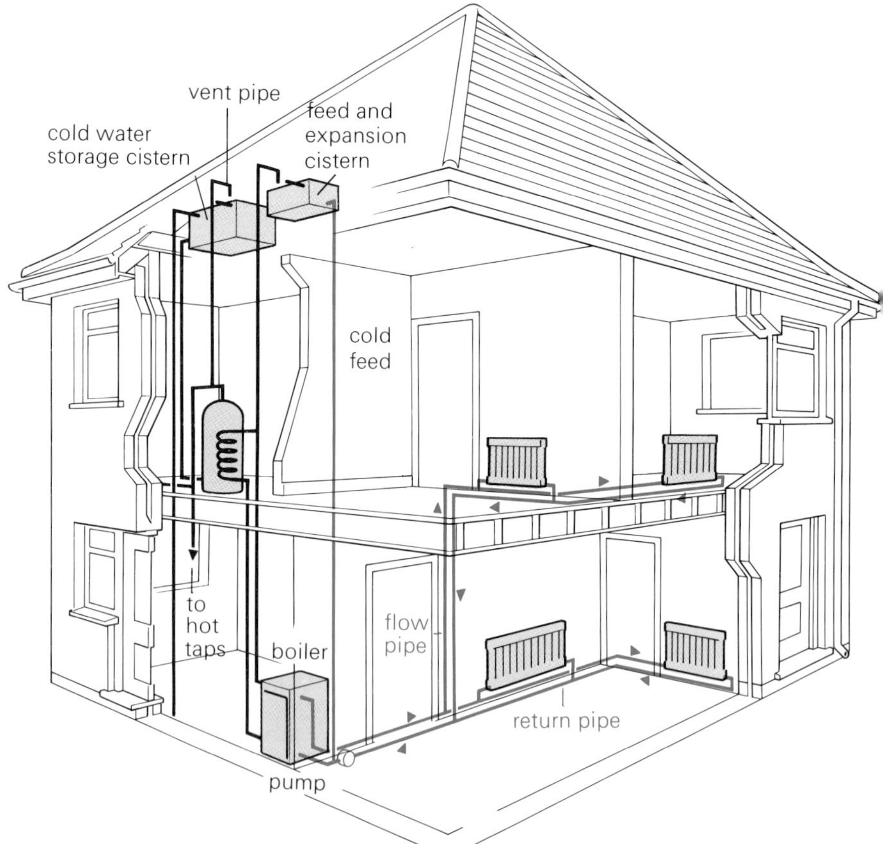


A two-pipe system using smallbore pipes can have several radiators on each branch and pipe runs can branch off other runs if the shared pipes are large enough.

tained inside a cylinder. The coil is connected by flow and return pipes to the boiler. Hot water from the boiler flows through the coil in the cylinder, and it gives up some of its heat to the tap water. The water in the system heating pipes and coil and the water which eventually flows to the taps are kept completely separate.

In many systems hot water circuits are not assisted by a pump, but rely on natural circulation. The cool water returning from the cylinder is little denser than the hotter water in the boiler and it therefore displaces the hotter water. The displaced water rises out of the boiler up to the hot water cylinder, where it becomes cooler and falls back down to the boiler to continue the cycle.

This *gravity* circulation is simple and, if properly designed, reliable. There is no pump to go wrong and electricity failures do not leave you without hot water. Solid fuel boilers must usually have some part of the system on gravity flow as, unlike other boilers, there is always some heat output from a solid fuel boiler, and this heat must have somewhere to go.

## Controlling the system

Automatic control makes a central heating system more convenient. Automatic controls can also mean that a system is run more economically, but only if they're used efficiently to keep the heating switched off for longer and thus to maintain the house at a lower average temperature. Using controls efficiently means regularly altering the settings to suit your activities. In the spring for instance, it should be possible to start cutting back on the programmed hours.

Automatic controls can also be used to protect a system. By fitting a thermostat with a frost setting you can ensure that the heating will come on if the temperature drops low enough to make frozen pipes a possibility.

Anything but the simplest time and temperature control has to be installed in association with motorised valves which can shut down or divert flow to various parts of the system. There are diverter valves which allow water to flow in one of two possible directions – either to the heating circuit or to the hot water circuit and two-way and three-way valves which allow flow through any or all of the outlets. These are necessary for separate control of the heating and hot water circuits. The motor in the valves enables control by electric devices such as a room thermostat, cylinder thermostat or timer – see pages 212–13.

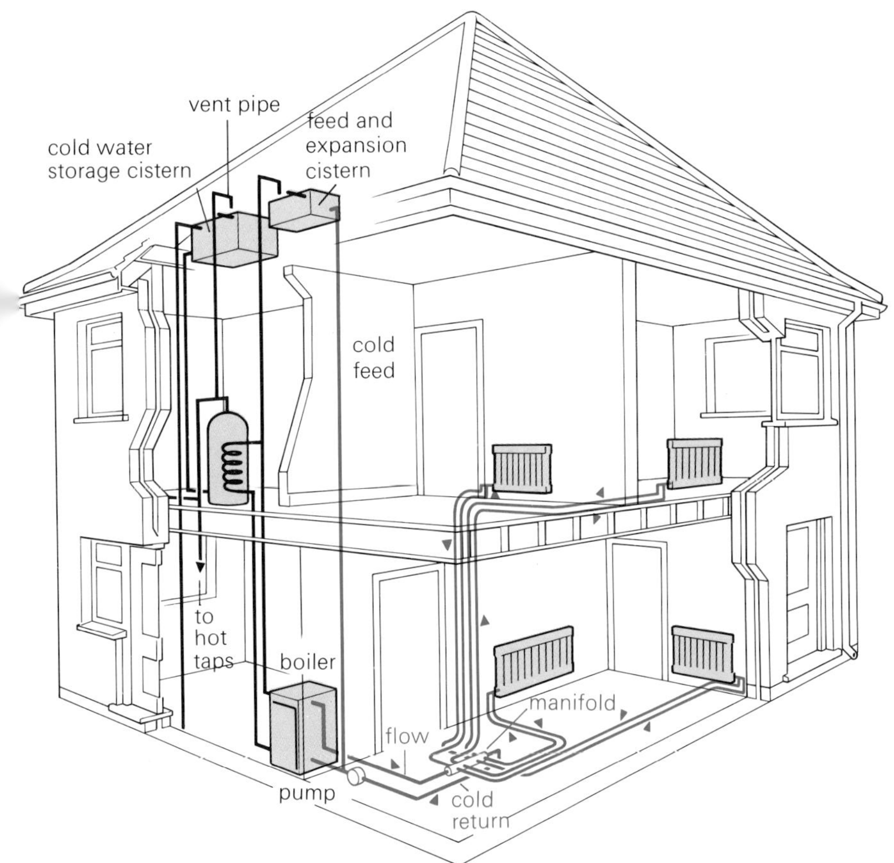


Microbore (or minibore) pipes can be used in a system like this where each radiator has its own pipes from and to a central fitting called a manifold.

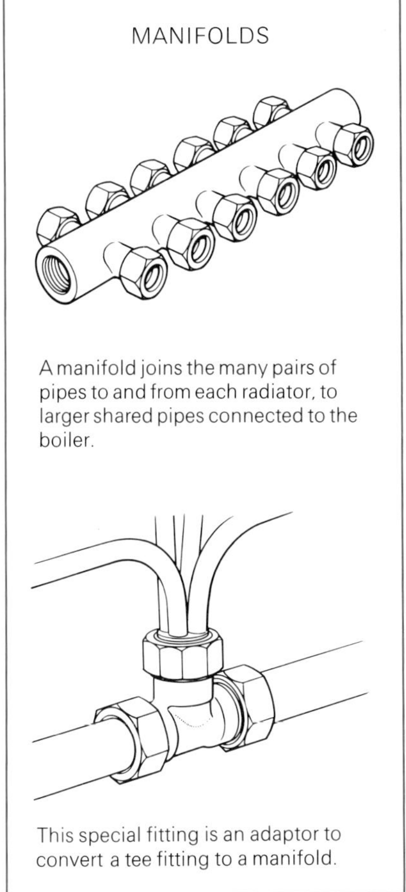


A manifold joins the many pairs of pipes to and from each radiator, to larger shared pipes connected to the boiler.

This special fitting is an adaptor to convert a tee fitting to a manifold.

# The components

Even if you're having a system taken off your hands and designed and installed for you, you might want to be involved with choosing the components, particularly the visible bits – like the radiators and the controls which you'll have to use regularly.

## Choosing a boiler

Your main decisions when choosing a boiler will be which fuel to use and then what heat output the boiler needs to suit your house requirements (see *Boiler sizing*, page 205). There are a few other features (as well as price and looks) which will help you decide between the various models available. However there is almost nothing to choose in efficiency between one brand of boiler and another: the running costs of a central heating system reflect mainly the cost of fuel used, and to some extent the accuracy of design and the type of controls fitted.

### Type of flue

Boilers that run on gas or oil may have either a conventional flue – where the exhaust gases go up some form of chimney, as required for a solid flue boiler – or a balanced flue – where the gases go straight out through an outside wall. Both types have their advantages and disadvantages.

**Balanced flue** The air for combustion is taken directly from outside the house, so no extra ventilation is needed in the room where the boiler is sited. However the boiler has to be sited on an outside wall, and there are restrictions on how close to windows and other obstacles it can be placed (see diagram). Balanced flue boilers cost more.

**Conventional flue** These boilers need a chimney. If a sound one exists where you want to site the boiler a conventional flue boiler can be cheaper than a balanced flue one. But old chimneys will need to be *lined* for a gas boiler and possibly also for other fuels to. This is relatively cheap for a gas boiler – a flexible stainless steel liner can be used – but can be very expensive for an oil or solid fuel boiler. Building a new chimney from scratch is even more expensive.

A conventional flue boiler also needs plenty of ventilation, for correct burning and for safety. Depending on boiler type and size an unrestricted opening of at least 600mm² may be needed – and in no circumstances must this opening be restricted.

### Burning method

This matters only for oil boilers. Two main methods are used to ignite the oil. The practical differences are that a *wall flame* boiler tends to be bigger, but a *pressure jet* boiler tends to make more noise. Once they were too noisy to site in a kitchen and were better sited in an outhouse, but modern pressure jet boilers are designed to be quieter.

### Stoking

Stoking solid fuel boilers can be a chore. Gravity-feed boilers incorporate a large hopper which feeds fuel down automatically on to the fire bed.

### Mounting

Many central heating boilers sit on the floor between kitchen units. Some are much smaller and are designed to be fixed to the wall. Wall-hung boilers are almost all gas fired. Solid fuel boilers are never wall hung.

### Back boilers

Combining a central heating boiler with a living room fire has both advantages and disadvantages. It is pos-

BALANCED FLUES

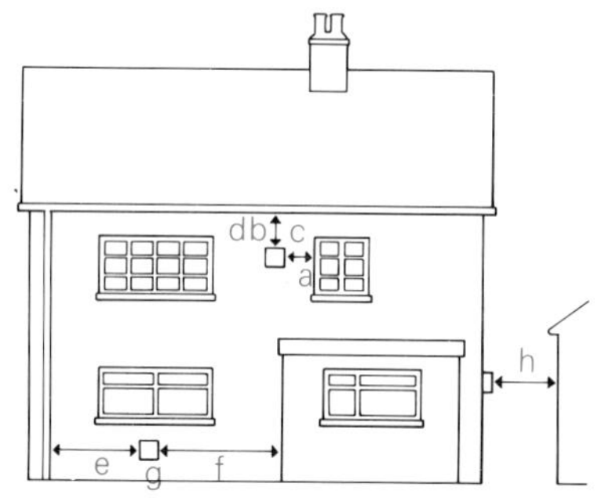


Dimensions for siting balanced flue terminals.

at least 300mm above ground or balcony (g), below eaves (c), gutters (b), and any opening – airbrick or window (a)

at least 600mm from a facing wall (h) (terminal or other surface), or any corner of the house (f) and below balconies (d).

at least 75mm from a vertical soil or drain pipe (e).

If the flue has a fanned draught some of these dimensions can be decreased, but if two fanned draught terminals face they must be 1.2m apart.

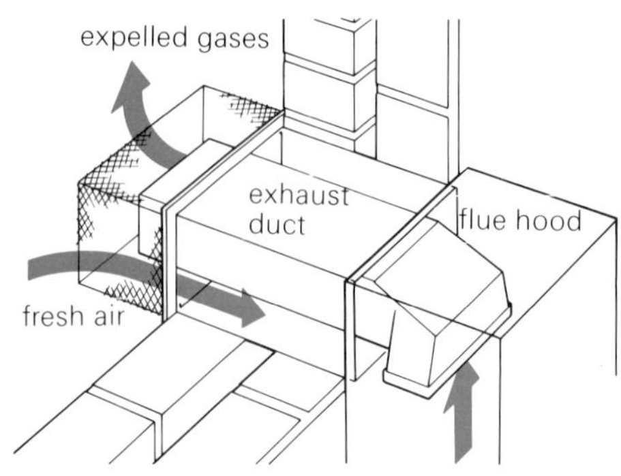


A balanced flue draws the necessary combustion air from outside.

sibly the only place for a conventional flue boiler without building a new chimney and the boiler is tucked away. But this site may not be the most convenient place for pipe runs (especially to the hot water cylinder) and it can be noisy.

With solid fuel-fired back boilers there are a couple of other snags – in a large house the heat output may not be enough, and they are not suitable for producing summer hot water. Gas-fired back boilers are really separate central heating boilers: the boiler and the fire part can be operated separately or together.

For a new house designed with low-energy requirements an electric boiler may be worth considering. The units are bulky, but no flue is needed and so they can be put anywhere in the house (provided the floor can take the weight), in a cupboard beneath the stairs for instance.

## CHOOSING RADIATORS

The important points governing the choice of radiators (or other heat emitters) are the heat output and the available wall space. These may over-rule any aesthetic considerations so it may be best to suspend decisions until the technical requirements have been worked out.

**Standard panel radiators** By far the most common type of heater used is the slightly corrugated steel *panel radiator*. These are relatively cheap, and are available in a huge range of heat outputs and different lengths and heights, to make the best use of the available wall space. They can be ordered to fit bay windows.

Where wall space is limited, you could fit *double panel* radiators – for the same frontal area these give greater heat output than single panel radiators (though less than twice as great). For even more heat per square metre of wall space, look for various forms of *convector radiator* – these have extra fins to increase the heating surface.

If you have the wall space, go for single panel radiators – £ for watt of heat output, they are the cheapest type. A long, low version should give the best heat distribution. Panel radiators don't all look alike, different manufacturers have slightly different styles.

**Exotic radiators** One or two firms make a variety of other designs – for example, smooth panel types, or slender, delicate versions of the old fashioned column radiator. If you want to use something exotic and intend to depart from the classic radiator position get the OK from an expert first.

**Convector heaters** All radiators give off a lot of their heat by convection, but convector heaters (not to be confused with convector radiators) give off nearly all their heat in this way with hardly any radiated heat. The heating element is enclosed in a box, often with a wooden finish. They occupy relatively little wall space, but they are rather deeper than panel radiators.

Most convector heaters have an electric fan, which moves air faster over the heating element and so increases heat output. At their highest setting they tend to be very noisy so choose one which will provide enough heat output for normal use at its *lowest* fan speed.

**Skirting heaters** A skirting heater is a long, low convector heater fixed in front, or in place, of the skirting board. The heat output is very low, so long lengths are needed.

The heat distribution is good, there are fewer cold draughts along the floor and you can feel as warm with lower air temperatures. Furniture placed in front of part of the heater doesn't affect heat output much. There is a tendency to make a ticking noise when heating up or cooling down.

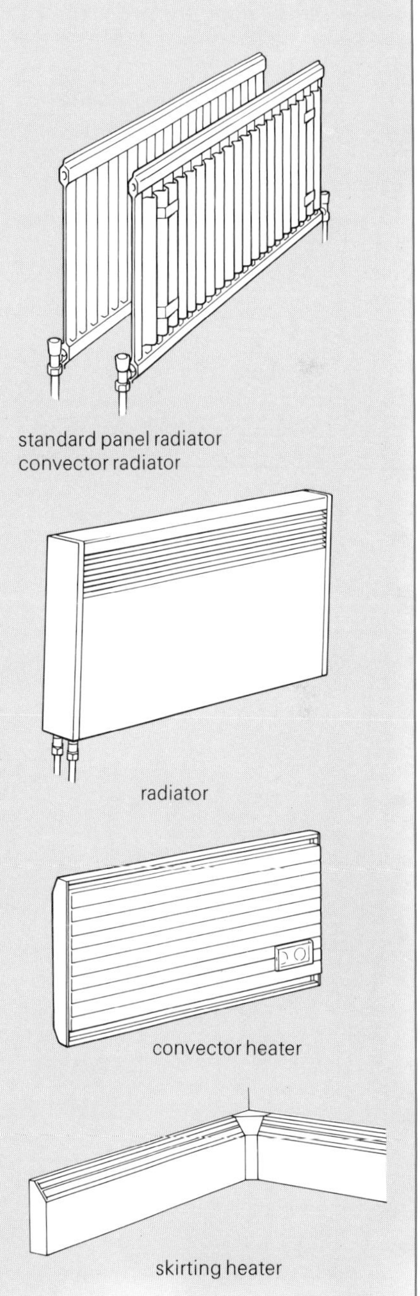
standard panel radiator
convector radiator
radiator
convector heater
skirting heater

## Choosing controls

Your choice will mostly depend on what the control can do, what it looks like and how much it costs. Getting the right control for the job is made easier by manufacturers who put together packages. These are well worth considering because it means the mixing and matching of controls and valves has been properly thought out. Professional designers and installers may offer a manufacturer's package.

## Buying

Unless someone else is installing the system, you will have to buy all the bits and pieces yourself. Although prices vary and shopping around can save quite large sums of money, it is unlikely that any one source will be the cheapest for everything. So it's much easier to check prices only on the major items.

You can buy central heating equipment from builders' and plumbers' merchants; from some d-i-y superstores and from the mail-order equipment sellers who will also design. If you use a mail-order firm for design, they will probably also supply you with an itemised shopping list for their components.

You'll be very lucky if you manage to forecast your needs totally accurately – in particular, you'll probably find that you need more of different pipe fittings. Some places will let you have fittings on sale or return. Check any return conditions carefully.

### CONTROLS

**Programmer** The commonest programmers for systems with gravity flow hot water circuits have two on and off periods in every 24 hours as well as a continuous on setting. They can be used for hot water only or hot water and heating. Most have clocks with tappets for setting the times. An override switch is useful.

Programmers for systems in which the hot water and heating can be separately timed usually have lights to indicate what is on or off when. The cheapest and all you really need have a clock with tappets allowing two on and two off periods, or a simple digital display with say, four on/off periods. More sophisticated digital versions are available and these have very many more settings.

**Room thermostats** Most thermostats are in Centigrade. Many have an integral room thermometer. The range is never wider than 0°C to 30°C – 5°C to 30°C is typical. Depending on what it's going to switch you may need a double-throw thermostat – see page 213.

**Thermostatic radiator valves (TRVs)** Most TRVs are angled valves to fit 15mm pipes, but straight versions are also available. Normally the sensor is in the valve head but remote sensors are also available for places where the valve head might not be able to sense true air temperature – behind long curtains for instance. Most valves are marked with a numerical scale, rather than temperature – this is because the actual temperature will depend on how and where the valve is used. Most valves have stops to prevent accidental altering.

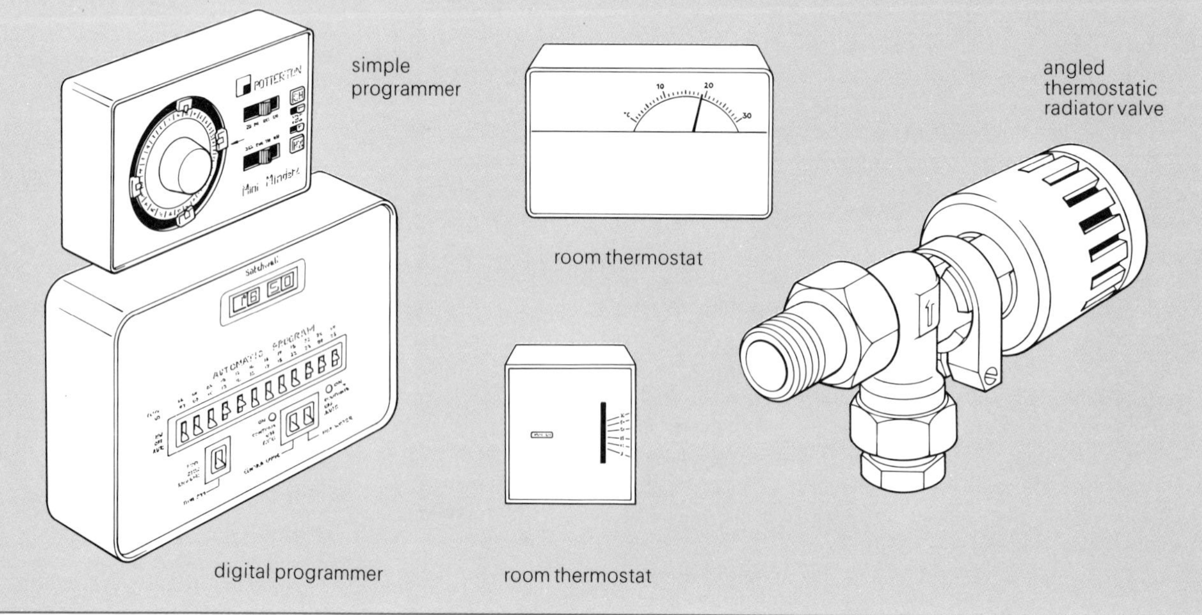

# Designing a system

The first stage in designing a heating system is to calculate the rate of heat loss from various parts of the house. The size (in terms of heat ouput) of any boiler, radiators or room heaters depends on this calculation.

Working out this heat loss isn't difficult – it's done in exactly the way as the first part of the insulation calculations, but as you have to make, and keep the results of, many minor and repetitive calculations it's worth collecting the information room by room on standard forms. These forms then give the detail required for drawing up some plans.

Much of the information is also relevant to individual room heaters but you wouldn't normally bother with a design for these.

## Plans and forms

Draw plans of each floor of your house. This is important for a number of reasons: they will help you visualise where radiators, pipe runs and so on will best go, they make it much easier to check the effects of changes to your designed system, and to calculate the quantities of materials needed. The plans can also act as an *aide mémoire* during design, to ensure that nothing is overlooked.

As well as plans, a couple of 'vertical' sections through the house will also be useful. Professional designers will also often show some form of skeleton three-dimensional view (usually an *isometric* plan which is drawn on special paper – there's an example on page 205), but these are rather complicated to draw and are not essential.

Plans and elevations should show walls, position and size of windows and doors; heights of window sills; types of floor and direction of floor joists (which run at right angles to the floor boards). Note also any obstructions to the pipe runs such as built-in cupboards, more-or-less permanent furniture and so on. You should indicate what the walls, ceilings and floors are made of. Measure up the house, and do the drawings on squared paper – work in metric units.

It is sensible to use a simple form to note down measurements and calculations as you carry them out: a sample form is given on page 204. Cross-checking is easier if you prepare a separate form for each room.

HOUSE PLANS FOR CENTRAL HEATING

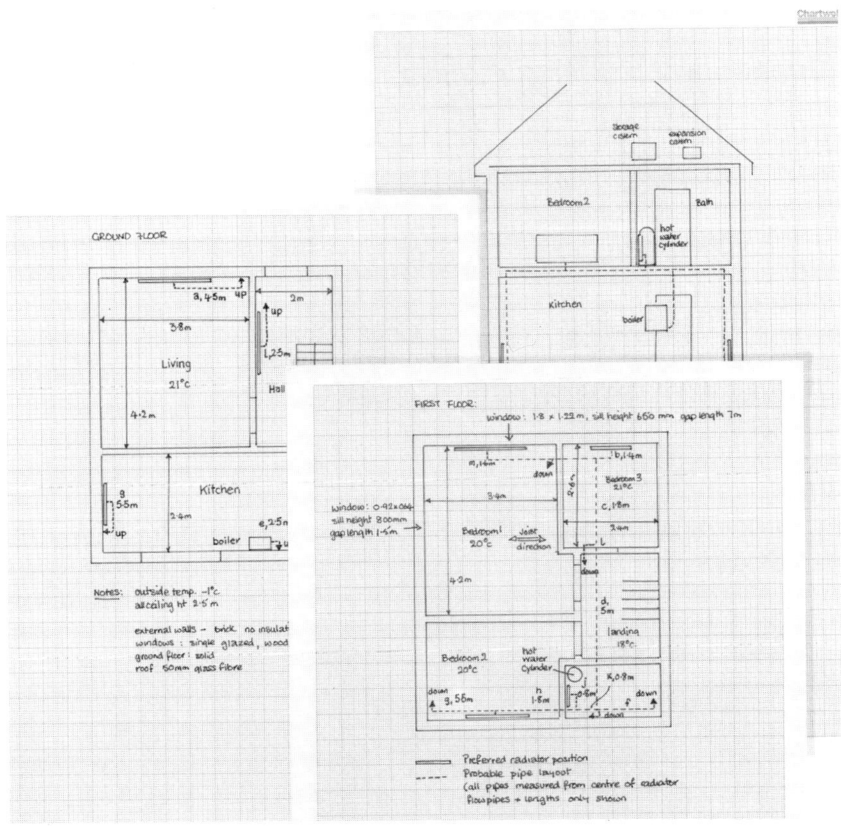


Plans and elevations are useful when it comes to visualising where the components can or should go, to calculate quantities and so on. Draw them accurately to scale, making walls and floors their true thickness not just single lines. Mark in any obstructions; show the lie of the joists; note the construction of the walls and so on.

Accurate plans are useful for many other jobs around the house, so photocopy a few spare sets for future use. A master set could be used to show the layout of all the pipes and cables in the house. It's also useful to mark the position of pipes and cables under the floor, in paint on the floor above.

## CALCULATING HEAT LOSS

The first stage is to calculate the *maximum* likely rate of heat loss from each room of the house. The radiators in each room can then be selected so that they will give off heat at this rate.

Add up the losses from conduction through each wall, window, door and so on when the room is as hot and the surroundings are as cold as they will ever be for any length of time, and add on an amount to cover losses through ventilation.

**Conducted losses**

The heat losses are calculated using the formula given on page 184. Table 1 on page 185 gives U values for different types of construction. The area of each part of the room will be noted on the plans. Maximum internal temperatures (called *design temperatures*) are a matter of choice. Many professional designers use a temperature of 21°C throughout the whole house. The recommended levels for each room are: living rooms (including dining rooms, bedsitting rooms, and so on) 21°C; bedrooms 18°C; kitchens, halls etc 16°C; bathrooms 22°C.

Remember these, are *maximum* design temperatures – it will always be possible to run the heating system so that rooms are cooler if you want them to be.

The external temperature used in this calculation should be the lowest it is likely to get for any length of time: minus 1°C is the figure usually taken. For walls between rooms, the external temperature is, of course, that of the room on the other side of the wall, which may be higher than the temperature of the room you are considering.

It is usual to assume, when calculating the heat loss for any particular room, that adjacent rooms will always be at their own particular design temperature. But, rather that just follow this rule, it is more sensible to think about how you intend to run the heating. For example, you might want to keep bedroom heating turned off until late in the evening, so bedrooms would generally be cooler than their design temperature. It is this lower temperature that you should use in calculating heat losses from ground floors, otherwise you might underestimate the losses and in doing so provide ground floor radiators that would be too small.

**Ventilation loss**

The amount of heat lost through cracks and gaps in doors, windows, etc, varies considerably from house to house and it is not possible to calculate it accurately. The heat lost depends on how much air moves out of the house. Many designers use a very basic rule of thumb and estimate of the number of times the volume of air in the house changes every hour:

- draughtproofed living rooms and bedrooms are estimated at one to one and half air changes per hour
- rooms with fireplaces at two to three and a half
- kitchens and bathrooms at two air changes
- very well-draughtproofed modern houses can be as low as three-quarters.

There's a more complicated method of calculation (which should give more accurate results) which involves using a number, called an *infiltration factor*, representing the rate of heat loss through a metre of gap around windows and doors – in effect, the infiltration factor is a kind of U value. If there are gaps on more than one wall of a room, the total heat lost is not simply the sum of the losses through each gap, but depends on the orientation of the different gaps and a correction factor has to be applied to the calculation. Infiltration factors and correction factors for weatherstripped doors and windows are given in Table 2 on page 206.

There is no point in trying to calculate the losses around less well draughtproofed window and door frames or through all the other gaps which are responsible for heat losses from a house. These should be sealed up to stop the losses.

The infiltration factors depend on the exposure of the building (sheltered, normal or exposed) as well as the type of window or door. Metal windows generally fit better than wooden ones and are more likely to have integral weatherstripping. External doors and centre-pivoted windows are the worst cases. Don't assume that non-opening windows will allow no infiltration often there are gaps in or around the frames which let air through if not filled.

### Insulating

Calculating the value of insulation is important at any time, but never more so than when you are considering a new heating system. Adding insulation at this stage should reduce the capital cost of the system – you will need a smaller boiler and perhaps fewer (or smaller) radiators. The savings you make on the system effectively make the insulation cheaper and so more cost effective. Think of all the insulation measures you could do and repeat your heat loss calculation (using a second set of forms) to find out how much this will reduce the size of your heating system.

# The layout

Having discovered how much heat is needed to supply to each room you can start thinking about the detailed layout: how many radiators you'll have and where to put them; how big the pipes need to be and where they'll run and so on. Then the hot water circuit has to be thought out and a pump chosen to suit the radiator system or radiator and hot water system, if you're going to pump that too. Finally the boiler can be sized. Sizing (and choosing) the radiators is virtually the last thing you do when you know how much heat the pipework will contribute.

### Positioning radiators

Ordinary central heating radiators, despite their name, provide much of their heat by circulating warm air round the room by natural convection. In order to get even temperature throughout a room, the best place for radiators is usually underneath windows, where the rising warm air will help to counteract the cold down draught that usually occurs near windows. Radiators positioned anywhere else (especially if on the wall opposite a window) can produce an uneven (and probably uncomfortable) heat distribution.

A fan convector heater, because it pushes air round the room, needn't be sited under a window. It can go on the opposite wall or on a wall at right angles to the window so that warm air moves across the cold zone.

Similarly, long, low radiators give a better heat distribution than tall ones (the ultimate being skirting heating).

In large rooms, you will get a better distribution of heat by using more than one radiator. For example, in a long, through room aim to have a radiator at each end.

Within all these constraints, try to position the radiators so that pipe runs will be as short, and direct, as possible.

### Pipe layout

Planning the layout of the pipes is largely a matter of making sure that the pipe runs are straightforward; that they will be easy to install; and can be easily hidden where you want them to be unobtrusive. It's worth experimenting with plans for different layouts and systems, perhaps mixing microbore and smallbore pipes, or trying a microbore-and-manifold layout. Consider each plan in terms of ease of installation and neatness of the result. Check the variation in cost of piping and fittings.

### Provisional pipe sizing

You cannot proceed too far with designing the layout until you've finally decided the *size* of pipe to use at each point of the run. The larger the pipe the more water (and thus heat) it can carry: each section of pipe has to be large enough to carry enough water to provide the heat that will be emitted by all of the radiators that are connected to that pipe – including all those that branch off it. So, because all the radiators, ultimately, are connected to them the pipes nearest the boiler have to have the largest diameter, (depending on your design these pipes might also have to carry the hot water circuit load); pipes nearest a single radiator have the smallest diameter.

Table 3 on page 207 lists pipe sizes for different radiator loads. Using this Table, you can experiment with plans for different pipe layouts. Altering which radiators are fed off which circuit, or adding and removing circuits can have an effect on the pipe sizes. Normally, a circuit using smallbore piping will have most runs in 15mm pipe, with perhaps just one long main run in 22mm, and only a small amount of 28mm pipe: note that Table 3 gives 'provisional' pipe sizes. This is because the various pipes have to be large enough to provide not only the heat for the radiator output, but also the heat that is lost from the pipes themselves. The amount of this loss depends on the length of piping, whether it is insulated or not, and on the pipe diameter – and until you have designed a layout these are unknown factors. The Table of provisional sizes makes a generous allowance for heat loss from pipes, so it is unlikely that your pipe sizes will turn out to be too small. (But it could happen if you are on the borderline between one pipe size and the next.) It may be that the allowances are too generous, leading you to use a bigger pipe size than necessary. So after the provisional design, go back over the layout, and check pipe sizes, this time calculating the actual pipe heat losses and checking that the pipe is the correct size for the actual total load (pipe losses and radiator emissions) that it is to carry.

Table 4 on page 207 gives the heat losses from different sizes of pipe, and the actual total load that each can carry.

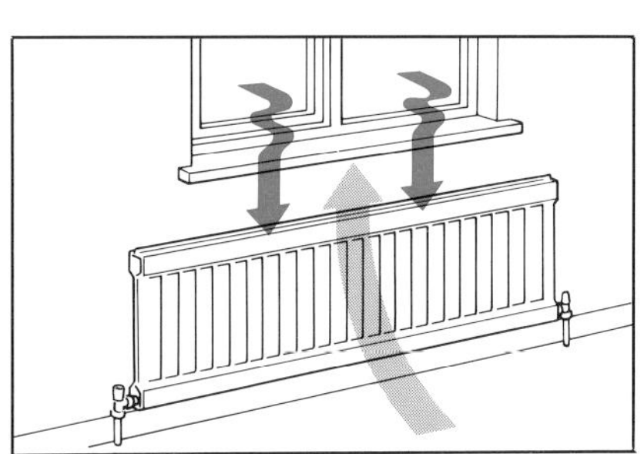

Panel radiators are best placed under windows to counteract the cold zone and downdraught caused by the window. Convectors can be placed elsewhere.

### Radiator outputs

The way the circuits are designed may mean you have to alter the required radiator outputs: it is sensible to make these alterations at this stage, because they may affect the results of the next calculations.

Radiators can cause staining on the

wall above. This can be prevented by fixing a narrow shelf above, and extending the full length of, the radiator. But this can cause a reduction in output from the radiator of up to ten per cent – so you should increase the calculated radiator size by up to ten per cent. Boxing-in a radiator will reduce its output even further, so would painting it with metallic paint (but ordinary household paints, of any colour, have little effect on the output).

The pipes within a room will also supply heat to that room – how much depends on the size of pipe and the total length that is exposed, but it could be anything up to 20 per cent of the heating requirements of the room – so if there is much exposed pipework in a room, you could reduce the radiator size to take account of it. Roughly, each metre of exposed pipe has an output of about 40 watts (Table 4 gives pipe losses more accurately). The heat emitted from pipes which run under floorboards, or are boxed in is usually ignored.

### Hot water circuit

The calculations for this circuit depend on whether the design is for gravity or pumped flow.

**Gravity flow** For this to work at all, the system has to be carefully designed and calculated. In fact hot water systems are rarely calculated from scratch: instead, the system is laid out following these simple design rules: the hot water cylinder should be no larger than 160 litres (most houses use 140 litres) and be fitted above the boiler – within a horizontal distance of 6m if it is on the floor above the boiler, or 2m if it is only just above. The piping connecting the two must be at least 28mm diameter; any horizontal pipe runs must slope up towards the cylinder by at least 1mm per metre (the greater the slope, the better).

Following this design the time taken for the boiler to reheat the contents of the cylinder will be between two and a half and four hours depending on the length of the pipe runs and the boiler size. If you cannot follow all the rules then you either have to calculate pipe sizes from scratch (which is not covered in this book) or use a pumped system.

**Pumped circuits** Again, elaborate calculations of pipe size are not normally carried out for a pumped hot water circuit. In most cases, the hot water piping also acts as part of the safety vent piping (see page 209) and so the pipe cannot be smaller than 22mm. It is rare that pipe greater than 22mm is required – this could reheat a 140 litre cylinder in 40 minutes (assuming the boiler could provide enough heat output).

### Pump sizing

The pump has to be capable of pushing water round the circuits fast enough so that the water can give off the right amount of heat. The speed at which a pump can push the water depends not only on the size of pump, but on the resistance the water meets in its travels – this resistance is greatest in narrow pipes, in long pipe runs and in runs with lots of pipe fittings or bends. Resistance also increases as the speed of the water through pipes increases. Modern pumps can cope with high resistances and still push water fast enough to cope with most normal heating loads. So it is not usually essential to go through the calculations for pump sizing.

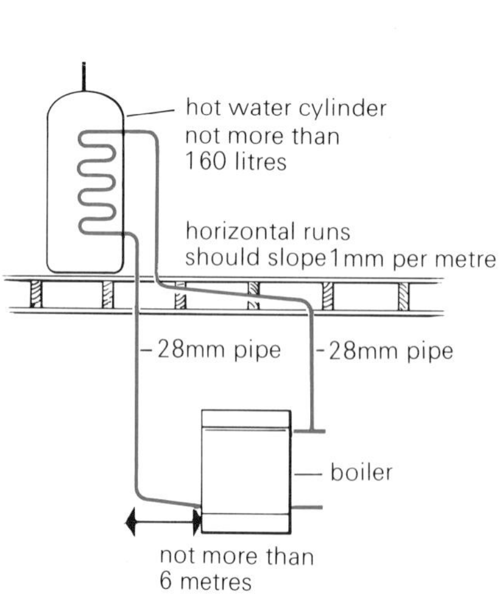

However, if your house is large, or your layout unusual, or if you intend to use much microbore piping (which has a particularly high resistance) it is sensible to go through the sums.

One circuit in the layout (a circuit is one unbroken line of pipe to and from any radiator back to the boiler) will have the greatest resistance: if the pump can overcome this resistance, it will be big enough to cope with all the other circuits, too. This *index circuit* will be the one with the greatest load and, or, the longest pipe length. It will probably be obvious which circuits *aren't* contenders for the index circuit; but there may be two or three that are possibles, and you will need to work out the resistances for each circuit to find out which is the biggest. Table 5 gives the resistance (more correctly, the pressure drop or pressure loss) per metre length of pipe – this depends on the total heat load of the circuit (the radiator load plus the losses from all the bits of pipe making up the circuit).

To this resistance the extra resistance in the run created by bends, elbows, tees and practice should be added. This is hardly ever specifically calculated – instead it is assumed that, in a normal domestic circuit, all these fittings have a resistance which is equivalent to extra piping a third the length of the circuit itself.

So the total resistance of a circuit is the appropriate pressure drop per metre for the diameter of pipe and the heat load it is carrying multiplied by the *equivalent length* of the pipe circuit (the actual length plus a third the actual length).

The resistance that a particular pump can overcome depends on the rate at which it has to push water through the pipes – and this depends in turn on the total heat load. The rate is usually expressed in terms of the volume of water passed, in litres, per second – and in normal domestic work, this is simply the total heat load in watts divided by the number 41,800. Sometimes, the rate is



A gravity flow hot-water system.

expressed as mass flow rate – the *weight* of water passed, in kilogrames per second. But as one kilogram of water occupies a volume of one litre, the result is the same whether it is expressed in kilograms or litres.

Manufacturers' literature and central heating catalogues will show a graph of each pump's 'duty' – the maximum resistance it can overcome at different flow rates. If your calculations show that the circuit's resistance is lower than this at your calculated flow rate, then the pump will be big enough. If not, you will have to think again.

There are few domestic central heating pumps widely available, and those that are have much the same characteristics. So if your calculations show that your circuit has too high a resistance, it is best to redesign the pipe layout (by splitting the pipe runs into more circuits, each carrying a smaller load, or by increasing pipe sizes) than to look for a larger pump. Most pumps are 'variable head', so you can match (roughly) the pressure it will give to the resistance you have calculated it must overcome.

## Boiler sizing

The boiler clearly has to be big enough to cope with the load of all the radiators plus the pipework. But it is equally important that it's not oversized because most boilers are less efficient when not running flat out. The boiler may not have to supply the total designed load at anytime for several reasons.

For instance you might have had to select radiators a little larger than the room heat requirements – the boiler does not have to be big enough to cope with this oversizing. Nor does it have to cope with designed radiator oversizing – such as putting in larger radiators downstairs to allow for keeping the upstairs radiators off much of the time. Piping hidden under the floor will give off *some* useful heat even if it isn't possible to apportion this between rooms.

A greater possibility for reduction comes from *incidental gains* of heat from sources such as cookers, people, the sun and so on. These could provide enough incidental heat to cause a temperature rise of around three to five degrees. One way to calculate boiler size is therefore to calculate the heat loss through the outside walls, windows, and so on assuming that the boiler will have to provide a maximum temperature rise of, say 18°C. A better method is a compromise which allows that hidden pipe emissions may not provide much useful heat (so you include pipe losses in the sums), but makes a reduction for incidental gains of 15 per cent. With the results of these calculations go for a boiler with an output of the next size up – which will give you a margin of safety on size.

After calculating the boiler capacity necessary for the heating circuits an allowance generally has to be made for the hot water circuit. It is unnecessary to add on the full hot water demand – most of the year, the boiler will have some spare capacity. A maximum of a spare 2kW for hot water is probably enough.

If, after all these sums, the calculated output is borderline between two boiler sizes, but just creeps into the higher size, consider ways of reducing the necessary boiler output by around ten per cent – by adding more insulation for instance. The cost of doing this should be offset by buying and running a smaller boiler.

In the past many designers, as well as ignoring factors that could reduce the boiler size, then *added* an allowance of ten per cent or more, as much for luck as anything. This is no longer considered good design and if you're having a system designed for you it is worth checking that your designer's got this part of the design right.

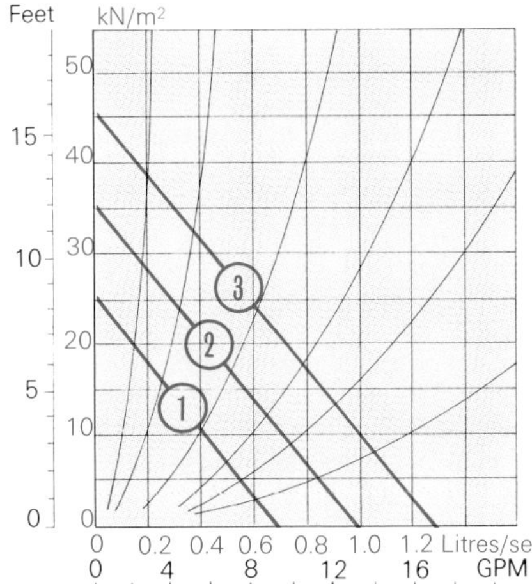


A graph of the pump duty gives the maximum resistance it can overcome at different flow rates.

## Radiator sizing

The correct size of radiator for a room (or the total size, if there's more than one) is one that has a heat output that is as large as the design heat loss of the room *plus* any increase due to how and where it is mounted, *less* an amount for any exposed pipework. A boiler also emits some heat which should be allowed for in the room where it is sited – the manufacturer's literature should give the allowance.

Central heating component catalogues, and radiator manufacturers, will provide figures showing the heat output for each type and size of radiator. But they usually do this only for one temperature difference between the radiator and the room – usually based on a room temperature of about 20°C, and a radiator temperature of about 75°C. If you are designing with different room temperatures, you will have to apply a correction factor – these will be listed in catalogues.

There may be several different radiators with heat outputs near the one you want. But despite the hundreds of sizes available, it is quite likely that there will not be one of exactly the output calculated. The usual choice is to select the next size up, on the grounds that this will certainly be big enough. Going one size up is a very good idea in a living room, but for other rooms, if the next size down is only slightly too small (say one or two per cent) then it makes sense to go for this – your calculations are unlikely to be accurate to more than a few per cent and the smaller radiator will be a little cheaper.

# Worked example

The plan shows a typical three bedroom house, with a combined kitchen and dining room. There is a gas supply. The *Heat loss chart* gives all the information needed to work out heat loss for bedroom 1.

### Calculating heat loss

The heat losses are worked out on one part of the room at a time – it is sensible to do windows, doors and so on before the walls in which they are set. For example in the bedroom, the front window has an area of 2·2 square metres, a U value of 4, and the temperature difference between inside and out is $20-(-1)=21°C$. So the heat loss through the window is $2{\cdot}2 \times 4 \times 21 = 185W$. To calculate the area of the front wall subtract the area of the window and then do its heat loss sum.

Note that, because the adjacent bedroom is warmer, there is a heat *gain* through one wall: this *reduces* the room's heating requirements, so it is shown as negative and is subtracted from the total heat loss. The same goes for the lounge below which is warmer than the bedroom: so the U value for heat flow upwards (1·6) is used, and the figure is negative. The other adjacent bedroom is at the same temperature, so there is neither heat gain nor loss.

### Ventilation losses

Using the infiltration method for this room with windows on any two walls gives a loss of 338W – see Chart 1.

Applying the easier 'guessed' ventilation rates (for a bedroom, an air-change rate of one) the loss would be: $1 \times 38{\cdot}3 \times 21 \times 0{\cdot}33 = 265W$.

### Layout

In this house, most radiators can go under the main windows of each room and this is best. The kitchen is narrow and best served by two radiators, as shown. To save floor space, the boiler is likely to be a small, wall-hung balanced flue model. A suitable spot needs to be found away from windows and doors.

**Pipe layout** The isometric plan shows a possible pipe layout. As the ground floors are solid, it is easiest to run all piping under the first floor floorboards, and drop pipes down to the ground floor radiators. There are three radiators at the front of the house, and it would be sensible to be able to feed them all off a long pipe stretching the length of the house, along the line of the landing – even better if this could be sized to feed the hall radiator, too. Another run will have to extend along the rear wall of the house, then down the side wall, to feed the left kitchen radiator: the

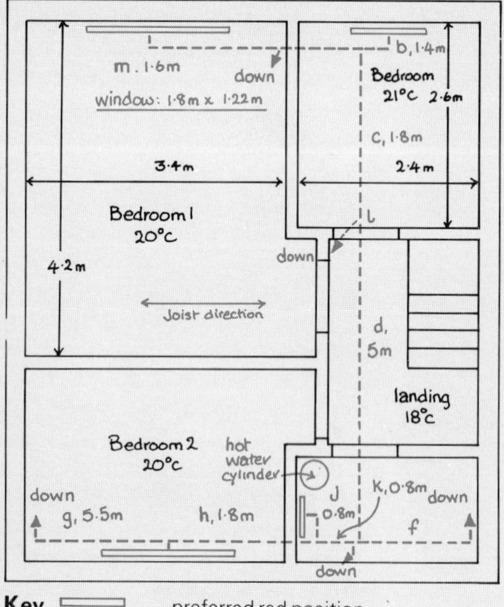


NOTES
outside temp −1°C
all ceiling heights are 2.5m
external walls – brick, no insulation
windows – single-glazed wood frame
ground floor – solid
roof insulation – 50mm glass fibre

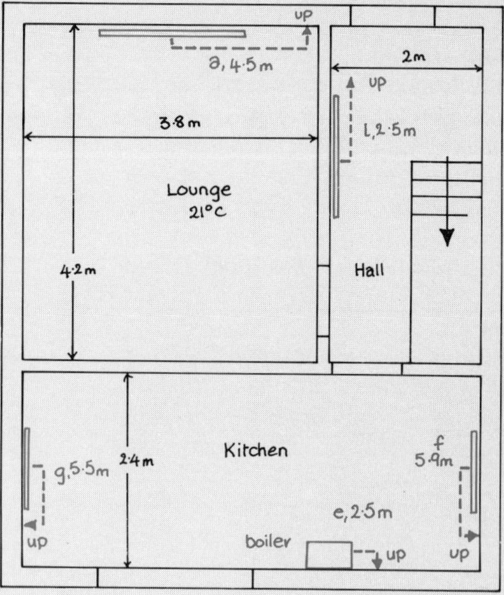


**Key** ▭ preferred rad position

----- probable layout. All pipes measured from centre of rad. Flow pipes only shown

House plans with preferred and provisional plans for the layout.

bathroom and bedroom 2 radiators could usefully branch off this run. The kitchen radiator on the right will have to be on a run of its own in this layout.

Each *stage* of the layout is identified by a letter. These are used on Chart 2 to determine the heating requirements of each stage. Table 3 (page 207) is used to pick the likely pipe size. Table 4 (page 207) is used to work out also the heat loss from the pipes themselves. On this Chart it's useful to note which pipes will emit useful heat (and allow you to scale down radiator sizes).

For example, pipe stage *a* supplies only the single lounge radiator – 2050W. Table 3 shows that this heating load can easily be carried by 15mm pipe. Table 4 shows that 15mm pipe has an emission of 43W per metre of its length. This is a two-pipe system, so that the *total* length of pipe in stage *a* is twice the distance from the branch to the radiator – 9m. So the total heat emission from stage *a* pipes is 9 × 43 = 387W. All this pipe is exposed on the living room walls, so the heat it gives off is useful, and the living room radiator need provide only 2050 – 387 = 1663W.

**Hot water** The hot water is on a gravity flow circuit designed according to the given rules for such a system. It would be relatively easy to pump the hot water circuit fitting a motorised valve for control and indeed if your boiler requires forced circulation or the boiler and cylinder cannot be properly sited, pumping will be necessary.

**Pump sizing** The next stage in a full design is to calculate the pressure drop in the circuit that the pump will have to overcome.

Working out the pressure loss is a little complicated, so over the page there is a stage-by-stage example.

**Boiler sizing** The total possible space heating load on the boiler is 9·6kW. But all this load is unlikely to be required at once, so a smaller boiler will usually be ample.

Following the sizing notes on page 203, reduce the space heating load by 15 per cent, which makes it 8·2kW. Then add the water heating load – not more than 2kW. And look for a boiler the next size up from 10·2kW.

**Radiator sizing** As an example of radiator sizing, look at bedroom 1. The heat requirement is 1289W. No piping is exposed, so no allowance is made for this; there will be no radiator shelf or boxing-in, so no change has to be made for these factors, either. There is room under the window sill for a radiator of up to 600mm high (allowing space for valves and connections) and up to 2500mm long: one radiator manufacturer's data sheet shows that there are several radiators of the right output that would fit.

However, the quoted outputs in this catalogue are based on a mean radiator temperature of 76·6°C and a room temperature of 21·2°C. This design uses the more usual radiator temperature of 75°C, and a room temperature of 20°C. The conversion table with the manufacturer's data

CHART 2

| Stage | What it feeds | Rooms' requirements W | Piping likely size mm. | Total length m | Emission W | Exposed? |
|---|---|---|---|---|---|---|
| A | Lounge only | 2050 | 15 | 9.0 | 387 | YES |
| B | Lounge and Bed1 | 3342 | 15 | 2.8 | 60 | NO |
| C | B a | | | | | |
| D | C a | | | | | |
| E | All | | | | | |
| F | Kit | | | | | |
| G | Kit | | | | | |
| H | G a | | | | | |
| J | Ba | | | | | |
| K | H a | | | | | |
| L | Ha | | | | | |
| M | Be | | | | | |

NOTES

Radiators c

Stage A – L

387W sma

Stage D – H

Smaller ma

Stage F and

of 22mm p

Smaller – sa

CHART 1

HEAT LOSS CHART

Room: Bedroom 1

| Surface | Size | Area | Temp. diff. °C | U-value W/m² °C | Heat Loss | Notes |
|---|---|---|---|---|---|---|
| Front Window | 1.8 × 1.22 | 2.2 | 21 | 4.0 | 185 | All windows single glazed. |
| Front wall (less front window) | 3.4 × 2.5 (–2.2). | 6.3 | 21 | 1.6 | 212 | All external walls cavity brick/brick |
| Side window | 0.92 × 0.64 | 0.6 | 21 | 4.0 | 50 | |
| Side wall (less side window) | 4.2 × 2.5 (–0.6) | 9.9 | 21 | 1.6 | 0 | Upstairs internal walls stand type. |
| Bed 2 wall | 3.0 × 2.5 | 9.5 | 0 | 1.6 | 0 | |
| Bed 3 wall | 3.0 × 2.5 | 7.5 | –1 | 1.6 | –12 | Bed 3 is warmer so there's a heat gain. |
| Landing door | 2.0 × 0.76 | 1.5 | 2 | 2.1 | 6 | |
| Landing wall (less door) | 1.6 × 2.5 (–1.5) | 2.5 | 2 | 1.6 | 8 | |
| Floor | 3.4 × 4.2 (plus door recess) | 15.3 | –1 | 1.6 | –24 | Downstairs is cooler so heat flow is upwards |
| Ceiling | 3.4 × 4.2 (plus door recess) | 15.3 | 21 | 0.6 | 193 | |

| | Crack length m | Temp. diff. | Factor | Heat Loss |
|---|---|---|---|---|
| Front window | 7 | 21 | 2.3 | 338 |
| Side window | 1.5 | 21 | 2.3 | 72 |

Walls are adjacent – 2/3 (total loss) is 2/3. (338 + 72) = 273

So use: 338.

TOTAL HEAT LOSS FOR ROOM: 1289 W

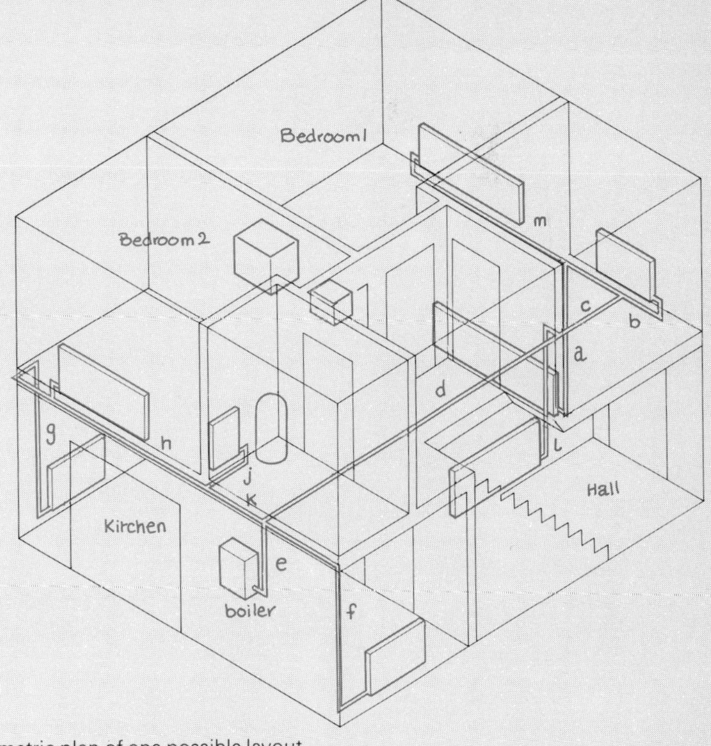


Isometric plan of one possible layout.

sheet shows that, in this case, the quoted outputs have to be multiplied by 0·98. Because length is no problem, a single panel radiator can be chosen. Of those 440mm high, the next size up from the required 1292W is 1348W, which will have a true output in this design of 1348W × 0·98 = 1321W – about 2 per cent over-sized, which is tolerable.

## Controls

As this system has a gravity flow hot water circuit, the simplest control package will suffice – programmer and room thermostat (or TRVs or a combination of both) wired to control pump *and* boiler. To keep running costs down a hot water cylinder thermostat wired to control the boiler should also be fitted.

## Pump sizing

First decide which is the likeliest *index circuit*. Then work out the pressure losses for each stage in that circuit and add them all together. If you cannot be sure which is the index circuit, then you will have to work out the pressure drop for all the circuits. This isn't as tedious as it sounds: most circuits share at least some pipe stages, so the extra amount of calculation required is not too great. Here, it is easy – the circuit a-b-c-d-e is both the longest and carries the greatest radiator loads.

The actual amount of heat that each pipe stage has to carry is the sum of all the heat loads that ultimately feed off it, plus its own pipe heat loss.

### Stage a

The radiator load is 1663W, and the pipe load 387W, making a total of 2050W. Look up Table 5. This gives the pressure drop through different sizes of pipe for different heating sizes of pipe for different heating loads. For example, with a heating load of 2090W, the pressure drop (see original) – in this case, a guess of 13kNm² seems reasonable.

The total pressure drop in the stage is this number multiplied by the pipe length – to take into account the resistance of the fittings, the actual length of pipe is multiplied by one and a third. Here, the actual length is 9m, so the equivalent length is $1\frac{1}{3} \times 9 = 11{\cdot}7$m. So the total pressure drop for this section is 11·7 × 130 = 1521, say **1·5kN/m²**.

### Stage b

This pipe supplies heat to stage *a* and also to stage *m*, which consists of the radiator in bedroom 1 plus the pipe connecting it to stage *b*.

So the heat load for *b* is:

| | |
|---|---|
| stage *a* load | 2050 |
| radiator, stage *m* | 1289 |
| pipe, stage *m* | 138 |
| pipe, stage *b* | 60 |
| **total** | **3537W** |

Note that the actual heat load on *b* is bigger than that provisionally worked out in the chart on page 205, because the heat loads of pipes which haven't been allowed to contribute to room heat requirements have been taken into account. However, a check with Table 4 shows that 15mm pipe can easily accommodate 3537W, so there is no need to change the provisional pipe sizing.

The pressure loss in 15mm pipe for a load of 3537W is about 335N/m² per metre length, and the equivalent length of pipe in stage *b* is $1\frac{1}{3} \times 2{\cdot}8 = 3{\cdot}6$m.

So the total pressure drop for stage *b* is: 335 × 3·6 = **1·2kN/m²**

### Stage c

This carries the whole of stage *b* heat load, its own pipe load, and the radiator load in bedroom 3 (there is probably also a little bit of pipe between the end of stage *c* and the bed 3 radiator, but this sort of thing can often be ignored).

Add up the loads:

| | |
|---|---|
| stage *b* load | 3537 |
| radiator, 3 bed | 616 |
| pipe, stage *c* | 155 |
| **total** | **4308W** |

Find out the pressure loss for this load: about 335N/m² per metre run. Work out the equivalent length of pipe run:

$1\frac{1}{3} \times 3{\cdot}6 = 4{\cdot}7$m

Calculate the total pressure drop:

4·7 × 335 = **1·6kN/m²**

### Stage d

This has to supply stage *l* (the hall radiator and its pipe) as well as *c*.

Add up the loads:

| | |
|---|---|
| stage *c* load | 4308 |
| radiator, stage *l* | 541 |
| pipe, stage *l* | 215 |
| pipe, stage *d* | 430 |
| **total** | **5494W** |

Pressure loss for this load: 721N/m²
Equivalent pipe length – 13m
So total pressure drop for stage *d*: **9·4kN/m²**

### Stage e

This carried stage *d*, plus all the remaining radiator and pipe loads.

Add up the remaining radiator loads:

| | |
|---|---|
| kitchen left | 632 |
| kitchen right | 632 |
| bed 2 | 829 |
| bath | 715 |
| **total** | **2808W** |

Add up the remaining pipe loads:

| | |
|---|---|
| stage *f* | 507 |
| *g* | 473 |
| *h* | 155 |
| *j* | 69 |
| *k* | 69 |
| **total** | **1273W** |

This is too great a load for 15mm pipe. For 22mm pipe, the pressure loss would be about 301N/m² per metre length. The equivalent length of stage *e* pipes is 3·9m. So the total pressure drop for this stage is **1·2kN/m²**.

**Total pressure drop** The total pressure drop throughout the whole circuit – the pressure that the pump will have to supply – is the sum of the pressure drops at each stage, which comes to **14·9kN/m²**

**Pump flow rate** The formula for this is simply the total heat load to be supplied by the pump – 9549W – divided by 41,800, which comes to 0·23 litres/sec.

So the pump has to supply 0·23 litres of water a second, against a head of 14·9kN – an easy job for most modern pumps.

**TABLE 1 : U values** – see page 185

**TABLE 2 : Infiltration factors for windows and doors** [1]

| | sheltered | normal | exposed |
|---|---|---|---|
| **WOODEN WINDOWS** | | | |
| **casement** | 1·2(0·5) | 2·3(0·9) | 4·1(1·6) |
| **centre-pivoted** | 1·4 (0·8) | 2·8(1·6) | 4·9(2·7) |
| **vertical sash** | 0·9(0·4) | 1·7(0·9) | 3·1(1·6) |
| **non-opening** [2] | 0·2(—) | 0·5 (—) | 0·8(—) |
| **METAL WINDOWS** | | | |
| **casement** | 0·8(0·4) | 1·5(0·9) | 2·6(1·6) |
| **centre-pivoted** | 1·0(0·6) | 2·0(1·1) | 3·6(2·0) |
| **EXTERNAL DOORS** | | | |
| **front (back) door** | 1·4(0·8) | 2·8(1·6) | 4·9(2·7) |
| **patio doors** | — (0·4) | — (0·7) | — (1·3) |

[1] Well-weatherstripped in brackets.
[2] Non-opening metal windows are the same.

### Using Table 2

Where there are gaps on more than one wall, calculate the heat loss for each wall separately, then work out what actually value to use in one of these ways.

Gaps on two adjacent walls – use the figure for the wall with the greater heat loss or two-thirds of the total heat loss, whichever is the larger.

Gaps on opposite walls – use the figure for the wall with the larger heat loss.

Gaps on three walls – use the figure for the worse two adjacent walls, or two-thirds of the total heat loss, whichever is the greater.

### TABLE 3 : Provisional pipe sizes

| total radiator output W | provisional pipe sizes mm |
|---|---|
| less than 800 | 6 |
| 800 to 1700 | 8 |
| 1700 to 3000 | 10 |
| 3000 to 6000 | 15 |
| 6000 to 11,000 | 22 |
| 11,000 to 18,000 | 28 |
| 18,000 to 28,000 | 35 |

### TABLE 4 : Actual pipe sizing

| pipe size | heat loss | | total load possible |
|---|---|---|---|
| | insulated | uninsulated | |
| mm | W | W | W |
| **6** | 17 | 4 | 960 |
| **8** | 23 | 6 | 2050 |
| **10** | 29 | 7 | 3550 |
| **15** | 43 | 11 | 7110 |
| **22** | 63 | 16 | 12,960 |
| **28** | 77 | 19 | 21,740 |
| **35** | 92 | 23 | 33,440 |

### TABLE 5: Pressure loss in pipes

| Load | Loss in a metre run | | | | | |
|---|---|---|---|---|---|---|
| | 6mm | 8mm | 10mm | 15mm | 22mm | 28mm |
| W | N/m² | N/m² | N/m² | N/m² | N/m² | N/m² |
| 290 | 810 | 182 | 46 | | | |
| 330 | 975 | 210 | 55 | | | |
| 380 | 1165 | 245 | 68 | | | |
| 420 | 1395 | 285 | 81 | 9 | | |
| 460 | 1625 | 325 | 94 | | | |
| 500 | 1885 | 360 | 107 | | | |
| 540 | 2165 | 405 | 120 | | | |
| 590 | 2475 | 460 | 133 | | | |
| 630 | 2800 | 525 | 145 | | | |
| 670 | 3155 | 595 | 164 | 18 | 3 | |
| 710 | 3535 | 665 | 180 | | | |
| 750 | 3930 | 740 | 195 | | | |
| 790 | 4350 | 815 | 215 | | | |
| 840 | 4800 | 903 | 234 | 27 | 4 | |
| 880 | 5330 | 990 | 253 | | | |
| 920 | 5780 | 1075 | 273 | | | |
| 960 | 6210 | 1165 | 293 | | | |
| 1000 | | 1260 | 313 | | | |
| 1050 | | 1350 | 338 | 40 | 6 | |
| 1250 | | | | 54 | 8 | 2·5 |
| 1300 | | 2010 | 520 | | | |
| 1460 | | | | 71 | 11 | 3·5 |
| 1550 | | 2755 | 754 | | | |
| 1670 | | | | 90 | 14 | 4 |
| 1800 | | 3585 | 1030 | | | |
| 1880 | | | | 110 | 17 | 5 |
| 2050 | | 4485 | 1325 | | | |
| 2090 | | | | 132 | 20 | 6 |
| 2300 | | | 1670 | 155 | 24 | 7 |
| 2510 | | | | 181 | 28 | 8 |
| 2550 | | | 2030 | | | |
| 2720 | | | | 209 | 32 | 9 |
| 2800 | | | 2140 | | | |
| 2930 | | | | 237 | 36 | 11 |
| 3050 | | | 2830 | | | |
| 3140 | | | | 267 | 41 | 12 |
| 3300 | | | 3280 | | | |
| 3340 | | | 3780 | 299 | 46 | 14 |
| 3550 | | | | 335 | 51 | 15 |
| 3760 | | | | 370 | 56 | 16 |
| 3970 | | | | 406 | 62 | 18 |

| Load | Loss in a metre run | | | | | |
|---|---|---|---|---|---|---|
| | 6mm | 8mm | 10mm | 15mm | 22mm | 28mm |
| W | N/m² | N/m² | N/m² | N/m² | N/m² | N/m² |
| 4180 | | | | 445 | 68 | 19 |
| 4600 | | | | 527 | 80 | 23 |
| 5020 | | | | 616 | 93 | 27 |
| 5430 | | | | 709 | 107 | 31 |
| 5850 | | | | 808 | 122 | 35 |
| 6270 | | | | | 137 | 40 |
| 6690 | | | | | 154 | 45 |
| 7110 | | | | | 171 | 50 |
| 7520 | | | | | 190 | 55 |
| 7940 | | | | | 210 | 60 |
| 8360 | | | | | 230 | 66 |
| 8780 | | | | | 250 | 72 |
| 9200 | | | | | 271 | 78 |
| 9610 | | | | | 294 | 85 |
| 10030 | | | | | 316 | 91 |
| 10450 | | | | | 340 | 98 |
| 10870 | | | | | 362 | 105 |
| 11290 | | | | | 390 | 113 |
| 11700 | | | | | 417 | 120 |
| 12120 | | | | | 443 | 128 |
| 12540 | | | | | 470 | 135 |
| 12960 | | | | | 500 | 144 |
| 13380 | | | | | 528 | 152 |
| 13790 | | | | | | 161 |
| 14210 | | | | | | 169 |
| 14630 | | | | | | 178 |
| 15050 | | | | | | 188 |
| 15470 | | | | | | 197 |
| 15880 | | | | | | 206 |
| 16300 | | | | | | 216 |
| 16720 | | | | | | 226 |
| 17140 | | | | | | 237 |
| 17560 | | | | | | 247 |
| 17970 | | | | | | 257 |
| 18390 | | | | | | 268 |
| 18810 | | | | | | 280 |
| 19230 | | | | | | 291 |
| 19650 | | | | | | 302 |
| 20060 | | | | | | 313 |
| 20900 | | | | | | 338 |
| 21740 | | | | | | 362 |

# The installation

Most of the problems with installing a central heating system are likely to be over the siting of boilers and the layout of the piping in the boiler area – so the instructions below concentrate on these problems which are part design/part installation. It is important always to follow manufacturer's instructions, especially where they differ from those given below.

## Help

If you need technical help or information while actually installing a system, try the firm who sold you the components, the system's designer, or the manufacturers. One job for which you might want a qualified person is checking the installation of a gas-fired, and perhaps oil-fired, boiler: this should cost relatively little. You might get a professional to do the actual connection to the gas supply.

**A Walls and floor around boilers** There are Building Regulations to be followed which concern mainly solid fuel boilers – domestic gas and oil boilers are usually designed so that they can be mounted on any wall or floor. Solid fuel boilers have to stand on a solid, non-combustible hearth at least 125mm thick and 840mm square. Usually a boiler will be within about 150mm of a wall at the back or sides – this wall has to be non-combustible and at least 75mm thick. There are different regulations for solid fuel appliances in fireplace recesses (eg room heaters); if the fireplace already exists then its structure will probably be approved.

**B Assembling and mounting the boiler** Follow the manufacturer's instructions.

**C Boiler connections** Tappings for joining pipes to the boiler are often larger than you will need, and can be made smaller by screwing in a 'black iron' male-to-female reducing bush. Iron fittings are still imperial sizes: the male end will be whatever size the boiler tappings are (check manufacturer's instructions); the female end will be the imperial equivalent of the pipe you will be connecting to it (1in for 28mm; ¾in for 22mm; ½in for 15mm).

Connect pipes to the tappings using a male-to-female compression (or capillary) fitting.

Sealing large threads near the boiler is best done with traditional hemp and jointing compound, rather than PTFE tape.

Many boilers have four tappings: often a sensible design is to use two for the heating circuit, two for a gravity flow hot water circuit. (The top tapping is always the flow; bottom the return.) Especially where the tappings face each other, it is often a good idea to increase the size of the last half metre of the heating circuit return pipe, this should help circulation in the hot water cylinder circuit.

Where there is only one return tapping and the hot water circuit is gravity-flow, joint the heating and hot water circuits together, at the boiler, using a *twin elbow* fitting, rather than an ordinary tee.

If the hot water circuit is pumped, then the layout will depend largely on the type of controls used – see page 212.

**D Pump** The usual position for a pump is close to the boiler, in the return pipe from heating circuit. Avoid the lowest part of the system where the pump would be prone to collect sludge and other debris.

Buy a pump fitted with valves, for ease of servicing. These are jointed to the pipes with compression fittings and the pump slides in between them. After checking for fit, remove the pump and valves, and replace with a piece of plain pipe (using compression fittings). Leave this pipe in place until the system has been filled and flushed out (see Commissioning – page 211). Then replace the pump: check that it is installed the right way round – there's usually an arrow to show the direction of water flow.

**E Cold feed connection** Make this connection close to the boiler, and between the boiler and the outlet from the pump. On some boilers, there is a special feed pipe connection point. Alternatively, where the boiler has four tappings and two are used for the hot water circuit, the connection can be anywhere in the return pipe from the hot water cylinder to the boiler. Feed pipes are usually 15mm diameter. Do *not* install any valves in any pipe between the boiler and the feed-and-expansion cistern.

**F Heating system vent pipe** Connect this close to the boiler on the main heating system flow pipe. Alternatively, where four tappings are used and with a gravity-fed hot water circuit, the connection can be made anywhere in the flow pipe to the hot water cylinder (note though that some experts prefer a connection low down close to the boiler). The vent pipe (and any length of pipe between the connection and the boiler if the vent pipe is not taken directly from the boiler) must be at least 22mm diameter. Do *not* install *any* valves in any pipe between the boiler and the end of the vent.

**G Feed-and-expansion cistern** This should be about 45 litres nominal (about 15 litres actual) capacity and is generally of rigid plastic: make sure it is suitable for use as a feed-and-expansion cistern. Connect it up in much the same way as a normal cold water storage cistern (page 293): fit a ball valve through one side near the top connected by a 15mm inlet pipe from the rising main (*not* from the storage cistern); a 22mm overflow at a slightly lower level; and a 15mm feed pipe sited about 50mm above the bottom. Fit a stop tap to the inlet pipe. Bend the ball valve down so that there is only about 100mm of water in the cistern when first filled: the water will expand a lot when heated. Tie down the cover to make it near airtight and thus reduce water loss and discourage the entry of bacteria. Insulate the cistern and feed pipe, especially if they are in the loft.

The cistern should preferably be at least 1m above the highest point (usually either the top of the radiators, or the heating coil in the hot water cylinder) of the heating system.

**H Height of vent** If the pump is close to the flow tapping of the boiler, water may be continually pumped over the 'crook' of the vent pipe into the cistern. To avoid this, move the pump. The alternative is to raise the height of the crook. In extreme cases, though, this might have to be as high as the head of the pump – a pressure of 10kN/m² is equivalent to a head of over 1m.

**I Safety valve** Most experts recommend that a pressure release safety valve should be fitted on the heating flow pipe, close to the boiler, whatever its type, this is particularly important with solid fuel.

**J Drain taps** At least one drain tap should be fitted at the lowest point of the system, and where a hose-pipe can be easily fitted to drain the contents out of doors. Down loops of pipes – such as downstairs radiators fed from upstairs circuits – need their own drain valves.

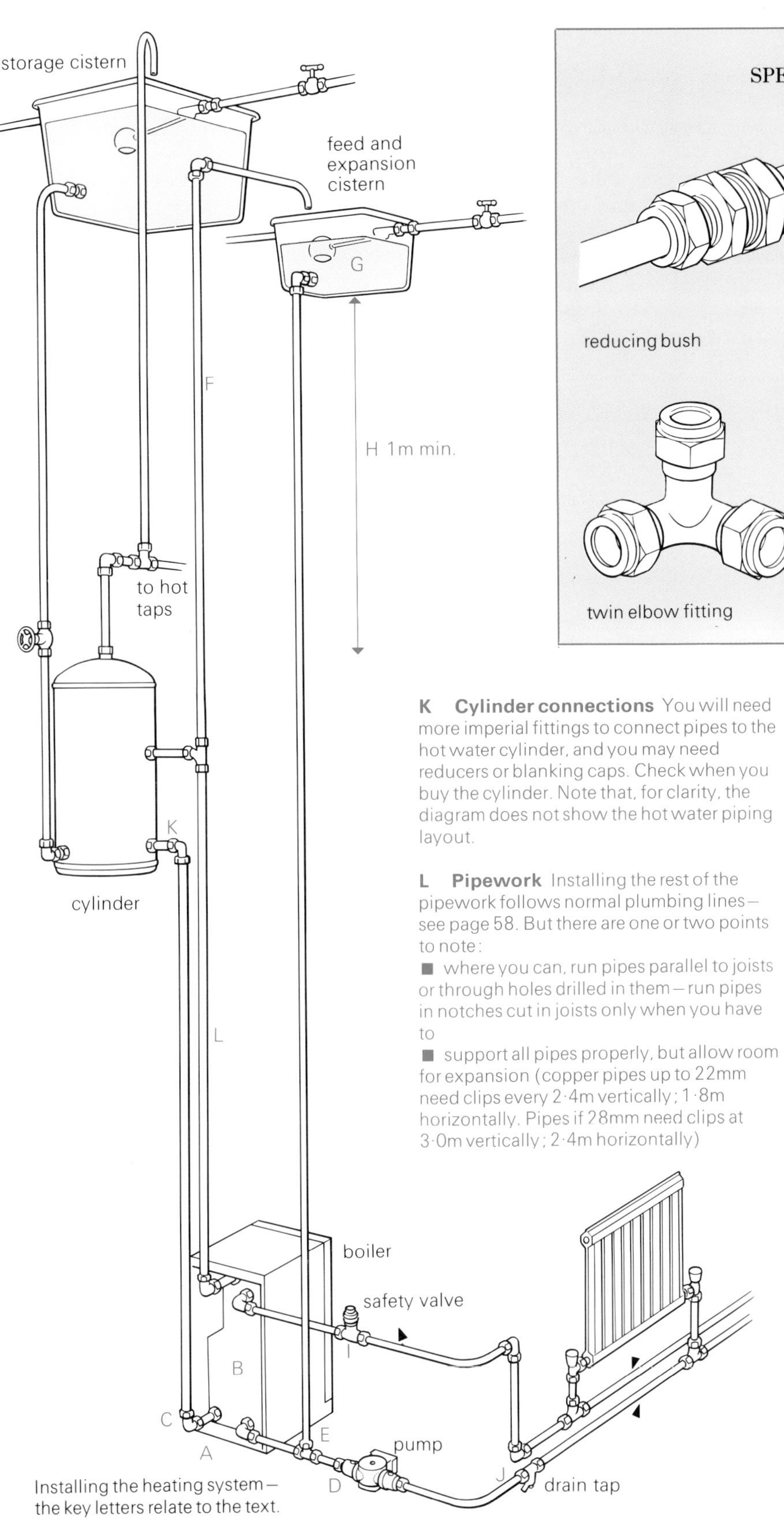


Installing the heating system – the key letters relate to the text.

**SPECIAL FITTINGS**

reducing bush

safety valve

twin elbow fitting

drain tap

**K Cylinder connections** You will need more imperial fittings to connect pipes to the hot water cylinder, and you may need reducers or blanking caps. Check when you buy the cylinder. Note that, for clarity, the diagram does not show the hot water piping layout.

**L Pipework** Installing the rest of the pipework follows normal plumbing lines – see page 58. But there are one or two points to note:

- where you can, run pipes parallel to joists or through holes drilled in them – run pipes in notches cut in joists only when you have to
- support all pipes properly, but allow room for expansion (copper pipes up to 22mm need clips every 2·4m vertically; 1·8m horizontally. Pipes if 28mm need clips at 3·0m vertically; 2·4m horizontally)
- to minimise noise from expansion and contraction, wrap lagging round pipes where they cross joists or pass through walls
- make sure pipes do not dip and rise too much – it could trap air. If anything, have one gentle rise or fall along a whole circuit. It is particularly important that gravity flow and return pipes to a hot water cylinder rise continuously towards the cylinder.

**Balanced flue**

A balanced flue is generally much easier to install than the conventional type (see over) but even so you must be very careful to get it right. Cut the hole for the balanced flue from the outside if possible as this will do less damage to the exterior brickwork – see page 120 for cutting holes. Remember that the cavity must be sealed. The position of the flue is controlled by the Building Regulations – see page 196 – so you need approval for the work.

The standard balanced flue terminal supplied with most boilers is telescopic and slides to take up wall thicknesses in the range 230mm to 380mm. This will suit most walls but for particularly thick house walls or the one brick thick walls of an outhouse or garage you will need to specify the appropriate size.

To fit a flue follow the manufacturer's instructions. Usually you slide the two pieces to the correct position for your walls thickness and tape the joint between sections. Then position the flue in the wall and hold it in place with the internal backplate which is screwed to the wall. The boiler flue outlet seals on to this plate.

## FLUES

The boiler connections to a prefabricated chimney vary from brand to brand: check with the chimney manufacturer of the system you are using.

With an existing chimney, first fit a length (at least 600mm) of heavy duty cast iron flue pipe or sheet steel if you can't get cast iron (usually with a white vitreous enamel finish) vertically to the boiler outlet; add a similar 135° bend with a soot door on top. All joints between flue pipes face upwards, are packed with asbestos string, and sealed with a thick layer of fire cement. Break into the chimney at the point the bend meets the wall, forming a hole at roughly the angle the pipe will enter. Cement a metal or asbestos-cement sleeve (about 15mm bigger in diameter than the flue pipe) into the hole and then feed the flue pipe into this. If you are not using a flexible liner, make sure the end of the flue pipe does not project into the flue.

If you are using a flexible metal liner, lower this down the chimney from the roof after removing the chimney pot. Push the liner into the socket end of the flue pipe. In some cases, for instance when the chimney is outside and therefore cold, you will have to provide a *condensate drain* at the lower end of the liner but this is unusual. A warm flue is much better. Check the details with your boiler manufacturer.

A fixing plate holds the top of the liner to the chimney stack – mortar this in place, then slide a terminal on top or rebuild.

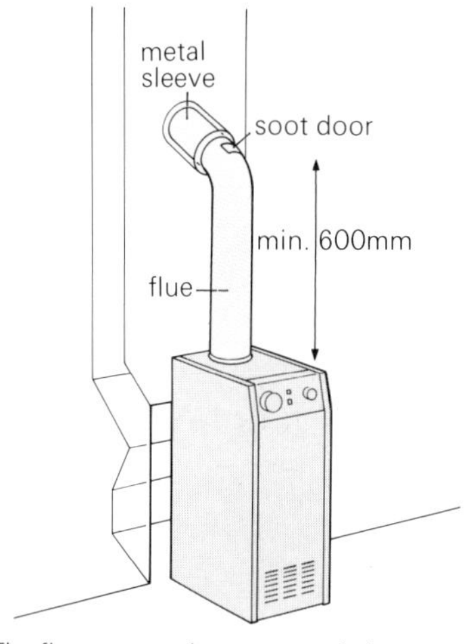


The flue connections to an existing chimney which needs no lining.

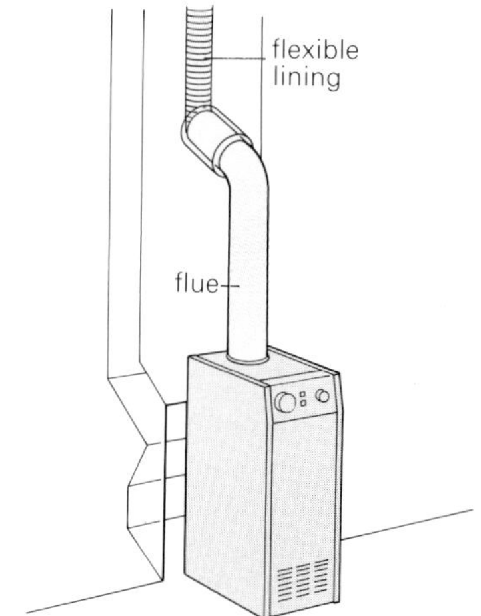


The flue connections when a flexible liner is required.

## Radiators

Hang the radiators on the walls before running the pipes – it makes pipe siting more accurate and gets the radiators out of the way.

First paint the backs and bottom edges of the radiators – these are difficult to get to after hanging. For outside walls consider putting radiator foil on the wall behind to reflect back heat.

Most radiators have four holes – *tappings*. The bottom tappings take valves. One (the lockshield valve) is set during installation so that the right amount of water flows through the radiator. The other (the wheel valve) can be turned to switch the radiator on and off. The valves are identical if you buy the same make (the wheel on a wheel valve can be swapped with the lockshield cover) so it doesn't matter which way round you put them, although it's usual to end up with the wheel valve on the flow pipe.

Fit the valves as shown in the drawings.

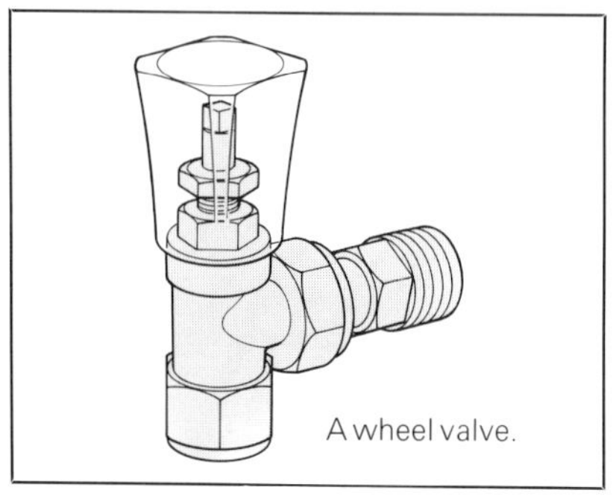

A wheel valve.

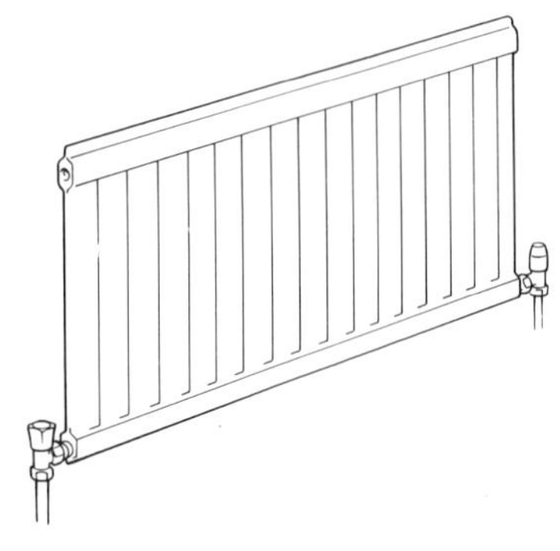

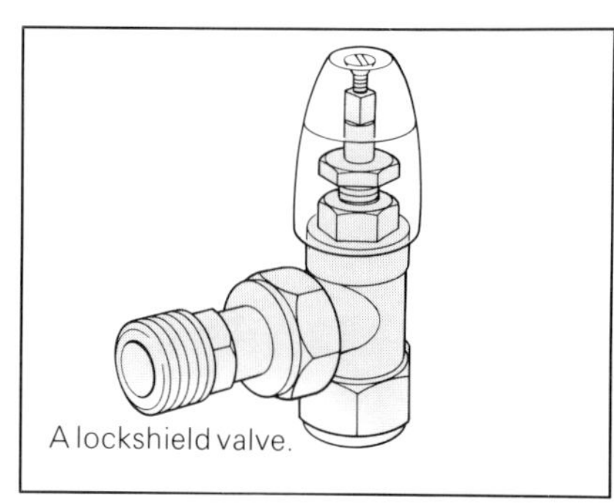

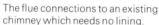

A lockshield valve.

INSTALLING A RADIATOR

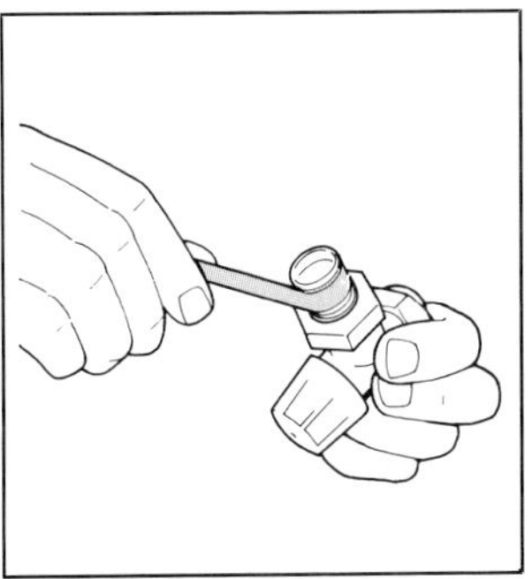
Wrap PTFE tape round the thread. Then undo the union.

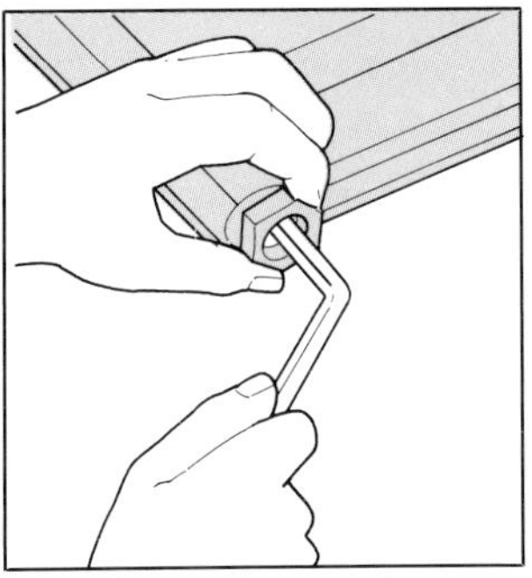
Screw into the lower radiator threaded tapping.

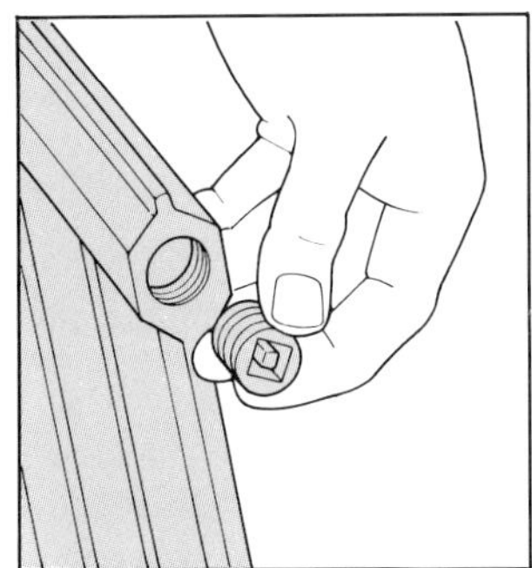
Wrap the air vent plug with PTFE tape and screw home.

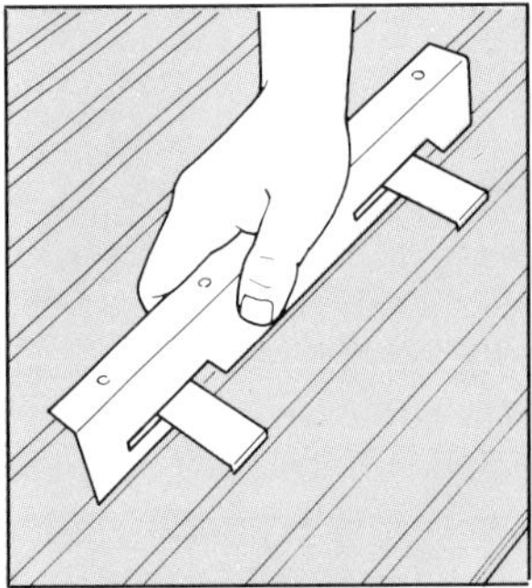
Clip the brackets in place and measure up for wall fixing.

The top tappings are fitted with an air venting plug at one end and a blank plug at the other.

To hang the radiator lay it on its face, clip in the brackets, and measure the positions of their fixing holes. Transfer these measurements to wall, making sure the radiators will be high enough up to clear skirting. Allow for connecting up pipes to the valves.

Fix the brackets so that the radiator will rise *slightly* to the air vent end.

## Commissioning the system

Check the whole installation carefully to make sure you haven't left any loose joints or open ends of pipe.

### Filling

Open all the radiator valves, but close all drain valves and radiator air vents. Open the inlet valve to the feed-and-expansion cistern and let the system fill – this may take some time. Check continually for leaks. Those at compression fittings can usually be stopped by gently tightening the nuts. With plastic and capillary fittings, you have to drain the water out of the system first – so provided the leak isn't too bad try to cope with it until all leaks have been found.

When the feed-and-expansion cistern starts to fill, it is time to *bleed* the radiators of any trapped air. Start at the lowest and furthest point of the system. With a radiator key, slowly release the plug in the radiator air vent – you should hear a hissing as the water forces the trapped air out. When water starts to come out of the air vent – at anything from a dribble to a spurt, quickly screw the plug home – have a cloth ready to soak up the water. Continue like this round the circuit – shortly after, the cistern should stop filling up. Check the level.

Close the inlet valve and drain the system in order to flush out any debris in the pipes. Attend to any leaks, then fill, bleed and flush again.

### Firing the boiler

Fit the pump (see stage D) and fill for the third time. As this is the last fill, add an anti-corrosion inhibitor to stabilise the water. It will help to reduce pump failure as well as reducing corrosion. The boiler can now be fired.

Let the water heat up, and start the pump running. Alter the variable head to the setting needed to overcome the circuit resistance. Check, so far as you can, that all controls are working properly, and that the pump is neither pushing water out through the vent pipe, nor sucking air in – to do this release the radiator air vent plugs, to check that they spill water.

### Balancing

You now have to alter the water flow through each of the radiators so that it matches the levels assumed during design – this is called *balancing*. If you fail to get it right, the system will not achieve the temperatures it is designed for. The basic assumption is that the difference in temperature between the water entering the radiator and that leaving the radiator is 10°C. (Usually, the flow temperature is 180°C, and the return 170°C giving a mean temperature of 175°C.)

You alter the temperature drop by adjusting the lockshield valves. Check the temperatures with two clip-on pipe thermometers, one on the pipework at each end of the radiator. Start with the radiator furthest away from the boiler, and check the flow temperature. If this is not 180°C, check the boiler thermostat setting and any other controls. Then gradually close the lockshield valve until the temperature drop is 10°C. Repeat for all other radiators, then check them all. You may have to go back and re-adjust some of them and that adjustment may in turn upset the balance of other radiators: balancing can be very fiddly work.

Whatever the outside temperature, you can get a rough idea of whether a system will reach its design temperatures by running the system at full belt without any thermostatic controls. The temperature the rooms reach should be higher than the design temperature by roughly *half* the level of the outside temperature (in Centigrade), plus 1°C. For instance room temperature reaches 27°C; design temp 20°C; outside temp 17°C. Difference 27°C – 20°C is 7°C, add the extra 1°C to get 8°C which is roughly half 17°C and therefore OK.

# Controls

The simplest control package which needs no extra valves and will work with a central heating system with hot water on gravity flow includes:

■ a programmer wired to turn the boiler on and off at pre-set times. Usually such a programmer can be set to switch the hot water and heating on together – it does this by switching on the pump as well as the boiler – or the hot water alone in which case the pump is not switched on. Heating alone is not available because the absence of any valves in the system means that the hot water and heating circuits cannot be isolated. The programmer should always be the master control so that heat is supplied only during timed on periods (regardless of what the other controls are demanding)

■ a boiler thermostat to turn the boiler off when the water in it reaches a pre-set maximum temperature and on again when the temperature drops

■ a thermostatic device to sense the air temperature in the heated rooms. This is often a single room thermostat – an electrical device which is wired to turn the pump off when the pre-set maximum is reached and on again when the air temperature drops. (When only the pump is switched off by the thermostat the boiler will still be on and during any timed on period heat will still go to the hot water circuit when necessary.)

An alternative is to have thermostatic radiator valves (TRVs) on all or just selected radiators. These replace the normal inlet valve. The valve closes as the air temperature rises and opens again as the air temperature falls, thus controlling the water flow. In this way it matches the heat output of the radiator to the room's need for heat.

There are lots of variations on this package, for instance a room thermostat downstairs could be used in conjunction with TRVs in the bedrooms. In which case the thermostat would be the master control.

### More sophistication

A good advance on the basic package is to include a further thermostatic device to give control over the hot water. Apart from anything else, this means that the hot water can be controlled at a safer temperature so that there is no danger of scalding water from the taps.

The extra control could be a thermostatic cylinder valve installed in the pipe back to the boiler. This senses the temperature of the water returning to the boiler and shuts off the flow when the required temperature is reached. An electrical temperature sensor clipped to the cylinder and wired to a motorised valve is a better choice, especially if the wiring is set up to turn off the boiler when heat is not required for either the heating or hot water circuit.

This is important; if only the pump is switched off when neither circuit needs heat, the boiler will continue to go on and off – called cycling – just to keep the water in it hot – an unnecessary waste. The motorised valve also allows separate time control of the hot water. A system with hot water temperature control is cheaper to run, especially in the summer.

## Fitting controls

Most of the possible problems associated with controls should be considered at the design stage when it's decided which of the many patterns of valve, thermostat switch and so on are needed for the type of control system that you want. How to wire them together also needs careful considering then.

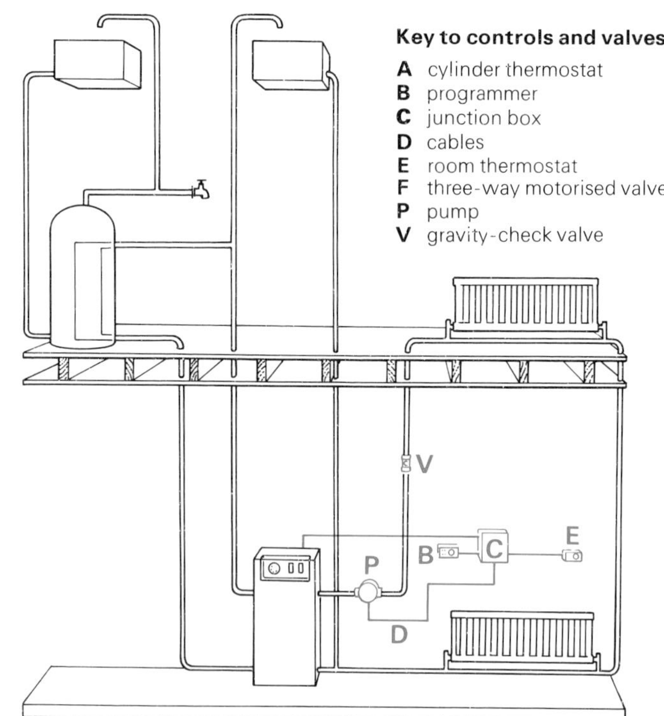


A simple control package with a programmer and room thermostat. The hot water circuit is not pumped and has no temperature control.

Using the manufacturer's control package helps to simplify this. An added advantage is that comprehensive wiring diagrams are usually included.

Control systems from different manufacturers vary quite a lot in how they are installed and wired up, so you must follow manufacturer's instructions. The details below give an idea.

The controls are keyed on the heating systems illustrated. The system on the right is most sophisticated: both the circuits are pumped; a motorised 3-way valve allows versatile control by the various thermostats and there is a programmer for overall time control.

### A Cylinder thermostat

This is the electrical temperature sensor type. It is usually held to the side of the hot water cylinder by means of a metal band – the best position is about a third the way up the side from the base. The alternative is a thermostatic valve in the return pipe from the cylinder.

### B Programmer

This is usually wall-mounted near the boiler or the hot-water cylinder. It doesn't really matter where, it just needs to be convenient. A programmer may need a mounting box.

### C Junction box

This is included to make the wiring up easier: all the cables from the various points in the system meet here. Special wiring centres supplied with instructions can be useful for this purpose. It needs to go where it can be worked on easily and, to keep wiring runs short, near to the main components (which probably means close to the boiler, pump, and motorised valve). The electricity supply cable is run from a fused connection unit fitted with the appropriate fuse – usually 3A. A gas boiler should be supplied from a plug (with appropriate fuse) and socket so that it can be rapidly disconnected.

### D Cables

The wiring diagrams will give details of the types of cable needed from the junction box to each component – these may be twin and earth: or special three-core with earth, four-core with earth, even five-core. All cables are at 240V, but carry little current. Four-core and five-core cables are normally specials. Otherwise normal wiring cable can be used except where heat-resisting ones are called for.

### E Room thermostat

As with a programmer, you may need to use a mounting box. Position the thermostat in the room that will need heat whenever the heating is on. The living room is often the best choice, some designers opt for the hall.

Experimenting with position is worthwhile (but you must take care that any temporary wiring is absolutely safe). In any event, the thermostat should be placed 1·5m or so above the floor, on an inside wall; where air can freely flow round it; and away from draughts, and heat sources – such as a radiator or direct sunshine through a window. A television can be a significant source of heat. If the thermostat is going to control a motorised valve it will need to be a double-throw switch.

### F Motorised valves

The position depends mainly on the pipe layout, a three-way valve as shown is likely to be close to the boiler. It may be easier to install two two-way valves. Check manufacturer's instructions to see if the orientation of the valve and its motor are important, and if so, run the connecting pipes so you can attach the valve the right way up.

### G Thermostatic radiator valve

These connect to the radiator and pipe in the same way as ordinary valves – they usually replace the handwheel valve on the flow pipe.

In a system where TRVs are fitted to all radiators the pump may find itself with nowhere to send its water if all the TRVs are shut off at once. A water-flow switch in the circuit will save wastage.

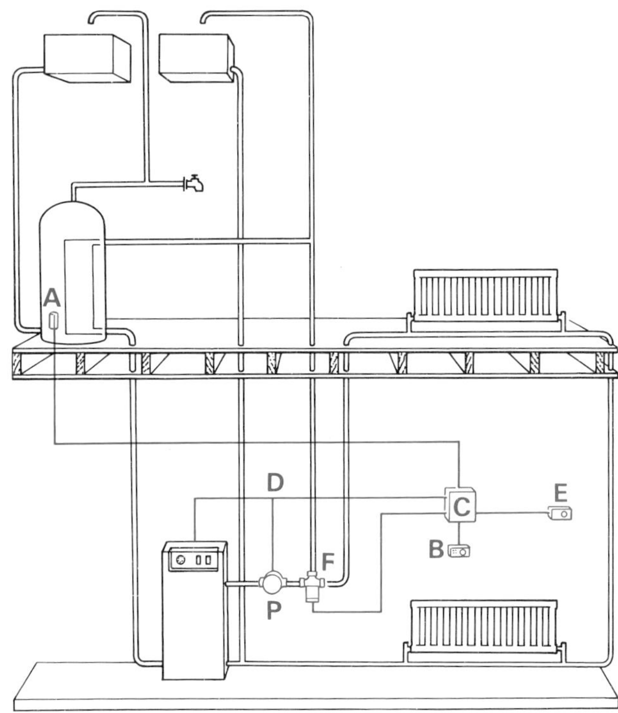

A more sophisticated control system with both hot water and heating circuits pumped.

# Moving a radiator

Before doing almost anything to a central heating system, the flow of water has to be stopped. Turn off the pump, switch off an oil or gas boiler, rake out the fire in a solid fuel boiler. Let the system cool down. Now you have a choice: the system can be drained – see below – or you can use a pipe freezing kit to form a plug of ice to stop the pipe. Kits are sold for do-it-yourselfers, but you get a much longer working time with a hired industrial kit which will be supplied with a much larger canister of freezing gas.

## Step-by-step

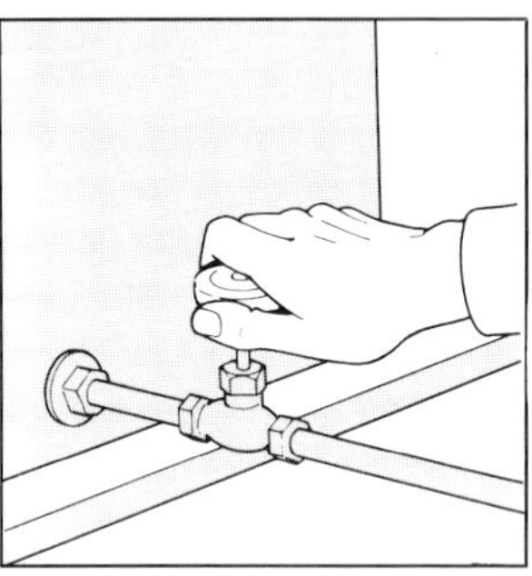

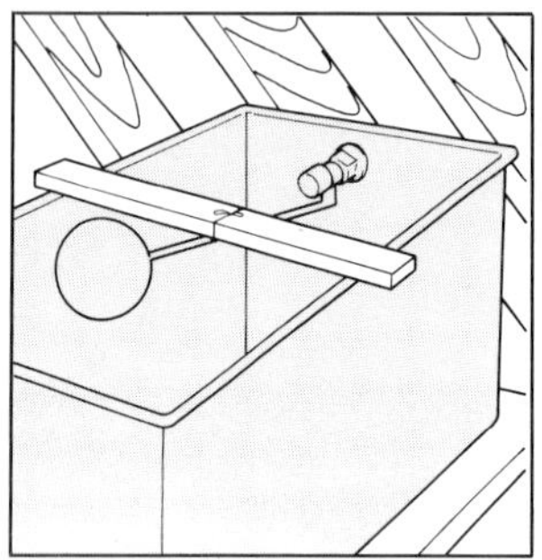

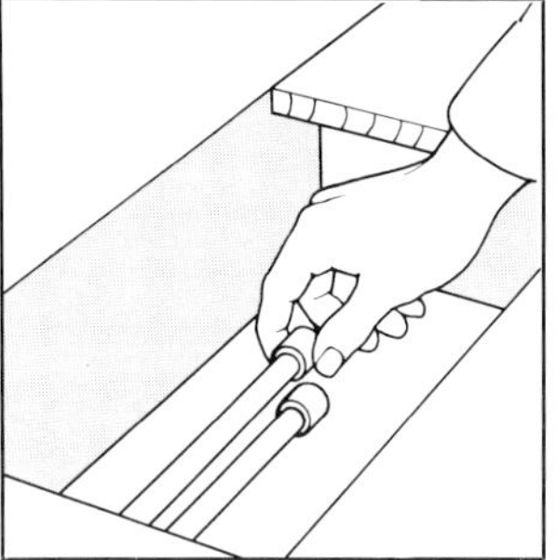

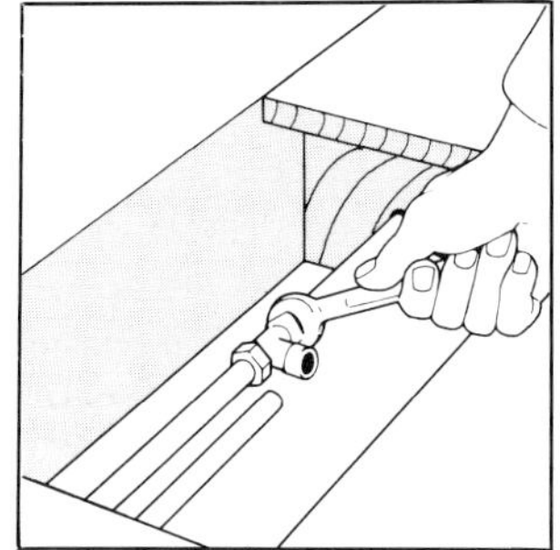

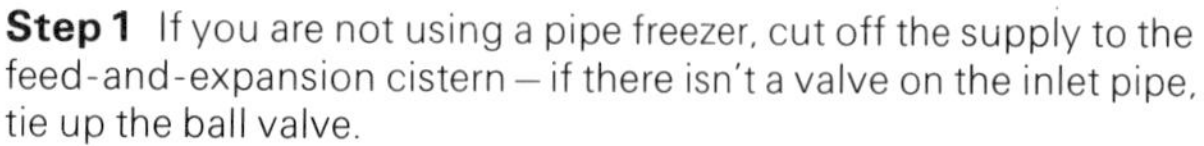

**Step 1** If you are not using a pipe freezer, cut off the supply to the feed-and-expansion cistern – if there isn't a valve on the inlet pipe, tie up the ball valve.

Push a hose pipe on to the drain cock – at the lowest point in the piping, usually by the boiler. Open the drain cock tap with a small spanner of the right size and let the system empty: this could take some time. Check for extra drain cocks at other low points in the system, and drain if necessary.

**Step 2A** A radiator re-sited near to its original position can remain on the same pipe branch. Disconnect the inlet pipes at the radiator by unbolting the radiator valve unions and lift it off its brackets. Re-hang in its new position – see page 210.

Re-route or extend the pipes from their former positions to the new site and connect up as usual. If the system was installed before the mid-70s, imperial piping may have been used – this is a slightly different size from the metric pipe and fittings used now. Compression and capillary adaptor fittings are available: these aren't needed for 15mm (imperial equivalent was ½in) compression fittings, so with 15mm pipe use compression fittings if you are in doubt.

**Step 2B** Moving a radiator more than a little way usually involves running a new branch at some point in the layout. You can do this providing the new branch is on the same circuit as the existing branch. If you want to move the radiator on to a different circuit, you should first check that the pipework at that point will be large enough. Disconnect the radiator and cut the pipework short so that it is hidden, for neatness. If the new branch is shorter, it may be worth cutting the pipes right back to the tee-piece and re-using them. Blank off the cut ends using compression or capillary caps. Re-mount the radiator in its new position.

Choose a convenient point on the pipe circuit for the new branch run. Cut the flow and return pipes and insert tee fittings of the appropriate size (the same as that of the pipes you are connecting to them). You may have to cut a small piece out of the pipes if there is not enough slack to accommodate the fitting. Connect branch pipes from the tees to the radiator.

## Extending a system

Before extending a central system by adding more radiators, you should check that boiler, pump and pipes have enough spare capacity – by going through the design calculations (see page 199 *et seq*) for the existing house and then adding on the design for the extension you want.

Most houses have over-sized systems (particularly boilers), so you might gamble on the calculations being unnecessary. However, you should at least check that the pipes in the circuit or circuits you intend to extend are large enough for all the radiators that will be connected to them (including of course the existing ones). If you don't have the original design of the system, use Table 3 (page 207) to find what heating loads different pipe sizes can reasonably take. Assume that single-panel radiators have an output of about 1350 watts per square metre of frontal area, and double panel ones around 2100 watts. If there isn't capacity to extend one circuit, there may well be enough to extend another. In extreme cases, you may well have to run the pipes for the extension nearly back to the boiler.

Once you have found a point to run a circuit from effectively, installation follows normal lines.

If possible install the same sort of radiators as in the rest of the system. Some experts say you shouldn't mix the types in one system. It's certainly better not to mix fan-assisted convector heaters with ordinary panel-type radiators.

# PART 3
# EXTENSIONS AND CONVERSIONS

# Chapter 8

# BUILDING AN EXTENSION

Extensions to existing properties come in all shapes and sizes, from a porch at the front or back door to a whole new wing. Depending on the size of the project the cost of the work is similarly wide-ranging – from under £500 to £20,000 or more. The costs depend on the size of the extension project and its complexity. In 1983 the typical cost for a square metre of a single-storey extension was around £300, with fittings and decorations on top. The extensions *Which?* readers told us about typically had a floor area between $14m^2$ and $21{\cdot}5m^2$. At 1983 prices these could have cost between £4,200 and £6,450.

The main reason for extending must always be that you want the extra space the extension will provide. But with such large sums of money involved it would be foolish not to think of the extension as a form of investment. This means considering what the extension might mean to the resale value of your house and whether it will affect the house's saleability – as outlined on pages 18 and 19.

## Making the most of an extension

The chances of an extension being good value as an investment are generally improved if:

- the house is not made substantially larger than others in the same road and immediate area (though this wouldn't matter in an area of very mixed property – a village for instance)
- the house is not made very tight on its plot of land – a minimum of one metre all round should be retained if possible
- the accommodation is balanced with the right amount of living space to match the bedrooms and vice versa.

Good design is also very important. In particular this means paying attention to:

- the look of the extension from outside. The best extensions look as if they were meant to be there either because they match the rest of the house or because they've been carefully designed not to match, but with an eye to architectural proportions and so on. Pitched roofs sloping one or both ways usually achieve this better than flat roofs
- the size and shape of rooms. Extending can create rooms which are too long and thin or rooms which receive inadequate natural light.
- access to rooms. Rooms which intercommunicate are best avoided, particularly adjoining bedrooms. Long corridors can also be detrimental to the layout as well as wasting a great deal of space
- where the windows go. The aspect to and from windows is important, having them where they'll overlook (or be overlooked by) a neighbour's window or another window in your own house is to be avoided. Try to retain bathroom and kitchen windows. These often get enclosed when an extension is added. Although acceptable in a flat, internal kitchens and internal *main* bathrooms don't add to a house's attraction – though you can often get away with a second bathroom as an internal room.

An extension that's well designed looks as if it was meant to be there. With most houses this is achieved by matching or blending in the new building. The illusion that an extension was always part of the house is achieved by following the architectural style of the existing structure and using the same materials, for the walls, windows and roof. If the wall materials prove difficult or expensive to match, painting, pebble-dashing, rendering and similar coatings can help to draw together the house and extension. If you're trying to match the extension to the rest of the house, windows should be the same style as well as material and it helps if they are installed at the same sill height with the detail around and above the new windows copied from the old. Other details peculiar to the existing structure are also worth continuing.

| | cost | value | selling |
|---|---|---|---|
| single-storey kitchen extension (20 sq m) | £6,000 | around 60% | improved |
| single-storey extension with glazed roof (15 sq m) | £3,300 | around 15% | possibly no improvement |
| two-storey extension (50 sq m) | £13,750 | around 100% | improved |

Extensions to three-bedroom semi-detached house. For Key to Table and explanation see pages 18 and 19.

## Two-storey extensions

Two-storey extensions have some advantages over single-storey ones: they can work out slightly cheaper on a £ per area gained basis and from the outside they can more easily be made to look like part of the original house. However, gaining access to the first floor of a new extension often means disrupting the first floor of the existing house and may mean that existing bedroom space has to be sacrificed for a corridor, so that the net gain is not as great as it seems.

Planning permission may be conditional on the external appearance of the new extension blending architecturally with the existing building.

The details and step-by-step guides in this chapter are for single-storey extensions – which are the most common and all that we would advise an amateur builder to attempt – however most of the information is also applicable to two-storey extensions.

A two-storey extension continues the roof line and blends well.

## Upper floor extensions

In some circumstances it may be possible to build over the top of an existing single-storey extension. If you want to do this you'll need to find out whether the additional weight will harm any part of the existing structure. Foundations which were designed and built to support only a single storey might not be capable of safely supporting additional loads, or may be sufficient only for a relatively lightweight extension such as a conservatory.

It is unlikely that you will be able to tell whether the existing foundations are adequate without taking professional advice. Some excavation may be necessary. If you are able to persuade your local building control officer to make an inspection, he will give his advice free. Building control officers are under no obligation to carry out an inspection of this sort, but some will do so. The BCO may be able to check from the original house plans kept in the office.

If the existing foundations are not capable of supporting any additional weight they must be improved or renewed before an upper floor can be constructed. Or, in certain cases, it's possible to add new columns outside the existing walls. The best course of action might be to demolish and reconstruct the walls which will have to bear the additional weight. The volume of any structure that is demolished and reconstructed does not have to be counted towards the permitted development volume limits.

Even if the foundations are adequate, the walls themselves may not provide adequate support.

The joists in the structure of the existing flat roof are unlikely to be sufficient to carry the load of a floor, so new joists (or a beam to shorten the span) will have to be introduced to support the new floor. (This usually has to happen for a loft conversion – details of the options are given on page 279.)

It is possible to build an extension solely at first floor level with the support being provided by means of

An extension at first floor level with garage/car port below.

columns, or piers, instead of walls. The space beneath can then be used as a carport. The piers would normally be masonry but could be other materials such as steel, reinforced concrete or timber. The thickness of the piers will depend on the material of which they are made and their height.

The underside of such an extension must be thermally insulated and have a layer of moisture-resistant material. As far as planning permission is concerned, the volume is deemed to be not only the solid part at first floor level, but also the open part at ground floor level.

## Planning permission

Planning permission will be required as outlined on page 22 for extensions larger than permitted development, extensions to listed buildings, buildings in a conservation area and buildings subject to an article 4 direction by the local authority (so check whether your house is any of these). Additions intended to extend forward of the building line also require permission – for a house on the corner plot this applies to extensions to the relevant side of the house as well as to the front.

## Other considerations

It's important when considering an extension not to firm up on the final plan too quickly. There are lots of things to think about – some of them design-related, others merely practical.

There's often a lot of useful information to be gained from friends and neighbours who have extended their properties recently. Most people are only too willing to tell. Talk to them and look at their extensions, particularly extensions to properties very similar to your own. Ask what their extensions are like to live in.

### Other jobs in the house

Try to see conversion and extension projects as a whole. This helps to avoid having to undo work already done and is also a practical approach, for instance rubble from demolished internal walls can provide hardcore for an extension floor.

### Co-ordinated dimensions

Building components – timber, plasterboard, window frames and so on – come in standard sizes, carpets and other floorcoverings supplied on a roll come in standard widths, kitchen units and bathroom fittings are based on co-ordinated modules. Check that things will fit. Ending up with a room a few centimetres too wide or too narrow, will be expensive and inconvenient.

### Access

An extension will often lead off another room, think about what this will mean to the way you can use the existing room. It's cheaper if access can be provided through an existing opening which will already have a support for the structure above.

Retaining existing supports makes the building work simpler, it may even be possible to turn it to your advantage. An enterprising design for extending beyond a bay window which supports a further bay on the floor above is to remove the windows and french doors but leave the bay columns and lintels in place. The columns can then be boxed in and decorated to become features of the room.

Leave making the access until the last possible moment. This will greatly reduce the amount of dirt carried into the house and will also mean the security and weathertightness of the main house is not breached for a long period of time.

### Provision for future work

It may be possible (and necessary financially) to extend in stages, creating in the first place a basic habitable structure, but making provision for further development when funds permit. This is probably most feasible for a d-i-y project. It could involve: building in lintels where you plan that a window or door will one day be required or leaving brick toothing protruding at corners so that a further extension can be easily tied in.

## Drawings

Whether you're intending to employ a builder or to build your extension yourself, professional help with designing will generally be invaluable – see *People who design* page 30.

When between you, you have decided what the extension will be like, the designer will produce the drawings for submission to the local authority. These drawings are important: they must show the BCO (and anyone else who needs to know – such as the lender of a loan) that the proposed scheme complies with the Building Regulations. A builder will use them as a basis for the quotation and to work from. You should make sure that they show your requirements precisely and correctly.

For a single-storey extension to a house, the drawings consist of a floor plan, views of the various sides of the building before and after the improvement – called elevations – and a cross-section through the building with details of foundations, roof and so on. Usually a location plan is required showing the position of the property in the district and also a plan showing the proposed extension in relation to the property and its ground including large trees with a note of the species.

The main plans and the elevations are normally drawn at a scale of 1 to 50, but the location plans are obviously to smaller scale. The way the construction is depicted on the drawings, the hatching and other symbols, is standardised.

These drawings are normally collated on one large sheet of paper – two at the most.

The building specification for a simple extension (or conversion) will usually be written on the same sheet of paper as the drawings. The specification takes the form of detailed construction notes: the notes provide extensive detail – for instance they state the type and depth of concrete to be used for the foundations and the grade of chipboard to be used for roofing. In many instances the specifications will make reference to British Stan-

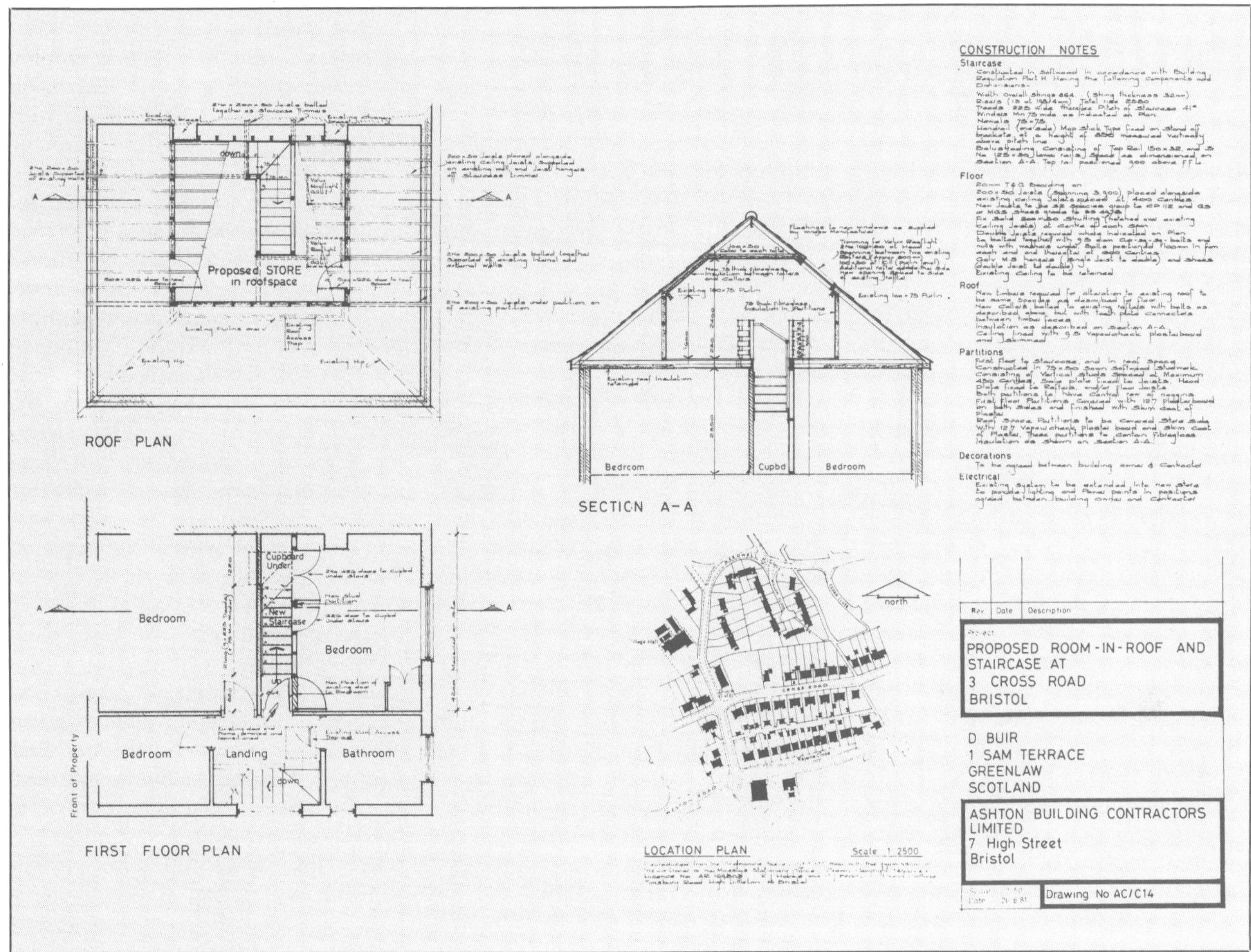


The designer's drawings include plans and sections.
The specification is usually written on the same sheet.

dard Specifications or British Standard Codes of Practice, as an indication that the proposed materials or method of building is to the standard required.

## Organising the site

If you're employing a builder who is supplying his own materials he should organise himself, but you might like to give some consideration to where things go so that they go where you want them and not where he does. You might restrict him to a particular area. For a d-i-y project it's essential to plan and prepare well beforehand. Good organisation means less physical effort, less confusion and a significant reduction in damaged or spoilt materials.

Store sand, ballast, cement, plaster where they will not get damp or contaminated. Be ready for deliveries – don't just hope that it won't rain and that you will find a space somewhere. Know where things are going and if appropriate what you propose to cover them with.

Window frames, timber and especially chipboard and plasterboard need storing under cover with good ventilation. Some things (but not timber) can be covered with polythene but plasterboard is easily damaged and awkward to handle. Store materials where they'll be accessible and safe from pilferage.

**Mixing** Provide a level area adjacent to the sand/ballast storage. This should be large enough to place a mixer or to mix by hand. It may be worth concreting a solid base for this purpose even if it is broken up when the extension is complete.

**Access** When the extension has reached damp-proof course level it pays to give serious consideration to building paths around it. They will be needed eventually: if they are built at this stage they make transportation for the materials around the side easier and safer, they provide a firm base for scaffolding and keep the site cleaner, reducing the amount of mud and dirt that is trampled into the existing home. To save spoiling its appearance the top surface of the path can be added later.

# Building Regulations

Many of the individual Building Regulations are involved in such a large project as a new extension. But although that sounds ominous, in practice a lot of the regulations require a standard of construction which, for a simple extension, is met almost automatically by following normal good building procedures.

The appropriate British Standard Codes of Practice (CoP's) are referred to where necessary in this chapter. It's useful to be familiar with the titles at least of these CoP's, as a professional designer will usually note them on the scale drawings, the BCO will look for their mention (along with relevant British Standard Specifications) as a sign that the finished construction will be deemed-to-satisfy and the builder (you if it's to be a d-i-y job) will need to refer to them.

Two groups of Regulations, those concerning structural fire precautions and those relating to the size and ventilation of rooms, deserve special and early consideration because they can have major implications on the design and type of extension built. In Scotland the regulations on Housing Standards would also be relevant. Although it will be your designer's responsibility to make sure the requirements of these Regulations are met in his drawings, it's helpful at least to understand how they might affect your ideas.

### Habitable rooms

Throughout all the Regulations mention is often made of habitable rooms and the Regulations are frequently more exacting in respect of such rooms. Rooms defined as habitable include living rooms, bedrooms, dining rooms and kitchens capable of being used as a breakfast or dining room.

### Window light

In *England and Wales* there is no requirement for any room to have window light, so provided there is something other than an opening window providing the necessary ventilation – see below – no room be it habitable or not *must* have a window. In practice, windows will invariably be provided.

In *Inner London* habitable rooms and kitchens must have windows opening directly to the open air and the total area of windows should be not less than one-tenth of the floor area. Bathrooms need not have windows if there is other means of proper ventilation to the satisfaction of the District Surveyer (DS).

In *Scotland* a daylighting window is required in kitchens, living rooms and all other habitable rooms. The glass area should be one-tenth of the floor area in a kitchen or living room (the largest apartment); one-fifteenth in any other habitable room.

### Ventilation

In *England and Wales* all habitable rooms, kitchens and sculleries must either have adequate mechanical ventilation, or have ventilation opening to the outside air with a total area of not less than one-twentieth of the floor area. Some part of the openings must be 1·75m or more above the floor. External doors count towards the total area of openings if there are other openings of minimum total area 10,000mm$^2$ which can be opened when the door is shut. This other opening can be a ventilator in the door itself.

Rooms containing a WC need either a ventilation opening to the outside air not less than one-twentieth of the floor area or mechanical ventilation discharging direct to the outside air and giving at least 3 air changes an hour. There are regulations requiring that a lobby or other space is provided between a room containing a WC and kitchen, scullery, habitable room (other than one used solely for sleeping or dressing) or a room used for business purposes.

In *Inner London* habitable rooms and kitchens must have windows with an openable area not less than one-twentieth of the floor area. The top of the openable window must be at least 1·75m above floor level. These rooms must have additional ventilation, normally an air brick at least 2,000mm$^2$ in area or an open fireplace with a flue at least 12,000mm$^2$.

The opening part of a bathroom window must be at least 0·18m$^2$ in area, if there is no other satisfactory means of ventilation. Staircases must also be ventilated.

In *Scotland* habitable rooms and kitchens must have a ventilation opening of one-twentieth the floor area and, if there is no flue, an opening of 6,500 mm$^2$. In addition unless a house is mechanically ventilated it must be designed with cross-ventilation.

In *all parts of the country* special attention must be given to the ventilation requirements when an appliance designed to burn solid-fuel or gas is installed in any room.

### Height of rooms

In *England and Wales* all habitable rooms must have a ceiling height of at least 2·3m, except under beams or in bay windows where the minimum headroom is reduced to 2 metres.

In *Inner London* 2·3m is the minimum for habitable rooms and kitchens.

In *Scotland* 2·3m is the usual height, but in some rooms some parts of the ceiling can be lower. For instance the main living room must be not less than 2·3m in height over nine-tenths of the floor area but can be not less than 2·1, over the remaining one-tenth of the area. There are separate regulations for kitchens, bathrooms and habitable rooms other than the main one. The limits for WC are lower: not less than 2·06m over three-quarters of the area and not less than 1·5m over the remainder. In *all parts of the country* there are special rules for rooms in roofs – see Chapter 10.

### Space outside windows

In *England and Wales* where an opening window provides the necessary ventilation to a room there are restrictions (as above) on its opening into an enclosed court. In addition the Regulations require a *zone of open space* outside the windows of habitable rooms. The zone is defined as a vertical shaft of space open to the sky.

For an extension the zone of open space has two implications: the windows of any habitable room in the extension must have its own unobstructed (though possibly overlapping) zones and it must not obstruct the zones of windows in the existing house so that the Regulations are contravened (or contravened more than they are already). Extensions intended to provide a kitchen, scullery, washroom, WC or bathroom are subject to slightly different Regulations. Such extensions can be built on to a house built before 1966 without regard to existing windows provided that there remains an open area of $9m^2$ adjacent to the house.

In *Inner London* 'open air' is all that is required outside a window – no zone or space is specified.

In *Scotland* 'open air' is all that is required outside windows. Where windows are sited overlooking an enclosed court or unenclosed court a zone of space (based on defined criteria) is required.

### External walls

External walls must comply with certain strict fire precaution regulations. The theory behind the rules is that a fire shall be prevented from spreading from one building to another across the boundary between. So it is the proximity to the boundary that determines the fire resistance required. Boundaries facing the external wall in question are the important ones, boundaries at right angles do not count even if nearer to the wall than the facing one. When the wall faces a street, river or canal the boundary line is taken as the imaginary centre line of that common land. Fire resistance is expressed as the length of time for which fire will be resisted.

In *England and Wales* an external wall which is within 1 metre of the facing boundary must be half-hour fire resistance from both inside and outside. There are restrictions on the sort of material which can be fixed to the outside – with particular reference to the combustibility. There can be no large openings – called unprotected areas. However, no account need be taken of:

- an unprotected area which has an area (or, if more than one, an aggregate area) exceeding 1 sq m (0·9m in Scotland), provided it is at least 4m (3·6m in Scotland) from any other unprotected area in the same side of the building.
- of an unprotected area which has an area not exceeding one-tenth of a square metre, provided that area is not less than 1·5m from any unprotected area in the same side of the building.

A wall 1m or more from a facing boundary need be half-hour fire resistant only from the inside. The outside can be covered with combustible material, though the total area of this and the area of other unprotected openings is still limited.

The maximum unprotected area permitted is the total permitted area in both the external wall of the extension and that of the house. In all cases, the critical distance on which the area depends is the distance between the boundary and the nearer of the two walls.

In *Scotland* the regulations are very similar to those in England and Wales, though the detail is sometimes slightly different.

In *Inner London* party walls and external walls of buildings within 1 metre of each other must be capable of resisting the action of fire for at least four hours (to be two hours each in the case of separate walls); there can be no openings in such walls.

Where adjacent buildings are more than 1 metre apart, normal solid or cavity wall construction will do, but the area of the openings should not exceed half the total area of the wall and there can be no openings in the walls of storeys above the ground floor storey which are closer than 900mm from the centre of a party wall or any facing boundary. If a boundary is substantially at right angles to a wall, openings can be nearer than 900mm but no less than 400mm.

The DS must approve the material and method of fixing any external cladding to a wall. The bye-laws are not specific, but large areas of combustible cladding would not normally be allowed within 900mm of a facing boundary or party wall.

**Unprotected area limits**

| If the least distance between the external wall and the boundary which it faces is [1] | and the length of that wall is not more than | the total unprotected area must not exceed |
|---|---|---|
| less than 1 metre | — | nil |
| 1m or more, but less than 2·5m [3] | 24m | 5·6 square metres |
| 2·5m [3] or more, but less than 6m | 24m | 15 square metres |
| 5m or more [4] | 12m [5] | NO LIMIT |
| 6m or more[2] | 24m[2] | NO LIMIT |

[1] Refer to the Regulations for walls that are not parallel to the boundary.
[2] If these dimensions are exceeded, this Table cannot be used, and complicated calculations are necessary. [3] 2·4m in Scotland.
[4] 4·9m in Scotland. [5] 12·5m in Scotland.

# Working off the ground

Whether your extension will be one or two (or more) storeys high, you will need some equipment for gaining access to the roof and upper walls. For a small ground floor extension with a flat roof you will be able to manage with trestles and boards, but for a taller extension, either a ground floor with pitched roof or two storeys, you'll probably need some scaffolding.

## Trestles

Adjustable steel trestles are available in sizes giving heights from about 500mm closed to 2·4m open: most trestles take up to four boards. Both boards and trestles are widely available for hire at reasonable rates.

## Scaffolding

The sort of scaffolding that's required for the average-sized two-storey house extension, is a relatively simple structure of scaffold tubes, connected together, and sometimes to the building, to give cross-linked support. Working platforms known as decks are created from scaffold boards laid across the supporting tubes. Ladders are used to climb from the ground to the first deck, and to higher decks.

For a brick extension scaffolding is first required when the walls are about 1·3m to 1·5m high. Above this height it's no longer possible for a bricklayer to work comfortably from the ground. The scaffold is set up so that the first deck is about three brick courses below the top of the part-built wall. From this platform the walls can be built up another 1·3m to 1·5m (up to 23 brick courses) and then a second higher deck has to be provided. For an extension built entirely of blocks, the scaffolding is required from about 1·8 metres and then at similar intervals to complete the building work.

The scaffolding tubes are all the same hollow galvanised steel section, but come in different lengths and have different names depending on their position in the scaffold. See Glossary – page 224 – for definitions of tubes, fittings and boards.

### Types of scaffolding

There are three main types of scaffolding which can be used for the construction of an extension, these are:

**Putlog scaffold** A putlog scaffold consists of a single row of standards parallel to the face of the building and set as far away from it as is necessary to accommodate a working platform of four or five boards with the inner edge of the platform as near to the wall as possible.

The standards are connected with a ledger fixed with double couplers and putlogs are fixed to the ledgers with single couplers. The flat end of the putlog tube is normally placed horizontally on the brickwork being built.

Where a putlog is required for a board support and it is opposite an opening in the building, such as a doorway or a window, the inside end of the putlog is supported on an underslung bridle tube between adjacent putlogs.

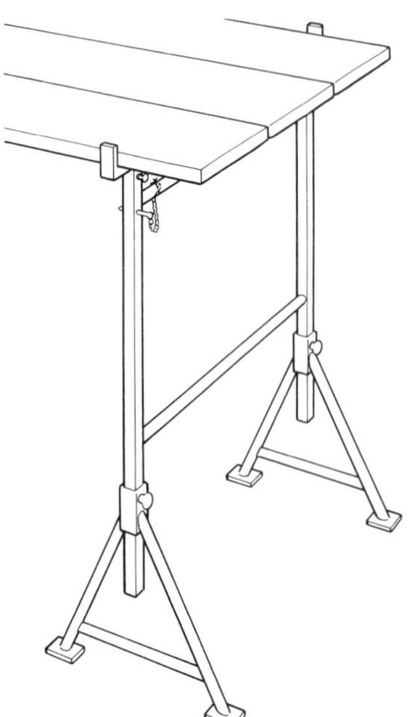

Trestles supporting boards are all you need for a single-storey extension with a flat roof.

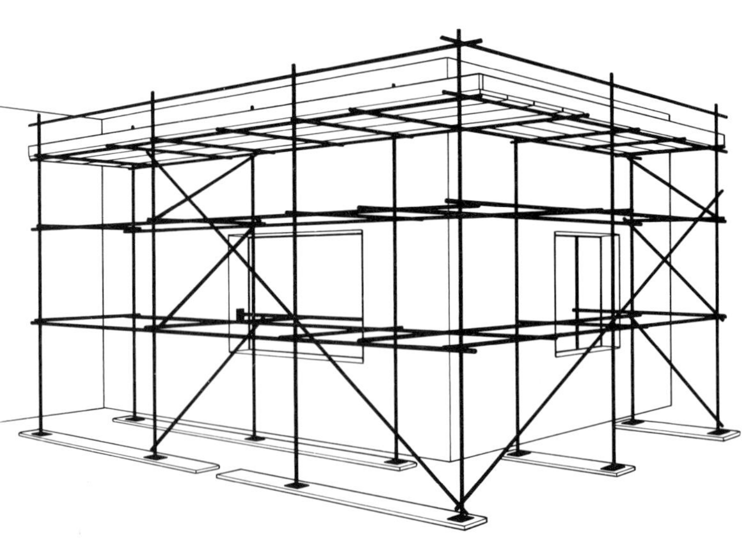

Independent tied scaffolding is self-supporting: it's the type most often used.

**Independent tied scaffold** An independent tied scaffold consists of a double row of standards parallel to the building. The inner row is set back about 300mm from the building face so that there is room for an inside scaffold board to be placed on the transoms projecting beyond the inner standards. The distance between the inside and outside standards should be sufficient to accommodate the required number of boards.

As with a putlog scaffold, the standards are connected with ledgers by means of double couplers and the transoms are fixed to both inside and outside ledgers with single couplers. Independent tied scaffold should have ledger bracing which is generally at alternate pairs of standards.

**System scaffold** There are many types of system scaffolds, all basically similar. They comprise of standard-sized components with pre-set fixing points. All levelling is carried out at the base of the scaffold by means of adjustable base jacks. Once the base has been levelled further lifts are erected simply by slotting more components on to the frame. As all system scaffolds are slightly different a complete set of instructions should be supplied, sufficient to ensure safe erection and use of scaffold.

**Scaffold widths and standard spacings**

| duty | use of scaffold | widths using 250mm boards | max. spacing between standards |
|---|---|---|---|
| inspection and very light duty | painting, inspection, stone cleaning and access | 3 boards | 2·7m |
| light duty | plastering, painting, glazing and pointing | 4 boards | 2·4m |
| general purpose | general building work | 5 boards | 2·1m |
| | window and mullion fixing, rendering, plastering | 4 boards +1 inside | |
| heavy duty | blockwork brickwork | 5 boards | 2·0m |
| | heavy cladding | 4 boards +1 inside | |

## Hiring

Most high street hire shops will be able to hire all the necessary components required to erect a scaffold. But, as scaffold equipment is a bulky item and can take up a lot of storage space, only a few will actually carry it as stock. The alternative is to use one of the major scaffolding companies, who all have hire departments. As usual, it is advisable to get quotes from at least three companies as hire rates vary from company to company. Also make sure that the cost of transport is included.

### How much?

The major scaffold companies will have trained staff to calculate the exact quantities (ie number of standards, ledger, transomes etc) required. You will need to present details of your extension – ideally the plans, otherwise a sketch with dimensions. Mark on the drawings any obstructions, narrow spaces or difficulties of access. Tell the company representative about any special requirements you might have, such as brickguards or standards in two pieces for easier handling.

### Cost

The cost of hiring scaffold components is dependent on how long the equipment is needed. Most companies will hire materials only on a four week basis, so if the scaffold was required for 10 weeks it would have to be hired for a period of 12 weeks. Make sure that the scaffold is returned within the hire period, two days over and a full four week charge may be required. When calculating the length of time the scaffold will be required, allow some extra time for unforeseen delays such as bad weather.

As a guide to the cost of a scaffold companies can quote the cost per square – multiply the total length in metres by the height in metres and divide by 9·3. This will give the number of squares of scaffold required.

For example, if the extension is 2·4m long front and rear, and 9m along the flank and is 5·5m high:

$$5.5 \times 13.8 = 75.9 \div 9.3 = 8.2 \text{ squares}$$

## Who'll build the scaffold

You can choose whether to build your own scaffolding or to employ contractors (who will normally be employees of the same firm who hire out the equipment). Equipment hired on a contractor-build basis is usually slightly cheaper than a straight hire, but then you have to pay labour charges on top.

As the most difficult part of erecting scaffolding is setting out, consider getting a scaffold contractor to base out the scaffolding with further lifts to be built by the hirer.

## DEFINITIONS OF COMPONENTS

**TUBES**

**Standard** – A vertical tube.

**Ledger** – A longitudinal tube fixed to standards and running parallel to the face of the building. It acts as a support for the putlogs and transoms.

**Transom** – A tube spanning across ledgers to form the support for boards.

**Putlog** – A tube with a flat end, to rest on part of the brickwork.

**Brace** – A tube placed diagonally with respect to the vertical or horizontal members of the scaffold and fixed to them to afford stability.

**Bridle** – A horizontal tube fixed across an opening in the building to support the inner end of a putlog.

**Guardrail** – A horizontal tube fixed to the outside standards to prevent people falling from the deck.

**Toeboard** – A scaffold board placed and fixed vertically on the outside edge of the deck to prevent materials falling.

**FITTINGS**

**Double coupler** – A loadbearing fitting used to join tubes together at right angles.

**Single (or putlog coupler)** – A fitting used for fixing putlogs or transoms to ledgers.

**Spigot or joint pin** – An internal fitting to join one tube to another – normally used for standards.

**Sleeve coupler** – An external coupler used to joint one tube to another coaxially – normally used for horizontal tubes.

**Swivel coupler** – A coupler used for joining tube together at an angle other than a right angle.

**Base plate** – A metal plate used for distributing the load from a standard.

**Sole plate** – A timber spreader (normally a length of scaffold board) used to distribute the load from a base plate to the ground.

**Protective tube end cap** – A plastic cap which fits over the end of a tube to enable tube to butt brickwork without causing damage.

**Boards** – A timber plank, nominially 38mm thick, used to create a working platform or deck. Boards are typically supplied in lengths of 3·9m and are 250mm wide.

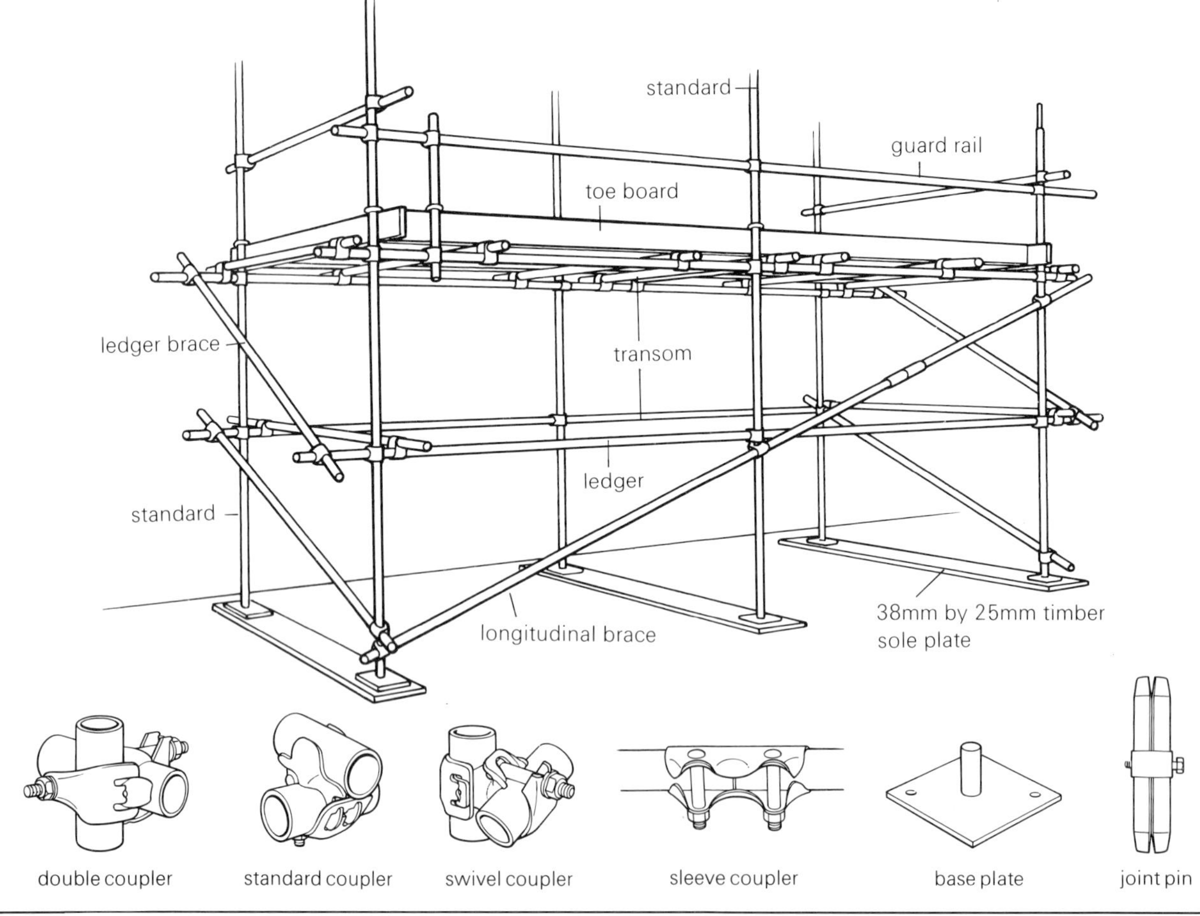

## Ground preparation

It is essential that the ground on which the scaffold is built is adequate in strength, to support not only the weight of the scaffold, but also the loads it will carry.

On concrete (which must be 100mm thick) the scaffold can be built by pitching the standard on base plates only. On any other surface – especially made-up ground (ground that has recently been dug out and back-filled – for the foundations perhaps), turf or sloping ground – timber sole plates beneath the base plates are necessary, to provide a greater area to distribute the load. Before placing each sole plate, the ground beneath must be compacted to ensure that there are no cavities and to provide a firm level surface. Generally on a hard surface, such as asphalt or compacted made-up ground, a 1·8m scaffold board, placed at right angles to the building, is adequate to support a pair of standards.

On softer surfaces such as loose soil or turf it is advisable to use a double thickness of boards (placed one on top of the other). The spacing between each pair of standards varies according to the purpose for which the scaffolding is built (see page 223).

## Safety

Although a scaffold is easier and safer to work from than many other types of access equipment. There are still some hazards:

- the scaffold may collapse, especially if it has been incorrectly erected or if critical tubes are removed
- people can fall from the scaffold
- materials can fall from the scaffold.

In all three instances, should anyone be injured, or damage caused, any claim for compensation could be the responsibility of the person who erected the scaffold.

Great care should be taken in checking the scaffold when it is first erected and at regular intervals – see Checklist. This applies to scaffold built by contractors as well as do-it-yourself scaffolding, as keeping the scaffold in a good and safe order is the responsibility of the person for whom the scaffold was supplied. Special care should be taken when other people have been working on or near the scaffold – a window fixer for instance may have removed tubes or ties to get better access to his work and failed to replace them.

To prevent materials from falling from the scaffold additional equipment can be hired such as brick-guards, when attached to the guard-rail these provide a mesh screen down to the toe board. They're often worth having if there will be frequent passers by.

In some cases it may be necessary to obtain a pavement licence and the scaffold should comply with the local authority requirements for lighting and hoardings.

In extreme cases, such as when the scaffold is erected adjacent to a busy pavement, or where the public may be at risk, it may be advisable to take out some extra public liability insurance.

Children pose a special problem. Many have been injured, either through falling or by causing the scaffold to collapse after climbing up scaffolding. They will shin up standards or a ladder left at ground level. It is essential to remove and secure all ground level ladders (preferably out of sight) whenever scaffolds are left unattended. This is also a sensible precaution from the point of stopping burglars who might otherwise gain easy access via the scaffold.

It is easy to slip on wet boards or wet ladder rungs, so don't work on a scaffold in the rain or very soon after rain. Wear suitable stout shoes or boots with soles that do not readily slip.

### SAFETY CHECKLIST

Whether the scaffold is contractor-built or self-built or a mixture of both, there are some checks to be made when the scaffold is first based out, at subsequent lifts and whenever the scaffold is used. A good contractor will make these checks himself, but you should double check that:

- ☑ the ground is well compacted
- ☑ sole plates and base plates are used
- ☑ the spacing between pairs of standards is not too great – see Table
- ☑ there is sufficient bracing – check both ledger and face bracing
- ☑ the transoms supporting the boards are spread not more than 1·5m apart
- ☑ adequate ties are fixed
- ☑ toe boards and guardrails are fixed to all positions where a person or materials could fall 1·8m or more
- ☑ that ladders are in place and firmly fixed – by wire lashing at the top
- ☑ all couplings are secure and that the scaffolding is not at all shaky.

# Erecting scaffolding

Independent tied scaffold is the sort most commonly used and because it is independent and carefully braced and put together with fittings that require a spanner to undo, it's generally recognised as the 'safest' sort of scaffold, least open to abuse. For this reason it's probably the best choice for a do-it-yourselfer and the one covered in the Guide.

Before you start collect together the appropriate tools and someone to help you with the lifting.

**Tools for scaffolding**

- a $\frac{7}{16}$th Whitworth spanner or a special swingover spanner, which can be hired with the scaffolding

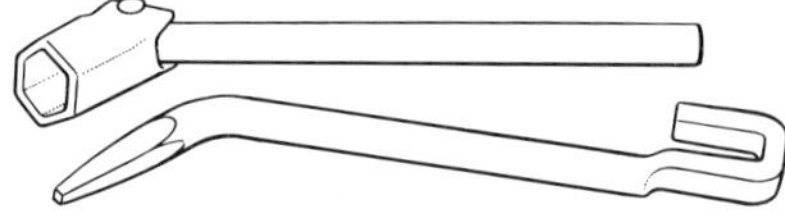

- a 250mm to 300mm spirit level
- a steel tape.

## Step-by-step

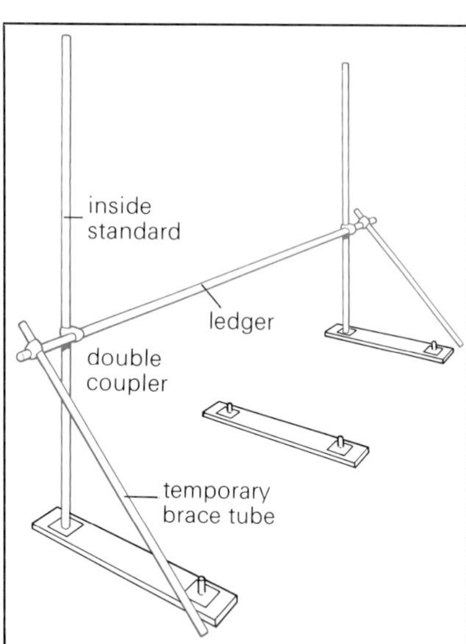


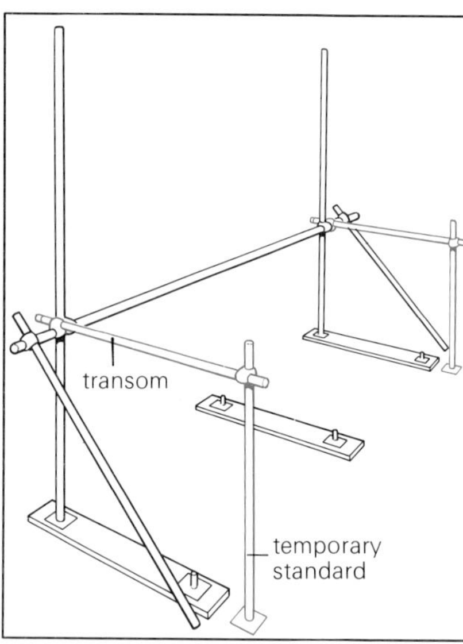


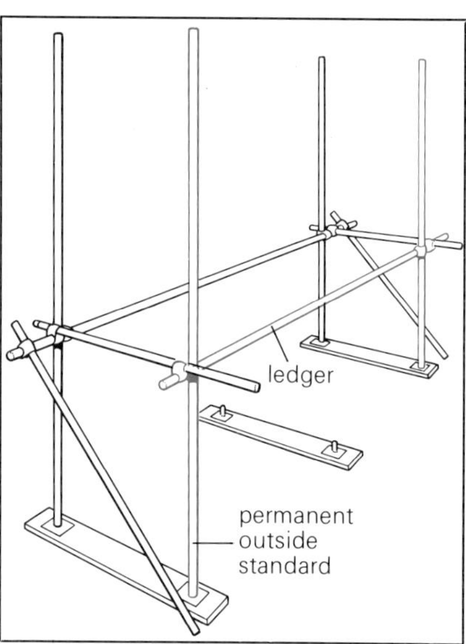


**Step 1** After preparing the ground, and setting out sole plates if necessary. Lay out the base plates and position the inside *standards* on to base plates leaving a gap between the brickwork and the bottom of the standards of 300mm. Connect double couplers to the standards at approximately three courses below the top of the brickwork, making sure that the cup on the front of the double coupler is to the bottom with the bolt to the top. With the standards leaning against the walls sit a *ledger* into the couplers and tighten. Using a spirit level adjust the ledger until it is horizontal. Place a *temporary brace tube* at either end of the ledger, at right angles to the building so that one end is on the ledger and the other wedged into the ground. Again with the use of a spirit level, one person at each end should pull the top of the standards away from the brickwork until they are vertical. Use single couplers to fix temporary brace tubes to the ledger to hold the standards plumb.

**Step 2** Cap a *transom* with a protective cap and fix to ledger, close to the standard, with a single coupler making sure that the cap is butting the brickwork. Support the other end of transom by means of a *temporary standard* connected with a single coupler and rested on the ground – with temporary packing to stop it sinking in. Level the transom before fixing. Repeat at the other end of the ledger.

**Step 3** Undersling an outside *ledger* between the transoms leaving a distance of 920mm between the inside and outside ledgers. Fix the *permanent outside standards* to the outside ledger with double couplers and plumb. Remove temporary standards.

**Step 4** *Ledger brace* the scaffold by fixing a tube from the inside ledger, with a double coupler, to the base of the outside standard with a swivel coupler. Ledger bracing should be fixed at alternate pairs of

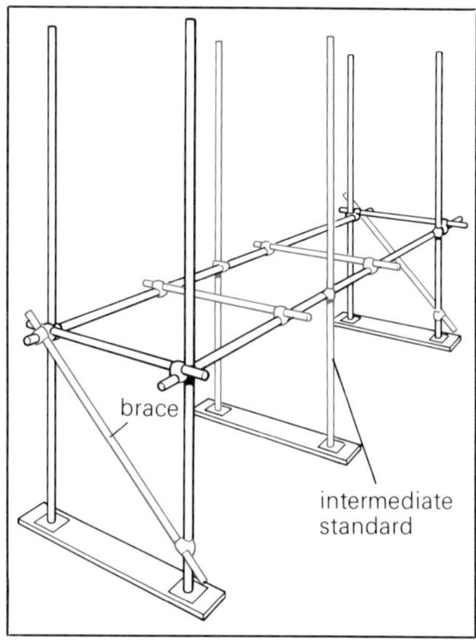

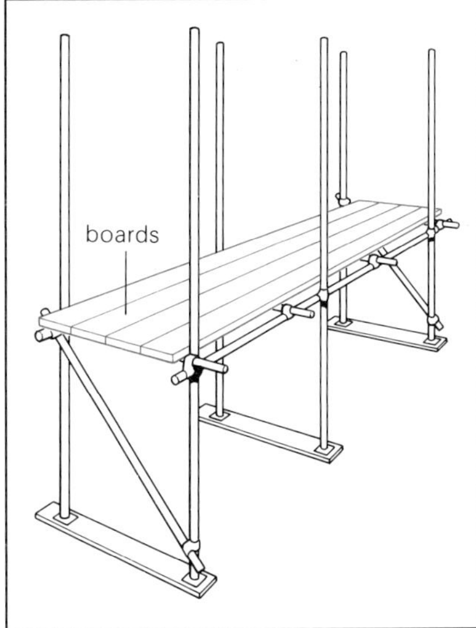


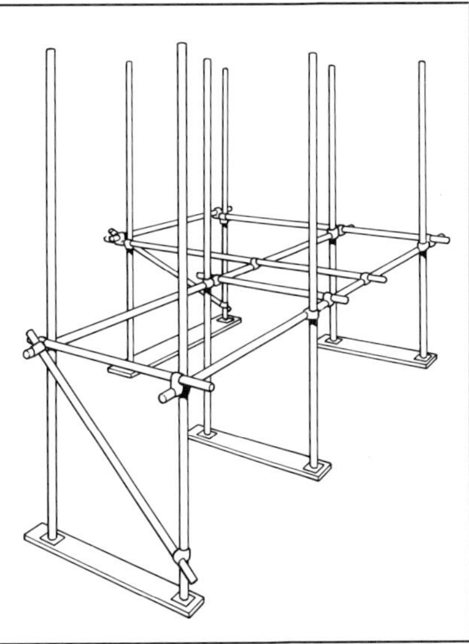

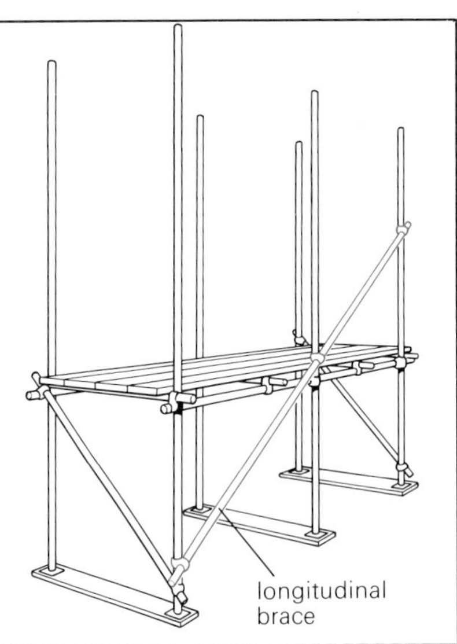


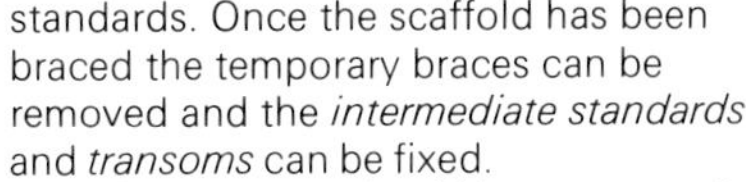

standards. Once the scaffold has been braced the temporary braces can be removed and the *intermediate standards* and *transoms* can be fixed.

**Step 5** Transoms should be connected to the ledgers with a single coupler. The transom at every brace (in practice every fourth one) should extend inwards and butt the brickwork and be capped with a plastic cap. The spacing of the transoms to support the boards varies according to the thickness and length used. When using boards 3·9m long there should be four transoms to each boards. You put up three transoms, then add the boards and fix the fourth transom to suit. As a general rule when using 38mm thick boards the maximum span between transoms should be no greater than 1·5m. To prevent tipping no board should overhang its end support by more than four times its thickness.

**Step 6** To return a scaffold at a corner run the inside and outside ledgers approximately 1·5m past the corner of the brickwork and support with temporary standards. Likewise run the ledgers from the return scaffold so that they sit on top of supported ledgers and fix with single couplers, again measuring 920mm between ledgers. Connect an outside standard and remove temporary standards.

**Step 7** To prevent movement along the face of the building longitudinal (or face) bracing should be fixed at an angle of 45° to the horizontal. Bracing connection should be made either to extended transoms by double couplers or to the outside of the standard with swivel couplers.

**Step 8** To erect the second and further lifts

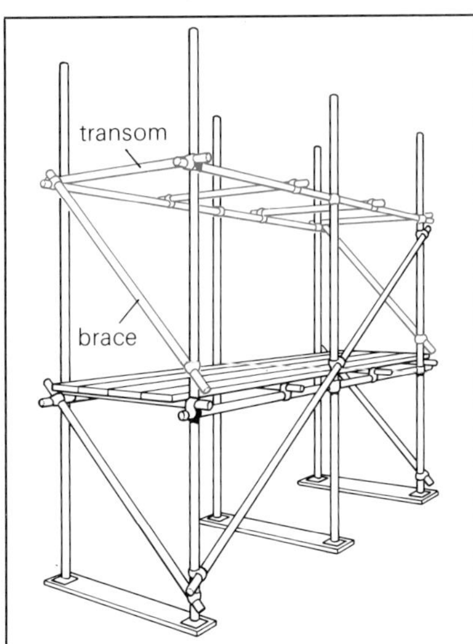


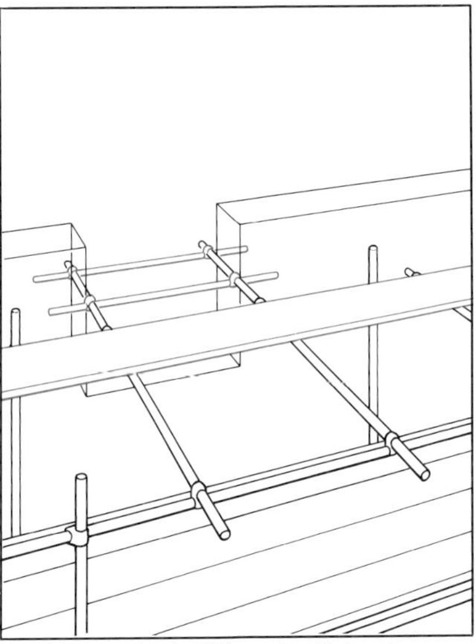

attach *ledgers* to the inside and outside standards and hold vertical with ledger bracing at the alternate pairs of standards – those already braced at the lower level. Place *transoms* across the ledgers and fix to the inside ledger, butting brickwork as on base lift. Before fixing a transom to the outside ledger plumb the outside standards. When the lift has been fully erected the scaffold boards may be lifted. Fit toeboards and guardrails.

**Step 9** Every scaffold should be securely tied into the building at intervals of approximately 3·7m vertically and 6·1m horizontally. It is tied into tubes set across window openings.

### Taking it down

To take the scaffolding down reverse the erection procedure until the base lift is all that remains standing. Strike out intermediate standards and transoms, leaving the nearest transom to the standards at each end of the ledgers. Remove the braces, pull the inside standards away from the wall at the bottom so that their tops lean against the building. Loosen the single coupler connecting the transom to the outside ledger and lean the outside standard against the building. Remove the transoms and ledgers and lower the standards to the ground.

### Extending tubes

To increase the length of the scaffold, ledgers can be joined together using sleeve couplers. Stagger the joints by using ledgers of different lengths so that the weak links are dispersed. Standards can be extended with joint pins between two tubes. Although it's generally better to use the longest tube possible, a do-it-yourselfer would find it easier to erect shorter standards. For a typical two storey extension about 5·5m high you might use standards made up from two 2·75m tubes and a 4·25m and 1·2m tube, staggering these in alternate pairs.

# Foundations

The essential requirement of any foundation, for whatever purpose, is that it should provide sufficient bearing capacity to support the self-weight of the structure (the dead load) together with any additional weight from the contents, snow, etc (the live load), without the risk of settlement or other movement.

This means not only extending down to a firm footing with sufficient area to take the lead, but reaching a depth where the ground will not be subject to shrinkage and swelling as its moisture varies or to frost heave in winter.

The onus is on the builder to ensure that the bearing capacity is sufficient to satisfy a Building Control Officer In theory this could mean having soil tests made, but for a home extension, garage or other single-storey domestic structure, this is rarely necessary. Normally the Building Control Office will have established guidelines based on soil surveys of their own areas, and will be able to advise on foundation depths or types for a given location. These are likely to be of a 'play it safe' nature, especially since the *Anns vs Merton* court decision held Building Control Officers liable for mistakes in judgement. It isn't unusual for the Building Control Officer to insist on a depth of 1 metre even on ground where considerably less would be adequate. Unless you can provide your own evidence, there isn't much you can do but comply.

Frost heave is unlikely to be a problem at depths greater than 500mm or so in Britain, but there are quite large areas of shrinkable clay, especially in southern England, where depths of more than a metre may be required, especially if there are large trees or shrubbery near the building or if any were recently close to the site and have been cut down or rooted out.

Another consideration is the possible presence of soluble sulphates in the soil or in ground water; these attack concrete made with ordinary Portland cement (OPC). Again, the local Building Control Office can usually give guidance. Protection is easily provided by using sulphate-resisting cement instead of OPC. Depending on the concentration of sulphate, it may also be necessary to increase the cement content.

For most purposes a simple strip foundation with a width approximately $1\frac{1}{2}$ to 2 times the thickness of a brick or concrete masonry wall is more than adequate. However, some ground conditions require special treatment such as a reinforced concrete slab or piles and reinforced ground beams.

The d-i-y builder can't tackle these, but strip foundations for an extension (or a simple ground slab for a light structure such as a conservatory or a prefabricated garage) are straightforward and present no real problems.

STRIP FOUNDATIONS

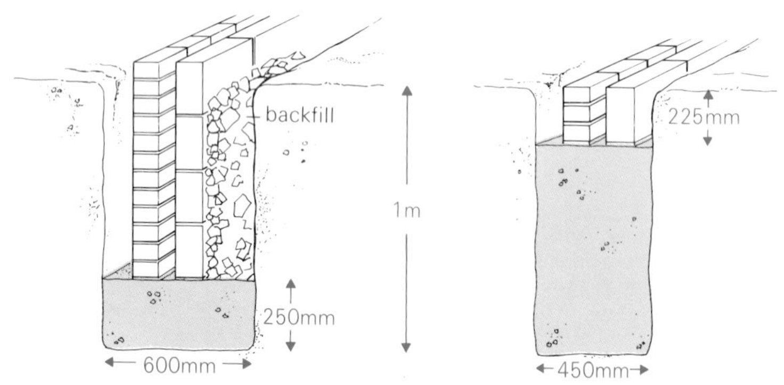


Strip foundations are traditionally built up in bricks and blocks.

Trench-fill foundations have concrete to about 225mm below ground level.

## Strip foundations

The traditional way of building the foundation is to excavate to the required depth, pour a footing of in-situ concrete 250mm to 300mm thick and build up to the damp-proof course (dpc) in brickwork. This is still common among builders, but it has several drawbacks. In order to provide enough space for working within the trench, the excavation needs to be 600mm wide or more, whereas 450 to 500mm is generally adequate for bearing purposes. It may be necessary to shore and brace the sides of the trench to prevent them from collapsing, and pumping may be needed to keep the trench dry. The trench also needs to be back-filled on the inside with sound material thoroughly compacted.

It takes less effort (and may be cheaper) to dig a trench only as wide as is necessary for structural purposes (this will vary depending on the subsoil) and to fill it, with ready-mix concrete to about 225mm (equivalent to three courses of brickwork or one of blockwork) below the finished ground level, leaving only a minimum of masonry to be laid up to dpc level.

When this trench-fill method is used, holes must be left for pipes and cables to enter the house below the top of the trench-fill concrete.

## Planning and preparation

Using the designer's ground plan of

the extension as a starting-point, prepare yourself a *working* plan drawing of the site and foundations to a scale large enough to be handy for fairly accurate readings. A simple pencil-and-ruler outline on squared paper is quite sufficient but make a point of writing in all dimensions – and double check all the measurements on the new plan.

The drawing should indicate not only the lines of the foundation (which will have the same centre lines as the walls) but any other relevant references or information. Wherever appropriate, indicate levels: the easiest way is to take the level of the dpc as zero (or datum) and indicate all others in millimetres plus or minus. Thus finished ground level might be −200, say, the top of the trench-fill −425 and the bottom of the trench −1200. Be sure to indicate locations and levels for any drains or services so that openings can be left in the foundations for them – see page 232.

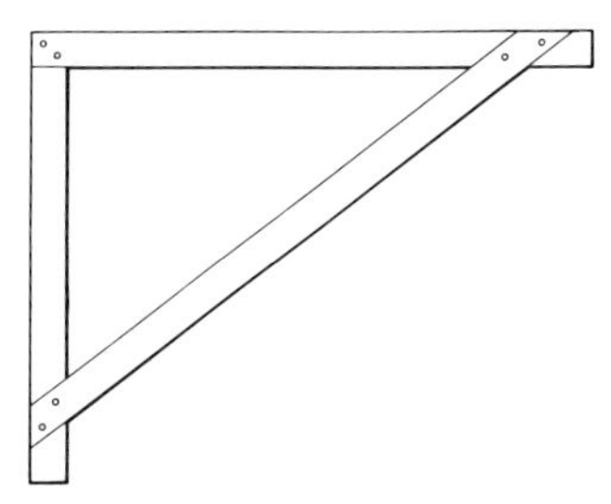

A builder's square.

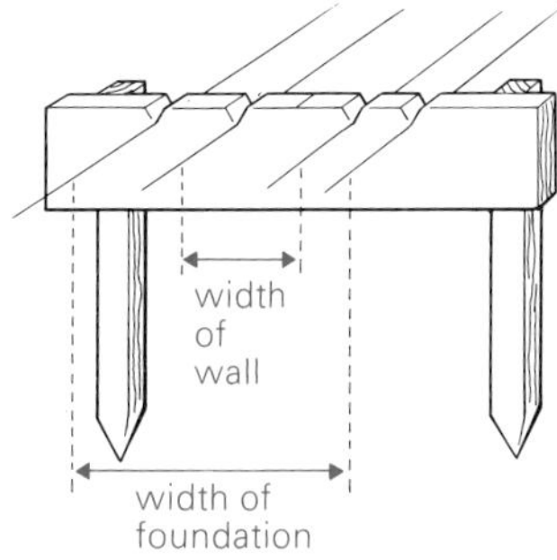


A profile board.

### Setting out

Exactly how and when you set out the work on the ground will depend to some extent on how excavation is to be done. If the site can be stripped down to firm sub-soil in advance, the setting out will be easier, but if you plan to hire an excavator and driver it may be more convenient to have the stripping, levelling and trenching done at the same time. In that case the main level and location pegs will have to be set out in advance, well outside the building lines where they won't be disturbed.

Start by setting out the building lines (the outer faces of the walls) using a builder's tape, stringlines and a home-made builder's square (timber strip fastened together in a 3:4:5 Pythagorean triangle – double-check the 90° angle with a carpenter's square before fastening the strips permanently).

Drive pegs at all corners, with a nail in the tops for pinpoint accuracy, but don't fasten the stringlines to them – extend the stringlines to pegs well outside the working area so that they cross directly over the corner nail: this way you can remove the corner pegs when the work starts and still locate the building lines and corners by the stringlines, which you can take down or set up as required.

Measuring from the building lines, locate the foundation lines next. The easiest way to do this is with 'profiles' – simple frames consisting of a batten nailed to uprights placed astride the building lines, far enough apart to straddle the foundations. Using the stringline set up first as a guide, cut a shallow notch corresponding to the building line in the top of the cross-bar, measure from this to locate the centreline, and from that locate notches for the inner face of the wall and for both sides of the foundation trench. With profiles set up outside all corners you can run stringlines as necessary for all subsequent work including the start of walling.

Next set the levels. Start from the existing dpc of the house: if the dpc in the extension is to be at the same level, work direct from the dpc, otherwise set a prime level to the new dpc level using the existing dpc as a reference.

The easiest way of setting levels over any great distance is with a water-tube level – a length of clear plastic tubing of the kind sold for home brewing, filled with water. Provided there are no bubbles in the tube, the bore is large enough (5mm or more) and the ends are open, the water level at both ends will be the same and accurate over any distance, even around corners. Using stoppers

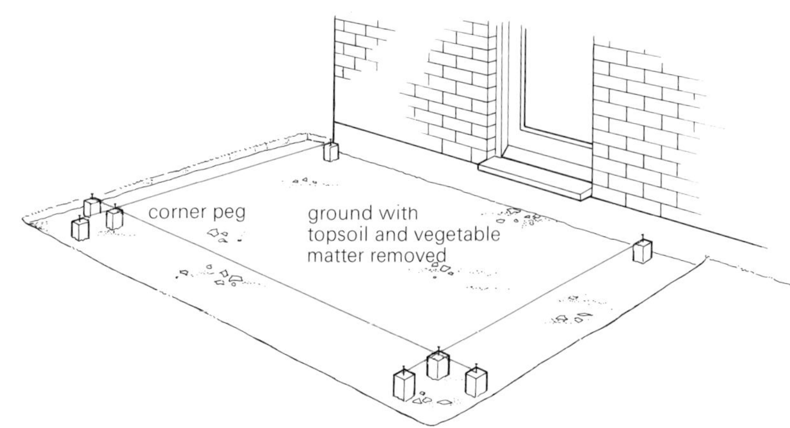


**Setting out** – pegs are placed at all corners with stringlines located to cross these pegs and extend to holding pegs well outside the working areas. Then profile boards are used to set the working lines.

whittled from wood (pieces of dowel tapered in a pencil sharpener will do) avoids the need to keep filling the tube and dye or food colour in the water make it easier to read.

For a level which can be used easily by one man, choose a suitable container and attach a length of clear tube – allow enough tube to be able to work in all directions without disturbing the container. Tape the tube to a metre stick (a softwood batten for instance). Rest the container on a level surface. Stand the stick on datum and mark the level of the water in the tube. Using a ruler add any other marks such as datum +50mm. Without disturbing the container move the stick to where you wish to set datum and adjust until the water in the tube is at the correct level.

Alternatively you can use a straight-edge and spirit level to transfer levels from one peg to another, but there is a risk of cumulative error from inaccuracies or misreading. You might instead borrow a dumpy level and staff.

Set key pegs around the outside of the working area, out of the way, to the datum level and use them to set other levels as required with temporary pegs – for the level of the stripped ground, for instance.

Rather than trying to drive pegs to exact level, it is simpler and just as accurate to use longer pegs, drive them in firmly, mark the transferred levels on the sides with a carpenter's pencil and saw the peg off squarely at the mark: to set a level higher or lower than the one you're working from, mark the peg at the same level and measure up or down before cutting off. (If the difference is so great as to be unnecessarily wasteful of timber – especially if the level to be set is below ground – measure down or up from a straight-edge or taut stringline spanning between a pair of pegs at the same level.)

SETTING LEVELS

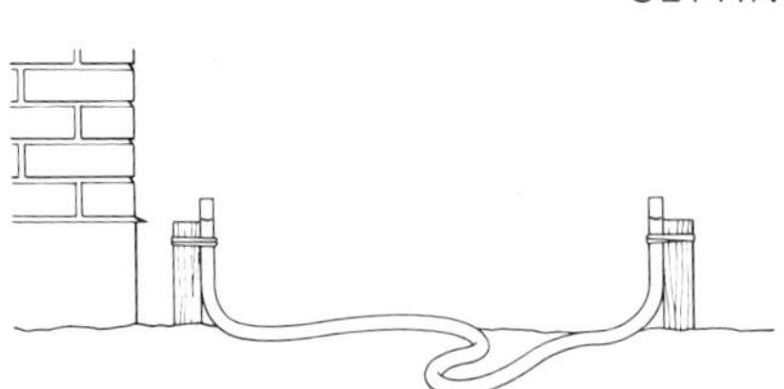

A water-tube level is accurate over any distance.

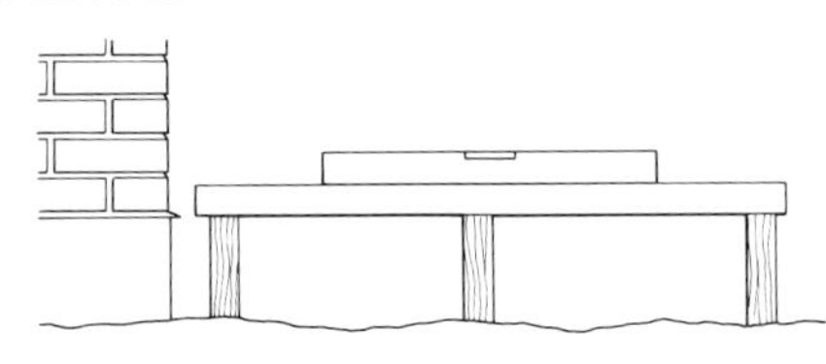

Using a straightedge and a level – there's a danger of cumulative errors.

**Excavating**

If it is possible to get a mechanical excavator on to the site this is by far the quickest and easiest approach, though the excavation will still have to be finished by hand. Make absolutely certain there are no buried drains or services in the way. Digging a trench entirely by hand is hard work and doing it right requires more than simple brawn (to stop the sides caving in for instance), so it is often worth while hiring someone else to do it.

The sides should be straight and vertical, and the bottom solid and reasonably level; all loose soil should be removed. The trench will normally have to be inspected and passed by a Building Control Officer before concreting; he may require changes depending on his assessment of the bearing capacity revealed by the excavation.

**Concreting**

Before placing the concrete, drive steel rods in the trench at intervals to mark the level of the top of the foundation (see Setting out, page 229). If a ready-mix truck can get alongside the job it should be possible to place some or all of the concrete direct from the

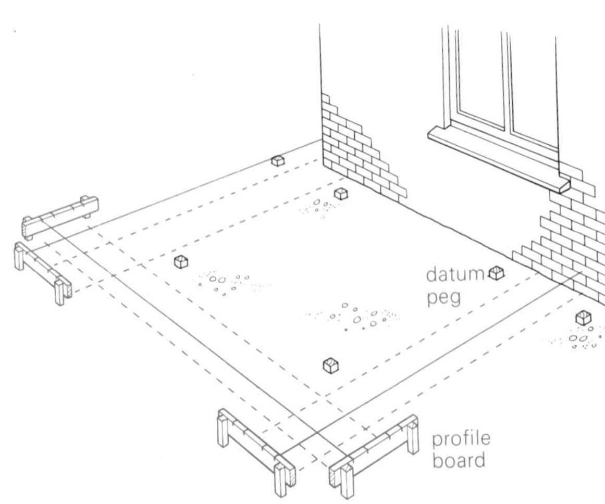



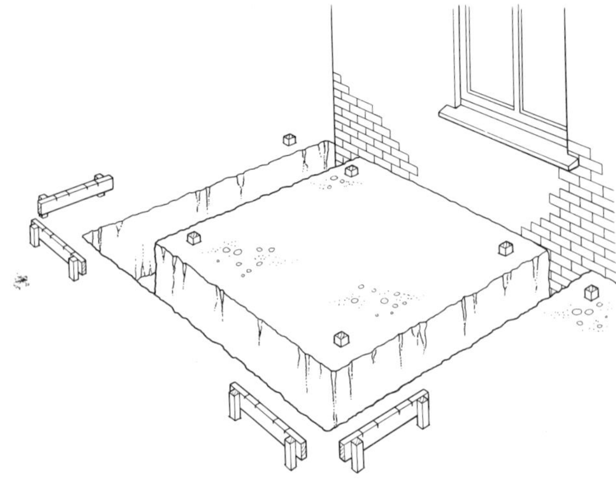

Profile boards are set outside the working area and used to locate the stringlines for the working lines. Key datum pegs are set outside the working area and used to set other levels with temporary pegs (which are later removed).

discharge chute: a chute can reach up to 3 metres from the rear centre of the truck. If the site is very far from vehicle access you could buy from a firm with a truck fitted with a concrete pump.

Otherwise concrete will have to be barrowed to the job and placed by hand (as it will if mixed on the site). To avoid caving in the edge of the trench, use a movable bridge of thick plywood or blockboard to span the trench – choose a board wide enough so that you can turn the barrow and tip straight into the trench – or place the sheet at the edge, empty the barrow on to it and then place the concrete by shovel.

Using a high-workability mix the concrete will be virtually self compacting; just the action of placing it in the trench will drive out most unwanted air and close any pockets, but it is a good idea to work along the bottom corners with the end of a piece of timber to ensure that the concrete is well packed in. Take particular care around service box-cuts and make sure the concrete fills completely under them.

To ensure thorough compactation at the top and obtain a reasonably level surface, use a tamping beam made up from a length of 50 × 150 timber with handles, compacting and striking off the concrete level with the tops of the steel rods (they can be left in place without harmful effect – timber stakes may not). Absolute accuracy isn't essential so long as the top of the foundation is level overall: minor irregularities can be taken up in the bedding mortar for the first few courses of bricks or blocks.

It isn't necessary to make any special provision for curing the concrete though it won't hurt to keep the surface damp or covered with polythene sheet, especially in hot, dry weather. If there is any likelihood of frost, however, protect the concrete from freezing with a layer of loose earth or plastic sheeting. Brick or block walling can be taken up to dpc level after a day or two.

### Aggressive soils

In many parts of Britain, especially in southern England, sulphates which are naturally present in the soil or ground water can attack concrete made with ordinary Portland cement. Harmful substances are also frequently present in 'made-up ground' which has been reclaimed with domestic or industrial waste: sulphates are particularly likely where ash, cinders and clinker have been used as land fill. Your best source of information is your Local Authority. The Building Control Officer may be able to recommend a 'deemed-to-satisfy' mix. If not, information and practical advice can be obtained from the Cement and Concrete Association (see page 314).

## BOXING OUT

If drains or other services will pass through the foundation, openings should be formed by 'boxing out'. Wedge a simple open-ended wooden box, a block of expanded styrene foam or any other suitable former across the trench where the opening is required before concreting. The former should be big enough to allow for some variation in the final position of the service pipe or duct. If the opening is close to the top of the foundation, the concrete can be dug out when it is stiff enough to hold its shape.

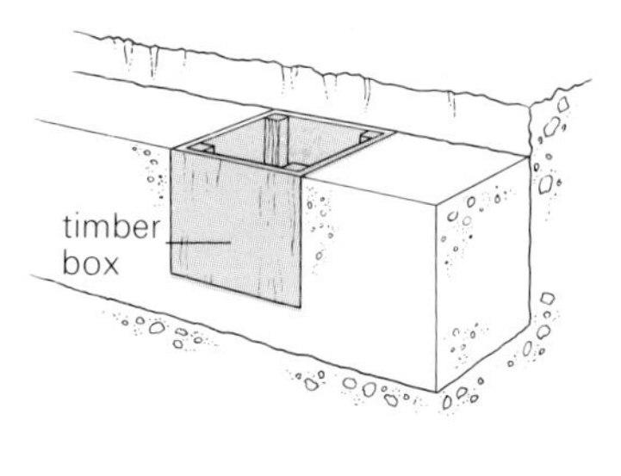


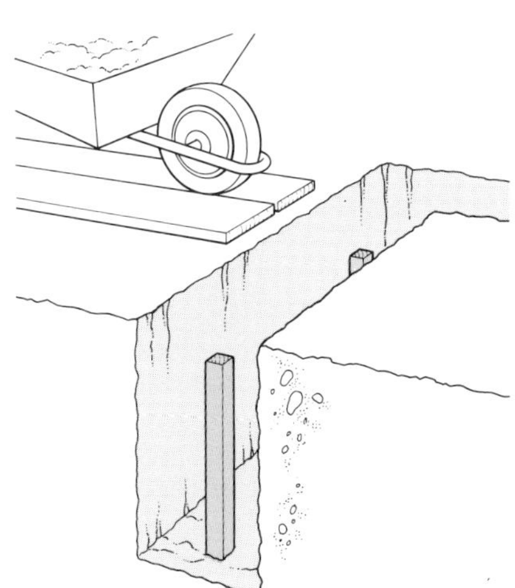

Use a board to protect the trench edges.

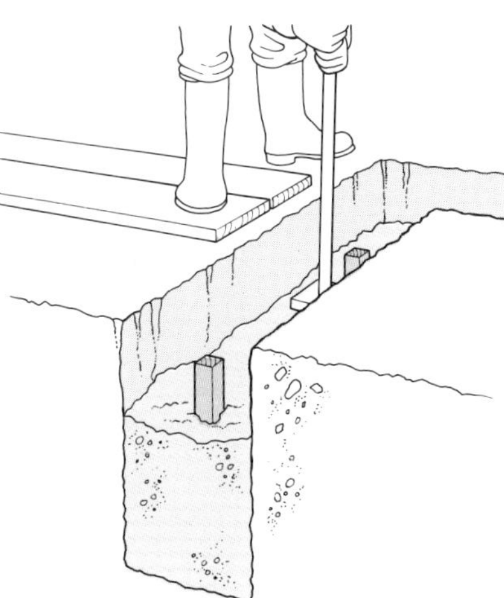

A high-workability mix needs compacting at the corners.

Use a tamping beam to level the top.

# Drains

Many ground floor extensions have to be constructed above or around existing drains and the extension itself may need new or extra drains. So, in the early stages of planning, it's important to establish where the existing drains run – see page 62. Check also for other buried services – electricity, gas and so on. You won't normally be allowed to build over a public sewer.

## Building over drains

If an existing drain runs under the site of the proposed extension or the run-in for a garage it need not be moved provided that it is protected so that it cannot be damaged by the additional loads which are likely to be placed over it.

How this is done depends on the type of pipe and how deeply it is buried. Stoneware pipes are more vulnerable than cast-iron ones and if a stoneware pipe is not very deep or is in poor condition it may be better to replace it. It may have to be surrounded by 150mm of concrete.

Inspection chambers and gully trap drains within the area to be built over, can be left, but must be fitted with an airtight cover bolted and screwed down so that it can be removed if necessary. It is possible to get a recessed cover for an inspection chamber which allows you to fit a permanent floor covering on the floor without covering over the inspection chamber – though if you do this the edges of the cover are usually visible. However a Building Control Officer usually requires that an inspection chamber inside a building is closed up permanently and replaced by a new one outside the building.

BUILDING OVER DRAINS

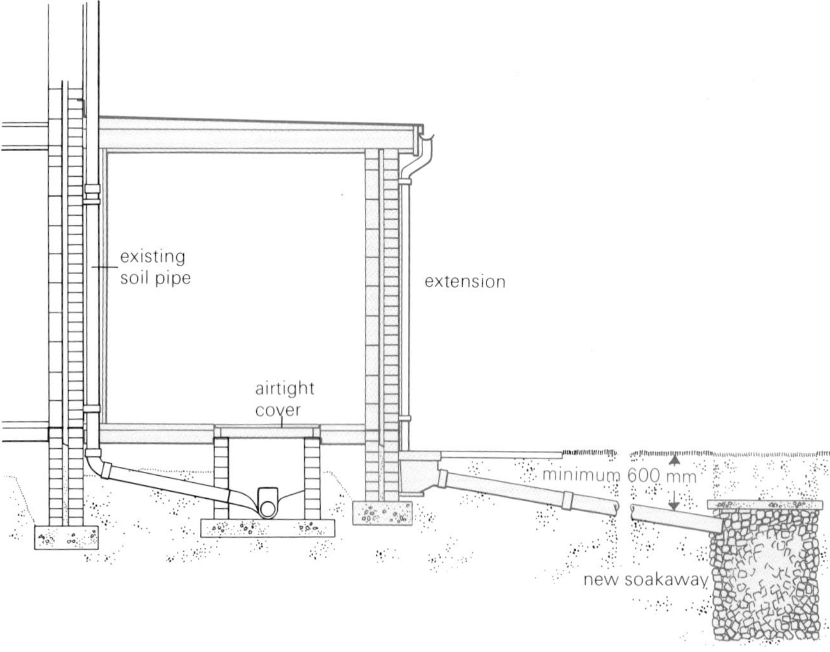


Where an existing drain runs under the site of an extension it need not usually be moved, but any inspection chamber or gully must usually be closed up and replaced.

### Land drains

Mapping the path of rain-water and surface-water drains leading to a soakaway or open drain isn't usually very easy, so such drains may not be discovered until digging commences. If the excavations do disturb existing land drains then it is necessary to replace them beyond the area of the extension.

## New drains

The way to go about laying drains and the material to choose for the pipeline depends partly on the type of subsoil and also on the attitude of the local BCO who must approve the plans. As well as inspecting the completed works, the BCO will probably also want to see the trench before the drain is laid, and to inspect the drain before it is covered up. He will almost certainly test the drain to see that it is watertight. It's the builder's responsibility to advise the BCO at the appropriate times.

## The layout

The drainage work involved with an extension generally does not involve laying a whole new system. Usually all that is entailed is a new branch drain, from say a new WC, or the moving, and perhaps extension, of an existing part of the drain.

The broad design details (points of connection, size, slope and so on) of the new drainage system should be included on the main plans for the extension – if you have employed a professional designer he should have given specifications. The final layout is then usually worked out by the person who'll lay the drain with the help of manufacturer's catalogues, which give details of the components available.

The design of a drainage system isn't simple – the size and the gradient of the pipe need careful consideration to ensure adequate self-cleansing flow

EXTENDING A SYSTEM

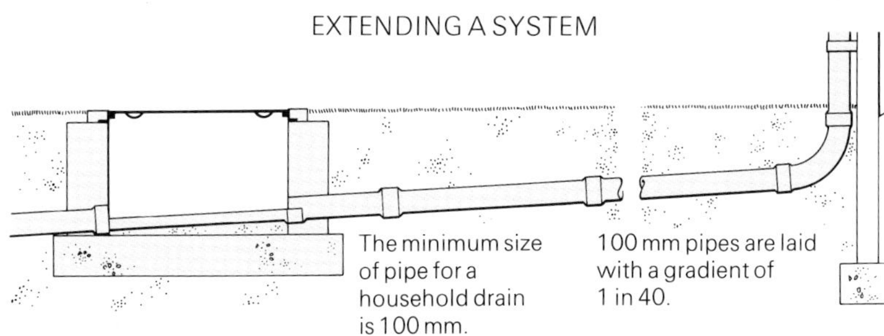
The minimum size of pipe for a household drain is 100 mm.
100 mm pipes are laid with a gradient of 1 in 40.

A new branch pipe can usually be joined at an existing inspection chamber.

without developing suction that could draw the water out of the traps. Generally the first thing to decide is where the new drain will connect to the existing system. It's usually easiest to make the connection at an existing inspection chamber. This is then the lowest level for the new branch (measured from the bottom of the pipe). The difference between this level and the level of the drain at the house end establishes the gradient of the new branch. Ideally drains should be laid no closer to the surface than about 600mm, but where the drain is connected to a house waste-pipe it is often closer to the surface.

The minimum size of pipe for a household drain is 100mm – these need to be laid with a gradient of 1 in 40 (though they will usually work adequately at shallower gradients – to a minimum of about 1 in 80). For larger loads (or shallower gradients) 150mm diameter pipes are used – these are best with a gradient of 1 in 60.

**A new inspection chamber**

The new branch may need its own inspection chamber or a new chamber may be needed where the new branch meets the existing drain. The features of a chamber are outlined on the drawing. In most cases using a pre-cast concrete chamber is the easiest way – there are also pre-cast bases which are useful if your junctions can be matched to the pre-cast layout. Some local authorities won't approve the use of pre-cast concrete chambers and require you to use engineering bricks, which are more expensive.

AN INSPECTION CHAMBER

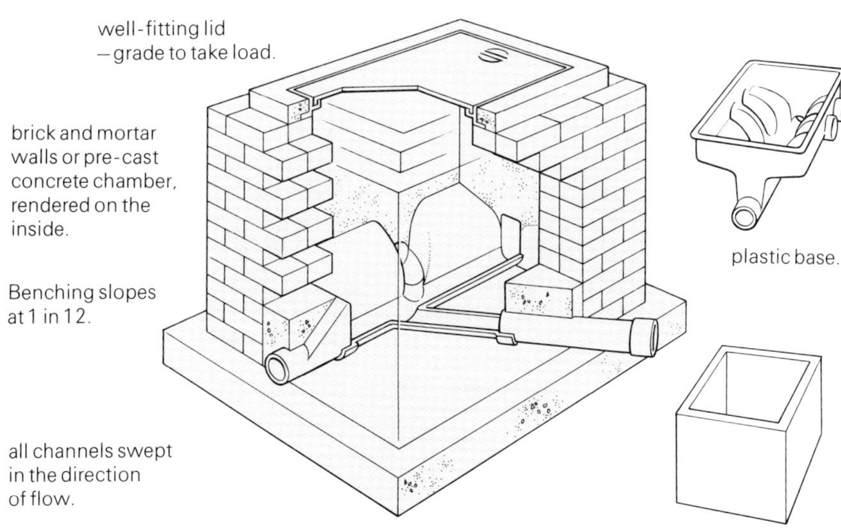
well-fitting lid
– grade to take load.
brick and mortar walls or pre-cast concrete chamber, rendered on the inside.
Benching slopes at 1 in 12.
all channels swept in the direction of flow.
plastic base.
pre-cast concrete chamber.

An inspection chamber in engineering brick.

## DRAIN MATERIALS

The main materials used for house drains are clay, pitch fibre and pvc. Unless the builder's used to cutting clay pipes or the layout can be planned so that no cutting is needed – pitch fibre or pvc pipes are the best choice. They can easily be cut and special fittings are available to join these to other materials where necessary.

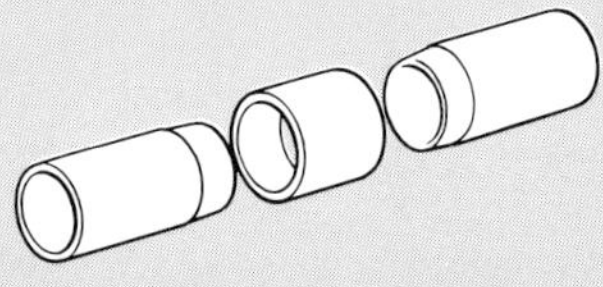

**Pitch fibre** Waste paper and other fibres soaked in pitch are used to make these pipes. The joints are usually formed with a plastic sleeve containing sealing rings – called snap rings – which snap into place as the sleeve is pushed into place.

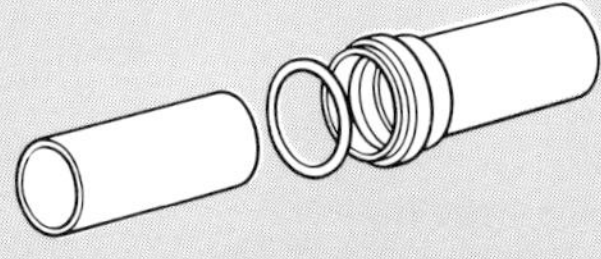

**PVC** Like plastic waste pipes, pvc drain pipes are joined either by sockets or sleeves containing sealing rings or by solvent welding. As well as pipe sections, there is a wide range of drainage fittings so that a complete system can easily be constructed in pvc – gullies and rodding points are particularly useful; inspection chambers are also available.

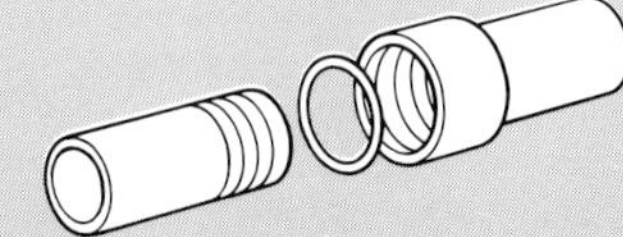

**Clay** Considerably heavier than the other materials, clay pipes are better for unstable ground and can be laid directly on the surface of the trench if the subsoil is suitable (clay and chalk soils probably wouldn't be). They're useful for drain runs close to load-bearing foundations where the drain has to be encased in concrete.

# Laying a PVC drain

## Step-by-step

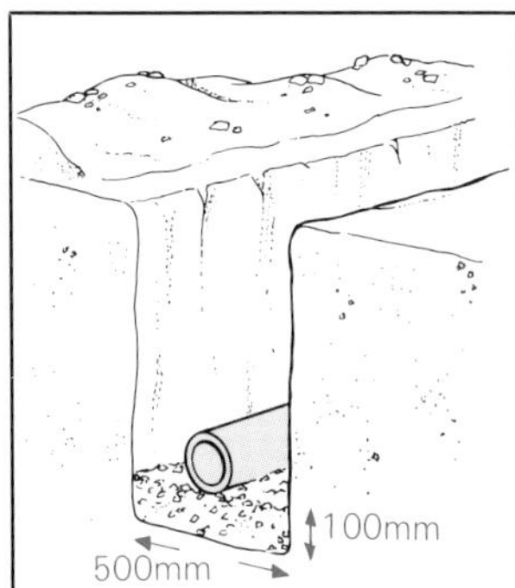


**Step 1** Dig the trench straight and wide enough to work in but not too wide – 500mm is adequate for a 100mm pipe. Start digging at the low point and work back up the trench. Check the levels using one of the methods on page 230. Allow 100mm extra depth for the bed material.

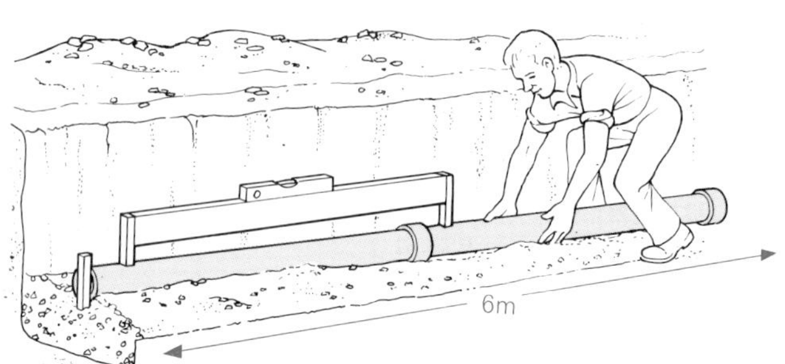

**Step 2** Working in sections up to about 6m long, lay the 100mm layer of fill (gravel about 10mm in diameter is usually recommended) and tamp it down to the right depth. Form a slope slightly shallower than required and fashion a small hollow in gravel where any joints will occur – this ensures that gravel doesn't get trapped in the joint as it's made.

**Step 3** Prepare the first section of pipe by fitting the supplied joint piece to one end and place it on the gravel bed. Stop the open end of this pipe with a piece of rag and use a stake to stop it getting pushed down the trench. Surround the pipe with more gravel and then, using a spirit level and a gauge board cut to the correct fall, lift the pipe until it's sloping correctly.

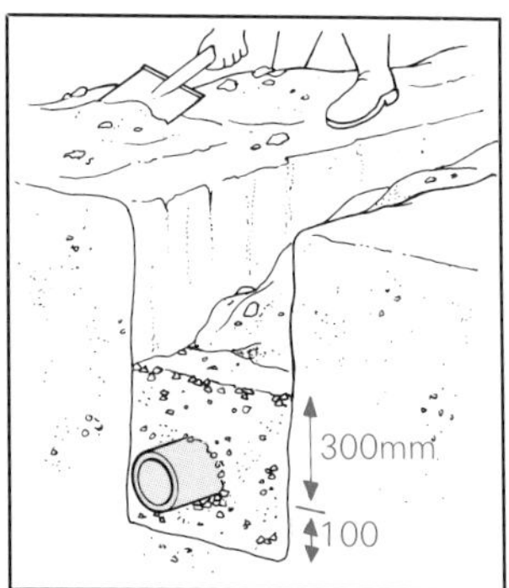


**Step 4** Prepare the next section of pipe with a joint piece and without disturbing the first section connect the two pieces of pipe. Follow the manufacturer's instructions for making the joint – lubrication (such as washing up liquid) can be helpful. Level as before.

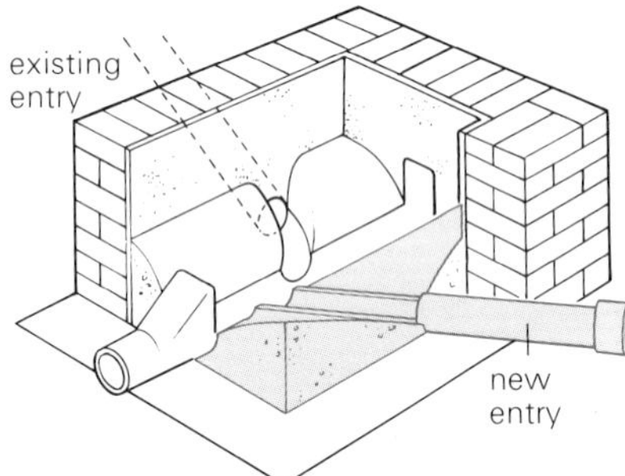


**Step 5** To join up with an existing inspection chamber break a hole in the wall of the chamber at the appropriate level and chop away the benching. Bed a branch channel in 1:1 cement and sand so that its end discharges over the main channel. Pass the last piece of branch pipe back through the hole and connect as the manufacturer instructs – these joints must be flexible to allow differential movement. Remake the benching to match the old. It should be smooth and slope at about 1 in 12.

**Step 6** The join to the house waste system will be a gully which should be supported with backfill or a wide radius bend at the base of the soil stack, which should be bedded in concrete at least 300mm below the ground level. The opening in a wall through which a drain passes must be capped with a lintel and be large enough to allow the clear passage of the drain surrounded by a protective duct, granular fill or expanded plastic.

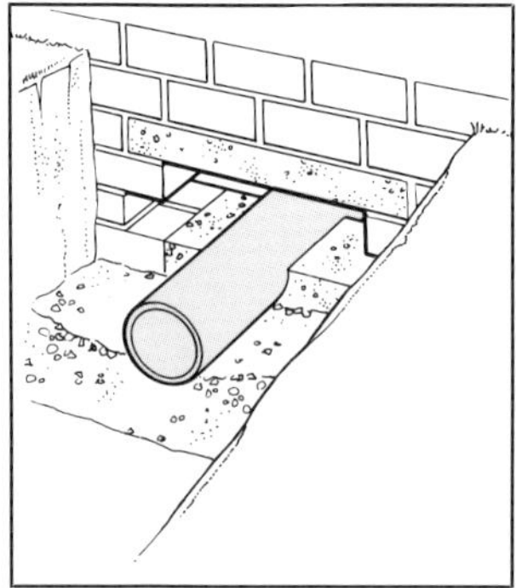

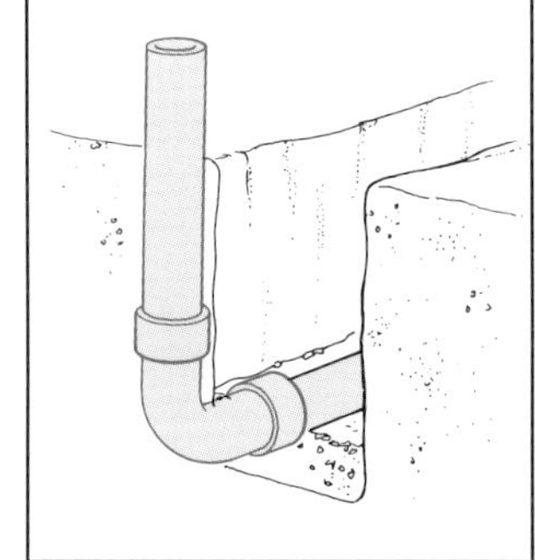

**Step 7** The BCO will test new drains. For your own tests you can hire air testing equipment or carry out a simpler test using water (which has the advantage that you'll be able to see where any leak occurs – it's also more stringent than the air test). Hire or buy drain stoppers and block off the new drain at all outlets. Fit a length of pipe vertically to the end of the existing pipe and fill the closed branch with water. After 30 minutes check the levels – to pass the test the amount of water lost from the drain should not exceed 0·05 litres per metre length of drain.

**Step 8** With the OK to proceed the drain trench can be backfilled. The first 300mm or so should be gravel or selected soil from the excavation. The top layer can be ordinary trench soil. Compact the filling in layers.

# Floors

The ground floor of an extension can be a solid concrete floor or a suspended construction of timber joists with flooring boards, laid on top. Of the two the solid floor is most common and unless there is a great depth below the floor – because the building is on a slope for instance – a concrete floor is usually the cheaper. However, if the ground quality is poor, a timber floor can offer the best solution.

## Laying a solid floor

Laying a concrete ground floor for an extension is very similar to constructing a slab base for a lightweight structure except that provision may have to be made for drains and services in the slab, and a framework is not needed as the extension walls contain the wet concrete. The major difference is that the slab is usually topped with a 'screed' of cement-sand mortar to obtain the final floor level and finish.

The purpose of using a screed is mainly to prevent damage to the surface of the floor during subsequent construction, and to get a better (more nearly level) surface. The screed can also be used to cover pipes and other service conduits.

Another reason for using a screed in commercial building, which doesn't necessarily apply to the d-i-y builder, is that floor finishing is traditionally the province of the plasterer, who comes on the job near the end; a roughly finished slab can be laid by labourers.

### Design

Where ground conditions are suitable, a simple unreinforced slab at least 100mm thick (often 125mm or 150mm is used) is all that is necessary; otherwise a suspended floor, or a reinforced ground slab designed to act as a suspended floor in case of settlement, will be required. The slab concrete should be CP20 or the mix-it-yourself equivalent, as for a base slab (page 38).

A damp-proof membrane (dpm) is required. There are several ways of laying a dpm, one is to install a 250 micron polythene or bitumen-polythene sheet under the slab and linked to the dpc in the walls. Or the dpm can be located on top of the slab below the screed, in sheet form or applied as a liquid (in several coats). A liquid dpm is painted up the walls to a height of about 300mm – so it is not suitable if the walls are to be fair-faced. When the dpm is placed like this it effectively eliminates any bond between the two layers and a thicker screed is required.

A screed laid directly on the slab so that it is partially bonded can be as thin as (but no thinner than) 38mm. The optimum thickness for a screed laid on a dpm is 60mm; a 65mm screed will allow pipes up to 15mm diameter to be buried in the screed.

The screed mix is 1 part cement to 3 parts 'sharp' concreting sand (*not* 'soft' bricklayer's sand).

### Underslab fill

It is usual to provide a 150mm fill of hardcore beneath the concrete. Extra fill may be necessary to bring the ground up to the slab base level.

If the depth is not excessive use hoggin (a mix of gravel and sand), crushed stone or a fairly dry 1:16 mix of cement and all-in aggregate (lean concrete). If deeper fill is required 'rejects' (oversized stones screened out of gravel) are ideal; you can also use builder's rubble such as broken brick – but remove plaster, wood, paper and other rubbish and break up large lumps with a sledgehammer.

The fill should be well-graded and placed in layers of 200mm or so. It should be well hammered down so that large pieces don't 'arch' and create voids. The deeper the fill the more important good compaction is. Finish off with a blinding layer of hoggin, sand or lean concrete to provide a smooth surface for the dpm. The blinding should be sufficient only to fill surface gaps.

### Shrinkage cracks

Narrow cracks may soon appear in the slab, especially if the floor area is large or the length is much greater than the width. This is the result of drying shrinkage in the concrete and so long as the cracks are fine and do not go on widening they can be ignored.

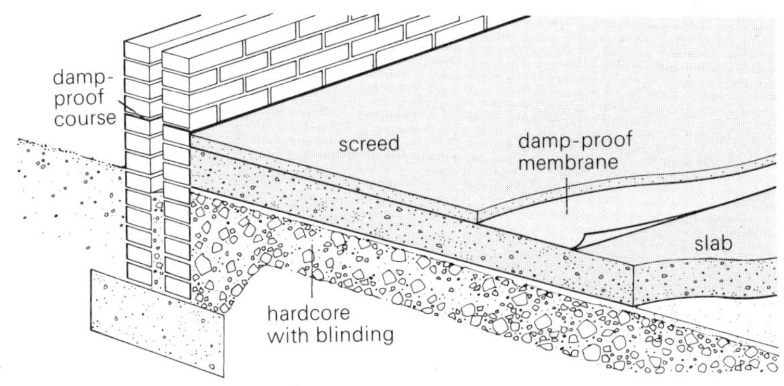


Where ground conditions are good a solid concrete floor is the cheapest construction.

# Laying a solid floor

## Step-by-step

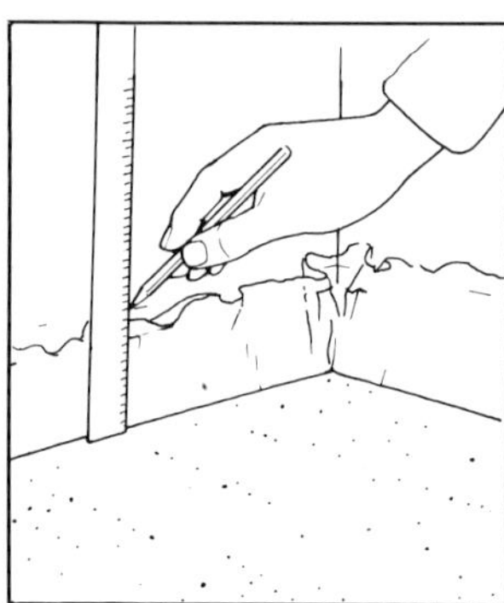

**Step 1** Remove all topsoil and vegetable matter. Drive pegs to floor level minus screed and slab thicknesses. When the walls have been built up to dpc level fill up to the tops of the stakes and remove the stakes. If you are going to use a sheet dpm, form a tray of sheeting – see page 235. Leave material projecting so that it can be folded out and lapped into the wall dpc, to make a continuous membrane. The dpm must be dressed-up around entries for pipes and cables. Care must be taken at corners to ensure that the dpm is tucked well in.

**Step 2** Using the masonry as the formwork, place and compact the concrete.

Place concrete round any projecting pipes first and compact it thoroughly before doing the main area.

**Step 3** After four to eight hours brush the 'as tamped' to finish vigorously with a stiff bristle broom to provide a key. Cure under polythene sheet for at least three days.

**Step 4** Carefully mark the finished level at intervals around the room for reference. Remove any spilled mortar or plaster from the surface of the slab and scrub thoroughly.

**Step 5** Mix the cement-sand mortar for the screed in fairly small batches, using just enough water so that a drop or two, but no more, is squeezed out when you clench a handful.

Dampen the floor and prime it with a cement-water slurry the consistency of double cream. To this you can add a bonding agent such as polyvinyl acetate (pva) or synthetic latex (styrene-butadiene rubber) following the instructions on the tin (pva should not be used in a bathroom or kitchen where the floor is likely to be frequently wet). Use the slurry to prime only as much floor area as you can cover with screed in 10 minutes if styrene-butadiene rubber is used; 20 minutes with pva.

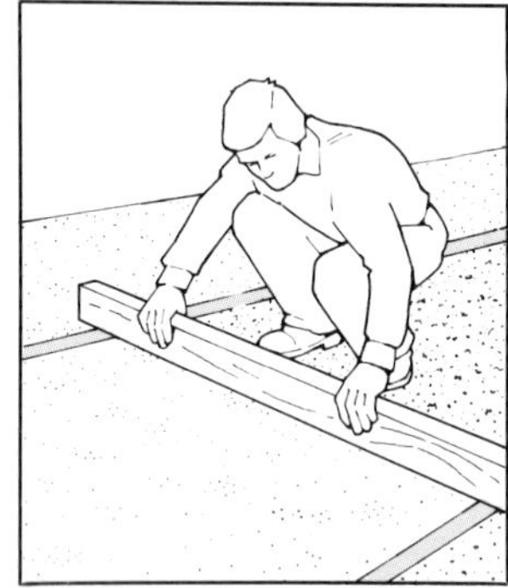

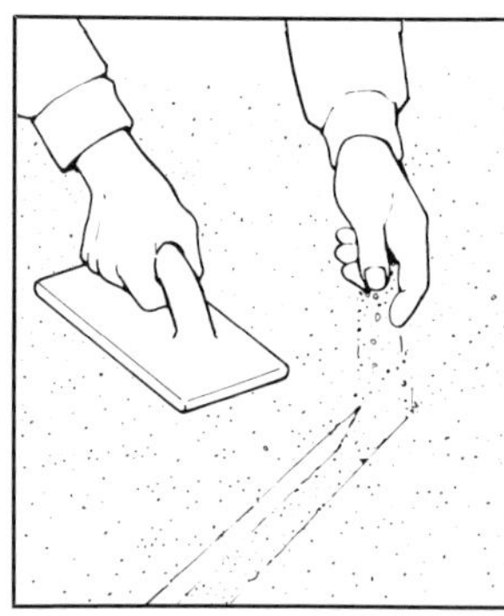

**Laying the screed**

For a do-it-yourselfer best results can be achieved by using 'screeding rails' – strips of timber batten about a metre long. This can be nailed or laid upon a bedding strip of mortar. Prime between the rails with the slurry, spread mortar and compact it level using a piece of timber drawn down the levelling rails. Remove the rails and make good with fresh mix and finish the floor with a wood float as you go.

When the screed has been laid around three sides work your way out of the room down the centre.

Curing under polythene sheet is recommended but if it is not practical dampen the screed at intervals for the first day or two with a fine mist spray. Don't do this if you've used a pva bonding agent. Be careful not to do this too soon or the water will cause pock marks. Dampened sacking can be useful.

Do not walk on wet screed and avoid heavy loads, especially point loads, for two or three weeks: boards can be used to protect the floor.

See page 84 for floor coverings. Some such as quarry tiles are laid in the screed.

## INSULATED FLOORS

The amount of heat lost through a ground-supported slab is relatively small compared with that lost elsewhere in a building. Nevertheless, you can save some energy and avoid cold feet by incorporating insulation during the construction of the new floor.

One way is to lay concrete 100mm thick as for a plain floor slab, over a damp-proof membrane. Then, before screeding, lay sheets of 50mm thick rigid extruded polystyrene foam insulation board (*not* ordinary styrene foam with a 'beady' internal structure). The boards simply 'float' on the slab – there is no need to fix them down to the slab.

An alternative method is to lay hollow clay blocks on the blinded hardcore under the slab concrete. Most heat loss is at the edges of a floor but this can be reduced by turning the blocks at the edge of the floor on their sides. The dpm goes over the concrete slab in the drawing, it could also go under.

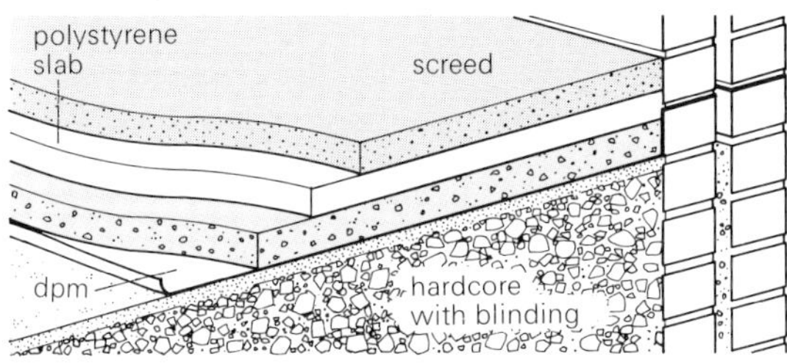


A 'floating' floor of polystyrene slabs as insulation.

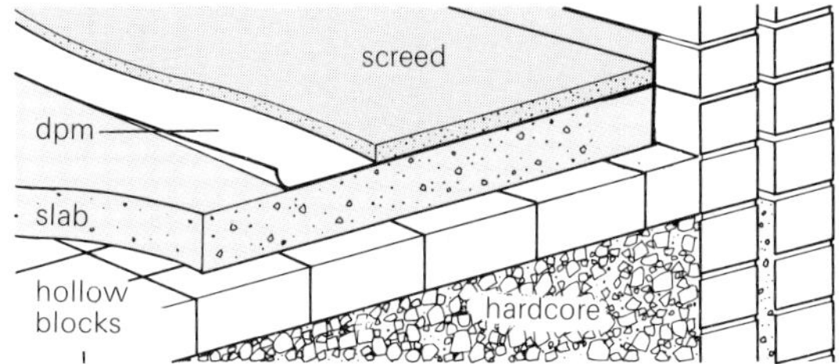


An alternative insulated floor construction using clay blocks.

# Laying a wooden floor

The drawings should contain the following information:

- the depth and width of the floor joists which are determined by the span between supports and the centres of the joists (see Table 1, page 238)
- the treatment of the ground beneath the floor
- the dimensions from the top of the ground cover to the underside of the suspended joists (not less than 100mm in Inner London, 125mm in England and Wales or 150mm in Scotland)
- the ventilation provision and the type and thickness of the floor decking (see Table 2)
- the position of the dpc.

## Ventilation

Under the Building Regulations the ventilation provision for the space under the floor is required to be 'adequate' in England and Wales and in Inner London. In Scotland it must be equal to 1500mm$^2$ of open area per metre run of external wall. (A typical clay air brick has an open area of 1290mm$^2$ for a 225mm by 75mm air brick and 2580mm$^2$ for a 225mm by 150mm air brick). It is important that air bricks are located on opposite sides of the building in order to obtain a flow of air through the whole area of the floor space. If possible install them on all walls, if on two sides only, arrange to fit air bricks close to the corners.

Providing there is adequate ventilation there is no requirement for the timber joists to be preservative-treated. However in view of the small cost of this and the complexity of possible further remedial work it is a worthwhile investment to ensure peace of mind. Two types of treatment are appropriate, copper chrome arsenate (CCA) water-borne preservatives applied by vacuum pressure impregnation, or spirit-based organic solvents which are applied by the double vacuum process. The timber should be purchased pretreated – the choice is most likely to depend upon which preservative treatment the timber merchant offers.

Buying untreated timber and brush treating it is a poor substitute, but brush treatment of any cut ends with a compatible preservative is advisable.

### Oversite concrete

Even with a suspended floor an underfloor layer of concrete is required by the Building Regulations. This concrete ground cover is cast after the foundation walls have been constructed and should finish level with or higher than the adjacent external ground. It is laid on a layer of sand or ash blinding over the subsoil, or if necessary on a fill of hardcore to make up the levels. A weak mix (1 part cement, 12 parts ballast) concrete is laid not less than 100mm thick (150mm in Inner London).

The joists are not installed until the building is watertight since if the floor joists were fitted prior to this stage they would normally be in the way and could be exposed to inclement weather for an unnecessary period of time.

The joist spacing (400mm or 600mm centres) is determined by the thickness of the floor decking (see Table 2).

**TABLE 1: Floor joist spans**

| joist span | general structural grade joists at 400mm centres size in millimetres | | | general structural grade joists at 600mm centres size in millimetres | | |
|---|---|---|---|---|---|---|
| 2·0 metres | 125 × 38 | | 100 × 50 | 150 × 38 | | 125 × 50 |
| 2·2 metres | 125 × 38 | | 125 × 50 | 150 × 38 | | 150 × 50 |
| 2·4 metres | 150 × 38 | 125 × 44 | 125 × 50 | 175 × 38 | 150 × 44 | 150 × 50 |
| 2·6 metres | 150 × 38 | 150 × 44 | 125 × 50 | 175 × 38 | 175 × 44 | 150 × 50 |
| 2·8 metres | 150 × 38 | 150 × 44 | 150 × 50 | 200 × 38 | 175 × 44 | 175 × 50 |
| 3·0 metres | 175 × 38 | 150 × 44 | 150 × 50 | 200 × 38 | 200 × 44 | 175 × 50 |
| 3·2 metres | 175 × 38 | 175 × 44 | 150 × 50 | | 200 × 44 | 200 × 50 |
| 3·4 metres | 200 × 38 | 175 × 44 | 175 × 50 | | | 200 × 50 |
| 3·6 metres | 200 × 38 | 200 × 44 | 175 × 50 | | | |
| 3·8 metres | | 200 × 44 | 200 × 50 | | | |
| 4·0 metres | | 200 × 44 | 200 × 50 | | | |
| 4·2 metres | | | 300 × 50 | | | |

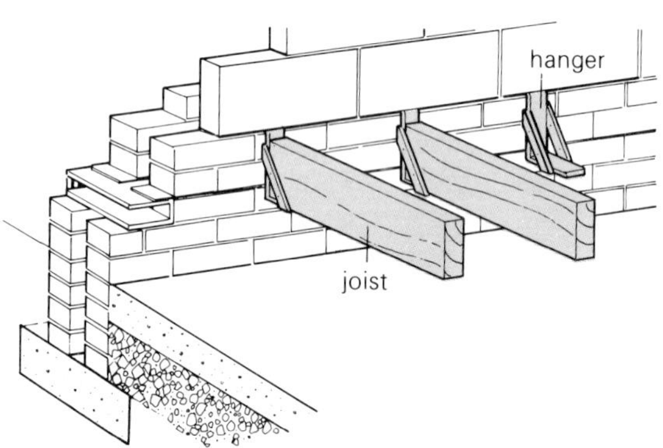


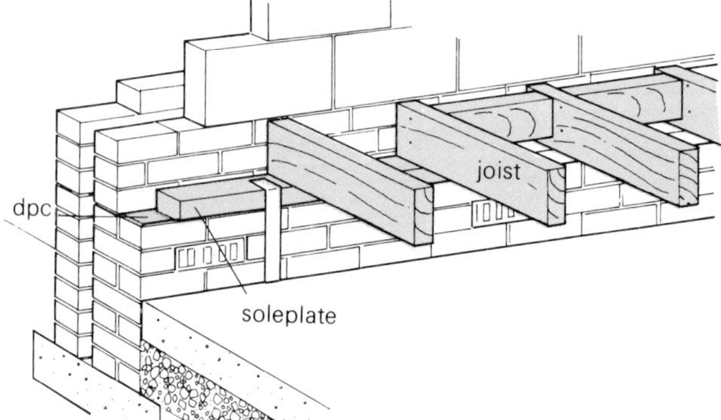


**Brick or block walls** If brick and block walls are to be used the floor joist hangers can be built into the wall at the appropriate height and centres and the wall then completed up to its finished height. The hanger must be fitted tight against the wall – no gap is allowed. The joists are placed in position and adjusted for level by packing with solid timber (preservative-treated). The joists are held in the hangers with 30mm nails through the side of the hanger.

Alternatively perimeter sleeper walls can be built and fitted with a dpc and a soleplate as outlined below.

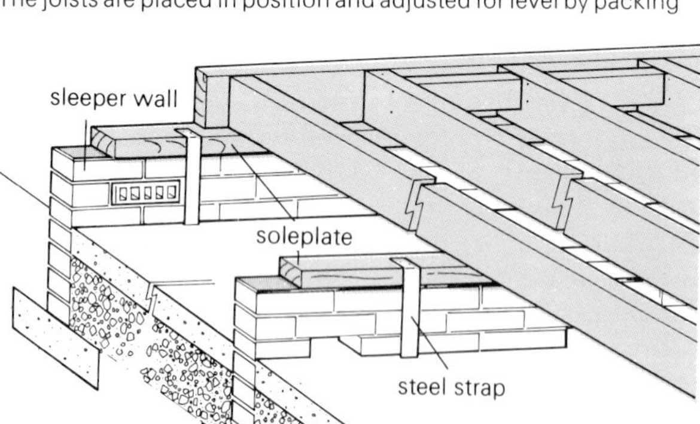


**Timber-framed walls** A soleplate should be fixed down to the foundation wall and any sleeper walls using galvanised steel straps or masonry nails. A dpc of 2,000 gauge (500 micron) polyethylene (or similar) is fixed between the wall and the soleplate. Care must be taken to ensure that the soleplates are level in themselves and with each other. To do this bed the plates on sand and cement mortar up to a maximum of 15mm thickness and check the level by lining through with a joist placed across and a builder's level.

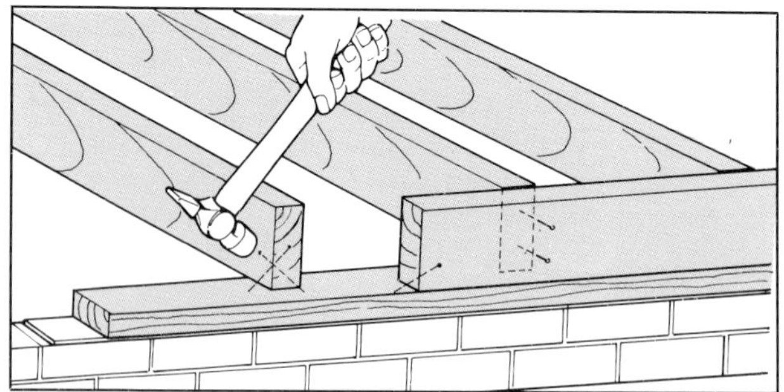

The joists are fixed by nailing diagonally through each side of the joists into the soleplate. A further joist – a header – should be fixed across the ends of the joists at the wall line. It is nailed into the ends of the joists and to the soleplate with nails approximately 100mm long, 8 gauge.

## TABLE 2: Floor decking

| joint spacing | minimum thickness | specification | typical fixing [1] |
|---|---|---|---|
| **Plywood** | | flooring-grade tongued and grooved plywood | fix with 50mm long annular ring nails at 150 centres along board edges and 300mm centres along intermediate joints |
| 400mm | 16mm | | |
| 600mm | 19mm | | |
| **Flooring-grade chipboard** | | flooring-grade chipboard type 2 or 2/3 to BS 5669 (1979) tongued and grooved all edges type 2 used in normal conditions type 2/3 in kitchens and bathrooms | boards should be conditioned by loose laying for 24 hours before fixing. Fix with long annular ring nails, 50mm for 18mm board; 63mm for 22mm board. Nail at 300mm centres along edges and 600mm centres along intermediate joints |
| 400mm | 18mm | | |
| 600mm | 22mm | | |
| **Softwood boards** | | tongued and grooved softwood boarding to BS 1297; normal board width 125mm | fix with lost head nails 40mm long for 16mm board; 50m long for 19mm board. Two nails for each board/ joist intersection. Nails not nearer than 20mm to board edge |
| 400mm | 16mm finished | | |
| 600mm | 19mm finished | | |

[1] many boards are marked to show which face is laid upwards and the direction of laying on the joists

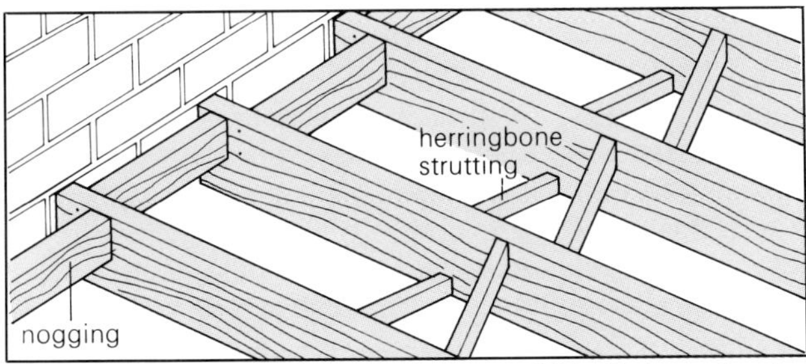


**Step 1** A series of short lengths of joist material (called noggings) is nailed between the joists to support the edges of the floor decking. Stagger these for easier fixing. If the span of the joists is more than 3 metres, similar noggings or herringbone strutting should be fixed at mid-span to stop the joists twisting.

**Step 2** Before the insulation and floor decking is fitted the main shell of the building should be relatively weathertight and the floor void must be cleared of *all* rubbish. Check that the airbricks are clear.

Any services to be laid in the floor space are fitted before laying the decking. It is preferable to avoid these if possible unless the space beneath the floor will be deep enough to give future access, or appropriate sections of the floor decking can be fixed as access panels. If water pipes are installed they should be insulated with pipe lagging

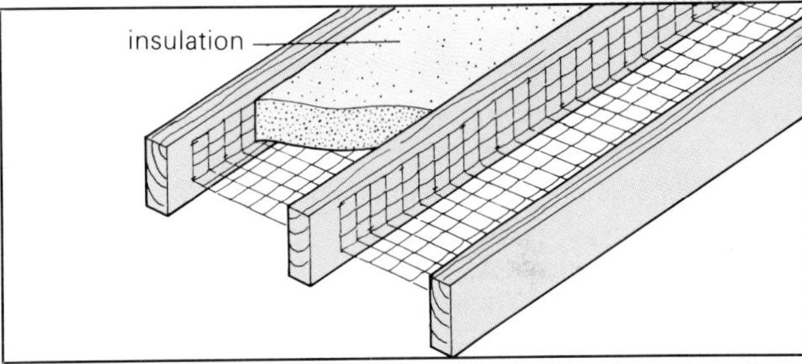


because the underfloor space will be cold. Fix all services where they cannot be perforated by nails when the floor decking is fixed.

While there is at present no mandatory requirement to insulate timber ground floors, the increased comfort and the comparative ease of installation makes it worthwhile. Fix a supporting layer of plastic or galvanised wire mesh in a series of 'U' forms between the joists by stapling or nailing it to the sides of the joist. The bottom of the mesh should be located so that the insulation is not compressed to less than its normal thickness. It is important that in the event of an accident, such as a radiator leak, any water running into the floor can pass through and be dried by the underfloor ventilation, so do not use a material to support the insulation which could contain the water. The insulation is then simply laid taking care not to block the airbricks

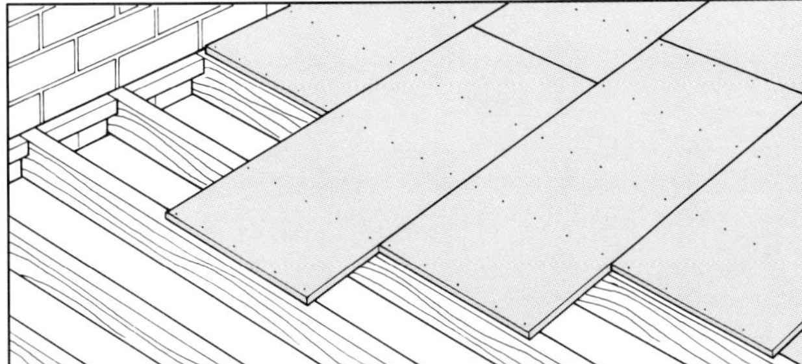

**Step 3** The floor decking can be chipboard or plywood sheathing, tongued and grooved softwood boarding or hardwood tongued and grooved strip flooring (see page 160). The thickness of the boards to be used will already have been decided to determine the joist spacing – Table 2. The edges of boards at the walls and any joints between board with square edges must be supported by joists or noggings of approximately 100mm by 50mm timber fixed by nailing through the joists into the nogging's end. Access panels can be easily

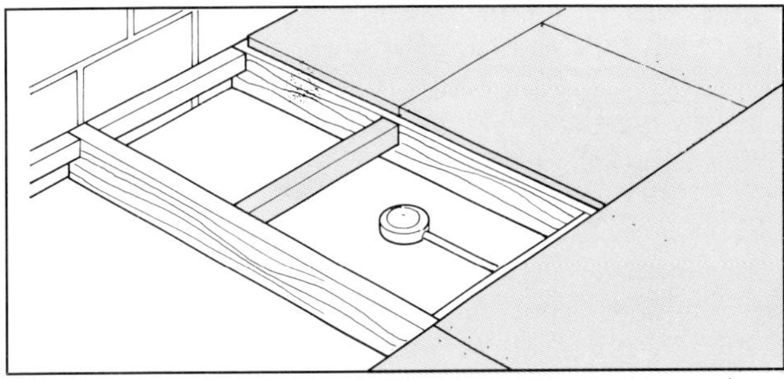

provided in a timber floor. They should be supported with noggings on all edges and fixed with countersunk screws 15mm longer than the board thickness in pre-drilled holes.

Where chipboard is used in rooms with a water supply – a kitchen or bathroom – it should be a moisture-resistant grade (Type II/III as specified in BS 5669:1979) – this would need to be noted in the specification.

# Walls

Choosing the materials to be used for the walls of an extension is usually one of the earliest decisions. It's an important choice which has a large influence on the cost and look of the extended building. Planning permission may depend on a match.

If you're aiming to match the existing walls you'll be tied to the existing material, but if you don't want a match (and sometimes it's better not to try for a match which would be unsatisfactory) your options are much wider. You could, for instance, go for a dramatic extension in glass and steel. However, for most people the choice will be brick, block or timber frame or a combination of these perhaps with an external finish such as tile hanging, rendering or weatherboarding.

Whatever material you choose for the walls, they should be constructed with a good level of insulation. Since 1982 the Building Regulations in England and Wales and Scotland (but not as yet in Inner London) have required the walls of new houses and extensions to have a maximum thermal transmission ('U') value of 0·6 W/m²°C – see page 185 for details on U values. To reach the standards required by the regulations some insulation usually has to be included in the wall. It's often worth going further than the regulations require.

## Cavity walls

The cavity wall in brick or block has two parallel walls or 'leaves' separated by a clear cavity at least 50mm wide. The two leaves are structurally independent and, except at window and doors, are physically connected only by wall ties, which keep the walls from bowing or bulging away from each other. Timber frame is another form of cavity construction.

The cavity allows any moisture penetrating the outer leaf–wind-driven rain, for example–to run down the inside face of the outer leaf and out through 'weepholes' rather than penetrating through to the interior face. The cavity also reduces heat transmission through the wall by allowing insulation material to be introduced.

## Solid walls

These days none of the old accepted methods of solid wall construction would meet the Regulations unless the walls were ludicrously thick – a plastered brick wall 220mm thick for instance has a U value of 2·1W/m²°C. A solid wall of ordinary concrete blocks is also well below standard, but 305mm thick solid blocks of ultra-light aerated concrete (500kg/m³), with an external render and a light-weight plastered interior face should be acceptable to most authorities. For a d-i-y extension this could be the easiest method of building masonry walls.

## Brick

Brick will often be the first choice for the outer leaf of a cavity wall. Most bricks are manufactured from clay, but there are also concrete bricks and calcium silicate (or sand-lime) bricks made from a mixture of hydrated lime with sand or crushed stone (or a mixture of both).

**Clay bricks** The clay bricks used for the exterior leaf of a house or an extension might be commons or facing bricks. The former are general-purpose bricks; the latter are general-purpose bricks made or selected to give an attractive appearance. Both types are available in an engineering grade which is strong and water-resistant and can be used for special purposes – exposed walls, foundations and dpc's, for instance.

Facing bricks can be further subdivided by appearance: rustic bricks are textured in some way during manufacture; sandfaced bricks have sand incorporated on the surface and this imparts a colour and texture to the surface. With these bricks the core material is often a different colour, if the applied finish is removed through mishandling, the core is exposed and the brick will look less than perfect. However, they are economic to use and durable provided there is good detailing to protect the wall – such as overhanging eaves.

Clay facing bricks can also be coloured throughout. These are generally higher quality than sandfaced facings and can be used in more exposed conditions. They are, however, more expensive.

All clay bricks are strong enough for small – one or two storey – build-

CAVITY WALLS

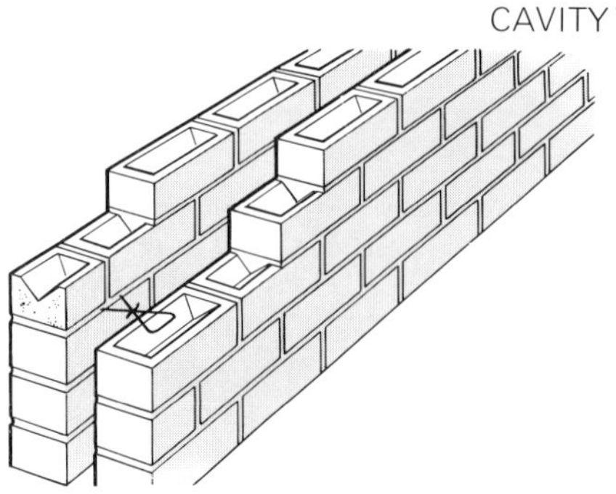

Facing brick outer leaf with inner wall of facing bricks needs partial or total cavity fill to meet the U value regulations

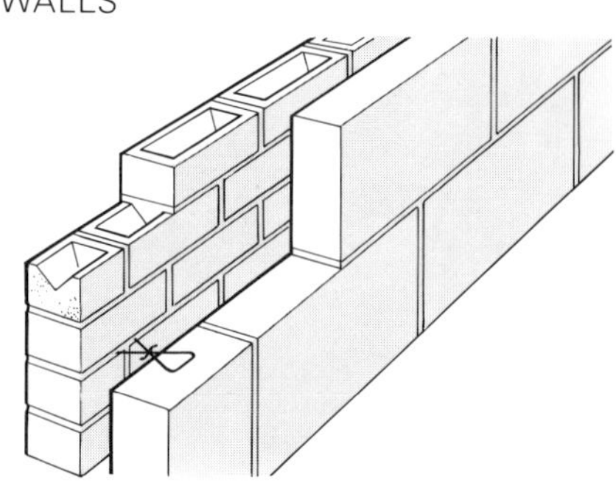

This is a common construction, a facing brick outer leaf and inner leaf of lightweight blocks – it also needs cavity fill.

ings, so for an extension durability is the thing to worry about: for external use you need ordinary quality bricks or, for exposed situations, specials (engineering bricks are specials).

The name of a brick may also indicate its provenance or method of manufacture, but this has little practical relevance. Some bricks have 'frogs', – an indentation in the top; others are solid, some have three large holes and others have many smaller holes. This is mainly to do with the manufacturing process and has little practical relevance.

**Calcium silicate bricks** Most of these bricks are coloured – usually plain colours ranging from white to chocolate brown. Like clay bricks, calcium silicate bricks range in quality from those which need some protection to those which are claimed by their manufacturer to withstand frost in any conditions or to be suitable for use in foundations.

**Concrete bricks** These are most widely available in parts of the country where there is no brick earth and therefore no brick works – they're quite common in Scotland, for instance. Unless your house is made of concrete bricks it is unlikely that you would want to use these in an extension as they are expensive and have no advantages over clay bricks. Concrete bricks may need frequent washing to remove lime efflorescence when they are first used.

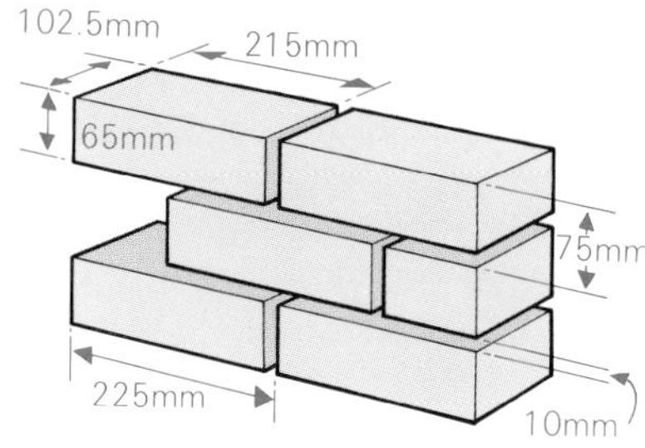


Including the allowance for 10mm joints a brick module is twice as long as it is wide and a third of its length high.

**Brick size**

The traditional size of brick was 9in by 4½in by 3in but most bricks now are actually 215mm by 102·5mm by 65mm (within the limits of manufacturing tolerance). Allowing a 10mm joint, the brick module then becomes 225mm by 112·5mm by 75mm. Modern bricks of this size will bond reasonably well with most existing brickwork although not perfectly in many instances. There are also a small number of 'metric' size bricks made 300mm by 100mm by 90mm and 200mm by 100mm by 90mm for example.

**Exposed brick**

This is currently popular as an internal finish. It saves plastering, but that doesn't mean it's a cheap choice: fairfaced brickwork, as this is called, needs to be built with care and therefore takes longer (and so costs more); the facing bricks used are generally much more expensive (perhaps three times more) than commons which can be used beneath plaster or plasterboard. However the costs of decorating in future years will be saved.

Special attention has to be given to the insulation, if the exterior leaf is also brick, cavity fill is needed to achieve a U value of less than 0·6. Also with fairfaced brickwork the electric cables to wall lighting points and light switches have to be planned early and run in the cavity and great care has to be taken throughout the progress of the work to prevent them being splashed with mortar or damaged in any other way. In use fairfaced brick walls can feel cold and do not absorb sound as well as plastered walls.

**Concrete block**

Lightweight concrete blocks with a plaster or plasterboard finish are very often used as the inner leaf of a cavity wall. They can also be used as the outer leaf, but in this position ordinary lightweight blocks need some protection. They can be: faced with tile hanging fixed on battens, cement and sand rendering, or painted. The disadvantage with applied finishes is that they are rarely permanently maintenance free. Usually, a painted finish will require a further application every five years or so and rendering will usually need maintenance after 15 to 20 years – possibly sooner if the specification and application are poor. It is essential that the rendering is prepared with the correct and accurate proportion mix of materials and that the blockwork or common brickwork is properly prepared to provide good adhesion. An incorrect mix and poor application will considerably shorten the life.

Most blocks are sufficiently loadbearing for use in an extension. Those with an Agrément certificate can be used below the dpc.

**Fairfaced blockwork** is also available but unless your existing building is built in fairfaced blockwork the use of this material is not likely to be suitable. For one thing the scale is often too big. There are concrete blocks to imitate real stone which are useful for stone houses and cottages.

**Timber**

Timber can be used as an external cladding for walls constructed of bricks or blocks. It can also be used as the inner load-bearing skin of an external wall.

Extensions constructed in timber frame require only fairly limited carpentry skills and tools. A timber-frame building is, if correctly designed and constructed, a durable permanent structure, easily insulated to a high standard. The dry construction obviates problems of drying out shrinkage. It can be two or three storeys in height, although only single-storey extensions are referred to in this book. Since most domestic buildings already comprise timber roofs and upper floors, the only major difference in a timber-frame building is that the structural walls and partitions are constructed of timber. The external appearance depends upon the cladding chosen–faced with brick or block it looks no different from a conventional building.

## Insulating cavity walls

There are three main ways to achieve a cavity wall with a U value of less than 0·6W/m²°C.

■ **full cavity insulation** The cavity is filled with foam, mineral fibre or polystyrene beads. If not expertly done, it can produce channels allowing water from the outer leaf to penetrate across the cavity, and is likely to produce a much wetter outer leaf (reducing its insulating value) by blocking escape of penetrating moisture down the cavity.

■ **partial cavity insulation** This takes the form of 'bats' of insulating material fixed to one face of the cavity (normally the inner one) to leave a clear cavity for drainage. A 25mm bat in a 50mm cavity will achieve the U=0·6 target with an otherwise conventional construction of 100mm brick outer leaf and 100mm aerated block and plaster inner leaf. Fixing the bats so they don't bridge the cavity adds complications to the construction process. The one leaf must be raised by the height of the bats ahead of the other leaf, and the bats have to be fitted between wall ties without leaving gaps, and without sagging across the remaining clear cavity. Work is often easier if the cavity is increased to 75mm.

■ **normal cavity construction** This will meet the regulations with a 100mm outer brick skin and 50mm cavity, if the inner leaf is a lightweight aerated blockwork not weighing more than 600kg/m³ and there is a 12mm layer of lightweight plaster. Several makers of lightweight blocks have introduced, since the announcement of the new regulations, blocks with a density of around 500kg/m³.

## Lintels

Another thing to think about is how the walls will be carried over any opening. A supporting lintel will be required and depending on the type chosen this will or will not show on the finished wall.

LINTELS

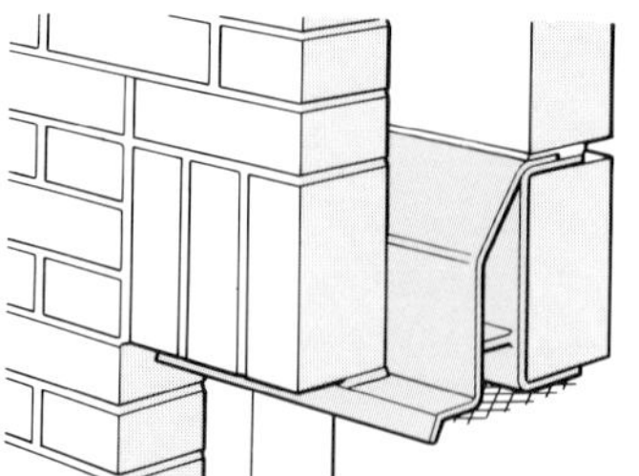

A combination galvanised steel lintel is water-shedding. The inner face usually has a key for plaster, plasterboard or battens for curtain rails.

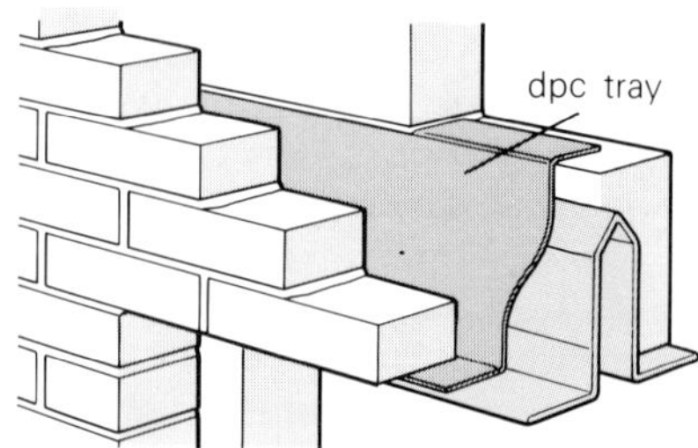


This type of galvanised steel lintel does not replace any masonry. It needs a separate tray to shed water – the tail of the tray should show outside.

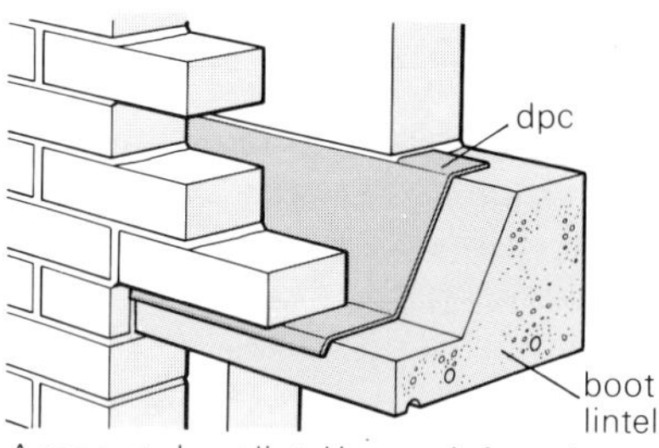


A concrete boot lintel has a reinforced toe to support the outer leaf. In a recessed window opening, this is hardly noticeable.

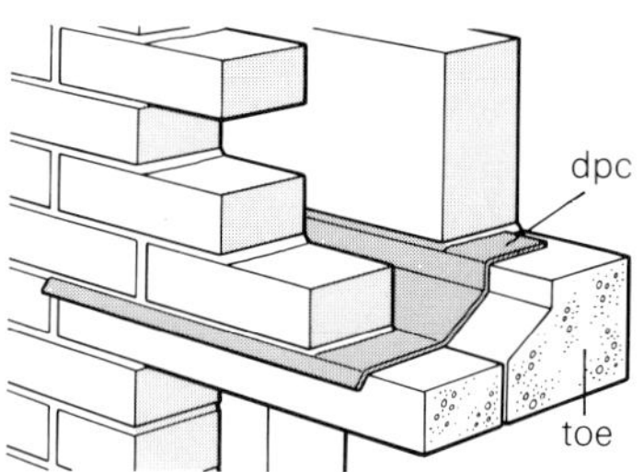


A concrete lintel in the inner leaf has a 50mm toe to close the cavity. The outer leaf is supported by a second rectangular lintel which shows on the finished wall.

### LINTELS

Lightweight galvanised steel, pre-cast, pre-stressed or reinforced concrete lintels are available more or less off the shelf for normal openings up to around 4·8m wide.

Galvanised steel lintels are the most popular: they have the advantage of being lighter and can support heavier loads over larger spans. They are made in profiles designed to support both leaves of a cavity wall, whereas concrete lintels are often installed separately in each leaf or, for better external appearance, are installed in the inner leaf only with an additional steel tray to support the outer leaf.

A disadvantage of steel lintels is their potential susceptibility to corrosion. Steel lintels may be galvanised before or after fabrication. In either case, it's very important not to damage the protective finish and any scratch must be made good. A coat of bituminious paint before installation is helpful. In some parts of the country (notably Scotland and Inner London) they need protection to ensure durability.

For fire protection, the BCO may want a steel lintel to be lined with plasterboard on the inside, whereas a concrete lintel can always be plastered over directly. It's worth giving some thought to curtain rail fixings on the inside. Concrete lintels can make fixing difficult–you need a hammer drill to get through them. Galvanised steel lintels must never be drilled into, but they are available with special provision for curtain rails.

# Constructing masonry walls

Building up the walls obviously requires some knowledge and skill in brick (or block) laying. You need considerable practice on simple jobs before attempting anything as ambitious as a brick extension. *The Which? Book of Do-it-yourself* covers bricklaying in some detail. Blocklaying technique is essentially the same. Masonry walls must be level and plumb – the maximum tolerance away from vertical for a one storey wall is 15mm in all or 6mm for each 1000mm.

## Up to dpc

To bring the walls up from the top of the trench-fill foundation, build up with leaves of the same thickness using materials acceptable for below dpc.

Take care with the setting-out. Set out the bottom courses of both leaves dry at first, using a 10mm wood shim as a joint spacing gauge to make sure everything fits. Use the bedding mortar at the bottom of the masonry to take out any irregularities in the level.

When the masonry reaches a level 150mm below the dpc, fill the cavity with well-compacted concrete. Chamfer the top of this fill to drain to the outer leaf and, provided the wall is not very exposed, omit the mortar in vertical joints to form weepholes in the outer leaf at intervals of about 1m. Finish the wall to dpc height (installing and sleeving air bricks if necessary). In the course one below the dpc set bricks dry at intervals in the outer leaf to allow the cavity to be cleaned later.

**Damp-proof course** A dpc is installed in each leaf. Normally a roll of bituminised felt is used, but slates or engineering bricks may be specified. The dpc must link to the damp-proof membrane in a solid floor – see page 236. To install a dpc, lay a full bed of mortar as for a 10mm joint and bed the dpc material firmly in it; rolled material may need weighting. Lap subsequent lengths by 100mm or so. Lay a further full bed of mortar so that the total joint-and-dpc thickness is about 20mm. The dpc should project slightly beyond the faces of the wall. It should be continuous under door sills, etc.

From the dpc carry the leaves up installing galvanised wall ties in the bedding courses 900mm apart (maximum) and every 450mm in height. The ends of the wall ties should be well bedded with the 'drip' – the offset bend or projection of twisted wire at the centre of the tie – pointing downward. Take great care to prevent mortar catching on the ties. A batten on wires which is lifted as work progresses is useful for this.

If the wall is to have partial-cavity insulation using 25mm bats, fit the first run of wall ties as near as possible to the dpc. Buy bats the right size or cut the bats to match exactly the vertical spacing between wall ties. Build the leaf to which the bat will be attached up the full height of the bat, fit and fix according to the manufacturer's instructions. Bring up the opposite leaf to match. If the clear cavity will be only 25mm wide, cleaning any extruded mortar from the cavity side of this leaf can be a bit tricky: it's much better to construct a cavity 75mm wide to leave a gap of 50mm.

When both leaves are level at the top of the insulation bat, repeat the whole sequence protecting the top of the installed bat with a batten to catch mortar. Raise the wall in 'lifts' of 1.2 metres and allow the mortar to harden for at least twelve hours before proceeding. Protect the part-built wall with plastic sheeting; if strong winds are likely, or there's a long expanse of wall, prop the walls.

A CAVITY WALL

Work at this level will be a guide for all that follows. Set the first courses dry and check the level and fit.

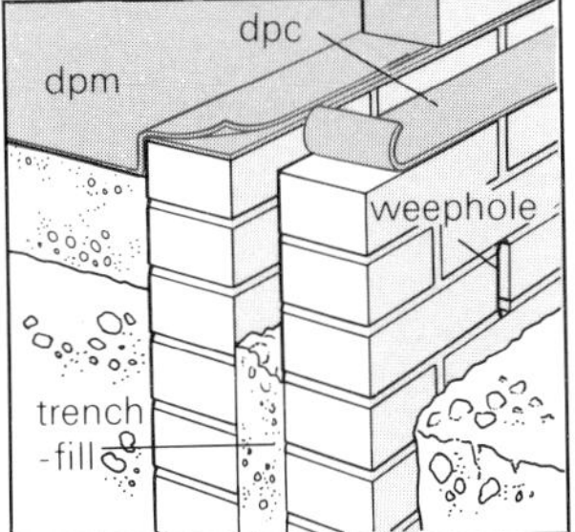


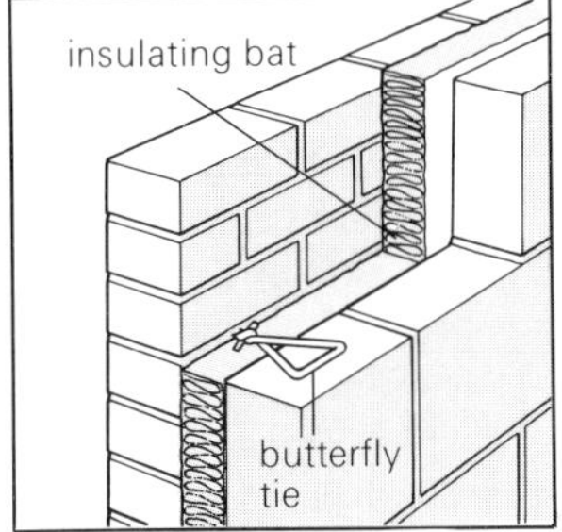


Partial-cavity insulation is provided by fitting bats between the wall ties and above the level of the dpc.

## Openings

Using lengths of timber, such as old scaffold boards, and short wooden stakes, prop the door and window frames in position – on the floor, or sill brickwork in the case of doors or on the wall when you reach sill height in the case of windows. The damp-proof membrane should be continuous under a door sill and a separate dpc should be installed beneath a window frame to seal the cavity. Build up around them, fitting a vertical dpc as you go. This should be wider than the cavity closure and should lap the undersill dpc.

Extra wall ties at 300mm intervals are needed round the opening. The windows can be fixed by any of the methods outlined on page 136. Fixing cramps are often the easiest, as they can be built into mortar joints as the wall goes up. Frames more than 1·2m wide also need head fixings. The frames can be held square as building work proceeds by nailing on temporary diagonal battens. Alternatively window frames can be used as formers and then removed for safe storage – in the dry – until the building is complete. The window is then installed like a replacement window.

If an outer leaf of facing brick is to be used, fit a galvanised steel combination lintel with a projecting tray to carry the outer leaf brickwork. These bricks can be laid to normal stretcher bond or as a straight soldier 'arch' of bricks on end for a more traditional appearance. For extra protection coat the lintel all round with bituminous paint. The lintel should have a good bearing on either side of the opening – at least 250mm – with a firm mortar bed. A horizontal dpc should be provided a course or two above the opening, extending right across the cavity and provided with weepholes sloping downwards to the outside (omit the weepholes in very exposed positions).

**Airbricks** If airbricks are installed in a cavity wall (to ventilate a timber floor) they should be sleeved to allow the air from outside to go directly into the building, instead of circulating in the cavity. An airbrick is fitted in each leaf and the sleeving is normally provided by four roofing slates bedded in the mortar courses around the bricks.

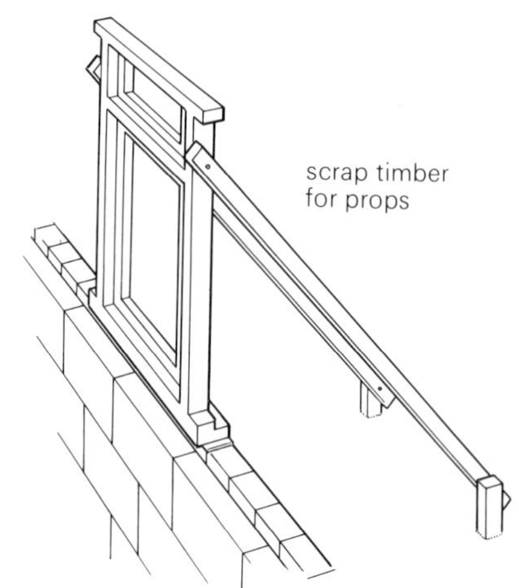


Frames can be installed as the building goes up or placed later when the building is complete.

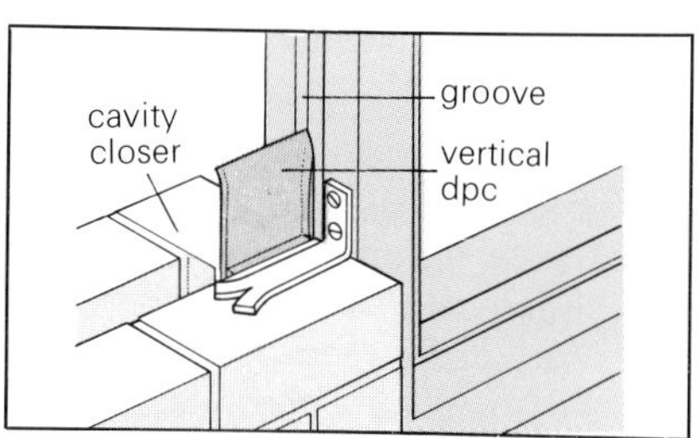


A dpc must be installed around the opening. Extra wall ties – at 300mm spacings – are also required for stability.

### LINKING TO THE MAIN STRUCTURE

New masonry can be bonded into the old by removing alternate courses (or blocks of four courses) from the existing wall and toothing the new brickwork in. You may be required to bond both leaves or just the outer one.

It is much easier, however, to build the new work independently and use ties of galvanised strap 3mm thick.

At 225mm intervals vertically along the centreline of each leaf, chisel out mortar from the existing joints and anchor the straps with a semi-dry mortar, or an epoxy mortar well rammed in.

The free ends should project at least 225mm. Fix strips of compressible bitumised felt, about 10mm narrower than the thickness of the leaf to the existing walls, with the straps projecting through it. Before bedding the straps in the mortar, coat them liberally with a heavy grease. This will allow for expansion and contraction without permitting sideways movement.

Mortar the ends of the bricks or blocks as they are laid against the bituminous felt, then rake out the joints, and later – when the work is complete – seal with a flexible polysulphide or silicone mastic.

## Internal walls

These are constructed as the external walls with appropriate foundations and dpc. They should be built at the same time and bonded in.

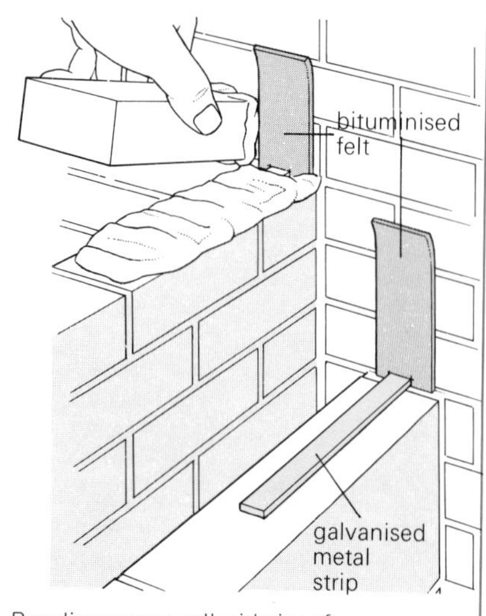


Bonding a new wall with ties of galvanised steel strap.

# Constructing timber-frame walls

The walls are framed up in softwood usually of nominal 100m by 50mm section. In practice this will be approximately 97mm by 47mm (or, if Canadian timber is used, 89mm by 38mm). Since the walls are designed to support the roof loads, the timber must be general structural (GS) grade; CLS construction grade for Canadian timber. The framework consists of top and bottom rails with verticals (called studs) at 600mm centres. This dimension is chosen to allow easy fixing of plywood sheathing and the plasterboard inner lining, which comes in 1200mm wide sheets. (Note: some plywood is still imported in 4′0″ (1220mm) wide sheets and will require trimming.) The plywood sheathing should normally be 9mm sheathing quality plywood. The height of the panels will depend on the height of the extension – bear in mind that the Building Regulations require a minimum finished ceiling height of 2·3m for habitable rooms.

It is strongly recommended that the timber for the stud framework is preservative treated and it should be ordered from the timber supplier in this form. The treatment can be either by water-borne copper/chrome/arsenate (CCA, commonly sold under the brand Tanalith as tanalized timber) or by spirit-based organic solvents. With timber treated with CCA sufficient time must be allowed for the timber to re-dry before use. All cut ends of timber should be treated by dipping or brushing with an appropriate preservative.

## The panels

When a concrete slab is used for the ground floor, the timber wall is built off a timber sole plate which is fixed down to perimeter wall (or the concrete slab). When a timber ground floor is used the wall panels are built directly from the header joist fixed across the ends of the joists – see page 238.

The wall panels can be made in a vertical position or laid flat on the floor of the building. The latter is perhaps easier and is therefore the method mainly dealt with here – although most of the details are the same in both cases. The size of panel which can be constructed on the ground depends on the arrangements for lifting and whether the plywood sheathing is fixed while the framework is laid flat or after it is erected. Plywood adds considerably to the panel weight: with plywood fixed, two people can lift and position a panel approximately 3·0m to 3·5m long; without plywood panels 4m or 5m long can be handled.

Cut the top and bottom rails of the panels to length and mark the bottom rail with the positions of the studs. The studs can then be cut to length and fixed in position by nailing through the bottom rail into the end grain of the studs with 2 No. 8 gauge 100mm nails. When nailing, take care to keep the faces of rails and studs as flush as possible and use a piece of plywood (or other square board) to keep the joints square. Mark the stud positions on the top rail, place it in position and double nail it to the studs, as for the bottom rail. If you're constructing the panel vertically the studs are skew-nailed at the bottom.

Check the overall height of the panel and cut the plywood sheathing to length as necessary. Depending upon whether there is help available to move the panel or not, the plywood will be fixed whilst the framework is laid flat or after it is erected.

Fix the plywood sheathing with 50mm long galvanised nails at 200mm centres making sure that the nails penetrate the intermediate studs.

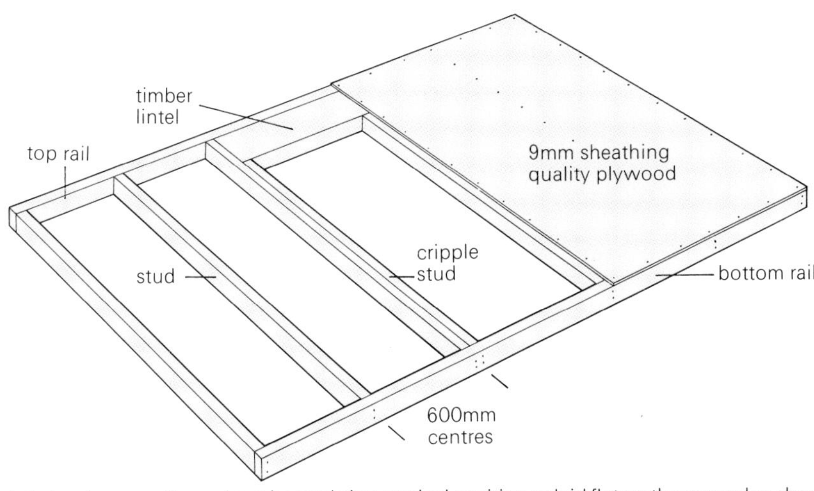


A timber frame wall panel can be made in a vertical position or laid flat on the ground as shown.

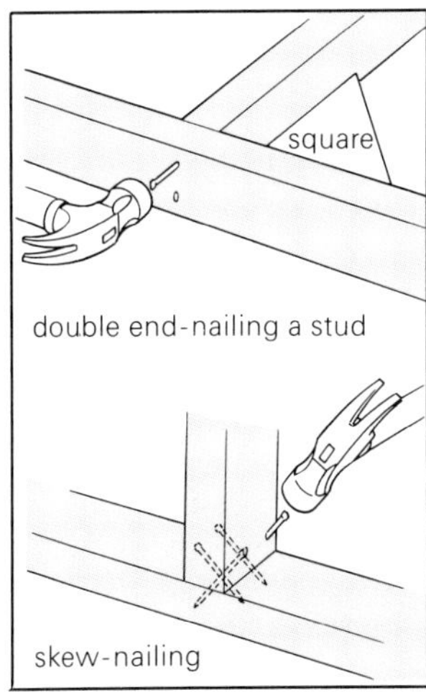

## Openings

Window and doorway openings are easily incorporated into panels during construction. For this purpose it is however necessary to differentiate between loadbearing panels – those supporting the roof structure (joists and trusses) – and non-loadbearing panels. Where panels are loadbearing the openings must be framed up with extra studs and a timber lintel across the top of the opening. Typical timber lintel sizes and the number of studs required are shown in the Table.

The studs should be nailed together with 8 gauge, 75mm long nails at 300mm centres. The lintel is supported by cutting short the inner stud or studs (called a cripple stud) to form a bearing, and then by nailing through the outer stud into the end of the lintel with 2 No. 8 gauge 100mm nails at each end.

Where panels are non-loadbearing, the opening can be spanned by a piece of stud section timber placed horizontally across the top of the opening. With another piece of similarly-sized timber at window sill level.

Unless you are certain of the exact sizes of window and door frames it is preferable to buy these and use them as formers for their openings allowing a tolerance of 5mm all around for the subsequent fitting and squaring. This method is usually better than fixing them into the panel as it is made since the window frame will probably need to project in front of the panel face to make a weatherproof joint with the external finish of the wall.

To fit door frames, it is normally necessary to cut away the bottom rail of the wall panel between cripple studs and this is done once the panel is in position. Remember to allow for this when measuring the height of the opening.

### Fixing the panels

As the panels are made they can be raised up to a vertical position, temporarily braced with spare pieces of timber, and nailed to the soleplate with 100mm 8 gauge nails at approximately 300mm centres. Subsequent

OPENINGS

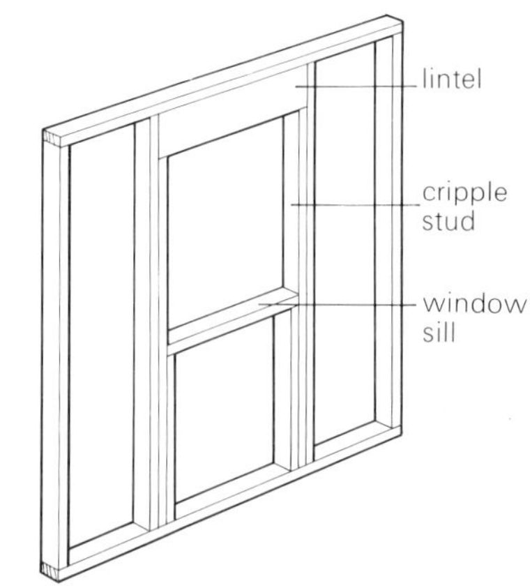


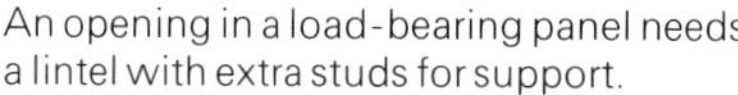
An opening in a load-bearing panel needs a lintel with extra studs for support.

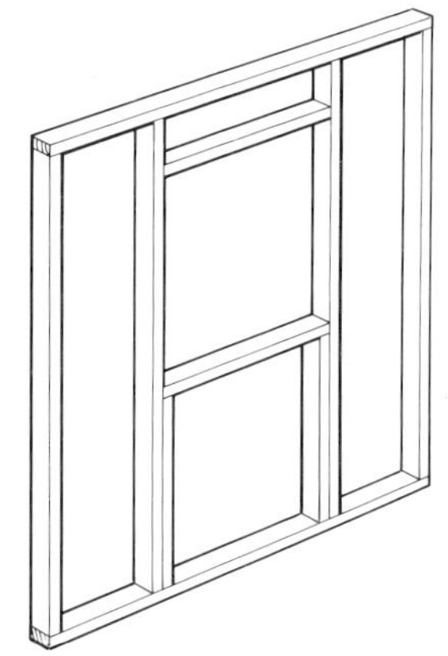

An opening in a non-load-bearing panel can be spanned by a piece of stud timber.

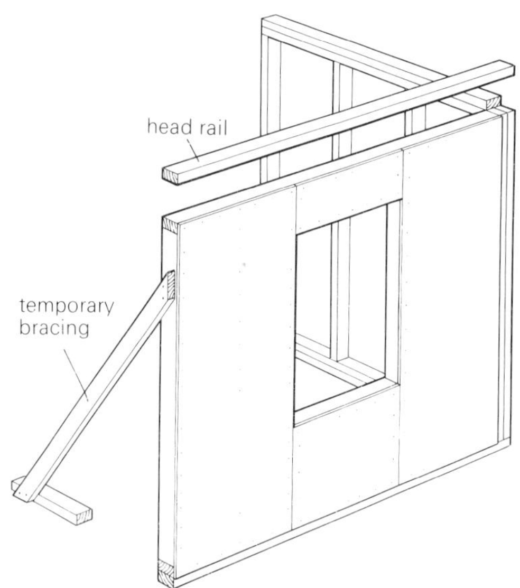


Panels are raised to position, temporarily braced and nailed to the soleplate and any adjoining panels.

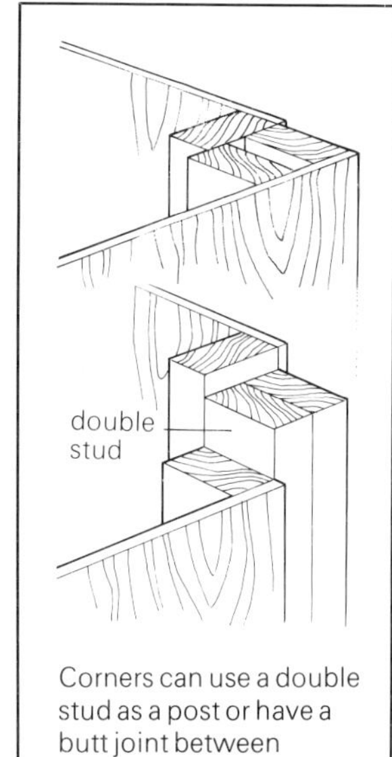


Corners can use a double stud as a post or have a butt joint between panels.

**Lintel sizes**

| Span of opening | number and size of lintel [1] | number of cripple studs | type of timber |
|---|---|---|---|
| up to 1·2m | 2 × 200mm by 38mm or<br>2 × 200mm by 50mm or<br>1 × 200mm by 75mm | 1 | softwood to general structural grade |
| up to 1·8m | 2 × 225mm by 38mm or<br>2 × 225mm by 50mm or<br>2 × 225mm by 75mm | 1 | softwood to general structural grade |
| up to 2·4m | 1 × 225mm by 75mm | 2 | hardwood (eg Keruing) |

[1] Choose a lintel size to match the panel thickness 38mm, 50mm or 75mm.

panels can be made and placed in position and nailed to the soleplate and the adjoining panels. Corners can be formed either by using a double stud as a post or by extending the length of one of the panels by the thickness of the adjacent wall.

### Linkage to the existing walls

Fixing a timber-framed extension to an existing wall is best achieved by plugging and screwing a vertical stud to the existing wall (having first removed any projections). The junction should be weatherproof and normally a damp-proof course is installed between the timber member and the wall. It is important to check that the existing wall is vertical and, if necessary, to pack out between the panel and the fixing stud before the panel is nailed to the stud.

### The head rail

Once all the panels are in place a head rail of the same size timber as the top rail should be nailed to the top edge of the panels around the entire building. Before fixing this, check for verticality and accuracy and adjust as required. The roof can then be constructed, the double head rail serving the same purpose as a wallplate (see Roofs – page 250). It is not necessary for the roof trusses or joists to be directly above wall studs, but any heavy loads, such as beams, should have studs beneath them. In extensions with large rooms (more than 5m or 6m wide) which will have a pitched roof, the top of the panels will need additional stiffening by means of diagonal bracing in the roof space. If the roof is flat the panels will normally be adequately rigid. Take professional advice.

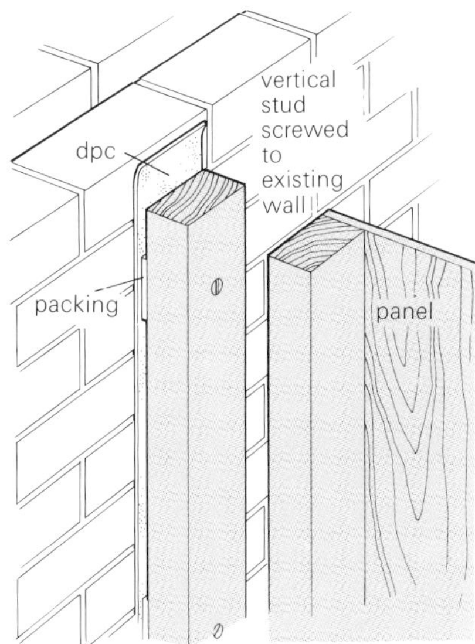


A timber frame extension is connected by screwing and plugging a vertical stud to the wall and nailing the first panel to the stud.

### Breather paper

It is normal practice to line the outer plywood face of the timber frame building with a breather paper or felt (to BS 4016) before fixing any type of cladding. This membrane is a special material which is waterproof, but is not impervious to water vapour. It is important that the correct material is used and that it is fixed with lapped joints using staples or large-headed tacks at 150mm centres.

## Finishing inside

As soon as the building is at a dry stage, with the roof on and glass or temporary polythene in the windows, work can commence internally. The plywood sheathing and its breather paper will give adequate weather resistance until the external finish is applied.

Any internal partitions (see page 126) can now be constructed. (But if internal partitions support the roof structure they should be built at the same time, in the same way as the loadbearing external walls including lintels over openings but without plywood sheathing.)

Where fixings will be required in the finished wall for things such as wall cupboards, basins and curtain tracks, short lengths of timber should be fixed between the studs.

Insulation can now be fitted into the wall panels; this can be the same type of mineral wool or glass fibre blanket insulation that is used for loft insulation. It should be tacked to the timber frame to hold it in place. It is important that it is fitted well and no spaces are left in the framing. Rigid plastic insulation should not be used.

Insulation is available in 60mm, 80mm, 90mm and 100mm thicknesses. The thicker the material the better the insulation standard, but all these in timber-frame construction have a performance better than the requirements of the Building Regulations. Once the insulation is in place, a vapour barrier of 500 gauge polythene sheeting is fixed to the inner face of the external wall. This is designed to prevent condensation within the wall panel. Joints in the polythene should be lapped over studs and the polythene sheets fixed with nails or staples at approximately 300mm centres, the joints can also be taped. Any holes or tears should be sealed.

It is easy to install electrical services in a timber-framed building by drilling small holes in studs and rails. If electrical services are run in the external walls, the vapour barrier should be taped around the cables where they pass through it.

The inner lining of 12·7mm plasterboard is required to give the structure its necessary fire resistance.

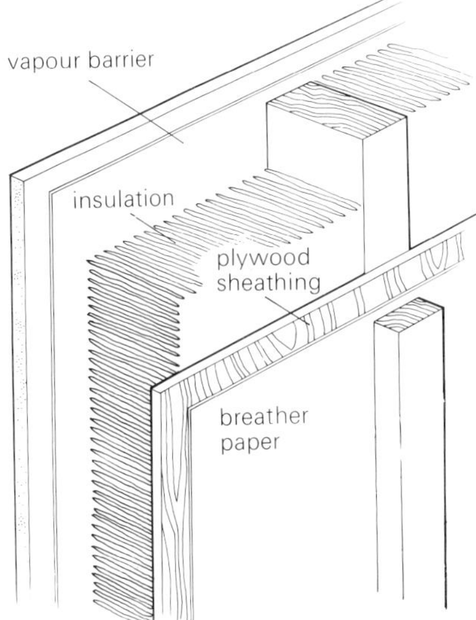


The outer face of the building is lined with breather paper fixed with staples or large-headed tacks.

## External finishes

Two types of external finish are appropriate to timber-framed structures, those which are fixed directly to the panels and those which are heavier with their own foundation and therefore only lightly tied back to the timber frame. Neither carries any load except its own weight.

For all types of cladding it is important that the detail of the window, door and wall junctions are carefully worked out and constructed for the building both to look and function correctly.

Detailed information is available from TRADA and CCA – see page 314.

When a wall is close to the site boundary, the external cladding must be non-combustible materials – see page 221.

### Lightweight claddings

Claddings fixed directly include timber boarding in various forms, suitable plywood sheathing, concrete, clay or asbestos cement tiles fixed to battens or cement render on wire mesh. Various metal or plastic board claddings are also available.

**Timber** Various profiles of timber cladding can be used to give a vertical or horizontal appearance. The timber can be hardwood or a durable or preservative-treated softwood. The Regulations in England and Wales require boarding to have a minimum thickness of 16mm; 21mm is required in Scotland for walls not subjected to severed expose conditions. Timber cladding should not be used within 150mm of the ground.

If V-jointed tongued and grooved boarding is used, it is important to use a type intended for external use. All boards should be fixed with just one nail at each fixing point to allow for movement.

Jagged shank or annular ring nails give better holding – they should be corrosion resistant. Nail length is approximately 2·5 times the board thickness.

Cladding can be painted or stained and should have one coat before it is fixed. Re-finishing paintwork is however a tedious process and in recent years the use of exterior wood stains has become more common. These have a service life of three to four years compared to five for good paint on well-prepared timber, but maintenance is much simpler usually requiring only washing down and applying further coats.

Varnish is not generally considered to be a good finish for external timber, it forms too hard a surface finish which deteriorates under weathering, in a couple of years and is then hard work to renovate.

Western red cedar cladding is durable without any surface treatment and in rural areas the timber weathers to an attractive silver grey colour. In urban areas however it tends to look dirty after a few years and its appearance is improved by a clear finish.

**Tile hanging** Clay, concrete or asbestos cement tiles are fixed to preservative-treated battens. They can be vulnerable to impact damage if used near ground level and care should be taken if they are to be used in this situation. The details round window and door openings are important and it can be difficult to achieve a neat solution around things like ventilators.

The horizontal battens should be at least 38mm by 19mm and nailed into the wall studs with 50mm galvanised nails. The batten centres depend upon the type of tile to be used – information should be obtained from the manufacturers.

**Render** Of the various lightweight claddings render is the one which requires the most skill in application. In compensation, the finished cladding can make the new extension blend well if the existing building also has render finish. It is important to have a cavity between the face of the timber wall panel and the back of the render and to achieve this 38mm by 50mm preservative-treated timber battens

CLADDING

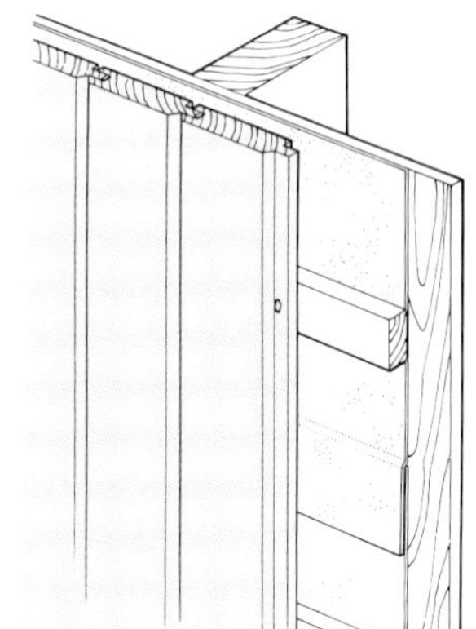
Vertical timber cladding.

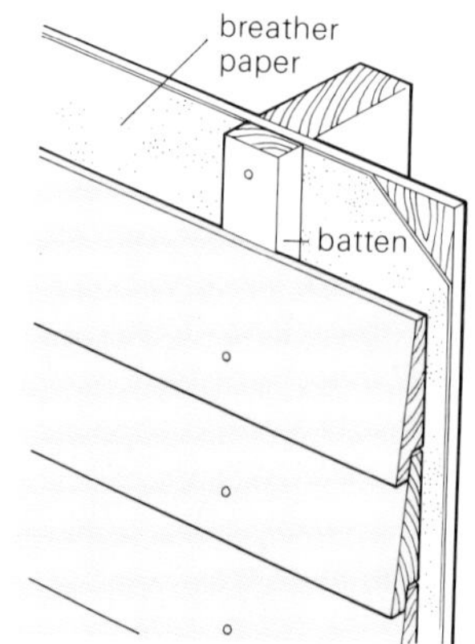

Horizontal timber cladding.

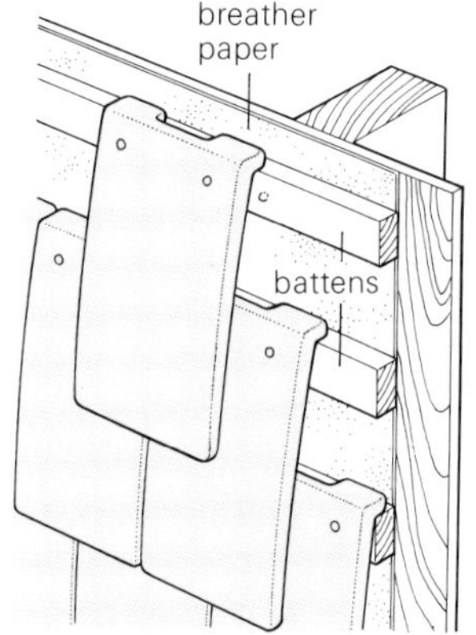

Tile hanging – detail is typical for concrete tiles.

should be fixed vertically over the breather paper at the stud positions and nailed into the studs of the wall frame with 75mm jagged shank galvanised nails.

Wire mesh is attached to the battens with staples in accordance with the manufacturer's recommendations as a base for the render. The mesh can be galvanised or stainless steel – some have a layer of building paper fixed to their back face to limit the amount of render pushed through the mesh.

The required render mix can vary dependent upon the locality and the type of sand used. Local knowledge is helpful in this respect although British Standard 5262: 1976 gives a specification for general use – see Table.

**Heavyweight claddings**

This group includes brickwork, concrete blockwork (either fairfaced or finished with cement render) and, in appropriate localities, coursed or random stonework (real or artificial). Claddings of brick and concrete block are built directly from the foundations as a single leaf and tied back to the timber frame with special flexible stainless steel ties. These are fixed with stainless steel nails into the timber studs at not more than 600mm centres horizontally and 450mm centres vertically.

When the brickwork or blockwork is carried over door and window openings there must be lintels incorporated to support it. These are quite separate from the lintels in the timber frame panels. Lintels can be avoided by stopping the masonry level with the top of the window opening and using lightweight cladding above.

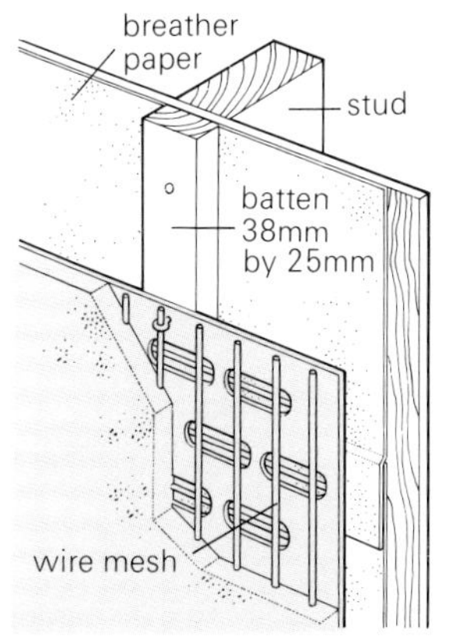


Although it looks simple a rendered finish is perhaps most difficult of all to apply.

BRICK CLADDING

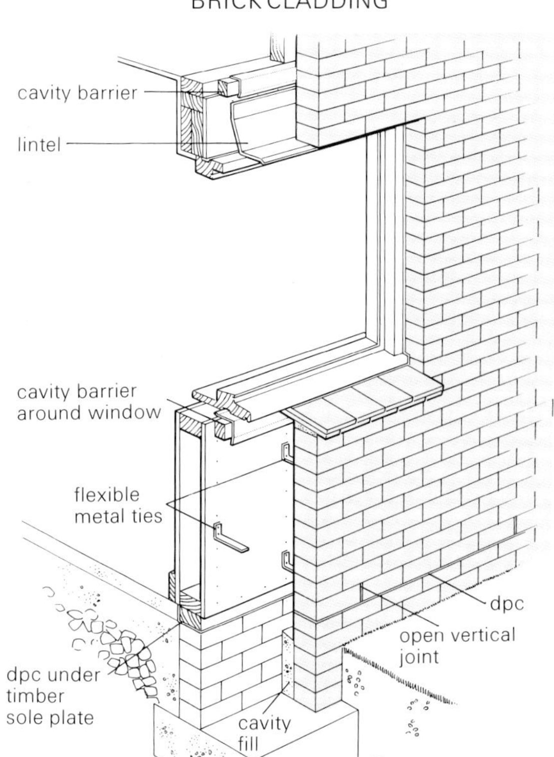


Brick (or block) cladding has its own foundations but is tied to the timber structure. Brick cladding can be used in combination with a lightweight cladding above windows.

## Cavity barriers

The Building Regulations require that the cavity formed between the outer cladding and the timber panel shall not be greater than 8m in any direction. To achieve this, preservative-treated timber 38mm broad and the cavity width deep are installed at 8m maximum centres or if the walls are less than 8m long at the corners of the building. Any small gaps in the cladding must be firestopped with non-combustible filler. A damp-proof course of 2000 gauge (500$\mu$m) polythene should be fixed between the back of the brickwork and the face of the timber cavity barrier, around all openings in the wall and at the junction of wall and roof–the eaves.

**Render mixes – parts by volume**

| | A cement | lime | sand | B cement | ready mixed lime/sand | (lime/sand ratio) | C cement | sand with plasticiser |
|---|---|---|---|---|---|---|---|---|
| coat 1 | 1 | 0–¼ | 3 | 1 | 3 | (1:12) | 1 | 3–4 |
| coat 2 | 1 | ½ | 4–4½ | 1 | 4–4½ | (1:9) | 1 | 5–6 |
| coat 3 | 1 | 1 | 5–6 | 1 | 5–6 | (1:6) | 1 | 7–8 |

# Roofs

The primary purpose of a roof is to provide a weatherproof covering for the room beneath. It must be waterproof, long-lasting, able to withstand extremes of temperature and able to withstand strong winds.

There are two types of roof construction, flat or pitched. A pitched roof may have a slope on both sides or slope in one direction only – sometimes called a lean-to roof.

Pitched roofs are architecturally superior. They cost more than a flat roof to construct (a *Which?* costing exercise in 1983, calculated the extra at about £50 a square metre of roof – perhaps £1000 on a medium-sized extension), but some experts reckon that the long-term maintenance costs of a flat roof are significantly higher than those of a pitched roof. Planning authorities often favour pitched roofs.

## Pitched roof

The combination of the relatively impervious nature of the roof covering and the slope prevents water passing through and forces it to drain off. Natural slates, clay, concrete and asbestos-cement tiles, and wooden shingles are used.

The most common variation for a pitched roof is to have a hipped end pitched at the same angle as the main roof. Its construction is more complex, but it is more weatherproof and it reduces the visual impact of a new building or an extension. A hipped roof is also used when light levels to neighbouring properties would be reduced by a gable end, or when a gable roof would throw unwanted areas of shadow around the new structure or, simply, block a view.

## Flat roof

A flat roof is inclined at a shallow angle so that water will run off to one side but for its waterproofing ability a flat roof relies on the surface being a totally impervious layer which will permit no water at all to pass through.

Most modern flat roofs are constructed from chipboard sheets (or other such boards) which form a semi-rigid underlayer covered and sealed, by 3 layers of bitumised felt or mineral felt topped with a layer of granite chips or fine gravel to protect the felt from degradation by the sun's rays.

Flat roof variations are concerned with improving the visual impact of the roof. This can be done by hiding it from view behind a brick parapet around the edge of the roof. Another way is to construct a short monopitch roof around the edges. Perhaps the best way to finish a flat roof is to make it project – say 300mm – beyond the outer face of the external walls. The overhang helps to prevent moisture penetration.

## Insulation

The newest regulations on thermal insulation for roofs set a maximum U value of 0·35 W/m²°C. For a pitched roof this is usually achieved by installing a layer of glass fibre insulation 100mm thick between the ceiling joists.

Insulating the ceiling below a pitched roof means that the chances of condensation in the loft space are

▲ The front pitch of the garage roof is continued to form a lean-to roof for the porch.

This extension has a flat roof with a mono-pitched edge to improve the appearance. ▶

THE TWO TYPES OF ROOF

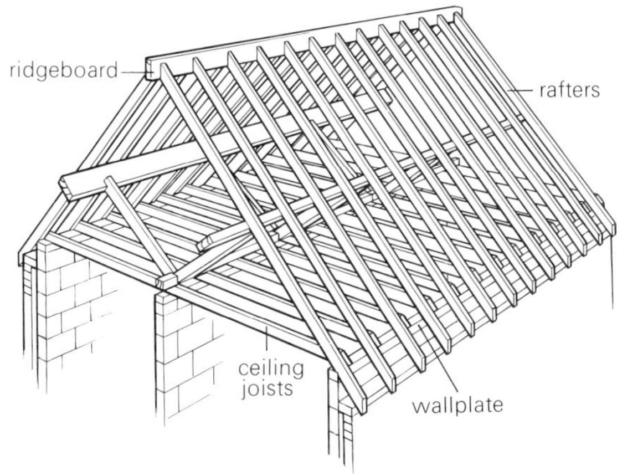

A pitched roof is architecturally superior and easier to insulate and to make weatherproof than a flat one.

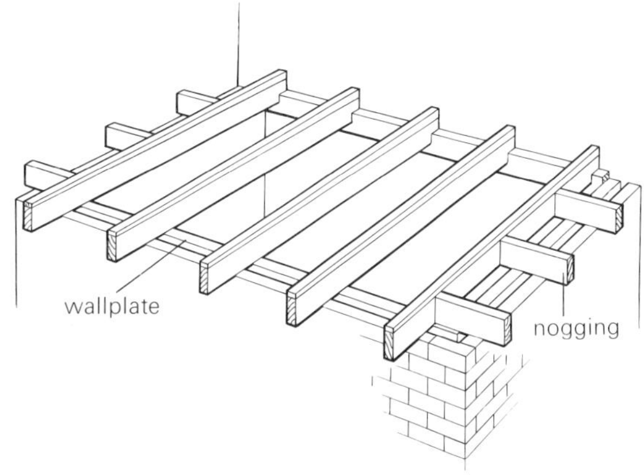


A flat roof needs good detailing if it is to last well without expensive maintenance.

increased. The ventilation must therefore be good and should be arranged to move the stagnant air at the eaves. In England and Wales the standard recommendation is a gap of 10mm at the eaves along opposite sides of the loft, or if this is not possible, regularly-spaced gaps to give an equivalent area; in Scotland ventilation is required for pitched roofs of less than 20 degrees only – the requirement then is for a 300 sq mm gap for each 300m length of eaves.

A flat roof can have the insulation above or below the roof deck. If the insulation is above it is called a warm roof; if below it is called a cold roof. The insulation should always be above a vapour barrier and if the vapour barrier is at ceiling level below a mat of insulation laid on the ceiling plasterboard, it's important that the air space behind is ventilated. The minimum ventilation is 1000mm² opening per metre run of eaves provided on opposite sides of the building to give a free flow of air. Wider roofs – 12m wide or more – need double the openings.

When the insulation is above the roof deck the vapour check is provided by bedding the insulation – usually a mineral fibre – on bitumen.

A flat roof with 100mm insulation has a U value of about 0·3 W/m²°C.

## Fixing the wallplates

Once the walls have reached full height the next job is to fit the wallplates. These timbers and all other roof timbers, including tile battens, should be preservative-treated with any cut ends brush-treated. The wallplates spread the downward load from the roof and they serve as a fixing plate to which the ceiling joists and rafters are attached. The plates usually consist of a length of rough-sawn timber of nominal 100mm by 50mm dimensions. It is essential that this timber is straight and true. Long lengths are best, if more than one length is used there should be a halving-joint.

The position of the wallplates depends on the type of roof: for a flat or mono-pitch extension roof which falls *away* from the house wall one wallplate is attached to the house wall and the second plate is positioned on top of the opposite wall; for a flat or mono-pitched extension roof that falls to a side wall and for a fully-pitched extension roof the wallplates are positioned on opposite side walls.

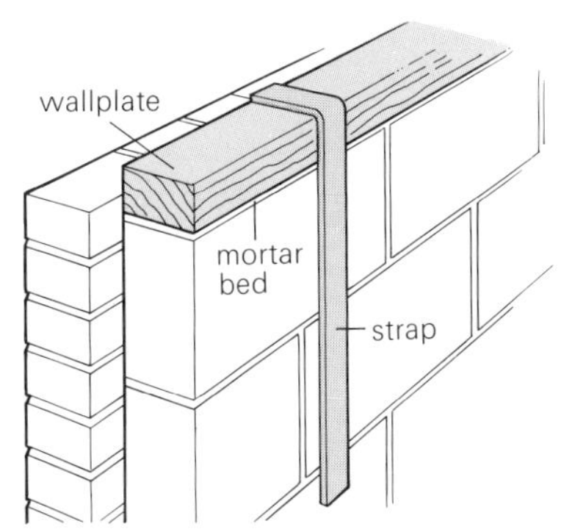


A wallplate is a dead straight timber bedded on mortar and strapped to the wall at 1·8m centres.

The wallplates should be installed at the same time to enable both plates to be made parallel and level in all directions.

To fix a wallplate on top of a wall, butter the top of the wall with mortar, lay the plate on top and tap it down until it is level. (Make sure that there are no voids in the mortar.)

Once the mortar bed has set the plate can be secured. If the building is in a sheltered position it is usually sufficient to secure the plate by driving nails or wall anchors through it into the top of the wall. In exposed locations steel straps are secured to the top of the plate and bent down the inner face of the wall for about 600mm – the strap ends are screwed to the wall. The wallplate fixings should not be more than 1·8m apart.

When one side of the extension roof meets an existing wall of the house wall anchors are used to fix a wallplate with its widest face to the wall.

# Constructing a pitched roof

After the wallplate, the ceiling joists are installed. Their primary purpose is to tie the ends of opposite rafters together to absorb the spreading load the roof exerts on the outside walls. The dimensions of the joists depends on the span of the room but for average-sized rooms they are usually nominally 100mm by 50mm – the extension design will give details.

Each joist is the same length, equal to the distance between the outside edges of the wallplate plus extra at each end to allow the joists to be cut flush with the rafters.

Mount them on edge, one at either end, with the rest positioned in between at a nominal centre line spacing of 400mm. Secure to the wallplate by skew-nailing twice from either side of the joist into the wallplate.

### The ridgeboard

The ridgeboard is the highest timber which runs along the length of the building midway from either wall. The rafters (which carry the weight of the roof covering) butt against it from either side. It usually takes the form of a straight board nominally 150mm by 25mm.

The height of the ridgeboard depends on the slope of the roof. This may be dictated by the need to match an existing roof line or by the type of tile or slate being used.

A number of operations have to be carried out before the ridge can be pitched. The ridgeboard has to be cut to the length of the extension. Rafters have to be cut at the appropriate angles and to the correct length and shape. A birdsmouth notch is cut in the lower end of each to form a seat on the wallplate. If the new roof merges at ridge level with the existing roof, the roof covering has to be stripped back around the join.

To install the ridgeboard support it in position by props resting of the ceiling joists. Butt the end against the

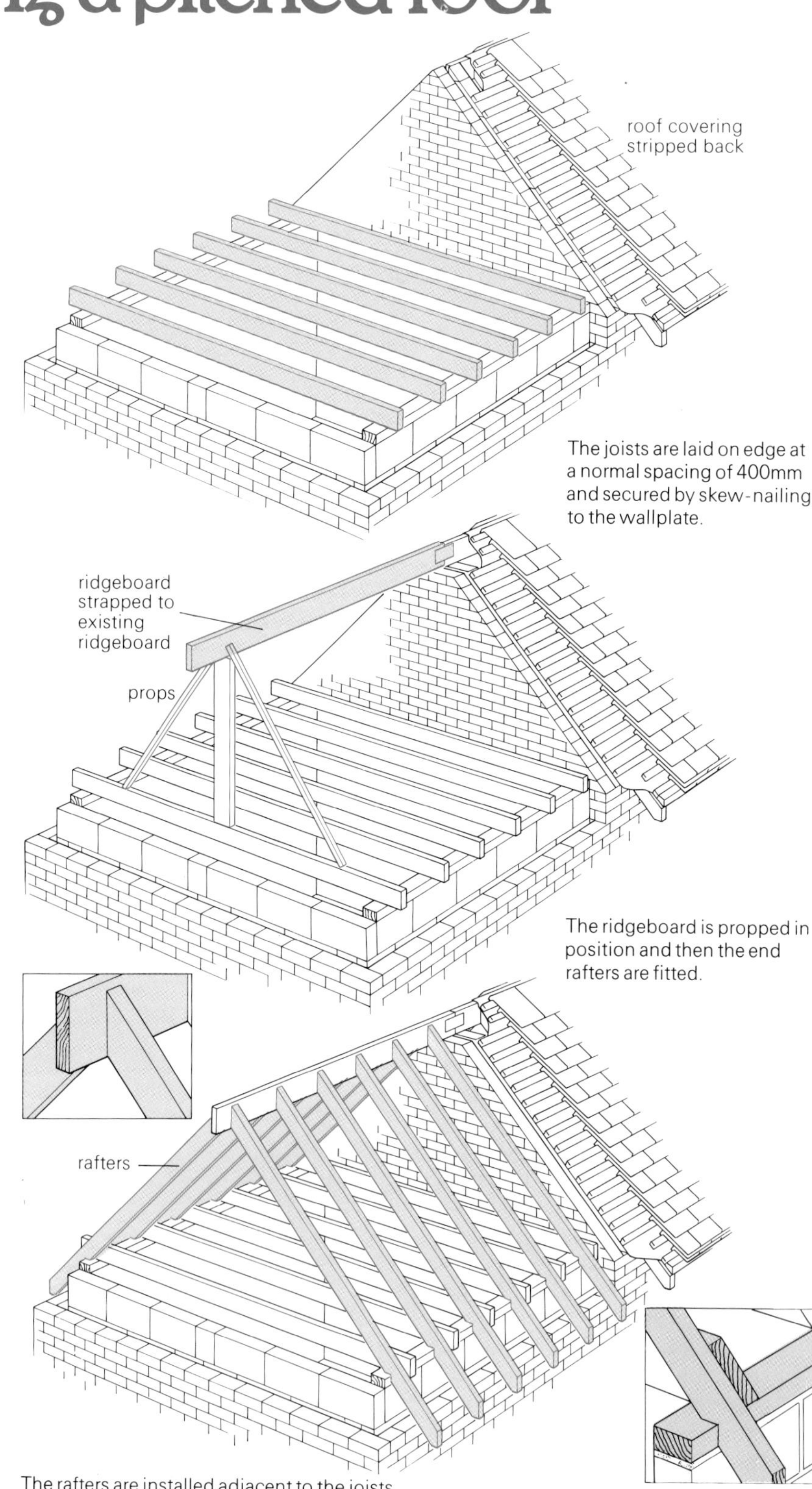


The joists are laid on edge at a normal spacing of 400mm and secured by skew-nailing to the wallplate.

The ridgeboard is propped in position and then the end rafters are fitted.

The rafters are installed adjacent to the joists.

house wall or the existing ridgeboard (if against an existing board the two are joined with steel straps screwed to both sides). The rafters, two at either end, can then be offered up and rested on the plate. Check for fit and nail firmly in place (taking care to ensure that the ridgeboard is level). Each rafter is skew-nailed to the wallplate, cross-nailed to the adjacent joist and through-nailed to the ridgeboard. If the rafters do not match exactly they are trimmed to fit.

The remaining rafters are then cut positioned adjacent to the ceiling joists, and nailed as for the first rafters.

On large roofs which have a wide span and long rafters, beams – known as purlins – are used to reduce the span of the rafters. On gable-ended roofs they are supported by the walls, usually on a corbel, but in a hipped roof they are jointed at the hips and act as a ring beam. If purlins are needed, they'll be shown on the roof specification that your designer prepares. Most extensions are small enough not to require them.

On an extension of cavity wall construction lay a course of bricks in the outer skin turned as headers to close the cavity and then build the brickwork to the top edge of the rafters.

EAVES DETAILS

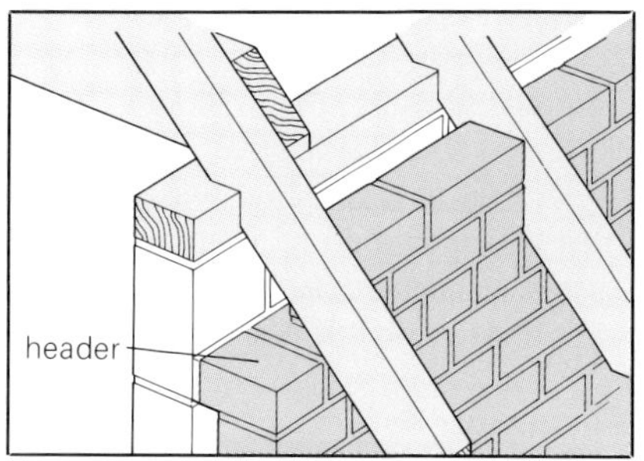


When the wall is a cavity construction, headers are used to close the cavity and the outer leaf is carried up to the rafters.

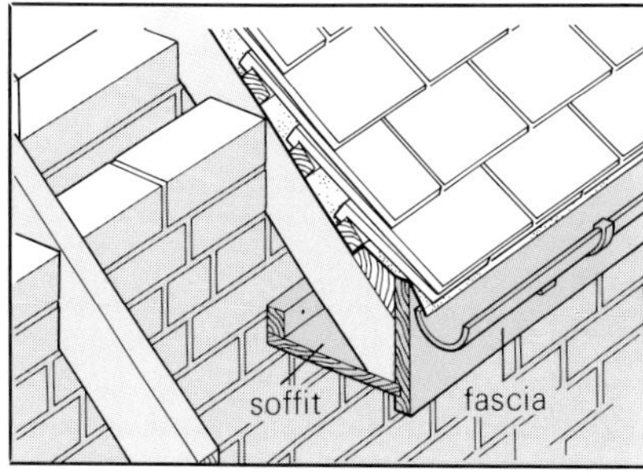


Soffit boards are fitted with the necessary gap for ventilation. The fascia board gives a neat edge and supports the guttering.

**Felt**

Roofing felt is reinforced with a layer of coarse hessian cloth; it is laid across the rafters. Start from the bottom and allow the bottom edge of felt to overlap the edge so that it will lap into the gutter when it is fitted. Nail the felt to the rafters using galvanised felt nails which have large heads. Allow it to loop slightly between the rafters; this forms a slight valley to drain any water which passes between the tiles. Each strip of felt should overlap the next one down the roof by at least 150mm. Arrange the top strip on one side to cover the ridgeboard and to overlap the top strip on the other side.

For a gable roof the next task is to fit the bargeboards which form the facing at the gable end to cover and protect the ends of the roof timbers and the wall below. These boards were traditionally wood, but now are often plastic, which does away with the need for painting a piece of the building that is high up and awkwardly placed. Cut the bargeboard end to the same rake as a rafter, but about 25mm longer. If there is no eaves projection nail it to the end of the ridgeboard at the top and secure it to the brickwork of the gable with masonry nails or screws and plugs. It's much sounder practice to have an eaves projection at the gable end, in which case, noggings are nailed to the roof rafters adjacent to the gable wall and built into the top of the gable wall.

The bargeboard is usually positioned so that the top of it will be level with the top of the tile battens when they are fitted but if plain clay tiles are to be used the board should be slightly higher.

## RAINWATER DISPERSAL

A soakaway can be constructed as a lined pit with holes in the lining – there are pre-cast concrete lining rings, but most domestic soakaways are simply a deep hole filled with hardcore (size range 10mm to 150mm) to within about 250mm of the top. The hardcore is then blinded or covered with a heavy duty polythene sheet and filled with soil to ground level. Where the pipe enters the soakaway it should be surrounded by large pieces of hardcore for good drainage.

The size of the hole depends on the permeability of the soil. The BCO may be able to advise on local conditions – in most cases 2m deep (measured from the bottom of the pipe) and 1·2m across would be sufficient.

To ensure that the sides of the hole do not fall in on the person digging use simple shutterings (150mm by 25mm boarding).

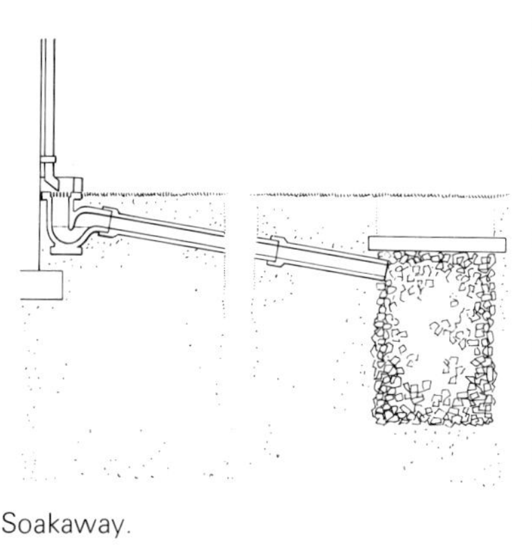

Soakaway.

## COVERING THE ROOF

Battens are nailed across the rafters over the felt. Batten size depends on the type of roof covering but for most applications 38mm by 19mm timber is adequate. The spacing of the battens (the gauge) depends on type and size of the slates or tiles being used. Cut a gauge batten to use as a measure or set chalk lines across the roof.

Plain or interlocking tiles have small projections called nibs which simply hook over the battens, but at least every fifth row on the main roof and all the tiles, on the edges, should also be nailed (or clipped). Tiles are usually placed left to right, bottom to top. Lay the end tiles on a good bed of mortar with a 50mm overhang. The mortar should squeeze between the tiles and is then struck off to give neat pointing.

Secure slates by nailing – nailing at the top on shallow roofs; centre-nailing on steeper roofs. Centre-nailing means less slates are needed and any subsequent repair is easier.

When tiling it is normal to stand on the battens, but stand directly over a rafter and take care that your shoes do not tear the felt. For roofs pitched at more than 30 degrees you need a roof ladder.

The tiling is finished with ridge tiles laid on a bed of weak mortar with a strip of roofing felt beneath each joint. The joints are pointed.

### Fascia and soffits

Before these boards can be fitted the alignment of the rafter ends and joists must be checked by means of a tightly-tied string and spirit level.

The soffit boards, which can be wood, asbestos or plastic, are often attached first – they should be arranged to allow the gap necessary for ventilation. Any joints in the soffit should be angled not butted. Secure by nailing up into the rafters or joists. Secure the fascia board by nailing into each rafter.

### Gutters

Most guttering used on domestic buildings is now plastic but cast or rolled aluminium guttering is useful where a match is required. The gutter is mounted in brackets screwed to the fascia with a slight fall to let the water drain. The fall is set by stretching a string at the required slope.

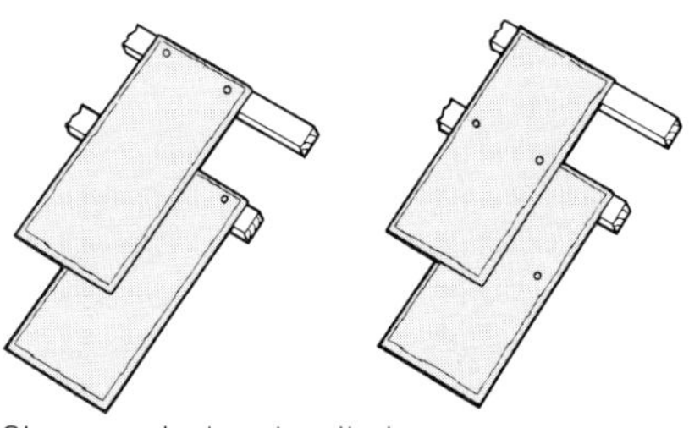
Slates can be head-nailed or centre-nailed' With head-nailing the overlap is great so more are needed on a roof.

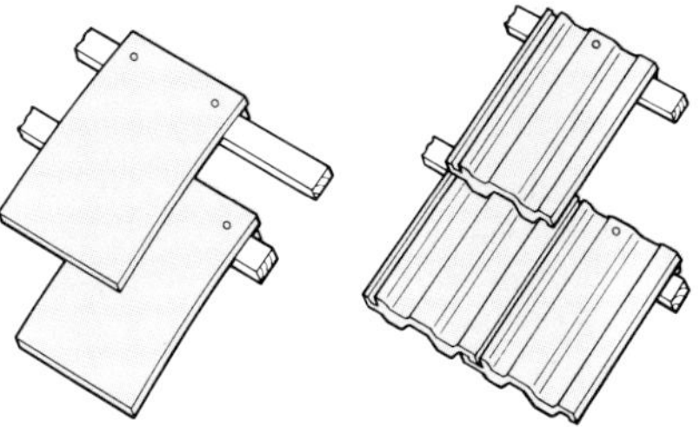
The lap between tiles and the gauge batten depends on the type of tile or slate.

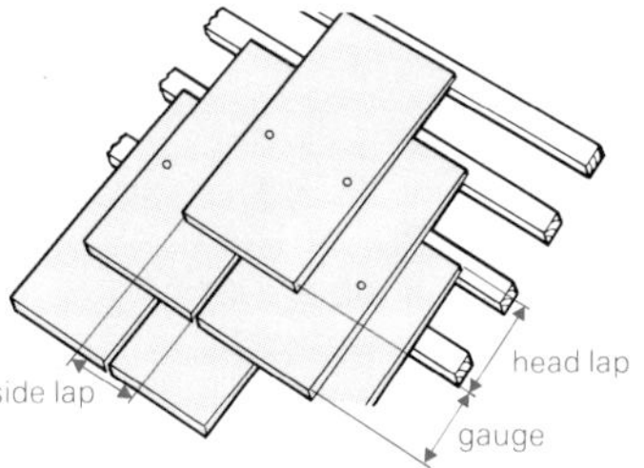

With the interlocking tiles the gauge equals the length minus the head lap.

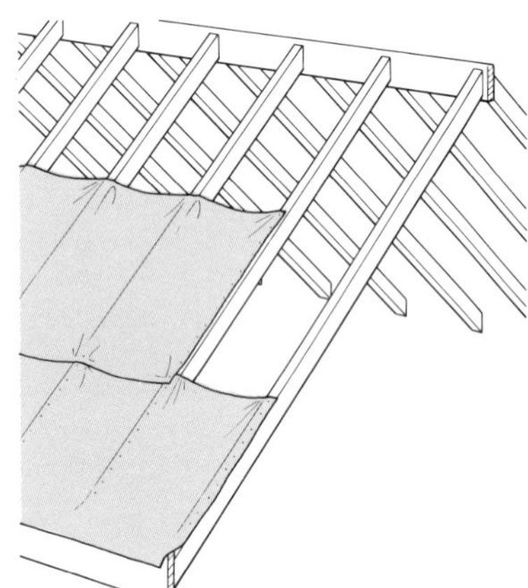
Roofing felt is laid across the rafters starting from the bottom. It is nailed with special large head nails and for good drainage dips a little between rafters.

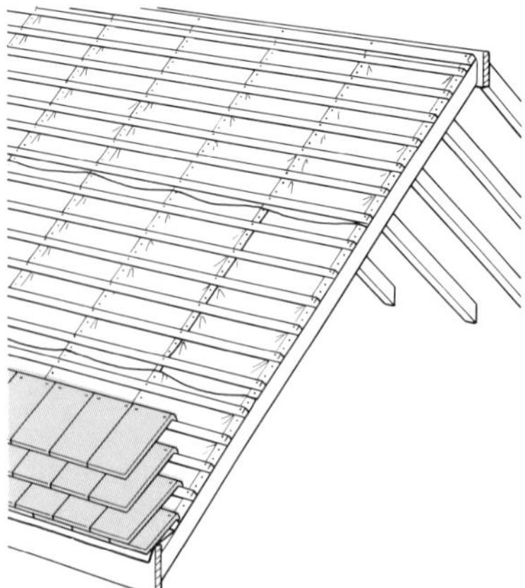
Plain tiles are hooked over the battens, and every fifth row on the main roof and all the eaves are nailed (or clipped) for additional security.

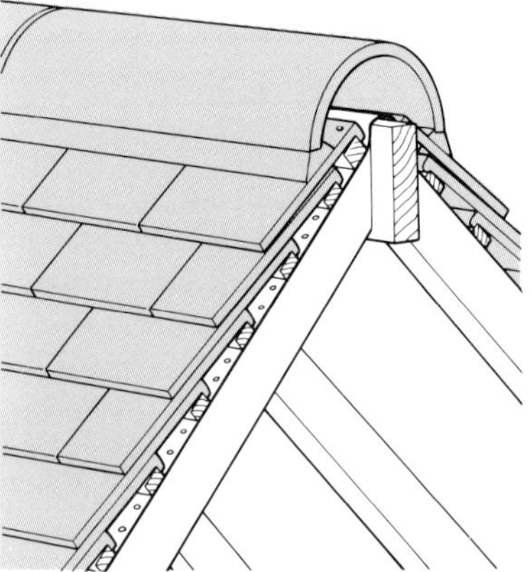
The ridge caps the heads of the tiles on either face. Ridge tiles are bedded on mortar with a strip of felt beneath joints. The joints are also pointed.

# Constructing a flat roof

The first two steps in constructing a flat roof are carried out as for a pitched roof, except that the ceiling joists are deeper. The timbers will normally be the same size as floor joists – typically 125mm or 150mm by 50mm. Flat roof joists are also longer than pitched roof joists as they overhang the wallplate to provide a fixing for the soffit board – on sides parallel to the joists, noggings are required for edge support. The details that follow are for a 'cold roof' with the insulation installed in the ceiling space below the deck.

Although in some cases the fall can be achieved by making the joists slope, it is more common to set the fall of the flat roof by nailing firring pieces across or to the top of the rafters – depending on the direction of fall. A firring piece is a tapered length of timber; timber merchants supply them cut to order.

The roof is boarded with plywood or chipboard sheets. If chipboard is used it is important to use a moisture-resistant grade type II/III – and to keep the chipboard dry at all times before it is covered. The boards are carried right to the edge of the ceiling rafters and nailed all round and to any rafter they cross.

A wood fillet 50mm by 50mm is nailed to the boarding on sides not served by the gutter and also along the edge that butts the house wall. This gives the roof a raised edge and prevents water draining off where it is not wanted. Nail the fascia board to the sides and ends of the joists. Finally nail the verge batten (a timber 25mm by 38mm) around the top of the fascia to form a slight overhang.

## Covering

Sweep the boards clean and start laying the first layer of felt at the centre of the lowest edge. To give this layer some flexibility it is nailed. Nail from the centre of the felt outwards at

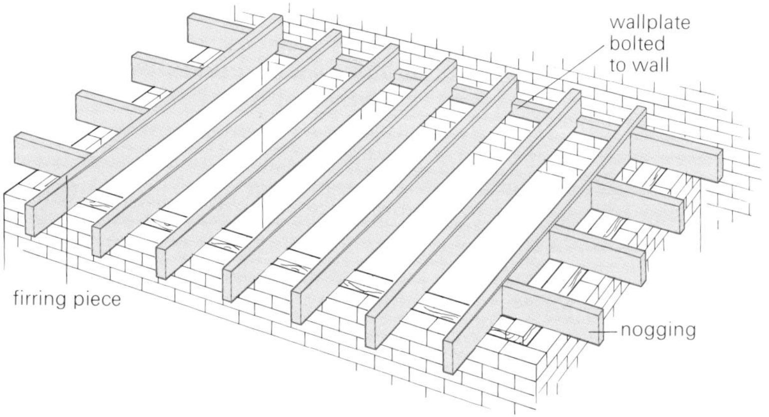


The ceiling joists are laid at 400mm (or 600mm) spacings. These joists overhang the wallplate on the outer edge and noggings are provided on the parallel edges.

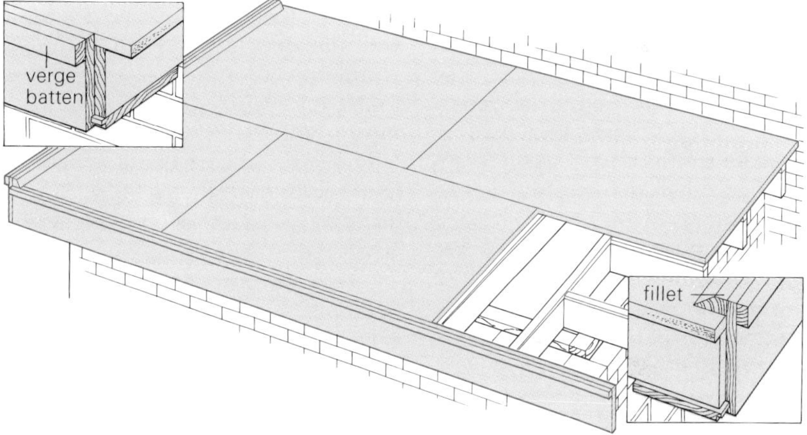


The roof is boarded with exterior plywood or moisture-resistant chipboard – the grade of board is important.

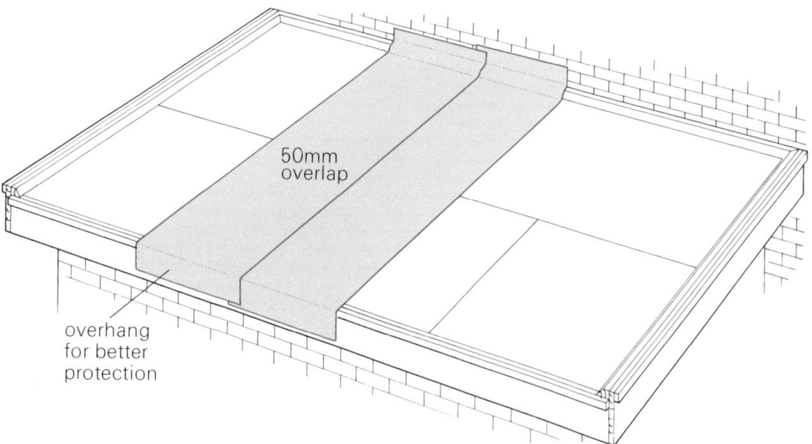


Three layers of felt are required. To give flexibility, the first layer is nailed roughly at 150mm intervals. Subsequent layers are firmly fixed on bitumastic compound.

roughly 150mm intervals. Overlap the strips by about 50mm.

At outside edges take the first layer of felt over the fillet and cut the felt flush with the inside edge of the verge batten. At edges adjacent to the main building cut the felt just short of the top of the fillet. At the corners of the roof fold the felt like a parcel corner before trimming.

At the gutter fascia cut a piece of felt about 250mm wide, nail it to the gutter fascia about 20mm from the top and fold it back on itself leaving a hang that will sit well inside the gutter. Attach the felt on to the top of the roof with bitumastic compound.

The second layer of felt is laid against these gutter fascia strips. Clean the roof, spread the bitumastic compound, start the first strip at an outside edge of the roof – allow for the fact that the overlaps in the first and second layers must not coincide and should be at least 50mm apart. Lay the felt on top of the bitumastic compound, tread it down and trim it. Repeat for the third layer, again laying the felt so that the overlaps in the layers do not coincide.

A verge batten felt finishes the edges. Lengths about 1·2m long by 350mm wide are fixed like the gutter felt with overlaps of at least 50mm.

The roof covering is completed by spreading more bitumastic and sprinkling stone chippings evenly over the roof. The last steps, fixing the soffit and arranging the guttering follow the final stages for a pitched roof. Ventilate the cavity, by fixing the soffit so that there is an air vent.

### The ceiling

The ceiling is constructed on the lines of the Guide on page 262. A vapour check *must* be provided, this is usually polythene sheet or foil-backed plasterboard. Thermal foil-backed plasterboard will improve the insulating properties and mean that the insulation in the cavity can be thinner. For instance, if a 32mm thermal board (12·7mm plasterboard and 27mm polystyrene) is used the mat need only be 80mm thick. This is desirable because it means there will be good space above the mat for ventilation.

## A waterproof joint

However the roof is constructed, the joint between the existing building and the new one has to be made weatherproof. This is a frequent source of trouble so it needs extra care.

For a roof which adjoins an existing house wall, a weathertight junction is made by using a 'flashing' strip which is secured to the existing building and overlaps the joint between the two buildings. Flashings are made of lead, zinc or aluminium alloy – all impermeable materials which are soft and easily bent and cut to shape.

The flashing is fixed after the roof has been completed and covered Remove the mortar to a depth of 25mm from the horizontal joint two brick courses up from where the two structures meet. It can be chipped out, using a plugging chisel and bolster or sawn with a brick saw. For a roof that pitches across the wall and therefore crosses several courses of masonry a brick saw can be used to cut the slot or stepped flashings (with a good overlap between each step) can be used.

Cut the appropriate length of flashing and insert one edge into the 25mm bed. Use small off-cuts of flashing as wedges to secure the flashing in the slot at approximately 300mm intervals. Fold the flashing down and form it against the wall to cover the joint and overlap the roof covering. Repoint the joint.

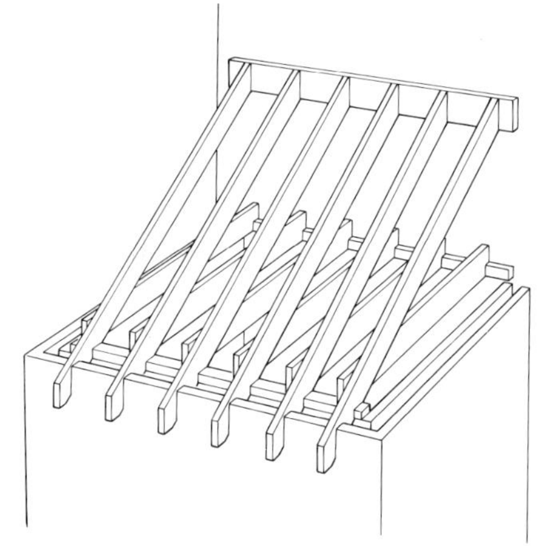

A lean-to (or mono-pitched) roof.

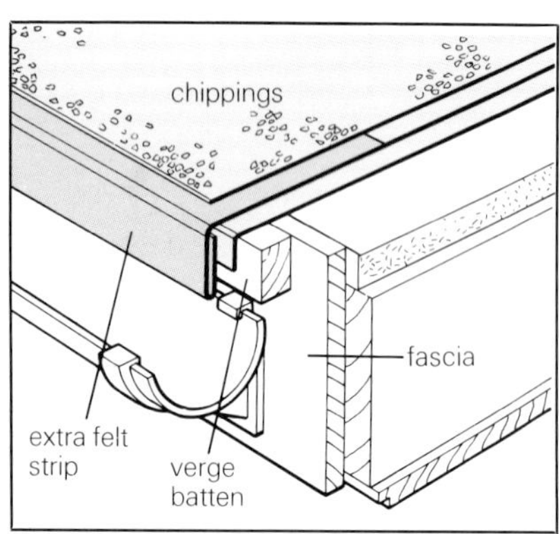


At the gutter edge an extra piece of felt, about 250mm wide, is fitted to overlap the main felt and hang into the gutter.

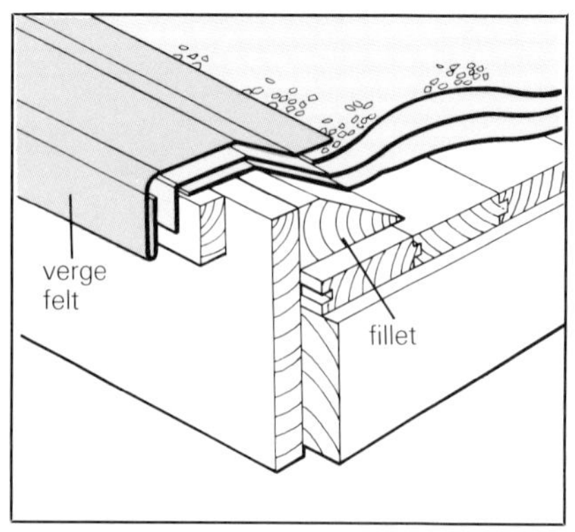


The verge felt is also fitted separately and cut flush with the fillet.

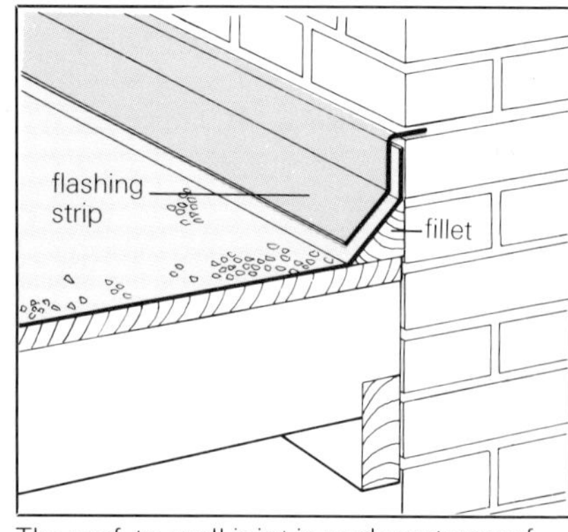


The roof-to-wall joint is made waterproof by flashing mortared into a raked-out joint.

# Electricity–a new circuit

Where an extension to an existing circuit won't do or isn't possible, you'll need a new circuit starting from its own fuse. If you have a consumer unit with spare ways it can be connected to this. If there is no spare way, a separate single switchfuse (or, better, a second consumer unit with provision for several new circuits) will be required and you'll have to call the Board in to connect the new unit. When you're connecting to a spare way in an existing box, just switch off the supply to the consumer unit.

## Installing the circuit

A new circuit would normally be a ring run in 2·5mm² twin and earth and protected by a 30 amp fuse. The theory is given on page 51 and the practical side on pages 52 and 53.

## A new consumer unit

Most new consumer units have a plastic or metal case, a third type has a hardwood frame with an open back and needs cable holes drilled and mounting on a non-combustible backing sheet.

Inside all units are fairly similar, depending on the type of fuse or MCB – see pages 48 and 49.

### Fitting

Before screwing the unit to the wall remove all the fuseholders (or MCB's), and connect the meter tails and the earth conductor. In most circumstances 16mm leads and a 6mm earth conductor will suffice for a 60 amp or 100 amp unit. Remove about 30 mm of outer sheathing and slightly less insulation – 25mm. Connect to the terminals of the main isolating switch, red to 'mains L' and black to 'mains N'. Connect the earth to the terminal block.

The circuit with the highest current rating goes to the fuse next to the main switch and so on down to fuses at the far end. The live connections are made either to the fuse holder or to an MCB which is then screwed into position. With ring circuits the two live conductors that form the ring are joined together first. The two neutrals and then the two earths are similarly joined and taken to their respective terminals – take special care that it is the two ends of the *same* circuit cable that are joined together.

The neutral and earth wires of each circuit are connected to their terminals in the same order as the live conductors. To complete the job, double-check the connections, fit the fuses, label the circuits, fit the cover and leave the main switch in the off position for the Board.

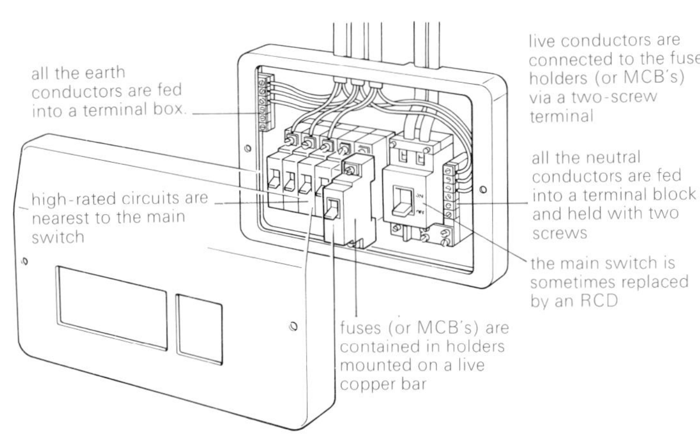

all the earth conductors are fed into a terminal box.
high-rated circuits are nearest to the main switch
live conductors are connected to the fuse holders (or MCB's) via a two-screw terminal
all the neutral conductors are fed into a terminal block and held with two screws
the main switch is sometimes replaced by an RCD
fuses (or MCB's) are contained in holders mounted on a live copper bar

Most consumer units have six ways; in this unit the circuits are protected by miniature circuit breakers.

### Removing a consumer unit

Once the electricity has been disconnected by the Board, remove the cover and the fuses from the existing unit. Release all the live conductors from their terminals and then remove the fuse holders. Label the cables as you remove them. Where the two conductors of a ring circuit are connected to one fuseway tape them together until they can be reconnected.

Release the neutral and earth conductors from their terminals. This leaves just the main switch to be disconnected and the old unit to be unscrewed from the wall.

## The Electricity Board

A consumer unit cannot be removed or replaced until the supply has been disconnected by the Electricity Board's electrician. The Boards are obliged to disconnect your consumer unit or fuse box from the mains at your request, but it must be in normal working hours and at least three days notice is needed. Only the Boards electrician may connect the supply. If a consumer unit is being replaced the job can normally be done in a day, so arrange for disconnection as early as possible and ask for reconnection at, say, 5.00pm. If a consumer unit is to be moved to a new position as well as replaced, you can organise things so that the new unit is wired up ready and then the Board's Electrician can disconnect the old and reconnect the new in the same visit.

The Board will carry out tests on any major new installation before they connect it to their supply. These tests won't necessarily indicate whether your installation is safe in all respects – see page 50.

# Lining the shell

At this stage in the construction of an extension, when the walls are up, the roof is on and the shell is ready to be finished, the various services are generally installed. You have almost carte blanche in deciding where these will go and it's worth being generous with sockets and so on, later on when the walls are lined and decorated changing your mind becomes much more expensive as well as disruptive.

**Lighting** Lighting to an extension can be: run from an existing lighting circuit (provided this doesn't overload the circuit) or installed as a new lighting circuit–see page 152.

It may be worthwhile providing the wiring for wall lights even though you might not intend to use them immediately. The end of the wires can be secured safely and neatly under small plastic covers.

**Power sockets** It costs very little more to have double sockets at each point rather than single sockets and it's also a widely held view that it is impossible to have *too* many sockets in a room. It is far better – tidier and safer – to plug into an adjacent socket than to have to run an extension lead from a socket over the other side of the room. You have most flexibility if the power supply to an extension is a new ring circuit; if it's installed as part of the existing ring (page 146) you may be limited on the number of sockets. If the cables are run as an unfused spur from a ring, only one double or single socket (or fixed outlet) is allowed.

**TV aerial sockets** Give some thought to the provision of a TV aerial socket in living rooms, bedrooms or even kitchens–see page 164.

**Plumbing** Any pipework will not be joined up to the fittings it will supply until the room has been lined and bathroom or kitchen equipment is installed, but some provision can be made while the room is still bare. Holes in the walls through which waste water pipes will pass can be made and pipes that will be hidden behind the lining can be installed.

**Central heating** Pipes to radiators can run behind the lining, along the skirting, in floor screed or under a suspended timber floor. Pipes under the floor should be kept well away from the perimeter of the room (to avoid carpet fixing nails). They must not touch.

All pipes should be tested and lagged (if under a suspended floor) before they are covered.

## Choice of linings

As the wall and ceiling linings can contribute to the insulating and fire resistance properties of a wall, the lining has to be considered at the planning stage and details are included on the drawings that are submitted for Building Regulations approval.

The commonest internal wall and ceiling finish for a new extension is undoubtedly plaster – applied either as a wet finish or by drylining with plasterboard (which may or may not have a plaster skim coat) – for a do-it-yourselfer drylining is probably easier. Nowadays almost all new ceilings are plasterboard.

The advantage of plastering over plasterboard is that you start with a flat surface and you don't have such a long drying out time as with a plaster undercoat – new brick walls which are plastered can take several months to dry out sufficiently for decorating. Plaster and plasterboard give a versatile inner finish which can be painted, papered or lined with wallboards or cladding. As non-combustible materials plaster and plasterboard are often used to contribute to the fire resistance of walls and ceilings.

Instead of lining with plasterboard, timber wallboards can be used. These are sheets of plywood or hardboard faced with a natural wood veneer or with plastic laminate printed to simulate natural wood. (In England and Wales – but not Inner London – and Scotland there are restrictions on their use over large areas of wall under the regulations concerning surface spread of flame.) Cladding with tongued and grooved softwood boards is another choice but its use over large areas can also be restricted.

Brick walls can be left fairfaced, but this is not a cheap alternative to lining and as the bricks will be on display they have to be laid with special care to achieve neat joints and no mortar staining. The bricks would normally be a facing grade which are considerably more expensive than commons.

### Existing walls

An extension nearly always turns an existing external wall into an internal wall, and this needs to be finished and decorated in the same way as the inside surfaces of the new walls. An external wall, particularly a north-facing one, may have collected algae, and these must be killed by the application of a suitable fungicide and brushed off, otherwise the algae may stain any subsequent decorations.

Some bricks used for external walls collect chemical salts on their outer surface, derived either from the bricks themselves or from the mortar. These salts should be brushed off at frequent intervals before plastering. In severe cases, the subsquent decoration of such a wall may have to be delayed for some months because paper or gloss paint would be blistered and damaged by the salts. So, until the efflorescence dies down, a permeable and cheap wall finish, such as emulsion, should be applied. Other remedies are outlined in the Basement section on page 310.

## Plastering

Plastering has always been regarded as one of the most difficult jobs for a do-it-yourselfer, but in 1979 *Which?* trials with do-it-yourself novice plasterers showed that, with adequate information and practice, amateurs could achieve an acceptable plaster finish. Recent years have seen the introduction of new plaster products which make plastering simpler. Some of these new products are meant for feathering in old plaster to new (one of the most difficult plastering jobs); others are complete plastering systems capable of forming thick coats – they come with instructions. Plastering can often be avoided by opting to use plasterboard instead.

Plastering can be messy work (so cover up things that need to be kept clean), but you should aim to work tidily keeping tools as clean as possible because set plaster can affect the rate at which fresh mix goes off.

## Types of plaster

There are two main types of traditional plaster – gypsum plaster and cement-based plaster.

**Gypsum** plasters are for use indoors on dry surfaces. Gypsum plasters are basically gypsum rock which has been crushed and then heated to drive off water. When the plaster is mixed with water, the crystals of calcium sulphate (gypsum) grow and lock into each other and to the surface – leaving a hard finish. Driving off different amounts of water, and adding different retarders, produces a range of gypsum plasters.

**Cement-based** plasters are usually used outside where they're called renders. They are occasionally used indoors – for example, when you plaster a wall after treatment for damp or in a shower compartment to be tiled. Cement render is made of cement, mixed with soft sand and can have lime in it (1:6:1 is a common mix for use on brickwork).

## Coats

Plasters are supplied as undercoat or finishing plasters.

**Undercoat** plasters are applied quite thickly – about 10mm – to level off uneven surfaces like bricks and blocks. There are several types of undercoat plasters available – designed to cope with surfaces which absorb different amounts of water. (If a surface absorbs water out of the plaster too quickly, the plaster will crack.) Cement-based undercoats should be allowed to dry out before applying a finishing coat since they shrink and crack slightly as they dry.

**Finishing** plasters are generally used over an undercoat plaster, but some are meant to be used on top of plasterboard. They give the smoothest finish. They should be applied thinly – up to about 5mm thick.

### Plasters available

Most of the gypsum plaster readily available is lightweight. This contains minerals like perlite or vermiculite – to make the plaster lighter and easier to use and warmer and more sound absorbing when on the walls.

Most of the plasters in builders' merchants are made by British Gypsum whose brand names are Carlite, Sirapite and Thistle – though their plasters are sold under other brand names as well. The only other brand name that's common is Limelite plaster made by Tilling Construction Services (Tilcon).

**For a brick or block extension wall** you would use Carlite. This is the most widely available brand of lightweight gypsum plaster. There are several types of Carlite undercoat plaster and a finishing plaster. *Carlite Browning* is an undercoat plaster for use on fairly absorbent surfaces – such as ordinary building bricks and lightweight blocks. the wall is dampened before applying the plaster. If the surface is very absorbent, the plaster may crack and so *Carlite Browning HSB* (high-section background) should be used or the surface should be sealed with a PVA emulsion (bonding agent) before plastering. *Carlite Bonding* is an undercoat plaster for use on plasterboard and surfaces such as engineering bricks which don't absorb much water. *Carlite Finish* is the finishing plaster which the manufacturers recommend for use on Carlite undercoats.

**Over a cement/sand overcoat** you use Sirapite. This is a gypsum finishing plaster mainly used on cement/sand undercoats – it shouldn't be used on plasterboard. It is slightly harder than the other gypsum plaster finishes and, because it sets slowly and so can be worked smoother, is particularly useful if you want to paint the plastered surface. Sirapite sets in two stages. About 15 minutes after mixing it will be too stiff to use, but you can then re-soften it (called retempering) by stirring in a little more water – you then have nearly two hours to use it.

**Over a cement-undercoat** (or Thistle Browning mixed with sand) you would use Thistle Finish. This is a non-lightweight gypsum plaster.

**For skim coats on plasterboard** use *Thistle Board Finish.* This is made specially for finishing coats (skim coats) on plasterboard. Since this plaster is applied only 5mm thick, the plasterboards must be flush where they join.

## How much plaster

Measure up the area you want to plaster. Allow about 6 kg a square metre for undercoat plaster, 2 kg a square metre for finishing plaster – the exact amount will vary with the plaster and the absorbency of the surface.

When applying an undercoat in two layers – of 5mm say – you will find that the second layer often requires less plaster than the first layer, provided that the first layer is still damp when you apply the second.

### Buying plaster

Almost all large quantities of plaster (50 kg bags) are sold through builders' merchants. Because gypsum plaster can deteriorate if it is stored for more than about two months, be careful what you're getting.

# Plastering/plasterboarding

Plaster is applied initially as screeds between wooden guides nailed to the surface to be plastered and kept in line with packing between the guides and wall where necessary. Guides are about 25mm wide and as thick as you want the plaster undercoat to be – typically 10mm.

Prepare the wall by raking out mortar joints to a depth of 6mm and then fix the guides about 400mm apart and dampen the wall.

## Step-by-step

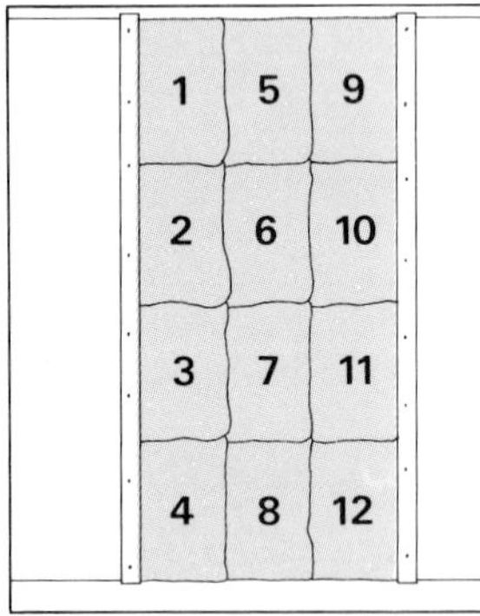


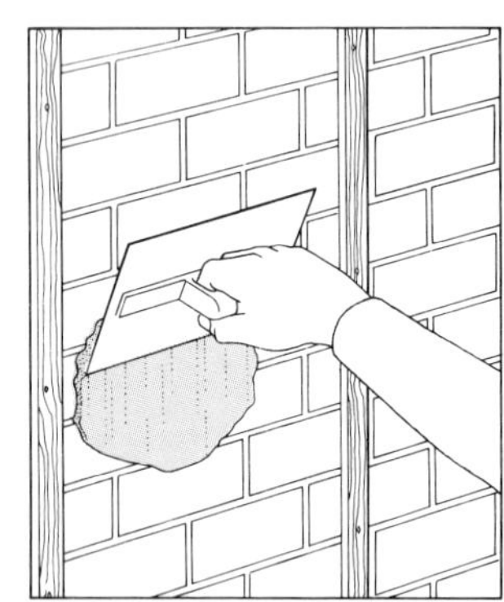

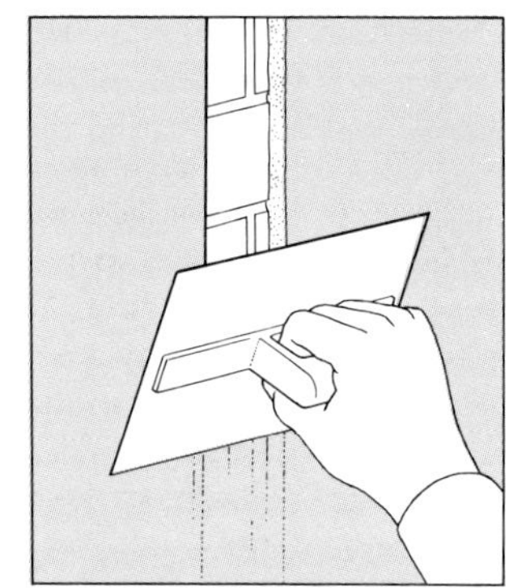

**Step 1** Mix up a cupful of plaster to check that it hasn't deteriorated. If it begins to go stiff within half an hour, you'll probably need to buy some fresh plaster. (You'll have to modify this test for Sirapite which has two setting stages.)

Mix the plaster in a plastic container using fresh tap water – impure water can speed up the setting time. Add the plaster gradually to the water, stirring steadily with a stick until the consistency is creamy. The mix should be just thick enough so that it doesn't fall off the mixing stick but can still be tipped from the bucket. Remove any lumps and make sure the plaster at the bottom and sides of the bucket is mixed in well. Keep the bag of plaster absolutely dry. At first do not try to mix up more than about one-third of a bucketful – about 2 litres of water.

Tip the plaster on to a dampened wooden board – a spot board. Stand the spot board off the ground so that you don't have to bend over too much. Workable amounts of plaster are carried to the working area on a hawk. You can make your own out of a bit of plywood.

**Step 2** Start by transferring a lump of plaster about the size of your fist from the spot board to the hawk using the face of the trowel. (Once you get used to the feel of the plaster, you can handle larger loads on the hawk.)

To get the plaster from the hawk to the trowel, tilt the hawk towards you and, in one movement, push the plaster upwards off the hawk on to the face of the trowel.

Start at the bottom of region 1 if you're right-handed (region 9 if you're left-handed). Push the plaster firmly against the wall and move the trowel steadily upwards, keeping it at an angle of 45 degrees to the wall. The first layer should be no more than about 5mm thick. When coming to the end of the stroke, flatten the trowel towards the wall a little.

Don't work right up against the guides and keep them clean. If you get plaster on the guides wipe it off at once.

Reload the trowel and start again at the bottom of region 2. Where you meet up with plaster at the bottom of region 1, flatten the trowel off slightly and move it in an arc to the right (left if your left-handed). Never flatten the trowel completely against the plaster or you'll pull it all off.

At this stage, the plaster will not look flat or smooth and if you've pressed too hard it will be rippled. Don't worry, carry on applying the plaster. It's much more important to get the plaster on the wall before it begins to set. Let each layer set just stiff before starting the next and continue until the plaster is just thicker than the guides.

The plaster is ruled off while it is still wet. Make sure your rule is clean and damp. Push the rule on to the guides at right angles and slowly work upwards, 'sawing' the rule from side to side as you go.

Clean off any plaster that collects on the rule. Fill any hollows with a little more plaster and rule off again. The finished ruled surface should look a bit rough. If it's smooth, you may need to roughen it while it's setting – plasterers use a wooden trowel (float) with nails sticking out of it. After about two hours, the plaster should have set quite firmly. Remove the guides and fill the gaps.

**Step 3** With the finishing coat, controlling the thickness is the main problem. Work an area at a time – about 1m wide and $1\frac{1}{2}$m high.

Put on the finishing plaster in the same sequence as for undercoat, using the same techniques. When you've covered a strip smooth off by lightly running the trowel from the bottom to the top – hold it at an angle of about 20 degrees. Fill any small hollows as before. Carry on applying the plaster in vertical strips, smoothing each strip. Then leave the plaster until it becomes stiff. Check, by pressing it lightly with your fingers to see if it's hard enough to finish – if it sticks, it's still too soft.

Use a clean damp trowel to smooth off the whole area. By pushing hard at this stage any lumps or high spots can be levelled. Fill hollows. Wait 20 to 30 minutes and them dampen the plaster using a large painting brush and smooth off again. Don't apply too much water – it can alter the setting of the plaster making it dry with a powdery or flaky surface. When the plaster is dry, smooth any remaining lumps with a fine abrasive paper.

## Plasterboard lining

Plasterboard is gypsum plaster sandwiched between two sheets of heavy-duty lining paper. The long edges of the boards are also covered with paper but the ends are not. It is suitable only for use indoors.

Almost all plasterboard is made by British Gypsum. There are two main types: boards made for plastering over and boards which can be used with one face forward for plastering or the other face forward to take paint or wallpaper directly – dry lining.

### Dry lining boards

Dry lining boards have an ivory-coloured paper on one side which you can paint, and a grey paper on the other side for plastering. The only widely-available brand is Gyproc wallboard. This comes in thicknesses of 9.5mm and 12.7mm with either square edges or edges that are tapered or bevelled on the ivory face. Tapered-edge boards should be used for decorating when the joints are filled and scrimmed to give a smooth jointless surface. When bevelled-edge boards are used the joints are accentuated as a feature. Square-edge boards are by far the most widely available.

Wallboards are made in three widths and many different lengths, but the ones you're most likely to find in the shops are 2400mm by 1200mm and 1800mm by 900mm with square edges.

There are several other kinds of wallboard (which may have to be ordered). These include:

- **vapour-check wallboard** incorporates a layer of plastic film. It is useful for ceilings above kitchens and bathrooms which can benefit from a vapour check, as well as all other places where vapour check is required.
- **thermal wallboard** is backed with expanded polystyrene which is useful for extra insulation.

**Step-by-step**

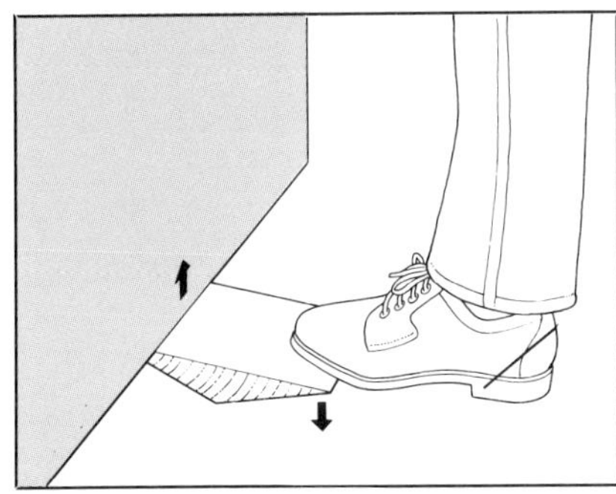

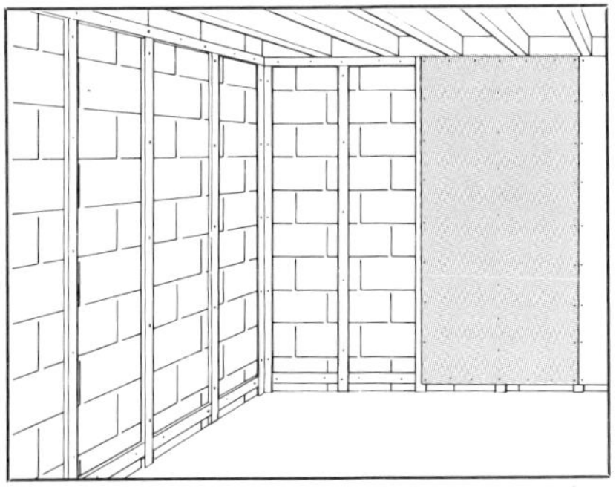

The easiest way to fix plasterboards to walls is to first fix wooden battens – not less than 25mm wide and 20mm deep – to the wall and then nail the plasterboards to these. Fix the boards vertically with the battens spaced a board's width apart. It helps if you fix horizontal battens about 25mm above floor level and about 25mm below ceiling height. The vertical battens can then be fixed in line using small wooden wedges between the wall and the battens. Extra battens can be fixed to the wall to support anything that is too heavy for the plasterboard.

All the plasterboard sheets must be positioned so that all joints lie along the battens. Cut the boards about 25mm shorter than the floor-to-ceiling height and lift them into position so that they press against the ceiling before nailing. Nail at least every 150mm along every batten, about 12mm from the edge of the board. Where walls may suffer from damp, use preservative-treated timber. For a one-man job a footlifter as shown is useful.

It is also possible to line walls by bonding polystyrene-backed plasterboard, with a vapour barrier, directly to the wall surface (there may be a further layer of plasterboard on the back, to give an insulation sandwich). Follow the manufacturer's fixing instructions properly, especially details on fixing the sheets to the wall to reduce fire risk, and on sealing joints to avoid condensation.

### SECOND FIXINGS

Second fixings is the building trade's term for the carpenter's second visit to install the internal woodwork, after the walls have been plastered or lined. Nails punched below the surface are generally used for fixing.

**Skirtings**, usually softwood, are available in a wide variety of sizes and profiles (so it should be possible to match existing woodwork). Plastic skirtings are also available with channels to house pipes and cables. Skirtings can be fixed to plugs set in raked-out joints, but it's better to install a batten – the thickness of the plaster – and plug the board to that.

**Architraves**, usually of wood, are mouldings which hide the joint between the plaster and a door frame. They are fixed to the edges of the door frame.

**Window boards** are traditionally wood, but plastic is increasingly being used. Sills usually locate in a rebate cut into the lower edge of the window frame and are fixed by masonry nails driven through the sill into the wall. Ceramic tiles and quarry tiles are another choice.

**Coving** There is a probability that a crack will develop at the joint between the ceiling and the wall. This can be masked by installing coving. Plain plaster coving is widely available, inexpensive and easy to handle. More expensive fibrous plaster cornices can be obtained made-to-measure or in a range of standard designs. There is also inexpensive (but less attractive) polystyrene coving.

Plaster coving is fixed by 'buttering' the contact faces with cove adhesive and then simply sliding into place. Heavier sections can be given extra support by nailing.

# Plasterboarding a ceiling

Plasterboard fixed to the ceiling is simply nailed to the underside of the joists. If the ceiling will be plastered a plastering-grade board is used, such as Thistle baseboard – a small board 9·5mm thick – or Gyproc lath – a narrow board 9·5mm or 12·7mm thick. Both these boards have a grey paper surface; there are insulation versions with a foil backing. The Guide gives details for constructing a plastered ceiling from either of these boards, but for a do-it-yourselfer a dry-lined ceiling, using wallboard ivory face down to receive decoration, is probably simpler. Although the joints then need more attention a plaster coat is not required.

Choose the thickness of board to suit the joist spacing: 9·5mm board for joists 450mm apart; 12·7mm board for joists 600mm apart. If a vapour check is required use a foil-backed board. Holes for ceiling roses can be made with a jigsaw or padsaw, before or after the boards are installed. In a ceiling with a vapour check any holes should be sealed.

A ceiling is normally lined or plastered before the walls are dealt with. Where a boarded ceiling meets a plastered wall (or vice versa), the joint should be sealed with pva adhesive before it is filled.

When wallboard is used on a ceiling the paper-covered edges are butted and cut edges are left with a 3mm gap and filled as normal.

## A hollow-joisted ceiling

A hollow-joisted ceiling has the joists left exposed and is an attractive alternative to a conventional ceiling. To achieve this the plasterboard is applied to the top face of the joists or, if that is not possible, to noggings and battens screwed between joists. The joists used for such an exposed ceiling would normally be planed all round timber, painted matt black or clear varnished.

If the ceiling height is critical, a hollow-joisted ceiling may be essential to meet the building regulations.

### Step-by-step

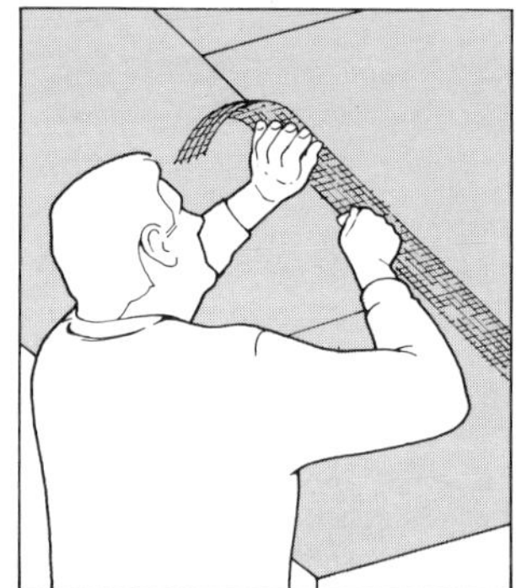

Both Gyproc lath and Thistle baseboard require support at the perimeter of the ceiling and noggings must be installed for this.

**Step 1** Starting from one corner of the room, nail the first board to the ceiling. You'll need a helper. One way to work is using the helper to support the board at one end while the nailer uses his head to hold up his end thus releasing both hands for nailing. Fix the boards with their long (paper-covered) edges at right angles to the joists. Start nailing from the centre of each board. Nail at 150mm spacings, 13mm in from the edge (to avoid edge damage) across the joists and then round the edges. Use galvanised nails 40mm for 12·7mm board; 30mm for 9·5mm board.

**Step 2** Allow a small gap of about 3mm between boards and fix the boards so that the joints are staggered across the ceiling. Normally you can achieve this by using the end cut from one row to start the next row. If this isn't practical because the cut piece is very short start the second row (and alternate rows thereafter) with a half board.

**Step 3** Fill all the joints between the boards and at the ceiling/wall edge with plaster, making a strip along the joint of 95mm. With baseboard all joints must be scrimmed; with Gyproc lath only the wall/ceiling angles need scrim. Cut lengths of jute (hessian scrim) to cover all the joints and, starting with the longest piece of scrim, open out each piece and press it on to the wet plaster. Do not overlap adjacent or butting scrims. For the ceiling/wall joint, fix the ceiling half of the strip first and then press the rest against the wall. The depressions over nails are spotted with filler to give a flush surface.

**Step 4** When the joints have set but not dried, plaster the boards. If the plasterboard joints are neat and flush, apply a single coat of plaster 5mm thick – usually Thistle Board Finish. For uneven joints you may need to apply two coats – Carling Bonding followed by a lightweight finishing plaster. See page 260 for finishing technique.

# Chapter 9
# PREFABRICATED EXTENSIONS

These days, most types of home extension, as well as most types of free-standing outbuildings – garages and sheds for instance – are available in prefabricated form. This means the building is supplied as a kit containing all, or nearly all, of the components needed in the construction. It can also mean that the method of construction is unconventional, using preformed concrete wall panels, for instance, rather than more traditional building materials These panels can be textured and coloured to look like brick, pebble-dash or rendering.

This chapter looks at four categories of prefabricated extension. The first three – porches, conservatories and sun rooms – are not regarded under the Building Regulations as habitable rooms, but can increase the area you have available under cover for storage or day-time use. Sun rooms and conservatories are most useful if you knock a connecting door through from the house. More substantial prefabricated extensions, with solid roofs and walls and higher standards of thermal insulation, are regarded as habitable space and can be built on as an extra room – a dining room, bathroom or bedroom, for instance – or as an enlargement of an existing room.

Sun rooms and the simpler types of conservatory are fairly inexpensive. In 1983 they cost £210 and £160 a square metre respectively when a builder carried out the erection. Surprisingly, the average cost of a substantial prefabricated extension is more than a conventional extension of the same size, though some brands are cheaper. A *Which?* costing exercise in 1983 calculated the cost of a habitable solid-walled prefabricated extension erected by professionals, at an average £430 a square metre; a small conventional extension would be about £400 a square metre.

A habitable prefabricated extension is unlikely to give the same investment return and increased saleability as a conventional one. Many are difficult to blend totally with the rest of the house and cannot usually be made to look as if they were always there.

This house has a custom-built extension with monopitched roof and a prefabricated sun room. Both are well matched to the style and materials of the main house.

# Window shopping

Since buying an extension 'off-the-peg', necessarily limits your freedom of choice when deciding the exact specifications you want your extension to have, you would probably consider going for a prefabricated type because it's quicker to put up, or because you think you may save money. Or perhaps you want to build the extension (or at least part of it) yourself and you're not confident of your ability to tackle a custom-built extension. Before you finally plump for a prefabricated building, these two factors – cost and the d-i-y element – are worth investigating fully.

## Working out the cost

In response to an enquiry about their products, most extension firms send out brochures describing the range of buildings they sell. In some cases, a price list, or a means of calculating prices, is included; in others the firm invites you to arrange for a representative to call to give estimates.

In any case, the range of sizes and options within many extension systems is very large, especially for habitable extensions. This makes pricing the whole job complicated and it's easy to overlook the cost of features which you think are standard but turn out to be optional extras.

First decide roughly the size of extension you want. Choose what sort of doors you want (single or double, hinged or sliding patio doors), and roughly the number and size of the windows. If you're thinking about buying a conservatory, decide on whether you need opening windows, louvre panels or roof vents. Some have staging (free-standing shelves around the edge).

When you have a fairly clear picture of the extension you're looking for, work out from the manufacturers' brochures how much each different system would cost. And note how close to your 'ideal' extension each different type is. With some extensions, features such as guttering, drainpipes, double glazing and patio doors come as standard; in others their cost is added to the basic price.

If you choose to have your extension erected by the manufacturer or a builder appointed by him, and this work is included in the price, make sure the work covers the building of foundations and floor (if it doesn't, reckon on from £30 a square metre for conservatories, from £60 for sun room and solid walled extensions, to have this work done). Check on the installation of rainwater drains and the complete construction of the roof. The price may or may not include any wiring or plumbing work.

As long as you're sure you can resist his sales talk, it's probably valuable to ask a representative to call. He can examine the site for any unusual features (such as drains) that will affect the cost of erecting the extension.

Of course, you can't compare the relative cost of different extensions unless you can compare them for quality, too. Prefabricated extensions are constructed from a wide variety of materials, many of which are best compared by close inspection. Most extension companies maintain display sites where you can see their buildings already erected. A visit is essential to make sure you'll be pleased with your own extension once it's built. A *Which?* report on some of the brands available was published in May 1983.

## The work involved

Even if you employ the extension company to erect your building for you, you may end up doing some of the work (like laying the foundations) yourself, or employing builders or other tradesmen to help. For those with enough skill, enthusiasm and

A prefabricated extension with tile-hung fascia and mock-brick panels.

spare time, the complete d-i-y building of an extension from a prefabricated kit may be an attractive proposition. However, before you embark on this option, make sure you're saving yourself enough money to make it worthwhile, and that you're capable of tackling the work involved.

The financial saving you can make by doing it yourself is complicated by the taxman: a prefabricated extension delivered in kit form for you to erect attracts VAT; the same extension built by the supplying company or subcontracted to a VAT – registered builder is zero-rated. Be careful to compare the *taxed* d-i-y cost with the *tax-free* cost plus building charges. For expensive, but fairly easily-erected buildings, like some conservatories, d-i-y construction may not be worth the bother. In other cases, a compromise may be the best solution. For example, you may decide to lay the foundations and install the drains and do any wiring and plumbing, while the extension company erects the walls and fits the roof. (Some companies do not in any case undertake foundation work.) Wiring and plumbing in a prefabricated extension are little different from these jobs in any other building. The foundations for a conservatory are just a simple concrete slab – see page 276.

A visit to a display site may help to assess whether you'd be capable of building a particular extension. The company may also be able to refer you to a previous customer who has taken the d-i-y option. An important factor in deciding which extension to go for is the clarity of the d-i-y instructions. *Which?* has found that they vary from very clear to non-existent. Study them before you commit yourself.

Although most companies assure potential customers that they'll need only average handyman skills, in most cases there are parts of the job that require more than one pair of hands.

A grand type of conservatory. ▲

A simple fully-glazed sun room. ▶

# Porches

An enclosed porch added to a front or back door has a number of advantages over a door opening straight into the house. It cuts down draughts and improves heat and sound insulation. If the outer door is locked, it can improve security. And a porch provides a useful area for taking off, and even storing, muddy boots. If it's glazed, it can be used as a small conservatory.

## Types of porch

The type of porch you will be able to build will depend to a large extent on the design of your house. If you've already got an open porch area, with the door recessed some way back from the wall of the house, you can enclose this by fitting a door frame flush with the outside wall. The frame may need only glazed panels to fit in with the porch opening, or some brickwork may be necessary to make a more private porch.

A fill-in porch of this kind is a feasible d-i-y project, made easier if you plan the design around the dimensions of standard-size windows, lintels and door frames – check these with local builders' merchants. Or you could get a joiner or builder to do the job for you.

If your door is already flush with the wall of the house and you can't (or don't want to), create an internal lobby, you'll have to build out. You may be considering adding a porch at the same time as planning a larger extension to your home. In this case, you have the opportunity of integrating the porch more fully with the design of the house than it would be if it were built on separately.

When planning the construction of a separate porch, the options are much the same as with larger ground floor extensions – you can get one designed and built by professionals (or do one or both of these jobs yourself) – see Chapter 8, or buy some sort of prefabricated porch for d-i-y or professional assembly.

## The choices

There are two broad types of prefabricated porch – those that are part custom-built and those that come in kit form in a range of standard sizes.

### Part custom-built

These porches are manufactured largely to your specifications and designed to fit the site where they're required, but there are some limitations on what you can have incorporated into the design. It may be that the company specialises in a certain building method (timber framing with insulating infill, for example) so although you can get any size or any door and window layout, the porch will be built using that method of construction. In other cases, porches are made up from panels of standard widths and heights and you are limited by the dimensions of these panels (solid, glazed or door-frame) in different combinations.

The choice of these styles of part custom-built porches is quite wide. They're available almost completely glazed with painted wooden frames; in hardwood with glass or timber panels; with solid walls consisting of insulating material sandwiched by plywood, plastered inside and rendered or faced with a simulated masonry finish on the outside. Roofs are nearly always flat, but a few firms offer a choice of roof styles – flat, sloping forwards or sloping on both sides of a central ridge.

Part custom-built porches are usually erected by the company themselves and they usually take care of Building Regulations approval and planning permission application, if these are necessary.

### Porch kits

These prefabricated porches are supplied in knock-down form, for erection by you or your chosen builder. Kits are often sold by mail order, though larger companies do have inspection sites.

Although porch kits are made up of standard factory-made panels, a cer-

Enclosing an open porch.

Typical kit porch.

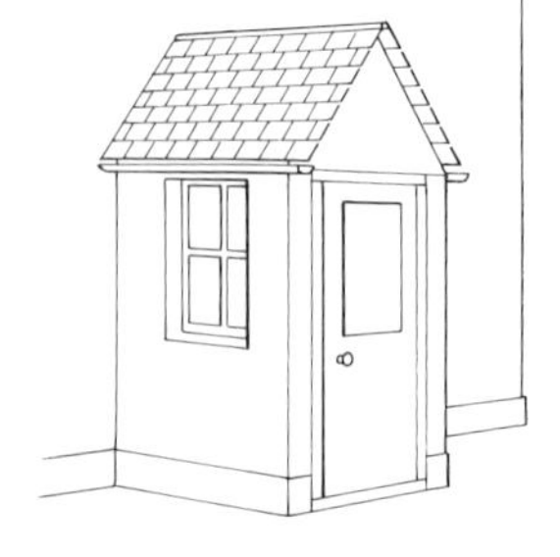

Brick with pitched roof.

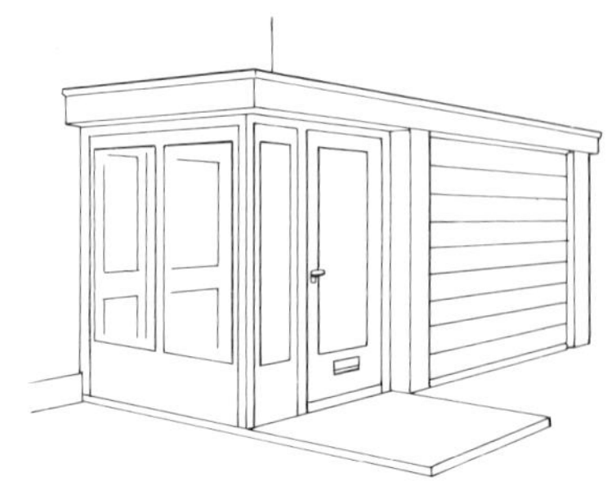

Part of a larger extension.

tain degree of variation is possible when you order. Flexibility varies from company to company. With some, you have quite a few widths and lengths to choose from as well as different heights. There are panel material options – glass of different types and thicknesses, timber and fire-wall materials, and optional louvre windows. With other firms, the porch design is less easy to vary, possibly with only two height options.

Despite this scope for individuality, most porches from kits look very similar. A typical construction measures about 1m by 2m and is erected on a concrete base. All three exposed sides are glazed with two glass panes divided by a horizontal bar, as is the door. There is a flat roof constructed of corrugated upvc sheeting or chipboard covered with roofing felt.

If you don't want an entirely glazed porch, there are more substantial porch kits. Another answer would be to turn to firms that sell house extensions in kit form, but don't necessarily market them as possible porches. Many of these extensions are of modular construction with the walls consisting of standard-sized bolt-together panels. An extension made up from just one or two such panels on each side would make a reasonably-sized porch. The minimum size you can order depends on which company you buy from, but most can supply panels to make up an extension less than 2m by 3m. From there, you can add panels (often in roughly 300mm steps) to any dimension you like.

In May 1980, *Handyman Which?* reported on six porch kits. The quality of materials they contained was found to be generally good, with the possible exception of the roofing materials which, in some cases, made effective weatherproofing difficult.

The amount of skill needed to erect the porches varied, but the more skill and knowledge you could put into construction, the better the results.

Once the concrete foundations had been laid, the porches took from four and a half hours to twelve and a half hours to erect. This assembly time didn't include the work involved in joining the porches to an adjoining house wall.

## RULES AND REGULATIONS

**Building Regulations**

In Scotland and Inner London you must submit the design of your porch for Building Regulations approval (page 24). In England and Wales, some types of porch have recently been exempted from the regulations. In these parts of the country, Building Regulations approval is not now needed for a porch with a floor area of two square metres or less, provided it is not built over an existing window or ventilator which is needed to keep the adjacent room within the regulations. The porch musn't be built over a flue or the draught inlet to a boiler or over a drain. If the proposed site includes a manhole, the cover must be a watertight one that conforms with the regulations.

If you want a porch larger in area than two square metres, or if there's any difficulty with windows, flues or drains, you must submit drawings of the porch you plan to build for approval. Most prefabricated porch suppliers will provide drawings.

Porches built within one metre of your property boundary must have the wall nearest the boundary made of fire-resistant material. Most prefabricated porch makers supply fire walls in standard sizes.

**Planning permission**

In England (including Inner London) and Wales permission has to be granted before you can start work on a porch which is more than three metres high, has a floor area larger than two square metres, or which will be built within two metres of a road or public footpath.

In Scotland the rules are once again different – you always need to obtain planning permission.

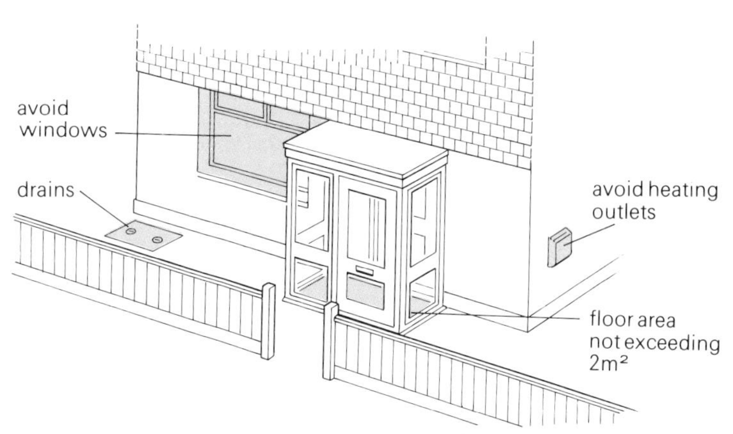


In England and Wales some porches are exempted from the need for Building Regulations approval provided the porch meets the requirements stated left and shown on the drawing.

# Building a porch

Part-custom built porches are usually erected by the company that makes them, though this arrangement may be flexible and you may be able to save some money by laying the foundations yourself – ask at the time of ordering. And there may be savings to be made by appointing a builder to do the work for you (see *Working out the cost* page 264). The cheapest kind of porch, though, is probably the one you build yourself, from a kit or from scratch. For such a small project you might manage without a professional designer. It shouldn't be too difficult to draw your own plans and get the necessary approval. A builder would probably draw his own plans too.

## Foundations

A simple concrete slab with damp-proof membrane (dpm) linked to that in the main house, is all that is required – see page 276. Take care not to block any airbrick under the door to be surrounded. This will be supplying ventilation to keep a suspended timber floor in good condition and you will need to move the brick or, simpler, provide a duct through the concrete slab to allow the ventilation to continue. Use a *clay drain pipe* bedded in the concrete and fit a grille at the end.

The floor can be brought up to house level (in which case you'll need to alter the threshold of the front door) or set to a level just below the threshold so that there's still a small step up and over the threshold – in which case the existing threshold can be left in place. A floated finish to the top of the slab will usually do, but if you want a better floor finish lay a screed over the slab when the porch is complete. The floor can be left bare or covered – see page 88.

A refinement you might consider is a door-mat well inside the door to take a door mat. Buy and measure the mat first and use a former of battens and hardboard to make the necessary dent in the top surface of the concrete. (You can also buy aluminium framed wells.)

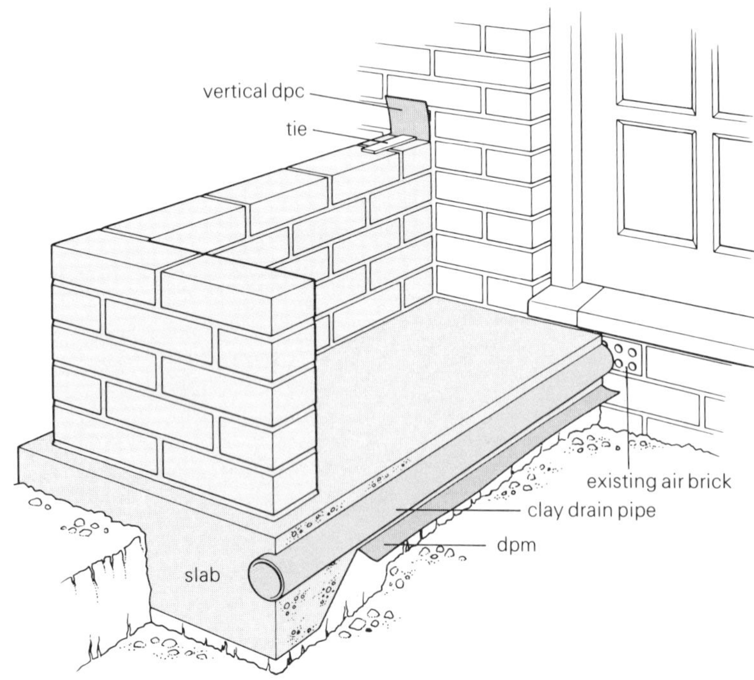


A porch can be built on a concrete slab, with thickened edges to support heavy walls.

## Walls

Solid walls of brick or block can be built on the concrete slab (the slab should have thickened edges if the masonry is more than 1m or so high). There is no need for a damp-proof course (dpc) beneath the wall as the dpm in the slab will halt rising moisture. A vertical dpc between the porch walls and the house wall is required.

The porch walls can be tied to the house wall – the method using dowels described on page 244 is easier than bonding in the bricks. For the sake of appearance, arrange the courses so that they line up.

A small project like this is a good way to learn brick (or block) laying, but timber-frame walls are probably easier to build. Panels can be constructed on site as described for a timber-framed extension (page 245). An alternative is to use standard-sized door and window frames screwed or bolted together. Some joinery firms suggest this and can provide a special sill.

## Roof

Most porches have a flat roof, but for such a small project a pitched roof of some sort is hardly more difficult or expensive to build and it may look much better. On the other hand, if there's a window above the porch or the porch is being added to a bungalow, there may not be room to fit a pitched roof. As a porch is not habitable space, the roof can be translucent – corrugated plastic perhaps – or, for better appearance, wired glass.

Whatever the type of roof there must be provision for drainage and the joint with the house wall must be well made – see page 256.

# Conservatories

The term 'conservatory' describes house extensions which are almost entirely glazed. The distinction between a conservatory and a sun room is not very marked, and many manufacturers use both words to describe the same building. In this Chapter 'sun room' describes extensions with a large window area, but with some solid wall area as well. Most have a corrugated plastic roof.

A conservatory isn't an alternative to a completely solid-walled habitable extension. An obvious drawback is that its use will be limited by the weather. On winter days an unheated conservatory which doesn't catch a lot of sun will be of limited use as a place to sit, and heating an area with such poor thermal insulation would be expensive. If you do decide to install some form of heating in your conservatory, a double-glazed type would be worth considering to cut down a little on heating bills. However, the double glazing normally offered for conservatories is the type with a secondary pane and this can be a condensation trap. In summer, a conservatory can get very hot, so opening lights, available as optional extras in some models, are worth considering.

A conservatory can be used entirely for the propogation of plants. Or you can increase its potential and make it more of a house extension by installing double doors between the conservatory and the house, using the area as part plant-house, part sun-room, part dining or sitting area.

## The choices

Conservatories are nearly all prefabricated to some extent, consisting of standard glazing bars supporting sheets of glass. A wide range of different types is available, from the ordinary lean-to greenhouse to the more luxurious palm house or orangery.

The grander type of conservatory is generally wood-framed and can lean against the wall of the house or be a wing extending from the house. Grander conservatories are often ornate with shaped windows, friezes at the level of the guttering and finials on the ridge.

Attractive as they are, grand wood-framed conservatories are not cheap, and most don't lend themselves to construction by an average handyman. Although some are available in knockdown form for do-it-yourselfers with better than average skill, most are erected on site by the manufacturer or by a builder appointed by them or by the client.

The more commonly-available, and less expensive, lean-to type of conservatory is a more likely option for someone on a restricted budget or a handyman wishing to do the building work himself.

Two types of conservatory – one is grand, ornate and expensive; the other a much simpler aluminium-framed lean-to.

Lean-to conservatories are usually aluminium framed, the glazing bars often treated with a bronze or white finish to prevent the metal oxidising. The commonest shape has a sloping roof which connects with the walls at curved eaves – these are usually glazed with flexible plastic. The glass is held in a groove in the glazing bars either with wire springs that push it against a soft plastic strip, or between two of these strips. Between adjacent bars, the wall may consist of two or three small panes which overlap each other like slates on a roof or, better, there may be one pane that stretches from base to eaves. Double glazing requires a special type of glazing bar, so you must start off with this type if you're considering adding a second layer of glass at a later date.

The glazing bars form a series of 'ribs' along the length of the conservatory. By varying the number of ribs, most conservatory systems can be adapted to make extensions of different lengths, from around 2·5m to 3·8m, though longer conservatories are available. Some systems include middle sections as extras – any number of these can be incorporated into the construction to produce a very long conservatory. Some manufacturers offer more than one width but most just offer one width (around 2·5m) and one or two ridge heights (around 2·3m and 2·6m). The height at the eaves is usually less – between 1·7m and 2·1m.

As with most prefabricated extensions, the number of options available makes ordering the conservatory you want a complicated job. And features which are standard with some systems are optional extras with others.

The features to look for are noted round the drawing. For each, decide whether you'd find it useful, then check the manufacturers' brochures and price lists.

## Building

For a do-it-yourselfer, one advantage of a lean-to conservatory is that it is fairly easy to put together. An important disincentive is that the cost of having a builder in to do it for you would not be much more than the VAT you have to pay on the same conservatory in kit form. However, if you can get around this problem, constructing a conservatory should be a fairly straightforward job.

The conservatory should be fixed to a concrete base (see page 276) or, to give added headroom, to a low brick wall laid around the edge of a concrete base. A dwarf wall lifts the glass panels above the level where they can easily be kicked.

The elements of aluminium conservatory elements are bolted together and the whole frame fixed with wall anchors to the base and the house wall. Adhesive flashing and silicone sealant are used for weatherproofing.

POINTS TO LOOK FOR

**Shades** To keep the sun off in very hot weather, and to improve insulation, some conservatories can be fitted with internal or external shades, which roll up like blinds when not in use.

**Vents and louvres** Opening windows in the roof are essential to control the temperature in summer. Louvres can be useful to increase ventilation further.

**Automatic openers** Temperature-sensitive pistons can be attached to some vents and louvres. These automatically increase ventilation as the temperature rises.

**Double glazing** requires a special type of glazing bar. The second set of glass panes can usually be bought separately, so double glazing can be fitted later.

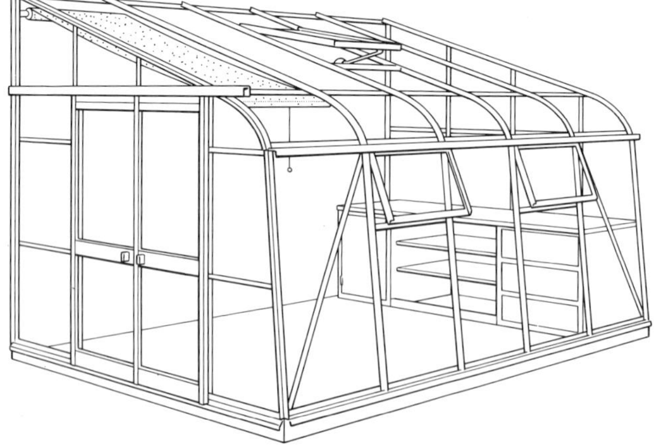

**Downpipes** In some conservatories, rainwater runs over the eaves and down the walls (this could damage the foundations). In others, there's a small gutter which can be connected to a downpipe.

**Staging and shelving** Intended for seed trays and plant pots, free standing staging or shelving attached to the walls can be bought to fit some conservatories.

**Doors** Doors can be sliding or hinged. They're usually situated in the end (or both ends) of the conservatory, though some are available with a door at the front. Some hinged doors have automatic closers.

**Base** The conservatory is fixed either directly on to a concrete base, or on to a special plastic, steel or wooden base frame. Some have pegs to anchor the conservatory to the ground.

# Sun rooms

Being part-glazed, part solid-walled and with a translucent roof, a sun room is intermediate between a conservatory and a habitable extension. A sun room has some of the advantages of a conservatory – it's relatively cheap, is easy and quick to build and, of course, gives you a room that will catch the sun and provide you with a good view of your surroundings. It has some of the advantages of a habitable room, too – heating a sun room to extend its use into early spring and late autumn is a feasible proposition. For evenings, you can fit blinds or curtains. Some have suspended ceilings as an extra (which helps to insulate the roof).

## Choices

Most sun rooms consist of a wooden framework with walls divided at about waist height between window above and wood panelling (usually western red cedar) below, though some models are available with the lower part of the wall finished in stone aggregate on concrete panels. Usually the walls are lined with plasterboard on the inside.

Above the windows and running the length of the sun room, is a plastic or wooden fascia. Sometimes this is quite deep, concealing guttering behind. In other cases it's a narrow strip, overhung by the roof, with guttering fixed directly on to it. The roof is made of corrugated translucent plastic supported on softwood rafters. The better roofs which are less prone to condensation have a double-skin of plastic, with a ventilated space between.

Look carefully at the method of glazing. The best have timber beading and a rubber seal.

Prefabricated sun rooms are usually built on a modular system and so many different lengths and widths can be obtained. Most systems allow you to build a sun room as small as 2m by 2m and as big as about 3m wide and 6m or 7m long. Most manufacturers offer a choice of two heights – generally around 2·2m and 2·5m.

When comparing prices, make sure each includes all the basic features you need, such as glass, roofing materials, flashing, sealants, and guttering – in some systems these are 'extras'.

Most manufacturers offer optional fire-resistant end walls. In order to satisfy the Building Regulations, any sun room built within a metre of the boundary of your property must have a fire resistant outward-facing wall.

## Building

When it comes to the construction of a prefabricated sun room, companies differ in what they offer. Most provide a construction service, employing their own builders or sub-contracting to local agents. In some cases, this service does not include the laying of the concrete base – you have to do this yourself or arrange for a builder to do it for you. To avoid any difficulties you may have in storing the sun room before it goes up, it's a good idea to make sure the base is complete before the sun room components are delivered.

The alternative is to build the whole thing yourself. Most companies offer this option and claim that it's easy for a handyman, following their instructions, to screw or bolt a modular prefabricated sun room together.

Once it is all together you seal the joints with the house wall with mastic and the roof with flashing.

Sun rooms are part glazed, part solid walled with a translucent roof. The lower panels can be replaced with glazing to create more of a conservatory atmosphere.

# Solid-walled prefabs

For habitable space the traditionally-built kind of extension has a number of important advantages over a prefabricated building. It's easier to match the extension to the house because they can both be built the same way from the same materials. And the design can be more flexible and therefore imaginative.

To a greater or lesser extent, this is sacrificed if you go for a prefabricated system. There's only a narrow choice of floor plans and roofs are nearly always flat, and you may have to compromise over the match between the wall material of your extension and that of your house. Prefabricated extensions are all one-storey, so are out of the question if you're considering expanding your house on two levels. And most important of all, they usually don't turn out to be any cheaper or to be any easier to organise and build or have built.

However, if you're satisfied with the specifications offered by a prefabricated extension, you may feel the advantages of an easy-to-buy off-the-peg building outweigh the various snags.

◀ An extension in mock brick with a uPVC fascia. Replaces an old lean-to greenhouse to create habitable space which could be used as a dining area.

## The choices

Extensions which can be used as habitable rooms can usually be built with one, two or three new walls – to fill in a yard, or an internal corner formed between two walls of the house, or as a block added on to the house wall. The same building systems can also be used to make free-standing buildings.

Construction methods are very varied. Many prefabricated extensions are supported by a frame (either timber or steel) to the outside of which is fixed some sort of cladding – cedar panelling, rendered boards, over-lapping concrete tiles or concrete slabs

This similar habitable extension has rendered walls and a tile-hung fascia. ▼

EXTENSIONS

Two-sided extension installed against two external walls.

L-shaped extension to fit alongside the house and partly round the back.

Extension built out from the main house. wall.

finished to look like brickwork or pebbledash. Alternatively, the walls may consist of structural concrete panels, either stretching from floor to roof or made up of smaller sections, without any supporting frame. Such panels are generally bolted together and bolted to the base and walls of the house. A variety of exterior finishes is available – mock brickwork of various colours, render or pebbledash aggregate.

Inside the extension, a wall cavity is filled with glass fibre or polystyrene insulation, to bring it up to Building Regulations specifications for thermal insulation – page 240. The insulation is covered with a vapour-proof skin to help reduce condensation, and finished with plasterboard and plaster. As with sun rooms, a habitable room extension within a metre of the boundary must have a fire wall, and all systems include fire walls for this purpose.

Roofs consist of felt-covered chipboard or plywood decking supported on timber joists and finished with insulating infill and a plasterboard ceiling. The roof is usually surrounded by a high fascia – timber, tiled or plastic – which conceals the rainwater guttering.

The dimensions of your extension are limited by the width of the modules from which it's constructed. However, these units are usually quite narrow, so you can specify an extension to within about 0·5m of your ideal size. Most systems are extremely flexible about the shape of the building – you can have any proportion of length and width, or sometimes even specify an L-shaped extension with an internal corner.

Most manufacturers offer a choice of window and door styles, frame materials and sizes, and you also have the choice of how many windows you want, and where they are to be sited. There may be restrictions on the number and positioning of windows – too many together may not provide enough support for the roof, and there are limits to how much glazing you can have and still satisfy the insulation requirements of the Building Regulations – if you want a great deal of glazing a sun room or conservatory is a better choice.

Window frames may be timber, plastic, plastic-coated timber or aluminium. Some systems offer a choice between two of these materials, others don't. The same is true of glazing – double glazing is usually standard; you sometimes get the option of single glazing. There's usually a choice of styles of window – fixed or hinged, though some extensions aren't available with completely opening windows but only with a large fixed pane topped by a horizontally-opening light. You can occasionally choose

CONSTRUCTION DETAIL

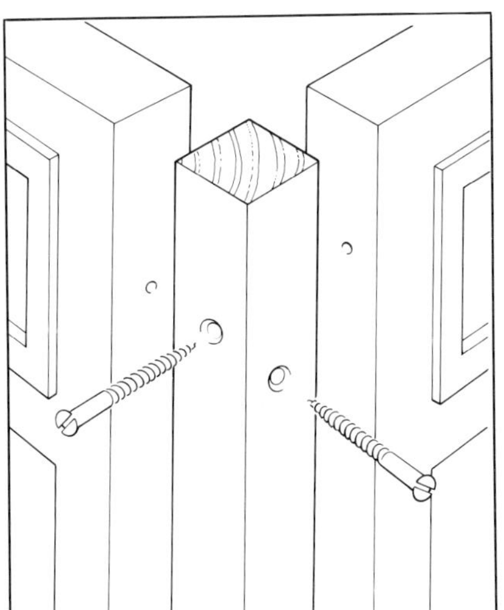

A frame, of timber or steel, is bolted or screwed together and to the house. Cladding is fixed to the outside.

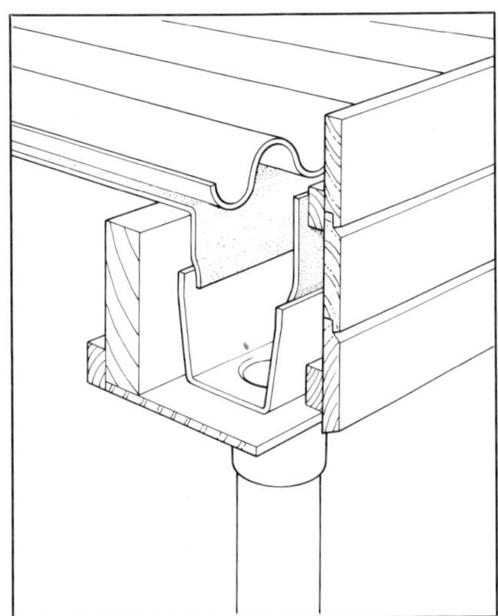

The gutter may be hidden behind the fascia, which may be timber, white plastic or tiles.

Georgian-style windows with glazing bars and bullion glass.

Doors are usually either fully glazed or glazed with two panels. Frames are found in the same materials as windows, and there's usually a choice of hinged or sliding, and single or double (patio) width.

The huge number of design possibilities available by choosing different combinations of all these options makes ordering the extension you want sound complicated. But most extension companies produce order forms which are quite easy to follow and could be used to cost the type of extension you'd like and compare prices between different companies. Most companies operate a system of sales representatives who can visit you to help you work out which options you want and how much the whole extension will cost.

In comparing prices, you should read all the small print to make sure there are no 'hidden extras'. One company, for example, may not provide roofing felt with their extension while another might. It pays to study the brochures very carefully. The sample specification form shows what you need to think about and could be a basis for a cost check.

The other important aspect to bear in mind when choosing an extension is who's going to build it. Building a prefabricated extension consists of a number of fairly routine stages, and different companies provide different degrees of aid at each of the stages. You may find that a particular firm offers more than one 'plan'. These will involve different degrees of involvement by you and the company; obviously the more the company undertakes the more you pay.

The best way to approach the problem is to decide which of the stages outlined below you're prepared to tackle yourself and which you'd prefer to pay the extension company to do for you. Then go for the firm that offers the right service for you at the most reasonable price.

In comparing different prefabricated extension systems for specifications and price, you would be well advised to contact a builder at the same time and ask what it would cost to have a similar structure built in brick, block or timber-framing.

**BLACKBERRY**
**e·x·t·e·n·s·i·o·n·s**

**order form**

WALL, DOOR & WINDOW UNITS

Wall units are 600mm wide, window units are available in three widths: 600mm, 900mm and 1800mm; doors are 900mm wide or 1500mm wide (double opening or patio doors). Heights available are 2.6m and 2.8m. Corner posts add 150mm to the external length of the wall.

| | number required | price each | £ | p |
|---|---|---|---|---|
| Corner posts | | £48.00 | | |
| Wall units (rendered) | | £68.00 | | |
| Wall units (brick or tiled) | | £76.00 | | |
| Window units 600mm (timber) | | £108.00 | | |
| Window units 900mm (timber) | | £158.00 | | |
| Window units 1800mm (timber) | | £310.00 | | |
| Add 15% of window price for double glazing | | – | | |
| Single door (timber – add £53 for aluminium) | | £173.00 | | |
| Double door (timber – add £96 for aluminium) | | £214.00 | | |
| Aluminium patio door (double glazed) | | £395.00 | | |
| For aluminium windows add £10 per 100mm width | | – | | |
| Add £10 per metre of wall length for extra height<br>Standard height ☐ Extra height ☐ | | | | |

ROOF & FASCIA

Solid roof is £50 per square metre
Price includes standard fascia. Add £5 per metre for western red cedar boards

OPTIONAL EXTRAS

| | | | | |
|---|---|---|---|---|
| Fire resistant wall (tick box if required) | ☐ | no extra | - | - |
| PVC translucent roof (price on application) | | | | |
| Bow window (price on application) | | | | |
| Venetian blinds (600mm £14; 900mm £20; 1800mm £38; cream only) | | | | |
| Extra for opening windows (600mm £23; 900mm £31) | | | | |

**All prices shown are exclusive of V.A.T.**

BLACKBERRY EXTENSIONS
Unit 4
Westhope Industrial Estate
Ferrywell
Loanshire CP32 8QT
Tel: Ferrywell (0926) 5412

Payment will be made by:-

| | | | |
|---|---|---|---|
| 1 Building Soc Advance | | 2 | |
| 3 Cash | | 4 Credit Sale | |
| 5 Access Card | | 6 Barclay Card | |
| Credit Card Number | | Credit Card Amount | |

NB Discount of 5% if balance paid before______

TOTAL CASH PRICE ______
VALUE ADDED TAX ______
ERECTION (see separate sheet) ______
TOTAL PRICE ______
LESS DEPOSIT ______
BALANCE ______

er form

Ferrywell
Loanshire CP32 8QT
Tel: Ferrywell (0926) 5412

Cash | Credit Sale
5 Access Card | 6 Barclay Card
Credit Card Number | Credit Card Amount

TOTAL PRICE
LESS DEPOSIT
BALANCE

NB Discount of 5% if balance paid before______

Use the manufacturer's order forms to compare prices between brands. Check the small print for hidden extras.

**Red tape** The design and specifications of a prefabricated extension need Building Regulations approval and, probably, planning permission before they're built – see page 218. Getting these approvals involves contacting your local authority offices, filling in forms and submitting architectural drawings and specifications of the building materials you propose to use. You will also require a building plan, showing the position of the extension on your property, doors, windows, drains and fences. And you'll need a plan to show the position of your property in relation to the others in your street, with the site of the new extension marked on it.

The extension company will usually provide the technical drawings; the rest can be done by you or, at a price, by them.

Although the extension supplier will make drawings specially for your extension, the accompanying specifications will usually be a standard format and may not give sufficient detail on some aspect of your particular building. Be prepared for the Building Control Officer to have some questions about the construction. Don't let this put you off seeking approval yourself; the BCO has asked for extra detail in about two-thirds of the applications *Which?* members have submitted for Building Regulations approval for extensions.

**Construction** There are a number of different ways in which the extension can be built.

■ *By you* The company delivers the materials; you (with a little help from your friends) construct the foundations and erect the extension yourself. You need confidence for this option and have to be a better-than-average handyman. The snag with this type of plan is that you have to pay VAT on the cost of the materials.

■ *By a builder working for you* As far as the extension company is concerned, this option is almost the same as the last: they deliver the materials, while you organise the rest. The company may help you to find a builder locally who has some experience in prefabricated extensions (possibly in their own range of extensions), but you arrange the estimates and dates, you pay the builder and check that he's doing a good job. You still pay VAT on the materials unless the builder is registered for VAT in which case he can buy the materials for you and reclaim the VAT.

■ *By the extension company* A few of the biggest companies retain their own tradesmen. This is probably the most satisfactory option (though it may be expensive) because the builders are likely to be experienced at erecting their own extensions and, should you be dissatisfied with the standard of work, you have direct recourse to the extension company.

In comparing different prefabricated extension systems for specifications and price, you would be well advised to contact a builder at the same time and ask what it would cost to have a similar structure built in brick, block or timber-framing.

▲ An extension with concrete wall panels made to look like brick.

▶ An extension made of pebble-dashed concrete panels.

# Slab foundations

There is usually no need to construct deep foundations for a light prefabricated extension or a sectional garage or outbuilding, and often none are needed even for a more substantial structure such as a detached garage or a carport with masonry walls. Provided the soil is firm and free from settlement a simple ground-supported slab 100mm thick will usually be sufficient. However if brick or block walls up to one storey are to be built on the slab, the edge of the slab should be thicker than the rest.

Whether a slab will suffice for Building Regulations compliance depends on the purpose of the structure, and in the case of one adjoining and communicating with a house this may be a matter of local interpretation, so check before submitting drawings specifying a slab.

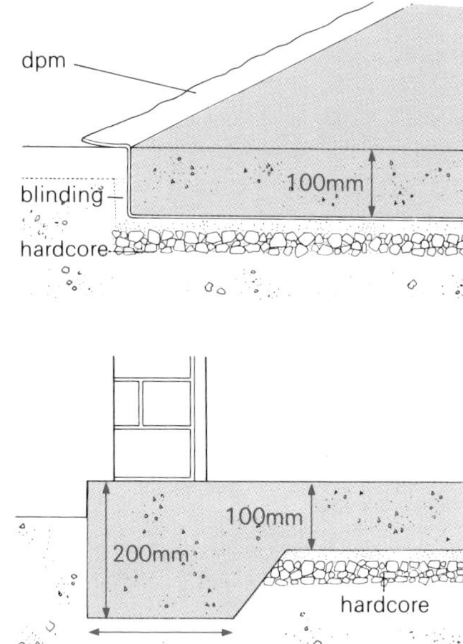


A simple ground-supported slab and a slab with thickened edges.

## Design

For a very light-framed structure such as an aluminium conservatory or sun room a plain unreinforced slab 100mm thick will normally be adequate. On firm, well-compacted soil free from vegetable matter the slab can often be laid directly on levelled ground. To give added stability on clayey or peaty soil, or to make up levels, a base of sound, well-compacted hardcore will be required: it should also be at least 100mm thick.

If brick or block walls higher than about 600mm are to be built on the slab, the depth will need to be increased to 200mm at the edges of the slab. The thickened portion should be twice the maximum width of the wall and on the same centre line. The transition from the thicker to thinner portions of the slab should be tapered smoothly, not stepped.

Depending on the use of the extension or building, a polythene or bitumen-polythene damp-proof membrane (dpm) may be needed between the soil or sub-base and the slab itself: it should extend up around the edges to tie in with the damp-proof course (dpc) between the slab and the walls.

### Setting out and preparation

Strip topsoil and all vegetable matter; set out building lines and levels as described on page 229. Trim the surface

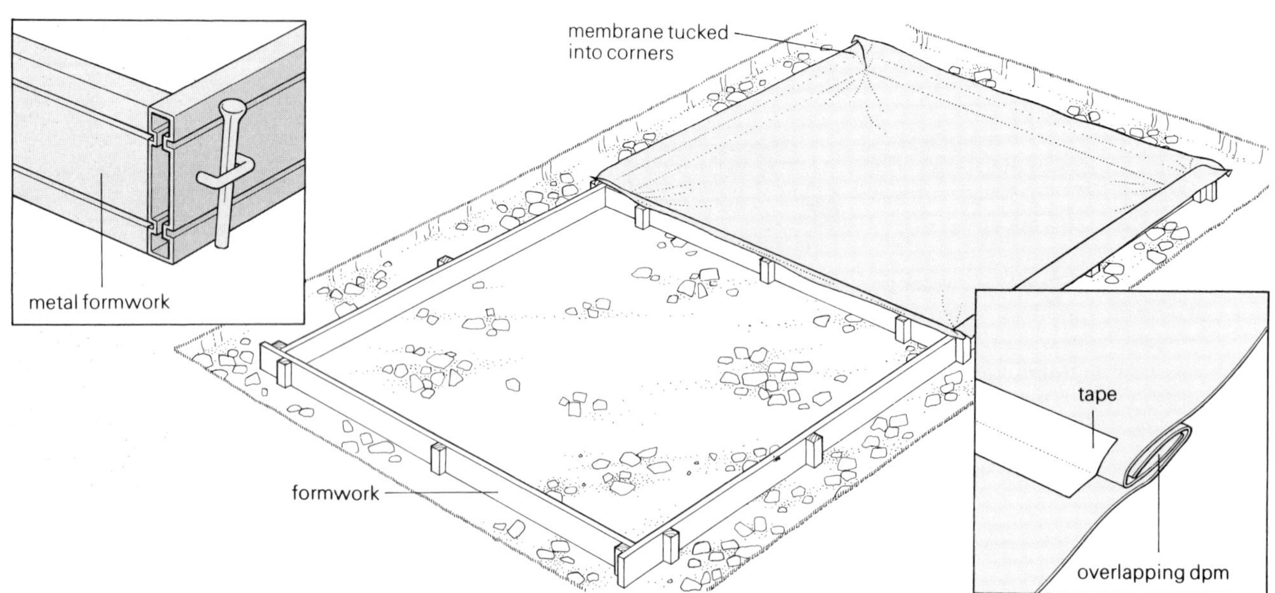


Simple side forms of smooth timber (or steel) contain the concrete while it hardens.

to finished slab level minus slab thickness and the depth of hardcore if any is required. Compact well with a tamper or roller (an old car tyre, bounced up and down, makes a good rolling tamper).

Spread and thoroughly compact sub-base material if you need it.

The cleared ground and sub-base should extend 200mm or so outside the slab boundary to allow for fixing down the side forms.

**Side forms**

Simple side forms will be needed to contain the concrete until it hardens; they will also serve as levels for compacting and finishing the slab.

Side forms can be constructed from smooth 25mm timber, as wide as the depth of the slab, set on edge and fixed to 50mm square timber pegs driven firmly into the ground: set the forms, not the pegs, to the required level and trim any projecting pegs flush with the forms.

Hiring steel *road* forms is a considerably cheaper alternative, if you can locate a nearby source (see 'Contractor's plant hire' or 'Formwork and shuttering' in Yellow Pages). These are available in 100mm or 150mm face height in 3m lengths and come with steel fixing pins. Steel forms are not fixed vertically to the stakes, and they must therefore be levelled with scrap timber or pads of concrete.

**Damp-proof membrane**

Lay 250 micron polythene sheeting or bitumen-polythene sandwich dpm material to form a 'tray' lining the formwork. (The bitumen-polythene type has the advantage of being self-sealing if small punctures occur during construction.)

Interfold any seams and seal them with heavy-duty polythene tape; tuck and fold the sheeting neatly into the angle between the base and the forms, and into the corners of the formwork. Leave enough at the edges to meet and overlap the wall dpc.

## Concreting

Use a mix of 1 part cement, 2 parts sand and 3 parts 20mm coarse aggregate (or 1 part cement and 4 parts combined aggregate) – see page 38. The equivalent ready-mix is C20P to BS5328 (minimum cement content 300kg/m³), but the quantity required will not usually be great enough to justify paying a part-load surcharge to get this. (Do *not* use this mix for a carport floor; it's best not to use it for a garage floor either – see page 298).

Spread the concrete evenly and strike off to a level 10mm to 15mm above the tops of the forms. Compact thoroughly with a timber tamping beam (50mm by 150mm with rough handles), raising and dropping it while advancing half the thickness of the beam each time. Strike off any excess with a side-to-side sawing motion. (If there is no excess the concrete is probably undercompacted; add a bit more to bring it up to depth and go over it again.)

Unless rigid ceramic, concrete or terrazzo tiles are to be laid on the floor (in which case leave the 'sawn' finish), finish with a wood or aluminium float to a sandpaper texture, or use a steel plasterer's trowel to smooth the fresh surface and then, for a smooth, almost polished surface, trowel again when the concrete has stiffened.

When the concrete has hardened sufficiently so as not to be marked, cover with polythene sheeting, weighted down with bricks around the edges and with a light sprinkling of sand on the top and leave to cure for at least three days. You can walk on the surface after this, but keep heavier loads off until the slab is a week or ten days old.

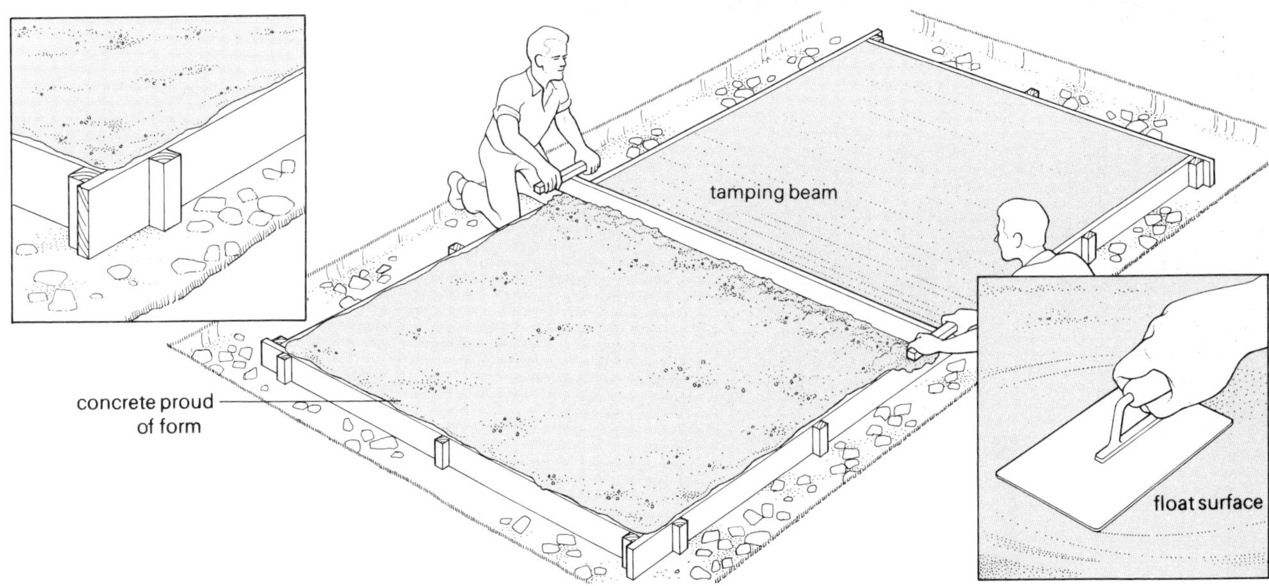


Fill to 10mm to 15mm above the frame. Compact the concrete thoroughly and strike off with a sawing motion. Float surface.

# Chapter 10

# LOFT CONVERSIONS

If your loft space is suitable a conversion is a fairly good way to provide extra accommodation. It has several advantages over a ground floor extension. One is the potential for increasing accommodation without losing any outside space. Others include the possibility of having a good view, the openness of which will often give better daylight levels and perhaps thermal gain from trapped sunshine. A loft room often has a feeling of separateness making it an ideal bolt-hole.

A full conversion means creating habitable space which complies with all the requirements of the Building Regulations. This is usually neither simple nor cheap – though £'s for each square metre a loft conversion is often cheaper than a ground floor extension. Also although you gain space in the loft you often lose a little from the floor below in fitting the staircase. An ugly or badly-planned loft conversion with poor access can actually detract from the value and saleability of a house, so it is important to make sensible choices and to spend the necessary money to provide a good conversion.

## Building regulations

All the structural work involved in a loft conversion and its implications for the house are governed by the Building Regulations and your plans must be submitted to the local authority for approval – see page 24.

## Planning permission

Whether or not you need planning permission for a loft conversion depends on a number of things. A conversion with roof windows usually needs permission only if it is installed in a house that is a listed building or part of a conservation area. Dormer windows – the type which stand out from the roof – always need permission in Scotland, and often do in other parts of the country – mainly because they have such a dramatic effect on the appearance of a house.

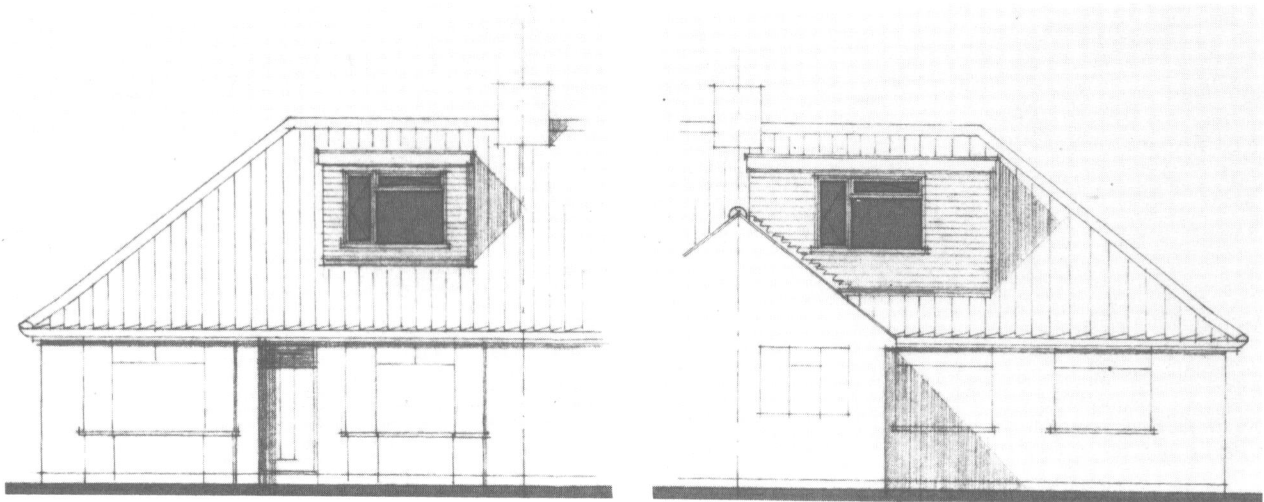

Bungalows are good candidates for loft conversions. A dormer gives necessary headroom.

# Is a conversion possible?

The main limitations on a loft conversion are the roof structure, the loft size and height and the house layout below.

## Roof structure

The roofs of most modern houses are constructed from factory-made triangular trussed rafters comprising light sections of timber joined by metal connectors and installed fairly close together – at 600mm centres. They are transported from the factory and fitted in one piece. If your roof is supported in this manner then a loft conversion is possible but would require an extensive rebuilding of the roof, using a different structural system. Any cutting and removing of members will weaken the roof structure. The low angle of pitch on most modern houses makes it even more complicated since to gain the required heights for habitable rooms the roof would need to be raised.

Before the factory-made trussed rafter roof was developed, roofs were built on site from heavier timber connected together in a series of triangles. The two inclined members act in compression, their roof loads creating a downward and outward thrust which is resisted by the third tie member fixed horizontally between the two ends. With these roofs it's often possible to change the construction without upsetting the existing balance.

There are many different pitched roof designs all based on the triangulation principle. Some are illustrated below.

ROOF STRUCTURES

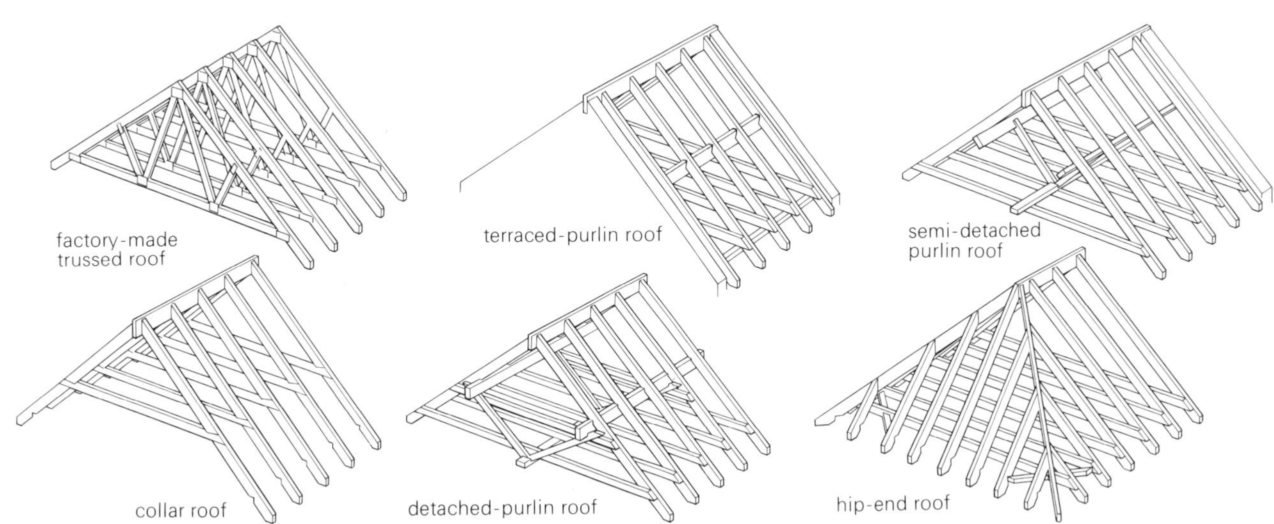


**modern lightweight trussed roof** This is made from light sections of timber connected by metal plates. There is no ridge. Each component is vital and a loft conversion is not often possible.

**close-coupled roof** This is the simplest form of triangulation; it's used for a small building with short span up to 5·5m. The joists are nailed both to the side of the roof rafters and to the wallplate and can be additionally supported from the ridge by hangers every third or fourth rafter with binders across the joist tops.

**collar roof** This is a slightly weaker version of the close couple roof with the ties commonly positioned one third of the height up the roof. The maximum span is 4·5m. The collar ties are traditionally dovetail-halved and nailed to the rafters but nowadays are usually just nailed. With the collars acting as ceiling joists the room below extends partially into the roof space. Usually there is not enough height in this sort of roof to create a new floor, but it may be possible to install a gallery of some sort in the room below.

**purlin roof** This can span up to 7·5m. There are many variations. In a terraced house the purlin ends are supported by the load-bearing separating (party) walls. These party walls should be built up to the roof covering to prevent the spread of fire and the purlins are then supported on brackets, metal hangers or corbels built out from the wall. In fact in many older terraced houses the walls are not built up to the roof and the purlins are supported on struts down to the wall. (Since these walls also act as fire barriers, a lender may require that they are extended up as one of the terms of a loan to buy such a house.)

**hips and gables** A roof can have gable ends which are simply continuations of the house walls or be hipped with a pitched end sloping to the edge wall. A hip roof often has extra strengthening timbers across the house corners.

## ROOF TIMBERS

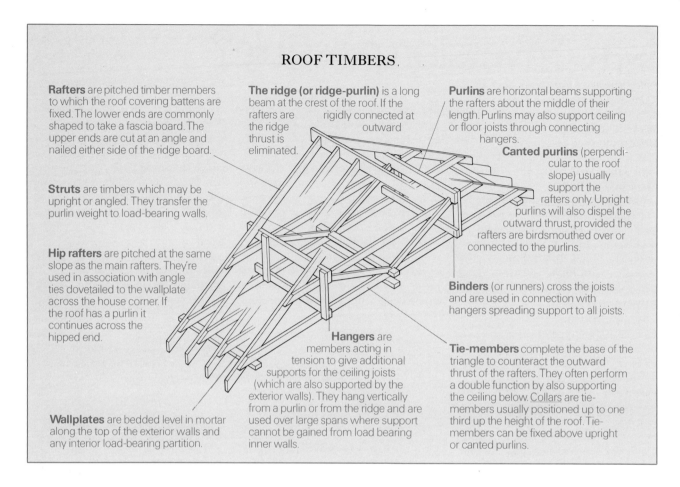

**Rafters** are pitched timber members to which the roof covering battens are fixed. The lower ends are commonly shaped to take a fascia board. The upper ends are cut at an angle and nailed either side of the ridge board.

**Struts** are timbers which may be upright or angled. They transfer the purlin weight to load-bearing walls.

**Hip rafters** are pitched at the same slope as the main rafters. They're used in association with angle ties dovetailed to the wallplate across the house corner. If the roof has a purlin it continues across the hipped end.

**Wallplates** are bedded level in mortar along the top of the exterior walls and any interior load-bearing partition.

**The ridge (or ridge-purlin)** is a long beam at the crest of the roof. If the rafters are rigidly connected at the ridge outward thrust is eliminated.

**Hangers** are members acting in tension to give additional supports for the ceiling joists (which are also supported by the exterior walls). They hang vertically from a purlin or from the ridge and are used over large spans where support cannot be gained from load bearing inner walls.

**Purlins** are horizontal beams supporting the rafters about the middle of their length. Purlins may also support ceiling or floor joists through connecting hangers.

**Canted purlins** (perpendicular to the roof slope) usually support the rafters only. Upright purlins will also dispel the outward thrust, provided the rafters are birdsmouthed over or connected to the purlins.

**Binders** (or runners) cross the joists and are used in connection with hangers spreading support to all joists.

**Tie-members** complete the base of the triangle to counteract the outward thrust of the rafters. They often perform a double function by also supporting the ceiling below. Collars are tie-members usually positioned up to one third up the height of the roof. Tie-members can be fixed above upright or canted purlins.

## Joining roof timbers

As many of the joints in a roof are in compression, they tend to hold together naturally and so roof timbers are connected and supported by remarkably simple joints – such as notches – or by metal brackets or connectors. Often skew nailing is sufficient to hold a timber in place. Where the strength of a simple joint is not enough, coach bolts are often used. There are many proprietary metal fixings.

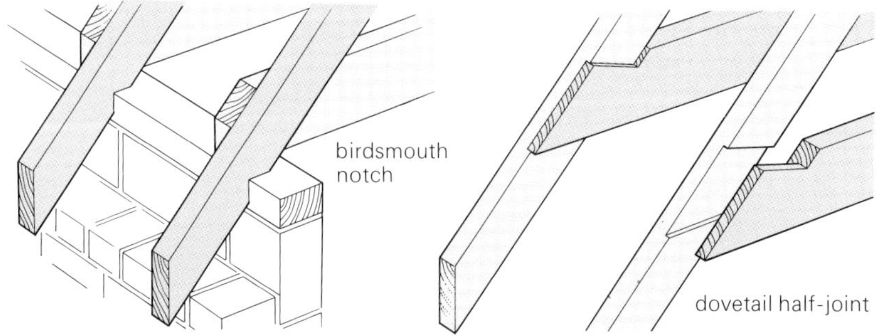


**A notch** is any cut in a timber to fit it over any other uncut timber – eg a rafter over a purlin or over a wallplate. In this situation the rafters normally have V-shaped notches.

**A birdsmouth cut** is a 90-degree notch. The joint is usually strengthened by nailing. It is used to notch a rafter over a wallplate or a purlin. The bevel of the cut is important and is generally calculated on a scale plan. The depth of the birdsmouth should not exceed half the depth of the rafter and must allow the rafter to pass unnotched over the outer wall.

**Skew nailing** is suitable for T-joints where the roof components meet at right-angles: for fixing trimmers (that won't bear great loads) or new framing uprights for instance. The nails are fitted from either side of the upright and to avoid displacing the joint the nails are banged home alternately. For timbers over 38mm, oval brad nails are used: they should be large enough to penetrate well into the timber, typically at least 50mm.

**Dovetail half-joint**–this joint can withstand sideways tension without the need for extra nails or bolts, though these are often used for extra strength. It's main use in roofs is to make a neat sturdy joint between a collar and a rafter, particularly when the roof structure will be visible from below. The housing is cut in the rafter to accept the peg of the collar.

## Loft size and height

The Building Regulations in England and Wales require that part of a habitable room in a loft space should be at least 2·3m high from the finished floor level to the finished ceiling. The area of the part at this 'full height' must be at least half the floor area on a plan measured at a height of 1·5m above the finished floor.

In Scotland the necessary height depends on the type of room created. When a habitable room, such as a bedroom is created, the height must be at least 2·3m from finished floor level over at least one-half of its floor area and not less than 1·9m over at least three-quarters of such area. In Inner London the height shall be not less than 2·3m, measured throughout at least half the floor area on a plan measured at a height of 1m above the finished floor.

The minimum roof dimensions required to provide sufficient space at the right height can be calculated by a formula (given in the *TRADA Book of Home Improvements and Conversions : Attic Conversion*), but for a particular roof it's simpler to climb up into the roof. You'll have to do this anyway to determine the roof structure.

To measure up the roof, prepare two battens, one 2·7m and the other the appropriate part-height for your part of the country plus a 30mm allowance for floor joists decking and plasterboard ceiling. Use these battens in conjunction with a vertical spirit level to mark out the outer floor area at part-height and the inner floor area with the roof at 2·7m. Mark the batten positions on the joists with chalk or a dab of white paint.

Measure these areas and transfer the sizes to a scale plan plotting the

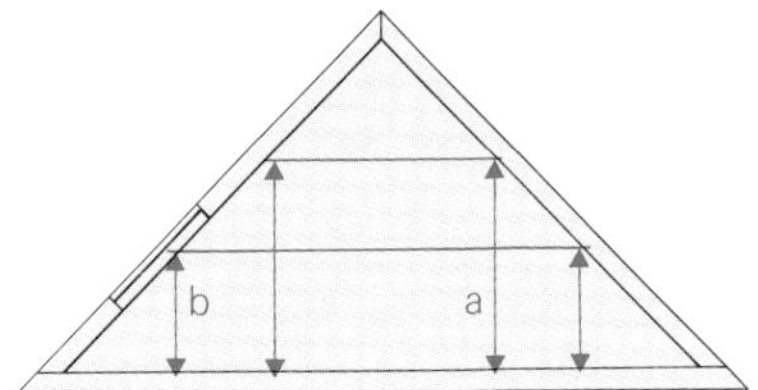


The Building Regulations require a minimum headroom (a) of 2·3m for habitable space, but for loft rooms the rules are relaxed to allow part of the space to be at a lower minimum (b) which varies around the UK– see text.

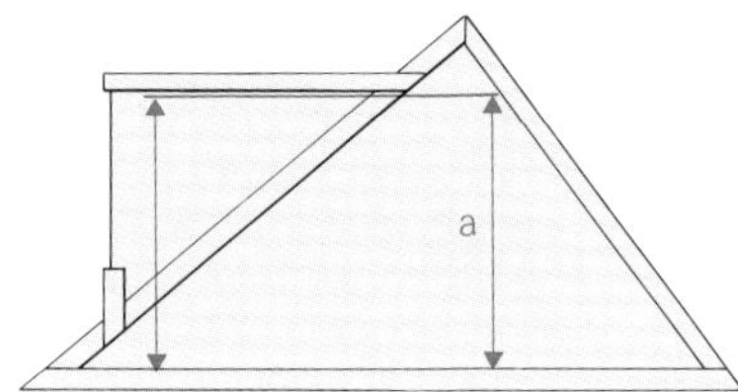


The necessary headroom of 2·3m is usually obtained by installing a dormer.

exact position of the corners relative to the house wall corners. Mark any obstructions such as chimney stacks, but note that chimney stacks don't count in the area calculation, you can consider the space as if they weren't there.

From the plan it will be possible to see if the inner area at full height and outer area at part height meet the requirements. If they don't, it may be possible to devise a way of using only part of the roof space for your conversion so that the ratio of part-height and full-height space improves. Otherwise it is almost certainly possible to satisfy the regulations by installing a dormer window which juts out from the roof to give the necessary headroom. Most loft conversions are carried out on this basis.

When thinking about the new space in a loft you need to remember that the floor area can determine the area of window the Regulations require – see Chapter 8. For this reason and to meet the rules for headroom height, it's often sensible to limit the floor area by installing vertical side walls on at least some sides of the new room. Partition walls are useful anyway to provide storage space and to mask off any plumbing left in the roof. They're also necessary when new deep purlins are fitted as roof supports. However, you usually won't need vertical walls all round the roof space and as sloping walls add character to the space it is worth retaining them where possible.

## House layout

The layout of the floor below the attic determines where the staircase will rise. In a two-storey house there will be a staircase up from the ground floor and it's often sensible and easiest to take the attic staircase up from this point – it may mean building a dormer window to give the necessary headroom above the stairs, especially if the roof is hipped and not gable end. If there isn't a stairwell, or you don't want to use it for some reason, the stairs will usually have to take an area from one of the rooms below.

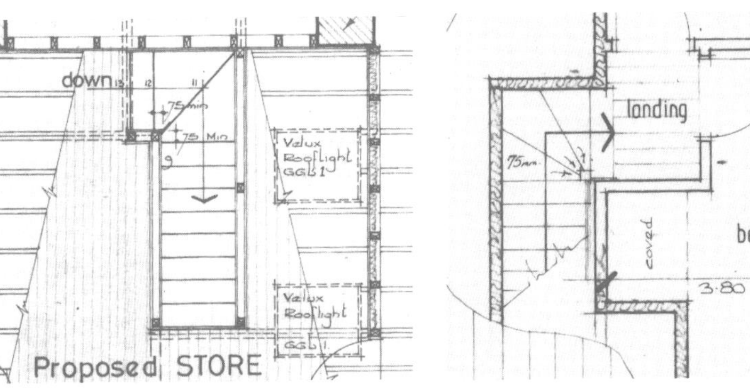


Amongst other things the house layout will determine where the staircase can rise. Within the existing stairwell is usually the best choice.

# Alterations to the structure

Changing the function of the attic from non-habitable to habitable space has several implications for the roof structure. Normally it will be necessary to remove some of the existing loadbearing timbers to open up the space and the designer must make sure that the loads are safely transfered via other structural members.

When a roof structure is altered the new support must always be installed before the old support is dismantled.

The existing floor joists are unlikely to be strong enough to take the increased loads and so will have to be replaced or upgraded. Timber trimmers to take the stair load may have to be installed. The stairwell enclosure and sometimes the floors below need to be upgraded in accordance with the regulations on fire resistance.

## New support for the roof

Occasionally it may be possible to build a room between struts and hangers of the existing roof, but such a room created within the existing structure is likely to be small and it's much more probable that some at least of the support timbers crossing the loft space will need to be removed. If a conversion includes a dormer window, then the purlin to which the support timbers are usually attached will, in any case, be repositioned. A common solution when a purlin is removed is to put in two new purlins – one at high level which will also support the new ceiling joists and the other at a lower level below the line of the new window sill. An alternative is to install a large floor beam which carries timber struts at close centres to support either a new purlin or the bottom frame timber of a dormer. This studwork is then boarded to create a wall of the new room. This solution is suitable for roofs with gables or loadbearing cross walls, but will not usually do for a hipped roof.

## Strengthening the floor

There are three main choices which a professional designer may adopt:

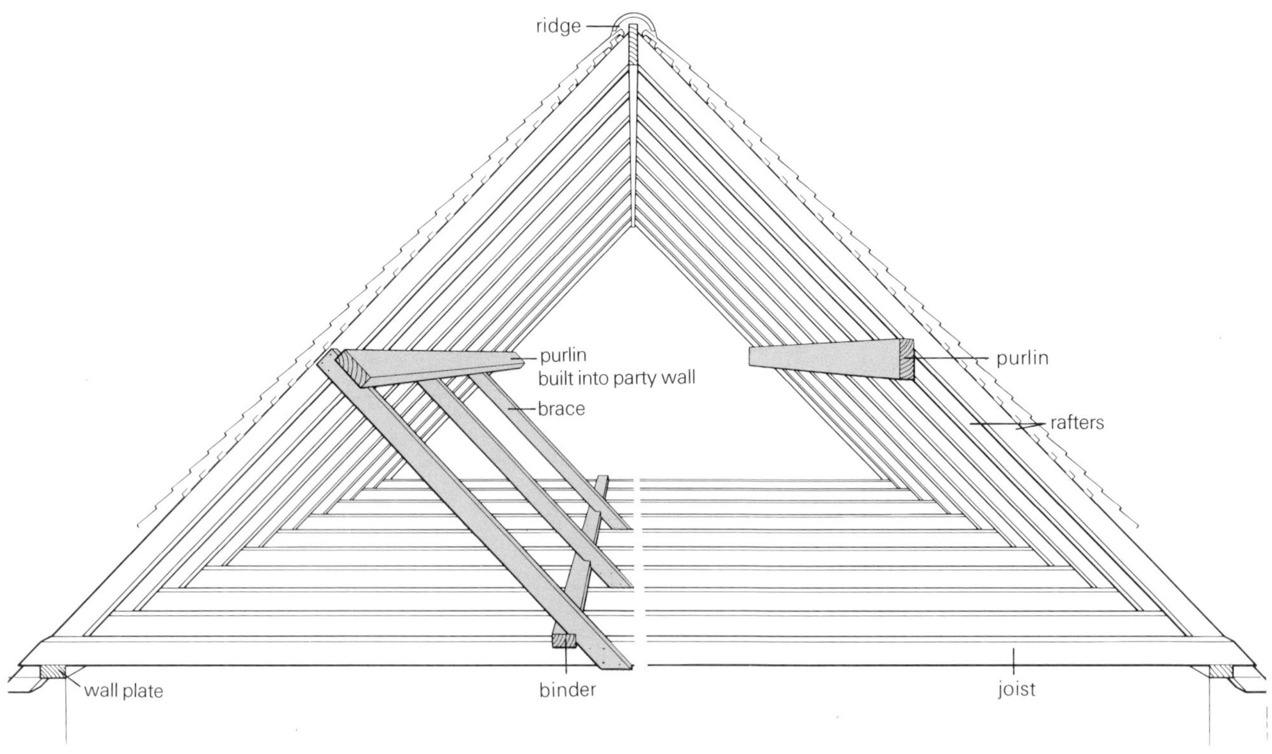


The roof timbers usually criss-cross the loft-space. To convert the space they need to be moved and the load redistributed.

**Doubling of existing joists** When the span is short and the joists relatively deep, it may be possible to bolt on joists of the same depth to share the increased load.

**New joists** The main disadvantage of adding intermediate joists is that an increased load is applied to the existing ceiling – which can cause cracking or serious damage. It's usually better to add a new set of floor-sized joists positioned with their bottom edge about 20mm above the ceiling. These then carry the full load without disturbing the existing structure. An additional advantage is that insulation for soundproofing can be installed between the two sets of joists.

Installing new joists will raise the existing floor level by at least 20mm, more if the new joists are deeper than the existing ones.

**Beams** Often the extra depth of the new joists doesn't matter, but even a couple of millimetres can be enough to cause the loft conversion to fail to meet the headroom regulations. In that case a more radical solution may be required – for instance a beam installed below the existing ceiling will reduce the joist span and the existing joists may then be sufficiently strong to support the new floor loads. A beam might also be used if for some reason new joists could not be fitted on an existing wallplate. If the beams cannot be fitted below the existing ceiling it may be possible to install them above the joists in the loft, outside the usable floor width.

The support for the new staircase will depend on the type of stairs. In the loft space the minimum support needed will be load-bearing trimmer joists across the ends of the opening.

## FIRE REGULATIONS

When a loft conversion has the effect of adding a storey to a house, the Building Regulations require that the period of fire resistance for structural elements is increased. For a bungalow this has little practical effect, but for a two-storey house which becomes a three-storey house it has many implications, particularly for the staircases – both new and existing.

A house with three (or more) storeys must have a protected staircase (including any hall or landing associated with the stair and any part of a floor linking stair flights) – see page 290.

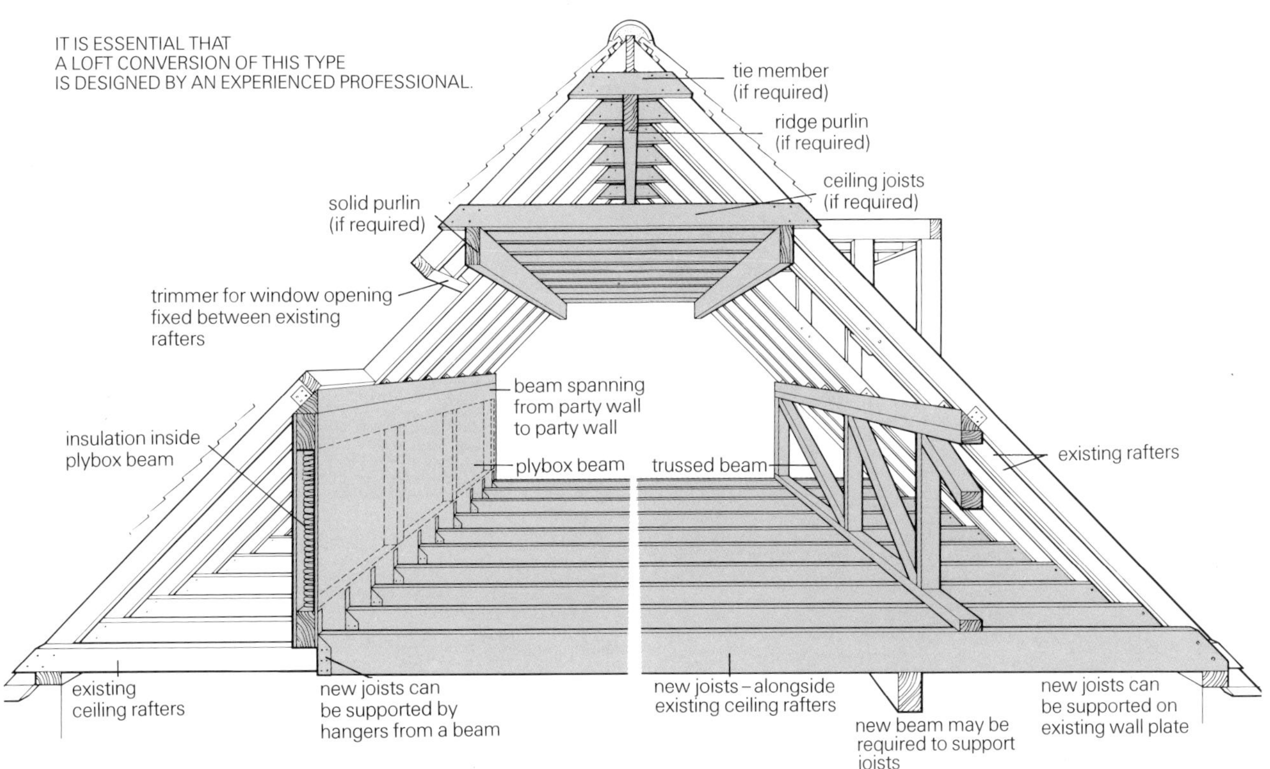


The load is redistributed on new beams and so the space can be opened up. New joists bear the weight of floor, furnishings and people.

# Letting in light

There are three main ways of providing window light in a loft conversion: an ordinary window can be installed in a gable end wall; a roof window can be fitted flush with the roof; a dormer can be built as a new roof structure around a standard window upstanding from the existing roof line. By itself a gable window will not usually provide enough light so it is usually in addition to main light and ventilation provided by one of the other two window types. The choice of whether to have roof windows or dormer windows is most likely to be made for you by the need to gain extra headroom. In a hip-end roof a dormer on the side of the roof is often the most practical way to achieve sufficient headroom for the rising staircase.

## Roof windows

If you are able to opt for roof windows, the commonest brand is Velux and these double-glazed timber windows are widely available in a number of standard types up to 1340mm by 1400mm. They have a pivoted sash which can be fully rotated to clean the outside. If the top of the window is within reach you can open the window by hand, otherwise a high-level opening gear is required which can be mechanised. There are also other accessories such as blinds and awnings.

## Dormer windows

The commonest dormer window is the flat-roofed version which sits part-way up the slope of a pitched roof.

A dormer that is supported by the roof is said to look better and is often more acceptable to planning authorities than a dormer which bears on the outer wall. But this sort of dormer, called a bay dormer, provides more space at habitable height. If a bay dormer is recessed then a balcony can be provided in front.

### Dormer roofs

A flat roof is the cheapest and easiest sort of construction and therefore the

Roof windows are suitable if the headroom is adequate. ▲ ▶

A lifted roof is pitched in the same direction as the main roof, but at a shallower angle (left). The curved roof of an eye-brow dormer is most suited to cottages (right). ▼

commonest. It is usually possible to have a pitched roof and pitching the roof usually looks much better. The simplest pitched roof is mono – pitched with a single slope in the same direction as the main roof, but at a shallower angle – this is sometimes called a lifted roof. A roof pitched on two sides of ridgeboard running back to the main roof can have a straight or hipped front.

Another choice, albeit unusual, is an *eyebrow roof* where the existing roof gently arches over the new windows.

### Dormer cladding

A dormer will be least obtrusive if it matches the materials used for the existing roof, which generally means tile or slate cladding for the dormer sides and walls – the cheeks. Glazed cheeks are another choice – though this will affect the dormer's fire resistance and will not be permitted for a dormer cheek close to the boundary between one property and the next.

The new windows should also match, in material and proportions, those already used in the main part of the house. As with all other alterations to a house, the match may be a requirement for planning permission.

Ease of maintenance is a major consideration for any high-level construction and so it is worth considering easy-to-maintain materials – such as plastic (uPVC) windows these can be made to match quite well with timber windows elsewhere in the house. Tile-hung cheeks are virtually maintenance free. The other main choice for the cheeks is cladding – which can be timber or plastic (pvc). Plastic should be maintenance-free and these days its outdoor performance is fairly well-proven over long periods. Painted or stained timber would need maintenance, but a timber such as Western Red Cedar needs no surface treatment and therefore no maintenance. Western Red Cedar will weather to an attractive silvery-grey, while plastic will look almost new.

## Patent glazing

Patent glazing is a fixed form of glazing using aluminium T-bar frames and overlapping panels of glass. It's a comparatively cheap way of letting in a lot of light and often used for studio lighting. The difficulty of cleaning outside can be a major limitation on its use. Large areas of glass also affect the fire resistance of a roof and its area is limited in roofs close to boundaries between properties.

## Soil pipes

Putting a window in the roof frequently disturbs the path of a soil pipe or means that the pipe must be moved or extended because it passes too close to the window. In Scotland the Building Regulations specify that the pipe is carried up to at least 600mm over the eaves (or gable) or the top of any window or other opening within a radius of 1·8m of the soil pipe, and that the pipe must terminate 900mm above or below the top of the chimney. In England and Wales it need only be positioned so 'as not to transmit foul air in such a manner as to become prejudicial to health or a nuisance', but in practice requirements similar to those in Scotland would apply. In Inner London there is no specific bye-law, but again sensible pre-cautions would be required to satisfy the District Surveyor that there is the necessary 'open air' outside the window.

The position of any existing soil pipe in relation to a new window needs careful thought at the designing stage, otherwise you can end up with a hideous configuration as the pipe bends its way around the new conversion. Soil pipes should be fitted with a wire balloon.

▲ A dormer window has been used to give height to an eaves conversion.

◀ This flat-roof dormer fits neatly into the right-angle between the main roof and a rear extension. The existing soil pipe has been re-routed and lengthened.

# Installing a roof window

If the headroom is satisfactory and the timbers are sound, a roof window can be used on any roof with a pitch between 20 degrees and 85 degrees – a special fitting is available for still lower angles.

For adequate light and ventilation, the window should be at least 10 per cent of the floor space (20 per cent for a roof window in Inner London), although more may be preferable. Although one large window may provide the glass area needed, it can often be less work to install two smaller ones side by side between the rafters and thus avoid cutting through them. Two small windows instead of one large one may also look better from outside. Since the windows are made in a range of standard sizes, check these from the manufacturer's catalogue to see the best way to arrange installation. The manufacturers also give details of the ideal height at which to position the windows so that you can see out.

There are a number of optional features which you may require. The most important of these are the flashings to prevent water penetration. There are different flashings to suit thin roof coverings, like slate or felt, and thick or profiled coverings, like tiles. Special flashings are required for very low-pitched roofs – between 10 degrees and 20 degrees. Where two or more windows are fitted beside each other, coupled flashings can be used to link them.

The windows themselves are double-glazed units with additional ventilator panels, but optional extras include a choice of glass, and external awnings and internal blinds to control the light. The sash is normally locked and released by a control bar at the top. If the window is set too high for the controls to be in reach, remote controls ranging from extension bars to electric operation can be specified. Since the sash can be rotated fully for cleaning, it is a good idea to specify an additional security lock, especially where young children are around. There is also a special version in which the sash can be opened fully to provide an emergency exit. Make sure the supplier has details of all the specifications you need.

To install a roof window it is not necessary to have access from outside the roof since all the work can be carried out from the loft. You should, however, make sure that the area below is cordoned off and post warning notices in case any slates or pieces of wood are accidentally dropped.

Before starting work on the roof, strip down the window to its basic timber frame. Remove the sash from its hinges by screwing in the release screw. Then unscrew the sectional aluminium edging from the timber.

ROOFWINDOWS

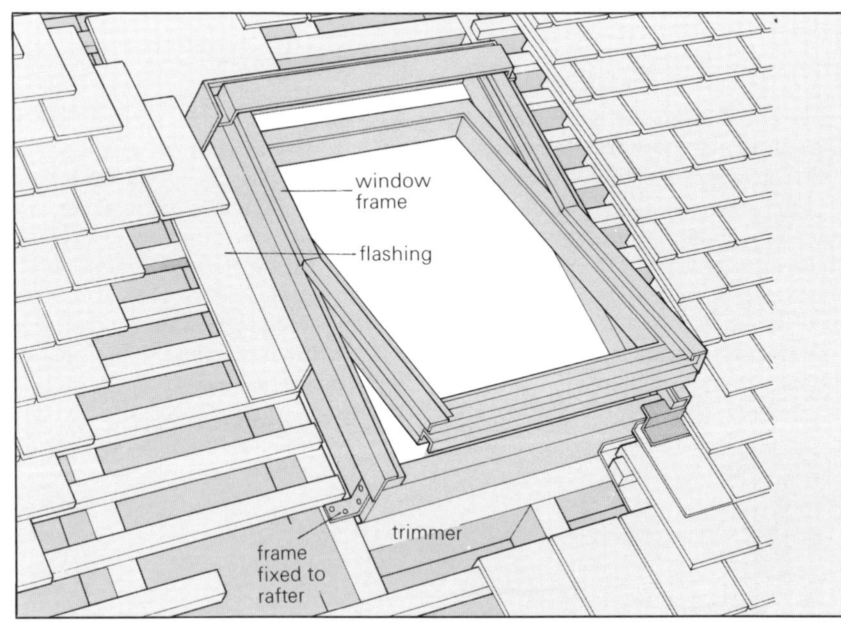


▲ To install a roof window you have to open the roof over a slightly larger area. Special flashings make the frame/roof joint watertight.

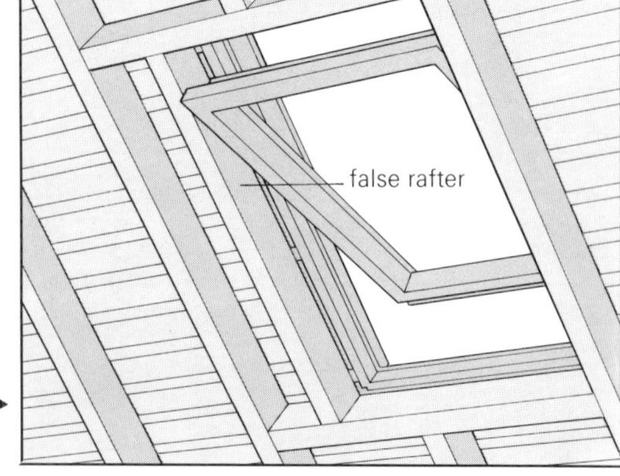


A false rafter may be required to support one edge of the window frame. ▶

## Step-by-step

**Step 1** Making all marks on the upper side of the rafters, mark the dimensions of the timber frame in position on the rafters. Trimmers made from timber of the same dimensions as the rafters will be needed top and bottom. Mark their position above and below the frame. To admit the maximum light, it's normal to arrange for a splay in the reveal above and below the window. To mark this, use a spirit level to mark a horizontal line below, and a vertical line above, the window, extending round the rafters from the marks you have just made.

Where a rafter will have to be cut, use a try-square to square a line around it, from the point where the splay line meets its lower side. The outer edges of the trimmers can then be aligned with the marks.

A clearance is needed at each side between the frame and the roof covering – the size depends on the type of flashing used. Mark this allowance out from the rafters and on the tile or slate battens. If the window is not being fixed between existing rafters, an additional false rafter will be needed on one side, mark this in position.

**Step 2** Open up a hole by removing the roof covering over a slightly larger area than marked. Cut through any roofing felt, and lift off the slates or tiles, using a slate ripper to cut the nails if necessary. Work from the centre of the area out.

If an existing rafter has to be cut, prop it temporarily above and below the opening with sturdy timber supports or adjustable steel props. Cut through the tile or slate battens fixed to it, then saw through the rafter along the marked lines. If it is long enough, you can probably use this timber for one or both trimmers, otherwise cut new timbers to span between the rafters and nail them in the marked trimmer positions – use nails long enough to pass through the first timber and at least 50mm into the butting timber. Take care to keep the opening square. the props can then safely be removed. If a false rafter is required, mark its position on the installed trimmers, measure its length, saw to size and then nail in position.

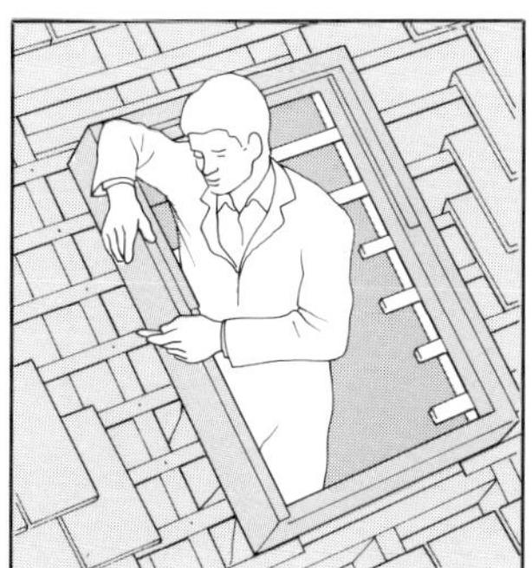

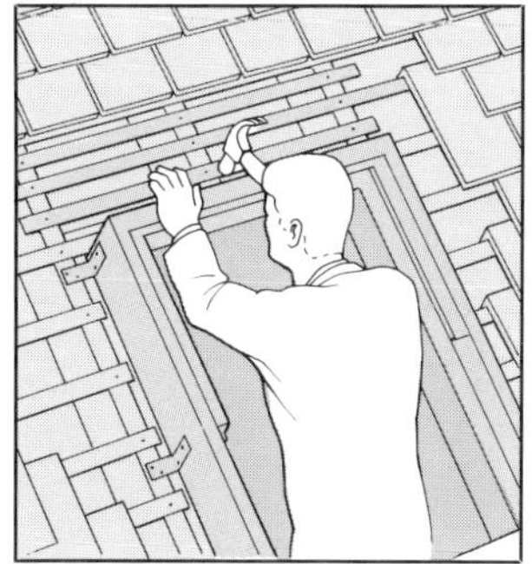

**Step 3** Trim the tile battens flush with the rafters on each side of the opening. Offer up the window frame to the opening. It must sit at the correct depth relative to the roof covering. This is indicated by a depth mark around the frame which should be aligned with the *surface* of the surrounding battens. It is fixed in position with metal angle brackets. Mark where these should be fitted to hold it at the correct depth, then screw them in place.

To support the top flashing, nail extra battens across the rafters above the frame, leaving about 20mm gaps between battens. The flashings can now be fitted, except where the roof covering is slate (see right). They are held to the frame by the aluminium edging pieces, which should be screwed back in place at this point. Fit the bottom section first, then the sides, and finally the top.

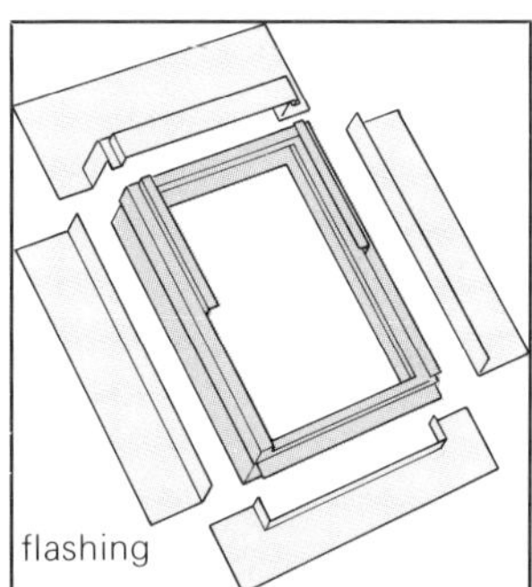

**Step 4** To finish off the opening, the roof covering around the frame is replaced. A weathertight seal is ensured only when the gap over the flashing is correct and to maintain this usually means that tiles or slates have to be cut to fit. Mark and cut accordingly. The easiest way to cut tiles without damage is with an angle grinder or disc

Refit them in position. If the tiles above the window have been cut short, they should be angled by fitting a tilting fillet below them. Below the window, dress the apron flashing down over the roof covering. At the sides, on a tiled roof, the tiles simply overhang the flashing. But where the roof covering is a thin material like slate, the flashing is in the form of short sections called soakers, which must be interleaved with the slates, starting from the bottom and working up to the top. This should be done before fitting the other flashings.

To finish off, replace the sash in the frame by refitting it to its hinges. Check that it opens and closes freely. The timber frame is prefinished with preservative, but it can be given a coat of sealer.

# Installing a dormer window

Dormer conversions must be individually designed and constructed with due respect for the relevant Building Regulations and need for planning permission. A professional design is essential and plans must be submitted for approval.

For ease of building, the general dimensions are best arranged to take advantage of standard-sized window units and the position of the existing rafters. Otherwise, most dormer construction is no more complicated than building any other roof structure of a similar type of material. Because of the loads involved, it is important to ensure that the frame timber sizes are adequate, and that the materials are sound.

In the first drawing below, the dormer frame is carried on a wallplate set on top of the house wall and on a heavy trimmer fixed between the rafters. The wall thus provides the main support for the window and lintel, and the dormer roof is carried by the lintel and the top trimmer. In some designs the side timbers supporting the cheeks are jointed to the rafters, in the drawing they are carried down and jointed to the roofing joists for additional support. In the flat-roofed design illustrated, firring pieces and boarding complete the timber construction. For a pitched roof a ridge and rafters would be added.

Timber sizes will be noted in your designer's drawings. The sizes – particularly the dimensions of the roof beam and lintel – are governed by the span and may need to be 200mm by 75mm or more on large dormers. Most of the other framing can usually be made from 100mm by 50mm timber, but for a very large structure, heavier timber may be needed.

The drawing below of a dormer fitted part-way up the roof slope shows its basic similarity to the bay dormer. Here, the structure is carried by the strengthened rafters at each side, and trimmers at the top and bottom. Once again, most of the structure can usually be made from 100mm by 50mm timber with 150mm by 100mm trimmers, but large dormers may require heavier framing.

## The installation

The Guide is for a flat-roofed bay dormer. The method for other dormers would be similar.

Unlike a roof window, which requires little more than basic hand tools, some special equipment is needed to build a dormer because you need access from outside the roof. To provide a safe base for work, scaffolding or a platform tower should be positioned against the wall in line with the dormer, with a roofing ladder secured to the ridge on either side of the planned opening. To avoid possible accidents, you should cordon off the area below and put up warning notices. Since the construction may take some time, it is essential to have some kind of waterproof covering.

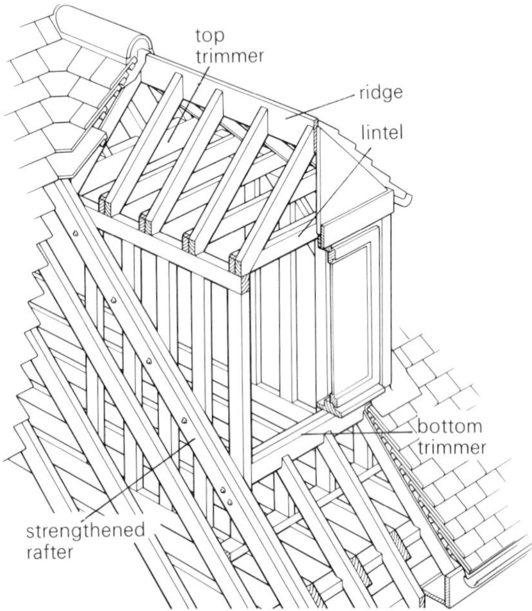


A dormer part-way up the roof slope is mostly supported by the main roof and the adjacent rafters will usually need strengthening.

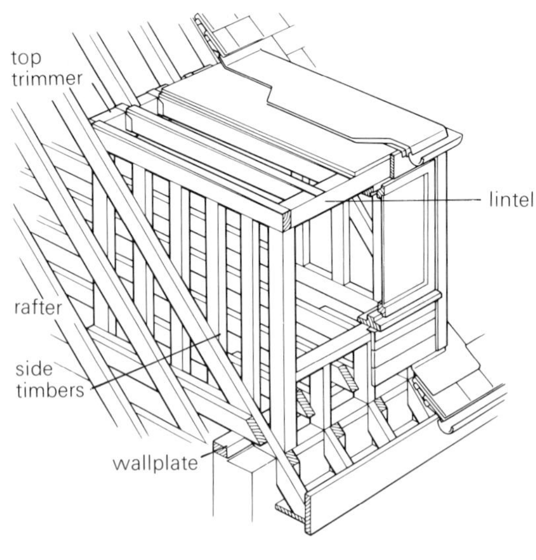


A bay dormer is mostly supported by the house wall. The main structural timbers are shown.

## Step-by-step

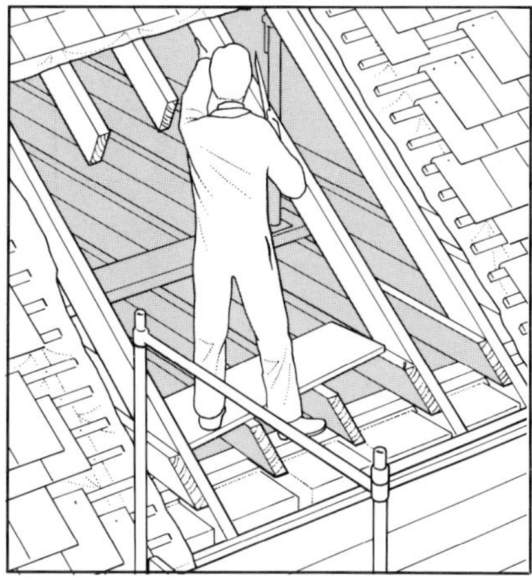

**Step 1** Mark out the position of the roof opening inside the loft. Before cutting timbers, the roof must be supported. Use two adjustable steel props under either the collar ties or a purlin above and brace these against heavy timbers laid across the joists.

Remove the slates or tiles, battens and felt over a slightly larger area than the frame will occupy. If the slates or tiles are removed intact, they can be re-used later for cladding the dormer. Then with the temporary props in place, cut through the rafters slightly below the position of the new top trimmer and remove them. Mark out and cut the end of each rafter to make a birdsmouth joint (see page 280) with the new top trimmer and nail this to the uncut rafters on each side – using nails that penetrate through the first timber and at least 50mm into the second.

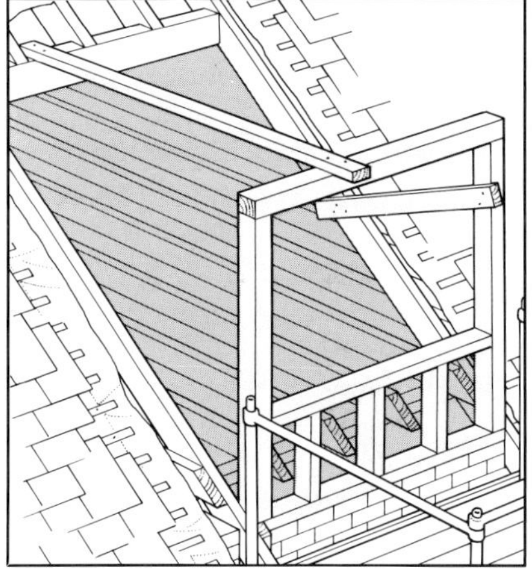

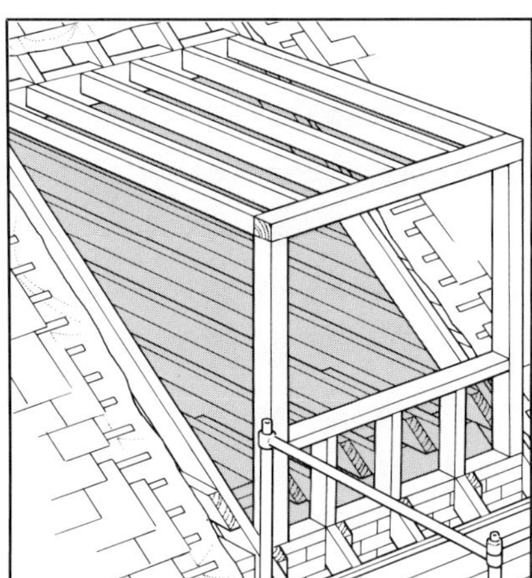

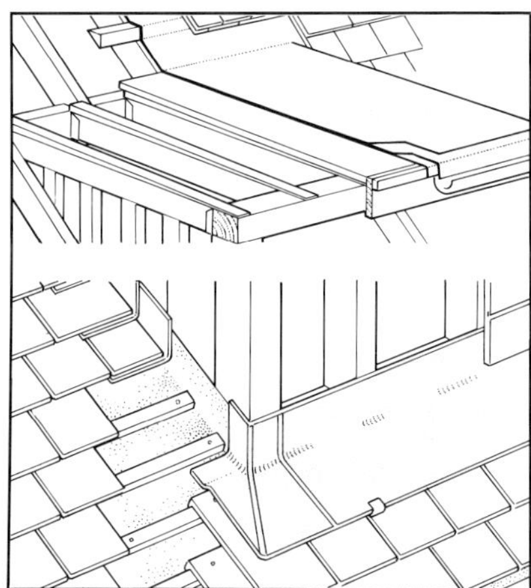

**Step 2** Make up the front frame, consisting of the lintel, wallplate, sill and two vertical struts. These can be skew-nailed together or joined with half-lap joints. Fix the frame in position by screwing or bolting the wallplate to the house wall and bolting the struts to the rafters on each side. Temporary braces should be fitted to hold it in position.

The roof is constructed like any flat roof – see page 255. The rafters are fitted between the lintel and the top trimmer. The easiest way is to use joist hangers. Nail the side timbers to the rafters at top and side and to the joists, if that is in the design. Nail the firring pieces to the rafters and board the whole dormer frame roof and cheeks.

Make good the existing roof covering around the opening, trimming the slates or tiles as necessary and fitting an apron flashing to the base of the window frame. Alternate the side tiles or slates with soakers (short sections of flashing interleaved with the slates) to form a waterproof flashing.

**Step 3** If the cheeks are to be clad with left-over slates or tiles from the original roof nail horizontal battens over the roofing felt at the appropriate spacing , then nail in position with the joints staggered in alternate rows.

The flat roof can be covered like any other roofing job, normally with three layers of bituminous felt. Take particular care that the main roof-to-dormer roof joint is made thoroughly waterproof with flashing. Depending on the design, a gutter may be fitted to a fascia board over the window.

To finish off the dormer, install the window frame in the normal way not forgetting the dpc – see page 136. Line the cheeks and ceiling with insulating material and board over with the lining which is used for the rest of the loft. This should incorporate a vapour barrier. There should be a gap of 25mm between the insulation and the lining. Paint or stain all exposed timber immediately.

# Providing access

As the Building Regulations on the dimensions of stairs are strict (see page 170), planning the staircase is an important part of the whole loft conversion design. The decisions made can make or mar the whole project and each case must usually be considered on its own merits. Stairs are normally straight or quarter-turn or half-turn. Spiral stairs are rarely a practicable choice for stairs to a conversion.

Usually the most convenient place for a staircase to a loft conversion is close to the existing stairs. With a straight flight this can be difficult since there's rarely enough room in the adjacent landing. A half-turn stair is often easier to fit because it can be installed as an extension to the existing staircase. Even in a bungalow where the staircase position is not fixed by any existing stairs, it's more economical on space on both floors to fit a staircase with at least a quarter turn to get the necessary height without travelling too far lengthways. A staircase that's greedy for space can take a large chunk from the floor area above, on the other hand, a straight flight, if it will fit, is usually cheapest and easiest to install.

Plans for a staircase to a loft conversion are often closely linked to the positioning of the dormer windows which are needed to give headroom for the stairs. It helps to be able to think and draw in 3-D, failing this it might be worth making a simple cardboard model of your plans or those a designer puts forward. The positions of windows relative to the new stairs needs consideration, if people will pass by low-level glass, it should be replaced with safety glass – toughened or laminated – or protected by a grille.

## Fire regulations

Basically the Building Regulations require a protective structure, which separates the stair from all other parts of the building. This structure is required to have half-hour fire resistance (for a three-storey house) and any door or other opening to a habitable room or kitchen must be fitted with a fire door.

Where an existing stair rises directly from a habitable room (such as a sitting-room) it is not necessary to build a half-hour separating partition around the stair, provided there is a half-hour wall between that room and any other habitable room or kitchen and that any doors in that wall are half-hour fire-resisting and self-closing. However, the first floor over this room and the new second is required to have half-hour fire resistance and may need upgrading. Most types of wall construction already have half-hour fire resistance, so they rarely need upgrading. When upgrading is required, a layer of plasterboard is usually sufficient. Fire resisting doors must withstand the passage of fire for at least half an hour, be self-closing (rising butt hinges usually meet with Building Control's approval) and any glazing must be Georgian wired glass.

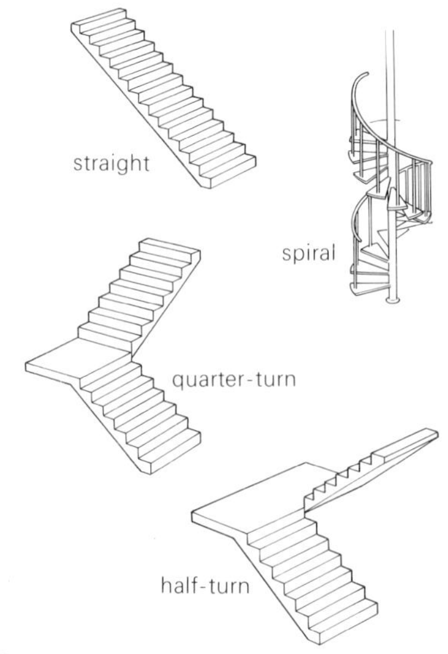

Types of staircase.

**Floors** Where floors need to be upgraded one of the easiest ways is to add a layer of plasterboard beneath the existing ceiling. It depends on the existing construction how thick the plasterboard is and whether this will suffice. Some floors can be upgraded by laying hardboard over.

### One room conversions

Where there is only one room proposed the requirements can be partially relaxed, but the new floor must have full half-hour fire resistance and all doors on all storeys from the hall or stairway must be self closing with any glazing in wired glass. The new room must have a window which can be used for an emergency escape. The existing first floor and new second floor must have at least half-hour fire resistance.

Where the new stair to a single room rises over the existing stair and is within the same enclosure – the new room must be fitted with a fire door set in an enclosure with half-hour fire resistance.

Where the new stair rises from an existing room on the first floor, it must be separated from that room and the rest of the house by a half-hour fire resistant enclosure, with fire door at either top or bottom. The walls and floor must have full half-hour fire resistance, with a fire door in a half-hour fire resistant enclosure at the top of the new stair.

### Installing the stairs

Installing stairs to a loft conversion is not a task to be undertaken lightly– see page 170.

A staircase up to a loft conversion is best installed after all the dirty work has been done. This saves whistling draughts, from an open roof structure and also contains the dirt. When the hole is made for the staircase opening it's sensible to use dust covers in the rooms below and to seal up doors.

## Loft ladders

In Scotland a ladder is not acceptable as access to a conversion. In England and Wales (and London) things aren't so clear cut. It is possible to argue that since the Regulations do not require a means of access between storeys, there is no requirement to have a fixed staircase, and a loft ladder (which is not a fixture) is therefore satisfactory. In practice the BCO may do his utmost to persuade you to have a proper staircase but may accept a ladder for converted space which is not intended for regular use – check with your local Building Control department.

If you are able to use a loft ladder or are carrying out a simple conversion for which a ladder will be adequate, there are basically two types to choose from – sliding and concertina. Most are aluminium.

Sliding ladders are the more widely available, are often considerably cheaper than concertina and in *Which?* tests were generally easier to operate and to climb. But concertina ladders need smaller hatchways and are neater, taking up less room in the loft when stored.

### The access hatch

A loft ladder is fitted in an access hatchway in the ceiling below the loft space. An access hatchway may be squeezed in between two adjacent joists or be a more generous two joist spacings wide with the middle joist cut back and trimmed.

Most sliding loft ladders need a hatchway between 550mm and 750mm long by between 400mm and 500mm wide. So to fit a sliding loft ladder in a ceiling with joists at 400mm centres you need a trimmed hatchway, but for a ceiling with joists at 600mm centres you should be able to get away with a hatchway cut between adjacent joists.

If your existing ceiling has joists at 400mm spacings and the existing access hatch is between adjacent joists (or there's no existing hatch and in making one you'd prefer to avoid the daunting prospect of having to cut a joist), you may be able to find a concertina ladder which will fit.

**Step-by-step**

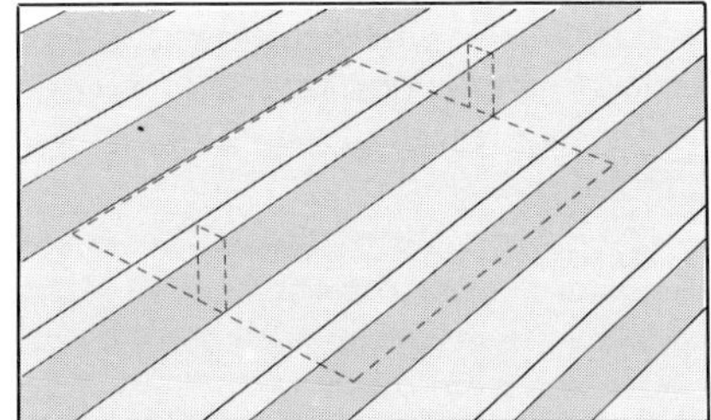

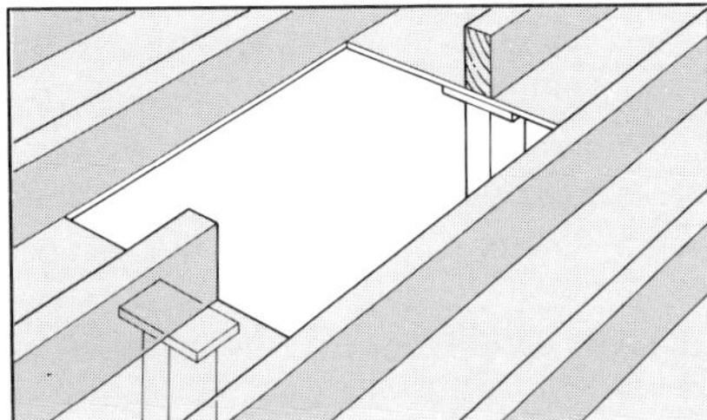

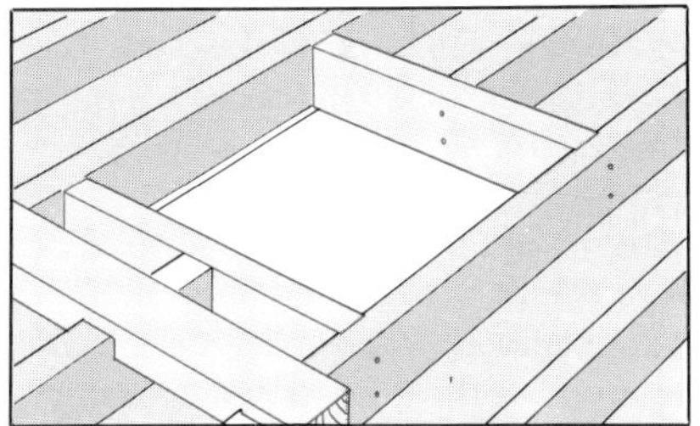

The way you set about creating a new hatchway will depend on whether you already have access to the loft space or not. If you don't have access you'll have to work from beneath the ceiling, finding the joists by tapping the ceiling and making pilot holes through the plaster or plasterboard. If you do have access you'll be able to work from above as well as below, which is much easier.

Choose a place for the opening where access from below will be safe and easy and there'll be room for a ladder extended to the floor at an angle of about 75°. Mark the hatchway outline on the ceiling with the long edge parallel to the joists and directly below the edge of a joist. (If you have access from above you can establish the edge of the joists by tapping nails down through the ceiling.) Ensure that the outline is square by checking that the diagonals are equal.

If a joist is to be cut it will need some temporary support at either end until it's trimmed and fitted. Adjustable steel props are best, but stout pieces of timber (at least 100mm by 50mm) could be used. Place a plank beneath the two supports to give a firm footing.

If you have access check whether there is any wiring or pipework that will be disturbed when the hatch is cut. If you don't have access consider the possible run of any nearby cables or pipes and cut carefully – with the electricity turned off as a precaution.

If you have access from above, any joist to be cut can be sawn through and pulled away and the trimmer can be fitted before the ceiling is cut. If there is no access the ceiling will have to be cut first. Proceed carefully, using a general purpose or keyhole saw and cutting as close to the joists as possible. Be prepared for a lot of debris to fall – lay a dust sheet and close adjacent doors; wear protective goggles to stop bits falling in your eyes (if you can work from above you'll have the opportunity to sweep up much of the dirt before cutting). Support the cut-out until all four edges have been cut, then it can be lowered gently without causing so much mess and without risking damage to the edges. Having a helper hold it up is the easiest way, in lieu of that make a net of cross-strings on nails.

Trimming joists (or trimmers) are cut from timbers the same size as the main joists – often the piece cut from the joist will do for one end – and are usually fixed in place with large wire nails through the main joists into the end of the trimmer and through the trimmer into the cut end of the joists. For joists 50mm wide, 100mm nails will normally do. A tusk-and-tenon joint makes a stronger fixing, or the trimmer can be notched over battens screwed to the main joists in addition to the nails. A 150mm by 25mm board notched over the cut joist on either side of the hatch completes the trimming.

To complete the hatch, you can line the opening with 100mm × 25mm planed timber nailed to the joists and trimmer and trim the opening with an architrave moulding mitred at the corner.

If a fold-away loft ladder is to be installed the hatchdoor will have to be hinged to open downwards and will need a latch which can be operated from below by the stick which is used to draw the ladder down – most ladders are supplied with this. Otherwise the door can rest on simple ledge created by the moulding.

**Enlarging a hatch** When enlarging a hatch you'll always have access from above to make things easier. When enlarging a hatch lengthways by moving back a trimmer, you'll need temporary support for the joist you're cutting back. Widening a hatch by trimming a joist is like making a new trimmed hatch.

# Services in the loft

You're unlikely to want a gas supply to a new loft conversion, but electricity will be essential and even if the new rooms themselves need no plumbing, there'll probably be a cold water cistern that needs moving and therefore alterations to the existing supply pipework. You may want to extend the central heating.

## Electricity

Most lofts are equipped with one light, often just a bare bulb in a battenholder screwed to one of the roof timbers with a light switch on the landing below or just inside the loft hatch. It's generally part of the upstairs lighting circuit. A new conversion will need more lights and some power sockets. If it's a large conversion it may be worth installing new circuits, one a ring circuit for power points, the other a new lighting circuit. Otherwise it may be possible to take a spur or spurs from the ring circuit on the floor below and extend the upstairs lighting circuit to give enough lighting points. Often the simplest solution is to install a new ring circuit which supplies the power points and has a fused spur for the lights.

For details of Electrical work see page 48 *et seq.* Also for:

- a new ring circuit page 257.
- a new lighting circuit page 152.
- a spur from the nearest ring circuit page 148.
- extending the existing lighting circuit page 152.

## Plumbing

Converting a loft usually means resiting the cold water cistern and therefore alterations to the existing supply pipework. If there's a wet central heating system – with radiators – there will usually also be a header tank in the loft space. Moving these won't be too difficult, the problem is where to resite them. If the new rooms are to have central heating, the header tank must be resited above the new radiators and if one of the new rooms is planned as a bathroom, or to be plumbed with a wash basin, the cold water cistern will also have to be raised. The height of the cistern isn't critical for ordinary taps, provided it is higher than the taps, but for a shower to have a reasonable spray the bottom of the cistern must be well above the shower rose. Though some showers can operate with a 0·3m or 0·6m head, shower-only mixers *Which?* has tested need 1m on average and bath/shower mixers need 4·5m. In a loft conversion this isn't easy to achieve and a shower in a loft room would often have to be pumped – see page 103.

### New positions

With a steeply pitched roof that can have a flat ceiling and still give sufficient headroom, it may be possible to move the cistern and any header tank to the apex of the roof. There they can be supported by new ceiling joists bolted to the rafters. Otherwise the cisterns can be moved to a wall, supported as high up as possible on a platform on wall brackets – and boxed in and insulated. Although it makes for a deep duct it looks better if the boxing framework is carried down to the floor and, if possible, across the wall too – the enclosed space can be used as storage.

Sometimes the cistern can be moved outside on top of a dormer or in the valley of a double pitched roof. But there are drawbacks to siting a cistern outside, access is difficult and the cistern and its pipes must be very well insulated and protected against the weather.

Noise could be a problem with a cistern in the loft, especially if it's sited in or above a bedroom. It may be worth raising the question of sound insulation specially with the designer of your conversion. Make sure your cistern is fitted with the correct ball-valve.

### A new bathroom

Given the limitation on a shower, a bath is usually a better solution for a new bathroom in a loft conversion, a bath can even be installed with one end tucked under a sloping roof provided there's sufficient headroom where you climb in and out. The position for the new bathroom is limited by the position of the existing soil pipe and so normally the best place for it is immediately above the bathroom on the floor below. An ordinary WC would have to go close to the existing soil pipe, but a shredder WC – see page 101 – gives more flexibility.

## Heating

If the central heating boiler has spare capacity and you're able to resite the header tank, running pipework and new radiators into the loft may be possible – see Chapter 7. Skirting radiators are a good choice for a loft conversion as they fit easily into the eaves space.

For a loft room that will be used intermittently, there may however be advantages in keeping the heating separate from the rest of the house and using individual room heaters of some sort to provide heat only when the room is occupied. If you plan to operate the heating like this, it makes sense to insulate the loft room below as well as above, so that heat provided to the storey below is not lost upstairs. If your loft was insulated before the conversion this simply means leaving the existing loft insulation between the floor of the new room and the ceilings of the room below. When the new room will be used continually, it's better to lift the old insulation and re-use it behind the lining to the new room, old insulation in the eaves space should be left.

## Moving a cistern

There are three main materials used for cisterns: galvanised steel, rigid plastic and flexible plastic. Plastic cisterns are lighter and much easier to handle than galvanised steel ones; most are circular – you can also get triangular ones.

Most water authorities require a new cold water storage cistern to have an *actual capacity* of 50 gallons (227 litres) which has a *nominal capacity* of about 70 gallons (310 litres).

To keep the water inside free from contamination, cisterns should have closely-fitting, but not airtight, lids. A suitable lid could be bought or made (it should be a material which is unaffected by condensation and mould).

Turn off the water supply at the mains, empty the old cistern by running cold taps in the bathroom and flushing WC's and bail out the water that remains in the bottom. Detach the old pipes – at the connections to the cistern or if you're replacing the cistern by sawing the pipes wherever is convenient for the new pipe run.

### The pipe runs

Moving a cistern means re-routing the supply pipes to and from it. As far as possible, you should aim to keep the pipes within the floor void or on inner walls – avoid the eaves of the roof as this is where it is coldest and freezing is most likely.

In many installations all the existing pipe-work will be copper and this can be extended in copper or in plastic. If the rising main is lead, or jointed to lead close to the cistern, consider having it stripped back to the point where it enters the house and replaced in one of the modern materials. In any case try to avoid having to make a joint to lead and get professional help if a joint has to be made.

### The pipe connections

Set the cistern in its new position on a firm platform of boards. Check that the supports will bear the weight – a couple of hundred kilograms for a full cistern. If you are taking the opportunity to fit a new cistern of plastic you'll need to make holes for the connections. The easiest way to do this is to heat a metal pipe of the appropriate size and use the hot pipe to melt a hole through the cistern wall – another way is to use a hole saw drill attachment or to use a drill with a twist drill bit to cut lots of little holes around the marked diameter of the pipe and then to smooth the hole with a half-round file. The rising main is connected near the top of the cistern to a ballvalve fitted to the cistern. The 28mm or 22mm supply pipes to the bathroom and to the hot water cylinder are connected about 50mm above the bottom of the cistern. An overflow pipe, at least 22mm in diameter, is connected roughly opposite the rising main inlet and about 20mm lower. When the ball valve is set the overflow outlet should be about 25mm above normal water level. Position the overflow through an exterior wall so that it discharges in a conspicuous position.

Pipes are connected to the cistern using tank connectors – a length of threaded pipe with a joint at one end. The connectors pass through the holes cut in the side of the cistern and are secured with a nut on either side. Use plastic washers to make the seal.

The supply of cold water to the cistern through the rising main is controlled by a ballvalve. A high-pressure type of valve is required and for a loft conversion it's worth investing in a valve with an approved silencer tube – the collapsible type which does not allow back-siphonage. The ballvalve is connected with washers – a plastic one backed by a metal one on either side of the cistern wall.

Pipes to and from the cistern should be well supported with pipe clips and blocks of wood. It's a good ideal to fit a gatevalve on all the inlets and outlets. Insulate the whole installation.

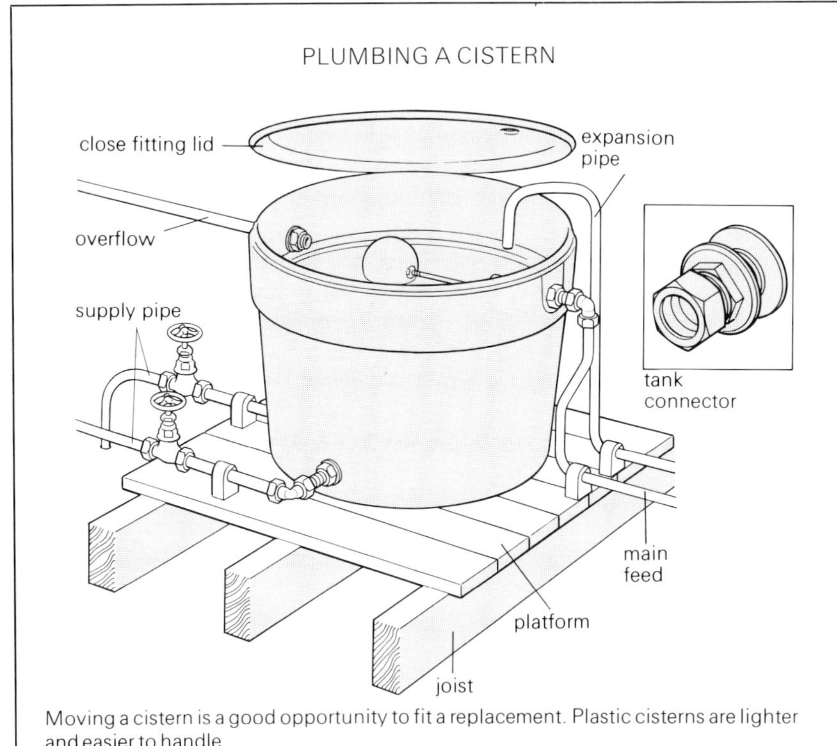

Moving a cistern is a good opportunity to fit a replacement. Plastic cisterns are lighter and easier to handle.

### Overhauling an old cistern

If a galvanised cistern is only slightly corroded, it may be possible to stave off having to fit a new one by removing old rust, thoroughly drying and coating the inside with an approved non-tainting bitumen paint.

# Lining the shell

Most loft conversions are lined with plasterboard to create the walls and ceilings of the new room and the methods of attaching the boards are the same as for ordinary ceilings (see page 262), partition walls (see page 126) and dry-lining (see page 261). Gable end walls can be dry-lined or wet plastered – see page 260. Wood cladding is another common choice for lining a loft room – see page 94.

## The flooring

The sooner the new floor can be laid in the loft space the better: the less chance anyone will have to lose balance on a joist and fall through the ceiling plaster. The whole floor usually has to wait until the electricity cables and any plumbing and central heating pipes have been laid – but it is often possible to floor at least part of the conversion before the services go in and thus to provide a solid platform to work from. Consider flooring the whole roof space not just the central area to be converted – this will allow storage behind the sidewalls.

For how to do it, see the Guide on page 237.

## The ceiling

The ceiling joists are usually attached to the rafters by bolts. The timber size will depend on the span–100mm by 50mm is typical. The space above this sort of flat ceiling is often useful to house a header water cistern for loft room plumbing or the central heating – in which case the appropriate joists should be sized to take the weight. The space is also worth having to conceal the roof ridge board (and any new beam that may have been necessary at the apex of the roof). It needn't be large, in fact there

LINING THE CONVERSION

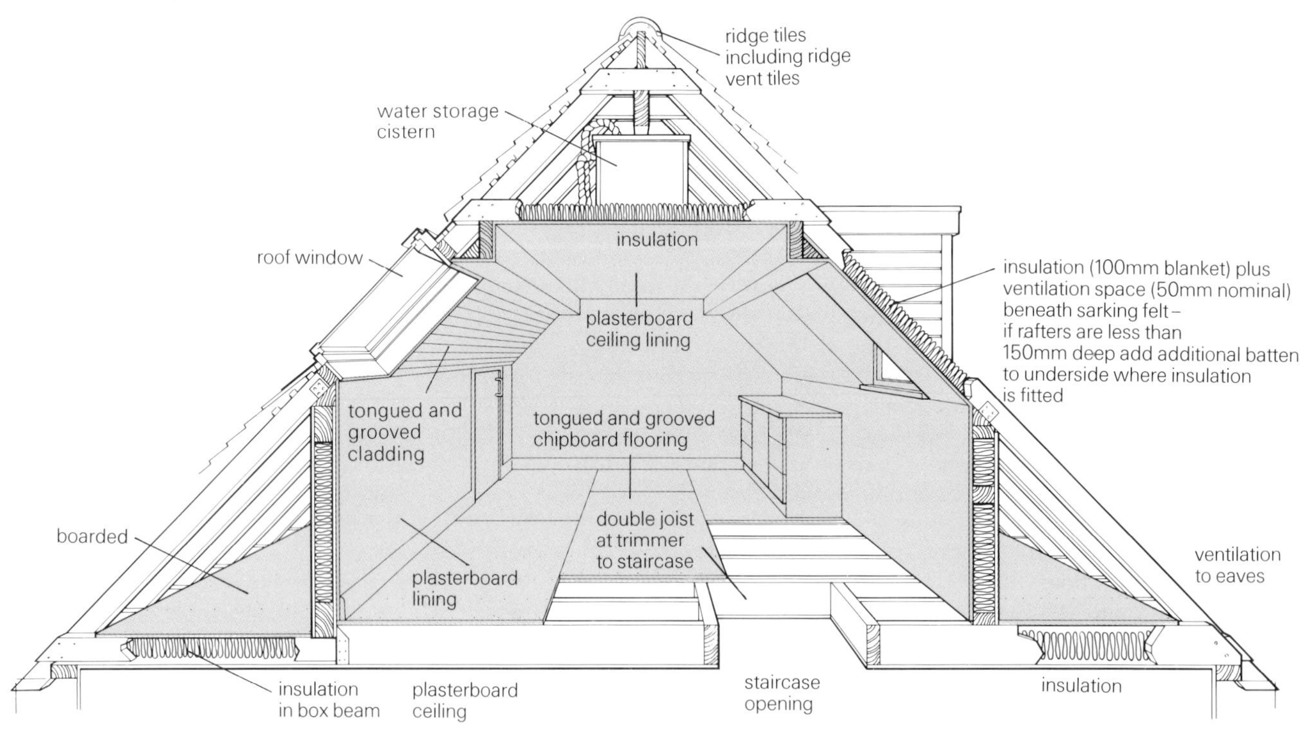


The walls and ceilings of a conversion are usually lined with plasterboard with a vapour barrier and insulation behind. Good ventilation is essential.

usually isn't enough headroom for a wide flat ceiling.

A ceiling on joists can be constructed by the normal method of nailing on to the bottom of joists. Or, if more headroom is needed or you want to use the joists as a feature of the room, the ceiling can be hollow-joisted with the boards laid from above. In this case the joists would normally be planed all round softwood and for a neater appearance they should be dovetail-half jointed to the rafters – see page 280.

When constructing a hollow-joisted ceiling, space to work in is likely to be restricted and it will usually be necessary to lift the boards on top of the joists before all the joists are set in place and access becomes difficult. Any cisterns that will be installed above the joists also need to be lifted into place early on.

Whether or not you intend to put a cistern or store things in the space above a loft ceiling, it's worth constructing a simple access hatch large enough to climb through – usually one joist will need to be cut and trimmed as for a main hatchway to a loft space.

## Walls

To some extent the choice as to whether the lower walls are vertical or sloping will be made for you by the type of conversion you have and whether your roof is hip or gable. But you're likely to be able to choose for at least some of the walls. Vertical walls are convenient because they create useful storage space behind. It's a good idea to carry the floor boarding into these cupboards and if there is no insulation already, to insulate the gap between the existing ceiling and this new floor.

Eaves storage is often used as a walk-in junk room with an access door through the partition wall, but it's also possible to create shelved storage, or hanging storage, in the space with front-opening – hinged or sliding – cupboard doors. This may be a built-in fitment or simply a piece of furniture recessed into the wall. Radiators can also be recessed.

It may be possible to make a feature of the roof support timber as here.

Sloping walls also have advantages. Although there's no concealed storage the low-level area is well suited to built-in seating or low-level storage. The join between the wall and any such fittings will be acute and, as this is difficult to clean, it's a good idea to round it off with a curved moulding.

## Insulation

Whether the ceiling and walls is attached directly to the rafters or fixed to joists and studwork, good insulation equivalent to at least 100mm of glass fibre insulating material is essential to keep the heat in in the heating season and out during the warm summer months. This much insulation meets the Building Regulations' requirement for a roof to have a U value of less than 0·35 W/m$^2$°C.

Insulating a flat ceiling is fairly simple, you can either drape an insulating blanket across the joists before fixing the plasterboard or climb up afterwards and install either blanket insulation or one of the loose-fill insulating materials between the joists. For vertical and sloping constructions you need to devise a way of preventing the insulation from slipping down. The easiest way is to use glass fibre blanket and tack it to the top of the framework.

## Ventilation

Any dry-lined wall or ceiling needs a vapour check to stop moisture penetrating through into the cold space behind. The space behind must also be ventilated. The easiest way to install a vapour barrier is to use plasterboard with a polyethylene backing and seal all joints with a waterproof tape. Alternatively a separate polyethylene sheet (preferably 125 mu, 500 gauge) can be fixed beneath the plasterboard. Joints should be over a timber member and lapped at least 100mm.

Ventilation gaps should be provided at the two opposite eaves equivalent to at least 25mm continuous slot (these gaps require mesh to keep out birds and large insects). The ventilation opening must be maintained above the sloping section of the ceiling and there should be a gap of at least 50mm between the top of the insulation and the underside of the roof. In addition to the eaves ventilation openings, it is recommended that ridge ventilators are also provided and the opening area for these should be equivalent to about 10mm continuous slot.

If ridge vents are not practical, an alternative is to provide air bricks to gable ends of the upper triangulated roof space.

# Chapter 11
# BUILDING A NEW GARAGE

A new garage can be detached, or an extension in its own right or integral in a larger extension. Much depends on the available space and the possible access for the car. If money is tight, or there's not quite enough room for a garage, a carport – basically a roof on piers – is an alternative.

A garage is usually a fairly inexpensive construction, always considerably cheaper than a habitable extension of the same size and similar outward appearance. The value of a garage is difficult to assess, most buyers paying over a certain price expect at least a single garage. Outside city centres, a semi-detached, let alone a detached, house or bungalow is an oddity without a garage.

But space may be a bigger consideration, if it is possible to get a car off the road and there's an area of land where a garage could easily be built (and would be permitted) the lack of a garage is less likely to affect the saleability of the house. In that situation the extra price a buyer might pay for a house with a garage that's already built would depend a lot on the garage itself, – what it looks like, how big it is and so on. It's unlikely to equal the full cost of installing the garage.

There are many firms offering prefabricated garages in timber or precast concrete. They normally provide an optional erection service but expect you to provide the floor slab and any foundations that are required. Usually a simple ground slab 100mm thick on firm soil (150mm on clay, peaty soil or other poor ground) is all that is required, but follow the supplier's advice. The alternative is to build your own, with brick or concrete block walls and either a home-built roof or a prefabricated timber or lightweight steel one.

## What size?

It's important not to be mean with garage space. It must be large enough to house the car comfortably. Ideally with room to open the car doors on both sides, as well as the boot and possibly also the bonnet. Even if you own a smaller car, it's as well to make provision for a large saloon car. For a single garage an internal size of 5·5m by 2·75m is a safe minimum; a double garage could be a little less than twice the width – perhaps 4·5m.

Most garages end up storing other bits and pieces – bikes, d-i-y and garden equipment, sacks of potatoes and so on – so allow an extra metre or so for these down one side or at the far end. Leave enough room to get things in and out without shifting the car. Consider also whether you want to make room to house other things or use the garage for other purposes. A garage can be a good place for a permanent workbench, it could also house a large freezer, a washing machine or tumble drier.

If you intend to make frequent use of a garage for other purposes – hobbies and so on – it's worth building a few comforts into the basic structure – better damp-proofing, extra insulation for the floor, walls or roof; better natural or artificial light; a more extensive wiring system and some provision for heating.

have at least 2m of headroom. A higher roof means you can store things aloft

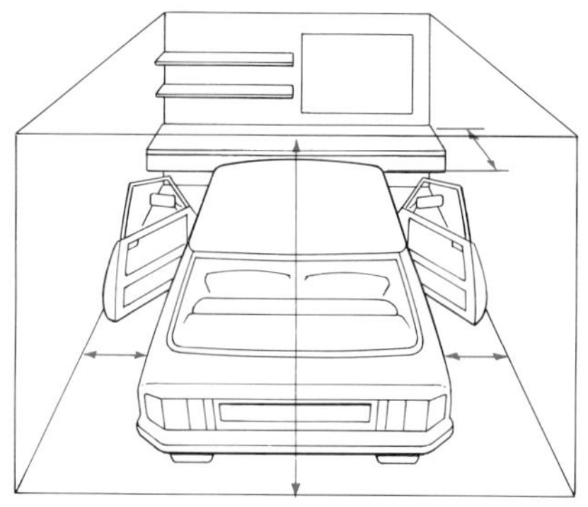

allow a metre or so at the end for storing old things. More if you want to put a workbench or something like a washing machine in the garage

a garage 5.5m long by 2·75m wide is a safe minimum to fit a large saloon car

Allow at least enough room to open doors and to walk beside the car.

## RULES AND REGULATIONS

**Planning permission**

If it's within 5 metres of the house, even a detached garage is counted as an extension for planning purposes, so if the volume of the proposed building exceeds the permitted development limits you will need to apply for permission. Permission will also be needed if the garage will extend forward of the existing building line. There may be a local ruling on whether a garage which totally obstructs access to the rear of the house is acceptable. If it isn't, the garage might have to be sited at the rear with a minimum of a metre gap between it and the nearest house wall, or built with a rear door and wide enough so that there's a passageway through the garage – which is maintained even when the car is there.

**Building Regulations**

The regulations on construction are considerably relaxed for most garages. For instance, there's no need for a damp-proof course in the floor, thermal insulation is not required. The walls may simply be lightweight panels – timber-frame for instance – which can be adequately supported on a simple concrete ground slab. The main limitations are the regulations concerning fire precautions.

**Fire precaution regulations**

The walls and roof must comply with certain fire precaution regulations. For a detached garage with a floor area of up to 30 square metres, the requirements depend mainly on whether the garage, all or part of it, is more than 2 metres away from the house walls or the nearest boundary. If it is more than two metres away, then in England and Wales its roof must comply with the regulations, but it is exempt from any of the other fire precaution regulations; in Scotland it does not need a Warrant. If within 2 metres, then as well as the roof complying, the walls must be constructed of non-combustible materials, such as bricks or blocks.

If a garage (not more than 40 square metres in area) is attached to the house and has a shared wall, that wall must have at least half-hour fire resistance – a brick wall 90mm thick or more will have this if it is not clad with combustible material. Any door through the wall into the house, must also be fire-resistant. It must be self-closing, and it's threshold has to be at least 100mm above the level of the garage floor.

Other openings – windows or ventilators – in the shared wall are best bricked up or covered permanently with fire-resistant shutters actuated by fusible links.

If you intend to have an integral garage in the lower half of a two-storey extension, the floor over the garage must be sufficiently fire-resistant – at least half hour. Depending on the type of floor construction, one way of achieving this is by constructing the ceiling of the garage with two sheets of 12.7mm plasterboard with the joints in the outer layer taped and filled.

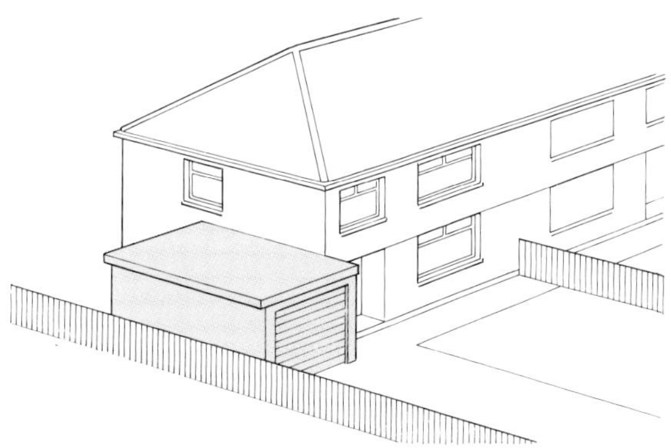

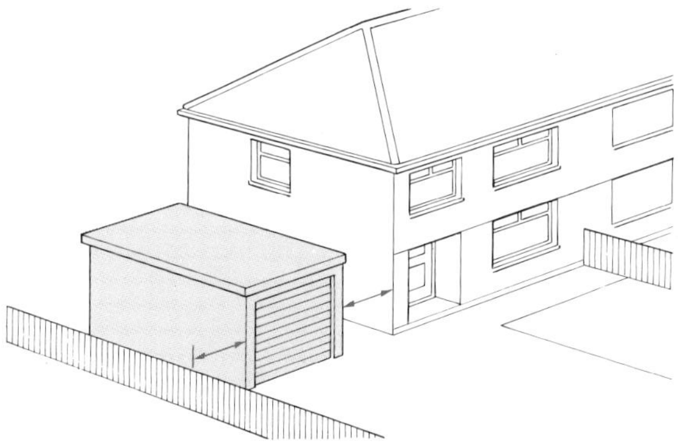

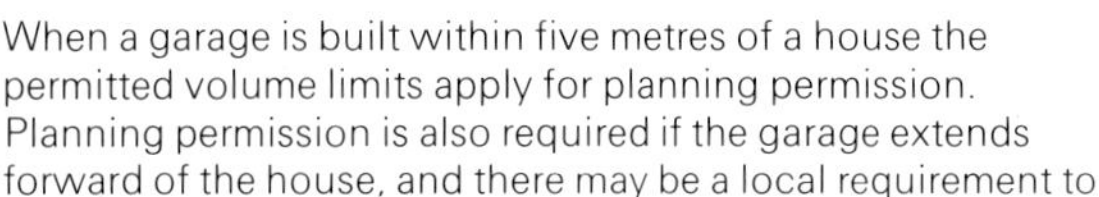

When a garage is built within five metres of a house the permitted volume limits apply for planning permission. Planning permission is also required if the garage extends forward of the house, and there may be a local requirement to retain rear access. Garages attached to the house, or within two metres of the house or boundary, are subject to more stringent fire regulations.

## Foundations and floor slab

Whether you need deep strip foundations or not will depend on the local interpretation of the Building Regulations. On good soil with a firm bearing a plain 100mm thick ground slab with the edges thickened to 200mm, as shown in the drawings, should be structurally adequate, so try for that first. See page 228 for strip foundations and page 276 for a simple ground slab with damp-proof membrane.

A good general-purpose concrete mix (C20P ready mix or 1:2:3 cement: sand: gravel if you mix your own) is fine for the floor slab, but any exposed paving outside the garage should be laid with the air-entrained mix described for a carport. There's no harm and there may be an advantage – especially in parts of the country with very cold winters – in using this mix for the floor of a garage as well. If the garage is built alongside the house an expansion joint is required between the slab and the house. With a plain ground slab the thickened edge should be twice as wide as the external wall thickness and centred under the walls.

Give the floor as smooth a finish as possible without making it slippery when wet: a coarse texture will make cleaning off oil drippings and other mess difficult. A 'sandpaper' texture produced by wood-floating when the concrete is partly hardened is just about right.

## Walls

Provided the fire precaution regulations are met, garage walls can be any material and need not meet any standard of thermal insulation. In most cases solid walls one block or one brick's width (sometimes called half-brick) thick will suffice, but a garage wall, constructed of bricks or blocks, should not be less than 90mm thick, and more than 2·5m high, piers at least 190mm square should be built at the corners of the building and at least every three metres (measured from centre to centre) to ensure good stability. If 150mm thick blocks are used, it will save cutting at the corners if the blocks can be laid to an off-centre running bond with the vertical joints offset by the thickness of the blocks rather than being centred on the blocks in the course below. The end walls are then easier to construct and provide the necessary stiffness at the corners.

If the garage is to have an exposed brickwork exterior, cavity walls can be just as easy to build as solid ones. Although insulation isn't usually important in a garage, dryness is, especially if workshop tools or domestic appliances are going to live there, and a cavity wall with a lightweight block inner leaf will keep rain penetration and condensation to a minimum.

Timber-frame walls are a fairly good choice for a garage more than two metres from a house or boundary. They are constructed in the same way as timber-frame walls for an extension and can be faced with most of the materials.

## Roofs

All the roof choices for an extension are possible for a garage (see Roofs page 250). A pitched roof is usually the most attractive although also the most expensive. If the triangle of the roof is left open to the garage, it can provide useful storage space. The cheapest type of roof is a gently pitched back slope of corrugated plastic or asbestos cement and this can be disguised to look satisfactory from the front by a short steeply pitched front slope – tiled (or slated) to match the house roof.

Flat roofs of bitumen felt on boards are usually in the middle price range – these can be disguised to the front by a parapet wall – a device which can be continued round the other walls too. A parapet will also disguise the necessary guttering for disposing of rainwater. For a simple garage many local authorities will accept discharge into a rainwater butt.

The fire precaution regulations also apply to roofs. A pitched roof covered with tiles or slates or corrugated sheets of galvanised steel or asbestos cement complies with the most stringent requirements. So does roofing felt on boarding, provided the required number of layers of the cor-

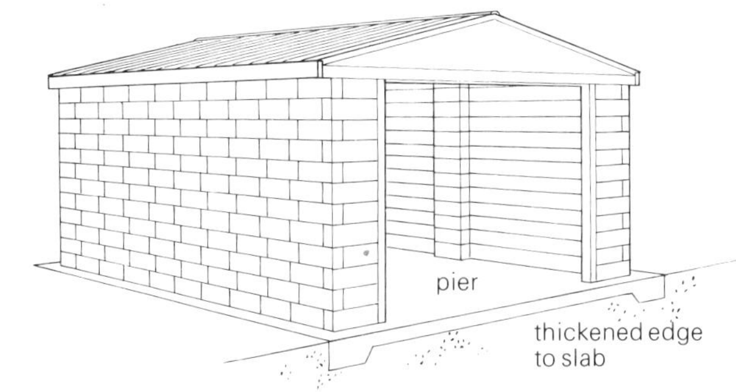


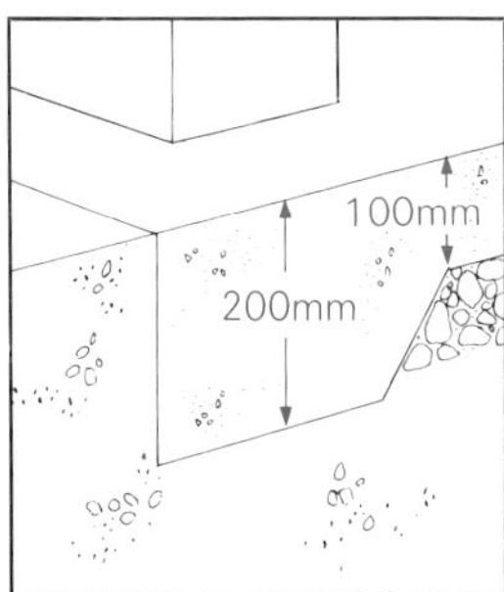


Use C20P or an air-entrained mix to make a 100mm slab with thickened edges.

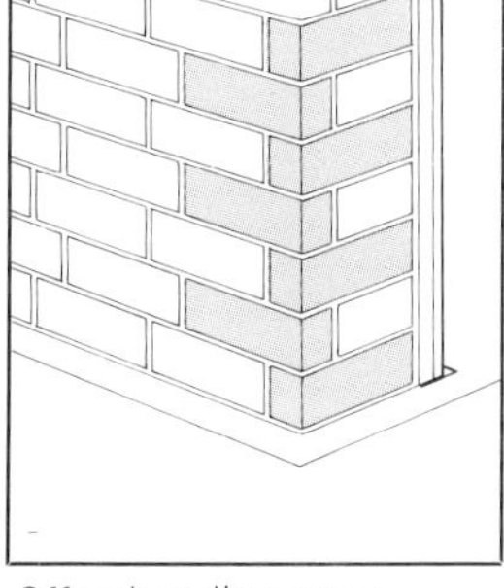

Offset bonding saves cutting at the ends of the wall.

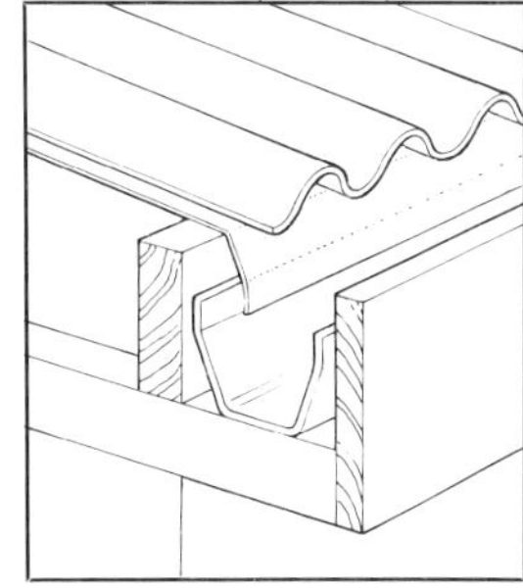

If the garage has a flat roof the gutters can be disguised behind a fascia.

rect grade of roofing felt is used. Translucent roofs are permitted: the site of the garage determines which grade of translucent materials can be used in order to confirm to the fire precaution regulations.

**Doors**

Modern garage doors are often the up-and-over type made of galvanised steel or aluminium – timber up-and-over doors are also available. When the counter-balanced springs (or weights) are properly adjusted, these doors require little effort to operate. Traditional double-hinged doors are also widely available and may look more acceptable in some circumstances.

Ready-made garage doors won't necessarily come in widths that match up neatly to a convenient number of brick block lengths – discrepancies can be more easily made up by adjusting the size of the framing timbers than trying to adapt the blockwork to the door dimensions.

The bottoms of door frames should be separated from the floor by pads of dpc material and be thoroughly treated with a wood preservative soaked well into the end grain.

## Prefabricated buildings

A wide variety of prefabricated garages are available. A package of component parts can be supplied and erected on a prepared base or the components can be supplied and delivered to the site for erection by you or a builder you've employed.

Cost, is the factor which usually influences the decision in favour of a prefabricated building. The site preparation, that is, the construction of the base, should be done well in advance of the delivery of the components so that these do not hinder the construction of the floor slab and so that assembly work can start as soon as the consignment arrives. At least 7, preferably 14, days should elapse to allow the concrete floor slab to harden sufficiently for the components to be placed in position without damage to the slab. While constructing the slab make arrangements for any surface water drains that will be required to take the roof rainwater to soakaways, if rainwater butts won't do.

If you are going to assemble the components yourself, take time in advance to study the manufacturer's plans and instructions and then follow them precisely.

The building size can be selected as required from a range of standard component panels that are available from each manufacturer. The panel sizes vary from one manufacturer to another but usually they will supply a 'package' comprising as many standard panels as required to provide a building as close to your requirements as their standard panels will allow. So a prefabricated garage can be a large or small; single or double. All are single storey. Most prefabricated garages are made from concrete.

The wall panels can be concrete furnished with special finishes, such as: imitation brickwork, exposed aggregate (in various colours or be simply smooth and lightly textured). Metal-framed structures with lightweight panels are available but are more vulnerable to impact damage.

Roofs are usually corrugated lightweight panels supported by concrete, metal or wood posts. There is usually a choice of windows and side doors. The choice of up-and-over or side-hung garage doors is often available.

Prefabricated carports generally comprise tubular metal posts with metal or wood roof supports carrying a lightweight corrugated plastic roof.

Most prefabricated building manufacturers will supply you with drawings as part of the package, for your own use and for the application for planning permission and Building Regulations approval. In addition to these you will need site and location plans.

A garage with a pitched roof has space for storage above.

A roof of corrugated plastic or asbestos-cement or felt can be disguised to the front with a short pitched slope.

# Building a carport

A carport is a simpler d-i-y proposition than a garage. The lean-to design shown here provides roof cover and a measure of protection from wind and driving rain without blocking the light: basically it's an enlarged porch and can provide the benefits of a porch as well as sheltering the car.

## Floor and foundations

In most cases a thickened-edge slab should provide the necessary foundation support for the screen block wall, but a strip footing isolated by an expansion joint may be required on some soils. An expansion joint is necessary between the slab and the house. Since there is no protection against freezing temperatures the floor should be laid with air-entrained ready-mix to reduce the risk of surface scaling from the combination of repeated freeze-thaw cycles and de-icing salts brought in from the road on the car underbody and tyres: specify a mix containing a minimum of 330kg of cement per cm and a 4 per cent entrained air content. To get the maximum cost benefit from ready-mix it makes sense to lay the carport floor at the same time as a drive. If ready-mix isn't a practical proposition, because you don't want enough to make ready mix worth while, use a cement-rich mix: $1:1\frac{1}{2}:2\frac{1}{2}$ cement: and sand: gravel or $1:3\frac{1}{2}$ cement: all-in ballast.

A screen wall can be built on an existing concrete drive or slab providing the existing base is well constructed and in good condition. It needs to be at least 100mm thick and the wall should stand 150mm or more from the slab edge or any expansion joint across the slab.

If the existing slab will not support a screen wall it may be possible to leave the main part as the car hardstanding, but break up a strip along the edge and prepare a proper foundation for the wall.

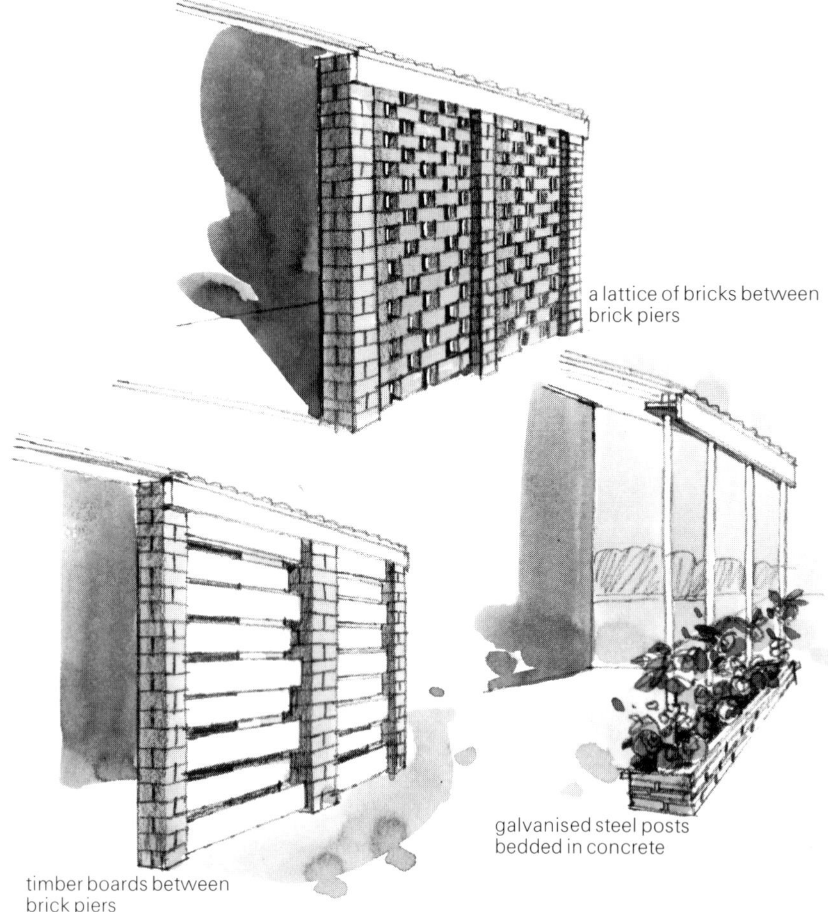

The walls can be almost anything you want – a honeycomb of bricks or a trellis support for plants for instance

## Screen wall

The wall is built from standard garden screen walling units. The piers should be at centres of not more than 3m and should be reinforced vertically with a length of 16mm deformed reinforcing bar in the hollow centres of the pier blocks. This is surrounded by concrete as the piers are built up. Concrete short lengths of bar into the slab edges or foundation on the centreline of the piers, leaving about 500mm projecting; the main lengths of bar can be tied to them with galvanized iron wire when wall construction is started. Bed ladder-type brickwork reinforcement in the horizontal joints at 600mm intervals (with the screen units shown, every other course of screen blocks and every third pier unit) to give added stiffness, as there is no true bonding between the blocks.

## Roof

This design has a simple roof with translucent plastic corrugated sheet covering on timber rafters. The main transverse timbers are shown resting directly on the piers: if a timber plate on top of the wall is used to spread the load, the timbers can be more closely spaced. The timbers are secured to the piers with ties embedded in the concrete infill.

### Variations on the walls

A concrete screen block wall is only one possibility for the side wall of a carport. Following the basic principles, bricks can be used in an open lattice design. An open side can be constructed from brick piers, timber posts or galvanised steel poles and any of these supports can be used with infill panels – of, for instance, trellis, woven fencing or corrugated plastic. The supports can be arranged with flower beds below and used for training plants.

Posts and poles need to be bedded in concrete with at least 600mm below ground, a wallplate or fascia board at roof level ties them together and provides a fixing for the gutter.

CONSTRUCTION DETAILS OF A CARPORT

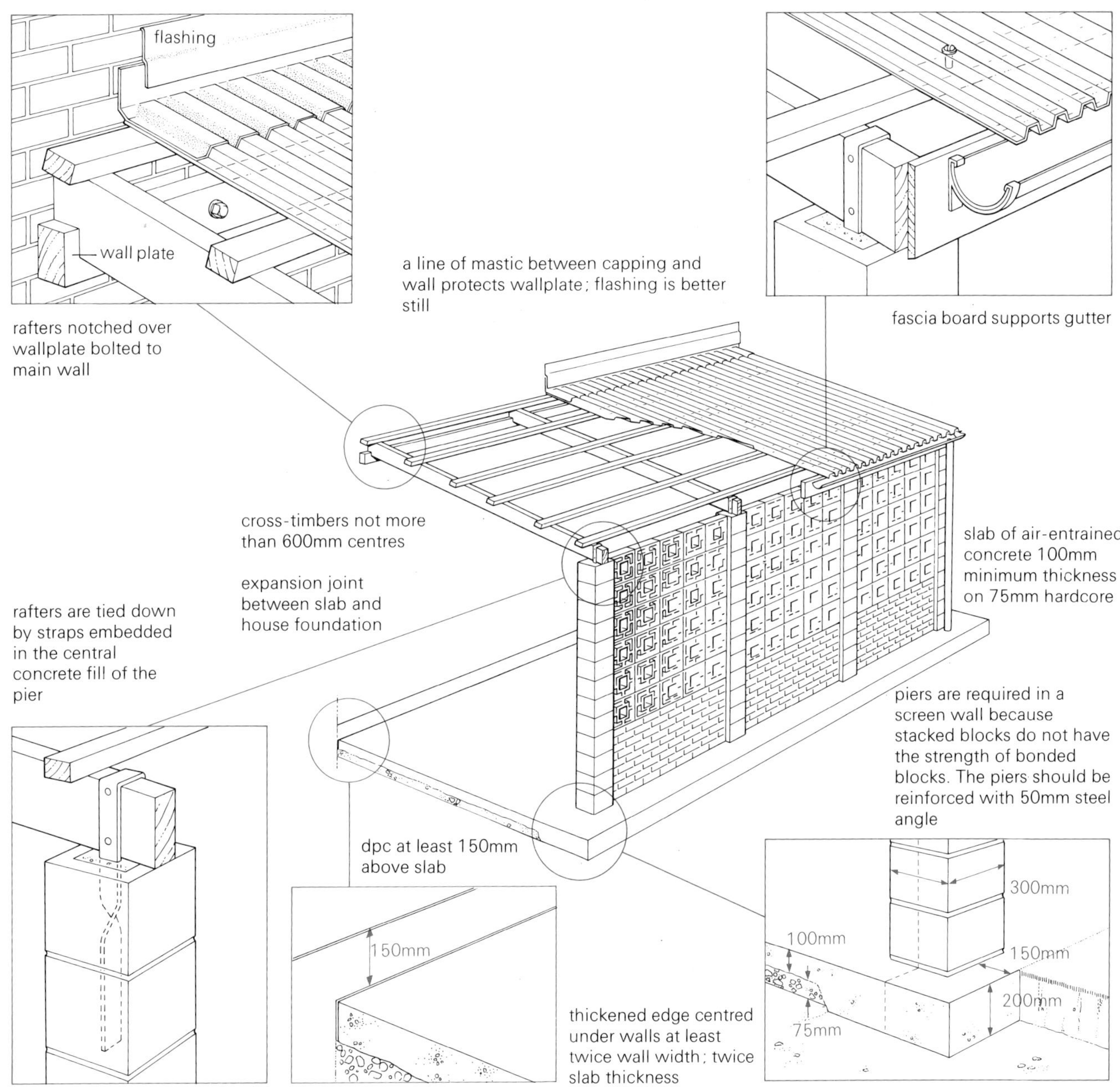
flashing
wall plate
rafters notched over wallplate bolted to main wall
a line of mastic between capping and wall protects wallplate; flashing is better still
fascia board supports gutter
cross-timbers not more than 600mm centres
expansion joint between slab and house foundation
rafters are tied down by straps embedded in the central concrete fill of the pier
slab of air-entrained concrete 100mm minimum thickness on 75mm hardcore
piers are required in a screen wall because stacked blocks do not have the strength of bonded blocks. The piers should be reinforced with 50mm steel angle
dpc at least 150mm above slab
150mm
thickened edge centred under walls at least twice wall width; twice slab thickness
300mm
100mm
150mm
200mm
75mm

A basic carport design which could be adapted to have different side walls.

# Electricity in outbuildings

If you intend to provide lighting or socket outlets in a separate garage, or any other outbuilding, then you must install a permanent fused supply. This can run from a spare fuseway in the existing consumer unit or from a new consumer unit (or switch fuse unit) installed alongside the existing one. Remember that any new consumer unit can be connected to the meter only by the Electricity Board. Any new circuits or individual sockets intended to provide power to electrical equipment to be used outside the house must be protected by a residual current device with an operating current of 30mA or less.

Much of work involved in outdoor electrics is normal electrical practice – see page 48 *et seq* – but between the house and the outbuilding special precautions are necessary.

Although an amateur electrician *could* carry out this work, only an experienced and competent person should attempt it. For other people it would be sensible to employ a professional to do the wiring, you could reduce the cost by doing any manual labour – digging trenches, erecting posts and so on – yourself.

## Special cables

Standard 2·5mm² twin and earthed pvc-sheathed cable can be used outdoors, but it has to be installed in impact-resisting conduit. *Mineral-insulated copper-sheathed* (MICS) is a special cable which can be used out of doors. It is available as twin-core cables surrounded by metal which acts as the earth connection. MICS has a copper sheath and looks like slender metal tube: for use outside it must be pvc covered; it is available with orange, black or white covering. Special clamping cable glands are needed at each end of the cable to grip the metal sheath or armouring, and form the earth connection.

The joints *must* be made correctly as earth continuity is essential. With MICS seals are also required to make the joints watertight. It's best to buy MICS with these (and glands if required) already fitted. Specialist electrical retailers should be willing to prepare MICS cable. A gland is like a compression plumbing fitting: the body of the gland and an 'olive' is fitted to the cable before fitting the seal and is then passed into the metal box, locked into the hole in the side of the box by a nut and the second part of the fitting which passes over the cable and is screwed down on the first section.

### Circuit sizing

In any circuit, the size of cable you need depends on the maximum likely load and the length of cable used in the circuit (the longer the cable, the bigger the *voltage drop* along it and so the bigger the cable needs to be). For the vast majority of indoor circuits, voltage drop is not a problem, but outside circuits are often much longer and then voltage drop does need considering.

Mineral-insulated copper-sheathed (MICS) cable.

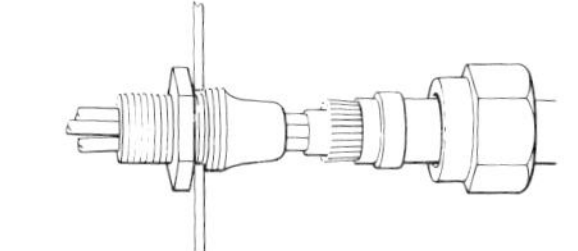

Armoured pvc-insulated-and-sheathed.

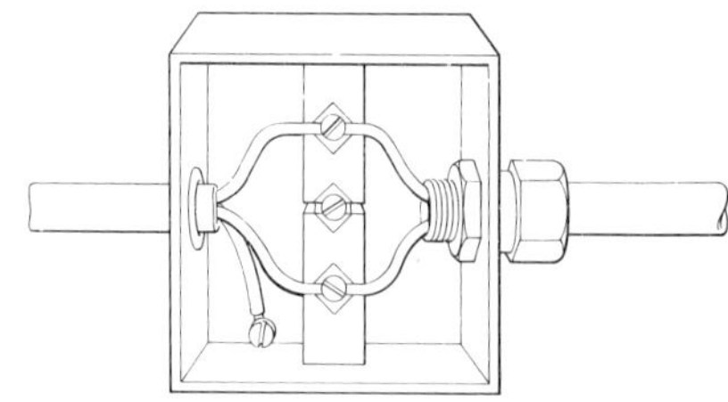

External cable in MICS (or the alternative armoured-pvc) is connected in the house to a pvc cable from the consumer unit and then runs unbroken to the outbuilding.

As examples, here are some typical jobs with the type and size of cable you might need. They assume that the circuit will be protected by a cartridge fuse or MCB–not a rewireable fuse – and that the cable is not bunched with other cables at any point and does not run through any insulation.

■ supplying power and light to a detached garage–total cable length not more than 22m (floor area not more than 50m²).

Fuse rating 30amps; cable 4mm² MICS; 4mm² ordinary pvc insulated.

■ supplying power to a greenhouse –total cable length not more than 29m (floor area not greater than 20m²).

Fuse rating 20amps; cable 4mm² MICS; 4mm² ordinary pvc insulated.

■ supplying power points in the garden – total cable length not more than 17m.

Fuse rating 15amps; cable 1·5mm² MICS; 1·5mm² ordinary pvc insulated.

### Taking cable through a wall

The circuit cable from the consumer unit should come through the wall as close as possible to where it is needed. Where it passes through the wall the cable should be protected by plastic or galvanised steel conduit which is angled slightly downwards to the outside and fitted at the ends with grommets that prevent the cable chafing on the pipe ends. The supply cable should be in one continuous length from inside the main building to the outbuilding – there can be no joints anywhere along its length. Normally ordinary cable (sufficient in size to carry the necessary current) is taken from the consumer unit to a connection point – a junction box – close to where the special cable will leave the house.

## Cable routes

There are two possible routes cable can follow to an outbuilding; overhead (known as catenary wiring) or underground.

### Overhead wiring

If it's only a short distance between greenhouse or garage and house, say 5 metres or less, overhead wiring can be the easiest method of providing a circuit and you can use ordinary twin and earth cable – preferably black coloured. But cable run overhead will be visible and is not always easy to organise. The clearance height must be not less than 3·5m above the ground, or 5·2m above a car passageway.

The cable must be supported by a catenary wire – a galvanised steel wire – suspended above the ground. The cable is taped and clipped to this catenary wire so that it is not subjected to any stress or strain and it will withstand wind and storms.

The catenary wire is threaded through an eye bolt at either end of its length and it must be earthed to the main earthing point in the house and to the earth terminal in the garage or greenhouse.

Choose a place on the outside wall of the house where the catenary wire can be attached and another at the outbuilding end. To get the right height you may have to erect a timber post. This will have to be securely attached to the greenhouse or garage and if necessary braced. Use a preservative-treated post, allow at least a metre below ground and give this metre and a little bit more an extra soak in preservative before it is buried – the most vulnerable part of the post is at the soil/air interface. The post should have a cap or angled or domed head to shed water.

Screw an eyebolt into a large wallplug on the wall of the house and another eyebolt into the side of the post near its top. Where possible fit them higher than the minimum permitted height to allow for possible sagging – allow 450mm or so. Thread one end of the catenary wire through the eye of the eyebolt at the outbuilding end. Take about 375mm of the wire through the eye and tie it neatly off. Since this catenary wire will be under strain for many years a strong joint at each end is vital. If you are using a stranded wire a strong neatly tapered joint can be achieved by 'whipping' the individual strands of the wire. First, separate a single strand from the free end of the wire. Wrap this tightly round the wire and the free end. Turn the last 75mm of the strand length-wise in line with the wire and then select a second strand, wrapping this round the doubled wire and the free end of the first strand. Continue until all the strands are tied in. Pinch the end of the last strand tightly into position with pliers.

Repeat the procedure at the other end, and fit a cable tensioner – a turnbuckle – which can be adjusted to take up the slack.

A downward rainwater 'drip loop' of slack is left at each end of the cable, then it is attached to the catenary, using weatherproof insulating tape beneath buckle–type cable clips at each end and then intermediate buckle-type cable clips every 200mm or so.

ROUTING CABLE OVERHEAD

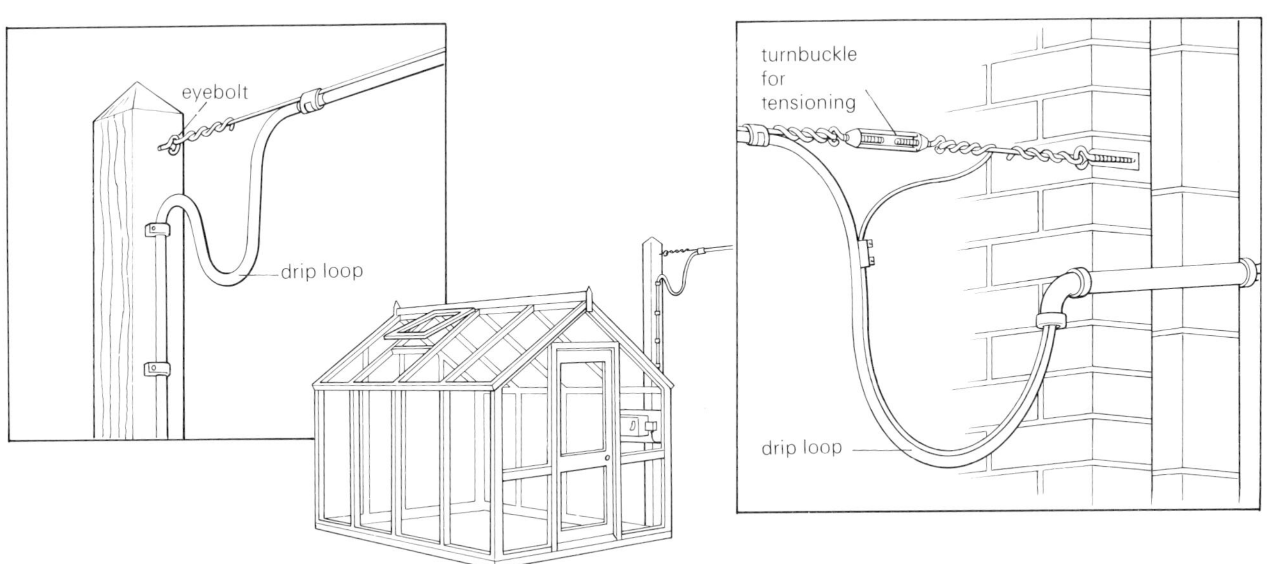


Ordinary pvc cable or MICS can be used overhead clipped to a catenary wire. Such an installation must be well above head height and must be secure against wind damage.

## RESIDUAL CURRENT DEVICES (RCD's)

An RCD to protect the whole house would be wired between the meter and the consumer unit or as part of the consumer unit – since you will need the Electricity Board to turn off the supply before such an RCD can be fitted, let them fit it.

To protect just one circuit use a more sensitive 30mA unit. Some consumer units have RCDs built in to protect certain circuits. RCDs to protect individual radial circuits (as most outdoor circuits are) are fitted on the circuit cable immediately *after* the consumer unit. The circuit earth connection must be complete, back to the consumer unit which may mean mounting the RCD in an *enclosure*. RCDs to protect a single socket are wired like any other socket and fit a double socket box.

## Underground wiring

Laying cables underground is the least obtrusive method of supplying electricity as they can be buried under a path or patio or even under a lawn or border, provided it is not likely to be disturbed. There the cable can be undisturbed for years and there is no danger of wind damage as there is with overhead wiring. Underground wiring is the best choice for long distances. The cable is buried deep enough for it not to be disturbed by digging–around 500mm below the surface will normally do.

MICS can be laid directly in the trench. Ordinary twin and earth can be used but must be protected by galvanised steel or hard plastic conduit with watertight joints.

The trench for the cable is usually dug a little over 500mm deep, but it should be deeper if it passes beneath ground that may be disturbed – a vegetable plot say. The trench needs to be about 300mm or so wide. As far as possible it should run in a straight line to the outbuilding so that its course can easily be discovered at a later date. It can be helpful to follow a marker of some sort – the edge of a path for instance. You might also map the route and paint it on a surface in the outbuilding.

If the house and outbuilding have suspended floors, the cable passes through the wall below the damp-proof course (dpc); if the floors are solid, access is more difficult and the cable has to be run up the side of the building, to pass through the wall above the level of the floor and above the dpc. Where cable has to be run up the wall at the house or outbuilding end of its run, it is clipped to the wall using exterior clips at approximately 250mm intervals. It must also be covered for extra protection and the top of a covering fixed vertically must be capped or sealed to prevent water trickling in.

After digging the trench compact the base, remove any stones and lay a thin cushion of sifted soil or fine sand. As a further protection for the cable cover it with concrete paving slaps or special concrete cable tiles before infilling the trench.

UNDERGROUND WIRING

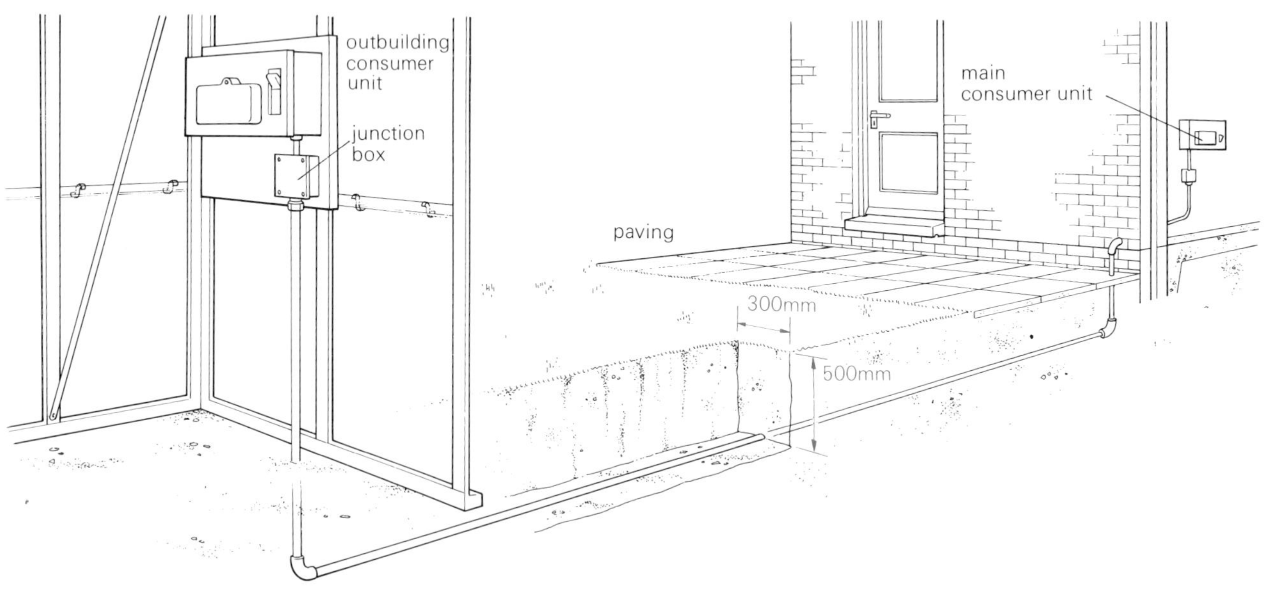


Wiring underground can be pvc cable in conduit or MICS. There must be no danger of disturbing the cable by digging.

## The outbuilding end

Where the cable enters the outbuilding it should end in another consumer unit (unless it is supplying only one socket or a light, in which case just a switch would be appropriate). The main switch in this unit makes it possible to isolate the circuit quickly and easily. Lighting circuits and ring or radial power circuits are wired separately from the consumer unit in the normal way. In protected dry places ordinary pvc twin and earth of the appropriate sizes can be used, but if for any reason the cable is vulnerable – for instance to attack by rodents – then the circuit should be continued with MICS cable or the ordinary pvc cable should be encased in rigid plastic conduit. If it is potentially damp, all fittings and outlets should be 1200mm above the floor.

For any fixed equipment that will be permanently connected, fused connection units are, as always, neater and safer. In an outbuilding, which is likely to be damp, there is a risk with a plug and socket of damp working between the two resulting in a blown fuse. Never use adaptors. It is a good idea to have connection units and sockets with red neon indicators to show when they are supplying electricity – especially for an outbuilding that is used infrequently.

A TYPICAL INSTALLATION

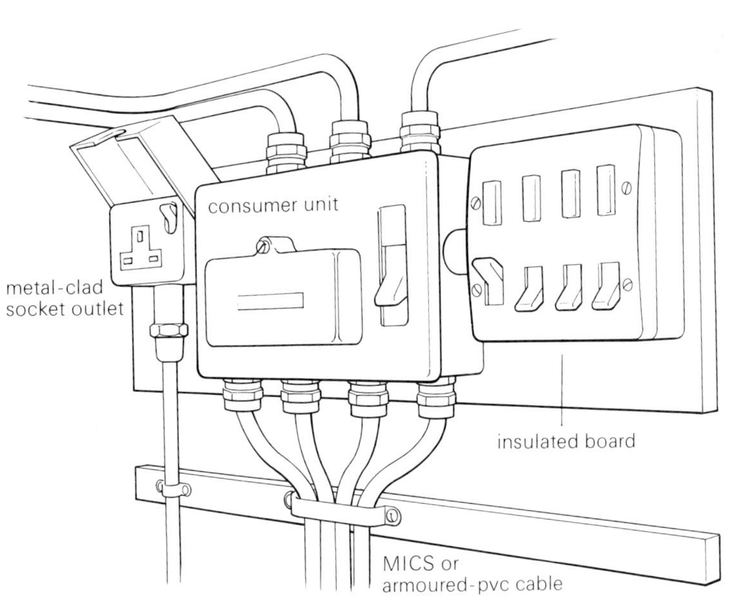


The cable to the outbuilding ends at a consumer unit, unless only one socket and light is to be supplied.

## Garden sockets

At the same time as installing a new circuit to an outbuilding you could take the opportunity to provide a socket for portable electrical equipment. However this must have its own supply cable from the consumer unit in the house or the one in the outbuilding. You cannot take a spur from the outbuilding supply cable on route to the outbuilding. The cable to the socket must be properly installed (like a supply cable to an outbuilding) and should also be protected by a residual current device with an operating current of 30mA or less.

An outdoor socket outlet must be fixed to a wall (not a fence) or to a stout post set in concrete with at least 600mm of its length below ground.

GARDEN SOCKETS

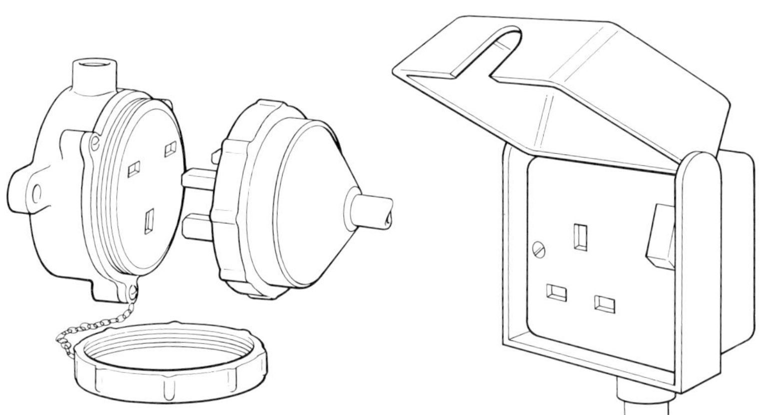

A weatherproof outdoor socket outlet must be installed at least 150mm above ground.

A standard socket outlet can be used in a sheltered position with a protective cover.

The socket height should not be less than 150mm above ground level – preferably more – especially if there is a risk of flooding or a covering of snow.

A standard socket outlet (preferably the more robust metal-clad type) can be used outdoors if the site is not exposed, but it must be set inside a protective cover with a weatherproof flap – these are available purpose-made. It's better to use a weatherproof socket made for the purpose. For one socket the current capacity of the supply cable and fuse is 15A or sometimes 16A.

# Chapter 12

# CONVERTING OTHER SPACE

Apart from the loft there are possibly two other main areas in a house which might usefully be converted to habitable space – garages and basements.

Converting existing space will almost always be cheaper than an extension built from scratch, but conversion work is never easy and for an amateur there could be many problems, especially when the structure of the building has to be altered in some way. Professional advice will always be useful, not least because each conversion will have problems peculiar to its own situation and the professional may be able to suggest a solution that you would never have thought of. This chapter deals with the main considerations for converting an integral garage or a basement.

An integral garage is often ripe for conversion. Here the conversion could combine with an enclosed porch.

A conversion for storage, as here, needs to be damp free.

The open well outside a basement has been roofed with translucent material to provide a useful covered area.

Sound outbuildings can often be converted, but many improvements may be required to make one habitable.

# Converting an integral garage

Houses and bungalows are sometimes built with an integral garage, that is, a garage formed as part of the main structure. Such a garage is often ripe for conversion because the standard of building construction for an integral garage is nearly as high as for the house itself. So, if your house has an integral garage and you need some additional living accommodation, converting the garage space is an idea worth exploring. But don't think it's a cheap option, it will usually be cheaper to build a habitable extension than to convert an integral garage *and* provide a new garage.

## Planning permission

The necessary alterations to the front of the garage – replacing the garage doors with windows for instance – may need permission because the works materially affect the external appearance of the house. Any alteration to the front which extends beyond the existing building line will also need permission – a bay window for instance. It would therefore be sensible to check with the local authority before finalising any plans. Planning permission may well be needed for any new garage erected to replace the integral one.

## Building Regulations

Even if planning permission is not required you will need Building Regulations approval. The main Building Regulations involved are those dealing with special requirements for habitable rooms; the weather resistance and thermal insulation of the external walls; if the garage is single-storey, the thermal insulation of the roof and, if you choose a masonry wall, to replace the garage doors, the foundations to that new wall.

### Habitable rooms

The Building Regulations for habitable rooms are dealt with in detail in Chapter 8. Providing adequate window light and ventilation shouldn't be a problem. Most garages will already have one small window and normally a new window is fitted to fill at least part of the original garage entrance. As the garage would have been approached by a drive, the necessary open space outside the window is usually available.

Obtaining the required ceiling height of 2·3m may be more of a problem entailing raising the ceiling or lowering the floor. Neither of these is likely to be cheap. Even if the existing garage has sufficient headroom, remember that work carried out to improve the floor and ceiling may raise the floor and lower the ceiling, eating into the available height.

### Walls

The existing external wall of an integral garage of a house is likely to be the same as the rest of the house – normally a cavity wall or a solid wall at least one brick thick (225mm). In a bungalow however, the original builder may have saved money by building a half-brick wall (100mm wide).

None of these walls is likely to have been plastered and in all situations the U value would have to be improved to achieve the $0{\cdot}6W/m^2{}^\circ C$ now

DRY LINING

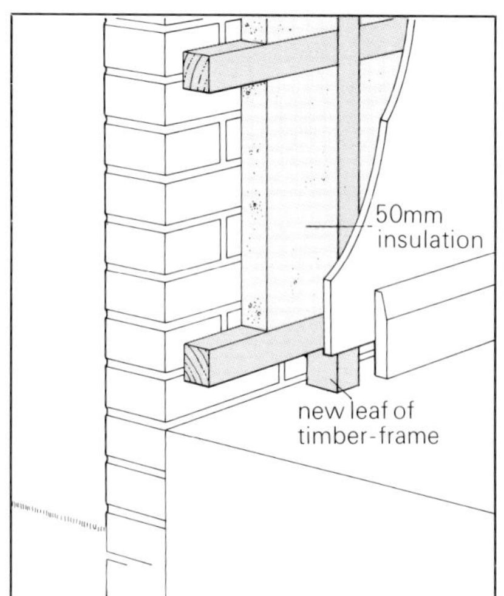

A half-brick wall will need a new leaf.

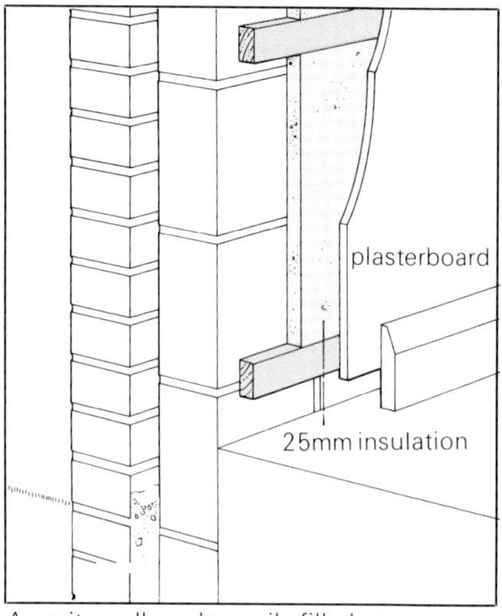

A cavity wall can be easily filled or dry-lined.

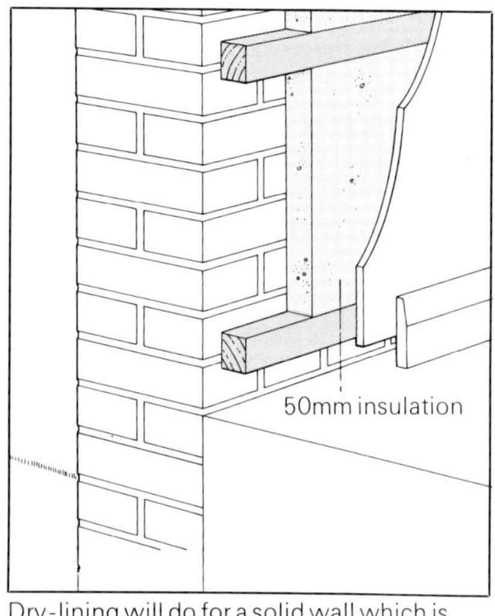

Dry-lining will do for a solid wall which is at least 220mm thick.

required under the Building Regulations. With a cavity wall the easiest way to achieve this might be to have cavity wall insulation installed in the whole house. The garage wall would then only need plastering – with a 16mm layer of plaster – or dry-lining to bring its thermal properties into line. Otherwise dry-lining with insulation in the space between the wall and the plasterboard is the answer – a cavity wall would need at least 25mm of insulation, a solid wall nominally 220mm (the traditional 9in thick wall) would need at least 50mm of mineral wool but 60mm of glass fibre blanket insulation.

Dry-lining could solve the insulation problem for a half-brick (105mm) solid wall, but with walls of this thickness moisture penetration would be a problem and a separate inner leaf is therefore required. This could be timber-frame (see page 245) or a leaf of concrete blocks. With timber-frame tieing the new leaf to the old could be a problem. You'd effectively be building a timber-frame wall back to front with the cladding completed before the framing. Building the frame as a timber stud partition taking its support from a headplate fixed to the joists of the floor above and a sole plate on the garage floor would get over the need to tie in – see page 126. If there is a simple coupled roof over the garage or any floor extends over only part of the garage it will be necessary to devise some other support for the head plate.

With a new leaf of blocks tieing in is easier, as you can install the ties as the new wall goes up, but the foundations might not be sufficient.

### Damp-proof course

Whatever the new leaf is made of it will need a damp-proof course at the base of the wall. The wall of an integral garage should already contain a damp-proof course (dpc) linked to the dpc in the walls of the rest of the house. But you will need to check and if there is none, one will have to be incorporated.

If internal partition walls are required, timber stud is again usually the most suitable – see page 126. If a more substantial partition to provide better sound insulation is required, 75mm lightweight blocks could be used but this again may need better foundations than the existing garage floor can provide – a block wall should be bonded to the garage walls or tied with metal straps.

### Replacing the doors

The wall which is to replace the garage doors could be almost any material which is compatible with the rest of the building. The beam over the garage doors ensures the structural integrity of the building above and all that is usually necessary, is for the opening to be filled in. The infill could be:

**Masonry** This could be block or brick construction to the same standard as the other external walls. Probably the easiest masonry construction would be some sort of solid wall. Bonding the new wall to the piers either side would be the main problem, it may be better not to bond. Firm foundations are also required.

**Timber frame** If a timber frame construction is chosen the concrete floor of the garage will normally be sufficient foundation and this is a good reason for choosing it. The frame of the garage door can be left in place and a new panel fixed to this. A dpc will be required below the soleplate of the timber infill. External cladding would complete the wall.

**Glass** A wall of glass is effectively a window and the Building Regulations limit the area of window openings to a percentage of the total wall area. For single-glazed windows up to 25 per cent of the total wall area is allowed, but windows can be larger if they are glazed with more panes of glass to improve their insulating. When fitting a new window it costs proportionally little more to buy and fit one which is double-glazed so it usually makes sense to do so. A double-glazed patio door (fitted with safety glass) is a possibility to fill the opening. A threshold would then have to be constructed.

### Floors

A garage will have been designed and constructed to take the weight of a car so the floor will certainly be strong enough for people and furniture. It will normally be solid concrete and, provided it is in good sound condition, it can be left in place. An existing garage floor may or may not include a damp-proof membrane. If there is not one, one which links to the dpc in the surrounding walls will be required. The easiest way to provide this is to apply a liquid damp-proofing solution over the slab and paint this up the walls to link with the damp-proof course in the walls. This should be done before lining or plastering the room. If the existing floor surface is bad, lay a new screed over the dpm – see page 236.

If an existing concrete floor is to remain, any car engine oil needs to be removed with a suitable proprietary solution before a water-proof membrane or screed is applied.

While working on the existing floor it may be worth upgrading its thermal properties (though there's no regulation requiring this). A floating floor of polystyrene is one way to do this – see page 189.

## Converting a detached garage

When a detached garage or any other outbuilding is to be converted to a self-contained independent dwelling, planning permission is always necessary. For a conversion for extra accommodation for the use of your family you need 'change of use' approval.

Needless to say, Building Regulations approval is necessary. Outbuildings are usually fairly basic in their construction and the amenities that they provide. So, a great deal of design and construction work is necessary to bring the building up to a habitable standard. Providing all the necessary services is usually a big expense. Professional advice is essential.

# Converting a basement

The conversion of a basement into habitable accommodation usually means solving a damp problem – in extreme case, penetrating water. Even when a basement doesn't suffer from penetrating damp, it frequently suffers from condensation due to lack of heating and ventilation – mainly because of inadequate windows. Whether a basement conversion is intended to provide habitable space or simply extra storage or a work area, these problems will have to be overcome.

## Dampness

Basements should be waterproofed when constructed and in new houses this is done by wrapping the area underground in a waterproof membrane contained within a masonry or concrete sandwich for protection. If a basement should then leak it means that the waterproof membrane has been damaged in some way. Repairing this membrane is a major operation requiring special expertise and should definitely not be attempted by anyone with a less than thorough knowledge of building construction. Often the level of the water in the ground will be above the floor of the basement and, if the floor or the walls were opened up, flooding could occur.

Where signs of dampness are less serious, it may be possible to install an internal damp-proof membrane for the floor and walls. The only sure cure however is to repair the membrane or install one where none exists.

## Signs and tests for damp

Water seeping, even running, from the walls will alert you to serious damp. But walls and floors which *appear* to be dry may be suffering from damp which is evaporating away. Such damp should be obvious under anything standing on the floor (or leaning against the walls). (You can check by placing a piece of foil or plastic on the floor or wall and seeing if moisture collects behind.)

Before you go ahead, even with a simple (and fairly cheap) d-i-y waterproofing scheme, some professional advice could be invaluable. A chartered building surveyor will undertake this sort of work for a fee. Or you can take advantage of the *free* survey and estimates offered by firms who undertake damp remedial work.

### Damp tests

The quickest and most practical way to investigate dampness is to use an electrical moisture meter. This normally takes a surface reading, but can be used with deep wall probes to sample deeper in the wall if necessary, or it may be possible to knock out a brick to get a deeper reading. The meter readings need careful interpretation because if there is a high concentration of soluble salts in the wall – the reading can be high, even when the wall is not actually very damp. (Tests on scrapings of the wall plaster can establish the presence of salts.)

Examine any survey report with care – the cause of damp is often difficult to diagnose and some people err on the safe side by recommending treatment for the problem when it does not exist.

## Dealing with damp from inside

Internal damp-proof treatments can at best only mask the damp and many have the effect of driving the damp up the wall and accelerating rot in things above – like window frames. Nevertheless these short-term damp-proof treatments can be useful.

### Dry-lining

The most satisfactory cover up can be

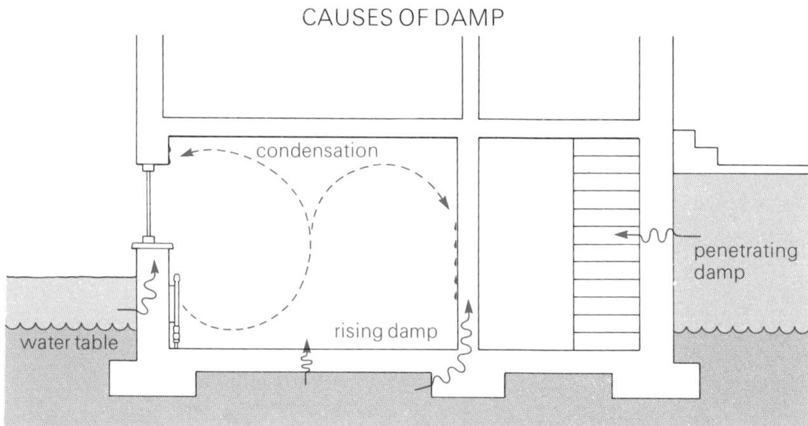


Damp is often a problem in a basement; it may be condensation due to poor heating and ventilation, but rising damp and penetrating damp are common causes. Any damp problem is difficult and expensive to cure.

done by dry-lining the walls. This is done exactly as any other dry-lining, but the battens *must* be treated with preservative and the wall surface and the back of the lining boards should be treated with a fungicide. Lining boards should incorporate a vapour-check. If using plasterboard, use a vapour-check grade and sealed joints or staple polythene to the battens before nailing on the plasterboards. Normally 50mm thick battens will be used and this will provide a cavity to stop the passage of moisture. The cavity can be ventilated by leaving a small gap top and bottom to allow air to circulate behind.

An advantage of dry-lining is that it can be done over a plastered wall, other methods of lining from inside usually require any existing plaster to be stripped.

### Bitumen lathing

Bitumen lathing is a corrugated sheet of pitch fibre which is impervious to moisture. The corrugations in the sheet allow air to pass behind the lathing and is important that the ends are open to allow this. The strips of lathing should be installed so that there is a slight gap between the bottom of the lathing and the floor and with a similar gap at ceiling height. (If the floor is boarded on joists the lathing can be taken below the floor to allow the air circulating there access to behind the lathing.) The lathing is fixed to a wall stripped of plaster with the corrugations running up and down the wall and adjacent strips overlapping about 75mm. It should be nailed at 150mm intervals. Breaks in the lathing around light switches and so on should be avoided (one way round this is to fit ceiling switches), if a break can't be avoided, seal around the opening with mastic.

### Brush-on damp-proofing

Bitumen can also be the base of an emulsion for brushing on to the stripped wall surface. There are similar products based on rubber/tar.

These brush-on sealers are usually applied in two or three coats. They're applied very thickly – a litre covering only 1 or 2 square metres of wall surface. The first coats are allowed to dry, but the last coat is covered with a thin layer of sharp sand while the emulsion is still sticky. This sandy surface then serves as a key for the subsequent plaster.

As this method of damp-proofing seals the moisture in, it's important to link the coating with any damp-proof membrane in the floor.

There are other brush-on treatments. Chlorinated rubber paints can be used if the water is not putting pressure on the walls and where efflorescence (the depositing of white salts on the surface) is not a problem. Products based on polyurethane resins can be used on wet masonry where they react with water to form an impervious hard layer.

Before any brush-on treatment is applied the wall should be brushed down to remove any crumbling mortar or masonry and thoroughly dried.

### Basement floor

A damp floor will need a damp-proof membrane. This could be a sheet of polythene with a concrete screed laid over or a liquid dpm which is painted over the existing floor. Neither of these methods will work on a brick-on-earth floor which will need breaking up and replacing with concrete – see page 85. If the floor has to be broken up you must get professional advice as the excavations could easily disturb the foundations.

## Lack of light

Many basements have small windows and so suffer from lack of light. Enlarging the windows may be possible if there is an open well outside the basement, but often there is no such well and it isn't possible to make the windows larger. One way to get light to a basement is to remove some of the floor above, but this is a job for professionals. Artificial lighting is the cheapest solution – used with skill, it can make up for lost daylight but it may not satisfy the Building Regulations.

### Removing moisture

If damp is masked, but not removed there will still be high humidity in the basement. An extractor fan will improve the ventilation, but remember air to replace the extracted air may be drawn in from elsewhere in the house and the air that's drawn in may already have high humidity. A dehumidifier, which is basically a refrigerator in reverse, may be the answer. Dehumidifiers work by cooling the air so that any water vapour carried is condensed and can then be collected and discharged (perhaps by a pump) to the outside. They can be free-standing units for one room or connected in association with a house ventilation system.

With bitumen lathing a gap is left top and bottom to allow ventilation through the corrugations. The lath is plastered over.

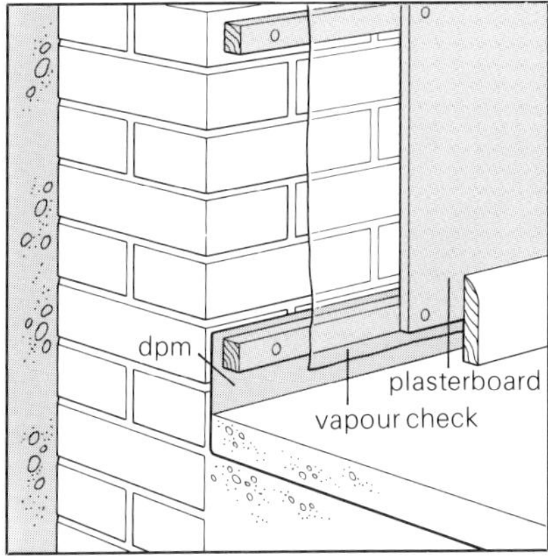


An advantage of dry-lining a damp wall is that any existing plaster need not be removed.

# Contract with a builder

Even for a small job, it is *strongly* advisable to have a written agreement showing exactly what work is to be carried out, the conditions on which it is to be carried out and the price. This can be done by the exchange of letters confirming what was discussed, but it is usually better to have a formal contract. Far too many people proceed without a contract and although nine times out of ten this is not a problem, it can only make things more difficult if disagreements do arise.

The best sort of contract for a small job, even an extension, is one where an overall contract price is agreed to cover the job as specified. The builder cannot charge more than this unless a clause is included to cover increases in the cost of materials after the date of signing the contract.

If you have consulted an architect, surveyor or other consultant, he will advise you about the type and content of a contract to suit your circumstances. He will probably offer you his professional organisation's printed form of agreement for minor building works.

An architectural or similar consultant or a solicitor will prepare a building agreement for a small fee.

If you do not put forward any form of contract, a builder's quotation may contain his standard terms and conditions. These will form the basis of a contract if you accept him for the job and produce no other formal contract.

The following are clauses which could be adopted for a fixed price contract.

1. The builder shall carry out and complete the work in strict accordance with the drawing and specification attached hereto, in a good and workmanlike manner and to the reasonable satisfaction of the employer for the sum of ........................(£...)

2. Possession of the site will be given to the builder on .....(day)....(month)....(year) He shall commence work immediately after such possession, shall regularly proceed with the work, and shall complete the work by .....(day)....(month)....(year) subject only to changes agreed according to the provision of clause 6 below.

3. If the builder shall fail or neglect to complete the work on or before the date in clause 2, he agrees to pay the employer (by way of damages, and not by way of penalty) the sum of ............. for every week or part of a week during which the completion is delayed.

4. The builder shall, within fourteen days of completing the work, and at his own expense, remove all tools, surplus materials and rubbish from the site and leave it in a clean and tidy condition.

5. The builder shall comply with all prevailing rules, regulations, laws and bye-laws relating to the works; he shall pay all fees legally due in connection with them and shall be responsible for giving all necessary notices, and arranging for inspections to take place.

6. No variation to the work described in clause 1 shall invalidate the contract, but any such variation, whether by addition, omission, or substitution, together with the cost and effect on the date of completion, shall be agreed in writing between the employer and the builder before the variation is carried out, and the contract price stated in clause 1 and the date of completion stated in clause 2 shall be altered accordingly.

7. The builder shall have or take out insurance indemnifying the employer for all loss, claims or proceedings arising out of or in the course of the execution of the contract, and for all costs and charges incurred in relation to the investigation or settling of such claims.

8. The builder shall be responsible for insuring the work in the joint names of himself and the employer for loss or damage by fire for the full value from the date of commencement until possession is taken.

9. The builder shall make good at his own expense any damage caused by him, his agents or his employees or by any sub-contractor.

10. The builder shall make good at his own expense any defects, shrinkages or other faults which may appear within six months from the completion of the works arising from materials or workmanship not in accordance with the contract.

11. The following prices for execution of work or the supply of materials are for payment to the parties stated:

provisional items £
(list)

prime cost sums £
(list)

12. The employer shall pay to the builder 95 per cent of the sum mentioned in clause 1, or such other sum as may have been agreed in accordance with clause 6, upon the submission by the builder of the final account following the completion of the work, the balance to be paid by the employer to the builder at the expiration of six months from the date of completion of the work or when all defects have been made good in accordance with clause 10, whichever is the later.

13. The employer and the builder agree that should any dispute or difference arise between them out of the work, either party shall give to the other written notice of such dispute or difference and at the same time shall refer the matter to an arbitrator agreed by both parties, whose decision shall be final and binding on both parties.

## The clauses

Clauses not mentioned below are self explanatory.

**Clause 1** If the builder does not complete the work to your reasonable satisfaction he commits a breach of contract and lays himself open to a claim for damages. If a professional will be engaged to supervise the work, the clause could stipulate that the work must be carried out to his reasonable satisfaction as your representative.

**Clause 2** Factors which could be agreed as reasonable cause for delay would be unseasonably bad weather or specified parts of materials unexpectedly becoming unobtainable, for instance, if the supplier of a special type of brick goes bankrupt and the brick cannot readily be obtained from elsewhere.

**Clause 3** This is intended to ensure that the work is completed by the agreed date or that you are paid something in compensation if it is not. This sum is referred to as 'damages' it is meant as recompense for additional expenses caused by the builder failing to complete on time. You could reasonably withold an amount for damages if a delay in completion caused additional expenses such as hotel, garaging or furniture storage bills. You have to estimate beforehand how much a delay would genuinely cost you, so that a figure can be put into the contract, to be agreed by the builder. Note that these expenses do have to be genuine you cannot claim cash just as a penalty for a delay in completion.

**Clause 6** These provisions should be observed most strictly. The lack of written agreement of the cost or value of variations to contracted work is one of the commonest reason for arguments after work is completed. In the event of any variation – however small – you should, having first discussed the details with the builder, confirm the variation in duplicate, including the amended contract price and completion date, and each keep one of the copies, signed by both.

This procedure may seem unnecessary at the time but it could save a lot of trouble later.

**Clause 7** The builder should have this insurance. Most builders have a blanket policy which covers all the projects on which they are working at any one time. Don't be afraid to check that the builder has current third party liability insurance and employer's liability insurance: this is one way of finding out the 'cowboys' who can afford to undercut reputable firms because they don't have overheads like insurance.

**Clause 8** This clause is important if you don't extend your existing house insurance policy to include fire damage to the new work. (You should however inform your insurers that you are extending your house, before the work starts.) Fire insurance for the extension should be the builder's responsibility until you move in. The insurance policy should be in your joint names, then, if the building is completely destroyed by fire, for instance, and the insurance company pays the insured sum to the builder, he cannot abscond without handing any over to you.

**Clause 10** This clause has the effect of asking a builder to guarantee both his workmanship and the materials used. The period stated could be less than six months, but think hard about employing a builder who will not agree to a minimum of three months.

**Clause 11** Where applicable this would be followed by a table listing what are referred to as provisional items and prime cost sums. Provisional items are optional features or fittings which, at the beginning of the scheme, you are not sure whether you want to have (if they are eventually not carried out, the appropriate sum should be deducted from the final price for the job – note though that a designer's fee will be a percentage based on the total cost of executing the design, including things that are not installed). A provisional item can also be work the extent of which the builder cannot assess properly until some work has started.

Prime cost (or PC) sums refer to work that will be subcontracted (such as the electrical work and plumbing). A sum is reserved but you will be charged their actual cost, which may turn out to be more, or less. You can yourself quote the amounts to be allocated for payment to specified firms of individuals for supplying a particular piece of equipment. The reason for having prime cost items in the contract is to make sure that they are included in the overall price for the whole job. If you know the cost of a fitting that you want, you can fill in the sum yourself.

If you subsequently change your mind about a prime cost item, this constitutes a variation to the contract – see Clause 6.

Decorations may be dealt with as a provisional or prime cost item. Even if you intend to do the decorating yourself, certain items should be specified, such as priming or woodwork to ensure that it is adequately protected from weather during construction.

If there are many provisional items or PC sums, list them on a separate sheet attached to the contract, and refer to the list in this clause.

**Clause 12** The agreed sum is not due until the work is completed. The builder may ask for *stage payments*. Interim payments are acceptable, if they're not made the builder may have to borrow and may charge you the interest. If the arrangement is to pay at specified stages of the work (the foundations completed, walls up, roof on), the payment should be a *percentage* of the contract price and not based on the value of the work done.

*Never* pay anything before the work starts.

Whatever arrangement is chosen, it should be stated clearly in the contract. It is also wise to stipulate that you will retain 5 per cent of the total price for a specified period after completion.

**Clause 13** This allows for the nomination of an independent arbitrator in the event of any dispute between the builder and yourself. You can agree that such an arbitrator should be appointed by an independent body, such as the Chartered Institute of Arbitrators (see page 314), or if you prefer, you can nominate someone in particular as arbitrator – check that your nominee agrees to this.

Some contracts include a clause allowing for the contract to be terminated in certain circumstances – if you (or the builder) became bankrupt, for example, or if you failed to make any agreed interim payment.

# Useful addresses

Most of the organisations below are noted in the book as a useful source of further information or as the first step in finding a tradesman (most will also pursue complaints about their members). Where an organisation is not specifically noted elsewhere, there is a brief note here of the help they can offer.

## Mainly information

**The BBC Engineering Information Dept.**, Broadcasting House, London W1A 1AA.

**The Brick Advisory Centre** is in the London Building Centre, 26 Store Street, London WC1E 7BT.

**The British Ready Mixed Concrete Association (BRMCA)**, Shepperton House, Green Lane, Shepperton, Middlesex TW17 8DN. They will also provide names and addresses of ready mix depots in their authorisation scheme.

**The Building Centres**, 26 Store Street, London WC1 and also in other major towns. These centres maintain exhibits of building materials with related literature.

**The Building Research Establishment (BRE)**. Carries out research and development. The BRE operates an Advisory Service (a fee is charged for site investigations). For information on damp and building materials contact The Building Research Station, Bucknalls Green, Garston, Watford, Herts. For information on wood, rot and woodworm, contact the Princes Risborough Laboratory, Aylesbury, Bucks.

**The Cement and Concrete Association**, Wexham Springs, Wexham, Slough SL3 6PL. They have some very good d-i-y leaflets and books.

**The Chartered Institution of Building Services**, Delta House, 222 Balham High Road, London SW12 9BS.

**The Copper Development Association**, Orchard House, Mutton Lane, Potters Bar, Hertfordshire EN6 3AP.

**The Design Council**, 28 Haymarket, London SW1Y 4SU.

**Eurisol – UK, The Association of British Manufacturers of Mineral Insulating Fibres**, St Paul's House, Edison Road, Bromley, Kent BR2 OEP.

**Fidor, Fibre Building Board Development Organisation Ltd.**, 1 Hanworth Road, Feltham, Middlesex TW13 5AF. Offer an advisory service on hardboards and other fibre building boards.

**The Glass and Glazing Federation**, 6 Mount Row, London W1Y 6DY. A list of their members in your area. Also advice on any type of flat glass, including mirrors.

**Her Majesty's Stationery Office**, London Region, Atlantic House, Holborn Viaduct, London EC1. They sell HMSO publications. Most bookshops will order.

**The IBA Engineering Information Services**, Crawley Court, Winchester, Hants. SO21 2QA.

**The National Fireplace Council** and *The National Fireplace Council Manufacturers Association,* PO Box 5, Stoke on Trent (NFCMA) Also at the same address *The Wood and Solid Fuel Association of Retailers and Manufacturers (WDRM) and The National Association of Chimney Sweeps* (NACS).

**The National Home Enlargement Bureau (NHEB)**, PO Box 67, High Wycombe, Bucks HP15 6XP. A non-profit making organisation which aims to give help on home enlargements. Have lists of builders, builders' merchants and insurance brokers in your area. They also run the Bonded Builder Scheme page 32.

**The Solid Fuel Advisory Service (SFAS)**. Head office is at Hobart House, Grosvenor Place, London SW1 but contact first your local office which is listed in the telephone directory.

**The Timber Research and Development Association (TRADA)**, Hughenden Valley, High Wycombe, Bucks HP14 4ND. They will answer simple problems you have about wood and wood-based sheet materials. A charge will be made if investigation is necessary. There are regional offices at Cambridge, Dublin, Evesham, Exeter, Glasow, Manchester and Weatherby.

**Scottish Association of Consumer Advice Bureaux**, 80 Nicolson Street, Edinburgh EH8 9EW.

## Mainly members' lists

**The Architects Registration Council for the UK**, 73 Hallam Street, London W1. Large libraries should have this list.

**The Confederation for the Registration of Gas Installers**. There are various regional offices – see local telephone directory.

**The Electrical Contractors' Association (ECA)**, ESCA House, 34 Palace Court, Bayswater, London W2 4HY. In Scotland they are at 23 Heriot Row, Edinburgh EH3 6W.

**The Federation of Master Builders (FMB)**, 33 John Street, London WC1N 2BB.

**The Faculty of Architects and Surveyors**, 15 St Mary Street, Chippenham, Wiltshire SN15 3JN

**The Chartered Institute of Arbitrators**, 75 Cannon Street, London EC4N 5BH.

**The Incorporated Association of Architect and Surveyors (IAAS)**, Jubilee House, Billing Brook Road, Weston Favell, Northampton.

**The Institute of Domestic Heating and Environmental Engineers**, 93 High Road, Benfleet, Essex.

**The Institute of Plumbing**, Scottish Mutual House, North Street, Hornchurch, Essex RM11 1RU.

**The Institution of Structural Engineers**, 11 Belgrave Street, London, SW1X 8BH.

**The National Association of Plumbing, Heating and Mechanical Services Contractors**, 6 Gate Street, London WC2A 3HX.

**The National Federation of Building Trades Employers**, 82 New Cavendish Street, London W1

**The National Federation of Roofing Contractors**, 15 Soho Square, London W1V 5FB.

**The National Institute of Carpet Fitters**, 17/21 George Street, Croydon CR9 1J2.

**The National Inspection Council for Electrical Installation Contracting (NICEIC)**, 237 Kennington Lane, London SE11 5QJ. Their list of approved contractors is also available in libraries, Citizen's Advice Bureaux and Electricity Board Showrooms.

**The Royal Institute of British Architects (RIBA)**, Clients Advisory Service, 66 Portland Place, London W1N 4AD.

**The Royal Institution of Chartered Surveyors (RICS)**, Information Centre, 12 Great George Street, London SW1P 3AD. In Scotland: 7 Manor Place, Edinburgh EH3 7DN.

**The Scottish & Northern Ireland Plumbing Employers Federation**, 2 Walker Street, Edinburgh WH3 7LB.

**The Society of Industrial Artists and Designers**, (SIAD) Designers Register, 12 Carlton House Terrace, London SW1Y 5AH.

# Index

## A



## B



## C



## D

*The publishers acknowledge permission to publish photographs as follows:*

Amdega Limited, 265, 269

Banbury Homes and Gardens Limited, 275

Blacknell Buildings Limited, 272(3)

Bowater Ripper Limited, 138

British Telecom, 173

Camera Press Limited, 114, 125(2), 175, 306

Crescount Loft Conversions Ltd, 284(2)

The Design Council, 17

Leo Ferrante, 13(2)

Susan Griggs Agency Limited, 16

Halls Homes & Gardens, 269

Harry Hebditch Limited, 271

Hepworth Astraseal, 138

H. Burbridge & Son Limited, 168

Marley Buildings Limited, 263, 264, 275, 299

MK Ltd, 179

W. H. Newson & Sons Limited, 125

Jessica Strang, 114, 115, 138, 167, 175(2), 295, 307(2)

Velux, 284(2)

David Wallis, 15, 16, 17, 217(2), 250, 285(2), 299

S. Wernick & Sons Limited, 271

Elizabeth Whiting & Associates, 10, 11, 12, 13, 14(2), 15, 65(3), 125, 295